McCary's
Human
Sexuality

McCary's Human Sexuality

Fourth Edition

James Leslie McCary, Ph.D.
Formerly Professor of Psychology
University of Houston

Stephen P. McCary, Ph.D.
Private Practice, Houston, Texas

Wadsworth Publishing Company
Belmont, California
A Division of Wadsworth, Inc.

Health Editor: Marshall Aronson
Production Editor: Judith McKibben
Cover Design: Cynthia Bassett
Cover Photograph: David Wasserman

Part and Chapter Opening Photo Credits

Page 2, United Press International; 4, 490, German Information Center; 28, Serena Nada; 36, 62, Norwegian Information Service; 38, 118, 278, 336, Erika Stone; 84, Pablo Picasso, *Pregnant Woman* (1950) Collection, The Museum of Modern Art, New York, Gift of Mrs. Bertram Smith; 102, The Bettmann Archive, Inc.; 172, Ed Lettau/Photo Researchers, Inc; 174, Dianne Baasch; 197, 383, Charles Gatewood; 226, Asia News Center; 236, copyright, Joel Gordon, 1979; 252, Richard Frieman/Photo Researchers, Inc.; 318, Ginger Chih; 340, 364, Randy Matusow; 444, 464, copyright, Michael Hanulak/Photo Researchers, Inc.; 492, Hugh Rogers/Monkmeyer Press Photo Service; 538, Dr. John Money/Johns Hopkins Hospital.

Printed in the United States of America
1 2 3 4 5 6 7 8 9 10—86 85 84 83 82

Library of Congress Cataloging in Publication Data

McCary, James Leslie.
  McCary's human sexuality.

  Bibliography: p.
  Includes index.
  1. Sex. 2. Hygiene, Sexual. I. McCary, Stephen P. II. Title. III. Title: Human sexuality.
  HQ21.M463 1982   613.9'5   81-12925
  ISBN 0-534-01108-X   AACR2

*Dedicated to those people
who wish both to better understand
their own sexual needs and behavior
and to be more accepting of their neighbor
whose sexual attitudes and behavior
might be different from their own*

Preface

The scientific and professional study of human sexuality continues at a rapid pace. If there is anything I have learned in revising this book, it is that the study of human sexuality is not a simple or static phenomenon. The innovative approaches to studying this area of human behavior progress in an amazing and challenging manner. About the time that a particular phenomenon is understood, new data are produced to shake heretofore accepted facts and hypotheses. There is little doubt that new and startling changes will continue to occur and that human sexuality—a complex area of human behavior—will continue to be reshaped and remolded.

The purpose of this book is to provide the reader with a solid background and understanding of human sexuality. Basically, the approach of this book parallels that of the first three editions. Explorations of the physiological, psychological, and sociological parameters involved in sexuality are undertaken with an emphasis on the emotions that affect human sexual experience. Pedagogical aids—summaries and annotated bibliographies—have been added to support the learning process and to encourage further academic exploration.

It is my hope that this edition will prove helpful to the many college, university, graduate, professional, and lay audiences who have responded so gratifyingly to the first three editions. Individuals with an accurate and objective understanding of human sexuality have been shown to have more fulfilling and satisfying sex lives, to be more accepting of others, and to have healthier, more fulfilling relations with others. Thus, I hope that the reader's sexual and emotional adjustment can be enhanced by considering the information covered in this edition. I attempted to keep this book as readable as possible while still providing enough detail to eliminate much of the mystery and confusion in the sensitive area of human sexuality.

I owe a debt of gratitude to the many individuals who have contributed their wisdom and talents in helping to make this edition a reality. In particular, thanks are due Mary Elizabeth Sieber and Elizabeth Miremont Smith for their editorial contributions to the previous editions of this text. To Ralph Eichhorn, M.D., David Short, M.D., and Jack Skelley of D. Van Nostrand Company go a decided vote of thanks for their advice and help in the compilation of the previous editions of this text.

Credit is due to Glenn F. Sternes, Ph.D., Monte Bobele, Ph.D., and graduate student Larry Hanselka for their editorial assistance in compiling this edition. These three individuals added their creative ideas and personal contributions to the book in numerous thoughtful ways. Thanks are extended to secretaries Bee Busch and Carmen Perez for their assistance in typing this manuscript. They performed many of the agonizing and often thankless tasks required to put the finishing touches on a book. Without their help, the publication deadlines would have been extremely difficult to achieve. Editors Harriet Serenkin and Judith Joseph of D. Van Nostrand Company are also due a vote of thanks for their help throughout the production of this fourth edition.

To the following reviewers who added their constructive ideas and insights regarding this edition, heartfelt thanks are due: Arlene Privette, Clemson University; Burton Weiss, Drexel University; Jerrald Floyd, Northern Illinois University; Larry K. McKane, California State Polytechnic University, Pomona; Patrick Duddy, Kingstown State College; Mark Schwartz, the Masters and Johnson Institute; Mary Jean Wallace; Miner Chamberlin, University of North Florida; R. Nash, Marquette University; Alan Glaros, Wayne State University; and Jay Mancini, Virginia Polytechnic State University. It is with regret that all of their ideas could not be incorporated into this edition. Additionally, those who have read past editions provided helpful suggestions that are invaluable to this revision.

Finally, credit is especially due to the senior author of this edition for his contributions not only to this book, but also for his pioneering endeavors in the study of human sexuality. James L. McCary passed away before this edition was completed, but his contributions are evident to those who have read and used previous editions. I am grateful for the warm, close emotional ties he and I shared, and I value the professional association we developed as well. James L. McCary was a teacher, a counselor, and a friend to many; his loss remains great for those of us who knew him.

To my wife, Sandra, and to my mother, LaVirle McCary, I owe a debt of thanks that cannot be expressed fully or often enough. Without their support and encouragement—together with some prodding from other friends and family members—I would have found completion of this edition to be a much more arduous task.

My understanding, awareness, and appreciation of the complexities involved in human behavior have been enhanced by this research into human sexuality. It is hoped that through this book the reader can likewise learn to appreciate our heritage as sexual beings.

Stephen P. McCary, Ph.D.

Foreword

In the spring of 1966 my lecture travels took me to the University of Houston, where I spoke on human sexuality. There I met Dr. James Leslie McCary and his son, Stephen. Dr. James McCary was then teaching courses on human sexuality and working on a human sexuality text. We discussed the need for an adequate textbook and the value it would have for the then evolving discipline of sexual studies or sexology.

From 1966 on I occasionally met Dr. McCary at meetings, and in 1967 the first edition of *McCary's Human Sexuality* was published. I also read the second and third editions of *McCary's Human Sexuality* (1973 and 1978). It was with sadness that I learned of Dr. McCary's death in 1978, and I wondered at the time whether there would be a further edition of the text. So it is a pleasure to find that there is, under the direction of his son, Stephen.

I was also delighted to be asked to write a foreword for this edition. I believe if one peruses these editions, it is possible to obtain an overview of the development of human sexuality in the last fifteen years, and to see why sexology has become a discipline itself, rather than an offshoot of medicine, biology, psychology, or theology. All editions of *McCary's Human Sexuality* have both addressed contemporary attitudes and speculated on future developments. Each new edition has given more attention to the emotional and attitudinal qualities of human sexuality; in the third edition a new chapter, "Intimacy and Love," was added. Social and psychological concepts have been integrated into other chapters, and historical and cross-cultural facts have been incorporated into discussions. As the reader examines one edition after another, sexuality becomes a more positive, enjoyable, and life-enhancing quality of existence. It is no longer seen as something apart, but as an essential part of life.

Dr. James McCary and Stephen McCary have sought to move their readers away from the fears that prevent people from approaching their sexuality affirmatively, toward both personal and social fulfillment. Some of these fears, which rest on sheer ignorance, arose in the past because certain results of sexual relations, now readily controllable, were largely beyond control. The hope is that by providing adequate information—based on research findings—these fears will be dispelled.

Other fears rest on the strictures of fundamentalist religious teaching. Many citations are made to support this point, among them the fact that in Biblical times a menstruating woman was considered unclean and untouchable. The McCarys note that women were portrayed as "second-class citizens" in the Old Testament.

We can all be pleased that *McCary's Human Sexuality* continues as a source of sexual information and positive, open attitudes. A major concern of the McCarys has been the recognition of the need for greater flexibility in sexual patterns. While *McCary's Human Sexuality* is addressed particularly to college and university classes, all readers will profit by its affirmative attitudes toward responsible and thoughtful sexual expression. The McCarys have also voiced a concern for people whose sexual associations go beyond the conventional—those who are regarded as sexual variants. In this new edition there is a chapter on homosexuality.

The McCarys espouse a number of important principles in *McCary's Human Sexuality*: for example, humans are sexual beings from birth until death (although sexual manifestations change, of course, as one ages); and there is a very important interaction between our sexuality, attitudes, preferences, patterns of behavior, and the society in which we live. This interaction is demonstrated in such concerns as the promotion of sex education in schools, the discrimination against the poor as in the denial of abortion funding, the abolition of laws that support the stigma of illegitimacy, and the need for a reassessment of the entire legal approach to the regulation of sexual matters. Certainly there is no mistaking the values that the McCarys hold; they are direct and outspoken. I enjoy this feature of *McCary's Human Sexuality*; it is a quality that attracts me to the book. However, despite the advances of this edition, there is enough social dissension remaining on the topic of sex that future editions of *McCary's Human Sexuality* will be needed.

What specifically should the task of future editions be, in terms of the interaction of sexuality and society? I believe it is to arrive at an even fuller understanding of sexuality in relation to society.

Sex has always been a central part of life and it always will be. However, it has been associated with many factors that do not elevate sex, but rather detract from it. The mass media play upon sex in many different ways; sex is used for selling all kinds of consumer products, from automobiles to perfume. As a result, people often feel that their sex lives are inadequate by comparison with the models presented in the media and that their other interests are invalid. One consequence of this is that we can talk about sex in a titillating way but fall silent when serious communication is needed.

These are vast and complicated issues, but this and future editions of *McCary's Human Sexuality* can help us to resolve them by making us think about how to achieve the necessary integration of sexuality and society. This goal of integration will require the best efforts of all of us.

Lester A. Kirkendall

Brief Contents

Part Five   Sexual Complications   491

References
Glossary
Index

Detailed Contents

Part Three   The Sexual Act   173

Part Five   Sexual Complications   491

Part One
By Way of Introduction

*I*n the recent past, especially the last 15 years, significant advances have been made in the quality of sex education. Yet sex education at all levels continues to be unsatisfactory. Research and clinical experience attest to lingering problems in individual lives and relationships that are directly attributable to sexual ignorance and misinformation. Psychotherapists are finding that three-fourths of their patients with mild to severe emotional problems have sexual difficulties as well. They also find similar complications in half of the marital relationships coming to their attention. The problem of sexual maladjustment is not a casual one.

In Part One the causes and effects of sexual ignorance are discussed. Sex-related mythology, the extensiveness of which bears witness to the prevalence of such ignorance in our society, is also considered.

Since mental health, physical well-being, and sexual adjustment are strongly correlated, it is curious that opposition remains strong to the surest means of achieving the last-named—i.e., sex education. The obstacles to sex education, and the guilts and fears underlying it, are examined in the hope of dissolving them so that effective sex education may one day become the birthright of all people.

Why Sex Education?

1

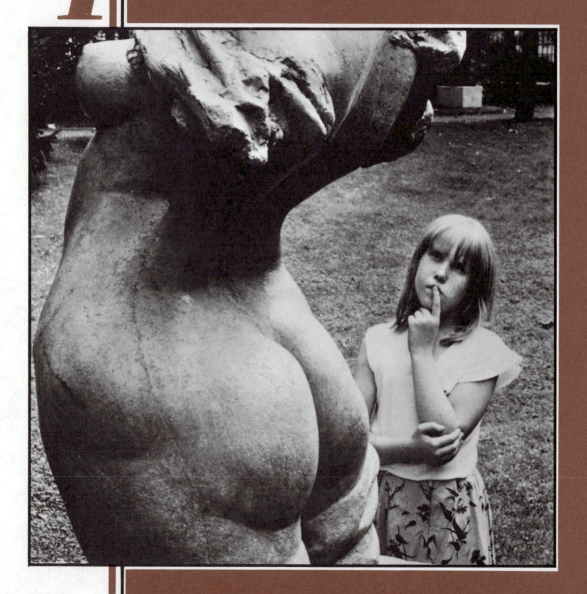

In the past 10 or 15 years the subject of sex has emerged (or was pushed) from its Victorian closet into broad daylight. There it has been examined and talked about as perhaps never before in history. Many behaviorists claim that a sexual revolution has occurred. But can one really accept that sexual ignorance and anxiety have appreciably lessened because of the modern environment of sexual frankness?

Without doubt great strides have been made toward more formal, adequate sex-education programs for the young and the reeducation of those not so young. Have we achieved, however, the final goal of a guilt-free, sufficiently broad understanding of sexuality to insure a greater fullness to our lives? Probably not, at least not yet. Too much sexual conflict and doubt persist—hence this book.

The late Ernie Pyle once said, "It ain't the things you don't know that make you a fool, it's the things you know that ain't so." Many people still desperately seek answers to sex-related problems from whatever sources are available, good or bad. When accurate information is not available, they accept misinformation for truth. This is especially true of the young. The failure of adults to discuss sex openly with youngsters endows sex with an unrealistic, magical quality, which

Figure 1.1   Sex Communication. Copyright 1976, G. B. Trudeau. Distributed by Universal Press Syndicate.

reinforces adolescent preoccupation with the subject. It also obstructs natural, legitimate sources of sex information, often forcing young people to seek warped sources to satisfy their normal curiosity.

Many factors significantly affect a child's emerging sexual attitudes and conduct: the way in which parents love, fondle, and hold the infant; the soothing or harsh sound of their voices; the feel of their skin; the smell of their bodies. Whether or not they realize it or intend to do so, parents begin children's sexual training in the earliest days of their lives. Even when parents avoid discussing sex altogether, children nevertheless detect their attitudes—stressful or happy—through silent communication (Calderone 1966).* Some of the most crucial aspects of sex education are thus taught unconsciously (SIECUS 1970). "Indeed, the way a boy's father lives, his self-esteem, and the way he treats his wife and children will constitute a boy's earliest sex education from his father" (Gadpaille 1971). Sexual interactions or rehearsal play among children and adolescents may help them in learning about and establishing healthy sexual relationships in their adult lives (Money 1980a).

* References are cited parenthetically in the text by author and date. For full documentation, see List of References at the end of the text.

Sexual ignorance breeds sexual anxiety, and the primary cause of both is simple. Adults in a position to instruct the young are all too often filled with sexual guilt. Further, they may be painfully uncertain about what they truly believe to be acceptable sexual behavior. In addition to their ignorance and conflict, they are often reluctant to admit to these shortcomings.

Few authorities in human behavior would deny that sexual adjustment is essential to maturity and successful adaptation to one's environment. Scientific investigations and clinical observations (Malcolm 1971; Thornburg 1970) confirm that sexual adjustment is positively correlated with well-timed, ongoing, accurate sex education presented in a wholesome manner. If properly educated themselves, today's young adults will be in a position to educate their own children properly in sexual matters. Only in this way can the cycle of sexual ignorance and anxiety be broken.

A Heritage of Confusion

In the field of human sexuality, lay people and scientists alike are often reluctant to consider new scientific findings. When new research appears to lend support to long-held prejudices, it is quickly accepted as scientifically accurate. But when it discounts tradition and cherished personal theories, the results tend to be dismissed as suspect, and its conclusions judged as distorted by sample and examiner bias. Such suspicious attitudes have been seen in certain public reactions to the work of the Alfred C. Kinsey investigators and of William H. Masters and Virginia E. Johnson. The Kinsey workers were especially harassed.

> There were attempts by the medical association in one city to bring suit on the ground that we were practicing medicine without a license, police interference in two or three cities, investigation by a sheriff in one rural area, and attempts to persuade the University's administration to stop the study, or to prevent the publication of the results, or to dismiss the senior author from his university connection, or to establish a censorship over all publication emanating from the study. [Kinsey *et al.* 1948]

A variety of social ills have been attributed to the sex research of Masters and Johnson—from spreading venereal disease to pushing the nation toward the brink of moral disaster. Persons holding rigidly to any value system become panic-stricken when it is challenged. Challenge to sexual or religious ethics (one typically founded on the other) appears to cause the most violent reaction of all.

Psychologist Albert Ellis (1961a, 1962) studied sex, love, marriage, and family relations in America by examining attitudes subtly expressed in advertisements, books, periodicals, and movies. He concluded that our inadequate sex education has caused neurotic repression and inhibition of normal sexual expression, seriously affecting our lives and behavior.

The growing sales of "nudie" magazines, the use of attractive males and females as seductive hucksters to sell everything from cigarettes to shoe polish to salad dressing, the suggestive ads for many films—all these are examples of how sex drives can be misdirected.

Parents too often suppose that if their children do not know about sex they will avoid it, and will consequently lead sexually pure lives. For example, parents will frequently withhold information on contraception and VD altogether, or will recount only the dangers and shame of illegitimate pregnancy and VD, expecting to keep their children from engaging in premarital coitus.

Yet history shows that fears of pregnancy and VD rarely deter anyone from premarital sex. In fact before the modern, quickly effective cures for venereal diseases were available and when these "social diseases" were greatly feared, people blithely had sex relations with partners whose freedom from infection was not known. Correlating fear of VD and its incidence, Rubin (1964a) showed that of psychologically normal men who had no fear of venereal infection, 15.4% contracted one of the diseases. Of those who had moderate fear, the percentage rose to 20.8%; and of those who had a very strong fear, 15.3% became infected.

Many girls become pregnant, of course, because of sexual ignorance. On the other hand, knowledge of contraception may be no assurance that a girl will protect herself in premarital coitus. A study (Settlage *et al.* 1973) made of 502 unmarried, never-pregnant girls aged 13 to 17 years seeking professional help in obtaining a contraceptive revealed that 61% had used no nonprescription preventive, although virtually all were coitally active. But the evidence is, fortunately, that sexually active teen-age girls are becoming more aware of the importance of contraception and are using it more often. Zelnik and Kantner (1977) have shown that in 1971 only 45% of sexually active girls aged 15 to 19 years used any method of contraception the last time they had intercourse. Of that sample, 16% used contraceptive pills (the Pill) or an intrauterine device (IUD). In 1976, by contrast, 63% of coitally active girls in this age group were using contraceptives, and 33% of them, the Pill or an IUD. Girls who do not themselves take contraceptive precautions usually do not insist that their partners do so. This recklessness exists despite the fact that half the boys and almost three-fourths of the girls express a real fear of pregnancy (Schofield *et al.* 1965).

Religious devotion offers no guarantees against premarital sex. Many unwanted pregnancies occur among the religiously devout who, despite their determination to "refrain from sin," lose control of their emotions and get caught up in the act of intercourse (Kinsey *et al.* 1953). But loss of control does not tell the whole story. Some religious girls feel that premarital sex in which contraceptives are used is more "sinful" than unprotected intercourse. Pregnancy resulting from premarital intercourse appears as just punishment for "having sinned" (Pohlman 1969). Furthermore, when young men know about contraception, they sometimes fail to use it because they are too embarrassed to make the necessary purchase or because making such a purchase in advance constitutes "planned sin" (Martinson 1960).

The World Health Organization (WHO) states that ignorance, not knowledge, of sexual matters is the cause of "sexual misadventure" (Calderone 1965). As an example, the head of Brazil's gynecological and obstetrics society lays his country's 50% illegitimacy birthrate, as well as soaring incidence of VD and abortion, squarely at the door of sexual ignorance. Neither home nor school, he says, offers any sex instruction to Brazil's youth, of whom 99% of the boys and about 60% of the girls have their first coitus between the ages of 11 and 15.

The impact of adequate early sex information on marriages can be judged from Clifford Kirkpatrick's analysis (1963) of the components of successful marital adjustment. The subjects of his survey ranked "adequate sex information in childhood" third in importance among the leading 10 factors considered fundamental to a successful marriage, falling behind only "happiness of parents' marriage" and "adequate length of acquaintanceship, courtship, and engagement."

Religion, Sex, and Marriage

Few people in the position to judge would deny that probably the greatest threat to psychosexual health is found in certain rigid, guilt-instilling religions. Leaders of such religions have succeeded remarkably well in

Figure 1.2 Sex Education. Copyright 1971, G. B. Trudeau. Distributed by Universal Press Syndicate.

training their followers in the belief that sex is dirty and animalistic, to be looked upon only as a necessary evil—with emphasis on the word *evil* (Duffy 1963). This attitude is clearly seen in the prudery of the Victorian era, when "decent" women, not daring to expect pleasure from the sexual act, endured it only because of their "duty" to their husbands.

Changes in attitudes toward sex and marriage that reflect changing needs, but often tag behind them, have occurred throughout history. Early Israelite tribes, for example, permitted polygynous* marriages, in which women were regarded as little more than chattel. Marriages were primarily of legal rather than of religious concern. Some men were left without female partners as a result of polygyny, and a more fair distribution of women became necessary. Thus monogamy evolved.

With the evolution of Mosaic laws, the foundation of present-day Judeo-Christian morality, marriage and sex gradually came to be regarded as belonging to a sphere higher than simple legality. Much of the ancient interpretation of these laws—indeed, the necessity for them in the first place—was based on the need for larger tribes. In this way a single justification for sexual activity was developed—procreation. By extension, sexual activity for any other purposes became an act of perversion.

The belief that women were unclean and untouchable during menstruation and for two days afterward (Leviticus 15) was undoubtedly based on the improbability of conception on those days. Man should not, therefore, waste his sperm lest he be punished by God for not attempting to add to the strength of his tribe.

It appears that the laws prohibiting bestiality and homosexuality were also aimed at conserving precious sperm. Significantly, the judgment against homosexuality between men was far more harsh than against lesbianism. Since there is no sperm loss in lesbianism, tribal growth was not threatened by it.

In prescientific times, the belief prevailed that females were imperfect males. Sperm were considered miniature men, women merely providing the "soil" in which the miniature men grew into maturity. The weaker sperm were thought to be deformed, therefore "growing into" girls. Thus the concept was formed that the female is inferior to the male. Any "loss" of semen, whether through intercourse during the menstrual flow, *coitus interruptus* (withdrawal of penis before ejaculation), or masturbation, were therefore viewed as mass murder of hundreds of thousands of potential men (Haring 1967).

Much has been written and damaging conclusions drawn concerning the biblical account (Genesis 38:9) of Onan's "spilling his seed on the ground." Onan was commanded by God to impregnate his deceased brother's wife, Tamar. He refused to do so, using *coitus interruptus* to prevent pregnancy, because any child Tamar bore would carry Onan's

* Definitions of technical vocabulary can be found in the Glossary of this book.

brother's name and not his own. (These were called Levirate marriages, designed to protect tribal lineage and property.) God was angered by Onan's defiance of his command and struck him dead.

Onan's sin—popularly called *onanism*—somehow became interpreted to mean birth control, and upon this rests certain religious teachings against birth control. Furthermore, some time during the 17th century the "spilling of seed" and masturbation became equated. Masturbation was thereafter condemned as a serious evil. All in all, the misinterpretations of this story have had severe repercussions on Western sexual stability.

The favored position of men in patriarchal societies apparently led to the inferior status traditionally accorded women. A typical example is the Old Testament view that when a woman gave birth to a male child she was "unclean" for 40 days. But when she gave birth to a female child she was "unclean" for 80 days (Leviticus 12).

Woman is portrayed not only as "second-class citizen" in some sections of the Old Testament but also as sexual temptress. Adam and Eve surrender to temptation, and the blame is laid on Eve. Lot and his daughters become involved in incest, and once more the burden for illicit sexuality is placed on woman—the daughters in this case. They allegedly had given Lot so much wine that he was incapable of knowing what he was doing and they seduced him. Although Lot appears absolved of any responsibility for these events, this biblical account is unconvincing. If he was so drunk as to be unaware of what he was doing, the chances are that he could not have performed sexually. For male sexual functioning is severely impaired by heavy drinking.

A glance at nonbiblical history will illustrate the evolution, good and bad, of sexual ethics and behavior. Prior to the 4th century B.C., Western civilizations, notably most of the Greek city-states, regarded sex according to a "naturalistic" philosophy—as a pleasure to be enjoyed. Those even attempting to lead a celibate life were looked upon with pity. But when Sparta, a Greek city-state with a very different set of values, overcame Athens, the Spartan philosophy of rigid self-discipline (which included avoidance of pleasure and luxury) almost destroyed the Greek culture that had taught "naturalism."

In his extraordinary conquest of the world in the 3rd century B.C., Alexander the Great opened many roads of cultural exchange. In consequence, the spiritual philosophies of India, Egypt, and Mesopotamia filtered into the Western world and gained a strong foothold. Rather than being a pleasure, sexual desire was now considered an evil to be overcome by self-denial. Salvation of the soul could be achieved only through control of fleshly pleasures. Celibacy was glorified. Sex thus fell under the shadow of guilt and condemnation long before the advent of Christianity. But because the New Testament was written during the latter part of this period, it was strongly influenced by the earlier spiritual attitudes (Rizzo 1968).

Jesus himself had little to say on the subject of sex, contrary to common belief. The vast majority of sexual restrictions associated with Christianity are actually outgrowths of the philosophies of later Christian theologians, formulated for the most part long after Christ's death. Paul was probably the first Christian to speak out specifically on sexual morality. He emphasized the need for marriage as a means of avoiding fornication, although he apparently considered sexual abstinence a more admirable goal in life.

St. Augustine (A.D. 354–430) probably has had as much impact on present-day sexual attitudes as any other theologian. His writings severely condemn nonmarital sexual outlets, including bestiality, homosexuality, and (especially) masturbation. In time the Roman Catholic Church came to idealize celibacy, with the highest level of male achievement being total rejection of all life's pleasures, while women could expect to reach their greatest glory only through perpetual virginity.

Virginity and purity were long regarded as one and the same. The virgin birth of Jesus, the springing of Athena full grown from Zeus's forehead, and the unusual origins of other deities are testimonials to that view (Anthony 1963). It is therefore not difficult to understand why concepts of sex and sin (impurity) are so closely bonded. When rigid sexual rules are not counterbalanced with a rationale for sexual morality, then guilt must be relied upon to control sexual behavior. Young people internalize these rigid ethics, the ridiculous as well as the sensible ones. And if they happen to break the rules—which is more often the case than not—then emotional stress is typically the result.

Of course, a marriage ceremony does not necessarily serve as a magician's wand to correct the "thou-shalt-not" and "sex-is-dirty-and-should-be-avoided" attitudes handed down by parents and society. Believing that sex equals sin, many brides and grooms eventually suffer from such unfortunate reactions as guilt, pain, frigidity, impotence, and premature ejaculation. It is too much to expect that the mere recitation of marriage vows can change sex from something evil into something good.

Although remnants of sexual rigidity are still evident in certain religions, these doctrines are, fortunately, being gradually analyzed with respect to their relevance to Our Town, U.S.A. In a good example of self-analysis, the United Methodists issued a policy statement in 1973 (Smith 1975), which stated in part:

> We support the development of school systems and innovative methods of education designed to assist each child toward full humanity. All children have the right to full sexual education, appropriate to their stage of development, that utilizes the best educational techniques and insights.

Further, the United Methodists engaged 100 sex educators from among their membership to teach 6000 young people and their parents during the initial two years of a sex-education program, which is expanding and strengthening yearly.

Breaking the Bonds of Sexual Fascism

Some people arbitrarily evaluate certain sexual behavior—their own, of course—as the only normal sexual behavior, and will go to great lengths to impose their views on others. Anyone who fails to comply with these arbitrary standards is considered an anti-Christ, pervert, or sexual inferior.

These "judges" are the world's sexual fascists (Ellis 1958). Most of them neither understand nor care, for instance, that women's response to sex relations is different from men's. They simply expect women to employ and respond to the same sexual techniques that are successful with men. They accept uncritically the traditional double standard of morality for men and women: girls must be virgins until marriage while boys are allowed, even expected, to have many premarital experiences. Women are much more to blame for having children out of wedlock than the men who father the babies.

A crucial factor in people's health and adjustment is the maintenance of "a reasonable degree of flexibility and freedom from fixation in the major aspects of their lives" (Ellis 1958). We do not expect everyone to like asparagus. And indeed we do not expect those who like it to want it all the time. When it comes to sex, however, the bigot's philosophy does not allow for any behavioral flexibility.

Any student of human sexual behavior soon recognizes the extreme difficulty of trying to define precisely what is, and what is not, sexual deviation. For instance, such noncoital activities as masturbation, petting, and oral-genital contact are often viewed in Western cultures as perversions. Yet masturbation is commonly practiced by most men and women, both single and married. Oral-genital contact occurs in most upper socioeconomic relationships. And most women prefer noncoital methods of stimulation to intercourse, and respond more intensely to them. There is evidence, in fact, that women experience oral-genital stimulation earlier in life than men (Cowart & Pollack 1979; Hite 1976; Kinsey *et al.* 1948, 1953; Masters & Johnson 1966).

The man-above coital position is not widely assumed anywhere except in a few Western countries. Among boys of Arab countries, masturbation is infrequently practiced and is less acceptable than homosexuality (Ellis 1960). These are only two examples of the significant differences in sexual behavior found interculturally. No one is justified in saying that the sexual practices of one culture are more proper and normal than those of another. Any valid program of sex education must, therefore, take individual differences in sexual tastes and pleasures into full account. No person or group has the moral (nor should have the legal) right to force its ethical views upon others any more than aesthetic or political ones.

Perhaps when we as a society mature to the point that we no longer feel compelled to impose our personal biases on others, we will develop—and generate—fewer emotional difficulties, including sexual ones.

Facts—and Arguments—About Sex Education

The Kinsey reports confirmed what educators had long known, that guilt feelings aroused by inadequate sex knowledge interfere with personal and marital adjustment. To be fully satisfying, sex must be guilt-free. Fortunately, a strong correlation has been shown to exist between adequate sex education and low levels of sexual guilt (S. P. McCary 1976; Ogren 1974). Sound mental health and a mind receptive to learning tend to go together; worry and anxiety hamper learning to the fullest of one's potential (Poffenberger 1959). Persons who have received a good sex education develop more appropriate defenses and are less anxious than those without one, since the latter tend to repress their anxiety by the self-defeating means of avoidance and denial (Wright & McCary 1969).

Those persons who are sexually knowledgeable are more capable of enjoying their sexual feelings and of deriving pleasure from many forms of sexual activity than are the less knowledgeable, who tend to restrain sexual impulses (Wright & McCary 1969). This difference is probably related to anxiety, which serves to inhibit freedom of sexual response: the greater the amount of accurate sex information, the less the anxiety (Barfield 1971). Masters and Johnson (1970) confirmed that sexual maladjustment among both men and women, when caused by sexual ignorance, is preventable through early, adequate sex education.

Specific physiological problems have been found to be related to sex education and to emotions. For example, most women who suffer from premenstrual tension and difficult menstruation have a family background of parents in conflict. And they typically received their sex education from their mothers, who presented the information in a disapproving way ("Medical Science Notes" 1961b).

David Mace, a former president of the Sex Information and Education Council of the U.S. (SIECUS) and long-time executive director of the American Association of Marriage and Family Counselors, commented:

A child who has been able to learn the basic facts about sex, to feel natural and comfortable about them, to hear the subject presented without embarrassment by at least one trustworthy adult, and to participate in the discussion of the subject with other children in a healthy and wholesome manner is the child who is going to cope effectively with his own emerging sexual feelings and needs. . . . The idea of "protecting" children from sexuality is . . . a myth, a *dangerous* myth. [1970]

The value of thorough sex-education programs in reducing the incidence of VD has been recognized for years (Rees & Zimmerman 1974). The American Social Health Association (Deschin 1962) conducted a careful study of the relationship between the two in a sampling of 600 teen-age VD patients. The association's primary conclusion was that these young people needed a more thorough knowledge of sex in general and VD in particular.

A good demonstration of this premise was the introduction of a course entitled "Family Life Education" in two junior and two senior public high schools in Washington, D.C. In one of these schools there had been 38 cases of gonorrhea the year before the course was introduced. During the school year that sex education was first taught, there were 22 cases, and in the next, only 16. By contrast, in a comparable high school in the District not offering this course, there were in the same two-year period 35 cases of gonorrhea one year and 40 the next. Realizing what was happening, the administration of this high school then instituted a sex-education program. In one year's time the incidence of gonorrhea decreased by almost 50% (Levine 1970).

Mandatory sex education and marriage and family programs have been instigated or planned in Maryland, Kentucky, and New Jersey. These programs have drawn upon the ideas of teachers, parents, and students. Course guides and materials have been devised for use in kindergarten through the twelfth grade. The focus of the programs has remained the junior and senior high school age groups, however, as opposition (particularly in New Jersey) from certain religious groups, Right to Life groups, and CURE (Citizens United for Responsible Education) led to dilution or elimination of the curriculum in the elementary grades. Nevertheless, important strides have been made in recent years toward establishing objective, factual, and appropriately timed sex-education programs for our youth (Francoeur & Hendrixson 1980).

Those Who Oppose Sex Education in the Schools, and Those Who Defend It

Sex education in the schools is endorsed not only by the public but by some of the country's most prestigious organizations as well. As examples: the Interfaith Commission on Marriage and Family Life (consisting of the Synagogue Council of America, the U.S. Catholic Conference, and the National Council of Churches); the National Congress of Parents and Teachers; the American Medical Association; the YMCA and YWCA; and the U.S. Department of Health and Human Services.

Despite endorsement by the majority, however, one cannot ignore the genuine concern of some parents that sex education might be presented in too dehumanized a fashion in the classroom; or that there is "too much too soon," most particularly for primary-school children. In a preliminary step to resolve this problem Stephen McCary (1976) presented 800 university students with a list of 100 sex-related terms and concepts (such as masturbation, menstruation, coitus, and orgasm), asking them to indicate the ages at which they had first heard the terms defined or had had the experience. It is known, of course, that sex information for the young is most often supplied by peer group members. Further, most of it is erroneous (and much harmful), or is tinged with guilt and shame. The findings of the McCary study, along with the findings of a follow-up study of 43 students at a Baptist university (S. P. McCary 1978), offer specific guidelines for the age at which students would best benefit from specific blocks of sex information. It would seem prudent to present the information in a formal sex-education program a year or so earlier than the students ordinarily learn it from their peers, thus allowing them to learn it accurately and in a wholesome atmosphere. Making these determinations is hampered, of course, by the sly tricks that memory plays, particularly in such emotion-charged areas as sexuality. But few schools or parents will permit the questioning of young children about sexual matters. Until this obstacle is overcome, recall of childhood experience must suffice. Information supplied by this and similar studies will go far in establishing the foundation for sex-education programs designed for specific age groups.

In school sex instruction, there is some danger that an unconscious cultural bias might filter into the program. Public-school courses are likely to reflect the most conservative ethical values of the community. Otherwise the courses will be condemned as immoral. In most parts of the country the prevailing ethic is Christian. But is this bias fair to other groups whose attitudes toward marriage, family, and sex may differ in many respects from Christian attitudes (Kushner 1976)? One can only sympathize with those school administrators whose programs and facilities are good, yet who are harassed by noisy groups (not necessarily parents) within the community whose motivations in opposing sex education may be misunderstanding, fear, ignorance, opportunism, or genuine concern.

Today the question of public-school sex education has become academic, the courts having ruled that such programs do not violate the constitutional rights of those parents who oppose them, and that a school district can conduct the courses in the interest of health, welfare, and morality ("Sex in the News" 1970). We do not always know what school children feel about sitting through sex-education courses. But their older brothers and sisters are emphatic—almost unanimously so—in wanting the programs in their high school and college curricula (Conley & O'Rourke 1973; Dearth 1974; Francoeur & Hendrixson 1980).

A particularly dangerous—and groundless—argument against sex education is that human sexuality is a simple phenomenon that one learns naturally. Formal instruction is therefore seen by its opponents as unnecessary because the presentation of factual information about sex might destroy its "mystery" and "sacredness," decreasing one's chances of future enjoyment of it (Vincent 1969).

Of all the arguments against school sex education, perhaps the most valid concerns the qualifications of those teaching it. Few institutions train people specifically to teach this most sensitive subject. Indeed, many of those teaching sex-education courses receive no special training beforehand. Consequently they are often forced to obtain much of their source material from nonprofessional sources. Because of personal embarrassment, some teach in a mechanical manner, or perhaps avoid subjects of real importance to their students. Certainly the attitudes, values, and behaviors of teachers towards their students and the subject matter can be as important as the content of the material taught (Dager & Harper 1959; Dager *et al.* 1966; Francoeur & Hendrixson 1980). Some teachers inject religious prejudice and personal guilt into their sex instruction, which probably does the students more harm than good.

Yet whatever the personal shortcomings of sex-education teachers, the implied suggestion in many arguments against sex education is particularly unfair—namely, that the instructor might be an unethical, perhaps morally depraved creature intent upon seducing the innocent from the path of virtue. The fact is that any teacher's ethical values are bound to filter into any subject that he or she teaches, whether it be sex education, mathematics, or literature. Imperfect sex-education programs and instruction are not limited to the public school. Private and parochial schools, colleges, universities, and medical schools often have equally ineffective programs, and for the same reasons that public schools do.

Sources of Sex Information

Some interesting relationships between the primary source of sex information and its accuracy emerged from investigations into the sex-education background of college students, conducted on the campus of a major southern university. When physicians and ministers gave the initial instruction, there was no relationship, either negative or positive, between source and accuracy. When the student's peer group or parents provided the information, there was an important *negative* correlation between source and accuracy. The only significant positive relationship involved those students whose instruction had come from formal classroom coursework or books of authenticated accuracy (Barfield & McCary 1969; S. P. McCary 1976).

Gagnon (1965) found that an overwhelming majority of both his male and female subjects expressed a preference for parents as the primary source of sex information for the young. About 90% of the subjects indicated a preference for the mother as a major source; 80% indicated the father; 60%, the family doctor; 40%, the school; 25%, the church; 25%, books; 10%, siblings. Only 5% preferred friends as a primary source. But preference and reality contrasted rather sharply. In actual fact friends had been the primary source of sex information for 53% of the male subjects and 35% of the women in this study. Mothers had been a source for 46% of the women, but for only 18% of the men. Fathers had been a source for 25% of the men, but almost no woman in the study had received any sex instruction from her father. This problem was highlighted in a 1977 Gallup poll that showed "getting along with and communicating with parents" to be the number two problem of U.S. teen-agers, ranking only slightly behind "drug use and abuse."

When mothers give sex instruction to their children, it is limited almost exclusively to the facts of menstruation and pregnancy. Details of intercourse, prostitution, and contraception, as examples, are much more frequently learned from peer groups than from any other source (Gagnon 1965; S. P. McCary 1976, 1978). School had been a source of sex information for only 8% of the adult men and 9% of the adult women surveyed in one study. But it had been a source for 38% of the adolescents (both boys and girls) surveyed, indicating that schools have assumed an increasingly important role in sex education during the past generation or so (Abelson *et al.* 1970).

A more recent study at a major northeastern university has provided results that generally support these findings. Bennett and Dickinson (1980) found their sample of college students preferred that parents be the primary source for sex information and sex education. However, most of the students reported that they had not learned about birth control, venereal disease, or sex in general from their parents. Instead, these students reported that their teachers had provided most of the information about birth control and venereal disease, while their peers had provided most of the information about sex in general. Media sources such as television, books, magazines, and movies, though making a lesser contribution, were also important sources of information for these students.

Young people are generally dissatisfied with the sex information available at both home and school. Parents, they feel, are frequently too embarrassed or uninformed to talk openly and meaningfully about sex, whereas information offered at school tends to be meaningless, sketchy, or ill-timed. Over 70% of adolescent boys and girls report that their parents cannot talk to them freely about sex (Sorenson 1973). But it would appear that young people are just as nervous about talking with their parents about sex as their parents are in talking with them. In fact, most people do not like to think of their parents as having any interest in sex. Parents primarily teach (or preach) the negative aspects of sex to their children: premarital coitus is wrong; premarital pregnancy, a disaster; masturbation, unhealthy;

Formal sex education program for unwed mothers. (Erika Stone)

VD, an ever-present danger. Children therefore deduce that sex is a distasteful and unpleasant thing for their parents, and that they engage in any sexual activity only minimally (Baron & Byrne 1977). This view apparently transcends adolescence because college students also tend to underestimate their parents' past and present sexual activities (Pocs & Godow 1977).

Which Source Is Best?

To argue whether or not sex education should be taught in our schools is actually futile, for it has always been taught in the schools, one way or another. The real question is whether sex is to be taught in the schoolyard or the schoolroom (J. L. McCary 1971). Further, as matters now stand, children have already acquired much of their sex education by the time they are of school age. Most of their sexual attitudes, or at least the foundations for them, are to a large degree formed by the time they are 3 or 4 (Auerbeck *et al.* 1976).

Factual sex information, even when presented in the schoolroom, has usually come too late to be of maximum use. By age 10, 69% of boys already know about pregnancy, 57% know about sexual intercourse, and 43% about masturbation. By age 14, almost all boys (92%–100%) know about these topics; most of them also know about prostitution. Two of the largest areas of ignorance concern contraception and VD (S. P. McCary 1976; Ramsey 1943; Thornburg 1970).

A study conducted at the University of North Carolina (Malcolm 1971) of the sexual habits and accuracy of sex knowledge of women students revealed that of the sexually active women, over 25% failed to answer *any* question correctly, only 59% answered half the questions correctly, and none answered all of them correctly. Of the less sexually active women, 80% answered half the questions correctly and 9% answered all correctly. The researchers were led to conclude that the more a women knows about sexual matters, the more responsible she is in her sexual behavior.

Parents concerned about their children's exposure to explicit sexual information should study the findings of the President's Commission on Obscenity and Pornography. When parents are their children's major source of sex information, the youngsters are not likely to learn about sex through pornography—or, for that matter, to be pornography patrons later on. Another important study, involving 600 teen-agers, showed that if a young-ster "obtained his sex knowledge from parents or adults with whom a positive identification exists, there appeared to be less tendency toward involvement in promiscuity" (Deschin 1963).

Those children whose primary source of sex information is friends are frequently exposed to pornography as part of their haphazard sex education (Elias 1970). By age 15 approximately 50% of all boys and girls report having seen pictures of or having read about at least five or more different forms of sexual activity, including sexual intercourse, oral-genital activity, homosexual behavior, and sadomasochistic acts. Well over half the 35 state departments of education studied by the President's Commission reported the belief that sensible and effective sex education would reduce the students' interest in pornography (Quality Educ. Dev. 1970).

Despite arguments to the contrary, the incidence of premarital sexual activity does not increase because of school sex education. In fact, quite the opposite appears to be true. Luffman and Parcel (1979), in studying the effects of a sex-education course on the attitudes of eighth-graders, found that these students developed more permissive and accepting attitudes toward the idea of sexual behavior in committed relationships. At the same time they developed less tolerant attitudes toward sexual behavior in less committed, casual relationships. Stephen McCary's study (1976) shows that college students whose concepts of sexuality were shaped in the classroom and from factual written material remain more conventional in their sexual attitudes and behavior than those students whose information came from such nonacademic sources as peers, doctors, parents, siblings, and church. In fact, marriage and family courses in which specific sex information is presented have proved to be a positive factor in reducing both divorce and premarital pregnancy rates (Quality Educ. Dev. 1970).

Sex education at the university level is no less valuable in its positive effects. A recent study of one such course (Gunderson 1976) demonstrated that, as expected, it had significantly enhanced the students' information. The course also acted to reduce sexual guilt, create a more tolerant attitude toward the sexual attitudes and behavior of others, and bring about a greater sense of responsibility for their own sexual behavior and the possible consequences of it. Further, male students tended to abandon the double standard, and female students, to reject it. Rather than weakening traditional moral standards, the course appeared to strengthen acceptance of monogamy and fidelity. It strengthened, as well, the view that premarital coitus should be reserved for persons whom one loves or with whom at least a strong emotional involvement exists.

The overall sexual activity of the students did not increase as a result of the course, except for the incidence of masturbation and response to pornography among women. Married students of the class (but not the unmarried ones) reported that their sexual activity had increased, primarily in greater experimentation with such extracoital activity as oral-genital contact and heightened response to pornography. Incidence of extramarital coitus, anal intercourse, and homosexual behavior *decreased* among the married subjects.

Other investigations of formal sex education (Godow & LaFave 1979; Rees & Zimmerman 1974; Zuckerman *et al.* 1976) have yielded similar results. Sex-education courses significantly shifted students' sexual *attitudes* in a more liberal direction, yet their premarital *behavior* remained unchanged. By contrast, informal sex education from such nonacademic sources as the peer group seems to prompt a greater incidence of premarital coitus because of peer pressure to try to appear "grown up" (Spanier 1976).

Sex information need not, of course, be obtained in a setting as formal as the schoolroom to be accurate. In one study, young unmarried patients at Yale Univeristy Hospital, who were pregnant for the first time and whose average age was 17, were separated into matched groups of equal numbers. One group was given instruction in the human reproductive systems and in birth-control methods. The second group received no such information. Within a year, 57% of those in the latter group reappeared at the hospital, pregnant a second time. By contrast, only 7% of the group that had been given sex instruction had a second pregnancy before they married (Guttmacher 1969; Rubin 1968).

In recent years the medical profession has become increasingly aware that physicians are in need of sex education and that the responsibility for providing it rests with the medical schools. A short time ago only 3 medical schools of the 110 in the U.S. included human sexuality in their curricula (Calderone 1971). Now almost all have done so (Lief 1974). Recent surveys indicate that about 80% of medical schools now have formal instruction in subject-matter areas related to human sexuality. However, only one-third of medical schools in the United States provide organized course material in the reproductive sciences (Lloyd 1980).

Excluding that part of human sexuality related to physiology, endocrinology and genetics, the average American physician may well be less knowledgeable about human sexuality than his patients (Sheppe 1976). Indeed, physicians often lack sufficient training or expertise to treat their patients effectively (Gregg & Ismach 1980). Yet it is typically to the physician that people first turn when there are sexual problems. Nearly 50% of the students canvassed at a Philadelphia medical school in 1961 thought that masturbation could lead to mental illness—and 20% of the faculty were of the same opinion (Greenbank 1961). Fortunately, only 15% of both female and male medical students today still believe that certain mental illnesses are caused by masturbation. But what about the patients of *those* budding physicians (Lief & Ebert 1974)?

Clinical psychologists, professional religious counselors, and social workers are often no better trained or informed than physicians. Thus it appears that, despite advances made in professional training in recent years, parents and young people cannot always rely on these professionals for the most up-to-date information about sexuality. These circumstances reinforce the argument that sex education should be offered in the schools, should begin early, and should continue through high school (Commission on Obscenity 1970).

Sex education for the mentally and physically handicapped has been even more neglected (or avoided) than for the nonhandicapped population, no doubt inflicting additional problems on already burdened minds and bodies. This need, however, has increasingly captured the attention of special-education and mental-health workers in recent years (Halstead *et al.* 1976; Spurr 1976). Fortunately, endorsement of such sex-education programs now appears much more frequently in professional literature than in the past.

A Suggested Approach to Sex Education

Van Emde Boas (1980) has provided a list of "ten commandments" for those parents who strive to provide sex education for their children. While this list of commandments may not be exhaustive, it provides a framework to consider issues pertinent to the sex-education process. A reworded version of Van Emde Boas' list follows:

1. Do not isolate sex education from other educational experiences and realize that sex-education begins in infancy.

2. Realize that our skin and our hands are perhaps our most important sensual and sexual organs.
3. Do not inhibit or negate open, spontaneous sex expressions in children.
4. Answer truthfully all questions posed by children, but do not answer in such detail as to go beyond their comprehension or understanding.
5. Realize that children learn through modeling and from real-life examples better than they do from written or spoken words.
6. Realize that sex education in the schools can only be an extension of the sex education provided in the home.
7. Realize that teaching the appropriate relational and emotional components of sexuality is as important as teaching the biological components.
8. Teach your children that sexual manipulation and exploitation of others is as reprehensible as other forms of manipulation or exploitation.
9. Teach your children that intimate and caring relationships are more meaningful and satisfying than casual and superficial sexual encounters.
10. Do not underestimate the importance of having discussions with your children about birth control matters.

To be well rounded, a sex-education course should be constructed to include several premises. First, dispassionate, accurate information about the physiological and psychological aspects of sex should be presented to all. Then the Judeo-Christian traditions within which we live should be understood and dealt with sensibly in the framework of present-day society. Relative freedom of expression in sexual matters is justifiable because of individual differences in sexual preferences. There are few absolutes in this world, and only bigots establish an inflexible code of sexual morality. Generally speaking, the consequences of a given act upon the individual or society are the best criteria by which to judge its morality (Kirkendall 1961a).

The only way our society is going to achieve proper sexual stability and mental health, which are undisputed requirements for maturity, is to instigate and persevere with a sound sex education for everyone. This goal means that those who are in a position to instruct would do well to admit freely to what they do not know, at the same time teaching that which they do know to be the truth. They must educate, not indoctrinate; teach facts, not fallacies; formulate a code of ethics, not preach strict self-denial; be objective, not subjective; be democratic, not autocratic; and seek knowledge, not emotionally biased constructs. This goal is difficult because most people have grown up in a culture filled with sexual ignorance and maladjustment, and with essentially negative attitudes toward sex. Richard Starnes in the *New York World Telegram and Sun* summed up this problem fairly well with his comment: "Never in history has a nation talked so much about prudery from a basically horizontal position."

The criteria for sex education as set forth by SIECUS and by the American Association of Sex Educators, Counselors, and Therapists

(AASECT) are excellent. Under the guidance of its founder and former executive director, Patricia Schiller, AASECT has become the recognized national professional organization for setting standards of training and certification of both sex educators and therapists. Application forms and details of qualification standards set for candidates aspiring to certification are available from the organization.* Mindful of the goals set by such organizations as SIECUS and AASECT, this book has been prepared with the specific purpose of helping its readers acquire a better knowledge of themselves and their sexuality. It is hoped, in addition, that the book will encourage readers to prepare others whom they teach—directly or indirectly—for a healthy, well-adjusted sex life.

Summary

Sexuality is part of our heritage from birth. Yet human beings do not know about sexuality from instinct; they must *learn* about the three main aspects of sexuality—the emotional, the physiological, and the psychological. At present, however, much of this sex education is unconscious, picked up at random from parents and peers, by what they say or don't say. This leads to confusion, ignorance, and guilt. Some individuals have gone to great lengths to repress this vital part of their existence. A proper sex education can aid in adjusting to life, and in breaking this cycle of ignorance and guilt.

The basis for many of our sexual beliefs, whether good or bad, correct or incorrect, is found in the teachings we receive in early life. These teachings, particularly those in history and religion, reflect concepts thousands of years old that may need to be reexamined in light of present circumstances. Sexual fascists, those with rigid views and inflexible attitudes, perpetuate this ignorance-guilt cycle, adding to the anxiety that exists for many people in our society. An open, understanding, and sensitive approach is needed to overcome the biases and bigotry about human sexuality. It is important to study the differences between cultures and to understand them as just that—differences—rather than putting strong value judgments on varied sexual behaviors.

Sex must be guilt-free in order to be really satisfying. Formal sex education programs are important ways to help people relieve their sexual anxieties and sexual guilt. Such programs, when presented by qualified and emotionally aware individuals in a thorough, objective manner, can help establish healthy attitudes and values. It falls upon such programs to carry

* AASECT, 600 Maryland Ave., S.W., Washington, D.C. 20024.

the responsibility, because other sources of sex information are inadequate, wrong, or come too late. Parents, teachers, physicians, and religious sources all have failed to provide the sex information young people need.

This chapter presented a sound sex education program, including physiological, psychological, and religious values. It provides a realistic alternative through which information can be given, information that is both relevant and appropriate to the educational and emotional development of young people.

Annotated Bibliography

Calderone, Mary S. and Johnson, Eric W. *The family book about sexuality.* New York: Harper and Row, 1981.

> This creatively written sex education text for the family covers all significant topics related to human sexuality and relationships, including giving and receiving love, sexuality and aging, marriage and family planning, variant behavior, and sex education programs. Important features include a bibliography of additional family readings and a listing of family planning and counseling services.

Clark, LeMon. *Where do babies come from? And how to keep them there!* Hicksville, New York: Exposition Press, 1978.

> This book addresses a wide range of topics related to teen-age sexuality including puberty and accompanying emotional and physical changes, masturbation, petting, nonmarital intercourse, marriage-divorce, birth control, abortion, venereal disease, and the importance of sex education. This sensitive and sensible book dispenses valuable information for teens and parents alike.

Comfort, Alex and Comfort, Jane. *The facts of love.* New York: Crown, 1979.

> This straightforward and sensitive book for young people covers the major topics of love and sex. The authors provide good treatment of difficult topics such as sexual morality, homosexuality, alcohol and drugs, pornography, venereal disease, and rape.

Kaplan, Helen Singer. *Making sense of sex.* New York: Simon and Schuster, 1979.

> Free of technical jargon, this book presents up-to-date, honest treatment of human sexuality for young people. Topics include sexual biology, sexual development, forms of sexual response, sexual problems, reproduction, birth control, venereal diseases, and love and sex.

McBride, Will and Fleischhauer-Hardt, Helga. *Show-Me!* New York: St. Martin's Press, 1975.

> An effective sex education tool for parents and teachers for use with children, this book presents basic sex information via explicit photographs accompanied by explanatory text.

Morrison, E. S., Starks, K., Hyndman, C. and Ronzis, N. *Growing up sexual.* New York: D. Van Nostrand, 1980.

> Based on anonymous autobiographical papers by students, this unique book tells in students' own words their feelings, thoughts, and experiences of sexual development. Topics include learning about sex, first sexual experiences, family styles, sex roles, self-image, contraceptive use, sexual exploitation, and personal sexual values. The young person particularly would benefit from this book, which has special applicability as a sex education tool.

Otto, H. A. (Ed.) *The new sex education.* Chicago: Follett, 1978.

> This volume is a comprehensive survey of the field of sex education by 28 leading authorities. The book examines current approaches to sex education, professional issues, clinics, and churches. Though intended as a source volume and text for sex educators, this book will also be of interest to the general public.

Rosenzweig, Norman and Pearsall, F. Paul (Eds.). *Sex education for the health professional: A curriculum guide.* New York: Grune and Stratton, 1978.

> This book presents the various approaches of leaders in the sex education field as related to the work of health care professionals. The book addresses several professional issues including legislation of sex education, deciding curriculum content, and sex education for special target audiences. Of special value is a table that summarizes audio-visual aids in sex education, their uses and availability.

Schiller, Patricia. *Creative approach to sex education and counseling (2nd ed.).* Chicago: Follett, 1977.

> This book addresses many topics in sex education and counseling including methods and techniques, developing communication skills, and problems in adolescence, marriage, the elderly and the handicapped. Model training programs are discussed as well as age-appropriate curriculum content. Written for the professional, this book would also interest the lay reader.

Smith, Peggy B. Sex education. In *Adolescent pregnancy: Perspectives for the health professional,* ed. P. Smith and D. Mumford. Boston: G. K. Hall, 1980.

> This article discusses the history of sex education and the utilization of schools and parents as sources of sex education. The author addresses the implementation of sex education in schools, important components of teacher training, and problems currently associated with sex education in schools and churches.

Sexual Myths and Fallacies

2

Sexual Physiology and Functioning

Sex Drive

Reproduction and Birth Control

Homosexuality

Sexual Disorders and Sexual Abnormalities: Real and Imagined

Sexual Offenses

. . . and Other Fallacies

When any aspect of the human condition becomes shrouded in ignorance and superstition, myths and fallacies spring up in abundance and obscure the truth. Myths are created to explain the inexplicable, and they persist because they preserve tradition and guard people from anxiety and insecurity; they serve as a shield, no matter how improbable they may be (Pomeroy 1977). They can be perpetrated not only laterally by members of the peer group, but also vertically by authorities in a position to educate.

Beliefs with no foundation in truth are by no means held only by the uneducated and unsophisticated. Highly educated professional people can hold a curious collection of sexual misconceptions. Error thus begets error, and illogical attitudes and information filter through all age, educational, and socioeconomic levels.

Because of the marked expansion and improvement in modern communications and the relative availability of more sexually explicit material, our society has become significantly more informed in sexual matters. People are more willing to reconsider previously unquestioned sexual mythology. At the same time, however, new myths are being created. For example, a few years ago it was erroneously thought that little could be done for those who suffer from sexual problems. Today,

29

as a result of open discussions of sexual dysfunctioning and methods of treatment, many have gone to the other extreme and falsely assume that sex problems can be easily cured by simple tricks (Pomeroy 1977). Once again, accurate sex education is the answer.

This book reflects the vital importance of obtaining valid sex information and teaching it in an honest, direct way. The material in the following chapters, presented in as open, objective a manner as possible, but with sensitivity, may help dispel much of the mythology that clouds the realities of sex. Some of the more common sexual myths and fallacies are listed below. The numbers shown after each one indicate the pages on which related facts can be found.

Sexual Physiology and Functioning

Nocturnal emissions ("wet dreams") indicate a sexual disorder. p. 80

Women do not experience nocturnal orgasms. pp. 369–370, 387

Women ejaculate, as men do. p. 93

Ejaculation and orgasm in men are one and the same phenomenon. p. 80

Simultaneous orgasms are more satisfactory than those experienced separately and are, moreover, necessary for sexual compatibility. p. 272

Sexologists are in agreement that there is a distinct difference between a vaginal and clitoral orgasm. pp. 255, 259, 519

During menstruation, women should not engage in sports; nor should they take a bath, shower, or shampoo their hair. p. 109

Menstruation begins earlier in girls living in the tropics than in girls living in cooler climates. p. 104

Lower animals menstruate just as humans do. p. 53

The absence of the hymen proves that a girl is not a virgin. p. 94

The presence of the hymen is positive evidence that a girl is a virgin. p. 94

The best health is enjoyed by those who abstain from sex. p. 281

Excellence of athletic performance is reduced by sexual intercourse the night before or the day of any athletic competition. p. 68

Diminishing function of the sex glands signals the end of the sex life of both men and women. pp. 322–325

Impotence in older men is always the result of physical factors. pp. 322, 325–326

The size of a man's penis can be judged by the size of his hands and feet. p. 68

A large penis is of great importance to a woman's sexual gratification. p. 69

The man with a large penis is more sexually potent than the man with a small penis. p. 69

Because of its calorie content, semen, if swallowed during fellatio, is fattening. p. 68

Sexual intercourse should be avoided during pregnancy. p. 130

The older man has no advantages over a younger one insofar as satisfactory coitus is concerned. p. 324

The uterus "sucks up" seminal fluid ejaculated into the vagina. p. 267

A woman's repeated sexual experiences with one man will leave a mark on a child later fathered by another man. p. 142

The purpose of menstruation is for the body to rid itself of an unfertilized egg. p. 106

If menstruation begins at an early age, menopause will occur early. p. 113

Regular douching is necessary to keep the vagina clean. p. 308

A woman does not need a Pap smear test until she has had a child or has reached middle age. p. 559

Breast development can be altered through exercise or use of salves. p. 166

Humans can get "hung up" (*i.e.*, experience *penis captivus*) during sexual intercourse. p. 72

Sex Drive

Each individual is allotted just so many sexual experiences; when they are used up, sexual activity is finished for that person. pp. 113–114, 211

Blacks have a greater sex drive than whites. p. 327

Alcohol is a sexual stimulant. pp. 11, 228

Marijuana is an aphrodisiac. p. 230

Sterilization reduces the sex drive of a man or woman. pp. 284, 287

Castration always destroys the sex drive completely. p. 287

The total or partial removal of the prostate reduces a man's sexual enjoyment, and will ultimately destroy his sexual capabilities. pp. 325, 567–568

Menopause or hysterectomy terminates a woman's sex life. pp. 322–323

Sexual desire and ability decrease markedly after the age of 40 to 50. p. 322*ff.*

Muscular men have the largest penises and make the best lovers. p. 691

A poor sexual adjustment in marriage inevitably spells its doom. p. 360

Reproduction and Birth Control

There is an absolutely "safe" period for sexual intercourse in which coitus cannot cause impregnation. pp. 88, 309–310

Vasectomies are 100% successful as a birth-control technique. p. 286

A couple must have simultaneous climaxes if conception is to occur. p. 295

A woman can become pregnant only through coitus or artificial insemination. pp. 127–128

Urination by a woman after coitus, or having sexual intercourse in a standing position will prevent pregnancy. pp. 246–248

Abortion, whether legal or criminal, is always dangerous. pp. 291–292

A woman may become pregnant if she swallows seminal fluid. p. 220

There must be two acts of sexual intercourse to produce twins, three for triplets, and so on. pp. 160–163

Sperm from one testicle will produce males, and from the other, females; or the ova from one ovary will produce males, and from the other, females. pp. 41, 127

The woman determines the sex of the child. pp. 41, 127

A woman's diet during pregnancy has a bearing on the sex of the child. p. 41

Scientists agree that the sex of a child to be conceived is a matter of pure chance, and nothing can be done to change the odds. pp. 75–76

A seventh-month baby has a better chance of survival than an eighth-month baby. p. 148

An unborn child can be "marked." p. 142

"Virgin birth" (parthenogenesis) does not occur in humans or animals. pp. 127–128

The birth-control pill will eventually cause a wide variety of ills in any woman using it for any length of time. p. 304

Humans and infrahuman animals can crossbreed. p. 143

Homosexuality

Homosexuals are a menace to society. pp. 456–458, 474–476

People are either totally homosexual or totally heterosexual. pp. 446–450

Childhood involvement with an adult homophile is an important causative factor in the individual's later becoming a homosexual. pp. 459–460

Men (and women) are homosexual because they were "born that way." p. 451

Hormonal imbalance is the chief cause of homosexuality. p. 453

Oral-genital sex between a man and a woman indicates homosexual tendencies. pp. 219, 372

Because of their sexual tendencies, homosexuals are more likely than heterosexuals to be disloyal to their country or cause. p. 458

The man who enjoys having his nipples stimulated has suppressed homosexual desires. pp. 206, 216

Any lesbian would prefer a man, if he were a "real man" and if he used the right technique. p. 455

Most prostitutes are lesbians. p. 433

Homosexuals are usually identifiable by their appearance. p. 454

Sexual Disorders and Sexual Abnormalities: Real and Imagined

Frequent masturbation has been known to lead to lunacy. pp. 22, 209–210

Masturbation can cause a number of physical manifestations, including warts, hair in the palms of the hands, pimples, acne, and, ultimately, impotence. pp. 210–211

Masturbation is a practice restricted almost exclusively to men. pp. 209, 367–369

Masturbation is a habit of the young and immature; its practice typically ceases after marriage. p. 211

Any person infected with gonorrhea will develop symptoms within seven days. p. 543

Vaginal-penile intercouse is the only normal method of having sex relations. pp. 218–220, 365ff.

Women who have strong sex drives, come to easy climax, and are capable of multiple orgasms are nymphomaniacs. p. 429

Nymphomaniacs and satyromaniacs abound in our society. pp. 429, 430

If one partner desires sex more often than the other, nothing can be done to make the couple sexually more compatible. pp. 218–220, 256

Premature ejaculation is due to physical circumstances. pp. 512, 513

Oral-genital sex is perverted and animalistic. pp. 219–220

Circumcision makes it difficult for a man to control ejaculation. p. 512

A transvestite and a transsexual are the same, and both are homosexuals. pp. 407, 408

Sexual Offenses

Sex offenders cannot be cured and are likely to continue their unacceptable behavior for the rest of their lives. pp. 413–414, 473

Persons who commit a series of minor sex crimes will quite likely become involved in more serious sex criminality if they are not arrested. pp. 404, 471–472

Being oversexed is a primary characteristic of sex offenders. p. 472

The typical sex molester of children is aggressive and potentially homicidal. p. 412

Sex offenders are typically unreligious. p. 413

Sexual molesters of children are usually over 65 years of age. pp. 412, 472–473

Pornography has a corruptive effect on people's minds and behavior, especially children's. pp. 415–416, 471

Pornography stimulates people to commit criminal sex acts. pp. 416–417

Pornography and obscenity lead to sexual excess and sexual acting out. pp. 417–719

Excessive exposure to pornographic material leads to an ever-increasing craving for pornography. pp. 417–418, 421

Married couples may legally engage in any type of sexual activity they mutually agree upon. p. 468

. . . and Other Fallacies

Physicians are generally well trained and emotionally equipped to deal with their patients' sexual problems. p. 22

The virginity of the woman is an important factor in the success of a marriage. pp. 344, 356–357

Nature compensates for the number of males killed during a time of war. p. 142

Since the human ovum is fertilized in the vagina, douching is a particularly effective contraceptive technique. pp. 88, 98, 307–308

Heart patients need not worry that sexual activity will be detrimental to their health, so long as they remain physically inactive and quiet during coitus. p. 332

Today's young adults are "going wild" sexually. pp. 346–347

Sex education has no place in our schools because it is a Communist plot to destroy the country from within and because it leads to: (1) sexual acting-out behavior; (2) a rise in promiscuity; (3) an increase in premarital pregnancy; etc. p. 14*ff*.

Annotated Bibliography

Ellis, Albert and Wolfe, Janet. The vaginal-clitoral orgasm controversy re-examined. In *The new sex education*, ed. H. Otto. Chicago: Follett, 1978.

This article examines the controversial notion that women experience both clitoral and vaginal orgasm types. The authors review literature relevant to the myth of vaginal-clitoral orgasm, discuss its bases and implications for sexual satisfaction, and present an argument against the use of terms "vaginal" and "clitoral" to refer to orgasm in women.

Hite, Shere. *The Hite report: A nationwide study on female sexuality.* New York: Macmillan, 1976.

This book reports results of a national survey of female sexuality, exploring women's sexual attitudes, feelings, experiences, and behavior. Topics include masturbation, orgasm, intercourse, sexual slavery, the sexual revolution, and aging and sexuality. Dispelling many myths related to female sexuality, this book would be of interest to the general reader.

Kuhn, Margaret E. Sexual myths surrounding the aged. In *Sex and the life cycle*, ed. W. Oaks, G. Melchiode, and I. Ficher. New York: Grune and Stratton, 1976.

This chapter examines the problem of agism in society and attempts to debunk several myths related to sexuality and the aged. This article would enlighten the lay reader as well as the health care professional.

McCary, James Leslie. *Sexual myths and fallacies.* New York: Van Nostrand, 1971.

This book presents frank discussion of 83 common misconceptions related to a wide variety of topics in human sexuality, including sexual physiology, sexual functioning, the sex drive, reproduction and birth control, homosexuality, sexual disorders, and sexual offenses. The author attempts to dispel sexual myths by presenting factual information taken from recent medical and psychological literature. This book would likely lead to increased understanding of human sexuality.

Masters, William H. and Johnson, Virginia E. *Homosexuality in perspective.* Boston: Little, Brown, 1979.

Based on the authors' research and clinical experience, this book attempts to dispel the many myths surrounding homosexuality and to establish a better understanding of homosexual behavior. The authors discuss treatment of sexual dysfunctions among homosexuals and report results of treatment of conversion or reversion. This book will be of interest to the lay reader as well as the professional.

Pietropinto, A. and Simenauer, J. *Beyond the male myth: A nationwide survey.* New York: Times Books, 1977.

Based on results of a major survey of male sexuality, this book reveals the sexual views, preferences, attitudes, feelings, and experiences of the contemporary American male. The authors attempt to explode several prevalent myths related to male sexuality.

Zilbergeld, B. *Male sexuality: A guide to sexual fulfillment.* Boston: Little, Brown and Company, 1978.

Honest and forthright, this book deals with many of the physical and emotional aspects of sex for men. Some topics covered include learning about sex, touching, masturbation, virginity and sexual abstinence, male sexual dysfunctions, male sexuality and aging, and medical and sex problems. This book will appeal to men of all ages.

Part Two
The Human Sexual System

Basic to the understanding of human sexuality is an accurate knowledge of sexual physiology and functioning—in effect, how the male and female sexual systems work. The process of sexual maturation, from prenatal life to the change of life, the creation of a child, and the physiology of sexual excitation are all fascinating aspects of human existence.

Chapter 3 discusses the effects of the endocrine system—hormones—on pre- and postnatal sexual development. The similarities and differences in the male and female sexual systems are then detailed in Chapters 4 and 5. Chapter 6 is devoted to the two dramatic occurrences in a woman's reproductive life, the menarche and menopause, and the male counterpart to the latter, the climacteric. Finally, the process of creating a new being, its prenatal development, and the birth process are described in Chapter 7.

Because mythology flourishes in these areas of human sexuality—especially in the subjects of menstruation and childbirth—a special effort has been made to dispel some of it. Interspersed in Part Two are some common fallacies pertaining to the subject matter, together with the facts refuting them.

The Role of the Endocrine System

Sexual maturation and reproduction, as well as sexual desire and function, are chiefly under the control of the glands of the endocrine system. These structures are called **ductless glands** or **glands of internal secretion.** Their products, known as **hormones,** are not secreted at the body's surface through ducts, as are saliva and sweat, for example. They enter directly in the bloodstream. Hormones are chemical messengers, sending information to specific organs in the body sensitive to their actions.

There are six known glands of internal secretory function,* in addition to the testes in the male and the ovaries in the female—and, during pregnancy, the placenta. Despite the minute quantities secreted into the bloodstream, hormones have profound effects on the body as a whole or on a very specific function of the body. Levels of hormones are maintained by sensitive control systems. Because they are excreted with the urine, their levels in the circulating blood tend to be held within loose boundaries, although there can be periods of dramatic changes within short periods of time (Schwartz *et al.* 1980).

* Pituitary, thyroid, parathyroid, pancreas, adrenal. The hypothalamus, which is part of the brain, also functions as a gland because it produces hormones.

39

The brain also exerts a vital influence on the coordination (or dysfunction) of human emotions and sexual behavior. The **cortex** or forebrain controls such superior functions as thought, memory, and ideation. It also controls motor impulse and action—in particular, voluntary behavior. In general, the higher the species of animal, the less the dependence upon rigid, stereotyped mating sequences resulting from hormonal influences.

The **mesencephalon** or midbrain, lying below the cortex, functions as the coordinating center of such behavior as feeding, sexual activity, and aggressive behavior. Within the midbrain lies the **hypothalamus,** which appears to function as a form of biological timing device. Interacting with the endocrine glands, it controls the onset of puberty, fertility cycles, and sexual arousal. Hormonal or electrical stimulation of the hypothalamus— whether natural or artificial—has a dramatic impact on emotional reaction, including sexual response. Clearly, then, well-coordinated interplay between the emotional impulses generated in the hypothalamus and the behavioral impulses generated by the cortex is essential to a well-ordered and satisfying sex life (Barclay 1971a).

Early Development of the Male and Female Genitalia

In very early prenatal life, the presence of certain hormones bring about the changes, or differentiation, of the embryonic sex-cell mass into female or male **genitalia** (internal and external sexual or reproductive organs). At puberty, other hormones are responsible for causing the individual to mature sexually, to become capable of functioning as a woman or man.

Despite what many people think, men and women are not vastly different creatures. Even the sexual systems, where the primary differences between male and female lie, are quite similar. From early embryonic through mature stages of human development, there are marked likenesses in both structure and function of the two systems. The completely developed genitalia of the adult man and woman maintain homologous (similar in embryologic origin) but modified structures and have complementary functions.

The development of the human sexual system is quite complicated. The genitalia of both sexes originate from the same anatomical structure or cell mass. In the early days of the embryonic stage—the first eight weeks after conception—the reproductive system appears to be merely an undifferentiated (structurally indistinguishable) genital thickening on the epithelium (posterior outer layer) of the embryonic body cavity. The differentiation into male or female results from hormonal signals initiated by the special chromosomal pattern established in the embryo at conception.

Although every ovum produced in the female bears only an X chromosome, each sperm cell produced in the male contains either one X (female) or one Y (male) chromosome. In a unique way, these sperm containing X- and Y-bearing chromosomes are produced in equivalent numbers. Of the approximately 200 million sperm contained in an average ejaculate, only one will penetrate and fertilize the female ovum or egg. If an X-bearing sperm fertilizes the ovum, an XX, or female, child is conceived; a Y-bearing sperm will produce an XY, or male child. Thus, the male germ cell is the sex determinant of the offspring.

Development of the Internal Genitalia

In their early formative periods, the **gonads** and **ducts** (internal sex organs) of both sexes follow an identical course of development and are sexually indistinguishable. Most of the structures in the embryonic reproductive system either disappear, degenerate, or are replaced by new structures long before the end of fetal life (Fig. 3.1). During the undifferentiated period, a gonad, or genital gland, originates from a genital ridge, which develops from the early epithelial cell mass. From the gonad of each embryo develop two systems of ducts, the **wolffian** and **müllerian,** before the true sex is established. These primitive genital ducts are the forerunners of specific sexual structures. Thus, all mammals in early embryonic life are bipotential since they have both sets of ducts. Under hormonal influence, however, the wolffian ducts will evolve into the male genitalia, and the müllerian, into the female.

The embryo's internal sexual transformation, first observable about six weeks after conception, starts with the differentiation of the gonad into male **testes** or female **ovaries.** Later in life these gonads produce procreative germ cells (the male sperm and the female ova) and are also involved in the hormonal activity of the body. After maleness or femaleness has been established by gonadal development, the ducts of the opposite sex for each embryo remain undeveloped or degenerate.

Development of the External Genitalia

The growth, development, and differentiation of the external genitalia of both sexes are similar to those of the internal genitalia (Fig. 3.2). The external genitalia arise at a common site, located between the umbilical cord and the tail of the embryo. This site becomes the genital tubercle. It is at first an undifferentiated area, then becomes a phalluslike projection that eventually develops into the male or female external sexual organs. In about the fourth week of prenatal life, the front area of the genital tubercle begins to form a vertical groove. This groove produces a separation of the anal pit from the genital ridge, the separating area being known as the primitive perineum.

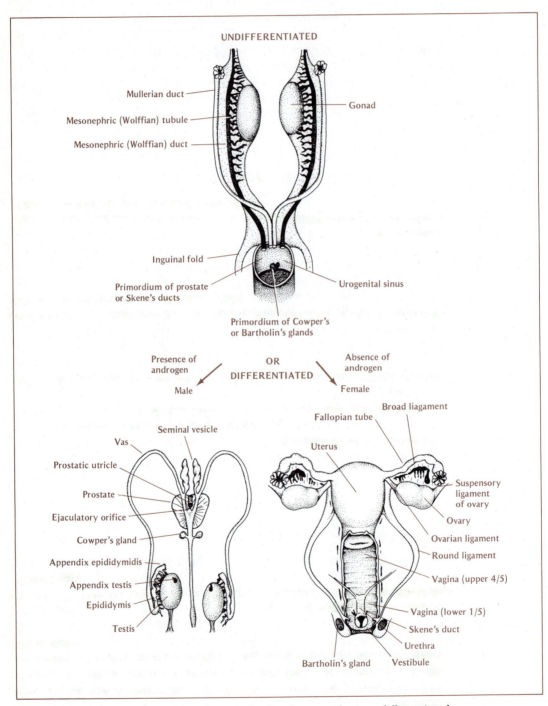

Figure 3.1   Internal male and female genitalia: Development from undifferentiated into differentiated stage.

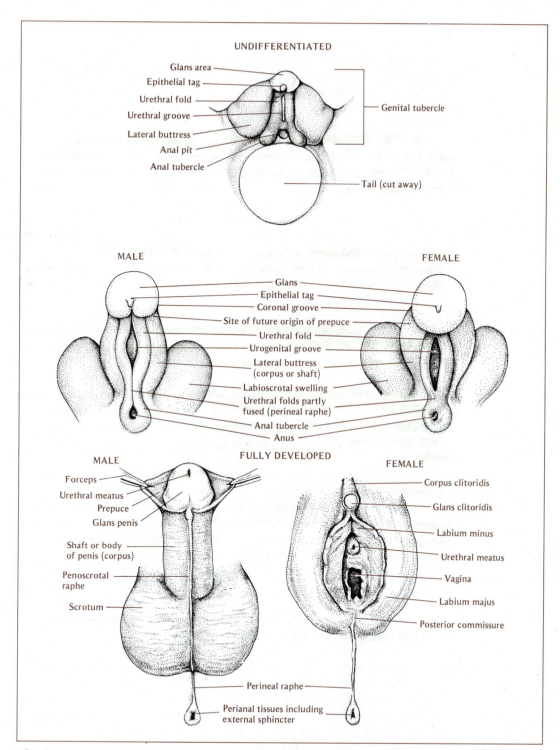

Figure 3.2 External male and female genitalia: Development from undifferentiated into differentiated stage.

In the male, the developing **penis** with its penile urethra parallels the development in the female of vagina, uterus, and intrauterine formations. The external genitalia are first recognizable at about the sixth week of embryonic formation, and for a period of some weeks they remain undifferentiated in appearance.

Two folds or swellings (labioscrotal swellings) develop on the elevated edges (lateral and parallel) of the urethral groove, and differentiate into the female labia majora (outer protective lips of the vaginal region) or into the male scrotal pouch. Once begun, genital development is rapid, and by the fourth month of embryonic life the sex of the fetus is recognizable.

The male embryo reaches a definitive stage about the tenth week when the edges of the urethral groove fold and grow together. The previously open urogenital sinus is now closed and transformed into a tubular urethra within the penis, the fused edge being referred to as the **penoscrotal raphe.** Rudimentary evidence of this fusion appears in the adult male as a scar line on the underside of the penis, running from the anus to the glans, or head of the penis. By the end of the third month the male urethra is fully formed. The prepuce (foreskin) develops over the glans of the penis simultaneously with the formation of the urethra. The outside opening of the urethra at the end of the penis is called the penile meatus.

The female external genitalia are slower to develop than those of the male. A phalluslike tubercle projection slowly develops into the body and glans of the clitoris, the most sensitive organ in the female sexual system. The developing labia majora continue upward to terminate in the mons veneris, or mons pubis, the fatty tissue at the upper exterior of the female genitalia.

In its early stages, the female's urethral groove follows the same pattern of formation as the male's. However, the groove never closes to form a tube. Instead, part of it deepens to fashion the vestibule, the area surrounding and including the opening of the vagina. The urethral folds do not unite in the female, and they gradually develop into the labia minora, the inner protective lips of the vagina.

The female urethra, or bladder outlet, is similar to the prostatic portion of the male urethra. It is just above the vagina, and both open into the vestibule. A prepuce, often referred to as the hood, also develops over the glans of the clitoris. **Vulva** is a collective name used for the whole of the external female genitalia, as is the term **pudendum.** Interestingly, the latter term derives from the Latin *pudere*, "to be ashamed," which clearly reflects the emotional conflict so often associated with sex throughout the centuries.

A peculiar and marked contrast exists in the differentiation process of the male and the female embryo. Although genetic sex is fixed at the instant of fertilization, the sex-related genes do not exert their influence until the fifth or sixth week of prenatal life. Prior to that time, all embryos appear to be morphologically bipotential. At the fifth or sixth week, however, the contrast between the sexes begins. In the genetically male embryo, the masculine sex tissue will develop only under the stimulus of the male hormone **androgen.** Normal development of the male embryonic cell mass, then, depends on the presence of androgen. If for any reason the male embryo is deprived of androgen, the müllerian system regresses with no development of the wolffian system, and the result is **hermaphroditism** (Money 1980b; Money & Ehrhardt, 1972). In the female embryo, however, no such hormonal addition is necessary, as the development of the female sexual structure occurs whether or not the female hormone estrogen is produced (Money 1968a; Salzman 1967).

In those rare cases in which the male embryo is, for one reason or another, deprived of sufficient androgen, the external genitalia do not fully differentiate into penis, foreskin, and scrotum, although the testes and other male internal accessory organs are present. Rather, they have undifferentiated external organs that may appear to be the homologous female sex organs: clitoris, clitoral hood, and labia minora and majora. The infant is assumed to be a girl and is reared as such, and the error may not be discovered until adolescence, when the production of primary sex hormones lead to the development of secondary sex characteristics such as beard growth or voice changes. (A discussion of genetic sex versus gender identity will be found in Chapter 17.)

A genetic female exposed *in utero* to excessive androgen may develop external genitalia that appear masculinized. The androgen is usually from a malfunctioning adrenal cortex. In some cases masculinization is a side effect of synthetic progestin injections given the mother to prevent miscarriage early in pregnancy. The result is a clitoris so enlarged that it is taken for a penis. If the genetic sex is discovered very early in the child's life, feminizing surgery (removal or modification of the enlarged clitoris) and hormonal therapy can bring about the correct sex-role assignment. If not discovered until the child's psychosexuality as a male has been firmly established, then the chromosomal XX person is reared as a male, and any appropriate surgical or hormonal procedures are completed (Money 1968a; Salzman 1967).

The condition in which a person is genetically a male or a female, but has the outward appearance of the opposite sex (or of both sexes), is called **male** or **female hermaphroditism.**

Androgen deprivation or gonadal failure may occur in adult life or in infancy as well as in prenatal life. The more severe cases of androgen deprivation are classified as primary—that is, of testicular origin—or secondary, in which the difficulties lie with the pituitary gland. Such conditions as destructive inflammatory diseases (mumps, syphilis, tuberculosis), X-ray irradiation, neoplasm, vitamin deficiency, and vascular disorders may restrict androgen production. The result is called **hypogonadism.**

If hypogonadism occurs during prepubertal life, the person may never become potent or develop a sex drive. If the disorder occurs in adult life after the person has engaged in normal sexual activity, he may possibly experience a loss of sexual desire and potency. Feelings of inadequacy and emotional symptoms indicative of depression may also result. Treatment for hypogonadism involves replacement hormone therapy, which helps in reversing the symptoms (Anderson 1970; Money 1980b; Money & Alexander 1967).

The Physical Changes of Pubescence

The second period of major hormonal influence on the development of the male and female sexual systems occurs during puberty. **Puberty** is that stage of life in which **secondary sexual characteristics** (those sexual ornaments which biologically signal the opposite sex) begin their development, and reproduction becomes possible. It is directly preceded by a period of rapid maturational change known as pubescence (also called pubic growth cycle). The changes that occur during this period are caused by gonadal hormones—androgen and estrogen.

The pubescent growth spurt is more a transition than a state, more a becoming than being. Sexual glands mature, and physiological differences between the sexes become more marked. Body chemistry, as well as physical appearance and functioning, become more distinctively male and female. As these differences widen, a girl becomes ready for womanhood and a boy for manhood.

There is no "typical" pubescence. Every boy and girl has his or her own periods of transition, and the range of individual differences is broad. Appearance and behavioral changes that immediately precede puberty occur later in boys than in girls, for whom development is more swift. Girls begin the rapid maturing process at about 10 to 12 years of age, approximately two years before boys do.

Generally speaking, a boy's physiological maturation moves more slowly and continues longer than a girl's. His greater physical size does not develop until after puberty. In fact, boys of 13 are usually smaller than girls of the same age. Most girls reach their full stature by their 16th year, while boys continue to grow in height until age 18 or later.

Pubescence is a period of "sexual awakening." While this by no means indicates that younger children have no sexual desires and interests, there is in pubescence a heightening and focusing of attention on sexual matters, and a changing of interests, attitudes, and emotions. It is a period met with mixed reactions by both sexes. Physical experimentation and new gratifications, such as masturbation, begin to occur or increase in frequency. A positive attitude toward one's biological sexual urge and condition, as well as an understanding of society's expectations for the newly emerging self, are essential to the emotional well-being of both sexes at this time.

Sexual Development in Pubescent Girls

The first evidences of pubescence in a girl are changes that occur in the breasts. The small conical buds increase in size, and the nipples begin to project forward. A girl now becomes quite aware of breasts not only because of the physical changes within her, but also because of cultural attitudes toward breast size.

Puberty: Girl or woman? (Jean Shapiro)

As development continues with the growth in size and sensitivity of breast tissue, the female body contour gradually rounds out and the pelvic area broadens. The bony structure of the pelvis widens, a growth of fatty pads develops on the hips, and the vaginal lining thickens. There then appears soft, downy, rather colorless pubic hair, and some axillary (underarm) hair growth. The pelvic hair thickens and coarsens, becoming curly and dark in color. It grows downward to the pubic area in an inverted triangular shape.

About two years after the breasts begin developing, and about one year after the appearance of pubic hair (at approximately 13 years of age), menstruation begins. The **menarche** is the beginning of menstrual functioning in a girl. But she cannot become pregnant until she starts **ovulation,** that is, until the ovaries commence releasing mature ova. This process usually does not take place until a year or so after menstruation first occurs. When a young girl's ovaries produce their first mature eggs, at about the age of 14, she has reached puberty.

There is considerable variation in the age at which girls reach the menarche because of individual differences in general health, developmental maturation, and heredity. In 1939, for example, at the age of 5, a Peruvian girl gave birth to a normal, healthy son. (Fathered by a mentally retarded teen-age stepbrother, the baby was delivered by caesarean section.) Despite the fact that the mother was so young, she was sexually mature, and physicians confirmed that she had menstruated since she was perhaps one month old.

Cases are on record in which a girl became pregnant and produced a child without ever having menstruated. The explanation appears to be that the girl, contrary to the usual sequence of events, released a mature ovum just before her menarche, and the resulting pregnancy delayed menstruation until after delivery.

Female genital changes continue to occur from pubescence on into adolescence. The thickened pelvic hair continues to spread. The mons pubis becomes prominent. The labia majora develop and become more fleshy, hiding the rest of the vulva, which is ordinarily visible during childhood. The labia minora also develop and grow.

The clitoris rapidly develops its extensive system of blood vessels at this time. The vagina turns a deeper red color, and its mucous lining becomes thicker, remaining so until the **menopause,** or "change of life," when it reverts to the thinness of childhood. Vaginal secretions now become acid. The uterus, which begins to grow rapidly when a girl reaches age 10 or so, doubles in size by her 18th year (although the wombs of 60% of 15-year-old girls have already reached their adult size).

It is interesting to note that, because of the influence of the mother's hormonal secretions, the uterus of a female infant is larger at birth than it will be again until the ovaries start to produce hormones as a prelude to the menarche. Because of the abrupt withdrawal of maternal hormones at the time of birth, the infant's uterus shrinks within a few days after birth. Sometimes the change is significant enough to result in vaginal spotting or staining. Although worrisome to parents, the discharge is usually of no consequence. Uterine size then remains constant until the ovaries begin their hormonal production. Pregnancies will later slightly increase the permanent size of the uterus.

When a girl is around 10, her ovaries begin to secrete female sex hormones (in particular, estrogen), and ovarian growth is rapid. At the time of the menarche, the ovaries are about one-third their adult size, reaching maximum size and weight by the age of 19 or 20.

The age at which girls begin to menstruate has dropped sharply in the last few centuries ("Sexual Maturity" 1961). In Germany, for example, the average age of menstrual onset was 16.6 years in 1795, but was only 14.5 years by 1920. In the United States in the late 1930s, the average age was 13.5, while data from the mid-1970s indicate a drop to 12.76 years (National Center for Health Statistics 1974). In all advanced countries, as a matter of fact, the average age at which the menarche occurs has been dropping about four months per decade (Tanner 1962, 1969), probably due to better nutrition leading to earlier achievement of the minimal weight needed for menarche. Some authorities conclude that approximately one-half of American girls become capable of bearing children when they are between 12.5 and 14.5 years of age.

There is strong evidence, however, that the age of puberty has leveled off after many years of gradually earlier onset (W. Sullivan 1971). By 1976 it had stabilized at 12 years, 9.5 months, according to the National Bureau of Health Statistics. At physical maturity the average 18-year-old American girl is 5 feet 4.5 inches tall and weighs 123 pounds.

Sexual Development in Pubescent Boys

A boy's pubic growth curve lasts from 4 to 7 years and parallels that of a girl's but, as we have noted, trails hers by a year or two. Progress to and through puberty varies considerably from boy to boy. Boys of today are considerably better developed physically than in the past. For example, in this country a 9-year-old boy today is 3.8 inches taller and 18.7 pounds heavier than a boy that age living in 1881 (Steinhaus 1963). The greatest variability in physical size and physiological development is observable at the age of 12 or 13, and growth continues until about age 18. The average 18-year-old American boy today is 5 feet, 9.5 inches tall and weighs 150 pounds. He can expect to grow another quarter to half inch in the next 4 years.

At the age of 11, a boy shows few outward signs of pubertal change. He may first blossom into a "fat period," often a forerunner of male pubescence. Penile erections occur spontaneously at this early age, but from various sources of stimulation, not all of which are necessarily sexual. By the age of 12, his penis and scrotum begin to increase in size, one of the earliest indicators of approaching puberty. Erections occur more often, but still spontaneously. While he might know about ejaculation, he has yet to experience it.

A boy's pubic hair commonly appears at the age of 13 or 14, following the spurt of genital growth by a year or so, although it is sometimes observed as early as the 12th year. For the average boy of 13 or 14, ejaculation is now possible. Secretion of sperm begins—a process parallel to ovulation in a girl, although neither sperm nor ova are necessarily mature. Growth of underarm and facial hair follows that of the pubic hair. **Nocturnal emissions** ("wet dreams") are now probable if a sexual outlet of another nature is not utilized.

Puberty: Boy or man? (Dean Hollyman/Photo Researchers, Inc.)

A change in voice occurs about the 14th or 15th year, due to the effects of testosterone on the larynx, so that the voice of a mature man is about an octave lower than that of a mature woman. The average age at which a boy's voice changes has dropped over the years. For example, at the time of the 18th-century Bach Boys' Choir in Leipzig, the average age of voice change was 18. In London in 1959, by contrast, it was 13.3 years (W. Sullivan 1971).

Glands and Hormones

Age alone is not responsible for the remarkable changes that make boys and girls sexually mature. As was brought out earlier, both sexual maturation and the stunting of sexual development are dependent upon sex hormones. The endocrine system is quite complex and contributes to many of the physiological functions and behavior patterns of humans. In this discussion, however, only those hormones that more or less directly influence sexual development and functioning will be considered.

The pituitary gland, located at the base of the brain, is about one-half the size of a thimble and contains three lobes: the anterior, the intermediary, and the posterior. The anterior pituitary lobe was once known as the "master gland," because it was thought to control and coordinate the functions of the other endocrine glands. It is now known, however, that the pituitary is under the control of the "releasing hormones" of the hypothalamus. The hypothalamus produces several hormone-like compounds that have a stimulating or inhibiting effect on the pituitary gland. One of these releasing hormones is gonadotropin-releasing factor (GRF). It controls the formation and release of two pituitary hormones concerned with sexual maturity and reproduction. Both the pituitary and the hypothalamus are therefore important to sexual growth and functioning. A properly functioning pituitary has a harmonizing influence on the other endocrine glands. If it functions abnormally, it can have a disturbing effect on any or all of them.

With regard to the gonads, the anterior lobe of the pituitary gland specifically controls both the cellular function concerned with the production of sperm and ova and endocrine secretion (C. W. Lloyd 1964). (See Fig. 3.3.) The anterior lobe secretes at least six hormones, three of which are directly related to reproduction. They are: (1) the follicle-stimulating hormone (FSH); (2) the luteinizing hormone (LH); (3) prolactin which stimulates the secretion of milk by the mammary glands following childbirth. These gonadotropic hormones exert great influence on the growth, development, and sexual activity of both males and females.

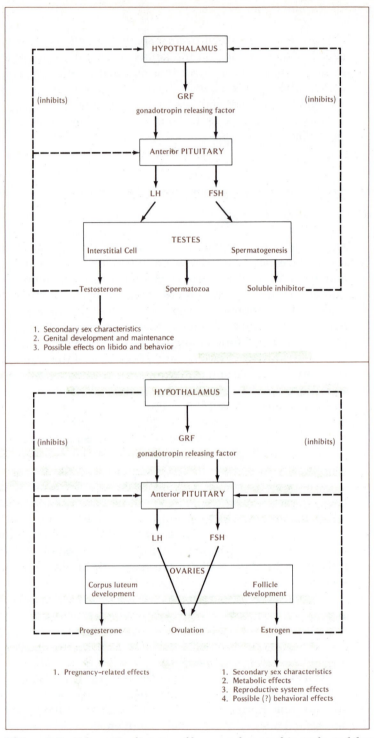

Figure 3.3 Schematic diagram of hormonal control in male and female.

The gonads, in addition to their other functions, produce sex hormones. On the basis of chemical and physiological differences, these hormones form three groups: the estrogenic hormone group, the progestational hormone group, and the androgenic hormone group. The action of these three hormonal groups differs greatly, although their chemical structure is quite similar. They are all classed as steroids, and each is a natural substance that is a basic component of living cells. Once the sex hormones have been used by the body, they are broken down and eliminated, usually in the urine.

Hormonal Activity in the Female

Estrogen (from the Greek *estro-:* to produce mad desire) is the hormone responsible for stimulating the sexual urge in a female animal's reproductive organs during estrus, her mating period (also called heat or rut). In human females (who do not experience estrus), estrogen seems to have little effect on sexual desire. Estrogen is essentially a growth hormone, highly important in the development of the body structure, the genital organs, and secondary sex characteristics. Estrogen also influences the menstrual cycle, which will be explained in a later section.

Humans and certain primates (for example, apes and Old World monkeys) have similar menstrual cycles. Other mammals do not menstruate, although the estrous discharge may resemble menstruation. Large amounts of estrogen in these lower female animals produce estrus when ovulation has occurred or is about to. It is also the time when these animals are most receptive to copulation. In human females, however, there seems to be no particular time during the menstrual cycle when all experience heightened sexual desire. Researchers (Udry & Morris 1977) have found that human sexual desire seems to be an individual idiosyncrasy, with previously reported "sexual peaks" dependent upon the method used to tabulate data. This lack of correlation between sexual receptivity and estrogen cycles points up a major difference between female humans and other mammals.

In the majority of women (unlike certain animals), ovarian hormones appear not to play a major role in regulating sex drive. In one study of women under the age of 40, 90% reported experiencing no change in sexual desire and functioning after the removal of both ovaries. The hormones produced by the pituitary and adrenal glands appear to play a vastly more important role in women's sex drive. To demonstrate: of 30 women, from whom these last glands had been removed as part of the treatment for breast cancer, none had maintained their preoperative sex drive. In 84% of them, it had vanished completely (Reichlin 1971). In the average woman, however, any temporary fluctuation in sexual responsiveness is apparently influenced more by emotional and other physical factors than by hormonal conditions (Luttge 1971).

Researchers have shown that certain neural centers of the brain are directly affected by sex hormones. For example, female test animals show an increase in smell acuity during certain stages of the estrus cycle. In female animals, body odors become much stronger during those days, which accounts for the attraction of male animals to them while they are in heat. Dense crowding of female mice can cause pseudopregnancies, a reaction that is prevented if their olfactory bulbs (organs sensitive to odors) are removed. Also, inseminated female mice will not become pregnant if they are made to smell the urine odor of a mature male mouse other than the one with which they have copulated (Parkes & Bruce 1961).

Studies of humans have revealed that women have greater smell acuity than men, and that their olfactory sensitivity is greatest midway between menstrual periods when estrogen levels are the highest. Smell acuity decreases after an ovariectomy, but can be restored through administration of estrogen.

As a part of a girl's developmental process, either the pituitary gland begins to secrete more of its follicle-stimulating hormone (FSH), or the ovaries develop to the point where they become more sensitive than before to the already existing level of FSH secretion. A third view is that pubertal development is brought about by the maturing of cells within the hypothalamus rather than by changes in either the ovary or the pituitary, "as both these glands are capable of adult function at birth if properly stimulated" (*Williams Obstetrics* 1961). Whatever the cause, FSH stimulates the growth of the immature ovaries and the ovarian follicles (small sacs, each containing an immature ovum), which, in turn, start the production of estrogen by the cells lining the cavity of each follicle. Among its other effects, estrogen inhibits the pituitary's production of FSH and causes the lining of the uterus to thicken in the first half of the menstrual cycle. The luteinizing hormone (LH) plays a role in the production of progesterone. In addition, when LH reaches a certain ratio in relation to FSH, it serves to trigger ovulation (*Williams Obstetrics* 1961).

Hormonal Activity in Ovulation, Menstruation, and Pregnancy.   When the LH-FSH ratio is such that ovulation occurs and an egg is discharged from a follicle, the remaining follicular cells multiply rapidly and fill the cavity of the follicle just ruptured. The new cell growth is yellow in color and is known as the corpus luteum, or yellow body. The corpus luteum begins to secrete **progesterone.** The corpus luteum also produces estrogen during the latter half of the menstrual cycle.

If fertilization and implantation do not occur, the corpus luteum begins to waste away by about the 27th day of the menstrual cycle and its secretion of progesterone begins to diminish. Progesterone is the reproduction hormone of primary importance in preparing the uterine lining for implantation of the fertilized egg and in maintaining the pregnancy itself.

In the process of degeneration, the corpus luteum shrinks rapidly and loses its yellow color, and the lutein cells are replaced by connective tissue. After a few weeks only a small white body, the corpus albicans, remains in the space that was once the location of the follicle. This cessation of the secretion of progesterone, together with the decrease of estrogen, causes a new production of pituitary gonadotropins, which stimulate another crop of ovarian follicles. The ovulatory growth cycle begins anew.

If the ovum is fertilized, the corpus luteum receives a signal not to degenerate from chorionic gonadotropin (HCG) released from the undeveloped placenta. The corpus luteum continues to secrete progesterone, which keeps the endometrium or uterine lining sensitized and ready to implant the blastocyst, a stage of development of the fertilized ovum, and to develop the membranes needed for the survival of the egg.

During pregnancy, the corpus luteum develops and grows until it may, at the peak of its hormone production, occupy as much as half of the ovary (Netter 1961). This endocrine tissue continues to function until about the fourth month of pregnancy. At that time the placenta takes over the necessary production of estrogen and progesterone and maintains this production for the remainder of gestation (the period of pregnancy).

Progesterone stimulates the secretion capabilities of the mammary glands of the pregnant woman, thus causing an enlargement of the breasts. A proper amount of progesterone is also necessary to prevent premature uterine contractions. In fact, progesterone hormonal therapy may be prescribed by the physician when there is a danger of spontaneous abortion, especially during the 10th to 16th week of pregnancy, when the threat of miscarriage is greatest. In a woman who is not pregnant, the production of abnormal levels of progesterone may produce dysmenorrhea (painful menstruation), premenstrual tension, and similar gynecological problems.

Hormonal Activity in the Male

The male sex hormone **testosterone** is produced in the testicles (although 5% of the total amount is produced by the adrenal glands), beginning in pubescence, when a boy's testicles grow and develop rapidly because of the pituitary gland's secretion of FSH. FSH acts to stimulate the seminiferous (sperm-producing) tubules to begin the process of **spermatogenesis,** the formation and development of spermatozoa or sperm. This is not the complete story, however. For although the germinal cell layers of the tubules become active at the time of pubescence, mature spermatozoa do not develop without the presence of LH, the pituitary gonadotropin that causes the testes to produce testosterone (see Fig. 3.3).

The chief function of LH in the male, however, appears to be the stimulation and maintenance of the interstitial cells of the testes in their production of the male gonadal (androgenic) hormone, testosterone (C. W.

Lloyd 1964). Testosterone is responsible for development and preservation of masculine secondary sexual characteristics, including facial and body hair, voice change, muscular and skeletal development, and sexual desire. (Testosterone does not determine whether a male's feelings of sexual desire or attraction will be directed toward same-sex or opposite-sex partners, but it does help stimulate libido.) Testosterone controls, as well, the development, size and function of male accessory organs (seminal vesicles, prostate, penis, and scrotum).

Apparently a healthy male body produces a more than ample supply of sex hormones for adequate sexual functioning. In proof of this, men with only one testicle reveal no evidence of hormonal deficiency. Even in men whose ejaculate contains as little as 60% of the normal hormonal content, the existing hormones are sufficient to sustain a normal, satisfactory sex life (Raboch 1970a; Weaver 1970).

Perhaps sensing the special function of the testicles that we now identify as hormonal, men have long tried to increase their sexual prowess by eating testicles—sometimes of a defeated enemy, sometimes of animals (Rubin 1965b).

As late as 1889, the renowned French physiologist Charles E. Brown-Sequard was, at the age of 72, apparently dissatisfied with his sexual vigor. He tried to outwit nature by injecting himself with extracts from the testicles of dogs. But despite the fact that he reported spectacular rejuvenation, any benefits he actually derived must surely have been the result of autosuggestion. For an injection of the extract from approximately 500 pounds of bull testicles would be needed to furnish what is considered an average dose of male sex hormones (Schering Corporation 1944)! The one thing that Brown-Sequard did accomplish, however, was to stimulate a considerable amount of research in this area. Since his time, well-controlled experimentations with hormones have shown that we are physically, mentally, and emotionally influenced by the action of our endocrine glands, and that our physical and emotional states may, in turn, affect the function of these glands.

Androgenic and estrogenic hormones are produced by both sexes—that is, a small amount of estrogen is to be found in the male, and a small amount of androgen in the female. The source of these hormones is thought to be in the gonads and adrenal glands. The urine excreted by normal men and women thus contains both types of hormones or their by-products.

Hormonal Imbalance and Hormonal Treatment

In adulthood, an excessive amount of androgen in a woman and too much estrogen in males can produce marked changes in secondary sexual characteristics. For example, the male who is given estrogen prior to transsexual surgery will notice some breast growth, fatty tissue deposits, and testicular shrinkage; a female with excess androgen becomes hirsute (Money & Ehrhardt 1972).

An imbalance in the natural hormonal state in an infant or growing child can produce deviations in primary sexual characteristics as well as changes in secondary characteristics. Hormonal therapy is often successful in adjusting the imbalance and correcting or preventing associated problems.

Women who have developed cancer are often successfully treated with male hormones injected to reduce the rate of growth and spread of the malignancy. Investigations indicate that it may be possible to reduce the death rate among men from heart attacks by as much as 50% in some instances when the female sex hormone estrogen is used in treatment. Estrogenic treatment, however, leaves the man with decreased erectile ability, lowered sex drive, and enlarged breasts ("Medical Science Notes" 1961a; "Science Notes" 1962).

By contrast, androgen treatment of women serves to enhance the sex drive, although it also has certain masculinizing effects (e.g., encouraging the growth of facial hair). After puberty, however, male and female hormones exert no influence on the individual's masculinity or femininity in the course of psychosexual development. Hormones cannot therefore be used successfully as a therapeutic tool in changing the sexual orientations and behavior of such people as homosexuals, transsexuals, and transvestites (Money 1968a).

Summary

The endocrine system plays a vital role in sexual maturation and reproduction, as well as in regulating sexual desire and function. The endocrine system and the brain have an important combined effect upon the coordination of human emotions and sexual behavior.

This chapter emphasized the many ways in which the male and female sexual systems are similar in structure and function. Cultural attitudes are probably more important than anatomy in determining "typical male" and "typical female" behavior. The internal genitalia, first recognizable about six weeks after conception, later differentiate into the male testes and the female ovaries. The external genitalia, observable initially in an undifferentiated state at the sixth week of embryonic formation, later develop into the male penis and scrotum or the female clitoris, labia majora, labia minora, and vestibule. The presence or absence of the hormone androgen significantly affects the direction this sexual development takes.

Much of this sexual differentiation occurs during prenatal development, but final maturation of the female and male systems occurs during puberty. Genital growth and development of secondary sexual characteristics occur in both sexes, together with menstruation and ovulation in girls and ejaculation and voice changes in boys. Generally, this physiological maturation and development takes place earlier in girls than it does in boys.

Hormones—including FSH, LH, and ISH, LTH, estrogen, progesterone and androgen—play a great role in sexual maturation and development. In women, FSH stimulates the growth of the immature ovaries and the ovarian follicles; LH helps the follicles to secrete estrogen; and LTH regulates the production of progesterone by the corpus luteum as well as prompting milk production in the breast following childbirth. Estrogen is primarily a growth hormone that also affects the functioning of the menstrual cycle. Progesterone is the reproduction hormone that prepares the uterine lining for implantation of the fertilized egg. In men, FSH stimulates the seminiferous or sperm-producing tubules to begin the process of spermatogenesis, and ICSH stimulates and maintains the interstitial cells of the testes in their production of the androgenic hormone testosterone. Testosterone induces and maintains the male secondary sex characteristics.

Hormonal imbalances sometimes occur, and hormone therapy can be employed to correct them through the appropriate use of androgen and estrogen. Although hormonal imbalances have their major impact during embryonic and fetal development, such imbalances also lead to deviations in primary and secondary sexual characteristics later in life. Relationships between hormonal imbalance and disease also have been detected.

Annotated Bibliography

Horton, Charles E. (Ed.) *Plastic and reconstructive surgery of the genital area.* Boston: Little, Brown, 1973.

> This well-illustrated, comprehensive source volume for plastic surgeons and other medical and allied health personnel covers psychological, developmental, and surgical aspects of genital surgery. Specific topics include history, genital surgery, embryology of male and female genitalia, genital anomalies, intersexuality and diagnosis of intersex problems, and surgical and psychiatric aspects of transsexualism.

Huff, Robert W. and Pauerstein, Carl J. *Human reproduction: Physiology and pathophysiology.* New York: Wiley, 1979.

> This text for medical students and practitioners contains detailed information

on human reproductive biology, gynecologic physiology, and pregnancy. Specific topics include male and female sexual differentiation, reproductive endocrinology, contraception and infertility, venereal disease, reproductive genetics, fetal growth, and management of normal and high-risk pregnancy. Pre-chapter objectives and self-test questions and answers facilitate learning.

Johnson, Martin and Everitt, Barry. *Essential reproduction.* Oxford, England: Blackwell Scientific Publications, 1980.

> This text discusses a wide range of topics related to reproductive biology, including genetics, sexual differentiation, endocrinology, ovarian and testicular function, puberty and the climacteric, hormones and sexual behavior, coitus and fertilization, pregnancy, parturition, and lactation. Though written for the student of the technicalities of reproduction, this book would be useful as a general reference.

Mazur, T. and Money, J. Prenatal influences and subsequent sexuality. In *Handbook of human sexuality,* ed. B. Wolman and J. Money. Englewood Cliffs, New Jersey: Prentice-Hall, 1980.

> This brief yet informative article discusses genetic and endocrinological influences in prenatal sexual development. Emphasis is placed on prenatal influences as they affect subsequent gender identity/role differentiation and development.

Mishell, Daniel R., Jr., and Davajan, Val. *Reproductive endocrinology: Infertility and contraception.* Philadelphia: F. A. Davis, 1979.

> This text for medical and allied health personnel integrates the latest clinical research findings related to normal and abnormal reproductive endocrinology, infertility, and contraception. Discussion includes topics related to puberty, gestation, menstruation, and the climacteric.

Money, John. *Love and love sickness: The science of sex, gender difference, and pair-bonding.* Baltimore: The Johns Hopkins University Press, 1980.

> This scholarly book encompasses a wide array of topics in human sexuality. Some general areas include the historical and cultural aspects of sexual behavior, factors influencing sexual orientation and pair-bonding, erotic sexuality, sexual taboos, and pornography. The author advances a new theory to guide understanding of sex differences based on the variety of factors contributing to gender identity and sex role. This book would appeal to the student, medical and allied health professional, and general academic reader.

Moore, Mary L. *Realities in childbearing.* Philadelphia: W. B. Saunders, 1978.

> Intended as a text for nursing students and other medical personnel, this book covers the various aspects of human reproductive physiology and the cultural, emotional, developmental, and environmental contexts of childbearing.

Shearman, Rodney P. *Human reproductive physiology (2nd ed.).* London: Blackwell Scientific Publications, 1979.

> This comprehensive text provides detailed information on most significant aspects of human reproduction, including genetics and cytogenetics, the physiology and function of testes and ovaries, pregnancy, and menopause. This book is designed for the student and medical and allied health professional.

Witters, Weldon and Jones-Witters, Patricia. *Human sexuality: A biological perspective.* New York: D. Van Nostrand, 1980.

This text approaches the various aspects of human sexuality from the biological standpoint. Topics of special interest include genetic engineering, hormonal control of sexuality, drugs affecting sexual function, surrogate parenthood, artificial insemination, cloning, and sex selection. The text is well illustrated and contains student performance objectives, but its appeal extends beyond the classroom.

The Male Sexual System

Centuries of observation and experimentation have demonstrated that living organisms, as far as present scientific competence can reveal, are produced exclusively by other, similar, living organisms. In higher orders of life—specifically, humans—the genetic continuation of the species depends ultimately upon some form of cooperative function and utilization of the reproductive glands and organs of the two sexes. At least these facts hold true today, even though there is some evidence that in the future scientists may be able to modify genetic and reproductive processes significantly.

In this and the next chapter are detailed the physiology and functions of human reproductive organs as we know them today.

The Male Genitalia

The Testicles

Of the male genital system (Fig. 4.1), the most important elements are the gonads, the **testicles** (also called **testes**), which develop as a pair in the abdominal cavity. The testicles descend shortly before or just

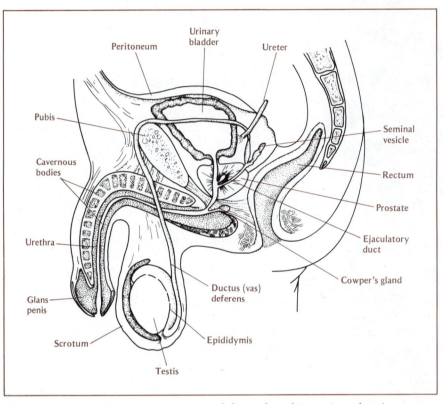

Figure 4.1   Schematic representation of the male pelvic region, showing organs of reproduction.

after birth into the **scrotum** (or scrotal sac), a loose pouch of skin that is an outpocket of the abdominal cavity. During the seventh month of fetal life, the testes pass through the inguinal canal, a passageway leading from the abdominal cavity into the scrotal pouch. After the descent, this opening is usually sealed off by a growth of connective tissue, and the body cavity and scrotum are henceforth separated.

Any of a variety of factors may cause the testicles not to descend in due time into the scrotum, in which case endocrine or surgical assistance is needed. It has been estimated that up to 3% of full-term male infants have undescended testicles at the time of birth (30% of male premature infants). Physicians generally agree that an undescended testicle should be corrected, if possible, by the time the boy is 4 or 5 years of age (Vaughan & McKay 1975).

Occasionally the inguinal ring fails to close after the descent of the testicles around the time of birth. Or it reopens when the boy or man is older—because of strain, muscular tear, or some other reason—resulting in an inguinal hernia. Sometimes a loop of the intestine may slip through the ring and into the scrotal pouch. If it is caught there, it is possible that its blood supply may be cut off and an operation becomes necessary.

The testicles are egg-shaped bodies that vary in size but in the adult are usually about 1.5 in. (4 cm) long and about 1 in. (2.5 cm) in diameter. The scrotum in which they are housed is supported by special muscles and tissues that act to regulate the temperature of the gonads. Ordinarily the scrotal temperature is slightly lower than that of the body itself. This lower temperature is necessary for sperm production. The supporting muscles and tissues act to contract the scrotum when the outside temperature is low, thus bringing the testicles closer to the warm body. They relax when the temperature is high, lowering the testicles away from the body. Long hot baths, prolonged use of athletic supporters, high fever, and the like have for centuries been thought to cause infertility, especially in men with a low sperm count to start with. A 2°C to 3°C increase in temperature does in fact occasionally result in temporary sterility in men, but fertility returns after a short time. However, there is little evidence of the success of prolonged hot baths as a contraceptive technique, though it is practiced in some countries.

Each testicle has within it about 250 lobules or compartments that contain, in turn, 1 to 3 winding and tightly coiled seminiferous tubules measuring 1 to 2 ft (0.3 to 0.6 m) each when uncoiled (Netter 1961). (See Fig. 4.2.) All told, the combined length of the tubules from both testicles measures several hundred yards. The walls of the tubules are lined with

Figure 4.2 Schematic representation of the testicle.

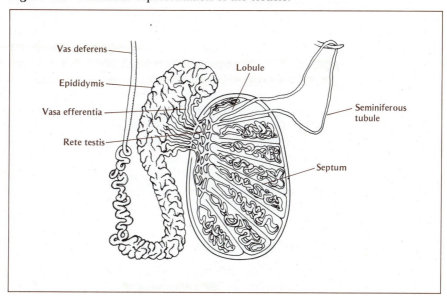

Vas deferens

Epididymis

Vasa efferentia

Rete testis

Lobule

Seminiferous tubule

Septum

germinal tissue, and it is here that the formation of sperm in the process of maturation known as **spermatogenesis** takes place.

The seminiferous tubules, some 1000 of them, meet at the corelike structure known as the rete testis, a network of vessels in the testicle located near the surface in its upper portion. This meshwork of tubes, fibers, and vessels empties into approximately 10 to 15 ducts, the vasa efferentia, through which the sperm are moved by means of peristalsis (successive waves of contractions) to the epididymis. The epididymis is a swelling attached to each testicle. Within, it is a compactly wound tube, approximately 20 ft (6 m) long, which serves as a chamber of maturation. Here the sperm may remain to ripen or mature for as long as six weeks, during which time they are nurtured by its lining. Those spermatozoa less fit to survive and to endure the long journey ahead are crowded toward the center of the tube. There they are less likely to live and are absorbed. The epididymis thus serves also as a selection chamber.

Sperm are transported by ciliary action through the epididymis into a connecting duct, the ductus deferens or vas deferens (commonly called the vas). About 18 in. (46 cm) in length, this tiny tube originates at the small end of the epididymis and passes upward into the abdominal cavity. The vas serves as a passageway for sperm and probably, as well, to store them, particularly at its upper end where it broadens into an enlarged portion called the ampulla. The ampulla connects with the seminal vesicle at a juncture that opens into the prostate gland.

To assess the size of a sperm, one has only to consider that it must travel 500 times its length in order to progress 1 in. (2.5 cm). This is equivalent to a man's swimming almost a mile ("Story of the Sperm" 1965).

The mature spermatozoa, or sperm—which were identified under a microscope as early as 1677—are relatively immobile until they mix with prostatic fluid to form the semen. Sperm are transported by the peristaltic and ciliary movements of the various tubes through which they pass into the two seminal vesicles, saclike structures lying behind the bladder.

The exact function of the seminal vesicles has been much debated. Some scientists have thought that they act only as storage compartments for spermatozoa. Today, the commonly accepted view is that they are glands specifically designed to produce a fructose-rich secretion that not only contributes to the volume of the ejaculatory fluid, but also activates the whiplike movements of the sperm's tails. Following coital ejaculation these lashing movements propel the sperm in their journey from the vagina toward the fallopian tubes.

The Prostate and the Ejaculatory Ducts

Immediately below the bladder, surrounding its neck and the upper part of the urethra, lies the **prostate gland** (Fig. 4.3). It is a firm body, weighing

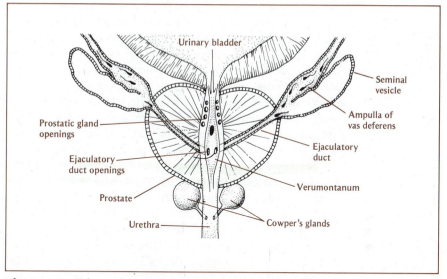

Figure 4.3 Schematic representation of the prostate gland, showing ejaculatory ducts opening into the urethra.

approximately two-thirds of an ounce. Made up of partially muscular, partially glandular matter, the mature prostate is in a continual state of activity. Part of its secretion is voided with the urine, while the remainder makes up the greater portion of the ejaculatory fluid.

That part of the prostatic secretion discharged at the time of ejaculation is a highly alkaline, thin, milky fluid that contains many substances, including proteins, calcium, citric acid, cholesterol, and various enzymes and acids (Mann 1954). The alkalinity of the secretion apparently helps the sperm move through acid areas at a rapid pace, since, for example, acid in the vaginal fluid will easily destroy them if they are left in contact with it even for a short time.

The prostate surrounds the ejaculatory ducts, which partially house the semen until its discharge. The **semen** is composed of spermatozoa and seminal fluid—secretions from the epididymis, seminal vesicles, prostate gland, and Cowper's (bulbo-urethral) glands. It should be pointed out that the consistency of seminal fluid varies from man to man, and that variations are to be expected in the same man from time to time. Sometimes the fluid is thick and almost gelatinlike, while another time it will be thin and somewhat watery, the determinant being, generally, the frequency of the man's ejaculations. Semen coagulates shortly after ejaculation, but liquefies about 20 minutes later (Clark 1965a).

The average amount of semen ejaculated is 4 cc, which weighs about 4 gm. Given the protein and fat contained in semen, the average ejaculate probably represents less than 36 calories. There is no convincing evidence, therefore, that a normal discharge of semen in any way "weakens" a man (Clark 1969a), as coaches have been known to argue, no doubt in an effort to get athletes tucked in bed (alone) at 8 o'clock on the night before a competition. (No less an authority on human sexuality than William Masters, himself a former athlete, once said that after a sexual experience athletes should be able to perform at maximum ability if they are allowed a sufficient recuperation period—one to five minutes!) Furthermore, it is a myth that a woman who swallows seminal fluid during oral sex will become inordinately fat or that she will become pregnant from swallowing the semen.

The Cowper's glands are two pea-sized structures situated slightly below the prostate at each side of the base of the penis. Along with the seminal vesicles and prostate, they make up a man's accessory reproductive glands. During sexual excitement, the Cowpers glands secrete an alkaline fluid that lubricates and neutralizes the acidity of the urethra for easy and safe passage of the semen. This thin fluid can be observed at the opening of the glans of the penis during sexual excitement and before ejaculation. The fluid does not ordinarily contain spermatozoa, but a few sperm do occasionally make their way into the fluid. It is therefore possible for a woman to be made pregnant by penetration even if the man does not actually ejaculate.

The Penis

Situated just below the Cowper's glands is the base of the **penis,** a cylindrical organ composed mostly of the erectile tissue. During sexual excitation, this tissue becomes engorged with blood, causing the penis to become erect and hard. In the adult male, the observable part of the average penis is from 2.5 to 4 in. (6.4 to 10 cm) long when flaccid (limp), slightly over 1 in. (2.5 cm) in diameter, and about 3.5 in. (9 cm) in circumference. The size, of course, varies considerably from man to man. When in a state of tumescence (erection), the average penis extends 5.5 to 6.5 in. (14 to 16.5 cm) in length, and becomes 1.5 in. (3.8 cm) in diameter and about 4.5 in. (11.5 cm) in circumference. Again, the size of the erect penis shows considerable variation from man to man.

There is little relationship between the size of a flaccid penis and its size when erect. And there is less relationship between penile and general body size than exists between the dimensions of other organs and the body (Masters & Johnson 1966). The measurement of a perfectly functioning erect penis can vary from 2 in. (5 cm) in one man to 10 in. (25 cm) in another, with one no less capable of coital performance than the other. Interestingly, Comfort (1980) notes that men believe penis size is a matter of special importance to women; women tend to report that other physical attributes, such as a man's legs or buttocks, are more attractive to them.

Men are often concerned about the size of their penises because childhood experiences have conditioned them to associate an adult's larger penis with strength and masculinity. When a boy so conditioned grows up, he may well think that to be a man of sexual prowess he must have an inordinately large phallus. Yet researchers generally agree that the size of a man's penis has relatively little to do with the pleasure experienced by either coital partner (Masters & Johnson 1966). There is increasing evidence, however, suggesting that, under conditions of similar coital techniques and positions (and based on both physical and fantasy factors), the larger penis may provide a woman with greater sexual enjoyment. One reason appears to be that many women also mistakenly equate the larger penis with greater masculinity. Another is that the larger penile circumference places greater pressure on the vaginal-ring muscles and is more likely to cause a pleasurable tugging of the labia minora. Further, the longer penis sometimes heightens pleasurable sensations with its thrusting against the cervix (Keller 1976). In some cases, of course, these same above-average penile dimensions can prove uncomfortable for a woman, detracting from her sensual enjoyment.

If a hormonal malfunction existed during boyhood, the size of a man's penis may have been adversely affected (Wood 1963). But unless there is some ongoing hormonal dysfunction, penile size has nothing to do with a man's ability to impregnate. The male hormone testosterone causes the penis to grow, the period of most rapid growth usually being between the ages of 11 and 14 years. If the testicles do not produce sufficient quantities of this hormone, the penis will remain small unless the boy receives hormonal therapy. However, in the man who has suffered no hormonal deficiencies during adolescence, the size of the penis is fixed by heredity. In rare instances surgical procedures have been employed to enlarge abnormally small penises (Dailey 1980a).

Scientists at the Sexological Institute of Prague, Czechoslovakia, have investigated the relationship between penile size, male hormone functioning, and potency. Their sampling consisted of 34 adult male subjects, most of whom were aged 25 to 35. Their hormonal secretions had been deficient during the critical adolescent years of sexual development and their flaccid penile length was consequently under 2.2 in. (5.6 cm). Through hormonal treatment, size was increased within a few months to the normal 2.5 to 4 in. (6.5 to 10 cm) (Raboch 1970b). Of the subject population in this study, potency disturbances rarely affected those men whose flaccid penises were shorter than 2.4 in. (6.1 cm) and narrower than 0.8 in. (2 cm), further evidence that male impotence has very little to do with a small penis. One surprising incidental finding in this investigation was that the penises of both effeminate and noneffeminate homosexuals were longer and wider than those of the control group of heterosexual men.

The erect penis is of inverted triangular shape. The shaft is made up of three cylindrical spongy bodies composed of erectile tissue: two larger bodies on top, and one smaller body below. The two top bodies are known as the corpora cavernosa penis, and the single body below is called corpus spongiosum or corpora cavernosum urethrae. The lower body houses the urethral canal, which passes through the length of the penis. A band of tissue called the Buck's fascia encircles the three bodies and separates the upper two from the lower one. This sheet of fascia is a continuation of the tissue joining the penis to the symphysis (connective juncture) of the pubic bone and the perineal and related muscles.

Large arteries feed blood to the spongy erectile tissue of the penis, especially its top part. As the spongy structures fill with blood, the penis becomes erect. Erection is lost when blood leaves the penis through veins faster than it flows in through arteries.

The glans (Latin: acorn) is the smooth conelike head of the penis (Fig. 4.4). It is by far the most sexually sensitive and excitable part of a man's body. Its surface is filled with nerve endings, especially at the corona, the crownlike ridge at the back edge of the glans where the glans drops down to join the shaft of the penis. The corona, particularly at the frenum, is a primary source of sexual pleasure and excitement when stimulated properly. The glans is a continuation of the corpus spongiosum. At its tip end is a meatus, the external opening of the urethra.

Figure 4.4   Glans penis and foreskin, showing position of the frenum.

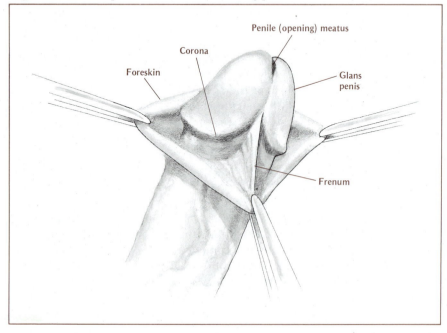

The shaft of the penis is covered by a loose skin which is continuous with that of the scrotum. This looseness of the skin allows free movement and full erection when the penis elongates and enlarges as it becomes engorged with blood. Near the tip of the penis, the skin is no longer attached to the organ directly, but encompasses the glans, usually hanging loosely. This fold of skin, which covers the glans but may be pulled back from it, is known as the prepuce or foreskin. It is attached to the glans on the lower surface by a thin midline tissue called the frenum.

For hygienic, functional, and in certain instances, religious reasons a portion of the prepuce covering the glans is frequently removed surgically in a procedure known as **circumcision,** usually just after birth while the infant is still in the hospital. When circumcision is performed after adulthood, the reasons are usually physical, such as a torn or brittle frenum, a too-tight and unretractable foreskin, or recurring, resistant infections such as herpes (Persky 1975).

Just behind the glans, under the corona and on each side of the frenum, are the Tyson's glands. They are modified sebaceous (suet-oily) glands, the secretions of which, together with cells shed from the glans and corona, form a cheeselike substance known as **smegma** (Fig. 4.5). If the prepuce is tight over the glans, smegma can collect and emit a foul odor. The area can also become a breeding ground for bacteria.

One of the main purposes of circumcision is to prevent the accu-

Figure 4.5   Representation of the penis, showing a collection of smegma.

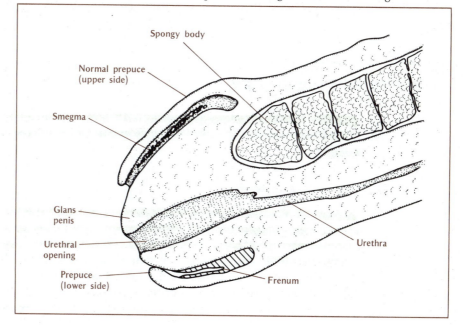

mulation of smegma. Another compelling reason is that research has demonstrated an inverse relationship between circumcision and penile cancer. An investigation of cases of penile cancer at one general hospital revealed that incidence among Catholics and Protestants, who comprised 67% of the hospital's patients, was 94%, whereas among the 30% patient population who were Jewish, the incidence was only 3% (Licklider 1961). This study tends to support the belief that circumcision prevents accumulation of smegma, which apparently encourages penile cancer. However, the American Academy of Pediatrics has formally stated that there are no valid medical grounds for routine circumcising of the newborn.

A surprisingly persistent myth in human sexuality is that of **penis captivus**—that humans can get "hung up" in sexual intercourse. This notion may result from observing the behavior of animals and attributing the same possibility to humans. Further, most people have heard stories of couples who became locked together while copulating, the services of a physician being required before the penis could be released. The story is characteristically sworn to be true and as having happened to a friend (or to a friend of a friend), although no one has ever witnessed the phenomenon or experienced it. It is, of course, possible for a woman to experience sudden strong muscle spasms of the vagina (**vaginismus**) during intercourse, and the vagina may momentarily tighten around her partner's penis. But even in these circumstances, the pain or fear that a man would experience would cause loss of erection, permitting easy withdrawal of the penis. There are no scientifically verified cases of *penis captivus* among humans in modern medical literature (Dengrove 1965).

Male Sexual Functioning

Delivery of mature male germ cells into the female vagina typically requires three male functions: spermatogenesis, penile erection, and ejaculation of semen.

Spermatogenesis

The germinal epithelium or lining of the seminiferous tubules contains two types of cells: spermatogenic, which eventually produce mature sperm, and sustentacular, or cells of Sertoli, which nurture the sperm at various stages of development. The space between the tubules is filled with interstitial tissue that, when stimulated by the luteinizing hormone of the pituitary gland, produces the male sex hormone testosterone (Figs. 4.6, 4.7).

As a boy grows older and hormonal function increases, the inner

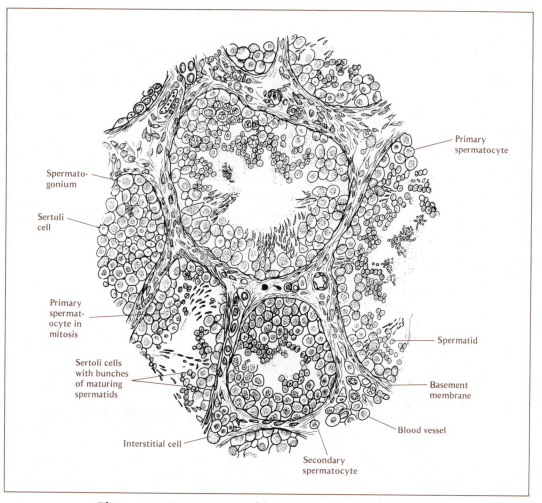

Figure 4.6 Representation of the human testis with seminiferous tubules, showing various stages of spermatogenesis. Interstitial cells, where male sex hormones are produced, are also shown.

surface of the seminiferous tubules yields an increasing number of cells known as primitive spermatogonia. These make up the first stage of spermatogenesis. (The first spermatogonia appear in the human testes during the fifth month of intrauterine life, but remain dormant until puberty [Baker 1972].) Spermatogenesis begins when a boy is about 11, although the age varies considerably, as can be judged by the different times at which puberty is reached. The median age in American boys of first ejaculation is between about 12.5 and 14 years. As with all averages, however, there is wide variation in the extremes. Kinsey *et al.* (1948) reported many cases of

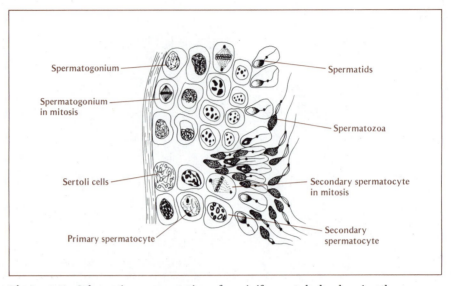

Figure 4.7   Schematic representation of seminiferous tubule, showing the process of spermatogenesis.

boys who experienced early-childhood orgasm. Reports of proven spermatogenesis in boys 4 to 6 years of age have also been published (C. W. Lloyd 1964), as well as one case of a 7-year-old father of a living child (Oliven 1974).

Through the unique process of mitosis, or ordinary cell division, each spermatogonium divides and produces two daughter cells, both containing the full component of 46 chromosomes. One is another spermatogonium, which remains at the surface of the tubule ready to split again, thus perpetuating formation of future spermatogonia. The other is a primary spermatocyte, which constitutes the next stage of spermatogenesis. The primary spermatocyte is a large cell that moves toward the center opening or lumen of the tubule. It undergoes meiotic cell division (meiosis or reduction division), producing two smaller secondary spermatocytes. In reduction division—primary spermatocyte to two secondary spermatocytes—the number of chromosomes in each cell is reduced to 23: 22 autosomal, or nonsex, chromosomes plus an X or female chromosome in one secondary spermatocyte, and 22 similar nonsex chromosomes plus a Y or male in the other. X and Y sperm are thus produced in equal numbers.

The secondary spermatocytes immediately cleave or split by mitotic division to form the last primitive male germinal cells, the spermatids. Spermatids develop, without cell division, into the mature spermatozoa, or fully formed sperm cells, each of which has only 23 chromosomes. Spermatogenesis proceeds to the spermatid stage after a boy is approxi-

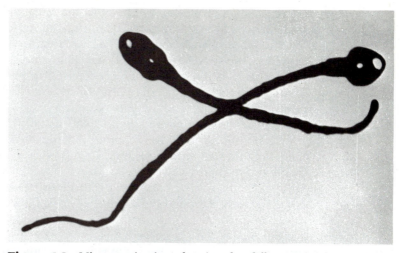

Figure 4.8 Microscopic view showing the difference between X-bearing sperm (with larger, oval-shaped head) and Y-bearing sperm (with smaller head, longer tail). Photograph courtesy Landrum B. Shettles.

mately 12 years old. Until then the lack of ICSH hormones blocks development beyond the secondary spermatocyte stage. The testes now grow rapidly because of marked enlargement of the seminiferous tubules, this germinal activity increasing as the boy advances to his mid-teens. At about age 15 or 16, he is usually capable of full spermatogenesis. The total process of spermatogenesis, from spermatogonium to mature spermatozoa, takes about 64 days. It is a continuing and continuous process in the normal healthy adult male.

In very recent years, noticeable differences between X (female) and Y (male) sperm have been reported (Figs. 4.8, 4.9). The Y sperm have been

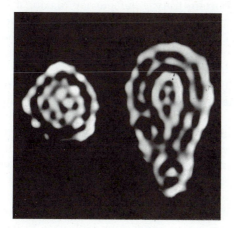

Figure 4.9 Microscopic view showing chromosomal arrangements of Y (male) sperm, left; and of X (female) sperm, right. (Original magnification ×1000.) Photograph courtesy Landrum B. Shettles.

alleged to have a small round-headed body with a long tail, the X sperm a large oval-shaped body and short tail. Landrum B. Shettles (1960, 1964, 1972), a leading researcher in this field, believes that, by use of this and other information, the sex of a child can largely be removed from the realm of chance. His theory is that sex can be predetermined by controlling the time of coitus and by following certain prescribed procedures.

The difference in shape and mobility of X and Y sperm has been noted by other researchers, in London and Berlin ("Babymaking" 1974). However, other scientists do not agree on the reported differences between X and Y sperm, stating that they cannot be distinguished by size or mass, shape, or electric charge (Rothschild 1960).

To outline Shettles's theory: ordinarily each ejaculate contains millions of both X and Y sperm, although the number of sperm per ejaculate tends to diminish as frequency of intercourse increases. Although the reason is not known, the higher the sperm count is, the greater the proportion of male sperm; conversely, the lower the sperm count, the greater the proportion of female sperm.

It is reasonable to assume that the smaller-headed, longer-tailed Y sperm would move from vagina to ovum at a faster rate than X sperm do. It is also reasonable to assume that the larger-headed, heavier female sperm are stronger and will live longer—or will at least maintain their vigor longer—than the male sperm.

For a couple wishing a boy, Shettles suggests that a preliminary alkaline douche be taken by the wife (two tablespoons of baking soda in a quart of water), that there be as deep penetration as possible at the time of ejaculation, that the woman experience an orgasm during the sex act, and that the couple abstain from intercourse until just *after* the time the wife expects to ovulate. The alkaline douche neutralizes the acid environment of the vagina, as does the woman's mucous secretion at the time of her orgasm, thus lessening the threat to the weaker male-producing sperm. The deep penetration shortens the vaginal journey, making it less hazardous to the male sperm. Abstinence appears to increase the proportion of male sperm, for one reason or another. Also, timing intercourse to follow ovulation allows the lighter, faster-moving male-producing sperm a better chance to reach the waiting egg first.

For a couple wishing a girl, Shettles suggests that a preliminary acid douche be taken (two tablespoons of vinegar to a quart of water), that there be shallow penetration at the time of ejaculation, and that the woman not experience orgasm at the time of the sex act. There should be no abstinence from intercourse. Intercourse should take place as usual until a day or so before ovulation is expected *and then cease*, so that the weaker male sperm will die off before the egg appears (Shettles 1972).

Incidentally, some geneticists theorize that the parent who is under less stress than the other at the time of intercourse is more likely to reproduce his or her own sex in conception (Schuster & Schuster 1972).

For some reason that is not clear, artificial insemination results in a marked preponderance of males. When the semen to be thus used is allowed to stand in a container for a time before being injected into the uterus, the heavier (by about 4%) X sperm settle to the bottom of the container, whereas the lighter Y sperm rise to the top. Samples of the top third of such a collection of semen reveal an approximate 80% Y content, whereas the lower third contains about 80% X sperm. The middle third contains roughly equal amounts of male and female sperm (Kleegman 1964).

Since X and Y sperm are produced in equal numbers, there is speculation as to why the normal conception ratio of males to females is, curiously, about 160 to 100 (Shettles 1964). The implantation ratio of male to female zygotes (newly fertilized ova) has been estimated at about 120 to 100, and the birth rate of boy to girl infants is approximately 105 to 100.

If it is true, as Shettles contends (1960, 1964, 1972), that the head of the male-producing sperm (Y) is smaller than that of the X (female) sperm, and if the motility of the Y sperm is superior to that of the X, the larger number of males conceived may perhaps thus be explained. A smaller-headed, more agile Y sperm would have a better chance to propel itself to and through the egg's covering before a larger-headed, less agile female-producing sperm.

The evidence is substantial that human sperm may live under ideal conditions for as long as 14 days after ejaculation. Once deposited in the female genital tract, however, they weaken rapidly and their length of survival is questionable. But researchers generally agree that the fertilizing capability of sperm lasts for only one or two days following their deposit in the vagina. The ability to fertilize is also impaired if their motility is poor or if abnormalities—giant, dwarf, or poorly modeled sperm or sperm with more than one head or tail—exceed 35% (Williams 1974). The results of recent research into the use of caffeine to increase sperm motility and longevity have offered renewed hope to couples deprived of children because of sluggish or short-lived sperm (Schoenfeld 1975).

Erection

Although the penis is ordinarily erect at the time of ejaculation, it is not necessary for it to be so. The penis, however, must be at least partially erect if it is to penetrate the vagina and thus be capable of impregnating. Of course, a woman can become pregnant without penetration—for example, through artificial insemination—but in the present discussion only the usual method of impregnation is implied.

Erection of the penis, which is controlled by nerves in the spinal cord at the lower end of the central nervous system, involves the synchronization of several reactions. These reactions are brought about by several forces working separately or together: friction at the surface of the penis and/or surrounding areas, which sends impulses to the sacral area of the spinal cord; sexual thoughts, dreams, odors, etc., causing impulses to be sent to the spinal area from the brain; stimulation of the sexual system by sex hormones; and impulses from full ejaculatory ducts.

Dilation of the arteries that feed blood to the penis results in engorgement of the spongy tissue. This dilation is followed or accompanied by a simultaneous tonic (contractile) spasm of the muscles at the base of the penis near the anus, which prevents the blood from draining out through the veins (Fig. 4.10).

The action of the brain appears to serve as a modification or control of the spinal reflex center, rather than as the most essential factor in producing erections. For example, mild electrical stimulation applied to laboratory animals at the lower spinal cord and/or to the nerves passing between the lower spinal cord and the arteries of the penis produced erections and ejaculations (Stiller 1962).

So long as there is proper and sufficient stimulation from the nerve endings of the penis, and proper and sufficient impulses from the brain, a man will maintain his erection. It should be recognized that inappropriate

Figure 4.10   Representation of the penis, showing the flow of blood. The spongy bodies, composed of erectile tissue, fill with blood to bring about an erection.

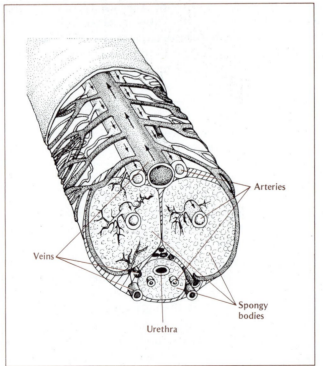

impulses—for example, such severe stimulation of the penis that excessive pain results, or a disturbed emotional state, such as fear, guilt, depression, or shame—can cause an erection to collapse or can prevent its occurring in the first place. Interestingly, however, Wolchik *et al.* (1980) have presented preliminary evidence suggesting that emotional states such as mild anxiety or anger may actually lead to increased sexual arousal.

Nevertheless, emotional difficulties are the most frequent cause of loss of erection, and of impotence as well. It is understandable that a man who fails to have a satisfying erection, then worries over his "failure" and about his abilities the next time he attempts intercourse, may be establishing a vicious circle of failure in his sexual behavior.

Considerable discussion has been devoted in other sections of this book (and in other books as well) to erections, or the lack of them, in adult men. Little is said of erections in young boys. But they do occur, and little attempt is made to understand what is a normal physiological phenomenon. An unwise parent's response will be perhaps to slap the exploring hand of the little boy or to shame him in some other way. Erections occur even in the newborn.

Ejaculation

Ordinarily, erection sets the stage for ejaculation. The stimulation of the penile glans, the presence of sex hormones in the blood, impulses from taut seminal vesicles and ejaculatory ducts, nerve responses from odors, and sexual thoughts are messages which stimulate the brain to bring about and maintain an erection, as well as to build up impulses in the ejaculatory center of the lower spinal cord. These impulses then travel to the section of the lower spine where, along with stimulation from the other areas mentioned, they build up to a threshold at which there is a sudden triggering of the process called ejaculation.

First there is a peristalsis of the ampulla of the vas deferens, the seminal vesicles, and the ejaculatory ducts, which moves the ejaculatory fluid containing the sperm to the membranous part of the urethral tract. Second, there is an accompanying *clonic spasm* (alternating contraction and relaxation) in the urogenital muscles, which discharges the semen by spurting it through and out the penis. This physical reaction is accompanied by a distinct and highly pleasurable sensation known as *orgasm*, to which a later chapter of this book is devoted.

The strength of the ejaculatory force varies from man to man. Some men ejaculate with such force that the discharged semen may travel three feet or more beyond the penile opening, while the semen of others may travel only a few inches, or simply ooze from the urethra. The strength of the force usually depends upon such factors as general health, age, degree of sexual stimulation, and the condition of the prostate. Most men report that semen is ejaculated with little force, although they sometimes tend to correlate the subjective pleasures of orgasm with the force of ejaculation.

It is perhaps coincidental that ejaculation and orgasm occur together. Ejaculation can occur in paraplegics, for example, if the spinal lesion is high enough not to have damaged the nerve area directly responsible for emission. But the paraplegic's ejaculation is unaccompanied by the subjective sensation of orgasm. Studies show that about 65% of paraplegics are capable of complete erections and another 20%, of partial erections; about 30% of the latter are able to have successful intercourse. Despite ejaculation, however, the fertility rate of these men is extremely low, because the spinal lesion in some manner impairs or destroys spermatogenic function. Paraplegic men may have sensuous thoughts and also may have dreams of vivid orgasmic imagery despite their inability to experience the sensation of orgasm (Money 1960, 1970a; Pepmiller 1980).

The sensation of orgasm is the result of impulses from the triggered area of the lower spinal cord reaching the brain. Both erection and ejaculation may occur without any physical stimulation. The prime example is nocturnal emission, which is the result primarily, if not exclusively, of erotic dreams. The dreams may have been preceded by prolonged abstinence, but in many instances they occur to sexually active people who, despite recent orgasm, may become so aroused by some new erotic stimuli that they seek another orgasm through coitus or masturbation, or experience one during sleep. This nocturnal response can occur night after night, especially among better-educated young men, who appear more responsive than others to psychological erotic stimuli ("Answers" 1972). Furthermore, both men and women have been known to have orgasms from erotic thoughts alone or from stimulation of nongenital areas, such as the lips and breasts (Masters & Johnson 1966).

Stimulation of the nerves of the ejaculatory center to the threshold of response does more than initiate ejaculation. Ejaculation itself causes the previously dilated arteries to narrow, so that less blood flows to the penis than is drained off through the veins. The penis thus returns to its flaccid state shortly after ejaculation.

Summary

The main components of the male sexual system are the testes, the scrotum, and the penis. The testes, housed in the scrotum, contain seminiferous tubules in which spermatogenesis takes place. Sperm then move through the testes and the vasa efferentia by peristaltic movements, and from the epididymis to the vas deferens by ciliary movements. The vas deferens connects with the seminal vesicles, the prostate gland, and the Cowper's glands. These organs produce fluids that combine with sperm to make semen. Below the Cowper's glands is the penis, an organ primarily composed of erectile tissue. The glans, or smooth conelike head of the penis, is the highly sensitive area that is covered by the foreskin or prepuce. The glans is exposed normally only during erection of the penis; it may be exposed continuously when the prepuce has been removed surgically. This common operation is usually performed just after birth in a procedure known as circumcision.

Spermatogenesis is an important male function that leads to the development of mature male germ cells. Through the process of mitosis and meiosis, spermatogenesis proceeds from spermatogonium to mature spermatozoon. Mature human sperm have half the full complement of 46 chromosomes: 22 autosomes and one sex chromosome, labeled X or Y, which determines the sex of the child at conception. X and Y sperm are produced in equal numbers. Certain physical differences in X and Y sperm have been reported, and these differences can be capitalized upon in helping couples give birth to children of the sex they desire.

Erection of the penis, which ordinarily occurs prior to ejaculation, is controlled by nerves in the lower spinal cord. The brain is not the most essential feature in producing erections; rather, it serves to modify the spinal reflex center. Emotional factors also influence whether a man maintains or loses his erection.

Ejaculation, together with the sensation known as orgasm, occurs with the following sequence of events: (1) peristalsis of the ampulla of the vas deferens, the seminal vesicles, and the ejaculatory ducts; (2) clonic spasm in the urogenital muscles which causes the semen to be discharged. Although many men associate orgasm and ejaculation, ejaculation, orgasm, and erection need not necessarily accompany one another, as shown in cases of physical injury or disease, or in cases involving erotic thoughts and nocturnal emissions.

Annotated Bibliography

Calderone, Mary S. and Johnson, Eric W. *The family book about sexuality.* New York: Harper and Row, 1981.
> This creatively written sex education text for the family covers all significant topics related to human sexuality and relationships, including giving and receiving love, sexuality and aging, marriage and family planning, variant

behavior, and sex education programs. Important features include a bibliography of additional family readings and a listing of family planning and counseling services.

Chesterman, John and Marten, Michael. *Man to man.* New York: Paddington Press, 1980.

Clear, straightforward, and free of medical jargon, this book answers many questions men ask concerning health and sexuality. Topics such as sexual variance, homosexuality, and venereal disease are discussed frankly and honestly.

Huff, Robert W. and Pauerstein, Carl J. *Human reproduction: Physiology and pathophysiology.* New York: Wiley, 1979.

This text for medical students and practitioners contains detailed information on human reproductive biology, gynecologic physiology, and pregnancy. Specific topics include male and female sexual differentiation, reproductive endocrinology, contraception and infertility, venereal disease, reproductive genetics, fetal growth, and management of normal and high-risk pregnancy. Pre-chapter objectives and self-test questions and answers facilitate learning.

Johnson, Martin and Everitt, Barry. *Essential reproduction.* Oxford, England: Blackwell Scientific Publications, 1980.

This text discusses a wide range of topics related to reproductive biology, including genetics, sexual differentiation, endocrinology, ovarian and testicular function, puberty and the climacteric, hormones and sexual behavior, coitus and fertilization, pregnancy, parturition and lactation. Though written for the student of the technicalities of reproduction, this book would be useful as a general reference.

McCary, James Leslie. *Freedom and growth in marriage (2nd ed.).* New York: John Wiley and Sons, 1980.

This book for the student and general reader considers various aspects of marriage, dating and mate selection, focusing on implications for individual growth and freedom within the marriage relationship. The past and future of marriage are discussed, as well as relevant contemporary issues, alternatives to marriage, the nature of love, aspects of human sexuality, marital adjustment, and other topics.

Moore, Mary L. *Realities in childbearing.* Philadelphia: W. B. Saunders, 1978.

Intended as a text for nursing students and other medical personnel, this book covers the various aspects of human reproductive physiology and the cultural, emotional, developmental, and environmental contexts of childbearing.

Sandler, Jack, Myerson, Marilyn, and Kinder, Bill N. *Human sexuality: Current perspectives.* Tampa, Florida: Mariner, 1980.

This text presents a comprehensive perspective of the field of human sexuality. A wide range of topics is covered, including sexual anatomy and sexual response, aphrodisiacs and anaphrodisiacs, past and current sexual attitudes and behavior, sexual diseases and disorders, sexual dysfunctions, birth control, sexual health, and sex and the law. Though designed for the student, this book would serve as a valuable general reference.

Shearman, Rodney P. *Human reproductive physiology (2nd ed.).* London: Blackwell Scientific Publications, 1979.

> This comprehensive text provides detailed information on most significant aspects of human reproduction, including genetics and cytogenetics, the physiology and function of testes and ovaries, pregnancy, and menopause. This book is designed for the student and medical and allied health professional.

Witters, Weldon and Jones-Witters, Patricia. *Human sexuality: A biological perspective.* New York: D. Van Nostrand, 1980.

> This text approaches the various aspects of human sexuality from the biological standpoint. Topics of special interest include genetic engineering, hormonal control of sexuality, drugs affecting sexual function, surrogate parenthood, artificial insemination, cloning, and sex selection. The text is well illustrated and contains student performance objectives, but its appeal extends beyond the classroom.

Zilbergeld, B. *Male sexuality: A guide to sexual fulfillment.* Boston: Little, Brown and Company, 1978.

> Honest and forthright, this book deals with many of the physical and emotional aspects of sex for men. Some topics covered include learning about sex, touching, masturbation, virginity and sexual abstinence, male sexual dysfunctions, male sexuality and aging, and medical and sex problems. This book will appeal to men of all ages.

The Female Sexual System

The Female Genitalia

The internal female genital organs consist of two **ovaries,** two **uterine** or **fallopian tubes,** the **uterus** or **womb,** and the inner two-thirds of the **vagina** (Fig. 5.1). The first three are supported in the body cavity principally by two broad ligaments, composed of a double layer of peritoneal tissue, permitting independent movement of each organ.

The Ovaries

The ovaries, which produce *ova* or eggs, are homologous to the male testes. Ovarian hormones contribute to a woman's sexual desire, but primarily they prepare and maintain the uterus for implantation of the fertilized ovum. Located on either side of the uterus, the ovaries are pinkish-grey bodies roughly the size, shape, and weight of an unshelled almond. The stout ovarian ligament attaches ovary to uterus; the mesovarium, also peritoneal tissue, connects it to the broad ligament; a third fold of peritoneal tissue passes from ovary to pelvic wall (Fawcett 1963).

85

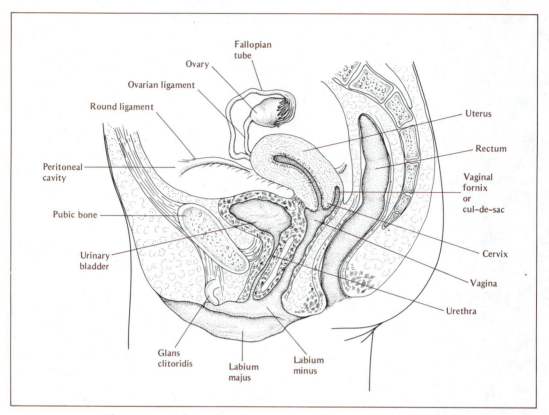

Figure 5.1   Schematic representation of the female pelvic region, showing organs of reproduction.

Within each ovary are a number of round vesicles called follicles. Each follicle houses an *oocyte* (an ovum in an early stage of development). At about the seventh month of a female's fetal life, there are about 7 million follicles in her ovaries (Baker 1972). At birth, the vast majority of them have disintegrated, leaving 200,000 to 400,000 follicles in each ovary (C. W. Lloyd 1964). With the body's growth, development, and subsequent hormonal secretions, some of the oocytes begin to ripen into mature ova, marking the beginning of puberty. At puberty, the number of oocytes has diminished to perhaps 100,000 to 200,000, the count steadily decreasing during a woman's reproductive years.

Each month, about midway through the menstrual cycle of the physically mature female, one follicle ruptures, discharging the ovum into the peritoneal cavity. This process is known as **ovulation.** (Perhaps 20 follicles ripen to the point of readiness for ovulation. Because of circulating gonadotropic hormones, however, only one of these follicles usually ruptures; the others degenerate.) Since the average woman is fertile for approximately 35 years and ovulates about 13 times every year, it can be seen that only 400 to 500 of the many thousands of oocytes are discharged. The numerous primitive follicles that reach only a certain stage of development and then disintegrate serve a purpose, however, in that, before degenerating, they are an important source of female hormones.

The follicles lie just beneath the ovary's cortex or outer layer (Fig. 5.2), and may be either primordial (not yet growing) or graafian (approaching the time when a mature ovum will erupt and be discharged). During their period of maturation, the follicles sink deeply toward the center or medulla of the ovary. The medulla consists of layers of stroma (soft tissue), which is abundantly supplied with blood vessels.

As the follicles grow, several layers separated by a clear membrane form around the ovum, creating tiny spaces between follicular cells which fill with fluid. These spaces eventually unite to form one larger space, called the antrum. The graafian follicle reaches a diameter of 12 to 15 mm and often occupies as much as one-fourth of the entire volume of the ovary. The rapid increase in follicular fluid and size exerts pressure, which ruptures the wall of the ovary, discharging the ovum from the follicular cavity in a wave of fluid.

In most cases, and in a manner that is still not clearly understood, the liberated ovum is drawn into the uterine tube on the same side of the woman's body. There are exceptions to this process, as there are with most biological phenomena, in that ova have been known to enter the uterine tube on the opposite side. Just how these journeys through the peritoneal cavity come about is something of a mystery.

Figure 5.2   Schematic representation of the ovary, showing developing follicles, mature follicle, and corpus luteum.

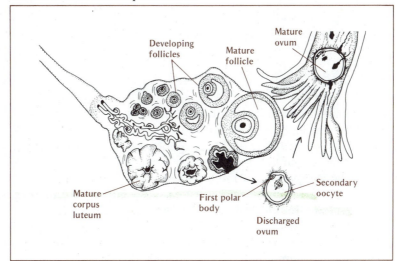

After the ovum is discharged from the ovary, the lining of the empty follicle grows inward and the vacated space is filled with corpus luteum. This new cell growth produces **progesterone,** the hormone so important in pregnancy. Ovulation is generally assumed to occur alternately in each ovary, but one ovary may in fact discharge several times in succession. A single egg is usually released at the time of ovulation, but two or more ova from one or more follicles may be discharged.

Hormonal measurements and clinical diagnostic procedures exist that can help determine whether a woman is approaching or is in the midst of ovulation. Measurements taken until the preovulatory peaks of estrogen and luteinizing hormone (LH) levels in the blood occur can aid in establishing that ovulation is imminent. Changes that occur in leucocyte alkaline phosphatase levels, vaginal cytology, cervical mucus, and basal body temperature also can help detect the time of ovulation (Eddy 1979). Thus, use of such procedures may aid women who have had difficulty in becoming pregnant.

The use of fertility drugs has enabled many women who were previously unable to ovulate to become fertile and have babies. Some of the drugs, however, cause several ova to mature and be discharged during the same ovulation period, resulting in a marked rise in the incidence of multiple births. In recent years there have been verified reports of exceptionally large multiple births, ranging in number from 7 children on several occasions, to one delivery of 8, one of 9, and one record delivery of 15 babies. In very large multiple births, the death rate is exceptionally high.

Women not taking fertility drugs may ovulate more than once a month under normal circumstances. An additional egg is especially likely to be discharged during a peak of sexual excitation, even during menstruation, perhaps explaining the high incidence of impregnation during the so-called "safe" period—the time of the menstrual month at which conception is considered least likely to occur (Neubardt 1968).

The Fallopian Tubes

One of the uterine or fallopian tubes (after Gabriello Fallopius, 1523–1562) conveys the egg from the ovary to the uterus. It is also the place where fertilization of the ovum normally occurs. Each of the uterine tubes is about 4 in. (10 cm) long and is suspended by a ligament, allowing each tube to extend from the upper and outer part of its side of the uterus to the ovary. The flanged part of the tube slightly cups over the ovary.

The fallopian tubes are divided into three sections: the intramural portion, the isthmus, and the ampulla (Fig. 5.3). The intramural portion is included within the uterine wall. Extending from it is a narrow isthmus, which broadens into the funnel-shaped ampulla. The end of the tube (infundibulum) is fringed with small fingerlike extensions called fimbriae,

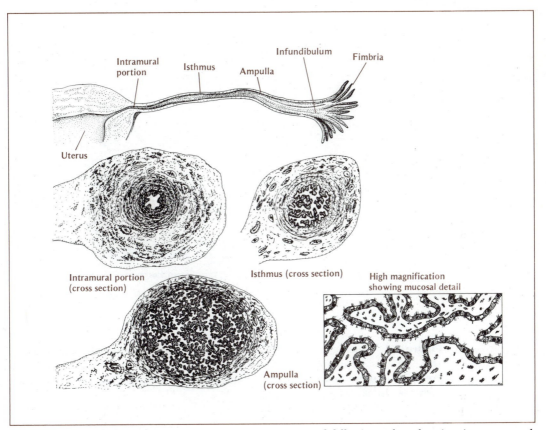

Figure 5.3 Schematic representation of fallopian tube, showing its gross and microscopic structure.

one or some of which may reach the ovary. Many cilia (tiny hairlike protrusions) extend from the tubal walls. These cilia act in a wavelike manner to sweep an ovum from the ampulla, where fertilization generally occurs, toward the uterus.

The Uterus

The uterus or womb is a hollow, thick-walled muscular organ shaped somewhat like a pear. In a mature woman, its size at the top measures approximately 2.5 by 2 in. (6.3 by 5 cm). It narrows to a diameter of about 1 in. (2.5 cm) at the cervix (neck) and is about 3 in. (7.5 cm) long. Situated in the pelvic cavity between the bladder and rectum, it hangs slightly below and between the fallopian tubes (Fig. 5.4).

The uterus is divided into two parts by its isthmus, a slight constriction near the center (to be distinguished from the isthmus of the fallopian tubes).

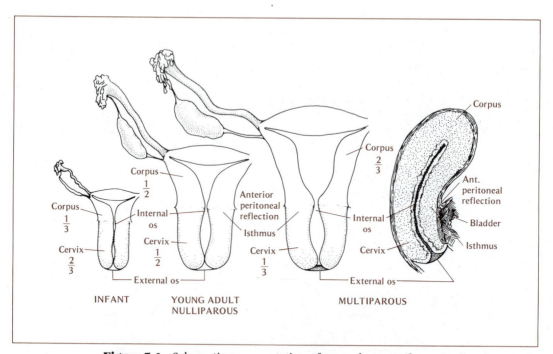

Figure 5.4 Schematic representation of normal uterus (front view) and append-ages, showing comparative size of infantile, adult nonparous (not having been pregnant) and multiparous (having been pregnant) uteri. Side view of multiparous uterus is also shown.

The larger portion—the corpus (body)—of the uterus lies above the second part, the cervix, which opens into the inner portion of the vagina. The opening of the cervix into the vagina is known as the external os, and its opening into the corpus is known as the internal os. (See Fig. 5.5)

The uterus is held in position by six ligaments: two broad ones extending from the uterus to the floor and wall of the pelvis; two round ones connecting the uterus near the openings of the fallopian tubes laterally to the pelvic walls; and the last two, the uterosacral ligaments, extending from the upper part of the cervix to the sacrum (the bone at the base of the vertebral column). When a woman stands erect with bladder and rectum empty, the uterus lies almost horizontal, with its fundus (upper end) forward, at a right angle to the vagina.

The walls of the uterus are particularly thick at the fundus, where the measurement may be 0.6 in. (1.5 cm) or more. The uterine walls are made up of three layers: the perimetrium (the outer layer or serosa), which consists of elastic fibrous tissue; the myometrium (the middle or muscular layer), which makes up most of the uterine wall, and which consists of bundles and layers of very strong smooth muscle cells; and the endometrium

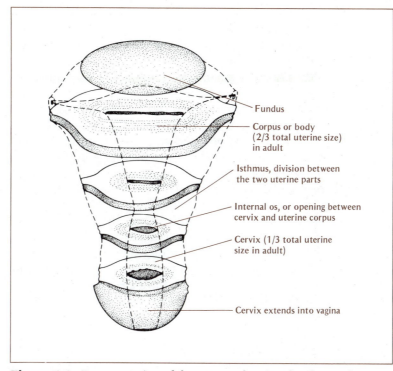

Fundus

Corpus or body
(2/3 total uterine size)
in adult

Isthmus, division between
the two uterine parts

Internal os, or opening between
cervix and uterine corpus

Cervix (1/3 total uterine
size in adult)

Cervix extends into vagina

Figure 5.5   Representation of the uterus, showing the shape of its cavity and the cervical canal.

(the inner layer or mucosa), consisting of tissue that thickens as the uterus prepares for implantation of a fertilized ovum, but that sloughs off at the time of menstruation, if fertilization does not occur.

Uterine musculature is complex and highly efficient. The muscle bundles combine the uterus and its tubes and ligaments into an interlacing system that produces certain contractions during the period just before ovulation when estrogen production is at its peak. It is thought that these coordinated contractions in some way move the flanged openings of the fallopian tubes into the proper position to receive the ovum when it is discharged.

The uterine walls contain longitudinal and circular muscle fibers that spiral and run through the walls in both clockwise and counterclockwise directions. The basketlike interweaving of the muscles allows the uterus both to stretch to gigantic proportions during pregnancy and to exert tremendous pressure by contracting downward during labor. Contraction of these muscles also takes place in the orgasmic phase of a woman's sexual response cycle (Masters & Johnson 1961b) and at certain times during menstruation, causing cramping in some women.

The cavity of the uterus is a flattened space that is little more than a slit, its total length being about 2.5 in. (6.3 cm). The flattened cavity narrows to a small opening at the internal os, and continues through the cervix as an opening smaller than a soda straw.

The **cervix** is smaller than the body of the uterus; the size ratio in mature women is about one to two. In the newborn the ratio is reversed, the cervix being about twice as large as the corpus. In young girls, the ratio is about one to one. Physicians often describe women as having an infantile uterus when the corpus and the cervix are nearly the same size; such women are frequently incapable of bearing children. The body of the uterus grows proportionately larger because of hormonal secretions that commence at puberty, while the growth of the cervix merely keeps pace with the growth rate of the rest of the body.

The cervix is more fibrous than the corpus of the uterus, and its palmate (foldlike) lining contains glands that produce a mucous secretion, once erroneously thought to attract sperm cells (Masters & Johnson 1966). About 0.3 to 0.5 in. (0.8 to 1.3 cm) of the cervix extends into the vagina, thus producing a passage for sperm. During pregnancy, the cervix is often closed by a mucous plug that prevents bacteria and other undesirable matter from entering the uterus, thereby reducing the possibility of infection.

The Vagina

The **vagina** is a muscular tube, capable of considerable dilation, which extends from just behind the cervix to an external opening in the vestibule of the vulva. About 3 in. (7.6 cm) long on the anterior or front wall, and about 3.5 in. (8.9 cm) on the posterior or back wall, the vagina extends upward in an approximately vertical manner in a standing woman, roughly at right angles to the uterus. It is the organ that receives the penis during the act of sexual intercourse.

The walls of the vagina are in contact with each other under ordinary conditions, and are made up of three layers: (1) the fibrous coat, a thin layer of elastic fibrous tissue, which serves not only as an aid to contraction but also as a connective tissue to other bodily tissues; (2) the muscular coat, a layer of smooth muscles that run primarily in a longitudinal direction, although there are also bundles of circular muscular fibers in the vaginal canal (for example, the sphincter muscle of striated fiber surrounding the external vaginal opening); and (3) the mucosa, which houses mucous crypts and many blood vessels. The mucosa's large folds give the vagina its wrinkled appearance. The entire area contains an intricate network of erectile tissue that serves to help dilate and close the vaginal canal (see Chapter 12).

The mucosal coat of the vagina contains no glands, as such, although mucous secretions of the uterine tissue sometimes aid in moistening the vagina. Vaginal lubrication, present during sexual excitement, is brought about by the vagina itself. It secretes a fluid through a process similar to sweating that remains something of a puzzle (Masters & Johnson 1966).

As sexual excitement builds and continues, small beads of "sweat" appear on the vaginal surface. Often the vaginal muscles contract suddenly, bringing the walls of the vagina together in such a way as to force the secretion out of the vagina in a spurting fashion. This secretion, along with the orgasmic platform contractions, is the foundation of the mistaken notion that women ejaculate as men do. However, the "sweat" merely serves as a lubricant to aid in penile penetration, making coitus easier to perform.

While it is generally recognized that women do not ejaculate as men do, Addiego *et al.* (1980) report isolated cases in which women have experienced an ejaculatory-type phenomenon. These investigators claim to have discovered evidence that "some women ejaculate a fluid which contains the product of the 'female prostate,' the system of paraurethral glands, including Skene's glands, which is homologous to the male prostate." Their evidence suggests that such responses occur most frequently from stimulation of the "Grafenberg spot," an area located on the "anterior wall of the vagina approximately 1 to 2 centimeters deeper in the vagina than the inner border of the pubic bone when the woman is lying in a supine position." Their report of the presence of ejaculatory-type responses in women will probably lead to further investigation by the scientific community.

Changes in the vagina occur with the birth of children. Also, the natural relaxation of muscles as a woman gets older often leads the vaginal muscles, no longer as firm or strong as before, to sag. The result may be a vagina that is too large to allow for the partner's fullest coital satisfaction. This condition is especially bothersome for a man who depends largely upon friction of the vaginal wall against the glans of his penis to stimulate his erogenous nerve endings and to supply the sexual impulses that result in an orgasm. Similarly, the condition can also be annoying to a woman who receives little or no physiological pleasure from penile penetration—the vagina contains very few nerve endings that give sexual pleasure—but who gains some psychological pleasure from penetration.

A woman with overly relaxed vaginal muscles can strengthen them by proper exercise (Clark 1963b; Witkin 1980). She is advised to contract the vaginal muscles as she would the urethral sphincter to halt urination midway. A series of 20 or so alternating contractions and relaxations should be repeated about 10 times a day. After a month of these exercises, a difference in the size of the vagina will probably be noticeable. The exercises are not necessarily time-consuming and can be done while the woman is busy with her daily activities. In recent years some women have begun to supplement or replace the exercises with the use of electronic aids to strengthen the vaginal muscles. A battery-operated, hand-held device known as the Vagette has been developed that specifically helps women to strengthen the pubococcygeal muscle (Dailey 1980b).

Scientific investigations of hundreds of women who have developed and strengthened their vaginal muscles revealed that many of them have subsequently experienced heightened sexual responsiveness and satisfaction. These observations have led some researchers to conclude that the proprioceptive nerve endings in the vaginal muscles, which are stimulated by the penis during coitus, possibly account for the concept of vaginal orgasm (Clark 1969b; Kegel 1953).

Formerly, relaxed vaginas were made smaller or tighter by surgical means. Such surgery is still performed, but only in extreme cases in which muscle damage is severe or other physiological difficulties exist.

The **hymen** or maidenhead is the fold of connective tissue that partially closes the external opening of the vagina. This tissue, if still intact, is usually ruptured by the first act of sexual intercourse. More often, however, the tissue is broken by accidents to the pubic area or by experimentation. A ruptured hymen, therefore, is certainly not *prima facie* evidence that a female is not a virgin. On the other hand, rare cases exist in which the hymen is so flexible or pliable that coitus can take place repeatedly without rupturing the tissue. An intact hymen at the time of marriage is extremely important to some women. Some cultures, for example, expect—even demand—that women be virginal at marriage, so their gynecologists frequently perform surgery to create an artificial hymen.

Pain accompanying first intercourse—frequently assumed to be a cause of frigidity—is often the result of hymenal rupture. If the hymen is intact, it would be wise to have a physician cut or remove it rather than risking the tissue's being torn by forceful penile penetration. In the case of an annular (ring-shaped) hymen, a doctor may suggest inserting and rotating the fingertips or using a small dilator, either of which will stretch the tissue and permit penile penetration without pain or difficulty. Obviously the hymenal tissue does not close off the vagina completely, since the menstrual flow is discharged as easily from virgins as from nonvirgins. The tissue is usually annular or perforated, or in some other way only partially covers the opening (Fig. 5.6). In those rare cases in which the vagina is completely sealed over, a minor operation before the onset of menstruation will solve the problem.

In addition to the pain of tearing the hymenal tissue, there is often pain during early, and especially first, sexual intercourse because of powerful contractions of the vaginal muscles—usually the result of fear and ignorance of the facts of coitus. If a woman is relaxed and unafraid, there is little reason why she cannot comfortably and pleasurably accommodate a very large penis, even though she has never before had sexual intercourse. Women under emotional stress, however, even though they

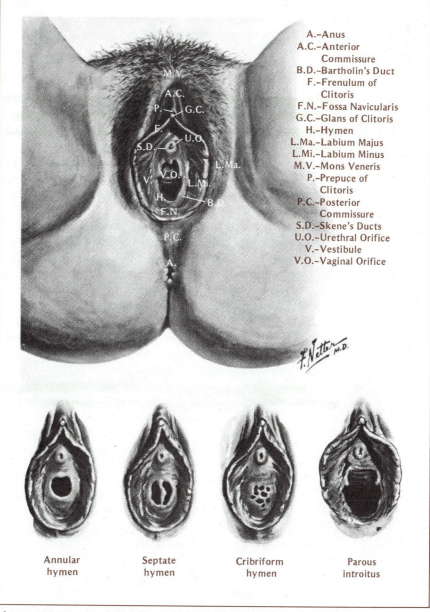

A.–Anus
A.C.–Anterior Commissure
B.D.–Bartholin's Duct
F.–Frenulum of Clitoris
F.N.–Fossa Navicularis
G.C.–Glans of Clitoris
H.–Hymen
L.Ma.–Labium Majus
L.Mi.–Labium Minus
M.V.–Mons Veneris
P.–Prepuce of Clitoris
P.C.–Posterior Commissure
S.D.–Skene's Ducts
U.O.–Urethral Orifice
V.–Vestibule
V.O.–Vaginal Orifice

| Annular hymen | Septate hymen | Cribriform hymen | Parous introitus |

Figure 5.6 External female genitalia, with comparison of four types of hymens. Adapted from an original painting by Frank H. Netter, M.D. from the CIBA COLLECTION OF MEDICAL ILLUSTRATIONS, copyright by CIBA Pharmaceutical Company, Division of CIBA-GEIGY Corporation.

might be highly experienced sexually, can experience these vaginal muscle spasms (a condition known as **vaginismus**), making forced penetration extremely painful or even impossible.

The Vulva

The external genital apparatus of a woman, known as the **vulva,** consists of the following visible parts or areas: the mons veneris (also called mons pubis), the labia majora (major or large outer lips), the labia minora (small inner lips), the clitoris, and the vestibule (Fig. 5.6).

The mons veneris or mons pubis is composed of pads of fatty tissue lying below the skin over the symphysis pubis (pubic bone). It is covered with springy, curly hair. This area houses certain nerve endings that when stimulated by weight, pressure, or similar conditions can produce sexual excitement. From this prominent mound, two longitudinal folds of skin bearing pubic hair extend to form the outer borders of the vulva.

These two folds of skin are the labia majora that enclose the vulval cleft (indentation). The lips are quite fatty; their inner sides contain sebaceous follicles and sweat glands but no hair.

The labia minora are also two longitudinal folds and are located within the major lips. Rich in blood vessels, nerve endings, and small sebaceous glands, they contain no hair or fat cells. These small lips form the lateral and lower borders of the vestibule. They fuse at the top to form the prepuce and to enclose the clitoris.

The **clitoris** is a small cylindrical erectile structure situated at the top of the vestibule and at the lower border of the symphysis pubis. It consists of two crura (leglike stalks) arising at the pubic bone and fusing together to form the body or shaft, terminating in the glans, which projects beyond the folds of the labia minora. The entire clitoris, except the glans, is underneath the upper part of the labia minora where its two lips join to form the frenulum clitoridis (clitoral prepuce or foreskin).

The body of the clitoris can be felt just beneath the prepuce that covers it. Unlike the penis, the clitoris does not hang free; only its glans is exposed. It contains two corpora cavernosa (spongy erectile structures), which are enclosed by a thick fibrous tissue. With stimulation, these bodies may engorge with blood and become erect. The clitoris is ordinarily less than 1 in. (2.5 cm) in length (although striking variations in its measurements are on record). When sexually stimulated it may enlarge considerably—to twice its flaccid size or more—especially in the diameter of its shaft.

The glans of the flaccid clitoris has a diameter of about 4 to 5 mm (Dickinson 1949). Like the glans of the penis, it contains an abundance of nerve endings and is the most sexually excitable area of a woman's body. Direct contact with the glans—such as the man's pubic bone rubbing against it—and indirect stimulation through pulling and tugging of the minor lips as the penis moves in and out of the vagina, are coital methods of bringing a woman to orgasm. Masters and Johnson (1966) have pointed out that, in self-manipulation of the clitoris, women stimulate to the side of it rather than stimulating it directly.

It is possible to remove the clitoris completely without destroying a woman's erotic sensations, pleasure, or, even, her orgasmic capability. The nerve supply to the vulval area is so great that large amounts of erogenous tissue may be removed without significantly decreasing sexual gratification. In fact, women may remain orgasmic after the entire vulval region has been removed by surgery. It appears, therefore, that frequency and intensity of sexual activity, including orgasm, are related less to anatomical size or the amount of tissue than to other factors, including psychological ones (Money 1970b).

Paralyzed women lose their capacity to respond orgasmically, but they may be sensitive to touching, stroking, or oral stimulation of their breasts, necks, or faces. Thus, emotionally gratifying sexual experiences can be attained by handicapped women (Pepmiller 1980).

Smegma, an accumulation of genital secretions, can collect under the prepuce covering the clitoris, resulting in abrasions and adhesions between it and the glans. Some specialists believe that this condition may cause severe pain when the clitoris enlarges during sexual excitement. Circumcision was a former remedy, but in present-day practice a probe is frequently used to separate the prepuce from the glans and to rid the area of the smelly, ragged lumps.

The vestibule is the cleft region enclosed by the labia minora. It houses the openings of the vagina and the urethra. This area also is rich in nerve endings and blood vessels, and is highly responsive to proper stimulation. The meatus of the urethra is located about halfway between the clitoris and the vagina and is, of course, the opening of the tube through which urine passes out of the body from the bladder. The greater vestibular glands, the Bartholin's glands, are situated on each side of the vaginal opening. Each secretes a drop or so of lubricating fluid during sexual excitement. Although this fluid was once thought to aid in penile penetration, recent research has shown that the secretion is too slight to be of significant benefit in vaginal lubrication (Masters & Johnson 1966).

Oogenesis

Oogenesis, the development of ova, corresponds to the male function of spermatogenesis. Although smaller than the period at the end of this sentence, the human ovum is a relatively large cell. It averages 0.13 mm in diameter and 0.000004 gm in weight, and is one of the largest of mammalian eggs (*Williams Obstetrics* 1961).

Oogenesis consists of four developmental stages: oogonium, primary oocyte, secondary oocyte, and mature ovum. In the first phase of development, the oogonium, or basic cell of the ovum, is enclosed in an ovarian follicle. It then develops into a primary oocyte, which is somewhat larger than the original cell. Just prior to ovulation, the primary oocyte undergoes a process known as reduction division, or meiosis. The paired chromosomes within the oocyte divide, with one of each pair going to each of the two daughter cells created by the division. The number of chromosomes in each daughter cell is therefore 23 rather than the usual 46.

One daughter cell, called the secondary oocyte, is much larger than the other because it retains practically all the cytoplasm, the material that maintains the life of the cell's nucleus, of the original cell. It is the secondary oocyte that unites with the male sperm, each contributing 23 chromosomes to make up the 46 common to human heritage. The second daughter cell, which is referred to as a polar body, has little function and ultimately degenerates.

In the course of ovulation the secondary oocyte moves from the follicle into the fallopian tube where fertilization, if it is to take place, usually occurs. The ovum is not considered to have reached full maturity, the fourth stage of oogenesis, until it is fertilized, for the developmental processes of the nucleus are not complete until then (Arey 1974).

Summary

This chapter focused on the main components of the female sexual system—the ovaries, fallopian tubes, uterus, and vagina. In a mature woman, the ovaries produce ova, or eggs, which are discharged monthly in a process known as ovulation. After an ovum is discharged from an ovary, progesterone, a hormone important in pregnancy, is produced. Fertilization of the ovum by the male sperm, if it occurs, takes place in one of the fallopian tubes. The ovum, fertilized or not, moves down toward the uterus—an organ divided into a corpus and a cervix. The fertilized egg becomes implanted in the endometrium of the uterus. If fertilization does not occur, the endometrium sloughs off during menstruation.

The vagina, or birth canal, extends from the cervix to an external opening, and is also the organ that receives the penis during sexual intercourse. Vaginal muscles that may have become too relaxed from aging or giving birth can be strengthened through proper exercise. Young women may have a hymen, a fold of connective tissue partially closing the vaginal entrance. This tissue, if not already broken, may require removal in order to facilitate sexual intercourse.

The vulva, or external genitalia, consist of the mons veneris, the labia majora, the labia minora, the clitoris, and the vestibule. The mons veneris is covered with springy, curly hair; the labia majora extend from the mons veneris to enclose the vulval cleft. The labia minora, located within the labia majora, fuse at the top to enclose the clitoris. The clitoris is the most sexually excitable area of a woman's body. Enclosed by the labia minora is the vestibule, the area of the vaginal and urethral openings.

Oogenesis, the female counterpart of spermatogenesis, consists of four stages: oogonium, primary oocyte, secondary oocyte, and mature ovum. It is the secondary oocyte that moves into the fallopian tube in the course of ovulation. Should the egg become fertilized, it reaches the fourth stage of oogenesis, where it is called a mature ovum.

Annotated Bibliography

Huff, Robert W. and Pauerstein, Carl J. *Human reproduction: Physiology and pathophysiology.* New York: Wiley, 1979.
> This text for medical students and practitioners contains detailed information on human reproductive biology, gynecologic physiology, and pregnancy. Specific topics include male and female sexual differentiation, reproductive endocrinology, contraception and infertility, venereal disease, reproductive genetics, fetal growth, and management of normal and high-risk pregnancy. Pre-chapter objectives and self-test questions and answers facilitate learning.

Johnson, Martin and Everitt, Barry. *Essential reproduction.* Oxford, England: Blackwell Scientific Publications, 1980.
> This text discusses a wide range of topics related to reproductive biology, including genetics, sexual differentiation, endocrinology, ovarian and testicular function, puberty and the climacteric, hormones and sexual behavior, coitus and fertilization, pregnancy, parturition, and lactation. Though written for the student of the technicalities of reproduction, this book would be useful as a general reference.

Kirkpatrick, M. (Ed.) *Women's sexual development: Explorations of inner space.* New York: Plenum Press, 1980.
> Articles in this volume discuss various significant topics related to female sexuality, including history of female sexuality, female sexual physiology, femininity, masturbation, lesbianism, father-daughter relationships, and sexual self-help. The book will appeal to a wide audience.

Lanson, Lucienne. *From woman to woman.* New York: Alfred Knopf, 1981.
> Written by a gynecologist for the general public, this book answers frequent questions concerning female sexual physiology, menstruation, sexual inter-

course, pregnancy, contraceptives, menopause, gynecological problems, and other areas. Language is straightforward and nontechnical.

McCary, James Leslie. *Freedom and growth in marriage (2nd ed.)*. New York: John Wiley and Sons, 1980.

This book for the student and general reader considers various aspects of marriage, dating and mate selection, focusing on implications for individual growth and freedom within the marriage relationship. The past and future of marriage are discussed, as well as relevant contemporary issues, alternatives to marriage, the nature of love, aspects of human sexuality, marital adjustment, and other topics.

Moore, Mary L. *Realities in childbearing*. Philadelphia: W. B. Saunders, 1978.

Intended as a text for nursing students and other medical personnel, this book covers the various aspects of human reproductive physiology and the cultural, emotional, developmental, and environmental contexts of childbearing.

Sandler, Jack, Myerson, Marilyn, and Kinder, Bill N. *Human sexuality: Current perspectives*. Tampa, Florida: Mariner, 1980.

This text presents a comprehensive perspective of the field of human sexuality. A wide range of topics is covered, including sexual anatomy and sexual response, aphrodisiacs and anaphrodisiacs, past and current sexual attitudes and behavior, sexual diseases and disorders, sexual dysfunctions, birth control, sexual health, and sex and the law. Though designed for the student, this book would serve as a valuable general reference.

Shearman, Rodney P. *Human reproductive physiology (2nd ed.)*. London: Blackwell Scientific Publications, 1979.

This comprehensive text provides detailed information on most significant aspects of human reproduction, including genetics and cytogenetics, the physiology and function of testes and ovaries, pregnancy, and menopause. This book is designed for the student and medical personnel.

Silber, Sherman J. *How to get pregnant*. New York: Charles Scribner's Sons, 1980.

This book discusses in simple terms a wide range of topics related to conception and contraception. Some subject areas include male and female reproductive physiology, tests of fertility, treatment of conditions causing infertility, artificial insemination and sperm-banking, test tube babies and cloning, and birth regulation and sterilization. This book is an excellent treatment of the topic for the general public.

Witters, Weldon and Jones-Witters, Patricia. *Human sexuality: A biological perspective*. New York: D. Van Nostrand, 1980.

This text approaches the various aspects of human sexuality from the biological standpoint. Topics of special interest include genetic engineering, hormonal control of sexuality, drugs affecting sexual function, surrogate parenthood, artificial insemination, cloning, and sex selection. The text is well illustrated and contains student performance objectives, but its appeal extends beyond the classroom.

Menstruation and the Climacteric

Two dramatic changes take place in a woman's reproductive life: menstruation, which usually begins in the early teens, and menopause, also called the climacteric or "change of life," which occurs some 35 years or so later.

Although menstruation and menopause are normal physiological events, both can cause great physical and psychological stress. Because of the change in a woman's hormonal structure and balance at menopause, physical difficulties are more typically associated with it than with menstruation. Physical distress during menstruation may be a serious problem for a few women, particularly young ones. But the main burden for some girls and women is psychological. The roots lie in negative attitudes toward menstruation that have persisted through many centuries and in many societies.

Menstruation

We have noted that most girls begin puberty between the ages of 11 and 15. Accompanying the development of breasts, reproductive organs, and secondary sexual characteristics is the **menarche, which is that point during puberty when a monthly uterine bleeding called menstruation** begins.

A widespread misconception is that menarche occurs earlier in girls living in the tropics than for girls living in milder climates. The truth is that menarche is controlled by heredity, although health and environment can influence it. A girl usually starts menstruating at about the same age her mother did. Identical twins typically begin menstruation within the same month. However, debilitating physical conditions such as anemia, malnutrition, and severe illness during late childhood may delay all maturational processes, including menstruation.

Girls living in countries with high living standards—for example, America, England, Germany, and Scandinavia—start menstruation at an earlier age than do girls in other parts of the world. While this comparison might be interpreted to mean that girls in cooler climates have earlier menarche than others, any difference is based on nutrition, not temperature. Furthermore, if hot weather were to bring on the menarche, one would expect the majority of girls to begin menstruation in the summer months. Yet in the U.S., only 25% of girls start their menstrual cycles during the summer (J. L. McCary 1971).

Altitude, however, is apparently related to growth and date of menarche. One study showed that girls from Denver, Colorado (5300 feet above sea level), averaged 7 pounds at birth and reached menarche at 13.1 years. A matched sampling of girls from Berkeley, California (sea level), averaged 7.5 pounds at birth and reached menarche at 12.8 years (W. Sullivan 1971).

The prepuberty growth spurt and the menarche are thought to be precipitated by the body's having reached a critical weight, regardless of age or height. The growth spurt apparently begins when a girl's weight reaches an average of 68 pounds, and menarche when she weighs about 106 pounds (W. Sullivan 1971).

Although the **menstrual cycle** (the lapse of time from the first day of one menstrual flow to the day before the next one) can vary from 21 to 90 days and still be physiologically normal, the typical range is approximately 24 to 32 days (Worley 1980). Young women, especially teen-agers, tend to have longer menstrual cycles than older women. A study of 30,655 menstrual cycles of 2,316 women showed that the average number of days in the cycles of 15- to 19-year-old girls is 30.8 days, while for women 40 to 44 years of age, the average cycle is 28.3 days. Furthermore, the duration of the menstrual cycle appears to vary more among teen-agers and premenopausal women than it does among women in their twenties and thirties (Chiazze et al. 1968). During the 30 to 35 years that a woman is capable of conception, she menstruates about 300 to 500 times.

Menstruation can occur without ovulation having taken place. In fact, the frequency of anovulation increases significantly when the length of the menstrual cycle falls under 23 days or goes beyond 38 days (Worley 1980).

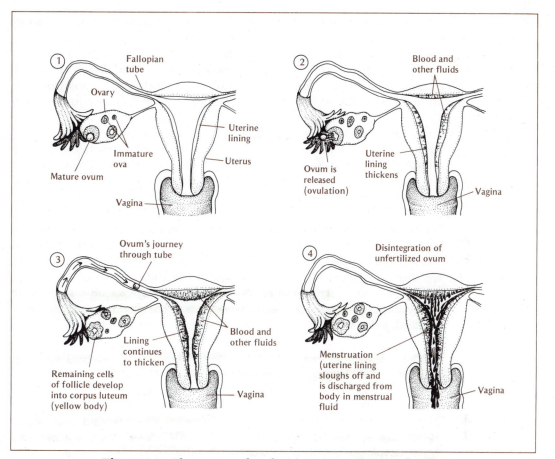

Figure 6.1 The menstrual cycle: (1) During early part of cycle, ovum matures in ovary; endometrium begins to thicken. (2) About 14 days after onset of last menstruation, mature ovum is released; endometrium is thick and spongy. (3) Ovum travels through fallopian tube; ruptured follicle develops into a glandular structure, the corpus luteum; blood and other fluids engorge uterine lining. (4) If ovum is not fertilized, endometrium breaks down and sloughs off in a form of bleeding (menstruation).

Nevertheless, the general purpose of the menstrual cycle is the preparation and maintenance of the uterus for the implantation of the fertilized egg (Fig. 6.1). The menstrual cycle can be divided into three phases: the destructive phase, the follicular phase, and the luteal phase. So that these phases may proceed normally, there must be a good balance between the central nervous system and the endocrine system.

Destructive Phase

Progesterone, which has prepared and maintained the uterine walls for implantation of the fertilized ovum, is withdrawn when the corpus luteum regresses. This withdrawal, or even a lowered concentration of the hormone, causes the **endometrium** (uterine lining) to break down, slough off, and be discharged from the body in a form of bleeding. The destructive phase usually lasts from 3 to 7 days, the average being 4 or 5. The discharge consists not only of blood, but also of other fluids and debris from the uterine wall in the form of mucus and fragments of endometrium, as well as dried epithelial cells from the vagina.

The amount of discharge during the destructive phase varies widely from woman to woman, and sometimes within the cycles of the same individual. On the average, however, the total discharge amounts to approximately one cupful (6 to 8 ounces), with the amount of actual blood loss on even the heaviest day of flow being only about one tablespoonful.

Menstrual Difficulties.   Almost every woman has suffered some menstrual problems. Fortunately, with medical attention and treatment with oral contraceptives, aspirin, codeine, or other appropriate drugs, many women are able to achieve symptomatic relief from their menstrual problems (Dingfelder 1980). Discomfort or pain occurring before menstruation is called the **premenstrual syndrome,** and that during menstruation itself, **dysmenorrhea.** The symptoms are the same. Among them are increased urination, dull pain in the lower abdomen, water retention, and acne. Fatigue, headaches, irritability, and depression are sometimes experienced in what is called **premenstrual tension.** These last changes may be related more to certain unfortunate attitudes toward sex in general, and menstruation specifically, than to women's biological clocks or "raging hormones" (McCary & Copeland 1976; Paige 1973). The most common complaint during menstruation itself is cramping in the pelvic area (called **spasmodic dysmenorrhea**), which is thought to be related to uterine spasms.

The body's toxicity increases as the uterine tissue dies and sloughs off. The bloodstream then picks up some of this toxic material and circulates it through the body, sometimes producing malaise and fatigue. Further, the marked decrease of progesterone in the body just before menstruation produces an imbalance between it and estrogen. This hormonal imbalance is believed to cause the physical and emotional reactions described above.

Recently, a new problem called **toxic shock syndrome** has come to the attention of health officials. The disease, which is apparently rare, is sudden in onset and is characterized by symptoms such as vomiting, fever, diarrhea, a sunburnlike rash, and a quick drop of blood pressure. Shock may occur, affected women may be combative and disoriented and afflicted by muscle aches, conjunctivitis, sore throat, and respiratory and heart difficulties. The cause of the disease is unknown, but a bacterium, *staphylococcus aureus*, is suspected to play a role in the development of symptoms. The continuous use of tampons throughout the menstrual cycle may also be associated with the development of symptoms. Current thinking is that tampons may favor the growth of this bacterium in the vaginal canal or that toxin secreted by the bacterium may be absorbed from the uterus or vagina. Future research into this illness should lead to a better understanding of its causes and insights into its cure ("Toxic shock" 1980).

Generally speaking, the degree of premenstrual tension a woman experiences correlates with her general response to stress. The better she handles stress, the less upset she becomes just before menstruation, and the more easily she recovers from whatever stress occurs. Some women suffer almost unbearable premenstrual tension that appears to be associated with sodium imbalance and resulting water retention. Dramatic relief has been reported when treatment is instituted to rid the body of excess fluid (Neu & DiMascio 1974).

Several studies (Dalton 1968; H. S. Kaplan 1975; Parlee 1973) have reported a wide array of disorders in women during a consecutive 8-day period of each menstrual cycle: the 4 days just before the flow (usually thought of as the time of premenstrual tension) and the 4 days of the flow. The investigators report that more women die by suicide or accident, are admitted to hospitals with medical or psychiatric illness and conditions requiring surgery, and get into trouble with the law during these 8 days than during any other 8-day period in the menstrual cycle. They also score lower on school and college examinations. However, the methodology employed in the data gathering and analysis in most of these studies has caused many scientists to question the validity of the findings (Parlee 1973).

Follicular Phase

After the menstrual flow stops, the uterine wall is very thin. At this time, as well, the breasts have decreased in size and have become somewhat soft, permitting easy examination by touch. Women are therefore encouraged to examine themselves during this time for the presence of lumps or other abnormal masses (Reyniak 1976).

Under the stimulation of estrogen, which is secreted by the follicles located in the ovaries, the uterine mucosa begins a growth process lasting about 9 days. Many follicles contain developing ova (hence the name of this phase), most of which cease to grow. Only one usually reaches maturity in a single cycle, the **graafian follicle**. Approaching the 14th day of the menstrual cycle, ovulation occurs. After the release of the ovum, the graafian follicle fills with corpus luteum and seals itself off with the aid of the luteinizing and luteotropic hormones secreted by the pituitary gland.

Luteal Phase

During the follicular phase, the secretion of estrogen increases gradually. Estrogen concentration in the blood is at its maximum at the moment of ovulation. Following ovulation, the corpus luteum begins actively to secrete progesterone. Estrogen concentration decreases as progesterone begins preparing the uterus for the fertilized egg. The mucous membrane of the uterus becomes thicker and more vascular as small "lakes" of blood, called *lacunae,* are formed within the uterine endometrium. The lacunae provide nourishment for the ovum if it becomes fertilized and implants itself in the endometrium.

During the luteal phase, luteotropin and the ovarian hormones cause the amount of fluid in the breasts to increase, resulting in greater size and sensitivity. Premenstrual congestion and swelling of mucous membranes sometimes cause a retention of fluid and consequent temporary gain in weight of as much as 5 pounds.

Some women experience a decline in sexual desire during this phase, which many believe is caused by the inhibitory effects of progesterone. Furthermore, those few women suffering from constant and insatiable sex desire have reported relief when placed on progesterone treatment. Others argue that there is no clearcut evidence one way or the other concerning progesterone's effect on women's libido, that any changes in drive during the month are based on influences other than hormonal (Dmowski *et al.* 1974).

If conception does not occur during the menstrual cycle, the corpus luteum degenerates and the concentration of estrogen and progesterone decreases immensely. This sudden decrease in the amounts of both hormones is believed to bring about the destructive phase of menstruation, and the entire process then starts all over again.

Cyclical Sex Drive

Of 28 separate studies conducted over a great number of years and involving many subjects, the results of 13 revealed that a woman's sexual desire peaks just after the menstrual flow begins. Nine showed the peak to be just before the flow, and six midway in the cycle (Cavanagh 1969). These differences may be individual idiosyncrasies, or as Udry and Morris (1977) reported, due to the manner in which the data were tabulated.

There is evidence that men, as well as women, have cyclic changes in hormone production and consequently in emotional responses. For example, a 16-year study in Denmark, testing for amounts of male sex hormones in the urine, revealed a pronounced 30-day ebb-and-flow hormonal rhythm (Ramey 1972). Another study of the male emotional cycle showed that not only did men's emotions vary predictably in rhythm within a 24-hour period, but also in the larger rhythms of 4- to 6-week cycles. All the subjects denied that they were less or more friendly or irritable at different times of the cycle. Yet standardized psychological tests showed quite different reactions to life stresses at different periods in these time spans (Ramey 1972). Furthermore, there is some evidence that men's cycles are related to accident proneness and efficiency.

That men and women function within rhythmic cycles should not be difficult to understand. Any traveler weary from transoceanic flight and time change can attest to the discomfort and mood changes that occur when his or her circadian rhythm (internal clock) is disturbed. Why should we not be equally affected by other changes in rhythm?

Vicarious Menstruation and Other Phenomena

There are rare instances in which extragenital bleeding occurs during the menstrual flow. Called **vicarious menstruation,** such bleeding is usually from the nose, although it has been known to occur from the lungs, the retina of the eye, and so forth. This phenomenon is brought about by an endometrial **vasospasm** (sudden decrease in the size of the blood vessels) approximately 48 hours before the menstrual flow begins. There is disagreement over the cause of this phenomenon. Some relate it to **endometriosis,** an ectopic (misplaced) growth of the endometrial tissue lining the uterus. Others maintain that its causes are psychological. In 30% of the cases uterine bleeding is totally displaced, while in the rest the two flows occur simultaneously (Dalven 1964).

The part of the body most frequently involved in vicarious menstruation is the lining of the nose. It is therefore interesting to note that an indirect relationship appears to exist between nasal functions and sexual activity. The mucous membrane of the nose, for instance, frequently swells during sexual excitation, making nasal breathing difficult (Kinsey *et al.* 1953). Moreover, oral or nasal decongestants appear to have some effect on the uterine endometrium during the menstrual period, reducing discomfort and the flow as well (Alexander 1964). The Kinsey group (1953) pointed out the interesting similarity between a sneeze and an orgasm in physiologic buildup and explosive discharge of tensions.

Menstruation and Mythology

Activities

The general agreement among physicians is that women should carry on their usual activities during the menstrual period. Participating in sports, taking a bath or shower, or shampooing the hair at this time will not harm the reproductive organs. Neither will eating lemons or sipping cold drinks!

Good health is important to an uneventful, comfortable menstruation, and exercise is essential to good health. For example, a comparative study at a Des Moines high school of members of a girls' swimming team and of nonswimmers demonstrated that the swimmers suffered less frequently from dysmenorrhea than girls whose swimming activity was minimal.

There is no physiological reason for refraining from sexual intercourse during the menstrual flow. Nevertheless, most present-day cultures impose restrictions against the practice (or at least express distaste for it), and some medical authorities have gone so far as to suggest that coitus during menstruation will lead to physical distress. The research of Masters and Johnson (1966), however, has shown clearly that the fear of distress is unfounded and that sexual activity may have just the opposite effect on the woman: It may provide relief from pain or discomfort. Of the 331 women who took part in an "orgasm during menstruation" study, only 33 objected to sexual activity on religious or aesthetic grounds; 173 expressed desire for coitus, especially during the last half of the flow; and the remaining 125 had no special feelings one way or the other. Nonetheless, surveys have shown that only about one-fifth as many coital acts occur during the days of menstruation as occur during an equal number of days during other parts of the month.

To test the effect of intercourse on menstruating women, all the subjects in a special Masters and Johnson investigation achieved orgasm in a laboratory situation through self-stimulation. During the last part of the orgasmic phase, the observers noted via a speculum (an instrument used for looking into a body opening, such as the vagina) that menstrual fluid frequently spurted from the external cervical os under contractile pressure that was powerful enough to expel the fluid through the vagina without touching either the speculum or the vaginal walls. The explosive force can be accounted for by a sudden contraction of the uterine muscles, starting at the fundus and moving toward the cervix. Perhaps the sudden clearing of menstrual fluid from the uterus and the relaxation of uterine muscles after the series of orgasmic contractions account for the reports of reduced pelvic cramping and backache from women who experience orgasm shortly after the onset of menstruation.

Folklore and Taboos

From the earliest days of civilization, folklore and superstition have surrounded the perfectly normal event called menstruation. From myths have grown taboos. And these taboos, some women contend (Weideger 1976), are age-old devices whereby men, fearful of women's power, have kept women under control by instilling shame and self-hate in them. However the taboos came about—and the theories are many, including Freud's suggestion that menstrual blood arouses castration fears in men—they have indeed existed. The menstruating woman has been called unclean, declared unfit for coitus, segregated into menstrual huts, and even beaten if she came into the presence of men. One finds in Leviticus (Chap. 15), for instance:

> When a woman has a discharge of blood, her impurity shall last for seven days; anyone who touches her shall be unclean till evening.

Everything on which she lies or sits during her impurity shall be unclean. Anyone who touches her bed shall wash his clothes, bathe in water and remain unclean till evening. Whoever touches anything on which she sits shall wash his clothes, bathe in water and remain unclean till evening. If he is on the bed or seat where she is sitting, by touching it he shall become unclean till evening. If a man goes so far as to have intercourse with her and any of her discharge gets on to him, then he shall be unclean for seven days and every bed on which he lies down shall be unclean. [From *The New English Bible*]

As early as A.D. 60, the Roman historian Pliny declared that the mere presence of a menstruating woman will cause new wine to become sour, seeds to become sterile, fruit to fall from trees, and garden plants to become parched. Furthermore, according to Pliny, menstrual fluid can blunt the edge of steel, kill a swarm of bees, instantly rust iron and brass (causing an offensive odor). If by chance dogs were to taste the menstrual flow, they would become mad, and their bite venomous and incurable. Ancient men (as well as modern ones, of course) needed scapegoats to blame for famine, pestilence, and other catastrophes. A menstruating woman, therefore, was adjudged to have the power to cause flowers to wilt by her touch and crops to fail just by passing the fields. This negativism was, and is, further strengthened by the universal fear of blood, since blood is associated with violence, injury, and death. These attitudes, although much diluted and altered, have filtered down through the centuries. Small wonder, then, that couples shy away from sexual intercourse during menses.

An expert in the field of folklore, F. M. Paulsen of George Peabody College, has collected a list of myths about menstruation. Some of the more intriguing are these:

1. If a soiled menstrual pad is picked up or handled by a man, from that time onward the woman who wore the pad will be an easy victim of sexual advances.
2. If an impotent man performs cunnilingus on a menstruating woman, his potency will be restored.
3. A frigid woman can be brought to numerous orgasms if she has sexual intercourse during her period.
4. Well-trained domestic animals will not respond to directions from a woman who is menstruating.
5. Dogs fed by a menstruating woman will develop worms.
6. Plucking pubic hair at night will assure the woman a painless menstrual period.
7. Shaving armpits or legs during menstruation will cause the woman to become weak and listless and will result in a difficult menstruation.
8. A menstruating woman's hair will not "take" a permanent wave, and kinky hair cannot be straightened during the menstrual period.
9. A soiled menstrual pad placed under a woman's pillow each time she

has intercourse will prevent her becoming pregnant. An unused pad under the pillow will assist a woman in becoming pregnant.

10. If menstrual cramps disappear while a woman is petting, the pain is likely to be transmitted to her lover.

Incredible as it may seem to some, these myths were gathered primarily from present-day college students in various parts of the United States.

The Climacteric or Menopause

When the average woman reaches the age of 45 to 50, her ovaries cease to produce and liberate ova, and the uterus gradually stops the monthly process of shedding and rebuilding its lining. This cessation of the menstrual cycle is called the **climacteric** or **menopause,** and its duration does not usually exceed two years. But as long as any menstrual periods occur at all, however irregularly, the possibility of ovulation and of conception remains. If a woman has not had a menstrual period for a year, on the other hand, she can be reasonably sure that ovulation has finally ceased and that conception is impossible. Childbirth after age 50 is extremely rare. During the last 100 years, only about 25 authenticated cases of women past 50 giving birth to normal babies have been recorded. The record for being the oldest woman to give birth to a child was set by a 59-year-old California woman in the mid-1970s.

The climacteric can be quite disturbing, and sometimes filled with considerable emotional upset. Because of greatly improved techniques of hormonal therapy and other medication, however, most if not all of these reactions can now be avoided or corrected. Tranquilizers and short-term psychotherapy can also be used in treatment, so that menopausal difficulties are not nearly so troublesome as they have been in the past.

The ever-decreasing natural supply of estrogen at menopause has been associated with various physical problems, including fatty arterial deposits, resulting in blood-clot formation, and the development of disorders in bone metabolism (M. E. Davis 1973). Estrogen therapy appears to reverse these pathologies. Furthermore, it has been highly successful in correcting some of the more classic symptoms of the menopause itself. Such post-menopausal symptoms as excessive dryness of the vagina and shrinkage of the external genitalia respond to it as well.

Because of its ability to reverse at least some of these conditions, estrogen has gained a reputation for slowing down the general aging process. It has been widely prescribed since the 1960s—by 1975, 25 million prescriptions were being written each year. Serious objections, however, have recently been voiced against routine administration of estrogen.

Doctors and hospital technicians began observing an alarming increase in patients with cancer of the uterine endometrium. The initial results of two studies, comparing women who have and have not had estrogen therapy, showed that the former's chances of developing uterine cancer are between 5 and 14 times higher. The risk apparently increases with the number of years of taking the hormone (Smith *et al.* 1975; Ziel & Finkle 1975). The relationship of estrogen to breast cancer is not at present clear, if indeed any relationship exists at all.

Estrogen therapy is valuable in controlling the serious complications of menopause. But its use thereafter must be guarded. Certainly, one should be aware that estrogen does not seem to have any real value in reversing the ravages of age.

The hormonal imbalance occurring in menopause causes instability in the vasomotor system and, consequently, changes from time to time in the diameter of the blood vessels. These changes permit more blood to flow at one time—inducing "hot flashes"—and less at another. Hot flashes last from a second or so to several minutes and can occur several times a day. Hot flashes of short duration may occur because of the physical effects of sudden changes in temperature or excessive alcoholic consumption or the psychological effects of anger or anxiety. Hot flashes of longer duration probably result from problems related to estrogen secretion (Labrum 1980; Riedman 1961).

Other symptoms associated with menopause are fatigue, dizziness, migraine headaches, chest and neck pains, insomnia, excessive desire for sleep, and depression. The chance that the climacteric will produce any mental disturbance is about 1 in 50,000. Only about 25% of all menopausal women have any sort of distressful emotional symptoms (Riedman 1961). Whether a woman will experience menopausal symptoms appears to depend first on her basic personality pattern, and second on general environmental factors and situational stresses (Easley 1974; Labrum 1980). Generally speaking, the better the mental health of the woman before the climacteric, the fewer unpleasant symptoms she will have when it occurs (Coleman 1972).

The median age for the onset of menopause advanced from 46.6 years in 1853 to 50.1 years in 1965 ("Growing Older" 1965). It has been observed that women who start menstruation earlier in life than average will continue menstruating longer. These findings seem to hold in other spheres of individual sexual life as well (Kinsey *et al.* 1948, 1953). For instance, people who begin erotic activity at an earlier age than average appear to maintain their sexual vigor longer. Furthermore, men and women who engage in frequent sexual activity are able to continue the activity later in life than those who do not.

As a man grows older he, too, undergoes certain physical changes. The testes shrivel a bit and are less firm. Sperm production slackens, because the testicular tubules begin degenerating. The prostate gland becomes enlarged, and the ejaculatory fluid thinner and less copious. The production of male sex hormones slows up, and certain physical responses at the time of orgasm are weaker. Symptoms of depression or paranoia sometimes accompany the physical changes of the climacteric, and can affect men and women alike.

Some men undergo a climacteric, but usually not until they are about 55 years old. When it does occur, it is typically part of the fear, common to middle age, of aging and death—of time's running out (Ramey 1972). The climacteric may cause men some reduction in sexual vigor and interest because of the depressive or other negative emotional conditions it can produce, but it appears to be less traumatic for them than for women.

Summary

Menstruation is the monthly uterine bleeding that usually begins when a young woman is in her early teens. Heredity, general health, and environmental circumstances help determine when a girl will begin menarche (start menstruating).

The purpose of the menstrual cycle is to help prepare and maintain the uterus for implantation of the fertilized egg. The menstrual cycle can be divided into three phases: The destructive phase occurs when progesterone is withdrawn with the regression of the corpus luteum. Withdrawal of progesterone causes the uterine lining to break down and be discharged through menstruation. Menstrual difficulties, including the premenstrual syndrome, dysmenorrhea, and toxic shock syndrome, may occur due to problems associated with this first phase. During the follicular phase, the secretion of estrogen increases until its highest concentration is reached at ovulation. During the luteal phase, the corpus luteum begins to secrete progesterone, and this hormone prepares the uterus to receive the fertilized egg. If conception does not occur, both estrogen and progesterone decrease and the cycle starts anew. These changes in hormone production are sometimes cited as having effects upon a woman's sex drive and emotional responses.

Other forms of extragenital bleeding, such as vicarious menstruation and endometriosis, can also occur. Under normal circumstances, women are encouraged to carry on their usual activities—including sex—during menstruation. Women appear to fare better when they continue with vigorous lives rather than succumbing to the usual mild physical discomfort or to the emotional effects of the mythology surrounding menstruation.

The cessation of the menstrual cycle happens to most women between the ages of 45 to 50 and signals the climacteric or menopause. At this time ovulation (and the possibility of conception) ends. During the menopause, usually lasting a few years, women can experience more pronounced emotional upset, and physical symptoms including hot flashes, fatigue, dizziness, chest and neck pain, and migraine headaches. Estrogen therapy helps control the serious problems associated with menopause. Generally, the better the mental health of the woman, the better she is able to adjust when the climacteric occurs.

Men can also experience emotional and physical changes as they grow older. They may experience depression or paranoia accompanying the physical changes, which include a slackening in sperm production, an enlargement of the prostate gland, and weakened orgasmic response.

Annotated Bibliography

Berman, Ellen M. and Lief, Harold I. Sex and the aging process. In *Sex and the life cycle*, ed. W. Oaks, G. Melchiode, and I. Ficher. New York: Grune and Stratton, 1976.
>   This article addresses several important topics related to sexuality and the elderly, including stresses common to aging, physiology of sex and aging, sex and the older married couple, sex and the older single person, and sexual dysfunctions among the aged.

Dan, Alice J., Graham, Effie A., and Beecher, Carol P. *The menstrual cycle: A synthesis of interdisciplinary research.* New York: Springer, 1980.
>   This book integrates current knowledge in various disciplines toward greater understanding of the menstrual cycle. Empirical, theoretical, and methodological articles address many relevant topics, including historical perspective on menstrual cycle research, menstrual stress, mood cycles, endocrinological changes, dysmenorrhea, and hysterectomy. This is a technical book intended mainly for the medical student and health professional.

Johnson, Martin and Everitt, Barry. *Essential reproduction.* Oxford, England: Blackwell Scientific Publications, 1980.
>   This text discusses a wide range of topics related to reproductive biology, including genetics, sexual differentiation, endocrinology, ovarian and testicular function, puberty and the climacteric, hormones and sexual behavior, coitus and fertilization, pregnancy, parturition and lactation. Though written for the student of the technicalities of reproduction, this book would be useful as a general reference.

Lanson, Lucienne. *From woman to woman.* New York: Alfred Knopf, 1981.
>   Written by a gynecologist for the general public, this book answers frequent questions concerning female sexual physiology, menstruation, sexual inter-

course, pregnancy, contraceptives, menopause, gynecological problems, and other areas. Language is straightforward and nontechnical.

Mishell, Daniel R., Jr., and Davajan, Val. *Reproductive endocrinology: Infertility and contraception.* Philadelphia: F. A. Davis, 1979.

This text for medical and allied health professionals integrates the latest clinical research findings related to normal and abnormal reproductive endocrinology, infertility, and contraception. Discussion includes topics related to puberty, gestation, menstruation, and the climacteric.

Rose, Louisa (Ed.). *The menopause book.* New York: Hawthorne Books, 1977.

This important book for women of all ages features articles by leading women in the health care professions. The book offers current information on menopause, its symptoms and accompanying changes, its emotional aspects, hormones, hysterectomy, breast cancer, and sex at menopause. Of special interest is a general directory of nationwide health centers, publications, and educational and employment resources.

Shearman, Rodney P. *Human reproductive physiology (2nd ed.).* London: Blackwell Scientific Publications, 1979.

This comprehensive text provides detailed information on most significant aspects of human reproduction, including genetics and cytogenetics, the physiology and function of testes and ovaries, pregnancy, and menopause. This book is designed for the student and medical personnel.

Utian, Wulf H. *Menopause in modern practice: A guide to clinical practice.* New York: Appleton-Century-Crofts, 1980.

Intended for the medical clinician, this book covers various clinical aspects of menopause, including etiology, endocrinology, physiology, and pharmacotherapy. The book also addresses the practical aspects of clinical care.

Wolman, Benjamin B. (Ed.). *Psychological aspects of gynecology and obstetrics.* Oradell, New Jersey: Medical Economics Company, 1978.

This book features articles by renowned contributors concerning psychological considerations in obstetrics and gynecology. Topics include changing roles, female sexual dysfunctions, puberty, contraception and fertility, the middle years and the climacteric, pregnancy and complications, and many others. Special issues such as rape crisis and breast cancer are discussed. The book was written for students and medical practitioners, but many articles will appeal to the general audience.

Fertilization, Prenatal Development, and Birth

7

Fertilization and Pregnancy (Gestation)

Fertilization means simply the union of the male and female germ cells or gametes—the sperm and ovum—to create a single cell from which the new being develops. It is indeed amazing that, given the millions of sperm contained in a single ejaculate, only one penetrates the ovum. Once it has entered, an immediate change occurs in the covering of the egg that blocks the entry of other sperm. On extremely rare occasions penetration by more than one sperm takes place. But development thereafter is abnormal, and spontaneous abortion follows (Newth 1973).

After penetration, the sperm's head and tail separate. The tail disintegrates and the head grows into the **male pronucleus,** which contains the paternal contribution of 23 chromosomes. This then joins the **female pronucleus** (nucleus of the secondary oocyte), containing the 23 maternal chromosomes, at the center of the ovum. The chromosomes form 22 matching pairs of autosomes (nonsex chromosomes) plus the sex-determining pair (XX or XY). The result is a fertilized egg containing the full count of 46 chromosomes common to all human cells. Chromosomes, found in the nucleus of every cell, are long filaments consisting of or containing hundreds, perhaps thousands, of genes. **Genes,** the elementary particles of heredity, are strung together by direct attachment to each other or to a fibrous protein thread (Metz 1963; Muller 1963).

Prenatal life can be divided into three periods (Arey 1974). The first, the period of the ovum, encompasses the conceptus (product of conception) as zygote and blastocyst, and lasts one week from fertilization. The second is the period of the embryo, the 2nd through 8th week. This period is characterized by the evolution of the placenta, the organ of attachment between embryo and mother, and by the appearance in primitive form of external bodily features and principal organs. The third, the period of the fetus, extends from the 3rd month to birth, during which time tissues and organs continue their differentiation and attain the ability to perform specialized functions.

The **zygote** created by the fusion of the ovum and sperm undergoes rapid mitotic cell division in which each cell receives 46 chromosomes identical to those of the parent cell. In a process of segmentation called cleavage, first 2 cells are formed, then 4, then 8, and so on, all of them remaining within the fixed outer bounds of the zygote. Despite the rapid increase in cell count, the overall size of the cell mass and the volume of protoplasm remain unchanged (Miller & Leavell 1972).

When cell division has produced a solid ball of approximately 12 cells—about day 3 after fertilization—the conceptus is called a morula. It continues its leisurely journey through the fallopian tube toward the uterus; and after further division has produced about 16 cells, an inequality in cellular size is observable. The outer layer of the conceptus, called the trophoblast, now consists of small cells which surround a few somewhat larger cells called the embryoblast or inner cell mass. These inner cells eventually develop into the fetus itself. The trophoblast develops into the fetus's extra embryonic membranes—for example, the body stalk, later the umbilical cord (Newth 1973).

At about day 4, the conceptus begins to accumulate intercellular fluid, creating a hollow sphere one cell thick, referred to as a **blastocyst.** The larger cells within the cavity now clump together at one side of the inner wall and, at approximately days 7 to 9, the blastocyst makes contact with the uterine wall (Fig. 7.1). The trophoblast erodes the uterine mucosa, or lining, possibly through the combined action of blastocystic enzymes and changes in the endometrial tissue. Implantation is complete by about day 14. A scheme of the hormonal activity involved in these events is shown in Fig. 7.2.

Implantation completed, the inner cell mass within the conceptus forms two layers, the ectoderm and the endoderm, in such a manner that

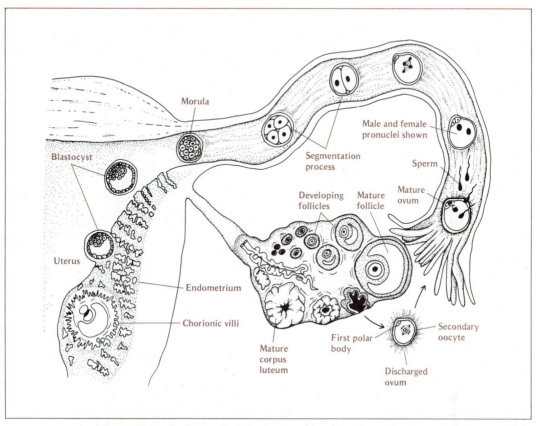

Figure 7.1   Ovulation, fertilization, and implantation of human egg (cross section).

two cavities take shape simultaneously. Later a third germ layer, the mesoderm, makes its appearance between the two. These three germ layers make up the embryonic disc from which all bodily components of the fetus develop.

Ectoderm, endoderm, and mesoderm begin a complicated process of differentiation. In time, the developing fetus's nervous system, sense organs, mouth cavity, and skin will evolve from the ectoderm. From the endoderm will come the digestive and respiratory systems. From the mesoderm will evolve the muscular, skeletal, circulatory, excretory, and sexual or reproductive systems (Arey 1974; Steen & Montagu 1959).

After the conceptus is implanted, small fingerlike protrusions, the chorionic villi, grow outward into the maternal tissue from the chorion, the protective envelope surrounding the embryo. Eventually these villi are limited to the point of junction between embryo and uterus.

During the first 14 days of gestation, the embryo does not have a functioning circulatory system. It obtains nourishment primarily by osmosis.

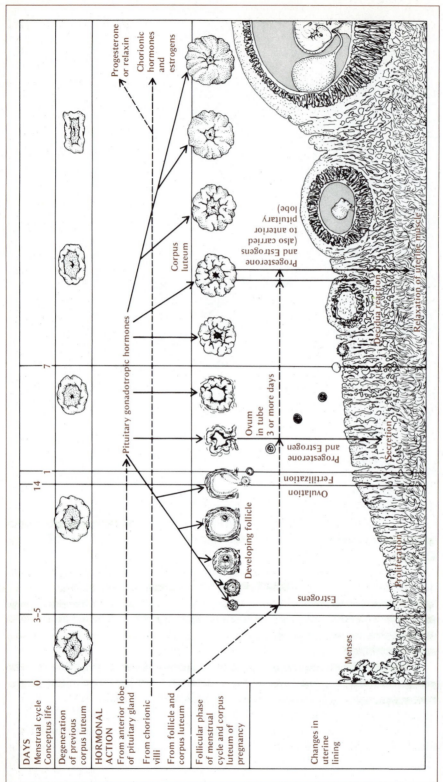

Figure 7.2 Hormonal cycle in which conception has occurred.

Then peripheral membranes, which are the means of obtaining food and oxygen and of eliminating wastes, form about the third week of embryonic life. Since these membranes are not incorporated within the body of the embryo or fetus, and are discarded at the time of birth, they are called extraembryonic or fetal membranes. The membranes include the yolk sac, body stalk, amnion, and chorion (Fig. 7.3).

Although virtually no yolk accumulates in the human embryo, a yolk sac is formed just as if a yolk existed. It is the forerunner of the primitive digestive tract. As the embryo develops, there is a progressive constriction of the yolk sac until it is connected to the embryo only by a threadlike structure called the body stalk, which eventually becomes incorporated into the umbilical cord.

The **amnion** is a thin, tough, transparent membrane. The cavity (amniotic sac) formed by this membrane appears before the body of the embryo has taken a definite shape. It is filled with a clear watery fluid called the **amniotic fluid.** The developing embryo is suspended in this fluid by its umbilical cord.

Amniotic fluid has several important functions. It equalizes the pressure around the embryo, thus protecting it from jolts and mechanical injuries. It prevents the embryo from forming adhesions to the amnion, which could result in malformations. It permits changes in fetal posture, and acts as a hydrostatic wedge to aid childbirth by helping to dilate the neck of the uterus. At about the 5th month of pregnancy, the fetus usually begins to swallow some of the amniotic fluid. The infant's first bowel movements, consequently, are a discharge of this liquid. The baby's

Figure 7.3   Schematic representation of implanted embryo.

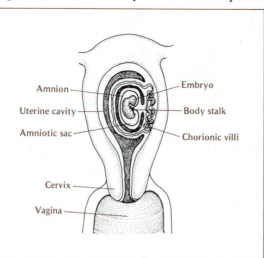

respiratory passages may have to be cleared of some of the fluid after birth in order for normal respiration to begin.

The disc-shaped, highly vascular **placenta,** which forms on the inner surface of the uterus, is the special organ of interchange between embryo and mother. Although it develops from uterine mucosa and the external surface of the chorion, it is largely composed of fetal tissue. Placental growth is rapid until the 5th month of pregnancy, when it has reached its greatest relative size (about 50% of the inner surface of the uterus). Fully developed, it is about 6 to 7 in. (15 to 18 cm) in diameter and weighs between 1 and 2 lb. It is over 1 in. (2.5 cm) thick at its thickest part, thinner at its edges. Interestingly, there is a high correlation between fetal and placental size (Liggins 1972). The placental villi are steeped in maternal blood, which enters the spaces about the villi by means of small blood vessels (Fig. 7.4). As the blood drains back into the veins of the uterus, it is replaced by fresh blood from the uterine arteries.

Figure 7.4 Schematic representation of placenta's attachment to uterine wall, showing interchange between maternal and fetal blood vessels through the tiny chorionic villi.

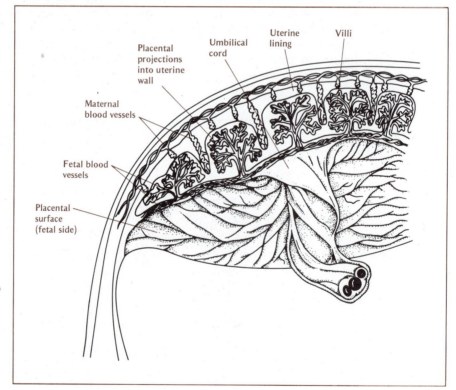

From the beginning of development, the fetal and maternal blood systems are separate entities. While both maternal and fetal blood circulate within the placenta, they are kept separate by the walls of the umbilical blood vessels. This separation may be thought of as a sievelike arrangement, with interchange of food, oxygen, and waste products occurring by diffusion and absorption.

Fetal blood absorbs food and oxygen. It also eliminates carbon dioxide and other metabolic waste products, which are taken into the mother's blood and eventually expelled by her along with her own waste products. Although this separation works effectively in separating the maternal and fetal blood systems, and substantial maternal-fetal blood exchanges are very rare, a few fetal blood cells do cross this barrier and enter the mother's blood system. It is not known whether the reverse is true. The presence of fetal blood cells in maternal blood may trigger an antigen reaction in cases of maternal-fetal Rh incompatibility.

While the cellular sieve between the two blood systems generally prevents the passage of bacteria and other disease germs, recent findings have shown that many more substances are capable of crossing than were thought. These include antibiotics, certain viruses, and some disease germs, such as *Treponema pallidum*, which causes syphilis.

During the 5th week of pregnancy, the **umbilical cord** is formed from the body stalk and other extraembryonic membranes. The fully developed cord ranges from 5 to 27 inches, with an average length of about 20 in. (51 cm), which is also the average length of a full-term fetus. It is actually a continuation of the fetal body (the point of its attachment is marked by the navel), and connects the fetus to the placenta. Blood is pumped to and from the placenta by the fetal heart through two arteries and one vein.

Unusual Fertilization and Implantation

Egg and sperm typically unite in the fallopian tube, after which the zygote becomes implanted in the uterine wall. There are, however, several exceptions to this pattern. Fertilization can be achieved by other means and implantation can occur in other sites. Some of these unusual conceptions proceed to a full-term pregnancy and delivery of a healthy, normal baby. Others are so abnormal that pregnancy cannot continue to term.

Artificial Insemination.   One method of solving the problem of infertility is artificial insemination (AI). In this process, sperm of the husband (AIH) are artificially placed into his wife's vagina or uterus when conception is considered most likely to occur. Or the sperm of the donor (AID), rather than those of the husband, are inserted.

Artificial insemination has been practiced in animal husbandry for years. As early as the 14th century, Arabic tribes are said to have secretly used semen from an inferior breed of stallions to impregnate the thoroughbred mares of their enemies (Lehfeldt 1961a). Today, AI is regularly used to build up the bloodlines of various species of animals. Semen can easily be refrigerated and shipped. One thoroughbred bull can therefore sire calves by many cows with a single ejaculate.

Artificial insemination of humans has been performed in this country since the turn of the century. Donor sperm can produce pregnancy 60% to 80% of the time, whereas when the husband's sperm is artificially introduced it is successful only 5% of the time. The difference between these percentages is understandable when one considers that the husband's sperm, for whatever reason, were incapable of producing pregnancy by coition in the first place. Whether conceived by AID or AIH, it is noteworthy that such children are at no greater risk for congenital defects than are children in the overall population. Furthermore, there is no greater incidence of spontaneous abortion among conceptions resulting from artificial insemination (Lehfeldt 1961a; Shapiro 1980).

In 1955, the Society for the Study of Sterility passed almost unanimously a resolution approving AID, with the stipulation that the procedure must be in harmony with the medical opinion of the physician and the ethics of both partners. Undoubtedly this resolution has contributed significantly to the increase in AI pregnancies in the United States (Lehfeldt 1961a; G. P. Smith 1970). One investigator estimates that about 10,000 children are born every year as the result of AID. An unknown number of children, though probably fewer, are born each year through AIH (Shapiro 1980). In 1956, Pope Puis XII stated firmly that the Roman Catholic Church opposes both AID and AIH. The Roman Catholic Church will, however, permit "assisted insemination," whereby an instrument is used to push the sperm toward and into the cervix after the semen has been deposited during marital intercourse.

Semen can be stored for long periods by freezing it, along with protective chemicals, in liquid nitrogen. Healthy babies have been born from both AIH and AID conceptions in which the sperm used came from a sperm bank where they had been frozen and stored for as long as two years. The use of frozen semen has a lower success rate than the use of fresh semen. But the use of frozen semen has advantages. Donor characteristics can be more carefully selected, screening of specimens can be done to eliminate the possibility of passing on sexually transmitted diseases, and it is more convenient (Kleegman *et al.* 1970; Shapiro 1980; Sherman 1965).

In recent years the idea of using donor surrogate mothers has received more media and public attention. There has been at least one reported incident of a woman's volunteering to be anonymously impregnated by AID (for an overall fee of $10,000) because the wife of the man involved was unable to conceive and he wanted a child genetically his own. He placed an advertisement for a volunteer, and received 160 replies.

Ovum Transplantation. Ovum transplantation, though now still in the experimental stage, is another way in which women may some day become pregnant. The procedure would be particularly helpful to a woman who ovulates but whose fallopian tubes are blocked, preventing passage of the ovum. The woman's own ovum could be fertilized artificially in a laboratory, then transferred into her uterus. Or the fertilized ovum of another woman could be transplanted to a host mother.

Zygote transfer is not new among lower animals, and its commercial vaule in improving livestock strains is great. But the problems of transplantation—legally, ethically, and technically—are far more complex in humans than in animals.

Parthenogenesis. Parthenogenesis means the "fertilization" and development of an ovum without any previous contact with a sperm.

In 1896 French scientists manipulated the birth of young to virgin sea urchins. Since that time experimentation with various animals has shown that many stimuli will start the process of development just as if the egg had been fertilized in the usual manner. A high percentage of the eggs of virgin turkey hens undergo parthenogenesis in experimental circumstances, although the early death rate among the hatched birds is very high.

An obvious question arises: Is this phenomenon possible in human beings? Investigators, past and present, disagree widely on the subject. One thing is certain, however. If parthenogenesis were to occur, the offspring would always be female. Since women have only one type of sex-determining chromosome (X), only the X chromosome could be passed on. Furthermore, a child born of parthenogenesis would be a replication of her mother (except for the role of recessive genes), since her heredity would be based solely on the mother's genes ("From the Editor's Scrapbook" 1968b).

Landrum B. Shettles observed in a study of 400 human ova that the first stages of development processes had begun in three of these eggs, even though there could have been no contact with sperm. It would therefore seem that, if developmental processes in the human ovum can begin spontaneously, they would be able to continue to term (Herrick 1962). Clearly, a great deal of further research is needed before the mysteries and possibility of parthenogenesis are understood.

The phrase "virgin birth" ordinarily conveys the idea of human pregnancy and subsequent birth without previous intercourse and fertilization. In this context, the possibility of a true virgin birth has never been scientifically established. Impregnation without penile penetration, however, is a real possibility. If, for instance, a man ejaculates on his partner's vulva during sex play, sperm could enter the vagina opening and make their way into the uterus. The same is true if he were to ejaculate, get semen on his hands, and soon thereafter manually manipulate the woman's genitals (especially if he inserted a finger into the vagina). If impregnation were to result in either of these instances, and if the woman had never had sexual intercourse, the subsequent parturition might accurately be called a "virgin birth."

Fertilization outside the Fallopian Tube.   Physicians have recorded many cases in which women reporting for surgery shortly after intercourse were found to have sperm in the fluid of the peritoneum (the membranous lining of the abdominal wall). The assumption that an ovum must be in the fallopian tube to be fertilized is therefore doubtful.

Ectopic Pregnancy.   Ectopic pregnancy is the implantation of a fertilized ovum in any place other than the lining of the uterus. It is, therefore, a misplaced pregnancy. About 2% of human ovum implantations are ectopic and 96% of these implant in the fallopian tubes (McLaren 1972). This is what is called **tubal pregnancy**.

Tubal pregnancies usually terminate themselves in one of two ways. The embryo or fetus may be expelled into the abdominal cavity through the natural opening of the fallopian tube. Or it may be expelled through a rupture in the wall of the tube into the cavity. Rupture poses the greater threat to the mother. Because of the acute shock and extensive bleeding involved, it is an important cause of maternal deaths (Netter 1961; *Williams Obstetrics* 1961).

If the embryo is young enough at the time of its abortion into the abdominal cavity, it may be absorbed by the mother's system. Otherwise, surgery will be required to remove it and to repair or to remove the injured fallopian tube and stop the bleeding. A tubal pregnancy is difficult to diagnose. But if a woman has missed a menstrual period and experiences any unusual vaginal bleeding or pain (especially if the pain is on one side only of the abdomen), she should see her obstetrician immediately. Given these symptoms, it is possible that the doctor can diagnose the condition before a rupture or abortion occurs.

A far less common form of ectopic implantation is an abdominal pregnancy, which occurs only once in 15,000 pregnancies (*Williams Obstetrics* 1961). In these cases the fertilized egg becomes attached to some ectopic endometrial tissue within the abdominal cavity and is nourished as if it were in the uterus.

Some abdominal pregnancies continue to term, in which case the delivery must be performed surgically. The danger to the mother is grave. Furthermore, there is a high incidence of malformation among these infants and rarely does one survive (*Williams Obstetrics* 1961).

When an abdominal pregnancy is not recognized and the fetus dies, it causes an irritation that accelerates calcium production by the mother. A large deposit of calcium salts (bone-building material) forms around the dead fetus, encasing the "foreign" object and protecting the woman's body from being poisoned by it. The whole mass becomes calcified and results in what is called a "stone baby" (lithopedion), which may not be discovered and removed for several years, if ever.

Ovarian and cervical pregnancies are even rarer forms of ectopic implantation. There are recorded in medical history a few instances of pregnancies that occurred after a hysterectomy (surgical removal of the uterus). All involved some misplaced endometrial tissue wherein the fertilized ovum implanted itself; none of the fetuses survived. In a recent case a fetus developed in the cul-de-sac of the vagina. The woman's ovaries and fallopian tubes had been left untouched at the time of her hysterectomy and, in some unexplained way, an egg became fertilized and implanted itself in the vagina (Hanes 1964).

Signs of and Tests for Pregnancy

The signs of pregnancy may be divided into three classes. The presumptive signs are the first to be noticed—cessation of the menses; morning sickness; changes in the size and fullness of the breasts and development of a dark coloration of the areolae (the pigmented areas around the nipples); fatigue; frequency of urination; and discoloration of cervical mucous membranes. These signs are not conclusive and they vary from woman to woman.

The probable signs consist of an increase in the size of the uterus; considerable softening of the cervix, beginning with the 2nd month of pregnancy; enlargement of the abdomen at about the 3rd month, when the enlarged uterus can be felt through the abdominal wall; and intermittent contractions of the uterus.

The positive signs, any one of which confirms pregnancy, are fetal heartbeats, which the examining physician can hear and count; active fetal movements, noticeable at the 5th month (although some such sensations may be experienced earlier) (*Williams Obstetrics* 1961).

Women quite understandably do not wish to wait several months to determine if they are pregnant. Nor is it advisable for them to do so, in the best interest of their own health and that of their babies. Most women therefore undergo endocrine tests, which can give accurate proof of pregnancy approximately 3 weeks after implantation, or about 6 weeks after the last menstrual period. (Test results any earlier are unreliable because the hormonal secretion is too slight.) The endocrine substance that yields laboratory proof of pregnancy is the chorionic gonadotropic hormone secreted from the earliest days of implantation by the chorionic villi protruding from the implanted embryo. This hormone is found in the urine of a pregnant woman, a sample of which is used in the popular pregnancy test known as the **agglutination (clumping) test.**

The Pregnant Woman

Activity during Pregnancy

Much has been written about the dangers of travel, exercise, sexual intercourse, and driving during pregnancy. These activities are not dangerous under usual, normal circumstances for the healthy woman, especially when done moderately and sensibly. In fact, they are often beneficial to the expectant mother (Javert 1960; Rosen 1980; Rutledge 1964). During recent wars, pregnant women traveled by many modes of transportation, much of it uncomfortable, for hundreds of miles in order to be with their husbands. Yet they had a lower miscarriage rate than women who stayed home. The emotional satisfaction of joining their husbands, even though it entailed considerable traveling, probably contributed to the good health of these young women.

Coitus during gestation is ordinarily permitted and even encouraged by obstetricians until approximately the final 6 weeks (Javert 1960; Rosen 1980) (see Fig. 7.5). After this time, when intercourse may become impossible

Figure 7.5 Diagram showing practicality of intercourse even in advanced pregnancy. Dotted line demonstrates angle at which penis may be introduced into vagina.

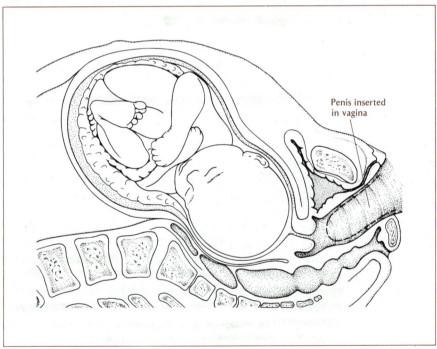

Penis inserted
in vagina

because of the woman's abdominal size, sexual relief through such means as mutual genital stimulation is valuable to both partners and to the relationship. As a matter of fact, it is during his wife's pregnancy and shortly thereafter that a man is most likely to seek extramarital outlets if no sexual release is otherwise available to him (Masters & Johnson 1966). Precautions must, of course, be taken in regard to sexual as well as other activities during pregnancy. The woman's obstetrician is the best person to offer guidance in these matters.

One effect of orgasm may prompt obstetricians to warn patients to avoid it during late pregnancy. Oxytocin, a chemical released from the maternal pituitary gland in the late stages of labor, aids birth by stimulating the more forceful uterine contractions necessary to expel the fetus. Evidence shows that oxytocin is also released during female orgasm. The chemical has no apparent effect on the nonpregnant uterus. But some specialists believe that the combined effects of oxytocin and the uterine contractions of strong and satisfying orgasms may be sufficiently powerful to start labor prematurely (Fox 1973; Rosen 1980), although results of other studies do not support this conclusion (Wagner & Solberg 1974).

Women often have questions as to how their pregnancies will affect their sexual desires and activities. An important study of pregnancy and female sexuality (Wagner & Solberg 1974) reveals that most of the women subjects experienced a loss of sexual desire during pregnancy. While frequency of intercourse decreased only slightly in the first and second trimesters, there was a dramatic decline in the 7th, 8th, and 9th months. The decline in incidence doubled with each passing month. As pregnancy progressed, frequency and intensity of orgasm and frequency of multiple orgasms also declined. These findings held true whether excitation came from coitus, manual or oral stimulation by the partner, or masturbation. One reason for a decrease in forms of sexual activity other than coitus was that fewer than 2% of these women's doctors had suggested sexual substitutes for intercourse. Only 10% had been told by their physicians about other sexual positions that might be used for more comfort during pregnancy.

Rosen (1980) also reports that couples abstain from or limit their sexual interactions as pregnancy progresses. However, some women experience an increase in sexual desire during pregnancy. A combination of physiological and psychological factors may account for increased sexual interest by these pregnant women.

Consumption of Food and Drugs during Pregnancy

Weight Gain.   Underweight newborns have a higher mortality rate than heavier infants because of circulatory and respiratory difficulties. Their prematurity rate is double that of larger infants (Montagu 1963). The 85,000 babies born annually weighing less than 4.5 pounds are at "grave risk" of physical and mental impairment, according to the National Foundation/ March of Dimes:

> Authorities now believe that the practice of discouraging a gain of more than 10–15 pounds has contributed to the large number of low birth weight infants and high U.S. infant mortality rates. Recent studies indicate a weight gain of 20–25 pounds is desirable. Women who are underweight at the time of conception and adolescents whose reproductive efficiency is least should gain even more.

Smoking.   The dangers of smoking are so serious that all cigarette packets are now required by law to carry health-hazard warnings, and tobacco advertisements are banned from radio and TV. The damaging effects of smoking on a fetus that were long suspected have now been made more clear (Fielding 1978; Montagu 1963).

American Cancer Society's anti-smoking poster. (Courtesy American Cancer Society)

Tobacco smoke contains over 4000 chemical substances. Many of these, such as nicotine and tars, are harmful. That the smoker does not inhale offers little protection, as chemicals can be absorbed through the membranes of the mouth as well as by inhalation. These facts should be enough to discourage any pregnant woman from smoking. Carbon monoxide generated by smoking interferes with the transport of oxygen to the fetus, which results in a slowdown in fetal growth and leads to an increased risk of both *in utero* and neonatal deaths. This risk is concentrated in the 20th to 28th weeks of gestation and is due to the increased risk of premature labor and delivery. Mothers who smoked less than one pack a day increased the perinatal mortality rate (stillbirth or death within the first month) by 20 percent; those who smoked more than a pack a day increased the rate by 35 percent (Fielding 1978). The increase in perinatal mortality rate is often due to *abruptio placentae,* a premature separation of the placenta from the uterine wall. Smoking damages the uterine arteries; it may also lead to dead areas within the placenta, tending to lower the blood supply and aid in this detachment.

It seems that these risks are also associated with how much and how long the mother smoked before pregnancy. Smoking, even before pregnancy, may damage the small arteries in the uterus, leading to permanent changes that affect future pregnancies. Women who smoke before pregnancy have increased risks of developing *placenta previa* (low implantation in the uterus), which leads to premature detachment of the placenta and miscarriage (Update 1979).

One good note, in regard to smoking, is that women smokers who are already pregnant may still provide a small yet critical benefit to their unborn baby by not smoking during the 48 hours preceding delivery. Davies (Medical World News 1979) found that mothers who quit just two days prior to giving birth had 8% more oxygen available in their blood than mothers who continued smoking.

In studies of 5200 newborns (Ochsner 1976), perinatal mortality was found to be greater among those babies whose *fathers* smoked more than 10 cigarettes a day, even when the mother was a nonsmoker. Babies whose fathers were heavy smokers, furthermore, had twice the normally expected incidence of severe malformation. Ochsner also observed that male libido and spermatogenesis are both impaired by smoking, making it a possible factor in impotence and infertility.

Women who smoke cigarettes have been found less likely to become pregnant than nonsmokers ("Smoking" 1968). Women smokers have more menstrual difficulties than those who do not. Only 4% of nonsmokers age prematurely, compared with 66% of smokers. Only 2% of nonsmokers experience a premature menopause, whereas 20% of smokers do so. Butler and Goldstein (1973) studied the effect of maternal smoking on several thousand children, aged 7 to 11 years. They found slightly lower levels in reading, mathematics, and general ability among children whose mothers had smoked during pregnancy.

Alcohol.   The effects of alcohol on the unborn are not definitely known. But it has been claimed that the mother who exceeds a very moderate daily intake (one cocktail or two glasses of wine) in the last trimester of pregnancy threatens her baby by possibly creating an alcohol dependency. Other researchers (Clarren & Smith 1978; Clarren *et al.* 1978; Hanson *et al.* 1978) have presented data indicating that the developing baby may be adversely affected by the mother's alcohol intake as early as the time of conception and the first weeks of pregnancy. A predictable syndrome of abnormalities, called the **fetal alcohol syndrome,** may appear in the babies of mothers who drink during pregnancy. Abnormalities including central nervous system deficiencies, growth deficiencies, and facial disfigurements may occur in babies, particularly if their mothers are moderate or heavy users of alcohol. Certainly the evidence indicates that women who plan on having a child would be wise to eliminate or significantly modify their alcohol intake or at least consult their physicians regarding alcohol use during pregnancy.

Other Drugs.   The effects of other drugs on the unborn are equally unclear. Yet the FDA has issued warnings to doctors that certain widely used tranquilizers taken in early pregnancy can cause such birth defects as cleft lip. Even aspirin has been indicated as potentially dangerous, and recent evidence indicates that caffeine may have harmful effects on the developing baby ("Pregnant Women" 1980). The wisest course for the pregnant woman, then, is to discuss with her obstetrician *any* drug that she takes regularly.

Exposure to Infectious Disease during Pregnancy

Toxoplasmosis.   A number of diseases can affect the pregnant mother and her developing child. One disease that has received public attention in recent years is **toxoplasmosis.** This disease can be contracted by people who eat partially or poorly cooked meat or people who own cats and handle or dispose of cat feces. Adults can have no symptoms of the disease, or they may exhibit symptoms similar to mononucleosis. But pregnant mothers are advised that the disease may have serious consequences for their unborn children. Toxoplasmosis may cause intrauterine death of the fetus, or the child who survives the pregnancy may have problems such as central nervous system damage, mental deficiency, or chronic eye defects. Proper attention to dietary issues and personal hygiene may be important in avoiding exposure to toxoplasmosis. Medical consultation and follow-up is important in preventing or, if necessary, in treating this disease (Ledger 1980).

Sexual Diseases. Exposure to sexually transmitted diseases such as gonorrhea and syphilis and perplexing and difficult to treat infections such as genital herpesvirus can present significant problems for pregnant women and their unborn children. Fetal morbidity and fatality rates substantially increase, and maternal health problems often become more severe without medical care. Even though effective treatment strategies for some diseases such as genital herpesvirus are still lacking, appropriate and well-timed medical attention can help in controlling symptoms and protecting the life of the child. If the mother has active vaginal lesions associated with herpesvirus at the time of labor and delivery, for instance, a caesarean section may be performed by the physician to protect the child. It is important that physicians and their pregnant patients take the time to explore whether the woman may have been exposed to a sexually transmitted disease or diseases so that appropriate treatment can be begun (Gregg & Ismach 1980; Knox et al. 1980; Ledger 1980). (Further discussion regarding sexually transmitted diseases can be found in Chapter 19, Sexual Diseases and Disorders.)

Rubella. Babies born to mothers exposed to rubella (German measles) run a grave risk of defect, particularly if the exposure occurs during the first trimester of pregnancy. Exposure to rubella may result in babies being born with such maladies as blindness, deafness, heart defects, and mental retardation. Until there is universal immunization, all women who wish to become pregnant are advised to be tested to determine their susceptibility to rubella. If they are susceptible, they can be inoculated with rubella vaccine. However, it is important that women not be pregnant and that they not become pregnant for three months after receiving the vaccine.

Since rubella vaccine contains a live modified form of the virus and since there is evidence that the virus can cross into the placenta, pregnant or soon-to-be pregnant women are advised not to receive the vaccine. Inoculation of children is another method that has been employed as part of the effort to reduce the risks of widespread rubella epidemics and thus the possibility of child-bearing women being exposed to the disease. The success of this approach, besides providing protection for the inoculated children, has been limited at best in preventing the spread of rubella (Knox *et at.* 1980; Ledger 1980; Shepard & Lemire 1980).

Disorders and Disease States and Pregnancy

Rh Factor. A disorder that has special implications for fetal development involves an incompatibility in the parents' Rh blood factors. Most people, about 85%, have the Rh factor in their blood; their blood type is Rh positive. People who lack the Rh factor are Rh negative. There is no danger to the developing fetus when both parents are Rh positive or Rh negative; nor is there any special problem encountered when the mother has the Rh factor and the father lacks it. When the mother is Rh negative and the father is Rh positive, however, there are potential problems for the fetus. In this instance, the Rh negative mother develops antibodies against the Rh factor present in the fetus's blood cells. These antibodies attack the red blood cells of the fetus and lead to a type of anemia that may be fatal to the child. A drug known as rhogam can be administered to the Rh negative woman and is usually effective in controlling the problems associated with Rh incompatibility. The drug is administered within three days of the birth, miscarriage, or abortion of an Rh-positive child. First children are usually not affected by Rh blood incompatibilities, but children of subsequent pregnancies can be affected if the mother is not inoculated (Queenan 1980; Sandler *et al.* 1980).

Toxemia.   Toxemia is a disease state of pregnancy that may be difficult or impossible to prevent, although severe symptoms can be eased or prevented if a woman receives appropriate medical care. The symptoms of toxemia—which can affect the mother as well as the developing fetus—include increased blood pressure, body fluid retention, and protein loss. The initial stage of toxemia, known as preeclampsia, is characterized by a significant increase in blood pressure and by swelling in parts of the body such as the face and the hands. If these symptoms are not attended to, the disease may progress into the next stage, known as eclampsia. In eclampsia there may be a dramatic increase in blood pressure; coma, convulsions, and even death may occur. Antihypertensive drugs such as hydralazine hydrochloride and anticonvulsant drugs such as magnesium sulfate may be employed with severe symptoms. Fortunately, with continual medical care and follow-up, toxemia can usually be monitored and controlled (Cefalo 1979; "Danger Zone Pregnancies" 1979; Diamond & Karlen 1980).

Diabetes.   Diabetes is another problem that deserves special attention during pregnancy. Since both the mother and the developing fetus can be adversely affected, it is important that diabetics, "borderline" diabetics, or any woman suspected of having this disease be followed closely during pregnancy. Careful control of the mother's blood sugar levels through regulation of insulin and diet requirements and attention to the mother's tolerance for stress and physical activity are important. Diabetic mothers are more likely than nondiabetic mothers to experience stillbirths or to give birth to infants with respiratory problems, malformations, and other medical complications, especially without appropriate prenatal care ("Danger Zone Pregnancies" 1979; Gabbe 1979; Goldstein 1980).

Thyroid Problems.   Thyroid problems, including hyperthyroidism (excessive thyroid functioning) and hypothyroidism (deficient thyroid functioning), may be issues of special concern during pregnancy. Untreated hyperthyroidism may not mean any special threat to the mother, but symptoms such as nervousness, weight loss, heart irregularities and palpitations, protrusion of the eyeballs, heat intolerance, diarrhea, and excessive growth of the thyroid gland may occur. The risk to the child may be a premature birth, with its increased chances of disease or death. Hypothyroidism in the mother may result from dietary deficiencies of iodine, thyroid malfunctioning, and inborn problems in metabolism. The hypothyroid child will often have problems in physical and/or mental development. Since medical treatment and follow-up can frequently alleviate the problems of hyperthyroidism and hypothyroidism, attention to them is especially important during pregnancy (Mestman 1980).

Prematurity. Whenever premature labor and delivery become an issue, regardless of the precipitating causes, concern for the development and well-being of the child becomes of paramount importance. Premature infants are more susceptible to gastrointestinal tract damage, heart problems, respiratory problems, mental retardation, and cerebral palsy. Thus, physicians are concerned with helping expectant mothers to accomplish a full-term delivery so that they can more likely give birth to healthy, properly developed infants. Physicians have prescribed sedatives, bed rest, and hormone inhibitors to patients who have been prone to premature labor and delivery. Sometimes they have sewed or stitched up an expectant mother's cervix to help get the infant closer to a full-term delivery.

The Food and Drug Administration, or the FDA, has approved the use of a medication known as ritodrine hydrochloride to help treat women prone to premature labor. Ritodrine has been used successfully in Europe and in experimental tests with women in the United States. The drug, which inhibits or delays labor by relaxing the uterine muscles, has side effects that include tremors, nervousness, palpitations, and increased heart rate. However, in cases of premature labor in which other medical complications are not affecting either the developing fetus or the mother, ritodrine may prove to be invaluable for prolonging gestation time ("Buying Precious Time" 1980).

Age of Mother and Family Size

Most women have their first babies between the ages of 20 and 24, although there have been verified reports of births to a girl as young as 5 and a woman as old as 59. Women past 40 who wish to have children appear to have as good a chance as younger women of giving birth to a live infant (Posner *et al.* 1961). Older women are well advised to consult a geneticist or obstetrician before deliberately conceiving or the evidence is that they stand in greater danger than younger women of producing a defective infant. There is also a greater incidence of **caesarean sections** (surgical deliveries) among older women (8% as compared with a general average of 3%). And a study of 27.7 million births, conducted by the Metropolitan Life Insurance Company, showed that multiple births are most likely to occur in women between the ages of 35 and 39.

The latest Census Bureau data ("Birth Rate" 1981) indicate that the American birth rate continues to decline and is presently 2.2 children per family. This rate is just above the "zero growth" rate of 2.1 children per family that Japan and many European countries have achieved. There has been a sharp decline from 1967, when the average number of children desired by married women of child-bearing years was 2.9 children. This decline seems in part because of economic uncertainties and in part because of the tendency for couples to wait longer before having children. Only 30% of women of child-bearing age had their first child before 21. On the other hand, women are not waiting too long—only 7.4% of women have their first child after age 30. These data do not apply to American women of Hispanic origin, who continue having large families at early ages.

Early childbearing, whether in or out of marriage, is increasing in all parts of the world, presenting serious health and socioeconomic problems. The younger the teen-age mother is, for example, the more likely that her baby will be premature, that its birth weight will be too low, and that it will die in its first year. Furthermore, the complications of pregnancy and childbirth are greater for the teen-age mother herself. The pregnancy-related death rate is 60% higher among girls who become pregnant before they are 15 than among mothers in their early 20s (13% higher among those 15 to 19 years old). It is the case of a child giving birth to a child. Yet about 70% of teen-age mothers under the age of 15 get *no* prenatal care during their first trimester of pregnancy, three times the number of 20- to 24-year-old mothers (Alan Guttmacher Institute 1976).

Family size, of course, varies enormously. Childless marriages are rather commonplace. But there is also a Russian couple whose marriage was "blessed" with 69 children born in 27 confinements—16 sets of twins, 7 sets of triplets, and 4 sets of quadruplets ("News of the Month" 1961b).

Genetic Screening and Experimentation

The National Foundation/March of Dimes estimates that 7% of all infants suffer from some form of birth defect.* This means that 250,000 babies are born each year with physical or mental impairment of varying severity. Past estimates suggest that 20% of birth defects are inherited, 20% are environ-

---

* The National Foundation has several excellent booklets and audiovisual aids on birth defects, which may be obtained by contacting a local chapter or the national headquarters: Box 2000, White Plains, N.Y. 10602. Medical professionals may write the Professional Educational Department for the "International Directory of Genetic Services."

mentally caused (infection, drugs, radiation, etc.), and 60% appear to be the result of an interaction between the two, although more definitive research in this area is needed. Risk of defect is greater in multiple births, when the mother is diabetic or has a history of repeated miscarriages, and when she is under age 18 or over age 35. The very young mother is underdeveloped herself, posing a nutritional threat to her child. And mothers over 35 bear more than 50% of babies with Down's syndrome (mongolism).

If there is concern that an unborn child might have a certain defect, **amniocentesis** can be performed. In this procedure, amniotic fluid is drawn off by means of a needle inserted through the pregnant woman's abdomen. The fluid will contain cells from the fetus that can be analyzed for such conditions as sickle-cell trait, thought to exist in 10% of American blacks, and cystic fibrosis, a genetic disease afflicting chiefly white people. Prenatal testing will also reveal Down's syndrome.

Amniocentesis is best performed during the 15th to 16th weeks of pregnancy. The procedure is most frequently performed when the expectant mother is over age 35 and when there is suspicion that chromosomal abnormalities, inborn problems in metabolism, or neural tube defects in the child may be involved. Amniocentesis carries certain risks for the mother and the fetus, but the diagnostic benefits usually outweigh the risks. A side benefit to amniocentesis, incidentally, is that the sex of the expected child can be determined (Elias 1980).

The most widely used genetic test, required by law in 43 states, is for **PKU (phenylketonuria),** done in very early infancy. PKU is treatable, but without treatment the child is doomed to irreversible mental retardation.

Gene transplantation is now a reality, at least in simple organisms like bacteria. But it has caused one of the most violent controversies in all of science. On the one hand, the ability to transfer genetic material from one cell to another of an entirely different species will permit biochemists to broaden their understanding of how cells (for example, cancer cells) reproduce. Perhaps genetic particles can be supplied which will cure such diseases as diabetes. Already, through a procedure called recombinant DNA, a bacterium has been created experimentally that one day may be able to absorb oil spills and then die without leaving pollution. But gene transplantation also poses serious dangers. It artificially creates a mutation, and mutations go on to reproduce themselves in the normal way. In the vein of science-fiction horror tales, critics foresee the creation of organisms never intended by nature, over which we will have no control. Many see a need for some form of federal control of genetic experimentation. Others see such a prospect as governmental invasion into scientific investigation and progress.

Cloning. Genetic technology has advanced so rapidly that many scientists think that the cloning, or exact duplication of a human being, is in the foreseeable future. Although clones of mammals have not yet been accomplished, much less humans, a frog was cloned in 1966 by Oxford University cell biologist, J. B. Gurdon. He replaced the nucleus of a frog ovum, having 23 chromosomes, with the nucleus of a body cell from a donor frog. The body cell nucleus, which had 46 chromosomes, then directed the growth of the cell into an embryo and finally a frog having the identical characteristics of the donor. Dr. Gurdon was able to replicate this 10 more times, although the 11 successful clones resulted from over 700 attempts ("Genetic Engineering" 1981).

Cloning has also been attempted through cell fusion. Two cells, one having its nucleus removed, are joined together with the aid of viruses in a laboratory culture. Cell fusion has been attempted with mice, but many abnormalities have resulted. Many problems are yet to be solved in this interesting and dramatic area of science.

Infertility (Sterility)

One-third of all U.S. couples have difficulty having children, either because they cannot conceive, or because the woman is unable to continue a pregnancy until a child is born (Westoff & Westoff 1971). Approximately one couple in 10 is never able to have children. When couples are purposely attempting to conceive a child, about 30% will succeed the first month, about 60% will have succeeded by the end of six months, and about 75% by the end of the first year.

A woman's age has a significant bearing on her ability to conceive. Natural fertility decreases progressively from her early 20s onward. If women aged 20 to 24 years are given a fertility rating of 100, women aged 25 to 29 years have a rating of 93 (or 93% of that of the younger women). Women aged 30 to 34 years have a rating of 85; those between 35 and 39 years, a rating of 69; those between 40 and 44 years, a rating of 35; and those between 45 and 49 years, a rating of 5 (Henry 1961).

Various diseases, including venereal infections and illnesses, such as mumps, can leave one permanently sterile. Injury, radiation exposure, or congenital defects can also leave one infertile. Alcohol or drug usage, inadequate nutrition, lack of rest or exercise, hormonal imbalances, or illness can sometimes cause temporary infertility. The difficulty in 30% of infertility cases is with the male, and males are probably responsible in an important contributory way in another 20% of cases (Amelar 1966; Clark 1959; "Infertility" 1979). Personality factors, sexual attitudes, and emotional stress may also underlie the fertility problems experienced by some couples (Mudd 1980).

Men often possess a low sperm count and sometimes have no active sperm at all, even though they are quite capable of having frequent and pleasurable intercourse. Some physicians consider a sperm count per ejaculation of less than 200 million too low for conception to result. But late research (Zuckerman *et al.* 1977) demonstrates that impregnation is possible with a count of 25 million. Below that number, impregnation is unlikely unless the sperm have especially high motility.

The effect that frequency of ejaculation has on sperm count and fertility is obviously a matter of individual variation. Generally speaking, the optimal time interval between ejaculations to insure maximum fertility is about 48 hours. Too much or too little sexual activity can negatively affect a man's fertility (Charny 1963; Masters & Johnson 1967). Recent experience indicates that, following the use of antidepressant drugs, sperm production is accelerated and fertility heightened. There is, as well, an increase in sex drive, energy, and interest (Kiev & Hackett 1968). On the other hand, there is evidence to indicate that exposure to excessive heat, such as that experienced when a man has a high fever or when he consistently takes hot baths, can adversely affect sperm production and sperm motility (Poulson 1980).

Heavy, prolonged use of marijuana is suspected of affecting male fertility by significantly reducing production of testosterone and sperm. The more marijuana smoked, the greater the reduction, although the effects appear to reverse in time if use is abandoned (Kolodny *et al.* 1974). Evidence also suggests that marijuana smoking affects female hormone levels because women may experience a disruption in the menstrual cycle (Smith 1980).

DES, or diethylstilbestrol, has been implicated as possibly causing vaginal cancer in female offspring and sterility in male offspring of women who have taken this drug. DES is a form of synthetic estrogen originally prescribed to pregnant women during the 1950s and 1960s to prevent miscarriages. The drug proved to be ineffective, but the adverse effects of DES are now being observed and studied more as the affected children have reached adulthood (Mazur 1980; "Possible Link" 1980).

Women can have any of several congenital defects or obstructions in their reproductive organs. They can also develop antibodies that eventually appear in the vagina and produce an immunity to sperm, making conception impossible (Masters & Johnson 1960b, 1961a, 1966). This immunity may be built up against the sperm of any man. But in some cases, the immunity may exist against one man's sperm but not another's ("Antibody's Role" 1964). It is not unusual for a couple to be unable to have children together, but for each to produce children with another partner.

A new development that holds hope for some infertile couples concerns the possibility of conceiving a **test tube baby.** An ovum can be extracted from the woman and fertilized, in a sterilized glass dish, with sperm from her husband. The fertilized egg can then be reimplanted in the woman's uterus so that the embryo can develop. World interest in the possibility of test tube babies came about with the birth of the first such baby in England on July 25, 1978. Moral, legal, and ethical issues underlying the medical technology of test tube babies are being debated, but test tube baby clinics are nevertheless being planned and opened to help many previously infertile couples to conceive ("Hospital" 1980).

Facts and Myths about Pregnancy

Male-Female Conception and Birth Ratios.   It is an established fact that many more males than females are conceived. But the female survival ratio is higher than that of the male. The conception ratio is about 160 males to 100 females; the zygote implantation ratio is about 120 males to 100 females; and the birth ratio is 105 males to 100 females.

After the shattering experiences of a war, people find some comfort in the notion that nature compensates for the men killed during hostilities by increasing, in some mystical way, the ratio of male to female births. Indeed, at first sight it seems that just such a miracle occurred after World Wars I and II when there was, in fact, an increase in the male birth ratio.

The noted biologist and anthropologist Ashley Montagu (1964) offers this explanation. During wartime people marry at a younger age. The younger mothers, being strong and healthy, provide fertilized ova—the greater number of which, as said before, are male—a good chance for implantation and survival. So they tend to give birth to a higher percentage of males. Furthermore, since these young mothers are separated from their husbands, the enforced spacing between births is longer than usual, leaving the women in a stronger physical condition to carry the next pregnancy to term and thereby increasing the likelihood of a male child.

Can an Unborn Child Be "Marked"?   Because of the close connection between fetus and mother, it is understandable why some people still assume that experiences such as a sudden shock or fright to the mother could cause a baby to be born with some physical or emotional "mark," most commonly a birthmark. This notion is, however, completely false, since there is no direct connection between the nervous systems or blood systems of mother and fetus.

What usually happens is that, when a child is born with an unusual birthmark—for example, a skin discoloration in the general shape of a bird—the parents' faulty memory processes cause them to "remember" an incident while the mother was pregnant wherein she was attacked or in some way frightened by a bird or something of similar shape.

Handicapped Women Cannot Have Children.   Paralyzed women may be able to bear children. With medical advice, care, and attention, handicapped women, like their physically normal sisters, can give birth to healthy children (Pepmiller 1980).

The Theory of Telegony. The influence of a "previous sire" on a later conception is a theory known as **telegony.** Despite its rather widespread acceptance among animal breeders and certain scientists, there is no scientific basis for the theory in either human or animal genetics. Inadequate knowledge of the laws of heredity or unscientific methods of observation and control in animal breeding have led some people to certain false conclusions—for example, that the offspring of the second partner might be affected by a woman's having had intercourse with an earlier partner or having been once impregnated by him.

A common occurrence that appears to give support to the telegony theory concerns female dogs. Bitches remain in heat for several days, during which time they may mate with several males. Because female dogs have a maddening capacity for escaping the watchful eye of their owners and mating with almost any male that happens along, it is quite possible for them to have a litter of puppies of which none resembles the intended sire. There is in this instance no carryover from the bitch's previous matings; it is simply that the puppies of the same litter have been sired by different dogs (Herrick 1959).

Can Humans and Infrahuman Animals Crossbreed? The belief that humans and animals can crossbreed continues to have some supporters. Not only is it impossible for humans to crossbreed with infrahuman animals, but interbreeding among the various genera of lower animals is equally impossible. It is true that members of different species of the same genus may produce crossbred offspring. For example, a man and an ape cannot interbreed, nor can an ape and a tiger. But two members of different species in the cat family, for example, can crossbreed.

Undoubtedly the wondrous creatures of Greek and Roman mythology—the centaurs, sphinxes, mermaids, and satyrs—has given credibility over the centuries to the myth that humans and lower animals can interbreed.

Pseudocyesis and Couvade. An interesting phenomenon known to occur in both humans and lower animals is **pseudocyesis** or **false pregnancy.** A woman, for example, will develop symptoms that are remarkably similar to those of true pregnancy. She may cease menstruating, be consistently nauseated, and gain a considerable amount of weight. In some instances the condition lingers for months before the symptoms disappear or are cleared up by psychotherapy. In extreme cases she will also develop a protruding abdomen and actually go into labor. But all that she "delivers" is an accumulation of air and fluids.

A related phenomenon is the practice of **couvade** among some primitive cultures. The man retires to bed during the woman's delivery and suffers in much the same manner as she does. In more sophisticated societies, the man will sometimes show some symptoms related to his partner's pregnancy. Expectant fathers have been known to become severely nauseated, vomit, and suffer abdominal pains. All the symptoms disappear after the woman has delivered their infant.

Prenatal Development

The development of children during the 9 months before birth is more rapid than at any other time during the entire life span. In the 20 years from birth to maturity, body weight will increase approximately 20 times. By comparison, in the 9 months between fertilization of the ovum and delivery of a fully developed baby, the increase in weight is about 6 billionfold. The most rapid period of growth for the human organism, then, is the early phase of prenatal life. From the time of fertilization to the end of the 1st month, the egg increases in weight by about a million percent (from 0.000004 gm to 0.04 gm). During the 2nd month, the weight increase is 7400%, dropping to an 1100% increase during the 3rd month, and to a comparatively insignificant increase of 30% during the final month (Figs. 7.6, 7.7, 7.8). The increase in rate of weight gain drops even more after birth. If this were not so, the infant would weigh from 160 to 170 pounds by the end of the first year of postnatal life (*Williams Obstetrics* 1961).

The following general outline of prenatal events from the 1st day of ovulation, assumed to be 14 days after the 1st day of the mother's last menstruation, is useful in obtaining a step-by-step view of fetal development (Arey 1974; Böving 1973; Hammond 1973; Miller & Leavell 1972; *Williams*

Figure 7.6   Human embryos, magnified 2.5 times. Ages from ovulation (left to right): 28 days, 31 days, 38 days, 39 days. Vertical lines indicate actual size. From Pritchard, J. A., and MacDonald, P. C., *Williams Obstetrics*, 15th ed., 1976. Courtesy of Appleton-Century-Crofts, Publishing Division, Prentice-Hall.

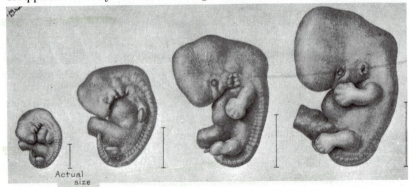

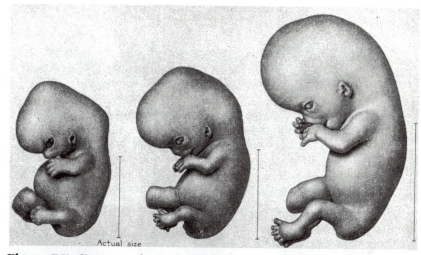

Actual size

Figure 7.7   Human embryos, magnified 1.9 times. Ages from ovulation: 6 to 7 weeks. Vertical lines indicate actual size. From Pritchard, J. A., and MacDonald, P. C., *Williams Obstetrics*, 15th ed., 1976. Courtesy of Appleton-Century-Crofts, Publishing Division, Prentice-Hall.

Obstetrics 1971). Experts are not in complete agreement regarding the exact sequence of these developmental changes. Table 7.1 gives a consensus of their views.

The baby's birth date can be predicted by calculating 280 days (40 weeks) from the first day of the mother's last menstruation, or 265 days (38 weeks) from ovulation and fertilization. Pinpointing the date of ovulation is, of course, the difficulty. Several investigators have shown that conception can take place on any day of a woman's monthly cycle, even during the mentrual flow, despite the generally accepted theory that women can become pregnant only during the 13th to 15th day of the cycle.

The period of gestation varies from birth to birth, even with the same woman, and according to the sex of the child. Women who engage in strenuous physical exercise may have their babies as much as 20 days earlier than less athletic women do. Girls are often born from 5 to 9 days earlier than boys. About 3% of pregnancies last 300 days or more (Clark 1967). The death rate among babies born after an overlong period of gestation is about three times that of babies delivered at normal term, probably because of the aging and withering of the placenta (Alexander 1965a). Most obstetricians will induce labor if they suspect placental shrinkage.

The size of babies at birth also varies considerably. The largest on record, born in Iran in February 1972, weighed 26.5 pounds, while the smallest surviving infant on record weighed less than 15 ounces at birth. Very large infants usually are delivered by caesarean section.

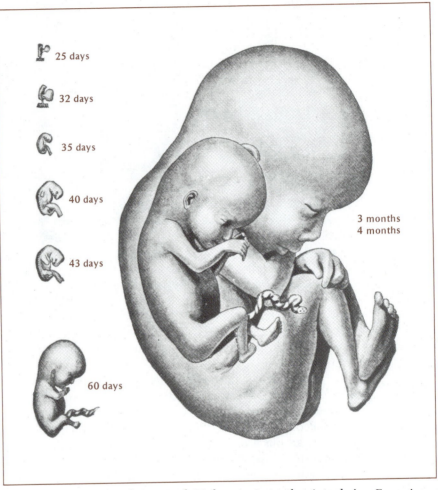

25 days

32 days

35 days

40 days

43 days

60 days

3 months
4 months

Figure 7.8 Human embryos aged 25 days to 4 months. Actual size. From Arey, *Developmental Anatomy*, 3rd ed. Philadelphia: W. B. Saunders Co., 1934.

Table 7.1. Human Prenatal Development

Days 1–3
  Zygote moves through fallopian tube toward uterus.
Days 4–5
  Conceptus floats freely in uterus in the form of a mass of cells (morula), which evolves into a hollow sphere (blastocyst).
Day 6
  After further cell division, the blastocyst attaches itself to the uterine wall and begins sinking into it (implantation).
Day 12
  Blastocyst lies wholly within uterine lining.

Table 7.1.   Human Prenatal Development (*Con't*)

Day 14

Implantation is complete. Conceptus is now called an embryo.

Days 14–21

Differentiation of the three primary germ layers—ectoderm, endoderm, and mesoderm—is completed.

The primitive backbone has developed. Neural groove is closing rapidly. Foregut (from which the pharynx, esophagus, stomach, and duodenum are derived) and hindgut (from which the colon is derived) begin to form. Heart tubes fuse. Respiratory groove appears. Oral membrane ruptures.

Days 21–28 (end of the 1st lunar month)

Enlarged brain area is plainly perceptible, the rapidly growing brain causing the disproportionately large head. Internal ear and eye structures are formed.

Other rudimentary sense organs, limb buds, and jaws appear. Heart—large and already divided into four chambers—is clearly visible under transparent membrane, and begins to beat. Liver tube is also prominent.

Blood vessels have formed and functional circulation begins.

2nd lunar month (weeks 5–8)

Embryo assumes more human appearance.

Face develops, including external structures of eyes, ears, nose.

Extremities are recognizable, fingers and toes distinguishable.

Head, now prominent, becomes more erect; neck is forming, back straightens.

Muscles rapidly differentiate throughout, assuming ultimate form and relationships.

Bone formation begins.

Between 6th to 8th week after fertilization, all organ rudiments are complete.

After 8th week, conceptus is called a fetus.

3rd lunar month (weeks 9–12)

Despite disproportionately large head, fetus has definite human appearance.

Nails begin forming on fingers and toes.

Urinary system exhibits some functioning.

Eyelids fuse; ears have moved up and are more level with eyes.

Fetus aborted at 10th week demonstrates spontaneous movements.

Local stimulus may produce squinting, opening of mouth, partial closing of fingers.

4th lunar month (weeks 13–16)

Fetus is capable of moving amniotic fluid in and out of respiratory tract.

Sex of fetus can easily be distinguished.

Body is becoming proportionately larger in relation to head.

Although incomplete, bones can be distinguished throughout body.

Gastrointestinal system is sufficiently functional to permit fetus to absorb water from swallowed amniotic fluid and to send unabsorbed material to lower colon (later to be discharged as meconium).

Table 7.1.   Human Prenatal Development (*Con't*)

Hair begins growing on head.

Fetus is about 8.5 in. (21.6 cm) long, and weighs about 6 oz.

5th lunar month (weeks 17–20)

Downy hair (lanugo) covers entire body.

Epidermis develops into layers.

Fetal movements can be felt and the heartbeat detected.

Fetus is approximately 12 in. (30 cm) long and weighs 1 lb. If born at this time, it might live for a few minutes, but cannot survive.

6th lunar month (weeks 21–24)

Fetus *in utero* can detect certain sounds.

Eyelashes and brows are visible.

Fetus is lean, but well proportioned.

If born at this time and given expert care, it has a 1-in-10 chance of survival.

*7th lunar month** (weeks 25–28)

Fetus is red, wrinkled, and rather old-looking.

Body is covered with greasy substance called *vernix caseosa*.

Eyelids reopen.

The fetus is about 16 in. (40 cm) long and weighs just under 4 lb.

8th lunar month (weeks 29–32)

Deposits of subcutaneous fat develop.

Testes in male fetus descend into scrotum from abdomen.

Sense of taste is now present.

Fetal length is about 18 in. (46 cm) and the weight somewhat over 5 lb.

A baby born at this time has a 90% chance of survival.

9th lunar month (weeks 33–36)

Skin redness fades. Wrinkles smooth out, as weight gain becomes rapid.

Nails reach tips of fingers and toes.

Full term (week 38)

Body is now plump.

Vernix caseosa still partially covers the body, but lanugo hair has fallen away.

At birth, infant weighs approximately 7 lb and is about 20 in. (50 cm) long.

Eyes react to light. They are slate-colored, not assuming final coloration until some weeks after birth.

Of infants born at this time, over 99% will survive.

---

* It is an old wives' tale that a 7-month fetus has a better chance of survival than an 8-month fetus. The notion stems from the fact that most allegedly 7-month infants are in reality full-term. As Dear Abby said, "The baby wasn't early; the wedding was just late!" The older the fetus is at birth, the better its chance for survival.

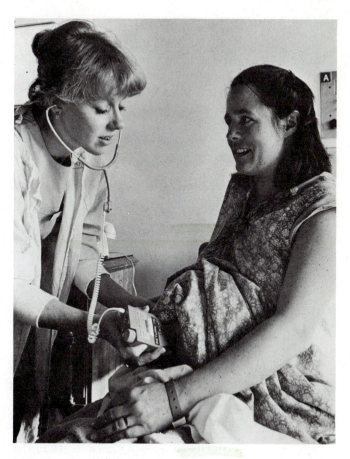

Good health begins with good prenatal care. (Jose Mercado, News and
Publications, Stanford University)

Birth

Now that some of the important issues concerning fertilization and prenatal
development have been discussed, an examination of the birth process will
be undertaken. This examination will focus on issues such as the time of
birth, the possible birth positions, the three stages of parturition, or
childbirth, the "new'" childbirth and midwifery, and multiple births.

Time of Birth

In some mammals, both day and time of birth seem based on certain
physiological factors. This phenomenon is less pronounced in humans. For
example, 8 or 9 out of 10 foals are born between 7 p.m. and 7 a.m., while

only 10% of human babies are born at night. The most common time of arrival of foals is between 3 a.m. and 4 a.m.; the least common, 3 p.m. The purpose of the circadian rhythms in the time of birth has apparently been lost in evolutionary history. But in the distant past they no doubt aided newborn animals by offering some added protection from predators (Liggins 1972). More babies are born in August and fewer in April than in other months.

Birth Positions

The manner and incidence of birth positions and presentations are as follows:

Longitudinal, accounting for over 99% of birth positions.
1. *Cephalic* or head presentations, which constitute 96% of all longitudinal births.
    a. Head bent downward with baby's chin on breastbone (Fig. 7.9).
    b. Head extended, face presenting.
    c. Head only slightly extended, brow presenting first.
2. *Breech* or buttocks presentations, accounting for 4% of all longitudinal births.
    a. *Frank,* the most common form; legs bent over abdomen with toes and shoulders touching and buttocks presenting over pelvis (Fig. 7.10).
    b. *Footling,* with the legs, held straight in a standing position, presenting first.
    c. *Full,* the rarest of the breech presentations; baby sitting cross-legged in mother's pelvis.

Transverse, occurring once in 200 births (Fig. 7.10). The fetus lies crosswise with a shoulder, arm, or hand entering the birth canal first. Either the fetus must be turned during labor, or a caesarean section is required.

Great pressure is, of course, exerted on a baby during delivery. In longitudinal cephalic presentations, the infant's head may be oddly molded in the birth process (Fig. 7.11), or the facial features may be bruised and swollen. The buttocks and genital area of an infant born in a breech presentation often becomes swollen and discolored during delivery. These conditions are understandably distressing to new parents. But the irregularities correct themselves within a few days of birth, and there is rarely permanent damage.

Although a breech presentation is rather unusual, almost 50% of infants assume this position prior to the seventh month of fetal life. Most infants in the breech position then make a 180° turn to the cephalic position before the ninth month. A fetus that does not make the turn can often be manipulated into the proper position during the later stages of pregnancy.

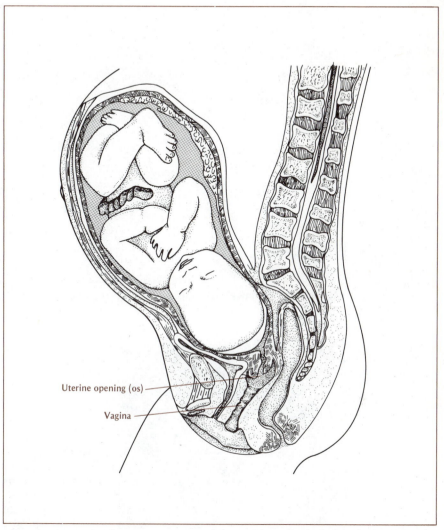

Uterine opening (os)

Vagina

Figure 7.9 Lateral representation of fetus in mother's pelvis in position for delivery.

Parturition

The First Stage. **Parturition,** the process of childbirth, takes place in three stages. The first stage can be recognized by any of three signs. First, powerful muscle contractions (called labor pains) may start, usually at intervals of 15 to 20 minutes. Each contraction lasts about 30 seconds. A second sign is the release of the mucous plug from the cervix, which will be flecked with

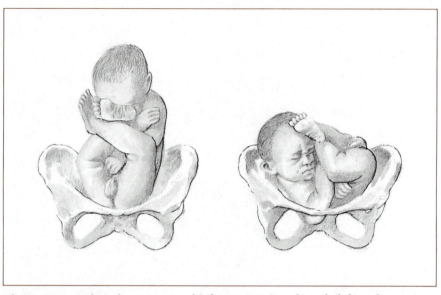

Figure 7.10   Relatively uncommon birth presentations: breech (left) and transverse (right).

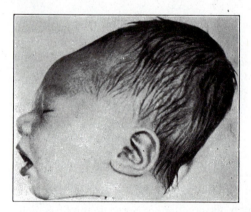

Figure 7.11   Molding of an infant's head at birth. From Eastman and Hellman, *Williams Obstetrics*, 13th ed., 1966. Courtesy of Appleton-Century-Crofts, Publishing Division, Prentice-Hall.

bright red blood. A third sign is the rupture of the amniotic membrane, which causes a flow of clear watery fluid from the vagina.

When any of these signs occurs, it is time to notify the obstetrician. The expectant mother should not then eat anything. After she checks into the hospital, she may spend a few hours in her room before it is time for the actual birth of the baby, unless there is some sort of emergency.

Initial labor contractions are usually relatively mild and rhythmic, but increase steadily in frequency, intensity, and duration. They finally occur every 3 to 4 minutes. Toward the end of labor, each contraction lasts a minute or more.

Labor contractions often feel as if they begin in the back and then move forward to the abdomen. This is primarily because the fetus is being pressed toward the back, as it has not yet made the turn into the vagina. Between contractions there is complete relaxation, a condition not found in most instances of muscle cramping.

The first stage of labor should produce a dilation of the cervix from its normal size (about ⅛ in. or 0.3 cm) to approximately 4 in. (10 cm), in order to permit the entry of the baby into and through the 4- to 5-in. (10- to 13-cm) long vagina. Each contraction pushes the baby downward, eventually with a force equal to 25 or 30 pounds of pressure. When the cervix is completely dilated, the first stage of labor has ended. This stage lasts about 16 hours for first babies, sometimes less, and about 8 hours in subsequent deliveries.

The Second Stage. The second stage of labor extends from complete cervical dilation until the baby is born. It lasts approximately 2 hours with first babies and about 1 hour in later deliveries. If the amniotic sac has not yet ruptured, the obstetrician will surgically rupture the membrane. The head of the fetus at this phase presses on the mother's lower vagina and bowel, the pressure producing a reflexive action of the muscles in that area that helps to expel the fetus. The infant is pushed along the birth canal with each contraction until its head appears at the external opening of the vagina (Fig. 7.12).

The mother is now placed on the delivery table with her knees bent and her thighs kept wide apart by leg supports. The genital area, abdomen, and inner thighs are thoroughly cleansed, and the region is covered with a sterile sheet containing an opening. The patient is usually catheterized (urine is withdrawn from the bladder by means of a tube inserted through the urethra) to be sure that there will be no accidental voiding while the baby passes through the vagina. Severe pressure on a full bladder, furthermore, could be injurious to the mother.

As the head of the fetus pushes forward during labor, the perineal tissue between vagina and rectum must stretch to an extreme degree. Frequently the opening to the vagina is not sufficiently elastic, and the emergence of the baby's head causes a tear. To prevent this, the obstetrician often performs an **episiotomy** (Fig. 7.13), cutting this tissue with scissors. The straight cut is simple to repair and heals rapidly.

The mother is now told to contract her abdominal muscles to create additional pressure. The obstetrician, meanwhile, may apply pressure on her abdomen. It is sometimes helpful in speeding up the birth process if the physician applies pressure on the chin of the infant through the thin tissue of the perineum.

When the infant's head emerges from the vagina, the physician holds it with both hands and gently guides it downward while one shoulder and

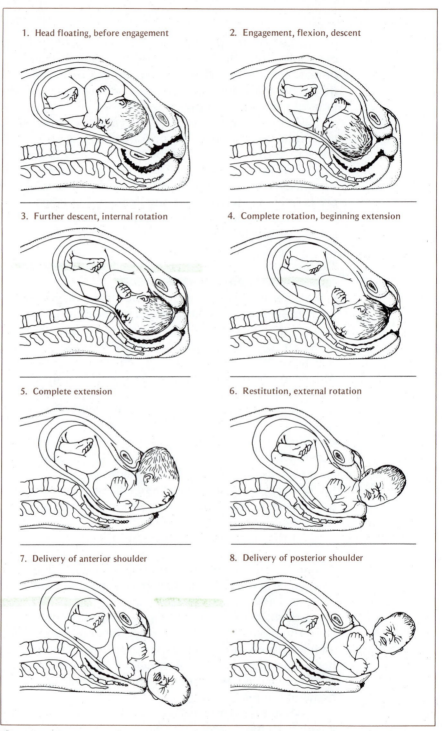

1. Head floating, before engagement

2. Engagement, flexion, descent

3. Further descent, internal rotation

4. Complete rotation, beginning extension

5. Complete extension

6. Restitution, external rotation

7. Delivery of anterior shoulder

8. Delivery of posterior shoulder

Figure 7.12   Principal movements of the fetus in process of labor and delivery.

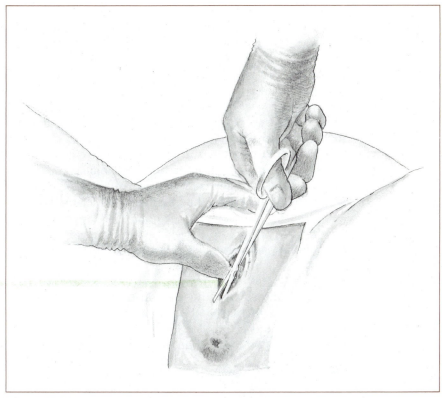

Figure 7.13 Scissors in position for an episiotomy.

then the other emerge. After the appearance of the head and shoulders, the rest is simple because the trunk and limbs are quite small in comparison. The baby sometimes emerges with a wrinkled appearance. This is because the bones of the head, which have not yet grown together, overlap, decreasing the size of the skull in order to facilitate the birth. The head will quickly return to its normal shape and the wrinkles will fill out.

As the head emerges, the obstetrician, using a bulb-type syringe, removes any blood, amniotic fluid, or watery mucus that may have accumulated in the infant's nose and mouth. To facilitate the first breath, some doctors still hold the infant upside down by the heels and slap the buttocks. But most physicians do not consider this necessary, since the change in temperature and atmospheric pressure is usually enough to cause breathing to start.

With an infant's first breath, a drastic change occurs in its circulatory and respiratory processes. Nourishment and oxygen had previously been supplied through the placenta by way of the umbilical cord. The same pressure and temperature changes that force the baby to breathe also create a vacuum in the chest cavity. This vacuum causes blood to be directed into the baby's pulmonary artery and lungs. Blood circulates to the heart through the pulmonary veins and fills the left chamber.

There is now no further need for an opening between the chambers and a flap of tissue closes the opening. It takes a few minutes for the process to be completed. During this time the baby is bluish in color, but as circulation is established in the pulmonary system the skin becomes pink. This process seldom fails. If it does, the result is a "blue baby." Fortunately, modern surgery can correct this abnormality.

Now that the infant is breathing the oxygen of the outside world, it no longer needs the placenta or the umbilical cord. Once the cord stops pulsating and the baby is breathing regularly, the cord is clamped and cut about 3 in. (8 cm) from the abdomen. The clamp is left in place until the stub dries up and separates. To eliminate any possibility of a gonorrheal or other eye infection, a weak silver nitrate solution or an ophthalmic ointment of penicillin is used in the newborn's eyes.

The Third Stage.   In the third stage of labor the placenta is delivered, about 15 minutes after the baby. Muscular contractions shrink the uterus and the area of placental attachment. The placenta detaches from the uterine wall and is expelled into the vagina within a short period—3 to 10 minutes (Fig. 7.14). The obstetrician sometimes presses the uterus downward

Figure 7.14   Appearance of the placenta immediately after its delivery.

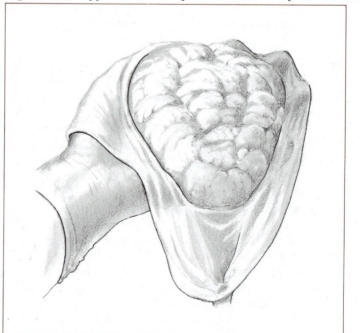

to facilitate expulsion. Occasionally these efforts are unsuccessful, and the physician must peel the placenta from the uterus. If an episiotomy was necessary, the obstetrician repairs it. The birth is now accomplished.

Other Delivery Procedures

Caesarean Section. A caesarean section is a surgical procedure whereby the baby is born through a low transverse incision in the abdomen wall and in the wall of the uterus. The popular but erroneous legend that Julius Caesar was delivered surgically gives the operation its name. Probably the term originated from an ancient Roman law, which was later incorporated into a legal code called Lex Caesarea. This statute was enacted to save children's lives by requiring that an operation be performed on a woman who died in the advanced stages of pregnancy.

In the past, the death rate among women undergoing this surgery was exceptionally high because of hemorrhage and infection. Today, however, death following a caesarean section is extremely rare, and a woman may have two or three babies this way. Indeed, caesarean delivery of five or six infants to the same mother is no longer highly unusual.

The caesarean procedure is used more frequently today than in the past. This is not because of convenience to patient or physician, but because improved techniques of detecting difficulties before birth reveal more instances in which normal delivery would endanger mother or child. Another reason is the increasing reluctance of doctors to use forceps to facilitate delivery.

Anesthetics in Childbirth. Because many women have been indoctrinated in the belief that childbirth is an event burdened with suffering and threat to life, their entire sex life is affected by fear of pregnancy and childbirth. Coitus develops overtones of unpleasantness and pain, and becomes something to be avoided.

Anthropologists have demonstrated that suffering during childbirth is related to the individual woman's expectations regarding the nature and severity of childbirth pains and the culture in which she lives (Melzack 1961). There is, to be sure, some pain from the uterine contractions and cervical expansion involved in childbirth. But extreme suffering is likely to be an outgrowth of cultural and emotional conditioning. An easy delivery is positively related to a woman's understanding the birth process, having confidence in her obstetrician, and having a secure relationship with her partner. The art of relaxation and the ability to free oneself from fear are also pertinent. An interesting illustration of childbirth uncomplicated by anxiety was provided by a Michigan woman who delivered a healthy infant weighing just under 8 pounds while she took an afternoon nap ("Sex in the News" 1967).

Maternal peace of mind and comfort can be greatly enhanced by the use of anesthetics in childbirth, or by the techniques of "the new childbirth" discussed in the next section. The art and science of anesthetics have become so refined that there is rarely an excuse nowadays for most of the fears traditionally related to delivery. Curiously, however, the initial reaction of the clergy to the use of anesthetics in childbirth was distinct opposition. They often quoted the biblical pronouncement against women from Genesis 3:16, "In sorrow thou shalt bring forth children." Some physicians judged the use of anesthetics in this connection as contrary to nature. Most of these objections were dispelled in the popular mind, however, when Queen Victoria was delivered of her seventh child with the aid of anesthetics (Beigel 1964). Some still argue, however, that a woman will not love her child unless she experiences pain during delivery. In fact, the evidence is that the mother who did not suffer severe pain in childbirth has greater love for her child than the woman who did suffer greatly and later, consciously or unconsciously, associates the child with a miserable experience. Recently, however, physicians have become more conservative in their use of anesthetics in childbirth. Increasing use of the new childbirth methods together with a concern over possible physical problems to the neonate, including brain damage, have led to less than automatic use of anesthesia in hospital delivery rooms.

The New Childbirth and Midwifery

The high incidence of maternal death put doctor and hospital in charge of virtually all confinements by the 1930s. Today the trend is moving in the direction of educating parents once more toward greater involvement in their child's birth.

Several techniques have been developed in recent years that aim at minimizing childbirth pain through programs of physical and psychological training prior to delivery, rather than through reliance on drugs. The first such technique was named **natural childbirth** by its originator, Grantly Dick-Read. These procedures today are more commonly called "prepared," "cooperative," or "controlled" childbirth. While opposed to the routine use of heavy sedation, followers of this approach in no way insist that a woman must do without light medication during labor or some form of anesthetic during the actual birth if it is necessary. The method also endorses avoiding the artificial rupture of the amniotic sac, since it acts as a cushion to prevent the fetal head from undue pressure during the birth process.

There are several programs of childbirth preparation, including hypnosis. The approach most favored in this country, however, is the **Lamaze method.** Originated in Russia and introduced to the Western world in 1951 by Fernand Lamaze, this procedure consists of classes for both expectant parents in which the physical and emotional changes occurring during

Parenthood: A labor of love. (Erika Stone)

pregnancy, labor, and delivery are outlined. They provide, as well, training in the muscle-control exercises and breathing techniques to be used during labor. The man learns how to assist the woman in her practice sessions at home and during delivery. The primary goal is to help her participate actively in the birth of her baby with a minimum of fear and pain. Presence of the man gives both a sense of complete sharing and adds to the well-being of the mother.

The **Leboyer method,** another new concept of delivery, concentrates on the infant's emergence into the world. Instead of being born into a confusion of bright lights, movement, cold metal scales, and harsh fabrics, the infant is introduced into a quiet, dimly lit room and placed immediately on the mother's belly to reestablish contact with her. The baby is then given a warm soothing bath, thus further muting the shock of the journey from the womb to the outside world (Leboyer 1975).

There are also campaigns urging a return to the use of trained midwives for uncomplicated deliveries and toward acceptance of delivery at home, so that childbirth becomes a more family-oriented event. Infant mortality is at its highest in the U.S. in the rural South (39 per 1000 live births). Lack of proper obstetrical care, malnutrition, and improper hygiene are the obvious causes. The University of Mississippi has therefore structured a far-reaching program to train registered nurses as midwives. They are given intensive obstetrical training, including pre- and postnatal care, after

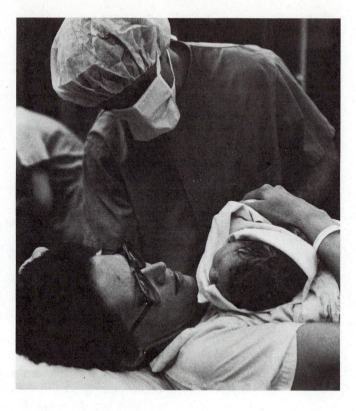

Childbirth as a shared family experience. (Erika Stone)

which they must serve one year in the rural South. Their patients' babies are delivered in a hospital, the midwife remaining with her patient throughout; a doctor and emergency services are immediately available, should complications arise.

But the change most popular across the country is toward natural childbirth. Those wishing further information on the subject should read *Thank You, Dr. Lamaze* by Marjorie Karmel, *Awake and Aware* by Irwin Chabon, *Childbirth with Hypnosis* by William S. Kroger, or *Our Bodies, Ourselves* by the Boston Women's Health Book Collective.

Multiple Births

Multiple births occur about once in every 80 to 89 deliveries (Carbary 1966; Trainer 1965; *Williams Obstetrics* 1961). Twins occur once in 80 births, triplets once in 80 × 80 (6400), and quadruplets once in 80 × 80 × 80 (512,000). Heredity, the age of the mother, and racial factors appear to be of significance, in that multiple births apparently occur more frequently in

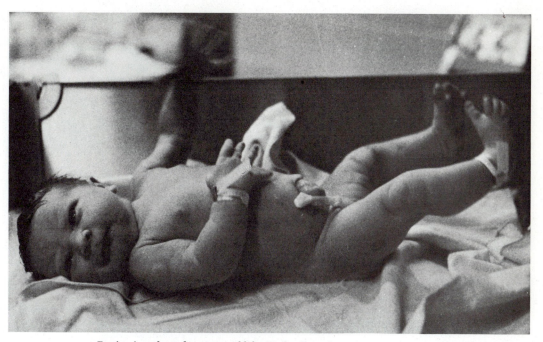

Beginning the adventure of life. (Erika Stone)

one family than in another, and to more women in their 30s than in their 20s. Blacks have more twins than do whites, who in turn have more twins than do Oriental women.

Identical twins develop from a single fertilized ovum that first divides and then separates into two beings which continue the process of cell division independently. Identical twins possess identical sets of chromosomes and are therefore always of the same sex. They have a single placenta and chorion, but each twin is ordinarily contained in its own amniotic sac and is nurtured through its own umbilical cord. There are rare cases in which twins share an amnion (Figs. 7.15, 7.16). Of identical twins, girls are more dissimilar in appearance than boys (Short 1972).

If the developing cell mass does not make a complete separation in the identical-twinning process, the result is **Siamese (or joined) twins.** Ordinarily only five such births occur in the world in any one year. But in a recent two-year period, 12 were born in three areas of Africa. None survived. No reason for so many of such births has been found.

Fraternal twins develop from two separate ova, both usually fertilized at about the same time. A single follicle may expel two or more mature ova, or ova in two or more follicles may develop to maturity simultaneously (*Williams Obstetrics* 1961). Fraternal twins can be of the same or different

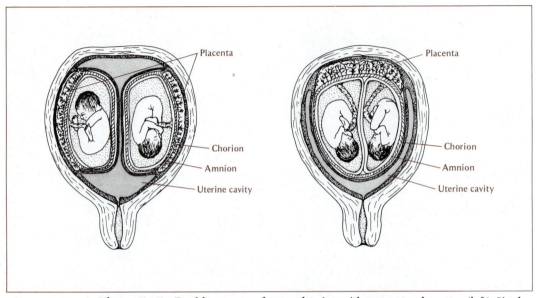

Figure 7.15   Double-ovum or fraternal twins with separate placentas (left). Single-ovum or identical twins with a common placenta (right).

sex. They have separate umbilical cords, chorions, and placentas. They bear no more resemblance to one another than siblings born separately.

The birth of most twins follows the usual pattern of parturition, although some interesting variations in the conception and birth process have occasionally occurred. For example, most twins arrive within a few minutes to an hour of each other. In infrequent cases, however, considerable time elapses between their births. In one instance, the twins arrived 48 days apart; in another, 30, with one infant born in December and the other in January. Mothers have given birth to twins of different races—fathered, naturally, by two men, the conceptions having taken place within a short time of each other. At least one birth has been recorded in which the twins, clearly fathered by different men, had different blood types (Carbary 1966).

Triplets may result from the fertilization of three different ova. More commonly, only two eggs are involved, one of which separates and then develops into identical twins. Quadruplets are for the most part the product of the fertilization of two ova, each of which separates and develops into a set of identical twins.

In multiple births, the percentage of males decreases with the number of children born. Among single births in one large sample, the percentage of males was 51.59%; among twins, 50.85%; among triplets, 49.54%; and among quadruplets, 46.48%. The explanation very likely is that from conception on, survival favors the female (*Williams Obstetrics* 1961).

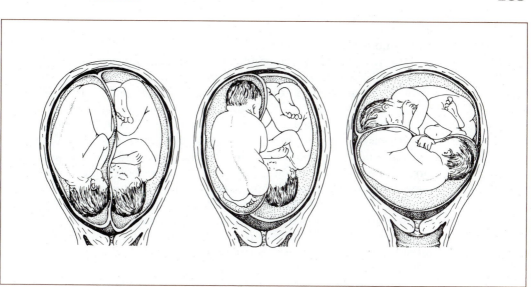

Figure 7.16   Various positions of twins in the uterus.

Viable twin pregnancies will terminate about 22 days earlier than viable single pregnancies, the average gestation period for twins being 37 weeks.

Lactation

Lactation refers to the production of milk in the mother's breasts following childbirth. The first secretion the nursing baby receives is **colostrum,** a substance present in the breast immediately after birth. The effect of colostrum on the newborn is not positively known, but it is of high protein content and is believed to contribute to the child's immunity to many infectious diseases during the early months of life (Steen & Montagu 1959). It possibly functions as a laxative, as well, helping to rid the infant's intestines of meconium (fecal matter consisting of mucus, bile, and epithelial threads). Colostrum disappears from the mother's breasts two or three days after delivery, and true milk replaces it.

After childbirth, the mother's pituitary gland begins to produce prolactin, a hormone that induces lactation. As the ducts leading to the nipples fill with milk, the breasts become swollen and congested. The mother usually experiences an uncomfortable sensation, or even pain, for a period of a day or so. The onset of lactation is often accompanied as well by such symptoms as fatigue, headache, and low-grade fever, for which the infant's sucking provides relief. Nursing also appears to initiate uterine contractions that help reduce the uterus to its normal size.

Certain substances consumed by the nursing mother, such as alcohol, strong sedatives, and vegetable cathartics, may adversely affect the infant. Alcohol concentration in the mother's milk, for example, is the same as in her blood. A nursing mother should not, therefore, consume alcohol or other questionable substances without first consulting her doctor.

Occasionally certain physiological difficulties are encountered in nursing a baby, in which case the physician can usually offer a solution. One of the most recurrent problems is an inverted nipple, a congenital anomaly resulting from fibrous bands holding the nipple in rather than allowing it to protrude in the normal manner. At the time of lactation, the mother may experience severe pain if the condition is not corrected. Sometimes a small suction cup may be used to draw out the nipple. In other instances nursing will correct the inversion; in still others, corrective surgery is required.

Breastfeeding tends to delay subsequent conception by prolonging postpartum amenorrhea (absence of menstruation). Prolactin suppresses ovulation, and postpartum prolactin levels differ significantly in mothers who nurse their babies and those who do not. In the latter, postpartum amenorrhea lasts only 3 to 4 months, whereas it persists in nursing mothers about 9 months or more (Jackson 1976). It should be borne in mind, however, that some women start another pregnancy without having menstruated following the preceding one (Tietze 1970). They become pregnant with the first ovulation after parturition. It has also been observed that nursing mothers return more rapidly to normal sexual interest after childbirth than other mothers do (Masters & Johnson 1966).

Formulas are available for those mothers who do not wish to breastfeed their infants, but in recent years breastfeeding has once again been encouraged by many physicians and allied health personnel for their patients. Proponents of breastfeeding point out that the nursing infant receives anti-infective and immunologic benefits and that both mother and child gain emotional benefits. Some advocates of breastfeeding suggest that breastfed infants have fewer problems with obesity, hypertension, and allergies than infants who are fed with formula (Robertson 1980). Of course, given other special lifestyle, career, physical, or emotional reasons, some women may still opt to formula feed their children.

While the incidence of breastfeeding has risen slightly in recent years, a great deal of apprehension remains in the mind of many women. One fear is that nursing will cause their breasts to sag, making the figure less attractive.

Women reveal anxiety over the shape and size of their breasts and often feel inferior if they consider their breasts too small. Indeed, brassiere-padding enterprises have benefited from this excessive concern over breast

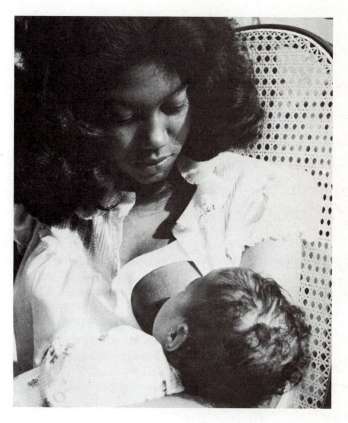

Breastfeeding: A way to establish the mother-infant bond. (Erika Stone)

size (if they have not deliberately encouraged it). It is little wonder that people consider breasts a symbol of ultimate sexuality in view of the emphasis placed on them in advertisements and clothing styles.

Plastic surgeons have devised ingenious methods for remolding breasts into desired shapes and sizes through the use of surgery, plastics, and silicone. Such cosmetic operations have now been fairly well perfected and many women—especially if some breast defect seriously impairs their attractiveness or self-image—reap considerable benefit from the surgery (Imber 1980; Zarem 1970). Women who have overly large breasts sometimes elect a surgical procedure known as a reduction mammaplasty in order to decrease breast size (Goin & Goin 1980).

Many people do not realize that the appeal of the breast varies widely from culture to culture and from era to era, and that breast size and shape have nothing to do with sexuality, except psychologically. Furthermore, large breasts are not even an advantage in lactation, because they often contain an excessive amount of fat tissue that can interfere with the function of the milk glands.

Breast development in a hormonally normal woman is largely a matter of heredity. Sagging of the breasts can to some degree be prevented by well-designed and properly fitted brassieres. However, a good posture, sensible nutrition, and proper hygiene remain the biggest assets to an attractive figure. A physician can offer the best advice for preventing breast-tissue breakdown during pregnancy, lactation, and weaning.

Because of the emphasis on breasts in our culture, many women are so afraid of breast cancer that they avoid proper physical examinations lest some malignancy be discovered that will necessitate radical mastectomy. Despite the fact that there are in some cases alternatives to radical surgery, the dread of mastectomy as a mutilation destructive to femininity causes some women literally to sacrifice their lives to their fears. Perhaps if these women realized that many lumps in the breast are not tumors and that most of those that are tumors are benign, they would not be so reluctant to seek medical treatment or advice (Witkin 1979).

It is a normal phenomenon for many of the lower mammals to have multiple breasts and a milk-line that the mammary glands follow. About 1% of human females have more than the normal two, making the condition less uncommon than many would believe (Netter 1961). There is usually only one extra breast in these cases; it is ordinarily nonfunctional and quite small, but it can be quite normally developed and functional. Men occasionally have breast development nearly identical to that of a normal woman. Surgery will usually remedy the problems of extra and abnormally oversized breasts (Netter 1961), thereby reducing or removing altogether the stress that "being different" creates.

Summary

Fertilization occurs when one of the male germ cells, or sperm, unites with the female germ cell, or ovum. The 22 autosomes, or non-sex chromosomes, and 1 sex chromosome that are within the sperm combine with the 22 autosomes and 1 sex chromosome that are in the egg, resulting in a fertilized egg containing 46 chromosomes, the number common to all human cells.

Prenatal life can be divided into three periods: (1) the period of the ovum, which lasts one week from fertilization; (2) the period of the embryo, which lasts from the second to eighth week of gestation; and (3) the period of the fetus, which lasts from the third month to birth. The fertilized egg, or zygote, undergoes mitotic cell division and in a process of division known as cleavage develops into a morula and then a blastocyst. The blastocyst implants itself in the endometrial tissue by about day 14. After implantation is completed, three germ layers—the ectoderm, the endoderm, and the mesoderm—combine to make up the embryonic disc from which all bodily components develop.

At about the third week of embryonic life, the extra-embryonic or fetal membranes—including the yolk sac, body stalk, amnion, and chorion—develop to protect and nourish the embryo and help in the elimination of waste. The placenta develops from the uterine mucosa, and the chorion and is largely composed of fetal tissue. The placenta is a special organ of interchange between embryo and mother. The fetal and maternal blood systems are separate, but food, oxygen, and waste products are interchangeable by diffusion and absorption. Some viruses, disease germs, and antibiotics can also cross between the blood systems. The umbilical cord develops during the fifth week of pregnancy and connects the fetus to the fetal portion of the placenta.

Other forms of fertilization and implantation than the usual uniting of egg and sperm and implantation of the zygote in the uterine wall are possible. Artificial insemination (AI) can be used to solve infertility problems. Sperm of a donor (AID), or sperm of the husband (AIH), can be placed in the woman's uterus when conception is considered most likely to occur. Ovum transplantation and parthenogenesis, development of an ovum without previous contact with sperm, are other possible alternatives. Ectopic, or misplaced pregnancies, lead to atypical areas of implantation of the fertilized egg. Tubal pregnancies, abdominal pregnancies, and ovarian and cervical pregnancies are forms of ectopic pregnancy.

The signs of pregnancy may be divided into three classes: (1) presumptive signs, including cessation of the menses, fatigue, morning sickness, and changes in the breast; (2) probable signs, including softening of the cervix and enlargement of the abdomen; and (3) positive signs, including fetal heartbeat and fetal movements. Tests for pregnancy, including the agglutination test, can give accurate proof of pregnancy soon after implantation occurs.

When women do become pregnant, they can continue to engage in normal activities, including travel, exercise, sexual intercourse, and driving. Consultation with an obstetrician is advisable, however, in determining what types of sexual activity might be appropriate as pregnancy progresses. Precautions can be taken to minimize problems such as premature labor and delivery. Medical follow-up of a woman's food consumption, smoking habits, alcoholic intake, and prescription and nonprescription drug usage is especially relevant during pregnancy.

Women who are exposed to diseases or disorders such as toxoplasmosis, gonorrhea, syphilis, herpesvirus, and Rh blood incompatibilities may be endangering their health as well as the health and development of their unborn children. Women who experience noninfectious disease states such as toxemia, diabetes, or thyroid problems also are advised to seek appropriate medical care. Teen-age mothers and mothers past age 40 may be particularly prone to complications during their pregnancies.

As many as one-third of couples experience difficulty in conceiving, and 1 in 10 couples are never able to have children. Disease states, injuries, congenital defects, alcohol or drug usage, hormonal inbalances, and emotional distress are factors that may contribute to fertility problems. The possibility of conceiving a "test-tube baby" may offer hope for some infertile couples.

Pregnancy is a human condition shrouded by mythology and by unusual, interesting phenomena. One myth is that a child can be "marked" as the result of some physical or emotional trauma experienced by the mother. Another myth, based on the theory of telegony, is that a "previous sire" can influence a later conception. Still another myth is that humans and lower animals can interbreed. Pseudocyesis and couvade are interesting phenomena related to pregnancy that have been observed occasionally in humans.

When genetic defects are thought to exist in the developing child, amniocentesis can be performed to determine whether or not there is a problem. Another genetic test, to rule out the presence of PKU, is done in early infancy. Gene transplantation and other forms of genetic experimentation offer intriguing possibilities as well as dilemmas for the future.

The prospective birth date of a baby can be estimated by calculating 280 days from the first day of the mother's last menstruation or by calculating 265 days from the time of ovulation. However, the period of gestation can vary even in the same mother. Most babies are born in cephalic or head presentations; breech and transverse presentations are rare.

The process of childbirth, known as parturition, takes place in three stages. The first stage can be recognized by the beginning of labor pains, the release of the mucous plug, or rupture of the amniotic membrane. The second stage of labor extends from complete cervical dilation until the baby is born. The third stage includes delivery of the placenta. When prebirth difficulties occur, a surgical procedure known as caesarean section can be performed to deliver the child. Anesthetics are often employed to relieve the discomfort experienced by the mother during the birth process.

Several programs of childbirth preparation have been developed that emphasize the use of educational methods and relaxation techniques. The Lamaze method is the most widely used in this country. Also returning to attention are ideas such as making use of trained midwives and allowing uncomplicated deliveries at home.

All conceptions do not necessarily end in single births. Multiple births— identical or fraternal twins, triplets or quadruplets—occur about once in every 80 to 89 deliveries. Heredity, the age of the mother, and race are factors that affect the incidence of multiple births.

Following childbirth, milk is produced in the mother's breasts in a process known as lactation. Prolactin is the hormone that induces lactation. At first, colostrum is secreted by the breast and received by the nursing baby, but two or three days after delivery, true milk is secreted.

Annotated Bibliography

Huff, Robert W. and Pauerstein, Carl J. *Human reproduction: Physiology and pathophysiology*. New York: Wiley, 1979.

> This text for medical students and practitioners contains detailed information on human reproductive biology, gynecologic physiology, and pregnancy. Specific topics include male and female sexual differentiation, reproductive endocrinology, contraception and infertility, venereal disease, reproductive genetics, fetal growth, and management of normal and high-risk pregnancy. Pre-chapter objectives and self-test questions and answers facilitate learning.

Johnson, Martin and Everitt, Barry. *Essential reproduction*. Oxford, England: Blackwell Scientific Publications, 1980.

> This text discusses a wide range of topics related to reproductive biology, including genetics, sexual differentiation, endocrinology, ovarian and testicular function, puberty and the climacteric, hormones and sexual behavior, coitus and fertilization, pregnancy, parturition and lactation. Though written for the student of the technicalities of reproduction, this book would be useful as a general reference.

Kitzinger, Sheila. *The complete book of pregnancy and childbirth*. New York: Alfred Knopf, 1980.

> This well-illustrated, comprehensive guide for the expectant mother delivers an abundance of information on pregnancy and childbirth. Topics of special interest include the effects of drugs and cigarettes during pregnancy, the changing marital relationship, sex during pregnancy, breast feeding, and postpartum exercises.

Lawrence, Ruth A. *Breast-feeding: A guide for the medical profession*. St. Louis, Missouri: C. V. Mosby, 1980.

> This detailed book is intended for health care professionals concerned with the clinical management of the nursing mother and her infant. A wealth of basic data is provided on the nutritional, biochemical, immunologic, psychological, and sociological aspects of breast feeding and lactation.

Money, John. *Love and love sickness: The science of sex, gender difference, and pair-bonding*. Baltimore: The Johns Hopkins University Press, 1980.

> This scholarly book encompasses a wide array of topics in human sexuality. Some general areas include the historical and cultural aspects of sexual behavior, factors influencing sexual orientation and pair-bonding, erotic sexuality, sexual taboos, and pornography. The author advances a new theory to guide understanding of sex differences based on the variety of factors

contributing to gender identity and sex role. This book would appeal to the student, medical and allied health professional, and general academic reader.

Oxorn, Harry. *Human labor and birth (4th ed.).* New York: Appleton-Century-Crofts, 1980.

Intended for practicing physicians and allied health care personnel, this informative book focuses on clinically relevant procedures and diagnosis in labor and childbirth. Problems in labor are covered with advice for treatment. Delivery phases are highlighted with emphasis on clinical management.

Queenan, John T. (Ed.) *A new life: Pregnancy, childbirth, and your child's first year.* New York: Van Nostrand Reinhold, 1979.

This comprehensive guide for expectant and new parents dispenses straight-forward information concerning pregnancy, childbirth, and infancy. The book is well-illustrated with color photographs and drawings.

Quilligan, E. J. and Kretchmer, N. (Eds.) *Fetal and maternal medicine.* New York: John Wiley and Sons, 1980.

This text presents detailed discussion of various clinically relevant aspects of perinatal medicine, focusing on basic concepts, systemic problems, and specific diseases affecting the mother and her child. Subject areas are expected to be of greatest concern to the practicing obstetrician and gynecologist.

Shearman, Rodney P. *Human reproductive physiology (2nd ed.).* London: Blackwell Scientific Publications, 1979.

This comprehensive text provides detailed information on the most significant aspects of human reproduction, including genetics and cytogenetics, the physiology and function of testes and ovaries, pregnancy, and menopause. This book is designed for the student and medical and allied health professional.

Witters, Weldon and Jones-Witters, Patricia. *Human sexuality: A biological perspective.* New York: D. Van Nostrand, 1980.

This text approaches the various aspects of human sexuality from the biological standpoint. Topics of special interest include genetic engineering, hormonal control of sexuality, drugs affecting sexual function, surrogate parenthood, artificial insemination, cloning, and sex selection. The text is well illustrated and contains student performance objectives, but its appeal extends beyond the classroom.

Wolman, Benjamin B. (Ed.). *Psychological aspects of gynecology and obstetrics.* Oradell, New Jersey: Medical Economics Company, 1978.

This book features articles by renowned contributors concerning psychological considerations in obstetrics and gynecology. Topics include changing roles, female sexual dysfunctions, puberty, contraception and fertility, the middle years and the climacteric, pregnancy and complications, and many others. Special issues such as rape crisis and breast cancer are discussed. The book was written for students and medical practitioners, but many articles will appeal to the general audience.

Part Three
The Sexual Act

In humans, a meaningful sexual relationship extends beyond physical intercourse to include emotional and intellectual components. In fact, sexual activity would quickly become humdrum if these other aspects were missing.

Fundamental to any lasting relationship are intimacy and love. In a sexual relationship, emotional closeness between a couple removes sex from being an act of mere copulation to a plane where many needs other than the sexual can be met. The means of achieving intimacy and keeping it alive are explored in Chapter 8. So also is the fear of closeness that compels many people to accept counterfeits rather than to reach out for the real thing.

Techniques of sexual arousal that men and women have found highly satisfying are described in Chapter 9. This information can heighten sexual pleasure during specific encounters and, in the long range, can help to keep ongoing relationships satisfying. The intriguing subject of substances alleged to intensify or decrease sexual desire is explored in Chapter 10, and the advantages and disadvantages of various coital positions are discussed in Chapter 11.

The peak of sexual excitement—orgasm—is explained in some detail in Chapter 12, because ignorance and a variety of emotional barriers often block orgasm itself or the full enjoyment of it. Freedom from fear of unwanted pregnancy and a couple's satisfaction with a birth-prevention technique contribute significantly to sexual fulfillment. Methods of birth control and the effectiveness of each are discussed in Chapter 13, so that readers can consider the options and choose the technique most suited to them.

Finally, the psychosexual aspects of aging are discussed in Chapter 14. This is a relatively neglected subject, but a very important one, since fear and embarrassment frequently hinder older people who might otherwise enjoy a satisfying sex life in their later years.

Intimacy and Love

Since the beginning of civilization the terror of loneliness has been one of humankind's great threats. People will go to incredible lengths to avoid loneliness and will pay an enormous price in money, property, time, and personal rights to prevent it. The most obvious and meaningful way to avoid loneliness is to establish and maintain intimate, constructive relationships with others. But the solution is far more complex than it would seem. For the road to intimacy is cluttered with many barriers arising from the individual's cultural background, personal needs, and private fears. The growth and survival of intimacy have a bleak prospect when either or both partners in a relationship have through the years internalized feelings of distrust, isolation, and rejection, or have developed the unfortunate protective mechanisms of withdrawal and withholding of self. These traits of alienation have become signs of our times.

Present-day feelings of distrust and isolation come from several sources: eroding social structures; blurring of male and female roles, which were once well defined; confusion over personal identity and goals; geographic changes forced by job transfers (the "average" American moves seven times in his/her lifetime, and changes professions three times), necessitating the difficult, often painful, process of forming new friendships; political unrest; and disillusionment over the integrity of governments. All have taken a heavy toll in personal security and confidence.

The ease of travel has expanded lists of acquaintances but has done little to improve the quality of friendship. The mass (and muddle) of communication have thrust a confusing assortment of voices and views into our lives without appreciably increasing the quality of our understanding of either ourselves or others. Far too many people feel, at least at times, that they stand on a curbstone, lonely bystanders watching the rest of the world pass by. Even in the midst of a crowd they feel miserably alone. They stand in paralyzing fear of rejection should they dare reveal themselves to others, because they cannot believe that anyone could like or love their real selves.

Yet they desperately need an intimate relationship and realize that personal disclosure is essential to its evolution. They therefore compromise by substituting masks and role-playing for self-revelation. The typical result is a shallow, unrewarding acquaintanceship with another person, not an honest, close bond.

Deeply satisfying intimate relationships among friends add immeasurably to human contentment. But when such a relationship exists between a man and a woman (or between homosexuals), love may grow from the intimacy and, from that, a sexual relationship that has meaning not remotely possible to couples less involved with one another.

For this reason it is important that the concepts of intimacy and love be examined in a book basically concerned with sexuality. Intimacy is the backbone of love. With intimacy in a loving relationship the potentials of sexual gratification are extraordinary. Intimacy is what it's all about.

Some Aspects of Intimacy

Perhaps this discussion should focus initially on what intimacy is *not*, for one of the barriers to achieving intimacy is accepting counterfeits for the real thing. Intimacy is not "togetherness." One can be with another person in the sense of closeness of bodies, yet live emotionally and mentally on separate planets. People can pass their entire lives very much in one another's physical presence, but never overcome the gap of spiritual separation. One is reminded of a noted film director who once remarked that his parents spent their married life lying side by side in iron coffins.

Nonintimate togetherness is railroad tracks running endlessly parallel but never touching. The missing part in parallel existence is not that the two persons are doing different things or even thinking separate thoughts or experiencing different responses. They are simply not *sharing* experiences, thoughts, or feelings. For body, mind, and emotions are all crucially involved in intimacy. A special kind of emotional bond exists between the two people who are involved in an intimate relationship. Such a relationship involves "an affectionate bond . . . composed of mutual caring, responsibility, trust, open communication . . . as well as the non-defended interchange of information about significant emotional events" (H. S. Kaplan 1979).

The Components of Intimacy

Many consider intimacy much more realistic than love in human relationships; certainly it is fundamental to love. Two basic requirements for the evolution of intimacy are time and privacy, because they provide the opportunity for development of its five primary components. In order of development, these are *choice, mutuality, reciprocity, trust,* and *delight* (Calderone 1972).

Two people meet; they like each other; they make overtures toward establishing a closer relationship by exchanging small confidences. The two have made a *choice*. The fact that each has made the same choice makes the act *mutual*. The choice must be a mutual one, since a unilateral choice would obviously exclude intimacy. In a truly intimate relationship, one cannot be more intimate than the other. More and more is revealed as the two grow in the confidence that they are understood by each other without having to apologize or defend. Each confides, understands, and gives equally to the other; *reciprocity* develops. Greater depths of feelings are then shared as each recognizes that the other's responses are consistent, nonjudgmental, and nondestructive. More and more is revealed as the two grow in confidence. With these revelations and acceptance *trust* grows. Intimacy can then expand to its limits: an unconditional acceptance of the other, exactly as he or she is, creating a relationship in which both partners can flourish and thus experience *delight* (Coutts 1973).

The delight of two people in one another "in an atmosphere of security based on mutuality, reciprocity, and trust . . . whatever their age or sex, this surely is what we all seek in human relationships yet do not all achieve, certainly never in quality, in our lives. . . ." If this sort of intimacy develops and persists over the years, neither major physical infirmities, nor aging, nor fading physical handsomeness, nor reduced sexual potency, nor even infidelity will destroy the relationship. "In intimacy two people are constantly saying to each other without words, 'I delight in you as a whole person and you delight me, and I can, I want to, I *may* express this delight in such and such ways' " (Calderone 1972).

Individual ranges of sensitivity, awareness of others, and emotionality vary enormously. The closer two people match in these respects, the greater the chances that true intimacy will evolve. If needs are similar, they can be met more easily, and there is little need to be apologetic about them. Intensity and marks of affection or tenderness are vastly important to a beginning relationship. But one must allow intimacy to develop subtly; "coming on too strong" can be as defeating as an attitude of distance and coldness (Coutts 1973).

Sharing and revealing of self—the supports of intimacy—are ongoing processes. They are not something done once, like a proclamation, and that is the end of it. They become, rather, a lifetime habit of looking inward, of trying to understand better oneself and others.

Many long-standing relationships (especially marriage) become stunted because sharing and self-revelation cease. Although confidences were shared at the beginning of the relationship, the habit of sharing tends to become selective, weakens, and is lost in the course of years. It becomes easier and easier for a couple to ignore disturbing feelings by refusing to admit that they exist or to avoid any unpleasantness by not talking about them. This is especially true when other troublesome aspects of living— jobs, children, community obligations—demand immediate attention.

One must also remember that one cannot develop intimacy with everyone. Some people simply are not on the same wavelength, so we should not become upset when initial reaching out is met with a blank stare. Because of the self-revelation involved, good judgment must be exercised when one seeks intimacy. One must feel justified in trusting the other, for there are those whom one truly cannot trust. They may be hostile and unforgiving by nature; or merely curious, not compassionate; or interested only in making themselves important to others by passing on newly learned confidences as gossipy tidbits. Disclosing oneself to someone whom one threatens is equally dangerous. And it is fruitless to disclose oneself to someone who is very insecure and finds one's honesty in disclosing fears and failures a terrifying reminder of his/her own weaknesses. An honest interchange of feelings would be impossible because the feedback would be warped.

It is also a mistake to assume that disclosing oneself to remote and uncommmunicative persons will encourage them to reveal more of themselves. Such personalities appear peaceable on the surface, but there may be no true empathy or spirit of cooperation. By doing or saying nothing, they may be expressing a subtle form of hostility and can cause much chaos in the lives of others (Coutts 1973).

To be able to like or love others (and to be likable and lovable ourselves) requires first that we like ourselves. Yet it is as difficult to accept emotionally as it is easy to accept intellectually that shortcomings and inappropriate behavior are as inescapable a part of the human condition as the heartbeat. All people, without exception, are physically, emotionally, and intellectually hobbled to one degree or another. *All people* includes you and me. It is the ultimate in unreality to expect perfection of any human being. The struggle toward perfection is destructive because it *is* so futile. It therefore comes as a tremendous relief when we can accept that human limitations exist, that making mistakes is normal, and that we are no less worthy of acceptance because of imperfection.

The partners in intimate relationships are assured of acceptance and do not have to defend their failures. Self-worth remains intact (although sometimes a little battered). Total acceptance by another person generates greater ego strength, leaving the individual more flexible and less demanding in other personal relationships. He or she becomes warmer, more tolerant, and more respectful toward others, as well as more assertive and honest. There is no necessity to screen thoughts or weigh words. Such a person is "less anxious, less defensive, and better able to throw off reactions that are inappropriate" (J. L. McCary 1975, 1980).

Those who are intimate tell each other the truth, and all of it. Each has the capacity to forgive, which in an intimate relationship is a fund that must be drawn upon periodically. The ability to laugh at one's own and the other's imperfections, but without ridiculing, must exist. Those who find it difficult to laugh often find it difficult to forgive as well.

Avoidance of Intimacy

With so much to be gained, why is intimacy deliberately avoided? Why is it so hard to achieve? Society is at fault, first of all, in that it conditions us to deny feelings, to play roles, and to please others even to the detriment of ourselves. A premium is placed on "playing it cool," always being in control of emotions. By expressing no feelings, we leave the impression of having none.

Second, as H. S. Kaplan (1979) points out, we as individuals are at fault. We tend too often to take passive, spectator roles rather than active, participatory roles in our interpersonal endeavors and we miss out in engaging in intimate interactions. Just as too many of us watch sports rather than actively participate in them, so too many of us engage in mechanical or lethargic sexual interactions rather than immerse ourselves in a full, intimate relationship. Sometimes we "find it easier to masturbate than to make love, to buy impersonal sex than to share love with a lover, to blot out the partner with drugs than to experience him/her fully."

Another barrier to intimacy is anger. It is an unacceptable emotion, we are told, so we go to great lengths to suppress, deny, and disguise it. But these efforts only mask anger; it lingers, and it destroys intimacy. The most successful means of getting rid of anger is, first, to admit to oneself that it exists. Next, one should express it directly to the person who aroused it, although in an acceptable manner, lest one generate yet another set of problems (J. L. McCary 1975, 1980). Constant fighting or bickering and efforts by one or both partners to bring up old grievances and complaints often lead to the demise of the love relationship. In contrast, well-chosen words and attempts by both partners to emphasize the positive aspects of the relationship generally lead to more effective, less defensive communication, and are more effective than abusive language and flying fists. The door to intimacy is more likely to be opened again once destructive anger and hostility are defused and communication is reestablished (Mace 1980).

Perhaps the most formidable of all barriers to intimacy is fear, notably fear of rejection. In revealing ourselves we dread the possible humiliation of appearing stupid, weak, unworthy. We too often assume that we stand as uniquely inferior creatures in a world almost wholly populated with exceptionally talented, intelligent, sophisticated, and beautiful people. We are curiously blind to the fact that the desirable others are also frightened, because they, too, have suffered failure.

Unconvinced that our unvarnished selves are likable, we abandon our true identity. We express opinions that we do not believe and emotions that we do not feel because we think they are the acceptable ones. We try to "snow" people rather than relate to them. As a result we eventually do not know who we really are ourselves. Neither does anyone else. By assuming these disguises we become phonies; intimacy is shortcircuited because it can exist only in an atmosphere of honesty.

The Game Called Courtship

Inappropriate efforts to establish intimacy are perhaps best exemplified in traditional courtship, American style. An unfolding male-female relationship can and should be an apprenticeship in intimacy, but more commonly only a superficial togetherness develops.

To assure acceptance—to avoid the misery of rejection—the lover usually presents his/her better self (as he or she sees it) by going to some pains to hide flaws. In such cases, real or total feelings are only minimally revealed or are suppressed entirely. Role-playing becomes a burden, loneliness deepens, and resentment at having to maintain a facade is often projected toward the loved one. Further, the lover's presentation of the image of perfection and, it follows, the expectation of it, arouse feelings of inadequacy in the partner. Fearing to look bad by comparison, he or she likewise begins role-playing.

So what emerges is two actors playing parts in which they are extremely uncomfortable. Each grows increasingly tense trying to guess what the other finds lovable and then twisting him- or herself into that image (Van Den Haag 1973). Both no doubt fervently wish that they could start again and be their genuine selves, however imperfect.

Fortunately many of today's young people recognize the phoniness of traditional courtship with its particular etiquette and rituals. They perceive it as destructive of the very thing they seek—intimacy. They resent

Courtship: An emergence of sensual and emotional awareness. (Kenneth Karp)

the "good-time, fixed-smile" dating game. But some of the efforts to restore naturalness to courtship have run contrary to the establishment of genuine intimacy (Bach & Deutsch 1973). Casual copulation and partner-swapping, as examples, do not bring people closer except, perhaps, physically. Honest communication is not necessarily achieved in strings of four-letter words, armchair psychoanalysis, and brutal verbal attacks delivered in the name of "truth." Our best interests are not always served by the sort of "honesty" that begins or ends with "I'm only saying this for your own good."

Many couples believe they have achieved closeness just because they are together constantly. But doing things side-by-side is not the same as sharing true feelings, which comes from having learned to trust one another. All they have achieved is temporary relief of the feelings of loneliness and depression common to adolescence and young adulthood through the illusion that love exists. What they actually feel in the constant physical closeness to one another is a strong sexual attraction. They are sharing little else.

A healthy substitute for the superficialities of traditional courtship is what might be called "the pairing system"—a getting-to-know-you period in which openness and honesty predominate in the couple's relationship. Fears and self-doubts, often very painful in this time of life, are trotted out and examined. Each finds wonderful relief in recognizing that the other is undergoing the same small agonies in the search for identity and the establishment of self-worth.

A bond develops as each demonstrates a feeling of responsibility for the other. Neither will violate the confidences and personal integrity of the other. This interaction creates trust, and once trust is established true intimacy is possible (Bach & Deutsch 1973).

Some Aspects of Love

Endless observations on the nature and quality of love have been made by poets, philosophers, behaviorists, and simpler folk. Yet despite the out-pouring of ink, words, tears, and even venom on the subject, a precise definition of love remains as elusive today as it was (no doubt) at the dawn of history. Because love has a tremendous range of meanings, and the need is enormous both to give and to receive it from birth until the day of death, it is one of the most complex, poorly understood facets of human existence.

Much has been said of the difference between loving and liking. Karl and Jeanetta Menninger (1959) suggest that there is no justification for the distinction. The two differ, they say, only in intensity. Both are positive attractions and feelings, although differently expressed. Some people are greatly threatened by the intense emotions associated with the very word *love*. They therefore avoid its use whenever possible, frequently substituting the word *like*, which to them does not convey the same menace.

Love in our culture tends to be defined according to intensity of feeling and how one should act when one believes oneself to be in love. Some use the word *love* so freely that it has little meaning; others invest the word with such enormous meaning that they may never be able to say honestly "I love." Still others consider the word such an irreversible commitment to another person that they become frightened by the enormity of the commitment and responsibilities involved. They therefore not only avoid *saying* the word, but avoid as well any but the shallowest of feelings.

To say "I love you" can have such a strongly personal meaning that individuals may use the words in entirely different ways. "I love you" may mean to one person "I *need* you" or "I need you to *need me*"; to another it may mean "I want your *approval*" or "I want to *control* you"; to still another, "I need to be *dependent upon you*" or "I want you to be *dependent upon me*"; or "I desire you *sexually*"; or "I *admire* certain things about you and would like to *have them for myself*"; or "I want to *use you* and your talents or prestige for my benefit." Or "I love you" may mean "I respect, admire, and love who you are, and want to *help you to continue to grow and benefit—to become*" (L. Benson 1974).

If "I love you" means any of the foregoing except the last, the words are being used as an exploitive tool. The "loved" person is regarded as an object or is used without consideration of his or her rights or needs. The "lover's" own gratification is the only concern. Such "love" relationships reflect serious deficiencies in these "lovers." They are so wrapped up in themselves and the fulfillment of their needs that they cannot possibly understand or give concern to the needs and desires of the other (L. Benson 1974).

Quality of Love

Maslow (1970) describes love as feelings of tenderness and affection for another person, accompanied by great excitement, elation, and even ecstasy. The loved one is perceived as clever, good, or attractive. There is a desire to please, and a delight in doing so. The wish to be constantly with that person is great, whether in work or in play, because any activity—no matter how humdrum—takes on special joy when it is shared. The lovers are amazed at the pleasure they find in things they had scarcely noticed before. They feel a uniquely enhanced vitality and intensity in everyday life, leading them to a more productive, active involvement in other spheres of their lives.

There is yearning when one or the other is absent; there is a longing to be closer and more intimate with that special person and to touch and embrace him or her. Usually there is a special sexual desire that can be aroused by no other person.

To love implies the ability to be alone without feeling lonely. To need another merely for company signifies dependency, not love. Meeting the legitimate emotional needs of another person is quite a different matter from trying to solve his or her emotional problems. In fact, neurotic mutual dependency is a basic marital problem (Fromm 1956; Lederer & Jackson 1968). Filling one's voids through another person rather than developing one's own resources is placing the other (and in the long haul, one's self) in bondage. This sort of dependency is as addictive as drugs. Love, by contrast, shares yet it frees. In mature love, sensitivity to the other's needs is constant and one gives unselfishly in order to enrich the other's life (McGinnis & Ayres 1976). Unselfishness is essential to a deep love, but only when it is mutual and neither partner sacrifices his or her integrity in the service of the other. Maslow (1970) made the point that he finds no intrinsic hostility between the sexes in healthy relationships, discounting the "war of the sexes" view held by many. Lovers are not silently angry opponents. To the contrary, they are best friends.

In discussing the hierarchies of two people's individual needs, Maslow (1970) suggests that in a loving relationship there is a pooling of basic needs into a single pattern, thereby expanding the individual egos to include both persons. Each learns to respond to the other's needs as to his or her own. Each experiences the other's happiness or pain as his or her own. In the same vein, Harry Stack Sullivan (1953) says that love exists "when the satisfaction or the security of another person becomes as significant to one as is one's own satisfaction or security. . . . "

Because it is a goal that must be strived for, mature and lasting love requires total commitment. Commitment arises from two kinds of feelings— responsiveness to the other, which is involuntary, and being responsible for the other, which is a conscious, acknowledged obligation. The interaction of two people in these circumstances "creates an overpowering sense of involvement and identification, of oneness, which some people call love, and it is the original source of commitment" (Masters & Johnson 1975).

It is dangerous folly to assume that the path of love is always smooth and blissful once a commitment is made. To the contrary, commitment lurches through "sharing, exploring, arguing, fighting, accusing, reassuring, touching, needing, loving, explaining, and the hurt of prolonged intimacy" (Coutts 1973). The ultimate success or failure of the relationship depends upon whether there is more pleasure than displeasure in the commitment, for certainly there will be both.

In the last analysis perhaps the qualities of the most fulfilling love to which we mortals can aspire is described in the 13th chapter of First Corinthians: "Love is patient, kind, non-envious, never boastful, not con-ceited, not rude, never selfish, not quick to take offense. Love holds no grudges and delights not in sin, but in truth. It believes, hopes, and endures all things. . . . There are three lasting values: faith, hope, and love. The greatest of these is love" (McCary & McElhaney 1971).

Falling in Love

Much is heard of "falling in love," a concept most psychologists reject. They contend that we do not fall in love, rather, we grow in love and love grows in us, beginning in infancy. Children first love their parents, then their playmates, then their teachers, and then other adults. It might be said that we grow in love as we grow in intimacy with another person, both processes requiring work, time, the willingness to risk pain, and the ability to be there when we are needed.

How does acquaintanceship progress to liking and then to love? The evolution is much the same as that of intimacy. When two people first meet they typically present themselves to each other with what they consider an acceptable mixture of conventional and personal ideals or opinions. That tentative step taken, they next express certain personal needs, which either clash with the other's or prove to be mutual. If too many views are in conflict, the relationship bogs down at the acquaintanceship level. But when personal needs are mutual and aspirations similar, a friendship can be launched. Even though there is initial satisfaction in the relationship, however, the couple tend to proceed cautiously, still concealing much of their real feelings.

As they become better acquainted and learn to trust one another, they disclose more and more of their deeper selves. They come to know the best and worst about each other. They like and accept one another either because or in spite of these revelations. The next step is profound identification or empathy with the other. The Menningers (1959) state that friendship merges into love at the point of this identification.

What is the particular attraction that draws a couple together in what they call love? A particular magic? Fate? Not really, because the choice on either side could have been made from an endless number of people with similar sociocultural characteristics. The factor of *chance* is the ultimate determinant. In addition to sufficient mutual physical attraction to permit them to start the relationship in the first place, the two people's backgrounds are sufficiently alike that communication is possible. They recognize feelings of rapport, which are then followed by increasing self-revelations. They develop "interdependent habit systems" (Reiss 1973); each now has someone to confide in, joke with, share feelings with. Finally they recognize that they fill each other's emotional needs—needs for affection, understanding of moods, respect, stimulation of ambition. They love each other. Some would say that they are "in love."

The distinction is often made between "loving" someone and "being in love." The first is usually interpreted to mean a deep concern for the welfare of a person; the second, a more intense romantic or sexual feeling for him or her. These emotions are not necessarily exclusive. They coexist in courtship, in the early part of many marriages, and, fortunately, in some marriages of long duration. It is when the romance, excitement, and "magic" disappear from the relationship, or significantly abate, that marriage counselors most often hear "I still love him [or her], but I'm just not 'in love' with him anymore." Disillusion over the loss of romantic love can threaten any long-standing relationship. It is particularly dangerous when the partners are immature or hold unreasonable expectations of the relationship, especially marriage. For feeling that they are no longer "in love" with their partners, many married people grant themselves the license to seek romance with another person—only to find the illusion-disillusion pattern repeated. Few people who have experienced intimacy with its full delight would deny that perhaps intimacy is the force that binds "loving" someone and being "in love" with someone.

Kinds of Love

Attempts to define love are inevitably full of value judgments. Idealists reject anything but "true love" (interestingly, "true hate" is seldom similarly considered). "Puppy love" is excluded; so is infatuation. (It is also interesting that infatuation is evaluated as such only in retrospect.) A sexually oriented love is dismissed as degrading, and romantic love as unrealistic. Yet as imperfect as these emotions may be in comparison with "true love," all have a place in the vast range of human experience.

To help sort out the many emotions clustered under the banner called love, many observers have broken the word down into categories or classifications. Murstein (1974), as an example, lists three kinds of love. The first, romantic love, is identified as "a strong emotional attachment to the opposite sex, a tendency toward idealization, and a marked physical attraction." The second is conjugal love, described as affection between couples who have been together some years. In this love, passion has evolved into deeper feelings of spirituality, respect, and contentment. Agape, the third kind of love, is described as a spontaneous, selfless giving, working toward developing the maximum potential of another or others.

Coutts (1973) describes five levels of loving. First is a love which more appropriately should be called *sentimentality*. It is extremely limited because it focuses on the self, on awareness of one's own feelings. It is centered on the needs of the lover, not those of the loved one. It may mean sympathy for the other, but not involvement, for the lover remains preoccupied with his or her own needs, fears, and insecurities.

Sentimentality may mean tolerance of the other, but it is rarely constructive love. Many people cannot care beyond the level of sentimentality because of their own unmet needs. They were taught to be insensitive to these needs, hence are incapable of being sensitive to them in others. They develop exploitive, demanding relationships which eventually drive the other away.

At the second level, love has risen above sentimentality through a growing awareness of both self and others. Sharing and caring develop and an intimacy emerges based on facts, not simply impressions. The third level is involvement, the product of caring and sharing. One sees what is needed and wants to offer it, even at the expenditure of considerable energy. The fourth level of loving is dedication. When the loved one is so significant that one is willing to make sacrifices for his or her needs, safety, and comfort, part of one's life is dedicated to that person. Dedicated relationships are powerful indeed.

The fifth and ultimate level of loving is commitment, in that it encompasses one's intellect, emotions, and body. It is the most powerful of all love relationships, involving, as it does, lasting awareness and involvement (Coutts 1973).

Romantic Love: Agony, Ecstasy, and Unreality

The love classically described in terms of agony and ecstasy, usually refers to romantic love. Despite all that has been said and written on the subject, it is small wonder that youth (and older people too, for that matter) are perplexed about what romantic love is really like and whether or not it can last. Their confusion grows when they look at the comfortable day-in-day-out nonpassionate relationship of their parents and compare it with the passionate and romantic love found in the great works of literature. Both affectionate marital love and passionate romantic love exist and both are valid. But can the second really endure over a long period of time? It cannot. The commonest attack on the concept of romantic love concerns its unreality, however enthralling, and the bitter disillusion that usually follows when couples marry in the attempt to perpetuate it.

"Love and Marriage . . ." the song goes. But *do* they go together like a horse and carriage? Van Den Haag (1973) doubts it, commenting that love is a "very unruly horse, far more apt to run away and overturn the carriage than to draw it." Romantic love was certainly not viewed historically as a rational ground for marriage and social stability. Except for a few societies—notably our own and those of northwest Europe in this century—marriage has traditionally been regarded as, primarily, the means of perpetuating the family, not the means of perpetuating romantic love. Certainly women hoped for a kindly man, a hard worker; men, for a good housekeeper and conscientious mother. No doubt both hoped for affection. But romantic love was a remote concept to them.

Some describe romantic love as a conditioned response. The love object is constantly paired with pleasurable feelings brought about by loving words, smiles, touches. Ultimately the very thought or sight of the loved person produces wonderfully pleasurable feelings. If the couple then enter into a long-term relationship such as marriage, life becomes pocked with a host of mundane, unromantic responsibilities. The ability to pair the partner with only pleasurable feelings obviously becomes impossible. Further, the endearing words and smiles, once so appealing, lose their impact. People become accustomed to accepting the rewarding behavior of their partners. Thus romantic love tends to weaken. The relationship, however, may well continue to be satisfying if a commitment based on something more solid exists, and if the couple continue to be supportive of each other (Bartz & Rasor 1972).

When most of us marry, the enchanted ideal is swiftly brought into focus as an imperfect reality. We must then either abandon the longing for romantic love, or shift the longing to another person. Because romantic love is so intensely pleasurable, many people understandably feel a great loss when it dissipates. Memory of the excitement and pleasure frequently propels a married person into an affair with another person, usually under highly favorable circumstances. The series of new intensely pleasurable events—the rewards—outweigh the rather stale, predictable routine of home life. Romantic love has blossomed anew. If the involved partner obtains a divorce and quickly marries the new love, he or she will quite likely find, with dismay, romantic love slipping away once more. And the whole process will have to start over again—and again (Bartz & Rasor 1972). If he or she does not divorce and remarry, time and daily living will dissolve the romantic ideal.

Much is heard about the role of love in all aspects of human behavior, especially human sexual behavior. The arguments range from "Sex is empty and animalistic without love" to "Sex can be fun and enjoyable without love." One thing we do know: Degrees of sexual gratification and quality of love in a stable relationship change. The longing typical of romantic love may be replaced by tenderness, gratitude, or affectionate companionship, or by indifference or hostility. But inevitably in long-term relationships romantic love will be replaced by other emotions.

Van Den Haag (1973) recommends marrying for affection rather than for romantic love. He defines affection as the acceptance of the unvarnished person rather than the enchanted image. Romantic love stresses the enchantment, the perfection of the love object; affection, the acceptance of an imperfect but unique person. Affection and romantic love differ, he says, as fulfillment does from desire. One may grow from the other, but affection has a better chance if it is not preceded by enchantment. For the disenchantment that typically follows fading romantic love may well turn to hostility.

In the view of Lederer and Jackson (1968), people do not marry for love: They merely like to *think* that they are in love. They may marry because they are blinded by the esctasy (from the Greek *ekstasis*, meaning to derange) of courtship; because society expects them to marry; because they need a parent substitute; because they are lonely and restless; because they seek economic security; because their parents push them into it; because they wish to fill a neurotic need.

Zastrow (1979) states that people become entangled in romantic love because they have irrational thoughts, beliefs, or "self-talk" about what love is. In romantic love there is a tendency to idealize, through one's self-talk or thinking, the attributes of one's lover. There is also a tendency to look to the lover to satisfy sexual desires and to make up for one's own feelings of insecurity and loneliness. Ironically, romantic love can be only maintained if there is "distance" between the lovers, because distance is required in order for the idealized, perfect image to be sustained. Rational love presents a striking contrast to romantic love because the "characteristics of a rational love relationship include being realistic in our appraisal of the loved one's attributes and qualities, knowing the loved one well, being clear about our own wants and goals in life, honest and open communication, and a respect and an admiration for the other person" (p. 55).

Although cynics say that marriage is the only game at which both players can lose, it still appears to hold the greatest potential (until something better comes along) for personal fulfillment, for protection against the aloneness that threatens all of us. Indeed, statistics show that, for whatever reasons, the married enjoy greater health and longer life than the unmarried. Cynics also point to the spiraling divorce rates (1 million divorces *vs.* 2 million marriages in 1975) as evidence that marriage as an institution has failed. But in truth marriage has not failed; rather, our expectations of it are unrealistic and make it unworkable.

Since romantic love depends upon the couple's not knowing very much that is real about the other, the types of early and ongoing relationships shared by an increasing number of young people today suggest that romantic love may be on its way out. Unlike their parents, young adults today often know each other too well to be caught by great surprises after setting up housekeeping together (Kernodle 1959). However, merely "living together" is a far cry from marriage or a true marriage-like relationship. The solidity of love cannot be proved until it has been tested in such ongoing responsibilities as car payments, housekeeping, and coping with illness.

Maintaining Love

"Love is appealing, but its practice is appallingly difficult" (Howe 1961). The most important tool in its practice is communication, however overworked the word has become in recent years. When communication is blocked the ground is fertile for misunderstanding, and the constructive energy of love can turn into resentment and hostility. A recent survey of over 20,000 women found that these respondents most missed open and honest communication of intimate thoughts and feelings in their relationships with their husbands. They claimed their husbands often showed little interest in "talking out feelings" and that empathy and understanding were missing ingredients in their relationships (Gittelson 1980).

Of course, communication means not only speaking words, but also listening attentively, using the other's name, watching the other's eyes closely, paying attention to facial expression, helping the other to express accurately what he or she is trying to say. Maintaining love presupposes that the intimacy discussed earlier exists and is nourished throughout the relationship with communication.

Communication is a skill, one that is not learned overnight. To listen does not mean merely to hear words, then to wait until the other has finished so that one can get on with one's own monologue. To speak, to make oneself understood, requires effort and practice. The process may be discouraging at first, but the rewards are enormous. Furthermore, the alternative is to leave the other second-guessing and the likelihood is that the deductions will be wrong. Through the constant challenge of communication, new life is constantly breathed into love and it is thus kept a growing emotion (Fromm 1956).

For love to endure, individuality must be maintained. Although nourished by the warmth and acceptance of the other, each must preserve independence and encourage it in the other, so that the potentials of both can develop. A woman's professional ambitions, for instance, must not be dampened by the unrealistic demand that she accept daily housework as woman's greatest fulfillment. A man should not be stifled by a woman who, rather than develop her own identity, hangs onto him as her window to the world. In these circumstances the couple are owning, restricting, and demanding each other in the name of love (O'Neill & O'Neill 1972).

Anne Morrow Lindbergh in her book *Gift from the Sea* (1965) touched on the concept of separateness in mature love:

> A good relationship has a pattern like a dance and is built on some of the same rules. The partners do not need to hold on tightly, because they move confidently in the same pattern, intricate but gay and swift and free, like a country dance of Mozart's. . . . There is no place here for the possessive clutch, the clinging arm, the heavy hand; only the barest touch in passing. Now arm in arm, now face to face, now back to back—it does not matter which. Because they know they are partners moving to the same rhythm, creating a pattern together, and being invisibly nourished by it.

Some Aspects of Love and Sex

Cultural conditioning often makes it very difficult for people, especially men, to enter into any close, loving relationship, including the sexual, with others. Little boys are often taught that to be tender and compassionate is to show characteristics of a "sissy"; little girls are admonished that it is "forward" to be warmly responsive. Growing up in an environment that restricts positive emotional responses makes it likely that the individual will learn to express only negative ones, such as anger and hostility.

Nonetheless, these people grow into adulthood with the abstract knowledge that some warm emotional exchanges are vital and expected in successful sexual interaction. But because they learned in their formative years to express only negative emotional repsonses, such people will actually start quarrels or fights with their sexual partner in order to express the only type of emotionality they understand. Men who have never learned how to express themselves, or who are afraid to do so, will often ignore the woman with whom they are sexually involved, or make belittling remarks to her. These men *want* to demonstrate their commitment but, not knowing how to use the appropriate positive emotions, use the only expressions that they are familiar with—the negative ones.

Married women often accuse their husbands of showing affection only when they have intercourse in mind; men deny this. What often happens is that the husband begins simply to show affection to his wife with no ulterior motive in mind; but in the process of expressing affection, especially if his wife responds warmly, he becomes sexually excited. The woman then judges only in terms of the final outcome.

Fortunately, both men and women can be taught to be receptive of close, warm, and loving relationships. If they have not acquired this knowledge through normal maturational processes and are too fearful of forming intimacies, help is available in several forms. (However, it is important to remember that complete agreement does not exist among behavioral scientists on how best to handle the complex of human problems.) When men and women recognize that free expression of affection is certainly nothing to fear, nor a barometer of weakness, all their relationships, including the sexual ones, will be much fuller and happier.

Rollo May (1969) points out that humans are the only creatures who copulate face to face, looking at their partners and baring their most tender and vulnerable parts. The intense scrutiny of the other's eyes; the sharing of the other's body, delight, and passion; the touching, the participation as a dual being, and the eventual separation into two individual selves—these elements comprise one of the most powerful acts in human experience.

Touching is vitally important in human relationships, although it is typically thought of merely as a means to an end (sexual intimacy). But it is increasingly apparent that the need to touch and be touched is an essential form of communication. It is an end in itself. Babies need it and will sicken and die without it. Older children express the need through rough-and-tumble playing; adolescents, through kissing, necking, and petting (Masters & Johnson 1975).

The psychological need for physical contact—touching, cuddling, stroking, and the tender response to them—is as great as, possibly greater than, sexual need. Indeed, it has been called the missing link between love and sex (Allen & Martin 1971). Furthermore, touching may be an important ingredient in helping eliminate general stress or depression. Human beings of all ages, backgrounds, and cultures respond in a friendlier, more loving, and emotionally healthful manner when they have had the opportunity to touch or stroke or to be touched and stroked by others. When there is a deprivation of touching or physical contact, *marasmus*, or a sense of "wasting away," may negatively affect us (Kirkendall 1980a).

Coitus cannot of itself be equated with total intimacy, although unfortunately it is the only form of intimacy that many ever achieve or even recognize. A dependence on copulation to express feelings overburdens sex with the task of supporting a relationship emotionally, a task that should, for success, be aided by many other aspects of living.

Good sex means more than the number and quality of climaxes, frequency of coitus, positions assumed, or techniques used. The best sex is not merely a physical response but a mature affirmation of love. "Sex removed from the positive influence of the total personality can become boring, unstimulating, and possibly immaterial" (Masters & Johnson 1975). When a couple's only intimacy is sexual, they are left alone to think and feel, their minds and hearts uninvolved in the coital act.

Sexuality in a concerned relationship takes three forms. First, each partner confirms that the other is admired, desired, and appreciated as a sexual being. Second, each confirms that the partner is not a sexual freak in his or her desires and performance, that each shares in the universality of sex. Third, they are assured that what they share sexually is special and unique (Masters & Johnson 1975).

Maslow (1970), speaking of self-actualizing people—those whose needs for belonging, love, status, and self-respect have been met—says that orgasm is both more and less important for them than for other people. Loving at a higher, committed level improves sex, he says, making its enjoyment more wholehearted. On the other hand, the love that partners bear for each other makes sexual frustration less acute when gratification is blocked. In other words, they do not need sexual expression so urgently, but can enjoy it more fully when it does occur.

An analogy has been drawn between an individual's involvement in work and in sex. In work, there are those who use their hands, and we call them laborers. Those who work with hands and head we call craftspeople. And those who work with hands, head, and heart are called artists. In coitus, sex can be used as a strictly physical experience, a monetary form of communication or self-identification. On a higher level, there is some degree of mental sharing and verbal communication which blend with the physical experience. At the highest level of sexuality, physical sensations and emotions are freely expressed and are fused with empathy and sensitivity toward the partner. This is true sexual intimacy (Fujimoto 1972).

The maturity, freedom, interdependence, and fulfillment to be found in a committed love relationship have not been better described than by Kahlil Gibran (1923)*:

> ... let there be spaces in your togetherness,
> And let the winds of the heavens dance between you.
> Love one another, but make not a bond of love:
> Let it rather be a moving sea between the shores of your souls.
> Fill each other's cup but drink not from one cup.
> Give one another of your bread but eat not from the same loaf.
> Sing and dance together and be joyous, but let each one of you be
>   alone,

Even as the strings of a lute are alone though they quiver with the
   same music.
Give your hearts, but not into each other's keeping.
For only the hand of Life can contain your hearts.
And stand together yet not too near together:
For the pillars of the temple stand apart,
And the oak tree and the cypress grow not in each other's shadow.

Summary

In order to overcome feelings of alienation and loneliness, men and women
often strive to establish and maintain close, intimate relationships with one
another. Intimacy is the backbone of love and adds an important dimension
to human relationships. Two basic requirements for the evolution of
intimacy are time and privacy, because they allow for the development of
its five primary components: choice, mutuality, reciprocity, trust, and
delight.

To be able to like or love others requires first that we like ourselves. Further,
it is important to recognize that all humans have limitations and that it is
unrealistic to expect perfection in any human being. Acceptance of flaws
in others and ourselves is therefore a prerequisite for the development of
intimate human relationships.

Unfortunately, many people avoid intimacy by denying feelings, playing
roles, and trying constantly to please others. Too often people take passive,
spectator roles rather than active, participatory roles in interpersonal
endeavors and miss engaging in intimate relationships. Destructive anger
and hostility destroy communication and interfere with the development
of intimacy. Fear, notably fear of rejection, causes people to avoid potentially
fulfilling intimate relationships.

Traditional courtship patterns frequently have led to superficial togetherness between men and women. Too often these patterns, composed of
empty rituals, lead to stereotyped interpersonal interaction and thus create
barriers to intimacy. The pairing system—a getting-to-know-you period in
which openness and honesty predominate—provides a healthier alternative
to the superficiality of traditional courtship.

Love remains one of the most complex, poorly understood aspects of
human existence. Some people use love falsely as a means of exploiting
another or becoming dependent upon that person. Mature forms of love

involve mutual respect, admiration, and the desire to help one another grow. Individuals who are in love are best friends committed to each other and to their relationship.

Most psychologists reject the idea that people "fall in love." Rather, people grow in love and love grows in them. Ideally, people "love" their partner and also have a sense of "being in love" with that partner. Intimacy is the force that links "loving" someone and "being in love" with someone.

Attempts have been made to define love in terms such as "puppy love," "true love," and "infatuation," all of which have a place in the vast range of human experience. One observer has described three kinds of love: romantic love, conjugal love, and agape. Another observer has described five levels of loving: sentimentality, awareness, involvement, dedication, and commitment. Romantic love is based on idealism, perfection, and passion. Ultimately, romantic love dissipates or fades away. Rational love is based on reality, acceptance of imperfection, and affection. Rational love is more likely to lead to fulfilling, long-lasting relationships. Mature love is maintained through open and honest communication. Mature love endures because the individuality or separateness of the man and woman is maintained.

Love involves tenderness and compassion as well as cuddling, stroking, and touching. When there is a deprivation of touching, marasmus or a sense of "wasting away" may overcome us. Sexual intimacy, at its highest level, is probably expressed best when physical sensations and emotions are fused with empathy and sensitivity toward the partner.

Annotated Bibliography

Butler, Robert N. and Lewis, Myrna I. *Love and sex after sixty: A guide for men and women in their later years.* New York: Harper and Row, 1976.

> This book is a helpful practical guide for the older person interested in maximizing satisfaction in marriage and relationships. The book contains expert treatment of many medical problems related to sex, learning new lovemaking patterns, dating, remarriage and children, and where to go for help.

Calderone, Mary S. and Johnson, Eric W. *The family book about sexuality.* New York: Harper and Row, 1981.

> This creatively written sex education text for the family covers all significant topics related to human sexuality and relationships, including giving and receiving love, sexuality and aging, marriage and family planning, variant behavior, and sex education programs. Important features include a bibliog-

raphy of additional family readings and a listing of family planning and counseling services.

Hamilton, Eleanor. *Partners in love: Lovingness, sex, and communication in marriage and relationships.* Cranbury, New Jersey: A. S. Barnes, 1980.

Stressing the need for love education, this book is designed for the general reader who wishes to enhance satisfaction in relationships. The book presents strategies to improve sexual pleasure and candidly discusses many factors affecting relationships, such as money, pregnancy, religion, and communication.

McCary, James Leslie. *Freedom and growth in marriage (2nd ed.).* New York: John Wiley and Sons, 1980.

This book for the student and general reader considers various aspects of marriage, dating and mate selection, focusing on implications for individual growth and freedom within the marriage relationship. The past and future of marriage are discussed, as well as relevant contemporary issues, alternatives to marriage, the nature of love, aspects of human sexuality, marital adjustment, and other topics.

Money, John. *Love and love sickness: The science of sex, gender difference, and pair-bonding.* Baltimore: The Johns Hopkins University Press, 1980.

This scholarly book encompasses a wide array of topics in human sexuality. Some general areas include the historical and cultural aspects of sexual behavior, factors influencing sexual orientation and pair-bonding, erotic sexuality, sexual taboos, and pornography. The author advances a new theory to guide understanding of sex differences based on the variety of factors contributing to gender identity and sex role. This book would appeal to the student, medical and allied health professional, and general academic reader.

Phillips, Debora and Judd, Robert. *Sexual confidence: Discovering the joys of intimacy.* Boston: Houghton Mifflin, 1980.

Written without technical language, this book is designed to help the adult reader unlearn myths related to love and sexuality, and to overcome sexual guilt and anxiety. The book suggests strategies to enhance intimacy and sexual satisfaction in relationships, and to deal with sexual problems.

Raley, Patricia E. *Making love: How to be your own sex therapist.* New York: The Dial Press, 1976.

This well-illustrated sexual self-help guide is intended for the adult reader of any sexual orientation who is interested in maximizing satisfaction in relationships. Systematic guidelines are provided for exploring sex history, sexual fantasy, sexual attitudes, sexual anatomy, arousal, orgasm, sexual communication, relationships with self and others, and other significant aspects of erotic life.

9

Techniques in Sexual Arousal

Although some fundamental differences between male and female responses to sexual stimuli exist, there is probably considerably less dissimilarity between the sexes than there is individual variation among members of the same sex (Kronhausen & Kronhausen 1965). For example, one study confirms that women like erotica, that their fantasies are as clear and self-arousing as men's, and that they are aroused by sexual descriptions just as men are (Heiman 1975).

Basically, the sex drive in women is as powerful as it is in men. But men and women may respond to different types of both psychological and physiological stimulation, and they respond to the same stimuli in a slightly different manner. Women have been conditioned for generations to inhibit their sexuality, if not deny it altogether, and to stifle their normal response. These culturally imposed inhibitions no doubt account for the popular misconception that women are less erotically responsive than men.

Sexual arousal in humans springs from psychological and from physiological sources. Such arousal usually begins with verbalization and indirect gestures (Eichenlaub 1961; Ellis 1963). In time, a couple usually build up their own private store of verbal endearments, which are then used advantageously to set the stage for satisfying sexual interplay.

197

Making the sexual partner aware that one enjoys his or her appearance, abilities, intellect, strengths, and the like is only half of a successful preliminary sexual interaction. The partner must also be made to know that he or she is enjoyed and appreciated as a lover.

To abandon oneself in an uninhibited expression of love and excitement, to have these manifestations eagerly accepted, to receive in turn spontaneous and equally unrestrained expressions of love, intimacy, and concern: these are the ingredients intrinsic to a sexual relationship in its deepest and fullest measure. Persons who confine their lovemaking activities merely to the search for orgasmic release soon learn that sex can become

Figures 9.1 and 9.2 Normal genitals of women and men are shown in a variety of shapes and sizes.

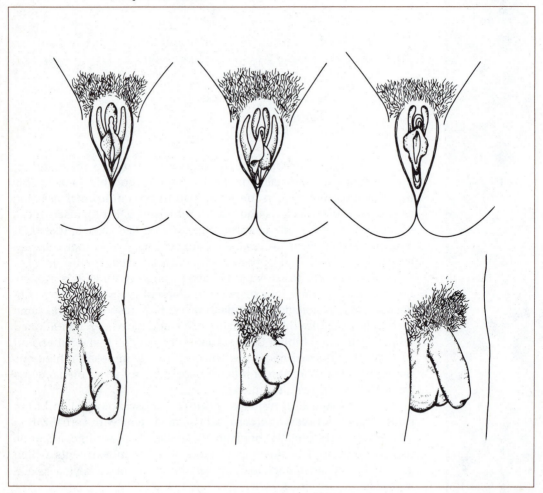

quite boring. The degree of pleasure and fulfillment derived from sex is great or small in direct proportion to what has been given. Those participating in sexual activity in a restricted, inhibited way, or simply to achieve the goal of orgasm, are cheating both themselves and their partners.

Many suggestions might be helpful in building a good sexual relationship. Three are particularly important: A couple will usually do well if they avoid sexual acts that are dangerous, antisocial, or unfulfilling to either of them. Once they have experimented sufficiently—perhaps with the help of good books on sexual techniques or even under the direction of a sex therapist—they should reject any activity they truly do not enjoy. And they should take great care to learn their partner's preferences and do everything reasonable to incorporate them in their sexual technique (Comfort 1972).

As one might expect, the more reckless and uninhibited the response (short of causing severe physical pain) a woman makes at the peak of sexual excitement, the more pleased most men are (Mozes 1959). Most men want a woman to express her excitement and involvement, and to leave little doubt that she has let herself go completely and has responded—authentically—exactly as she felt. This sort of open communication is not as difficult to achieve as it might sound. It can be assisted by actions such as rhythmical body movements accompanied by low moans and gasps, all building to an expressive crescendo at the moment of orgasm. But whatever form the communication takes, freedom of response and expression is the key.

Overcoming Sexual Inexperience

Sexual adjustment is best when there is an understanding and acceptance of one's self, of one's own body, and of one's sensual and sexual feelings (McCarthy *et al.* 1975). Special burdens are placed on a relationship when sexual inexperience is augmented by the unrealistic expectations of either partner. A person's anticipation of sexual expertise on the part of his/her partner frequently ignores the very real possibility that the partner, too, may be lacking in proper experience or even sound sex information.

In addition, it is unfortunate that the roles in male-female relationships fixed by custom are so difficult to shift. This is particularly so in a sexual relationship, in which the man is usually expected to be dominant and, above all, confident. The disparity between expectations on the one hand and experience on the other, together with the faulty sex education that both partners may have received, frequently paves the way for emotional stress that may eventually manifest itself in any of a variety of sexual problems.

Sexually inexperienced young people, therefore, are well advised to acquire as much dispassionate information about sexual techniques as they can from authoritative books, lectures, teachers, and the like. It might be pointed out that one's peer group seldom falls into this category. It is certainly true that entering a relationship with *only* academic information tends to make a couple's initial sexual experiences more mechanical than spontaneous. But their confidence will be greater than if they had no knowledge, or knowledge based on hearsay.

Effort on the man's part at taking charge in initial sexual encounters—even if he must act more confident than he feels—is sometimes necessary because of the society-bred dichotomy in the roles of men and women. Neither partner should be expected to assume more control in a relationship than the other. However, until men can overcome their *machismo* attitudes and women their passivity and dependency—that is, until the point of maturity is reached at which men and women share full partnership in every respect—men will too often be expected to "control the relationship," like it or not. Fortunately, in today's more enlightened society, women frequently have been able to take active, initiatory roles in sexual relationships and have been able to overcome many of the inhibiting influences of the past (James 1980).

Nevertheless, women who are victims of the myth that sex is the exclusive responsibility of the man and that the sexually assertive woman is "unfeminine" may not recognize that they should act in their own behalf. They may not know what to do or even how to go about trying to correct the problem if they are not adequately responsive sexually. For even with the "new sexual morality," many people, women especially, equate sex with sin, shame, and danger. And to be assertive often causes more anxiety and less satisfaction than being passive does (H. S. Kaplan 1974). Once frank communication, in addition to confidence and equality, is firmly established between partners, a couple may be able to help each other toward greater sexual fulfillment.

Maintaining a Good Sexual Relationship

A leading sexologist (DeMartino 1970) investigated the primary criticisms that a group of American and Canadian women offered to men's lovemaking abilities and techniques. Men, the women reported, are too selfish; they do not properly prepare a women for coitus, chiefly because there is insufficient sexual foreplay; men are in too much of a hurry; they want to "have sex," which of course differs significantly from making love.

In addition, the critics continue, men are not sufficiently concerned that the woman be sexually satisfied. If they do express concern, it often reflects more their own need to be recognized as a "great lover" than their genuine regard for the woman's needs. Men are not gentle in their approach; they are too crude, forceful, unromantic, or even violent during coitus. Men are unimaginative; their lovemaking techniques are far too mechanical and ritualistic. Men are much too inhibited in their sexual expression; their response is not free and spontaneous. They apparently feel that "letting themselves go" during coitus, especially at the time of orgasm, is an indication of weakness or unmanliness, that a "real man" should control his emotions and restrain his responses.

The Hite survey (1976) of women's sexual attitudes and behavior supports these criticisms. In this study women made the following statements:

> Most of the men I've slept with have had absolutely no idea of what I want or need and no interest in finding out.

> A little kiss, a little feel, a finger for arousal, a touch of breast and he's on top, wham it's over.

> They undress me and try to penetrate at once. It's horrible.

> In and out.

> They jumped on and rode.

> Most didn't seem to be aware that what brought them to climax was not what brought me to climax. That about sums it up.

> Foreplay, always too short, then penetration.

> Most were speed demons.

> Before my present lover, they would expect me to jump into the hay whenever they got horny, go through a perfunctory foreplay, enter me, thrust rapidly for fifteen to thirty seconds, shoot their wad, graciously condescend to "finish me" with their finger, roll away and let me sleep in the wet spot. It was monotonous, drill-like, and boring.

Pleasing One's Partner

For a man to become a good sex partner, or a better one, he must first be willing to admit that he does not know all there is to know about human sexuality. Many men, unfortunately, are unwilling to make this admission because it threatens their ego and masculine self-image. So entrenched in their sexual ignorance, they stumble along ineptly in their sexual relationships, lending much validity to the French adage that "there are no frigid women, just clumsy men."

A woman often has the romantic yet dangerously mistaken notion that her partner should anticipate her sexual needs with unerring accuracy. She therefore feels that she has no need to tell him what pleases her sexually. Almost every man wants to please his partner. But in his attempts to anticipate a woman's preferences, a man may make the wrong move and then be mutely condemned as an inept lover. When he does succeed in pleasing her, he is often, unfortunately, rewarded only by her silence (E. Hamilton 1971).

The old saying that "beauty is in the eye of the beholder" is true. Men with rough, rugged features and those with classic profiles, the muscular and aesthetically thin, the baldheads and bearded; women with large breasts and those with small ones, the thin and buxom, the svelte and naturally windblown: all turn *someone* on.

The sense of smell is almost as important in sexual stimulation as the sense of sight (Eichenlaub 1961). The physiological relationship between the tissues of the nose and sex organs has already been mentioned. Frequently, also, conditioning plays a role in the relationship between the sense of smell and sexuality. During the early days of a relationship, for example, the faint scent of a woman's perfume or a man's cologne or after-shave lotion may become associated with their developing love and sexual arousal. Later in the relationship, the same pleasant scent may well serve to reestablish the earlier excitement. Conditioning quite naturally involves many sensory elements other than smell. Almost anything that is associated with love and passion can be woven into the fabric of the couple's sexual interaction.

It cannot be said too often: Differences in individual sexual needs and desires are wide. Each person should therefore make every effort to discover what, precisely, offers his/her sexual partner the greatest pleasure, and to use this knowledge in developing a sexual technique.

Some women become especially aroused when their men wear a special cologne during sexual activity. Other women prefer a clean-scrubbed, natural odor. Unless a man has strong feelings about using or not using perfumed products, why would he not prepare himself in the manner most pleasing to the woman?

Some men enjoy the complete nudity of their sexual partners during both the sexual preliminaries and coitus itself. Some men, however, prefer women to dress in a special manner—perhaps to wear a garter belt or sheer black lingerie—in order to increase their sexual excitement. Unless a woman particularly objects to this mode of dress, why would she not want to make the little effort necessary to please and excite her partner?

These are perhaps trivial examples of cooperation within a relationship, but the point is that it is important to try to please one's sexual partner before, during, and after sexual activity. It is difficult enough to keep sexual interest fresh and lively in ongoing relationships, even when a conscious effort is made. If such an effort is lacking, sexual enjoyment is bound to suffer and, eventually, so will the overall relationship. Perhaps one reason a new sexual relationship seems more exciting than an old one after a few years is that a new partner is apt to make special efforts to please, sometimes even in so fundamental a matter as personal appearance.

As superfluous as it may seem, it is nonetheless important to emphasize the significance of a clean and attractive body in successful sexual interaction. While it is true that some people become sexually aroused by the smell and taste of a partner who is not freshly bathed, most people are far more stimulated by a partner whose body is immaculately clean, perhaps enhanced by the subtle fragrance of perfume or lotions.

It is, of course, expecting too much of a wife who holds an exacting job or has sole responsibility for highly active children to be consistently rested, seductive, and glamorous at bedtime. It is equally unreasonable to expect a tense, harassed husband always to act, or look, the role in bed of a cinematic idol. But, unfortunately, too many people after marriage stop making even minimal efforts to keep themselves interesting in the eyes of their partner. Disenchanted, they find their sex life growing stale. Worse, one or both begin to look elsewhere for the glamour they feel is missing in the marital relationship.

On another level, the qualities of courtesy, kindness, and sensitivity to the needs and desires of others, which are so fundamental to all successful human interaction, are particularly vital to sexual relationships. For example, to some women a particularly meaningful part of lovemaking is being talked to during the act. Men may not appreciate this need—a need for tenderness, essentially—or may fail to meet it, despite the woman's asking her lover to "talk to me." Unfortunately, one cannot suddenly teach another tenderness (Comfort 1972). It is a quality learned from early childhood experiences, from warm parental relationships, and through the years from satisfying everyday associations. Depending on the particular woman or the stage of lovemaking, the talk among couples varies from tender whispered utterances of love to quite earthy, unrestrained expressions that under other circumstances might be considered vulgar (E. Hamilton 1971).

Pace and Style

Pace as well as style is also a matter of individual taste. Most successful couples seem to proceed slowly and gently, with the goal of bringing gratification to one another rather than hurrying to satisfy their own needs. The best and certainly the least stressful way for each partner to determine the specific erotic desires of the other is to open the doors of candid communication. Neither partner is a mindreader, and even an unintentionally offensive gesture or clumsiness will tend to squelch the present response and to inhibit response in similar circumstances at a future time.

Variety

In a study investigating marital orgasm (Gebhard 1966), when only 1 to 10 minutes of sexual foreplay preceded coitus, 40% of wives reported that they "nearly always" reached orgasm; 50% did so when foreplay was extended to 15 or 20 minutes; and 60% achieved orgasm if foreplay was even longer. Furthermore, there was a higher rate of orgasm among those women whose husbands prolonged intromission. When intromission lasted less than a minute before ejaculation occurred, only about 25% of wives achieved orgasm "always" or "nearly always"; about 50% did so if intromission lasted 1 to 11 minutes; and about 65% did so if intromission lasted longer than 11 minutes. Virtually all the women were brought to the full extent of their orgasmic capacity if intromission lasted for 16 minutes or longer. The same investigation also revealed the incidental information that many marriages broken by separation or divorce had a history of short rather than long periods of coital intromission.

Variations in sexual approach and setting can add considerable spice to a relationship. Too often sex becomes a ritual, stale and unimaginative, engaged in mechnically or to relieve physical urgency. Men could add much to their partner's sexual gratification—hence their own—if they would heed the importance placed on certain aspects of female sexuality, such as those revealed in surveys like *The Hite Report* (1976). Only 30% of the sample reported that they could achieve orgasm regularly through coitus. But 87% of the women stated that they nevertheless liked and wanted vaginal peneration—even those who never reach orgasm during coitus. In addition to the closeness and affection associated with intercourse, penetration provided for the woman a soothing and fulfilling experience that orgasm alone could not give.

Ongoing sexual activity that brings a high level of enjoyment does not *have* to be varied, but it typically happens that way. When a couple stick too rigidly to one sexual position or technique, it is usually an indication of anxiety (Comfort 1972). Shortly after two people enter into a committed relationship, they begin reducing the time given to sex play, and coitus unfortunately tends to become increasingly routine. Furthermore, coitus is usually relegated to the end of the day, after all work is finished, the late TV news over, and the partners too tired for anything but a "quickie"—if that—after which they immediately fall to sleep. Couples who wish to preserve delight and vigor in their sexual interaction will work as consistently to bring novelty into sex as they do to keep other aspects of their relationship alive.

A little imagination can significantly improve a sexual relationship. A couple might have a secret weekend at a motel—even a local one if nothing else is feasible. Or lovemaking can begin in an unexpected part of the house, such as in the kitchen or atop the bar (a bed is not the only horizontal surface in a house). Novelty can add a "forbidden fruit" flavor to the relationship. A couple can make a game of writing on separate pieces of paper certain positions, acts, and unlikely (if possible, legal) sites for sexual activity that intrigue them. They can put them in three separate boxes, shake well, and pull one from each; then have at it. The combinations may be highly unusual, but they will seldom be dull.

A man who impulsively sweeps his sex partner into his arms in the middle of a happy afternoon and carries her off to the bedroom for a wild lovemaking interlude—or the couple who occasionally have intercourse while showering or visiting some isolated beach—or who engage in an impromptu act of coitus in the back seat of the car when revisiting a lover's lane of their courtship years—or the woman who surprises her partner by appearing in his study carrying two cold, very dry Martinis and wearing nothing but a smile—these couples are not likely to find sex dull, even after years of being together. Some couples find their sexual encounters enhanced or improved when the woman feels free enough to express her desires and to initiate the sexual interaction at least some of the time (James 1980).

Couples wanting to maintain sexual interest over a long period of time might wish to remember the negative effect that "too much too soon" can have on love play. A woman, for example, needs to recognize the charm and excitement of semi-nudity, especially in the early part of a sexual encounter (Neiger 1968a). It has been observed that pictures of partly clad females—especially where a portion of the anatomy is "accidentally" exposed—are more exciting to men than many of the more frankly sexual poses.

A woman can put this information to good use. She can become more seductive as an evening wears on through progressive undressing that does not become complete nudity. This "teasing" frequently will not only put her partner in a state of sexual readiness that evening but will also serve his fantasies in the future when personal contact between the couple may not be possible (Levitt & Brady 1965). Once the appropriate point in lovemaking has been reached, however, the woman must abandon the pretense of holding herself back from her partner. Her teasing abandoned, she should then enter into the sexual act as freely, openly, intently, and intensely as possible.

Playing soft music, using mirrors to observe the intimacies of the sex act, and perusing sensuous literature and art are other devices that help keep boredom out of the bedroom (Ellis 1960). The value of fantasy in augmenting sexual arousal should never be overlooked. It is superior to such commonly accepted techniques as erotic writings and photographs. In a recent study, Harris, Yulis, and LaCoste (1980) found that the ability to form clear and vivid images in fantasy was associated with self-reports of higher sexual arousability in both sexes. Another study (Baron & Byrne 1977) revealed that couples experienced greater sexual excitement when they relied on their own imaginings rather than on erotic books or pictures. Furthermore, the uninhibited couple share their sexual fantasies with one another (Comfort 1972). Caution must be used in such disclosures, however, because certain fantasies can be disturbing to some who are insecure (and jealous) or are nervous about the form of sexual activity the partner might be fantasizing.

The wish for variety in sexual life is normal. If this ideal is reached within marriage or other long-term relationships, there is considerably less likelihood that either partner will seek it elsewhere. Imagination and a willingness to experiment, together with an air of confidence and consideration, will serve most couples very well.

It must be stressed, however, that a certain degree of monotony will inevitably enter a sexual relationship of some duration, no matter how much the man and woman love each other or how much novelty they attempt to introduce into their sex life. Psychic stimulation of the sort that heretofore caused almost immediate erotic arousal becomes increasingly ineffective, and the man becomes more and more dependent on his partner's direct stimulation of his penis to help achieve an erection. Since men typically feel a threat to their masculinity when penile erections are sluggish, couples are well advised to use this very effective means of attaining sexual arousal (Lief *et al.* 1968).

It is for these very reasons that many marriage counselors recommend *planned romance*—setting aside a specific time for coitus when the couple can plan to be alone. Other counselors disagree, saying planning coitus ruins spontaneity. But total spontaneity in sexual activity disappears from most sexual relationships after a few weeks in any event, even under the most ideal of circumstances. It would therefore seem that planned coitus, at least some of the time, promises more relaxed enjoyment and is more cementing to the relationship than spontaneous sexual experiences in which either or both partners are not at their best, emotionally or physically.

The Erogenous Zones

Erogenous zones are those parts of the body possessing a large concentration of nerve endings (sometimes termed "sexual nerves") that, when stimulated, cause sexual arousal. These areas are numerous, and they are basically the same in man and woman—although there are, of course, individual variations in the areas producing excitement and in the degree of arousal.

Physical Stimulation

The most sensitive erogenous areas are the genitals and the areas surrounding them: the inner and outer regions of the thighs, the buttocks, and the abdomen. The nongenital erogenous zones extend over a large portion of the body, some areas being more sensitive than others. The breasts (particularly the nipples), armpits, navel, small of the back, shoulders, neck,

earlobes, scalp, eyelids, and especially the mouth, tongue, eyes, and nose
are all areas rich in nerve endings.

Sexual arousal takes place when messages are sent by the stimulated
sexual nerve endings to the brain, which in turn transmits them to the
centers of the lower spinal column controlling sexual impulses (Coleman
1972). A psychological or physical block at some point can delay or even
prevent sexual excitement. For example, messages of disapproval, unpleasantness, fear, pain, or injury can and often do delay or obstruct altogether
the channel to sexual centers, thus preventing arousal. On the other hand,
as has been mentioned, pleasant messages, such as a lovely sight, a gentle
word, a soft touch, an exotic scent, or a harmonious sound can easily evoke
sexual feelings. Pleasing sensory stimuli may produce erotic thoughts,
which in turn may cause penile erection and vaginal lubrication.

Although the erogenous zones appear to be a matter of heredity and,
in general, are common to all people, individual differences, largely the
result of conditioning are wide. Present scientific data indicate that there
are no abnormal erogenous regions, and those that are uncommon are so
simply as the result of individual background and experience. For example,
if a man were to tickle the sole of his partner's foot preceding each pleasant
act of coitus, sooner or later foot-tickling would come to be associated with
pleasurable intercourse. The sole of the foot would become a conditioned
erogenous zone for that particular woman. Should she later have coitus
with another person, however, the conditioned erogenous zone on the sole
of the foot might well appear abnormal to her new partner (Williamson
1961).

As with psychological factors that serve as strong erotic stimuli, mutual
experimentation and frank discussion are the best ways to discover which
areas are the most effective for individual sexual arousal (Caprio 1959; Ellis
1963). This is important precisely because of the marked degree of difference
in preferred methods of sexual arousal and the time required to become
aroused.

The genitals, the part of the body most responsive to stimulation,
contain millions of nerve endings concentrated in small regions of erectile-
type tissue. For a man the most sensitive part of the genitalia is the glans
or head of the penis, particularly the lower surface at the corona (ring) and
frenum. Probably the most meaningful sexual response that a woman can
show a man is her obvious enjoyment of his penis, and her willingness—
or, better, her desire—to fondle, play with, kiss, look at and take it in her
mouth as well as in her vagina. Such acts denote acceptance of the man,
and indicate to him that she enjoys and considers valuable a part of his
anatomy that is highly meaningful to him (E. Hamilton 1971).

The clitoris and its glans, catalysts of a woman's sexual excitation and
orgasm, contain a delicate network of nerve endings in erectile-type tissue
covered with mucous membrane. The clitoris is stimulated during coitus

by two mechanisms. First, there is pressure on the pubic area. The clitoris itself is involved in varying degrees, depending upon how the two bodies fit together and which sexual positions are used (the female-superior position is usually the most effective). Second, there is traction of the clitoral hood. The latter is thought to be the most important element in clitoral stimulation, as the minor lips tug at it with coital thrusting or other sexual maneuvering (H. S. Kaplan 1974). In the findings of a recent survey of women, only 35% expressed a preference for gentle, direct clitoral stimulation. The glans was "out of bounds" because of its ultra sensitivity (Devanesan 1975). The entire vulval area, especially the vestibule and labia minora, are also rich in nerve endings and are highly responsive to stimulation.

The walls of the vagina, with the exception of the anterior wall and the upper front area where the roots of the clitoris are located, are somewhat insensitive because they contain only a few nerve endings. The cervix is so insensitive that it sometimes can be cauterized or surgically cut without the aid of anesthetics (Hoch 1980; Sentnor & Hult 1961). Nevertheless, some women apparently do experience heightened sexual pleasure from penile pressure against the cervix as it, in turn, moves the uterus and its supporting broad ligaments. Both of the latter are encased in the peritoneal membrane, which has great sensitivity (Clark 1970a).

Some physiologists (Kegel 1953) believe that penile stimulation of the highly sensitive nerve endings in the pubococcygeal muscles encircling the vaginal opening generates great erotic pleasure. Women with weak vaginal muscles, according to these theorists, are perhaps unable to receive sexual satisfaction from coitus until these muscles are strengthened through the exercises described in Chapter 5. Furthermore, women often find that contracting the pubococcygeal muscles while thrusting produces erotic sensations that they perhaps have never before experienced (H. S. Kaplan 1975; Dailey 1980b).

It is well known that the lower side of the penis is particularly sensitive because of the network of nerves surrounding the urethra. The female urethra, the meatus of which is slightly above or forward of the vaginal opening, is supplied with similarly sensitive nerve endings. When the area of the vagina nearest the urethra is gently stimulated—for example, by the in-and-out penile movements of coitus—the woman may experience erotic sensations that can add immensely to her sexual pleasure (Clark 1970b).

The perineum of both man and woman is sensitive to manipulation. This area includes the anus and inner portions of the thighs, and extends from the anus to the lower region of the sexual organs. About half of all men and women, in fact, report that they experience erotic reactions to some form of anal stimulation (Kinsey *et al.* 1953). While the mouth, lips, and nose are widely recognized as highly erogenous areas, there is nonetheless considerable variation in the degree of their sensitivity, because of personal differences resulting primarily from conditioning and second-arily from differences in supplies of nerve endings. The breasts are another important erogenous zone common to both men and women. The nipples and areolae are especially responsive to several stimuli.

Developing One's Own Sexuality

Today more than ever before, the attitude is becoming accepted that both men and women have the right to seek as complete and satisfying sexual fulfillment as possible. It is reflected in many current books and articles, which discuss freely the importance of sexual completeness both in and out of marriage. No longer are the sexual needs of women considered subordinate to those of men. Men and women are encouraged to loosen their inhibitions and permit themselves complete sexual responsiveness (Comfort 1972).

Sexual responsiveness (or the lack of it) is largely learned. The basic biological inclinations exist, of course, in both men and women. But beyond these physiological basics, the peaks, nuances, and joys of sexuality are learned and refined through experience and experimentation. How better can one understand the fine points of sexual sensitivity and responsiveness than by experimenting with one's own body? All of us have done so throughout our lives. Unfortunately, however, guilt, shame, and fear learned from outside forces, as well as ignorance, have prevented many of us from experimenting as fully with our own bodies as is required to develop our sensuousness to its greatest extent. (And it seems only reasonable that one cannot fully appreciate, enjoy, and fulfill the sexuality of another person until one can enjoy and fulfill one's own.) Certain techniques are widely recognized as capable of leading almost anyone to new heights of sexual enjoyment and responsiveness.

Masturbation. Probably the most successful way of learning to respond to one's full sexual capacity is through self-stimulation. Masturbation is a perfectly normal, healthy act in boys and girls and in men and women, young and old. Nevertheless, it has long been a subject of great controversy, and discussions of it are often filled with ignorance, misinformation, superstition, and shame. It is scarcely surprising that many people, especially the naïve, come to believe that masturbation is an evil, abnormal, or, at best, infantile practice.

Only under extremely rare circumstances can masturbation be con-sidered a sexual abnormality, especially since the vast majority of both men and women practice it at one time or another (Kinsey *et al.* 1948, 1953). It should be viewed as a sexual problem only when it becomes, as it occasionally does, part of the behavior pattern of psychotic patients, or is utilized as the sole method of sexual outlet when other outlets are readily

Figure 9.3

available. Indeed, those who do not practice masturbation, or have never done so, are far more likely to be suffering from an emotional or sexual problem than those who have masturbatory experience. Suppression of the tendency to masturbate usually occurs when the individual's thinking regarding sexual matters is clouded with guilt, fear, and perplexity (Ellis 1958, 1960).

Long prior to the birth of Hippocrates down through the ages to 1900, the medical world remained largely ignorant of cause and effect in sexual behavior. Objectivity and a scientific approach were notoriously lacking in the few investigations that were made. Occasionally some brave scientific soul would reach out for enlightenment, but such people were rare. Struggles through these dark ages toward an understanding of human sexuality were dealt a near deathblow in the mid-18th century when S. A. D. Tissot of France wrote his *Onana, a Treatise on the Diseases Produced by Onanism*. Projecting his personal problems, to say nothing of his unique ignorance, into his writings, Tissot wrote of the viciousness of "self-abuse," attributing most of the known medical disorders—including consumption, epileptic seizures, gonorrhea, and insanity—to the loss of semen through masturbation. It was Tissot who introduced the foolish and totally unscientific idea that the loss of one drop of seminal fluid causes more bodily damage and weakness than the loss of 40 drops of blood (Dearborn 1966).

Hysteria over masturbation reached such a pitch in the late 19th century that "depraved" women who resorted to it were frequently forced by their families to submit to a clitoridectomy (the surgical removal of the clitoris) as a method of control. French medical men, furthermore, expressed their dismay at an occupational hazard peculiar to seamstresses: the masturbatory up-and-down movements of their legs as they treadled their sewing machines were apt to cause orgasms. In at least one establishment, a matron was appointed to circulate among the seamstresses to detect runaway machines as the women became caught up in this "horrible" by-product of their profession (Duffy 1963, 1964).

The arguments against masturbation are legion, time-worn—and invalid. These are some of the more hackneyed ones:

Only the immature person masturbates. Refutation: Masturbation provides about 50% of the total sexual outlet of unmarried college-educated men between the ages of 26 and 30. Among women, the incidence of masturbation to orgasm increases until middle age, after which time it remains about the same (Kinsey *et al.* 1948, 1953). Both middle-aged and older men and women masturbate. One study showed that 59% of unmarried women and 30% of the married ones between 50 and 79 years of age masturbate ("Sex Behavior" 1966). The act, therefore, can hardly be called immature.

Masturbation is unsocial or antisocial. Refutation: It is true, of course, that masturbation usually takes place when the person is alone. But other forms of sexual behavior, including coitus, likewise are rarely carried out in public view. If a shy or withdrawn person masturbates, he or she does not become introverted *because* of masturbation any more than an outgoing, popular person who masturbates becomes extroverted because of it.

Masturbating too frequently causes fatigue and physical debilitation. Refutation: The human body exerts excellent control over the amount of sexual activity the individual engages in. When one has reached the point of satiation, further sexual acivity becomes physically unpleasant, so it is virtually impossible to indulge in "too much sex." In any case, there is no logic in the premise that one form of sexual functioning more than another generates debility and fatigue. An orgasm is an orgasm, whether it is the result of coitus, heavy petting, or masturbation.

Sexual fantasies associated with masturbation are emotionally unhealthy. Refutation: Fantasy is a part of human existence. Few today would contest the argument that what is universal in human nature is also normal and acceptable. And of Kinsey's sample (1953), 65% of the women who reported masturbating used fantasy at least occasionally to enhance the pleasure of the act. Our conscious mental state involves a continuous flow of fantasy, sexual and otherwise, sometimes fleeting images, sometimes protracted, volitional daydreams.

Sexual fantasy does not occur only during masturbation. It can take place in the absence of any sexual activity whatever, in the course of coition, and in homosexual contact, as well as during masturbation (P. R. Sullivan 1969). Its effects can be beneficial, indifferent, or detrimental, regardless of what form of sexual activity (or inactivity) it accompanies. Thus the couple who have been titillated by sexual fantasies during the day will quite likely find coitus more exciting than usual that night. But when shy, inhibited young people allow endless romantic or sexual fantasy to prevent them from facing actual encounters with members of the opposite sex, the daydreaming cannot be called healthy.

All in all, it would seem more healthy than unhealthy that fantasy accompany masturbation. Otherwise, masturbation becomes a mechanical, somewhat dehumanized form of sexual release. On the other side of the coin, fantasy—with or without masturbation—would appear detrimental to a young person (particularly) if so much time is invested in its pursuit that schoolwork is left undone and grades drop.

Masturbation is sexually frustrating and not as satisfactory as sex relations with a partner. Refutation: Masturbation is frustrating only when one feels guilt or shame about it, or when one expects more from it than is reasonable. It is true that sexual relations are usually preferable to solitary masturbation. But if for some reason this is not possible or advisable, masturbation offers a satisfactory substitute in the release of sexual tension. In the case of some women, furthermore, masturbation may be the only means of achieving orgasm (Ellis 1958; Hite 1976; "M" 1971; P. R. Sullivan 1969). And women observed during various sexual acts in a laboratory setting reported that orgasms resulting from such direct but noncoital methods as masturbation were physiologically more satisfying than those produced coitally, although the latter were more satisfying emotionally (Masters & Johnson 1966).

In January 1976, the Vatican issued a declaration calling masturbation "a seriously disordered act." This position was immediately challenged in letters and other communications to the pope by the most respected and prestigious organizations and scientists in the field of human sexuality. And while the Vatican did not change its position, the subject was relegated to a quiet and unobtrusive position in Vatican affairs.

Certainly it is advisable, if an individual has anxieties concerning masturbation, and if self-stimulation causes extreme guilt, that it be avoided until the underlying psychological problem is corrected. Similarly, if one has extreme and severe guilt about head-scratching, one should also avoid head-scratching until the underlying psychological difficulty is solved.

The technique of masturbation customarily used by men is to grip the penis and move the hand back and forth at the desired pressure and tempo along the length of the penile shaft. The glans is stimulated somewhat as it is by in-and-out body movements during penile penetration of the vagina. The degree of pressure, the speed of stroking, and the use or nonuse of lubrication vary from man to man.

Hite (1976) found that 73% of women masturbate by stimulating the clitoris and vulva area by hand or vibrator while lying on their backs; 5.5% do so in a similar manner while lying on their stomachs; 4% by pressing or thrusting the vulval area (clitoris) against a soft object; 3% by rhythmically pressing thighs together; 2% by water massage of vulva and clitoris; 1.5% by vaginal insertion of some object, such as fingers, candles, vibrators, or dildoes (more than half these women had earlier manually stimulated the clitoris); and 11% used more than one of these methods.

Learning about Sensuality. Women can learn to heighten their sexual responsiveness through certain exercises. The woman who, because of a lifetime of sexual taboos and restrictions, is not freely responsive to sexual stimulation is advised to explore and experiment with her body to uncover its full sensitivity. She can begin by exercising her tactile senses while blindfolded. She can slowly and gently feel objects of different textures, allowing the resulting tactile sensations to become firmly fixed in her memory. She can then lightly stimulate various parts of her nude body with furry or fluffy material.

She is advised to relax by lingering in a hot bath while all stresses of the day float away. After delicately drying her body, she should stretch, roll, curl up, and otherwise maneuver herself in her bed, mist-sprayed with cologne, as she listens to music, with a flickering candle as the only source of light. She should follow this bit of self-indulgence by delicately rubbing and massaging her breasts, abdomen, and other curves of her body with her favorite lotion, all the while making herself as acutely aware as possible of the various tactile sensations that she is experiencing.

Since the mouth and tongue are highly important in lovemaking, the woman who wishes to develop her sensuousness should practice various flicking, stretching, clockwise, and counterclockwise movements of the tongue. These maneuvers can be practiced by running her tongue over her palms, between her fingers, and on her wrists and arms. She can also use an ice-cream cone, directing her tongue in various swirling patterns on the ice cream. This exercise not only enhances the finesse of tongue movement but also allows a woman to fantasize her own body's being thus caressed and stimulated by her lover.

The woman who wants to give and obtain the greatest pleasure from lovemaking must practice muscle control. She must learn techniques of strengthening, tightening, and controlling muscles of the vagina, abdomen, back, and gluteal area. She is also advised to learn to coordinate her body movements with those of her lover. One of the best ways that this can be accomplished is through dancing. She can close her eyes and allow her body to melt into his as they dance. She can concentrate on the feel of his body next to hers as they become attuned in rhythm, movement, and style ("J" 1969).

Learning to masturbate successfully is probably the most important step for the woman in learning to come to orgasm. She learns what is required of herself and of her lover to give her the fullest sexual response. In addition, learning to breathe in a manner to reduce muscular tension is a valuable lesson in training oneself to reach orgasm. Tension begins to build with inhalation but is released with exhalation. Proper breathing can remove muscular tension from the groin, the pelvis, and buttocks, producing a warm and tingling sense of aliveness in the genital area that can add significantly to sexual pleasure and orgasmic response. Freedom from muscular tension, coupled with free, uninhibited fantasy of an erotic subject that her sexual imaginativeness can conjure up, are essential "keys to sexual heaven" (E. Hamilton 1971).

Although men commonly achieve orgasm more easily than women, they can benefit no less than women from practice in the art of becoming more sensuous. The first step, again, is a positive attitude toward sex, sensuality, and sex knowledge. The second step is a realization that the hands and mouth are of primary importance in making love to a woman. A man must develop the muscle control important to the maintenance of lengthy acts of coitus. He should also master the techniques of cunnilingus (application of tongue or mouth to a woman's vulval area), in much the same manner as is prescribed for the aspiring sensuous woman.

A man wishing to heighten his sensual awareness is also urged to develop his tactile sensitivity, in much the same manner as that suggested for women. Men are sometimes slow to realize that tenderness, sensitivity, and delicacy, when coupled with firmness, usually bring far greater erotic pleasure to a woman than a rough, forceful approach ("M" 1971).

Forms of Heterosexual Arousal

Any sexual behavior between consenting adults is (or should be) permissible so long as certain criteria are met. The partners must, first of all, be capable and willing to assume responsibility for their behavior and its consequences. The behavior should not hurt anyone and should be out of the sight and sound of unwilling observers. The last criterion is that the behavior be pleasurable to the participants.

Among the most effective of all sexual stimulants are the hands, a fact that some tend to forget. Petting, foreplay, love play—whatever one chooses to call it—is the most satisfying when hands and fingers are freely employed. And while petting is the royal road to intercourse, it can also be highly pleasurable in its own right. Petting causes difficulty only when it is prolonged, producing distressful tissue congestion in the genital area that is not relieved by orgasm; or when it arouses guilt feelings. The evidence is that people who freely enjoy petting or extended foreplay are the ones most capable of responding freely and pleasurably to intercourse (Beigel 1952; Ellis 1958, 1960, 1963; Ficher 1979; Kinsey *et al.* 1953; Stone & Stone 1952).

Persons who are reluctant to involve themselves in sex play are often simply fearful that their partner will consider them too bold in their manner of sexual stimulation or response. The less inhibited of the two should start the coital foreplay, and then at the appropriate time should gently but firmly put the partner's hands and lips at the spots where they are most desired (Ellis 1963).

Sexual excitement is most easily heightened when a maneuver of advance and retreat is adopted (Eichenlaub 1961). Stimulation is instigated and then, after a brief buildup, withdrawn in a slightly teasing, tantalizing manner. Stimulation is begun again, carried to a more advanced point of excitement, and once more withdrawn. Quite naturally, timing is of the essence. Knowing just how long to continue advancing and retreating is the key to success in this lovemaking strategy. To continue beyond this point may very well be interpreted as rejection by the recipient, so that what started out to be a promising adventure ends in stress and unhappiness (Eichenlaub 1961).

In Masters and Johnson's training sessions to help sexually inadequate husbands and wives overcome their difficulties, great emphasis is placed on the couple's establishing a "sensate focus,'" which means that they learn to think and feel sensually. Each partner is taught to use, with varying degrees of finesse, hands and fingers to touch, stroke, massage, and fondle all parts of the mate's body. The purpose is not only to give the most meaningful and exciting erotic sensations possible to the partner, but also to enjoy oneself the matchless erotic pleasures growing out of an uninhibited tactile exploration of the total skin surface and body contours of a lover (Lehrman 1970; Masters & Johnson 1970).

With proper use of the hands, not only can sexual excitement be built up in one's partner, but one's own excitement can be brought to and maintained at the response level of the other person. As an example, the man's light stroking and caressing of his partner's body with his fingertips will build her sexual excitement faster than his own. But when he uses the palms of his hands, as well as his fingertips (along with other excitants such as darting tongue-kissing), his own excitement usually develops at about the same tempo as hers (Eichenlaub 1961; Ellis 1963; Van de Velde 1957). With this in mind, a man may pace the development of mutual excitement to achieve a synchronized crescendo.

Initial sexual excitement is brought about by light touch—not pressure—and the more intense and prolonged the sexual buildup, the greater the orgasmic response (Eichenlaub 1961; Masters & Johnson 1966). While at first the bodies of both the man and woman are stimulated with gentle, slow, generalized stroking, the caressing should gradually become more specific as sex play progresses. The general orientation of the stroking should be toward the erogenous zones, particularly the genitalia, the caressing done in the teasing advance—retreat—advance manner already described. It is of special importance that the genitals be stimulated lightly at first because of the sensitivity and tenderness of the area. As excitement increases, the man or the woman may wish the pressure to be heavier.

A woman's skin is often considerably more sensitive to the touch than a man's is, and care should be taken, especially with a sexually inexperienced woman, to avoid overstimulation (Eichenlaub 1961).

Exceptionally gentle caressing will gradually "awaken" the nerve endings of the genital region, and will condition the woman to welcome this manner of lovemaking as something pleasant and exciting. Fingertip stroking of the abdomen and inner thighs—with general movement in the direction of the genitals—will usually prepare a woman for more direct stimulation of the genitalia.

Breast manipulation is usually regarded as one of the most effective sexual stimulants for a woman. Indeed, a small percentage of women can be brought to orgasm by breast manipulation alone (Kinsey *et al.* 1953; Masters & Johnson 1966). Surprising to many is the fact that men can become as sexually excited from having their breasts stimulated as women (Kinsey *et al.* 1953; J. L. McCary 1966). That men enjoy this stimulation is a normal response, and the pleasure has a sound physiological basis.

In lovemaking, a man can gently massage his partner's breasts, interspersing the manipulation with a light brushing of the nipple and an occasional tweak of its sensitive tip. Caressing with the hands can very pleasurably be alternated with soft moist kisses and an exploring tongue. The tempo of the tongue's movements can be changed occasionally, to erotic advantage, allowing it to dart back and forth across the nipple in a tense, rapid-fire manner, before resuming once more the soft moist stimulation (Caprio 1959; Eichenlaub 1961; Ellis 1958, 1960, 1963).

The erogenous nerve endings in a man's breasts are limited to the nipples and areas immediately surrounding them. When a man's breast is stimulated by gently rolling the nipple between the thumb and finger, or by the sort of oral contact described in the previous paragraph, he is likely to experience the same sort of sexual desire and excitement that women do from the same techniques.

Kissing, like hand-fingertip caressing, can be varied in a teasing manner: open mouth, closed mouth; light lip pressure, heavy lip pressure; moist lips, dry lips, soft lips, nibbling teeth and lips; a darting, teasing tongue, a soft sensuous tongue. The lover's face and body should be covered with kisses as the point of action varies quickly, then slowly, from the lips to the eyes, hairline, earlobes, to the mouth again, to the breast, to the neck, to the abdomen, back to the lips. All the while, the tongue should also be participating in this exploration of the lover's body.

The kissing maneuver should be repeated again and again with increasing passion and delicate timing (Eichenlaub 1961; Ellis 1963; Van de Velde 1957; Vatsyayana 1962). Ordinarily, kissing of the mouth should precede kissing of other parts of the body, except perhaps the hands. It should be noted that having the palms of her hands kissed is a particularly exciting and stimulating experience for a woman (Eichenlaub 1961). There is also the psychological element of its being a rather courtly and tender gesture on the part of the man.

No matter what approach the man takes, his hands should seldom be motionless during the entire period of sex play. They should dart and slide over his partner's body—stroking, holding, caressing boldly and lightly, squeezing, and massaging—alternating strong palmar movements with light stroking of the fingertips. As he brings his partner to successive levels of arousal, he must take heed of the very thin and delicate tissue of the vulva and vagina. These areas should not be manually stimulated unless the man's fingernails are clipped and smooth, and the vulval region well moistened with either bodily secretions or with a commercial product, such as K–Y Sterile Lubricant. The clitoris, furthermore, is often too sensitive to accommodate direct and uninterrupted manipulation comfortably (Eichenlaub 1961). Knowing that the regions to the side and around the clitoris are the sites of stimulation preferred by most women who masturbate can be helpful to a man in his love play (Masters & Johnson 1966).

As mentioned earlier, sex play should be a gradual, slowly unfolding experience, especially for the woman. It has been suggested that kissing and manual stimulation of erogenous areas should be carried on for at least 15 minutes before intercourse itself commences, although some couples prefer longer, others shorter, periods of stimulation (Stone & Stone 1952). An overly protracted period of sex play, however, can actually interfere with maximum pleasure (Eichenlaub 1961). Kinsey and his associates report that many couples prefer sexual intercourse itself as a method of stimulation (Kinsey *et al.* 1948, 1953). Communication and good timing are once more essential; when both lovers are ready to proceed with coitus, they should let one another know.

There are many things a woman can do by way of lovemaking that will bring delight to her lover. She can initiate kissing or return his kisses passionately, stimulate his nipples orally and by fingertip and palmar manipulation, lightly rake her fingertips over his bare back, gently stimulate the scrotum and perineal area, and manipulate the penis with alternating light and heavy stroking (particularly at the glans and frenum). The woman, too, would do well to remember the importance of the teasing game of advance and retreat in the art of building up sexual excitement.

In her efforts to determine what sort of lovemaking brings the greatest pleasure to her partner, the woman might bear in mind individual differences. For example, while some men prefer a gentle stroking of the penis, others may desire heavy pressure and squeezing in such a manner that there is tugging at the scrotum and perineal area. She should let it be known that she thoroughly enjoys giving, as well as receiving, such pleasurable stimulation (Eichenlaub 1961).

In attempting to discover a pleasurable means of stimulating her partner's genitalia, a woman can often obtain a helpful guideline from any masturbatory techniques he may have used. If, for instance, a man stimulates himself with light, slow stroking of his penis, it is quite likely that he will welcome the same sort of caressing from his partner (Kronhausen & Kronhausen 1965).

Some women who masturbate insert their fingers into the vagina. Since they are so conditioned, these women will probably find it pleasurable if their partners arouse them in the same manner during sex play.

A vibrator can be of value in heightening the pleasure of a couple's sexual interaction. Some women apparently cannot achieve orgasm with penile penetration, nor indeed can some reach it through any of the techniques of stimulation already discussed. But direct clitoral and vulval arousal through the man's application of a vibrator as he fondles and kisses her seldom fails to bring a women to orgasm (Clark 1949; Ellis 1963).

A few women prefer the type of vibrator that the man attaches to the back of his hand. It allows him free movement of his fingers, to be sure, but most of the vibration is absorbed by his hand. Therefore, greater stimulation is possible from the application of a rubber-knobbed vibrator directly on or to the side of the clitoris. Or a battery-driven penis-shaped vibrator can be applied directly to the clitoral area or inserted into the vagina, if such stimulation is desired.

Use of the latter vibrator meets with great success in producing single or multiple orgasms in women who might otherwise be incapable of reaching such an intense level of response. The man also remains free to kiss, caress, and stimulate his partner in any other way he chooses. Marriage counselors frequently recommend vibrator stimulation for women who experience difficulty in reaching orgasm, and women without lovers who need sexual release. Few women fail to achieve an orgasm when they are properly stimulated with a vibrator, no matter what their previous history of sexual response has been. However, some couples find the vibrator too "mechanical" for their tastes. Some women fear that their orgasmic response to this sort of stimulation will be so intense that other methods will be pleasurable only to a lesser degree (Rubin 1964c).

It is important for a woman first using a vibrator to realize that she will remain "in control." Given time to get used to the vibrator, a woman can arrive at an appreciation of just what kinds of erotic sensations it can provide. While the vibrator can provide intense and pleasurable orgasms for many women, it need not overwhelm them or take over their sex lives (Steinhart 1980).

Another form of sexual activity that is far more popular than many realize is oral-genital stimulation. It is not a new phenomenon, for Kinsey's research (1948, 1953) showed that oral-genital contact had been experienced by at least 60% of married college-educated couples and by about 20% of the subjects who had completed high school and 10% of those who had a grade-school education. By the 1970s, the incidence of oral-genital sex had risen above 90% for married couples under age 25, whatever their educational status (Hunt 1974). That these figures are so high may be surprising, because society has tended to frown on this sort of sexual behavior. However, marriage counselors have long recognized its great value in the sex lives of many couples.

The prevailing negative attitude toward genital kissing is primarily an outgrowth of the fact that many people regard the genital region as "dirty." The proximity in the woman of the anus and the urethra to the genitals, and the fact that the male penis is both a seminal and a urinary outlet are the physiological factors that have given rise to the "dirtiness" concept in genital kissing. But these objections are not logical (Ellis 1960).

People seldom enjoy even kissing someone whose breath is reeking, to say nothing of entering into more intimate physical contact with someone who needs a bath. The same observations can be made of the genitals. Because the folds of skin that partially cover the surface of the genitals are natural receptacles for a collection of smegma and secretions, the region should be cleansed so that any offensive material or odor is removed. In the same fashion used to clean the ear, a finger can be moved in and around the folds of the genitalia to cleanse them. If a couple give this sort of attention to keeping themselves clean and pleasant-smelling, making whatever use is indicated of "personal hygiene" and cosmetic products, the objection to oral-genital contact on the grounds of "dirtiness" is less than valid.

Couples who engage in oral-genital contact generally agree that it is enjoyable to both man and woman, whether giving or receiving. The mouth and lips are erogenous zones for nearly all people. There is, in addition, an abundance of nerve endings in the tip of the nose. That these two areas of sensitivity universally exist no doubt accounts for mouth contact and nose-rubbing as the chief methods of "kissing" in our world, and for the fact that oral stimulation of the genitals is so pleasurable for many people (Sentnor

& Hult 1961; Williamson 1961). Furthermore, neurophysiological studies (MacLean 1965) have shown that there is a close relationship between the parts of the brain concerned with oral functions (amygdala) and those concerned with sexual functions (septum and rostral diencephalon). Stimulation of an area of the brain affecting oral activity will readily produce a "spillover" into areas governing genital function.

A couple may engage in mutual oral-genital contact during the early part of stimulation. Achieving simultaneous orgasms in this manner—or even prolonged simultaneous oral-genital stimulation—presents some of the same problems that simultaneous coital orgasm does. That is, neither partner can properly concentrate at the same time on him/herself and the partner to the fullest satisfaction of either while receiving such intense stimulation.

The clitoris usually receives the greatest measure of the man's attention during cunnilingus (from the Latin: *cunnus*, vulva; and *lingere*, to lick). Its sensitive glans can be stimulated in much the same manner as the nipples of the breasts are stimulated in mouth-tongue-breast contact. The tongue-stroking begins in a light, teasing manner with intermittent heavy, moist, bold tongue-stroking. Then the technique is varied to keep pace with the heightening sexual excitement. As the woman's climax nears, and if the couple wish to bring it about in this manner, the man should put into action the findings of Masters and Johnson (1966), which demonstrate that orgasm is best produced by a steady, constant stroking of the clitoral *area*. (At the height of sexual tension the clitoris withdraws under its hood, and direct contact can no longer be maintained in any case.) Other parts of the vulva, particularly the labia minora, are also sensitive to oral stimulation. Women who have experienced oral-genital stimulation report that the method is overwhelmingly pleasurable and effective, both as sex foreplay and as the primary avenue to achieving orgasm (Kronhausen & Kronhausen 1965).

Kinsey *et al.* (1948, 1953) have shown that women are less inclined to engage in fellatio (Latin: *fellare*, to suck) with their partners than men are to engage in cunnilingus with them. Any such reluctance is usually based on psychological blocks. If a woman will talk over the matter of fellatio carefully with her partner, she can usually overcome her objections and eventually may find the act quite pleasurable. Other women avoid fellatio in the mistaken notion that, if ejaculation occurs and they swallow the fluid, they could become pregnant. This is pure mythology, as there is no way in which seminal fluid could make its way from the alimentary canal to the reproductive tract.

The glans of the penis, especially at the frenum and contiguous areas, is highly sensitive to a woman's kisses and sucking, and to her warm, moist, now darting, now soft tongue. At the same time, she can also stroke the corpus of the penis with an up-and-down movement, occasionally fondling the testicles and scrotum. This technique of lovemaking can quickly bring the man to sexual heights that can easily terminate in orgasm.

Whether climax occurs as a result of manual stimulation, oral activity, or intercourse is a matter each couple must decide individually. The method best suited to the particular coital occasion should readily be adopted, with each participant expending his/her best efforts to bring about maximum satisfaction for the partner (Eichenlaub 1961).

Because of their individual and combined personalities and preferences, each couple needs to discover—through open discussion and experimentation—just what brings both of them the greatest erotic pleasure. What one couple finds exciting, another might find dull or even repulsive (Eichenlaub 1961). One person, for instance, might find highly pleasurable the application to the perineal area of crushed ice wrapped in a cloth at the time the paroxysms of orgasm commence, whereas another might find it a rather ludicrous experience (Eichenlaub 1961). Some couples have found that the application of certain mild chemicals, such as Mentholatum, to the glans of the penis or the vulval region (or even the use of the salve as a lubricant during coitus) enhances sexual pleasure, while others would find such a practice physically painful. Some desire anal stimulation or the insertion of fingers or small objects into the rectum during certain phases of the sexual response cycle. Others consider anal techniques unnecessary, repugnant, even barbaric. Whatever the sexual variation, it should be introduced spontaneously and with obvious desire by one participant, and tried willingly by the other.

Many handicapped persons learn to express themselves freely and give of themselves to their sexual partners. Those persons who have come to grips with their physical disabilities—whether the result of amputation or paralysis—often find satisfaction in being able to express their sexuality (both verbally and nonverbally) with their mates or partners. Uninhibited giving and receiving of sexual pleasure is by no means limited to physically normal individuals (Pepmiller 1980).

Successful sexual relations, no matter what the physical constitution of the man or woman may be, are *caring* relations, in which each partner is sensitive to the desires of the other. This caring, indeed, can continue well beyond the experiences of sexual arousal and release. For sex relations do not—or, rather, should not—end with orgasm (Eichenlaub 1961; Ellis 1963; Van de Velde 1957). Many couples find the interval after the sex act to be as pleasant and emotionally fulfilling as any other part of it. To hold each other in a close and lingering embrace, to discuss softly the delights of the experience they have just shared, to caress the lover's body with tender, sweeping movements of the hands, to doze and relax with intertwined bodies, all serve to aid in the emotional fulfillment. Other couples are completely overcome by the release of physical and emotional tension and are ready to drop off into a deep and restful sleep after a brief expression of love and appreciation. Lovers must give as careful attention to the partner's wishes concerning the period of resolution of sexual tensions as they do to each other's preferences in the matter of sexual foreplay.

The implications of this discussion are many. Sex is a pleasurable, significant part of marriage and other ongoing relationships. Thus both the man and woman should do everything possible to make it joyous and satisfying. Lovemaking can fulfill both psychological and physiological needs in a way that nothing else in a relationship can. The approaches are many, but one does not have a profound sexual experience without profound affection and loving feedback. Or as Comfort (1972) has said, a sexual encounter should be a completely satisfying and fulfilling link between "two affectionate people [who] emerge unanxious, rewarded, and ready for more." Sex can be a rather grim business in a relationship when it is unsatisfactory. But it can also be fun. A well-known and respected psychologist, A. H. Maslow (1954), summarized a healthy love relationship perceptively when he wrote:

> It is quite characteristic of self-actualizing people that they can enjoy themselves in love and in sex. Sex very frequently becomes a kind of game in which laughter is quite as common as panting. It is not the welfare of the species, or the task of reproduction, or the future development of mankind that attracts people to each other. The sex life of healthy people, in spite of the fact that it frequently reaches great peaks of ecstasy, is nevertheless also easily compared to the games of children and puppies. It is cheerful, humorous, and playful.

Summary

Fewer differences between the two sexes and the responses to sexual stimuli and erotica exist than most of us believe. Women have as powerful a sex drive as men and as great a need psychologically and physically to express their sexuality. Today, more women are taking active, initiatory roles in sexual relationships. As both men and women become better educated about sexual matters, they tend to share full partnership in every respect, and are more likely to achieve greater sexual fulfillment.

In order to enhance their sexual relationships, men and women are encouraged to take full advantage of their senses of sight, smell, and touch, for sensuality is multidimensional. Also to be included is communication, on both verbal and nonverbal levels; the way we communicate (in a sensual manner) can make us attractive and desirable sexual partners. People who follow a slow and gentle pace in their sexual interactions and who vary their approach in sexual settings avoid boredom. Adding novelty and a little imagination helps keep sexual relationships alive. Those men and women who use fantasies to augment their sexual arousal and are willing to experiment with one another are likely to have more vibrant and exciting relationships. As couples mature in their relationships, they can use *planned romance* to enjoy and cement their sexual interactions.

In their sexual interactions, couples enhance arousal through stimulation of the erogenous zones—those areas of the body possessing a large concentration of nerve endings. Erogenous zones include the genital areas, together with areas such as thighs, buttocks, or abdomen, and nongenital areas such as the breasts, neck, earlobes, and mouth. An especially sensitive area for the man is the glans of the penis, while for the woman it is the clitoris and its glans. Stimulation of other areas such as the urethra and the anus also leads to pleasurable sensations for many men and women.

Sexual responsiveness in both men and women is largely a learned phenomenon. One of the most important ways to learn full sexual response is through masturbation. Arguments against masturbation—that only immature people masturbate, that masturbation is antisocial, that masturbation causes fatigue or physical problems, that sexual problems associated with masturbation are unhealthy, or that masturbation is sexually frustrating and unsatisfying—are simply not true. People who learn about their own sensuality through masturbation, by exercising their tactile senses, and by learning erotic tongue movements and developing appropriate muscle control enhance their sexual relations.

When consenting adults do engage in sexual behavior, it is important that: (1) partners be willing to assume responsibility for their behavior and its consequences; (2) the partners engage in sex out of the sight and sound of unwilling observers; and (3) the partners engage in a pleasurable sexual interaction. If these three criteria are met, then couples are likely to enjoy activities such as petting or extended foreplay, breast manipulation, kissing, vibrator stimulation, cunnilingus, and fellatio. Uninhibited giving and receiving of sexual pleasure in the context of a tender, caring, sensitive, and yet cheerful relationship provide the ultimate in sexual arousal.

Annotated Bibliography

Bing, Elisabeth and Colman, Libby. *Making love during pregnancy.* New York: Bantam Books, 1977.
> This well-illustrated practical guide for expectant and new parents emphasizes sexual behavior during pregnancy. The guide also stresses education in prenatal development and changes in the woman's body during pregnancy.

McCary, James Leslie. *Freedom and growth in marriage (2nd ed.).* New York: John Wiley and Sons, 1980.

> This book for the student and general reader considers various aspects of marriage, dating and mate selection, focusing on implications for individual growth and freedom within the marriage relationship. The past and future of marriage are discussed, as well as relevant contemporary issues, alternatives to marriage, the nature of love, aspects of human sexuality, marital adjustment, and other topics.

Mooney, Thomas O., Cole, Theodore M., and Chilgren, Richard A. *Sexual options for paraplegics and quadriplegics.* Boston: Little, Brown, 1975.

> This book is a valuable guide for the spinal cord injured to sexual satisfaction. Stressing the importance of sexual expression, the book uses explicit photographs illustrating techniques in preparation for love-making, arousal, intercourse, and oral-genital and manual stimulation.

Phillips, Debora and Judd, Robert. *Sexual confidence: Discovering the joys of intimacy.* Boston: Houghton Mifflin, 1980.

> Written without technical language, this book is designed to help the adult reader unlearn myths related to love and sexuality and to overcome sexual guilt and anxiety. The book suggests strategies to enhance intimacy and sexual satisfaction in relationships, and to deal with sexual problems.

Raley, Patricia E. *Making love: How to be your own sex therapist.* New York: The Dial Press, 1976.

> This well-illustrated sexual self-help guide is intended for the adult reader of any sexual orientation who is interested in maximizing satisfaction in relationships. Systematic guidelines are provided for exploring sex history, sexual fantasy, sexual attitudes, sexual anatomy, arousal, orgasm, sexual communication, relationships with self and others, and other significant aspects of erotic life.

Aphrodisiacs and Anaphrodisiacs

10

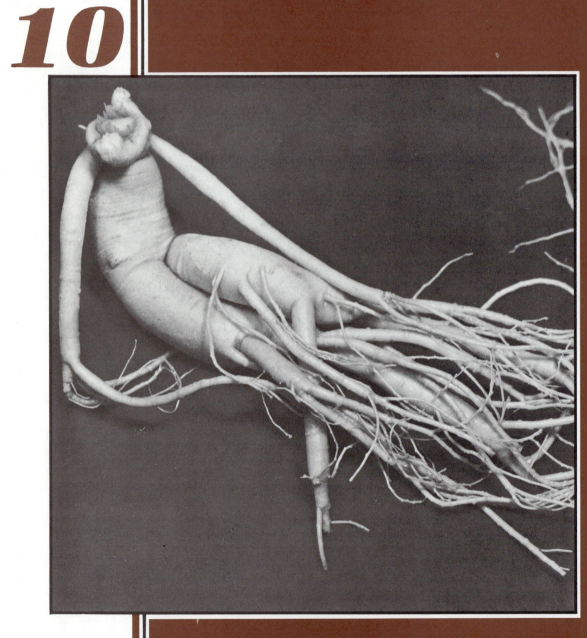

Aphrodisiacs
   Foods
   Drugs
   Hormones
Anaphrodisiacs

History is full of accounts of the efforts to control sexual appetite. Most often we have sought means of increasing sexual desire (**aphrodisiacs**). But there are also times when we seek ways to diminish it (**anaphrodisiacs**). Food, drugs, mechanical devices—the list is long and intriguing. But it is more a testament to the often desperate search for remedies than of their effectiveness.

Aphrodisiacs

Foods

High on the list of substances commonly thought to have sexually stimulating properties are certain foods. The notion that one food or another has erotic value springs from two sources: first, the rarity or newness of a food (such as the potato when it was first introduced in England); second, the "doctrine of signatures." In this second instance, sexual strength is assumed to come from eating foods resembling a sex organ—bananas and oysters, for instance, because of their superficial resemblance to the penis and testicles (MacDougald 1961).

The classic among these alleged aphrodisiacs, at least in our culture, is the oyster. But chemical analysis shows that it consists of water (75%), protein (10%), and carbohydrates (10%), plus small amounts of fat, sugar, and minerals—none of which can in any way affect sex drive or performance (Neiger 1968b). In one of the most obvious applications of the doctrine of signatures, many Chinese and Asiatic Indians place unshakable faith in the potency of powdered rhinoceros horn. (It is not hard to understand how the succinct word "horny" came to have a number of sexual connotations in the vernacular.)

That the shape of an unrelated object should endow it with aphrodisiac properties seems absurd to most of us. Why, then, do people continue to place unwarranted value on some foods as aphrodisiacs? First of all, it is often difficult to distinguish between fact and folklore. Few people are experts on the properties of various foods, fewer still on the physiology of sexual desire. The psychological impact, therefore, of *believing* that raw bull's testicles ("prairie oysters," as they are sometimes called), or clams, or celery, or tomatoes are aphrodisiacs is sometimes strong enough to produce, at least for a while, greater sexual desire and performance. The triumph, however temporary (and of the mind, at that), is attributed to a "wonder" food, and this discovery is passed on to the next person wishing to be transported to new heights of sexual experience.

In actuality, the libido of most people diminishes significantly after a meal, especially a heavy one. It has also been demonstrated that people who are overweight and who consistently overeat suffer from decreased sexual drive and ability.

The only persons for whom food can act as a true aphrodisiac, in a sense, are those whose hunger is severe and threatening. Studies made during World War II, for instance, showed that sexual drive decreased in direct proportion to the degree of hunger the individual was experiencing. As hunger became a more and more relentless companion, food became almost an obsession, crowding out sexual thoughts entirely (Frankl 1963; Keys 1952). (It has also been suggested that the reason so many Americans think of sex as the most important thing in the world is that they have never been hungry [Udry 1968].)

Drugs

The most famous of the alleged sexual stimulants is alcohol. But the truth is that alcohol, when taken in considerable quantity, is a depressant. It narcotizes the brain, thus retarding its reflexes, and dilates the blood vessels, thus interfering with the capacity for erection. Acting on the physical system, alcohol decreases sexual abilities. Further, recent research into the effects of long-term alcohol consumption shows that it drastically increases the production of a certain enzyme in the liver that destroys testosterone. In these tests, there was no compensatory increase in production of the hormone by the body (Rubin *et al.* 1976).

Despite its adverse physiological effects, however, alcohol does tend to relieve, temporarily, feelings of sexual guilt and fear, making some people less inhibited than they normally would be. A study of 20,000 well-educated, liberal men and women of high socioeconomic status revealed that almost 60% experienced greater sexual enjoyment afer drinking. Women seemed to be more affected than men, probably because they tend to be more sexually inhibited (Athanasiou *et al.* 1970). Removing inhibitions through alcohol consumption often more than counterbalances depressed physical reactions, as was shown in a survey made in Great Britain: 40% of both men and women reported that alcohol increased their sexual drive ("Alcohol and Sex" 1970).

It can generally be accepted, however, that if a person's sexual drive and ability increase after the use of alcohol, one of two forces (perhaps both) is at work: The stresses of daily living—possibly quite unrelated to sex—have acted as temporary inhibitors to sexual impulses, or some real emotional block exists in the area of sex (J. L. McCary 1971). Getting past the strains and crises of the moment or ridding oneself of emotional conflicts concerning sexuality would probably do more for sexual functioning than alcohol.

Another drug widely considered to be aphrodisiac is *cantharides* (Spanish fly), derived from the *Cantharis vesicatoria,* a beautiful beetle found in southern Europe. The insects are dried and heated until they disintegrate into a fine powder. Taken internally, the substance causes acute irritation of the genitourinary tract, specifically the mucous membrane of the urethra (MacDougald 1961). Accompanying this inflammation is a dilation of associated blood vessels, all of which produce a certain stimulation of the genitals. The drug can thus indeed produce penile erection, but usually without an increase in sexual desire. Furthermore, if taken in excessive doses, cantharides can cause violent illness or even death. The drug is not an effective sexual stimulant and is seldom used in modern medical practice.

A third drug to which aphrodisiac qualities are attributed is *yohimbine*, extracted from the bark of the yohimbé tree native to Africa. Its primary use in most nations has been as a diuretic and in the treatment of such disorders as neuritis and meningitis. But yohimbine also stimulates the lower-spine nerve centers controlling erection and has long been used by African natives for sexual arousal.

Claims are also made that certain potentially habituating drugs are aphrodisiac—hashish, opium, morphine, cocaine, marijuana, and LSD. Like alcohol, these drugs break down inhibitions, the cause of much sexual malfunctioning. But drugs taken in large enough quantities usually—like alcohol—have the effect, instead, of an anaphrodisiac.

Marijuana has gained many devotees as a sexual stimulant. In reality, however, its effect on the sex drive is at best only indirect. The drug distorts time perception and may produce the illusion that a sexual climax is somewhat prolonged. Also, it tends to make users extremely suggestible. Thus if they believe firmly that the drug is a sexual stimulant, it may well have that effect on them. As a true aphrodisiac, however, it is a failure (Churchill 1968). It appears to have neither a positive nor a negative effect on libidinal drive or performance (Mendelson 1976). But a sobering consideration comes from evidence presented by the American Medical Association that marijuana smokers have a higher incidence of impotence than nonusers (United Press International 1971a). Further, heavy use of marijuana has been shown to cause gynecomastia (femalelike breast development) in men (Harmon & Aliapoulios 1972).

Amphetamines and cocaine are drugs that act as brain center stimulants. Reports (unconfirmed) of their aphrodisiac properties have been made. But if, in fact, any increase in sensual pleasures follows their use, it most likely results from misplaced confidence in them or the loosening of excessive sexual controls rather than from their actual aphrodisiac properties. In any case, with continued use these drugs become addictive, and in time would inevitably diminish sexual capacity rather than enhance it (H. S. Kaplan 1974, 1979).

A drug that is reputed not so much to increase sex drive as to intensify orgasmic pleasure is amyl nitrite. Some people have reported that inhaling amyl nitrite at the instant of orgasm enhanced the pleasure of the experience. Apparently the drug relaxes the smooth muscles and consequently produces vasodilation of the genitourinary tract. But valid scientific data are lacking to confirm amyl nitrite as an aphrodisiac. Further, some of its side effects—dizziness, headaches, fainting—are known to be dangerous (H. S. Kaplan 1974, 1979) and have led, in rare cases, to death. Its use is clearly most ill-advised unless prescribed and directed by a physician (Louria 1970).

Certainly it seems logical to assume that the centers of the brain controlling sexual response can be influenced by various pharmacologic substances and other stimuli. To date, however, about the only effects that drugs appear to have on our sexual behavior are inhibitory rather than enhancing (H. S. Kaplan 1974, 1979). Because any drug is only one variable in the complex system of sexuality, its effect (or seeming effect) on any two people may differ vastly. Indeed, even the same person may experience quite different results from one episode to another in using the same drug in conjunction with sex. Table 10.1 lists the most common mood altering drugs together with experimental findings of their effects on the various phases of sexual response.

Table 10.1 Effects of Some Common Drugs on Human Sexual Response[a]

Drug	Medical Usage	Phase of Sexual Response Affected[b]		
		Desire	Excitement	Orgasm

Sedative-hypnotics
Alcohol
Barbiturates
Chloral
  hydrate
Methaqualone
  (Quaalude)
	For insomnia and to lower anxiety.	In low doses, may increase because of lessened inhibitions, although expectations may influence behavior. In high doses, decreased.	Prolonged with low doses due to decreased sensitivity or due to intimacy or shared feelings; impotence with high chronic alcohol and barbiturate use.	With high doses, inhibited.

Mild tranquilizers Librium Meprobamate Tranxene Valium	To reduce anxiety and muscle tension; also for convulsive states.	May be enhanced slightly due to lessened anxiety; diminished in high doses.	None reported.	With usual doses, no effect; with very high doses, orgasm delayed.
Narcotics Codeine Methadone Morphine	For relief from pain and control of diarrhea and coughing; for withdrawal from narcotics (methadone).	In high doses, absent.	With high doses, impotence.	With high dosage, inhibited.
Major tranquilizers Haldol Mellaril Stelazine Thorazine	Sedative effect for control of psychiatric disorders.	May be decreased in high doses. (Delay of ovulation and menstruation in females reported with Thorazine.)	Impotence is reported rarely; some erectile difficulties.	Inhibition of ejaculation and retrograde ejaculation reported with Mellaril.

Antidepressants
Tricyclics
  (Elavil,
  Tofranil)
MAO inhibitors
  (Marplan,
  Nardil,
  Norpramine)
	For depression.	Probably none.	None.	Very rare ejaculatory problems as side effects; some females report delay of orgasm.

Lithium carbonate	For manic states and possibly prevention of manic/depressive cycles.	Urgency and desire may be reduced.	Very rare potency problems as side effects.	

[a] Adapted from Kaplan (1979) and Sandler *et al.* (1980).
[b] Discussion of this triphasic model of sexual response is found in Chapter 20.

Hormones

Androgen is the only substance now known that can increase sexual interest, drive, and performance of both men and women. And when its administration proves effective, it does not appear to cause other behavioral changes. Androgen is a male hormone, but is produced by both sexes, and its natural secretion appears to control libidinous reaction in both. When androgen deficiency exists, especially in males, sexual interest and potency are impaired. Androgen replacement therapy in such cases will increase libido and performance. But if the sexual problem is not clearly related to androgen deficiency, the usefulness of this therapy to increase sexual desire is debatable (H. S. Kaplan 1979).

Another hormone known as the luteinizing hormone-releasing factor (LH-RF) apparently helps increase sexual desire. This hormone, a minute peptide molecule secreted within the brain, may enhance libido even when androgen therapy is ineffective. The clinical implications of this hormone have not as yet been fully realized. Thyroxine, a hormone used to correct hypothyroid states and to lift depression, also reportedly enhances desire. No mention of its effects on the excitement and orgasmic phases of sexual response has been reported (H. S. Kaplan 1979).

Erotic pictures; songs; literature; recordings of squeaking bedsprings accompanied by heavy breathing, moans, and gasps: All titillate the sexual interest and drive of some people. Marriage counselors frequently suggest pornographic films or books for couples whose sex life has become lackluster. When experience with erotic stimuli has been limited and infrequent, new sexual excitement and interest almost certainly will occur from increased exposure. But immunity to such stimulation develops rapidly if the exposure is overdone.

In sum, most claims regarding aphrodisiacs are based more on folklore than on scientific evidence. Alleged sexual stimulants are not likely to increase sex drive unless a psychological component of suggestion is present, or unless the individual is physically debilitated, in which case such treatment as hormonal therapy might be of benefit.

All in all, good health, plenty of rest and sleep, an adequate amount of exercise, and freedom from emotional tension remain the most effective aphrodisiacs (G. L. Kelly 1959; Rubin 1966b).

Anaphrodisiacs

Techniques used in an attempt to decrease sexual interest and drive have varied through the ages—from cold baths and going barefoot, as suggested by Plato and Aristotle (MacDougald 1961), to wearing chastity belts and penis cages, as suggested by the Romans and the British at one time, to the use of chemicals and tranquilizers.

The best known method for trying to decrease sexual appetite is the use of the chemical potassium nitrate, or saltpeter. Actually, this is an almost neutral chemical, except that it is a fairly effective diuretic, which perhaps accounts for its widespread but undeserved reputation as a sex deterrent. It is a failure as an anaphrodisiac.

Experimentation with the drug Ismelin (*guanethidine sulphate*), used in the treatment of high blood pressure, showed that erectile potency, ability to ejaculate, and intensity of climax were all reduced significantly by use of the drug. Side effects of stomach cramps, diarrhea, and general loss of physical energy were reported by half the subjects (Money & Yankowitz 1967).

Physicians occasionally prescribe certain tranquilizers and other drugs in an attempt to decrease sexual desire. Limited success has been reported. Some doctors shy away from their use, however, fearing that these drugs might have the same effect as alcohol: That is, removal or reduction of emotional blocks might produce results opposite to the desired ones by releasing even stronger sexual yearnings or unusual sexual behavior.

Male patients who are being treated with the female hormone estrogen for various maladies almost always experience a decrease or cessation in sexual drive and interest. By contrast, male hormones prescribed for women frequently have the opposite effect. Unfortunately, estrogen has an undesirable feminizing effect on men, while male hormones have a masculinizing effect on women (Neiger 1968b). Cyproterone acetate, an experimental drug used to treat compulsive sexual disorders, has reportedly led to a loss of libido in both genders, and in males to impotence, delay in ejaculation, and lessened volume of ejaculate. Cyproterone acetate is a hormone and works by antagonizing testosterone (H. S. Kaplan 1979).

Summary

Aphrodisiacs are foods, drugs, or devices that are used in an attempt to stimulate sexual desire. The "doctrine of signatures" assumes that sexual strength comes from eating foods resembling a sexual organ, such as bananas. Although foods such as oysters, clams, tomatoes, or even raw bull's testicles have been eaten in attempts to enhance sexual desire, any positive impact such foods have upon sexual desire is probably psychological.

The aphrodisiac qualities of drugs—including alcohol, cantharides or Spanish fly, yohimbine, hashish, opium, morphine, cocaine, marijuana,

LSD, and amyl nitrite—have been extolled by users. Again, however, the effects of such drugs in increasing sex drive are probably psychological. Typically, the physical effects of such drugs are inhibitory rather than enhancing. Sedative-hypnotic drugs, mild tranquilizers, narcotics, major tranquilizers, and antidepressants can, in high doses, have inhibitory or adverse effects on sexual response.

The hormone androgen increases interest, drive, and performance. Libido may also be enhanced by other hormones such as luteinizing hormone-releasing factor (LH-RF) and thyroxine. In general, however, good health, rest, exercise, and freedom from emotional tension remain the most effective aphrodisiacs.

Anaphrodisiacs are techniques and drugs that are used to decrease sexual interest and drive. Potassium nitrate, Ismelin, estrogen, and cyproterone acetate have been employed as anaphrodisiacs. The results of usage have been neutral (as for potassium nitrate) or of limited success, and have been compounded by the side effects of the drugs.

Annotated Bibliography

Kaplan, Helen Singer. *Disorders of sexual desire.* New York: Brunner/Mazel, 1979.

> The author uses detailed case studies drawn from her own experience as a clinician to demonstrate treatment of various sexual dysfunctions, especially problems of desire. Included in the Appendix are valuable tables covering the effects of drugs and physical illness on sexuality and the physical causes of dyspareunia. This is an excellent volume for the clinician.

McCary, James Leslie. *Freedom and growth in marriage (2nd ed.).* New York: John Wiley and Sons, 1980.

> This book for the student and general reader considers various aspects of marriage, dating and mate selection, focusing on implications for individual growth and freedom within the marriage relationship. The past and future of marriage are discussed, as well as relevant contemporary issues, alternatives to marriage, the nature of love, aspects of human sexuality, marital adjustment, and other topics.

Money, John. *Love and love sickness: The science of sex, gender difference, and pair-bonding.* Baltimore: Johns Hopkins University Press, 1980.

> This scholarly book encompasses a wide array of topics in human sexuality. Some general areas include the historical and cultural aspects of sexual behavior, factors influencing sexual orientation and pair-bonding, erotic sexuality, sexual taboos, and pornography. The author advances a new theory to guide understanding of sex differences based on the variety of factors influencing gender identity and sex role. This book would appeal to the student, medical and allied health professional, and general academic reader.

Sandler, Jack, Myerson, Marilyn, and Kinder, Bill N. *Human sexuality: Current perspectives.* Tampa, Florida: Mariner, 1980.

> This text presents a comprehensive perspective of the field of human sexuality. A wide range of topics is covered, including sexual anatomy and sexual response, aphrodisiacs and anaphrodisiacs, past and current sexual attitudes and behavior, sexual diseases and disorders, sexual dysfunctions, birth control, sexual health, and sex and the law. Though designed for the student, this book would serve as a valuable general reference.

Witters, Weldon and Jones-Witters, Patricia. *Human sexuality: A biological perspective.* New York: D. Van Nostrand, 1980.

> This text approaches the various aspects of human sexuality from the biological standpoint. Topics of special interest include genetic engineering, hormonal control of sexuality, drugs affecting sexual function, surrogate parenthood, artificial insemination, cloning, and sex selection. The text is well illustrated and contains student performance objectives, but its appeal extends beyond the classroom.

Positions in Sexual Intercourse

11

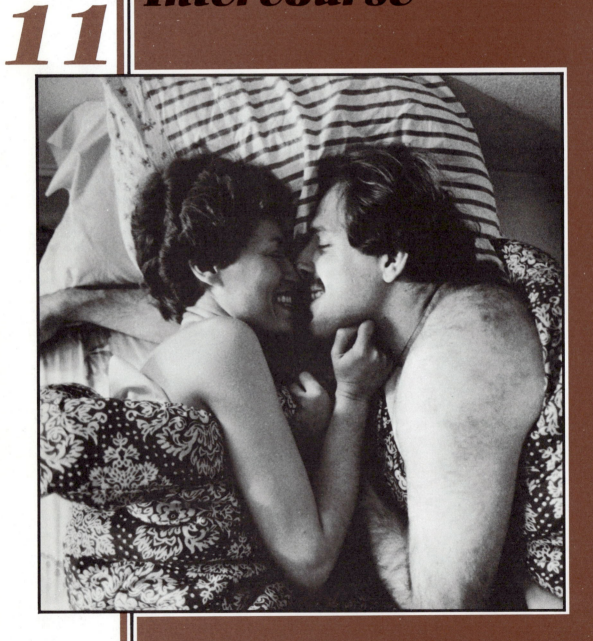

Face-to-Face, Man-Above Position

Face-to-Face, Woman-Above Position

Face-to-Face Side Position

Rear-Entry Position

Coital variation is almost limitless. It has been estimated that there are as many as 14,288,400 positions for cunniligus alone (Legman 1971)! No single coital position is more "normal" or "acceptable" than another. There are many positions, variations of them, and variations of the variations. All are at least of academic interest; many are challenging; and some simply cannot be achieved unless the partners are uniquely acrobatic.

This discussion will not focus on the number of possible coital positions. Rather, we shall aim at a broader understanding of the *reasons* for experimentation and the benefits to be derived from it. The four most basic positions will be described, and the advantages and disadvantages of each. With a little imagination and a healthy attitude toward sex and experimentation, the individual should be able to work out his or her own adaptations—and that is the way it should be.

Unlike lower animals, human beings must be taught, one way or another, how to conduct the act of sexual intercourse. Extensive research into sexual behavior has disproved the popular notion that the art of love comes naturally (Harlow & Harlow 1965). Even the elementary facts of coitus must be learned.

The sexual act involves two persons (usually) whose needs are equally important and require consideration. A couple's immediate happiness together and their future harmonious adjustment are often directly correlated to their skill in pleasurable coital techniques. Most of the "shoulds" and "should-nots" of sexual behavior are contingent on the mutual pleasure, comfort, and satisfaction of the two people involved—and upon those alone (Ellis 1958; J. L. McCary 1966). Experimentation and variation in coital positions therefore assume major importance as part of the effort to achieve fulfillment for each partner. Any and all positions of sexual intercourse that both partners find pleasurable should be freely enjoyed by them (Greenhill 1971).

The benefits of sexual experimentation are practical as well as emotional and intellectual. Variety in coital positions makes sexual activity more interesting and can prevent its becoming humdrum (Greenblat 1962). Equally important, some positions are more pleasurable to one partner than to the other, and it is vital that the preferences of each be learned. Masters and Johnson (1966) have found that the most intense and pleasurable sexual responses of both men and women occur when there is freedom from muscular tension and cramping during the coital act. Some sexual positions provide this freedom to a much greater degree than others.

In addition, the desirability of certain positions may alter from time to time, depending upon such conditions as health, weight, and pregnancy (J. L. McCary 1966; *Williams Obstetrics* 1961). Furthermore, some coital attitudes are more conducive to conception than others. Positions also vary according to whether coition is spontaneous or anticipated, whether it takes place in cramped or adequate space, and whether it occurs in absolute privacy or with some danger of discovery. The experience and the genital characteristics of each partner are also important determinants in choosing a position. In fact, there are about as many reasons for varying coital activity as there are coital positions.

Most couples do their sexual experimentation during the earlier years of their relationships, then settle on the one or two positions that best suit them (Eichenlaub 1961). If one partner has particular difficulty in becoming aroused or in reaching orgasm, experimenting with new positions is usually helpful. Often the position most enjoyed by a couple can be more easily assumed by their first taking a quite different one and then shifting or rolling into the desired one (Ellis 1960). For example, intromission can first be made in a face-to-face position; after penetration has taken place, the couple can then shift to a side-by-side position before orgasm is reached.

The sexual position of man atop woman is by far the most common one in European and American cultures. That this position is more popular in Western cultures can in part be traced back to the Christian teachings of St. Augustine. It was St. Augustine and some of the other early Christian leaders who taught that the man-atop-woman position was the only acceptable position for sexual intercourse (Bullough 1980). In other cultures, however, alternative sexual positions have been used and enjoyed through the centuries. As a matter of fact, "man above" was given the name "the missionary position" by amused Polynesians, who preferred to have intercourse while squatting (Comfort 1972). And the Kinsey group discovered drawings dating back as early as 3200 B.C. that most commonly depict the woman-atop position.

Face-to-Face, Man-Above Position

As stated, the face-to-face, man-above position (Fig. 11.1) is probably the most common one in our society. Most women express a preference for it, and until recently about 70% of American males had never experienced coitus in any other manner (DeMartino 1966; Kinsey *et al.* 1948). Indeed, laws exist in some states making it illegal and punishable for married couples to try sexual positions other than "normal" ones (Zehv 1969).

Ordinarily, vaginal-penile contact is quite easily achieved when the woman reclines on her back with legs apart and knees bent. She can shift her pelvis or perhaps place a small pillow under her buttocks to help adjust the slant of the vagina for easy and deep penetration. In this, as in all coital positions and positioning, it is usually advantageous for the woman to use her hands to guide the penis into the vagina. She is the best judge of the exact location of the vaginal opening and the angle of the vaginal canal. Her role in guiding the penis is important not only for ease of penetration, but also because of the psychological value of her indicating by this action a full and zestful participation in the sexual act (O'Conner 1969).

It is sometimes desirable for the woman to close her legs after entry, thus constricting the vaginal opening and walls, in order to provide more

Figure 11.1 Face-to-face coital position, man above.

friction against her partner's penis. This pressure against the base of the penis at full penetration helps him maintain erection.

The man partially supports himself on his elbows and knees to avoid putting his full weight on his partner. He is largely in control of the bodily rhythms, as his weight and size limit her to circular, up and down, and rocking pelvic movements. The man should try to keep contact with the clitoris by putting pressure on the upper part of his partner's vulva. Pressure on her pubic bone is helpful in that it sandwiches the clitoris between it and the point of the man's contact, which is usually at his pubic bone (Fig. 11.2). There are numerous variations on the man-astride position, such as the woman's pulling her knees to her shoulders, or locking her legs around her partner's body.

Figure 11.2   Representation of the erect penis inserted into the vagina.

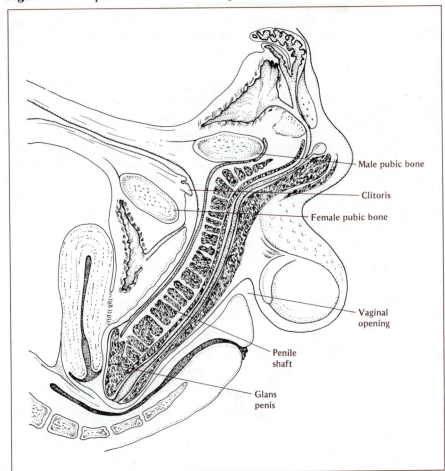

Advantages of the face-to-face, man-above position are many. In this posture, the woman is usually relaxed, and the man has the primary initiative; in our culture, this male-superior position appears to carry certain psychological advantages. Entry is simple, and any adaptations that bring pleasure to the couple can be made easily. It is convenient for couples who enjoy the man's pelvic thrust. In addition, the man can often maintain penetration after he has had an orgasm, and the position facilitates caressing, kissing, and affectionate intimacy between the two. It is an excellent position for impregnation, as the woman can keep her knees raised after the ejaculation (Ellis 1960; Greenblat 1962). Chances of impregnation are improved if she will maintain this position for about 20 minutes after ejaculation, allowing time for the sperm, retained deep in the vagina, to pass through the cervix into the uterus (Langmyhr 1976).

The disadvantages of the face-to-face, man-above position are the obverse of its advantages. The woman's movements and active participation may be too restricted. Penetration may be too deep for her comfort. It may also be uncomfortable for a woman with an obese or awkward partner, and it may be too acrobatic for older or stouter couples. The man-atop position increases muscle tension in the man since he is supporting his body weight, thus hastening his orgasm. Some men have difficulty in maintaining contact with their partner's clitoris in this position and find manual stimulation of it difficult. Since the man is raised on his hands and knees, however, the woman can stimulate her clitoris.

Male atop is considered the most sexually stimulating of all positions for a man, often making it difficult for him to control his orgasm. It is therefore usually not favored by sex therapists in the course of sex-dysfunction treatment.

Face-to-Face, Woman-Above Position

The woman-atop position (Fig. 11.3) is often assumed to give the woman a chance to depart from a "passive" position. She can govern contact with her clitoris and control the tempo of movement and depth of penetration. The position can also be modified so that the man rests on his elbows and draws up his knees for the woman to lean back on. Or if he lies on his back, his arms and hands are free to clasp and caress her. To accomplish intromission, the woman lowers her body, usually in a sitting position with knees bent, over her supine partner and guides his penis into her vagina. Couples may find it more pleasurable to achieve penetration in some other position, and then to turn or roll over gently, so that the penis does not slip from the vagina or orgasm occur in the process.

Figure 11.3   Face-to-face coital position, woman above.

The Dutch physician Van de Velde (1957) has declared that coitus with the woman astride "affords the summit in excitement and response, the acme of specific physical sexual pleasure, to both man and woman." Interestingly, in the 1930s and 40s, only 30% of married couples had tried this position. By 1975, however, 75% had at least occasionally experimented with it (Barbach 1976).

The advantages of the face-to-face, woman-above position are numerous and also vary with the individual (Witkin 1980). A woman possesses maximum control and freedom to express herself sexually. The position permits fullest penetration, yet she can avoid any discomfort or pain to herself because she regulates the depth of penile entry. Clitoral contact is easier in many cases, and the friction of erotic stimulation more intense. Furthermore, the woman does not have to contend with the man's weight. Consequently, she can control such pleasurable movements as pelvic thrusts, which both she and her partner may find most exciting. A man may be able to delay orgasm more successfully because little physical exertion or strain is imposed on him in this position. These facts may be of significance to him if his partner is slow to reach climax, or if he tends to ejaculate prematurely or is in poor health.

Sex therapists frequently have a couple use one of the variations of the face-to-face position—the woman in a squatting position above the man—in their training sessions to overcome sexual inadequacies (see p. 509*ff*). Their reason is that this position allows the man complete relaxation in coital activity and permits the woman to control the timing and movements, as required in certain phases of the treatment.

There are many further advantages. The man's hands are free to caress his partner's breasts or any other part of her body. The woman can rest full-length upon the man; this complete bodily contact often affords pleasure and excitement to both partners. The position is therefore especially useful when the woman is much smaller than the man. It also allows conversation and observation of facial expressions. Furthermore, a man frequently welcomes this position because the burden of coital movement is primarily the woman's, thereby permitting him to relax and abandon himself to the pleasures of erotic fantasy.

There are disadvantages, however. The man's freedom of movement and pelvic thrust may be too restricted for his tastes. Since he is not controlling the coital movements, his penis may persistently slip out of the vagina. The woman may find that penetration is too deep in this position, causing her pain. It is not a good position for impregnation, as the sperm are likely to seep out of the vagina after ejaculation. Neither is it a comfortable position during pregnancy (Eichenlaub 1961; Ellis 1960; Greenblat 1962; Van de Velde 1957; Vatsyayana 1962).

Many women do not enjoy such vigorous sexual participation. They may feel uncomfortable in such an "aggressive" role. Some men are of the persuasion that their masculinity is threatened if they assume a lower or "passive" position. These objections are obviously flawed outgrowths of sex-role ambiguity; any position is right as long as it brings pleasure to both partners.

Face-to-Face Side Position

Coitus can often be achieved more restfully when the partners are lying on their sides facing one another (Fig. 11.4). Both have complete freedom to maneuver arms, hands, and legs. Either can withdraw or otherwise control

Figure 11.4 Side coital position, face-to-face.

the movements of intercourse. The side position has many variations. Often the man may lie largely on his back with the woman resting on him (Hirsch 1951). The woman raises her upper leg and crosses it over the man in order to permit entry. Sometimes the couple begin in another position, then roll onto their sides. They are under little physical strain since neither is supporting the weight of the other. They can often go to sleep with contact maintained after coitus has ended (Eichenlaub 1961; Greenblat 1962; Vatsyayana 1962).

In addition to its relatively comfortable and restful nature, the side-by-side position carries further advantages. Its interlocking attitude allows maximum contact between the man's body and the woman's clitoris. The man can cradle his partner between his legs and hold her in close and continued contact. This position is especially helpful when conditions of fatigue, ill health, or obesity exist, or if one partner is considerably taller than the other. It is often a satisfactory position for coitus during the last months of pregnancy. Both partners—especially the man—can regulate pelvic thrusts and prolong sexual activity before orgasm. Penile withdrawal and reinsertion are possible without very much change of position or adjustment, and a steady coital rhythm can easily be sustained (Ellis 1960; Rosen 1980).

An important variation of the face-to-face side position is what has been described by Masters and Johnson as the *lateral coital position* (see Fig. 17.6). They have found that this position is reported to be "the most effective coital position available to man and woman, presuming there is an established marital-unit interest in mutual effectiveness of sexual performance" (Masters & Johnson 1970). It provides, in their opinion, the greatest flexibility for free sexual expression by both sexes because neither partner is pinned down. Its mutual freedom permits easy pelvic movement in any direction. The muscle cramping and tiring common to other positions are avoided because the partners do not have to support each other's or their own body weight. The position is especially effective for a woman, since she is free to engage in slow or rapid pelvic thrusting, according to the level of her sexual tensions. It is also the position in which a man can best develop and maintain ejaculatory control. Masters and Johnson maintain that couples choose this position 75% of the time once they have tried it.

The primary disadvantages of the side position are that, for some people, it is uncomfortable, it is difficult to effect entry, and it is not easy to provide sufficient stimulation to the vulval area. Other couples, preferring more vigorous coition, find the position inadequately stimulating, since it offers little possibility for deep pelvic thrusts and penetration. Movements may be difficult in the interlocking position because of restrictions placed on certain parts of the body.

Rear-Entry Position

The most usual variation of the rear-entry position is called "spoons." Both partners lie on their sides with the woman's back against the man's chest (Heiman *et al.* 1976). Or the woman can kneel, or lie on her stomach, as her partner enters her (Fig. 11.5). Also, the man can sit (on bed or chair) while the woman sits on his lap with her back to him. There are numerous other variations (Eichenlaub 1961; Ellis 1960; Vatsyayana 1962).

Entry from the rear when both partners are on their sides exacts less exertion from the woman and places less pressure on her than other coital attitudes. For this reason it is a position often recommended for coition in the advanced months of pregnancy. Rear entry is also restful for a man, as he can be more relaxed than when he is astride a woman. This posture shortens a woman's vagina, which may be advantageous since less of the penile shaft is required to effect deep penetration.

Because the woman's buttocks are in the way, not much of the penis can be introduced into the vagina in this position, but whatever the degree of penetration, it can be easily regulated by the man. Often the man finds the pressure of his partner's buttocks against his body quite exciting. Furthermore, his hands are left free to encircle her body and caress her

Figure 11.5   Rear-entry coital position.

breasts, clitoris, legs, etc. (Ellis 1960). Some women find the position painful, however, because penetration is deep in the foreshortened vagina. Others object to it because it seems unnatural and animalistic to them.

Side-by-side rear entry is particularly relaxing to a couple when either or both are tired, debilitated, old, or convalescent, although the entry is not always easy to make or maintain. Contact is usually lost after the man's orgasm. The position, furthermore, offers little assistance toward conception. For very stout persons, or for a man with a small penis, the side-rear position presents special difficulties (Eichenlaub 1961).

The knee-chest attitude is a more active form of rear-entry coitus. Both partners assume a kneeling position. The woman can rest her arms and head on pillow or bed, and her partner presses his body against her buttocks to effect entry. Sexual activity is usually quite vigorous in this position, especially for the man. This position is favorable to conception, because the semen remains in the vagina for a longer time and closer to the opening of the uterus than in other coital positions (Eichenlaub 1961; Greenblat 1962).

Although the rear-kneeling position is psychologically and physiologically exciting for some persons, it is objectionable to others, and for the same reasons—its novel and vigorous nature. One or both partners may object to rear entry because it lacks face-to-face intimacy, or because the nature of its approach becomes associated in their minds with anal intercourse, carrying with it (as it does for some people) repugnant overtones.

Another rear-entry coital posture is one in which the woman lies on her stomach and her partner attempts penetration while lying on top of her. It is awkward and not sufficiently pleasurable to be used by many couples (Ellis 1960).

For rear-entry sitting coition the man seats himself on the edge of a bed or chair and his partner sits down on his penis with her back to him. This variation of the face-to-face sitting position is greatly enjoyed by many couples because of the closeness of contact and freedom of movement it allows them both (Ellis 1960).

Sitting positions offer special coital variety and enjoyment to some couples. However, the deep penetration often resulting from them can prove uncomfortable or even harmful to the woman, so care should be used.

Again, variations on the four principal coital positions are infinite—sitting face-to-face; man standing between the legs of a woman whose torso is on a bed; or both standing (Fig. 11.6). But a detailed discussion of these will not serve present purposes, except to point out that the standing position does not prevent conception, as some couples mistakenly think. Some positions may be more favorable to conception than others, to be

Figure 11.6 Variations of the basic coital positions.

sure. But the movement of sperm toward and into the uterus after ejaculation cannot be stopped merely by having coitus in a standing (or any other) position. A related myth holds that if a woman urinates immediately after coitus she will not become pregnant. As with the standing position, semen may tend to flow from the vagina during urination, but some sperm can still easily make the upward journey to the uterus. And, of course, urine does not pass through the vagina, hence cannot wash out the sperm deposited there. This confusion perhaps arises because the urethra in the male's penis serves as the passageway for both semen and urine.

Emotionally secure, sexually uninhibited persons are capable of experimenting with the entire spectrum of human sexual expression, including coital positions. They should be governed only by their particular tastes, their imagination and dexterity, and the occasion at hand. These couples are much more likely to enjoy their sex life than those who are sexually hobbled (Zehv 1969).

A couple should take care, however, to avoid exaggerated concern for the "how" of sexual intercourse while they are engaging in it, or coitus may become artificial or mechanical. Coitus is not a gymnastic feat, an endurance contest, or an event for constant experimentation. It is, rather, a mutual act involving a wide range of techniques and postures. Whatever techniques of love play, sexual intercourse, and postcoital caressing found by a couple to bring mutual pleasure should be freely enjoyed by them.

Summary

Although many people believe that the art of loving comes naturally, research indicates that human beings must be taught how to engage in the act of sexual intercourse. Beyond the necessity of learning the elementary facts of coitus, however, there are benefits to be gained from having a knowledge of the variety of coital positions. Conditions such as health, weight, and pregnancy can influence which sexual positions are most comfortable and most pleasurable.

The face-to-face man-above position is the most common one used by couples in our society. Some advantages of this position are that in this position the woman is usually relaxed; the man has the primary initiative; entry is simple; kissing, caressing, and intimacy is facilitated; and it is a good position for impregnation. Some disadvantages are that the woman's movements may be too restricted; penetration may be too deep for the woman's comfort; the position is often uncomfortable for women in very late pregnancy; and the position may be too stimulating for a man, making it difficult for him to control his orgasm.

The face-to-face woman-above position has the advantage that the woman possesses maximum control and freedom to express herself sexually; the woman can regulate the depth of penile penetration; clitoral contact is easier to maintain; the woman does not have to contend with the man's weight; and the man can relax and control his orgasm more successfully. Some disadvantages of the position are that the man's freedom of movement may be too restricted; the man's penis may slip out of his partner's vagina; the position is not good for impregnation; the position can be uncomfortable during pregnancy; and some men and women may feel uncomfortable in exchanging "aggressive" and "passive" roles.

The face-to-face side position is advantageous in that it is a relatively comfortable and restful position; maximum contact can be maintained between the man's body and the woman's clitoris; it is a helpful position when conditions of fatigue, ill health, or obesity exist; it is a good position during the last month of pregnancy; and sexual activity can be prolonged in the position so as to delay orgasm. The lateral coital position is an important variation of the face-to-face side position. Some disadvantages of the side position are that it is difficult to effect entry in this position; stimulation is often inadequate in this position; and movements may be restrictive or difficult.

Variations of the rear-entry position include entry from the rear when both partners are on their sides, entry from the rear with knee-chest attitude, entry from the rear with the man lying on top of the woman, and rear-entry sitting coition. Some advantages of the rear-entry positions are that some couples find the positions relaxing as well as exciting; some of the positions can be used in the advanced months of pregnancy; and the man can freely touch and caress the woman's breasts, clitoris, or legs. Some disadvantages are that some couples find the position "unnatural" and "animalistic"; penetration can often be awkward or uncomfortable; and the positions do not allow for face-to-face intimacy.

Other variations of these four principal coital positions are possible. Couples who desire free and spontaneous relations can use their sexual knowledge and imagination to try a variety of positions to enhance their sexual lives.

Annotated Bibliography

Bing, Elisabeth and Colman, Libby. *Making love during pregnancy*. New York: Bantam Books, 1977.
> This well-illustrated practical guide for expectant and new parents emphasizes sexual behavior during pregnancy. The guide also stresses education in prenatal development and changes in the woman's body during pregnancy.

McCary, James Leslie. *Freedom and growth in marriage (2nd ed.).* New York: John Wiley and Sons, 1980.

> This book for the student and general reader considers various aspects of marriage, dating and mate selection, focusing on implications for individual growth and freedom within the marriage relationship. The past and future of marriage are discussed, as well as relevant contemporary issues, alternatives to marriage, the nature of love, aspects of human sexuality, marital adjustment, and other topics.

Mooney, Thomas O., Cole, Theodore M., and Chilgren, Richard A. *Sexual options for paraplegics and quadriplegics.* Boston: Little, Brown, 1975.

> This book is a valuable guide for the spinal cord injured to sexual satisfaction. Stressing the importance of sexual expression, the book uses explicit photographs illustrating techniques in preparation for love-making, arousal, intercourse, and oral-genital and manual stimulation.

Raley, Patricia E. *Making love: How to be your own sex therapist.* New York: The Dial Press, 1976.

> This well-illustrated sexual self-help guide is intended for the adult reader of any sexual orientation who is interested in maximizing satisfaction in relationships. Systematic guidelines are provided for exploring sex history, sexual fantasy, sexual attitudes, sexual anatomy, arousal, orgasm, sexual communication, relationships with self and others, and other significant aspects of erotic life.

Witters, Weldon and Jones-Witters, Patricia. *Human sexuality: A biological perspective.* New York: D. Van Nostrand, 1980.

> This text approaches the various aspects of human sexuality from the biological standpoint. Topics of special interest include genetic engineering, hormonal control of sexuality, drugs affecting sexual function, surrogate parenthood, artificial insemination, cloning, and sex selection. The text is well illustrated and contains student performance objectives, but its appeal extends beyond the classroom.

Orgasm

We have emphasized that the methods and techniques of sexual activity of individual people are many and that they produce varying degrees of pleasure. A method or technique is the "right" one only insofar as it is satisfactory and serves its purpose. What is "right" for one person may not be "right" for another. But no matter what techniques are employed or how intense the enjoyment is, the frequent (although certainly not the sole) goal in sexual activity is orgasm.

An **orgasm** is a highly pleasurable, tension-relieving, seizurelike response that is the summit of physical and emotional gratification in sexual activity. Comments made by the women surveyed in *The Hite Report* (1976), discussed more fully later, are broadly descriptive of the subjective sensations of orgasm:

> There are a few faint sparks, coming up to orgasm, and then I suddenly realize that it is going to catch fire, and then I concentrate all my energies, both physical and mental, to quickly bring on the climax—which turns out to be a moment suspended in time, a hot rush—a sudden breath-taking dousing of all the nerves of my body in Pleasure—I try to make the moment last— disappointment when it doesn't.

253

It starts down deep, somewhere in the "core," gets bigger, stronger, better, and more beautiful, until I'm just four square inches of ecstatic crotch area!!

There is an almost frantic itch–pain–pleasure in my vagina and clitoral area that seems almost insatiable, it is also extremely hot and I lose control of everything, then there is an explosion of unbelievable warmth and relief to the itch–pain–pleasure!

The charm of an orgasm is that, when it's there, all your concentration is on it, until a feeling of intense relief encompasses your whole body and mind—then when it's over, it's impossible to describe it accurately or catch any remnant of the feeling. So you go at it again and it seems all fresh and new again, but then the moment it's over it's as elusive as ever: pure amnesia seems to set in the minute you try to explain it.

Just before orgasm, my clitoris is burning and tingling and vibrating until there is a sudden orgasmic gush of heat and burning into the vagina also, that is followed all too suddenly by my contractions, the clapping of the walls together.

It feels like a balloon in the abdomen filling up and then exploding.

Although these descriptions were written by women, the best available evidence strongly indicates that orgasmic sensations are essentially the same for both sexes. The conclusions of the two best-known and most influential sex-research teams—the Kinsey group (1953) and Masters and Johnson (1966)—have emphasized the similarities, not the differences, between male and female human sexual behavior and response. Both research groups found that, of the few existing dissimilarities between male and female orgasm, the most significant is ejaculation, which accompanies male orgasm. To determine just how much alike (or unalike) male and female climaxes are, written descriptions by men and women of orgasms as they have personally experienced them were submitted to obstetricians, gynecologists, clinical psychologists, and medical students. None of these groups as a whole was successful in identifying the authors as male or female. Further, a female judge was no more successful in identifying a woman author than a male judge was (and conversely) (Proctor *et al.* 1974). These findings have been replicated by Vance and Wagner (1976).

What Is Orgasm?

The neurological and physiological structures and functions that give rise to sexual climax have been discussed in Chapters 4 and 5. Now we examine the particular physical changes involved in orgasm. Orgasmic response is marked by a rise in blood pressure and pulse rate, faster and deeper breathing, engorgement of special tissues with blood, and, finally, the explosive release of muscular and nervous tension. This release is followed by a rather quick return or *involution* of the body to its normal, nonstimulated state. The subjective sensation of orgasm is centered in the pelvic region: in the penis, prostate, and seminal vesicles of men; and in the clitoris, vagina, and uterus of women (DSM III 1980; Masters & Johnson 1966).

Orgasm is a highly individual, short-lived experience, lasting usually about 3 to 10 seconds, and has an intensity that many find difficult to understand. However, if another body need—for example, hunger—were to be satisfied in an equally short period of time, perhaps a similar intensity of reaction would be experienced.

Kinsey *et al.* (1953) found that only 70% of women achieved orgasm during their first year of marriage. However, 95% of the Kinsey female sample had reached orgasm at some later point in their lifetime. Today, many more women are sexually active and orgasmic before they marry, or become so in the early years of marriage. With each passing year of marriage, however, they become less orgasmic. The reason is almost always psychological and should be handled accordingly. It is nonetheless unfortunate that orgasm is usually singled out as the most important criterion of sexual satisfaction, and both partners tend to feel inadequate if the woman fails to achieve orgasm (Gebhard 1966). For women, especially, emotional intimacy, tenderness, closeness, and sharing of deep feelings with a loved one are infinitely more fulfilling than orgasms per se (Hite 1976).

Most specialists in human sexuality recognize that orgasm for *both* sexes is a total body response, although men apparently have a tendency to be more "genitally focused" than women (Brotman 1980; de Moya & de Moya 1973). Since some men and women achieve climax from fantasy alone, it appears unreasonable to categorize orgasms as being specifically related to penile, vaginal, clitoral, or other bodily regions. That which produces the strongest, most satisfying, and most soothing orgasm in one person may not be particularly satisfying to another. It simply cannot be said that all orgasms are basically the same (Butler 1976).

Achieving Orgasm

Because of the many nerve endings in the region of the clitoris and vulva, many women find that masturbation and other forms of direct stimulation, rather than coitus, bring them more orgasms, in faster succession, and with a more intense physical response. This point has been supported by research and by laboratory observation of women engaging in various sexual acts (Masters & Johnson 1966; Wilcox & Hager 1980). Coital orgasms, however, are considered more emotionally satisfying and vaginally soothing by some women (Hite 1976). Recent research indicates that stimulation of the anterior wall of the vagina may lead to highly pleasurable sensations or even orgasm for many women (Hoch 1980). Most men consistently report that they find it easier and more satisfying to achieve orgasm through coitus than through other methods.

A man usually achieves orgasm within about 4 minutes of intromission. A woman may require from 10 to 20 minutes of intercourse before she climaxes. With manual, electric vibrator, or oral-genital stimulation, a woman can usually reach orgasm in less than 4 minutes (Kinsey *et al.* 1953).

Kinds of Orgasm

After publication of their data and clinical findings, the Kinsey researchers found themselves criticized for their "fantastic tale" of multiple orgasms in women (Pomeroy 1966a). It has now been established that women are capable by natural endowment of multi-orgasm. Many, in fact, are able to have six or more orgasms during a single period of sexual activity (Masters & Johnson 1967). Kinsey and his co-workers (1953) reported that 14% of women regularly have multiple orgasms; and Masters and Johnson (1966) showed that, if the sexual stimulation producing a woman's first orgasm is continued, a second and a third orgasm—perhaps more—will follow. Furthermore, the women in the Masters and Johnson sampling reported that, subjectively, they found the second and third orgasmic responses to be more intense and more pleasurable than the first. Some women experience *status orgasmus,* which is sustained orgasmic response lasting at least 20 seconds and perhaps as long as a full minute. The physiological mechanism involved is not known, but the response is not believed to be the same as multiple orgasm (Jobaris & Money 1976).

Men are not nearly so capable as women of multiple orgasms. Only about 6% to 8% of men are able to have more than one orgasm during each sexual experience. And when the capacity exists, it is usually found only in very young men. Kinsey and his co-workers (1948) reported that the highest frequency of orgasms found in their study of men was 26 in a 24-hour period—the experience of a 13-year old boy. One adult male in their sample reported averaging 33 orgasms per week for over 30 years. Those men who have a second orgasm shortly after the first relate that the pleasure of the first is superior to that of the second, in direct contrast to women's subjective reports (Masters & Johnson 1966). Scientific interest in the male multiple orgasm has increased of late, with both behavioral scientists and physiologists turning to the laboratory for investigation. The capacity of a man to achieve multiple orgasms has been attributed primarily to expectations, learning, and "breaking old habits" (Tauris 1976).

Despite women's capacity for orgasm, the unfortunate fact remains that they do not, as has been pointed out earlier, reach orgasm as easily as men. In fact, failure to reach orgasm during coitus, despite full responsiveness to other forms of sexual stimulation, is the most common complaint of women seeking help from sex therapists (H. S. Kaplan 1974). Psychological blocks appear largely responsible for the difficulty.

The quality of an orgasm—that is, the intensity, length, and overall pleasure—may vary from one sex act to another. Recency and frequency of occurrence can influence the quality of the next sexual experience, as can such factors as anxiety, guilt, depression, anger, indifference toward one's partner, and distaste for one's surroundings. Not only can these factors affect the quality of the orgasm, but they can also, if strong enough, block the response altogether. Women report a greater variability in the subjective quality of their orgasms than do men (Marmor *et al.* 1971). Some women pass out at the time of orgasm (French poets of a certain era referred to the experience as *le petit mort*—"the little death"), and on rare occasions men do too. The experience is not unpleasant, but it could be a frightening one for a partner unacquainted with the phenomenon (Comfort 1972).

A few men experience orgasm without ejaculation, but that is a rare and special occurrence. Some men have retrograde ejaculations, which means that the semen is discharged into the bladder rather than through the penis (Fig. 12.1). Since external evidence is lacking, it appears that the

Figure 12.1 Schematic representation of normal ejaculation and retrograde ejaculation.

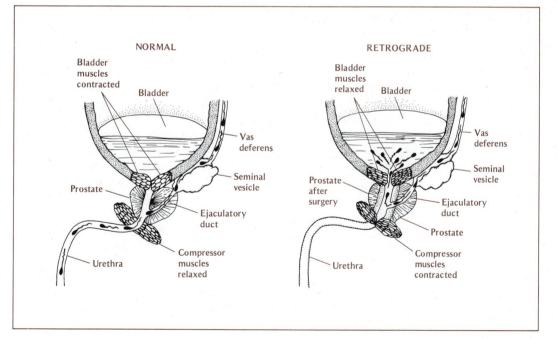

NORMAL

Bladder muscles contracted

Bladder

Vas deferens

Prostate

Seminal vesicle

Ejaculatory duct

Urethra

Compressor muscles relaxed

RETROGRADE

Bladder muscles relaxed

Bladder

Vas deferens

Prostate after surgery

Seminal vesicle

Ejaculatory duct

Prostate

Urethra

Compressor muscles contracted

man does not ejaculate, although in reality he does. "Dry orgasm" is another term applied to the absence of seminal discharge from the penis at the time of orgasm (Fellman 1975). This condition is caused by some abnormality at the junction of the ejaculatory ducts and urethra within the prostate. The condition can result from prostatic surgery, an accident, or some caprice of nature. About 80% of men who have undergone prostate surgery will experience retrograde ejaculation, although the sensation of orgasm remains quite normal (Hotchkiss 1971).

Sometimes drugs, especially tranquilizers ("From the Editor's Scrapbook" 1964; H. S. Kaplan 1979), may inhibit the ejaculatory centers, yet not affect the neural network involved in orgasm (see Table 10.1). In other instances, diabetes will inhibit ejaculation at the time of orgasm.

Ejaculatory anhedonia, which seldom appears in books on behavioral science, is the term given to ejaculation unaccompanied by orgasm. It can occur in physically normal men, in whom "the mechanics of sexual function are intact but ejaculation brings no pleasure" (Dormont 1975). When men experience climax but with little pleasure or sensation, the basis is rarely physiological, although such organic pathology as neuropathy or diabetes can cause it, as can certain drugs. Such diminished orgasmic pleasure is usually psychological in origin and reflects dissatisfaction with the sexual relationship, or emotional barriers such as fear, anxiety, aggression, hostility, fatigue, or boredom. Appropriate physical or psychological treatment can be of considerable aid in alleviating the difficulty (Lear 1972).

Incidence

The ease or difficulty with which various women achieve orgasm has been arranged along a continuum by Kaplan (1974). At one extreme is that handful of women—1% to 2% (J. L. McCary 1974)—who can reach orgasm with erotic fantasy alone. Then come those who reach orgasm by fantasy slightly augmented by a rhythmical pressing together of thighs to produce clitoral stimulation. Next there are women who become orgasmic in response to passionate kissing and the fondling of their breasts, but without genital touching. Following are those who, after sufficient arousal from foreplay, can reach a climax after only a few coital thrusts. At about the middle of the continuum are women who are orgasmic in the male-superior position after longer periods of coital thrusting; next, those who need the increased clitoral stimulation provided by the female-superior position; next, those who require their partner to supply additional, manual stimulation during coitus. Following are women who may even be capable of multiple orgasms, but who require direct clitoral stimulation orally or manually to achieve them. A large number of women fit into this category. Next on the continuum are women who (1) require lengthy, intense stimulation of the clitoris to reach a climax; (2) must fantasize along with this intense clitoral stimulation; (3) can masturbate to orgasm by themselves, but cannot achieve it through clitoral stimulation by a partner; and (4) can reach orgasm through prolonged application of a vibrator. At the other extreme of this continuum are those 10% or fewer women whose orgasmic response is totally inhibited, or nearly so.

New insights into female orgasm have been provided to the professional and lay world alike by Shere Hite (1976). In her sampling of 3019 women she found, for example, that masturbation was by far the most effective means of achieving orgasm. Further, the number of women who never experienced coital orgasm was five times greater among those who had never masturbated than among those who had.

Of the vast majority (82%) of women in the Hite study who stated that they masturbate, 95% easily and regularly reached orgasm. By contrast, only 30% were consistently capable of it in coitus. An additional 14% achieved orgasm through coitus, but only when penile thrusting was accompanied by manual stimulation of the clitoris. About 42% of the subjects regularly had orgasm during cunnilingus. In evaluating the strength of orgasms produced by direct clitoral stimulation versus that of orgasms produced coitally, more than twice as many women reported that the former were stronger. Almost half the women in the Hite sample stated that they masturbated to achieve orgasm after intercourse, or would have liked to do so, indicating that coitus was orgasmically ineffective or at least not completely satisfying. However, 87% of the women stated that they liked vaginal penetration whether or not they had ever achieved orgasm that way.

Hite's survey, like most such studies, leaves something to be desired in methodology and sampling. For example, 8% of her all-female sampling reported that they prefer sex with other women (3% preferred to enjoy sex alone; and 1%, to have no sex at all). Yet from the results of numerous other surveys, it has been generally concluded that lesbians constitute only 1.5% to 2% of the female population. *The Hite Report* nonetheless provides much useful information, which either supports earlier studies or throws new light on the problems of human relationships, especially the sexual one.

The Response Cycle

In their highly significant research projects Masters and Johnson (1960a; 1961b,c; 1962; 1963a,b; 1964; 1965a,b; 1966; W. H. Masters 1959, 1960) have described with scientific precision the physiological reactions men and women experience during the various phases of the human sexual response cycle. They found it convenient to divide sexual response into four phases: *excitement, plateau, orgasmic,* and *resolution*. Masters and Johnson demonstrated in a laboratory what clinicians and laypersons had only been able to surmise before—that a variety of physical and psychological stimuli can produce sexual excitement, and that adverse stimuli or a variation of stimulative techniques, can shorten, prolong, or interrupt erotic arousal.

When effective sexual stimulation is employed, the recipient enters the first or *excitement phase,* which varies in time from a few minutes to hours. The duration depends upon the effectiveness, intensity, and continuance of the techniques used, and upon the degree of freedom from adverse stimuli, whether physical or psychological. Generally speaking, the longer the excitement phase, the longer the last or resolution phase. These are the two longest phases of the sexual response cycle.

The second phase, the *plateau phase,* is intense but of short duration. And the third or *orgasmic phase* is extremely short, lasting from 3 to 10 seconds (sometimes longer in women). When the stimulation that was effective in evoking the excitement phase is continued, the plateau phase is reached. From this point, continuation of the same arousal techniques will (unless inhibiting circumstances arise) culminate in the peak of the sexual cycle, the orgasmic phase. During the last or *resolution phase,* the sexual system returns to its normal nonexcited state. The length of this phase is directly proportionate to that of the excitement phase.

There is little individual diversity in the pattern of men's response during the orgasmic phase. On the other hand, women—individually and as a group—display wide diversity, both in duration and intensity. Women who seldom or never experience orgasm are far more likely to control their spontaneous movements toward the end of coitus than are women who usually or always respond with orgasm (Adams 1966).

There is a significant difference in the response of men and women following coitus. After orgasm, the man enters the **refractory period** (a state of temporary resistance to sexual stimulation) of the resolution phase. Sexual stimulation that was previously effective and pleasurable now becomes futile and distasteful. Women, on the other hand, usually do not enter a refractory period (DSM III 1980). They generally remain capable of returning to earlier phases of the sexual response cycle. If the same sexual stimulation that produced the first orgasm is continued or reapplied, they may experience one or several more orgasms.

The duration of a given individual's orgasm is about the same whether it occurs as a result of coitus, manual or oral stimulation, or use of mechanical devices. There is great personal variation in the pleasure and intensity of orgasm, depending upon the individual's preferences in the matter of sexual stimulation.

The intensity of sexual arousal or orgasmic response can now be more accurately determined than in the past, when sexual excitement was measured primarily by subjective evaluation. Scientists have recently developed instruments for measuring changes in vaginal blood volume and pulse pressure as indices of female sexual arousal. For the male, instruments for measuring strength of penile erection have long been in existence, although they were not widely used in sex research (McCary & Copeland 1976). However, Masters and Johnson have perfected the use of instrumentation similar to the polygraph in their extensive physiological studies of the sexual response cycle, making their research results unique in the field.

Those wishing to study in greater detail the subject of the physiological responses in sexual expression are referred to the basic two-volume work on sexual behavior by Kinsey *et al.* (1948, 1953) and Masters and Johnson's *Human Sexual Response* (1966). The following material on the four phases of arousal is a summation of the latter.

The Female Sexual Response Cycle

Excitement Phase

As sexual tension builds, the nipples of the woman's breasts become erect. Venous blood is trapped in the breasts, causing them to enlarge by about 25% by the end of this phase. The areolae (dark pigmented area surrounding the nipples) swell noticeably. Veins of the breast become quite visible, forming the familiar "vascular tree." About 75% of sexually stimulated women develop a flush of the skin, known as the maculopapular sex flush. It begins in the regions of the stomach and throat and spreads to the breasts, the intensity usually being in direct proportion to the stimulation received.

Myotonia—tension of voluntary (and sometimes involuntary) muscles—begins and heightens during this phase, providing clear evidence that a woman's sexual response is not limited to her pelvic region; she responds with her entire body. As tension builds, her movements become more restless, forceful, and quick. During this and subsequent phases, rectal and buttocks muscles may involuntarily tense.

As sexual tensions mount, blood pressure increases from the normal 120/80 reading and heart rate from its usual 80 beats per minute.

The clitoris enlarges—although the *tumescence* (swelling or engorgement) may not be detected by the naked eye—and continues to do so throughout sexual stimulation. Direct stimulation of the clitoris produces more rapid and pronounced enlargement than indirect stimulation (fantasy, breast manipulation) does.

The woman's first anatomical response to sexual stimulation is a lubrication or "sweating" in the vaginal barrel, which begins from 10 to 30 seconds after physiological or psychological stimulation is begun (Fig. 12.2). (Contrary to earlier theories, the cervix is in no way responsible for vaginal lubrication.) As excitement continues, dilation and lengthening of the vagina occur, limited to the inner two-thirds of the barrel. The wrinkled surface

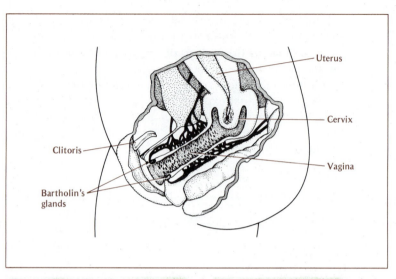

Figure 12.2   Female pelvic region, showing enlargement of vaginal blood vessels and "sweating" of vaginal walls during sexual arousal and climax.

smoothes out and the mucosa thins with expansion, making the vagina 25% larger than its nonstimulated dimensions. Its coloration becomes a deeper purple as excitement continues.

In the uterus, rapid, irregular contractions called fibrillation begin in the early part of the phase. Vasocongestion causes an increase in size; if stimulation persists for a prolonged period through this and the next phase, there may be a two- or threefold increase in size. As the excitement and plateau phases merge, the entire uterus is pulled upward into the lower abdomen, producing a ballooning or tenting effect in the inner two-thirds of the vagina.

In a woman who has not borne children, the labia majora thin out and become somewhat flattened. They elevate slightly upwards and outwards, flaring away from the vaginal opening. In a woman who has borne children, the major lips become greatly engorged with blood, often becoming two or three times their normal size. The labia minora (also called sex-skin) begin to enlarge, eventually becoming two or three times their normal thickness.

At most, the Bartholin's glands produce very little mucoid secretion— a few drops only—and then usually not until the very end of this or in the next phase. Contrary to earlier belief, therefore, the Bartholin's glands are not responsible for vaginal lubrication.

Plateau Phase

Breasts and areolae become their fullest and the sex flush its most intense during this phase.

Muscular tension is observable from head to toe. A woman frequently reacts with facial grimaces, flared nostrils, and marked strain of the mouth. The cords of the neck become rigid and stand erect, especially with the approach of orgasm. The back arches and thigh muscles become very tense. Late in the phase spastic contractions of hand and foot muscles are demonstrated in grasping, clawing movements. Muscles of the buttocks are often purposefully tensed in the striving for orgasm.

Heart rate may reach 110 to 175 beats per minute; the systolic blood-pressure reading may rise 20 to 60 mm Hg over normal, and the diastolic, 10 to 20 mm Hg above normal. Increased respiratory rate (heavy breathing) is first noticeable during this phase.

The clitoris exhibits its most singular response to sexual stimulation during the plateau phase (Fig. 12.3). With almost perfect consistency among all women, the clitoral body and glans withdraw from their normal pudendal overhang position and pull back deeply beneath the foreskin or hood. At the end of the plateau phase, just before orgasm, the retraction is so pronounced that the clitoris is reduced in length by at least 50%. If sexual stimulation is discontinued during the plateau phase, the clitoris will resume its normal overhang position; if stimulation is begun anew, it will again retract.

The outer third of the vagina, including its encircling musculature, becomes so distended with venous blood that its barrel is reduced in diameter by about 33%. The distended muscles contract with approaching

Figure 12.3 Representation of clitoris during sexual activity, showing (a) normal unstimulated state; (b) response during excitement and plateau phases; and (c) response at end of plateau phase and during orgasmic phase.

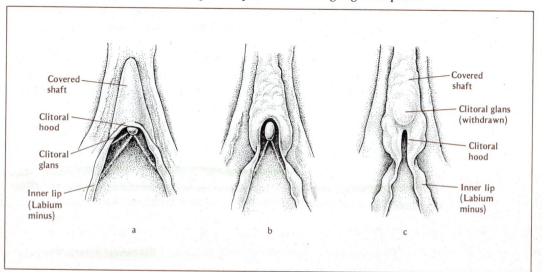

orgasm, causing the vagina to tighten around the inserted penis. This congested outer third of the vagina and the engorged labia monora have been given the name **orgasmic platform** by Masters and Johnson. The uterus elevates to its maximum potential, increasing the vaginal tenting effect, and uterine fibrillation intensifies.

The changes in both the labia majora and minora first observed in the excitement phase intensify. Coloration of the sex-skin in women who have not had children progresses from ashen pink to bright rose and, finally, to a scarlet hue. The minor lips of women who have had children may become an even darker wine color. The intensity of color change in both instances is directly related to the degree of sexual excitation, and a marked color change is evidence of impending orgasm.

Orgasmic Phase

Intensity of the sex flush and muscle tension are parallel with orgasmic intensity. The woman is so caught up in her orgasmic response that there is loss of voluntary muscular control. She is unaware of her physical movements, which are sometimes so violent that they cause aching and soreness the next day. The stronger the orgasm, the more completely the woman's whole body becomes involved in the release of physiological and psychological tensions. There are involuntary contractions of the perineal area, the rectum, and the lower abdomen. Flushing, slight facial swelling, and rib-cage expansion may also occur.

Involuntary contractions of the sphincter muscles of the rectum may occur at 0.8-second intervals during the orgasmic phase, especially if orgasm is intense. Involuntary distension of the external urethral opening may occur momentarily during this phase. Women occasionally feel an urge to urinate during or immediately following orgasm. There is possibly a loss of urine as sexual tension mounts, especially among women who have had children.

Heart rate elevates even further (usually to a higher degree in masturbation than in coition). Blood pressure continues to climb, perhaps reaching 200/120, although the rise is less than a man's during this phase. There is a direct correlation between intensity and duration of sexual tension and any respiratory change that occurs; normal breathing may double to 40 breaths a minute.

The clitoris remains retracted and unobservable beneath its hood during this phase. But the vagina demonstrates a unique reponse. The orgasmic platform contracts strongly at about 0.8-second intervals. There are at least 3 or 4 such contractions, and there may be as many as 15. The intervals lengthen after the first few contractions, and intensity also diminishes. The stronger the contractions and the greater the number of them, ordinarily the more powerful is orgasm. Uterine contractions begin

2 to 4 seconds after the first sensations of orgasm and are not unlike the initial contractions of childbirth labor. They typically begin at the top of the uterus and work their way downward to the cervix. For a comparison of the female genitalia in their unstimulated state and as they are during sexual excitement, see Figs. 12.4 and 12.5.

Resolution Phase

Almost all of a woman's organs and tissues quickly return to their nonstimulated state after orgasm. The sex flush disappears from the body in the reverse order of its appearance during the excitement and plateau phases. There is loss of nipple erection, but the breasts return more slowly to normal size; in a woman who has not borne children, they often remain enlarged 5 to 10 minutes after orgasm. If sexual stimulation is not continued or begun anew, muscular tension usually disappears completely within 5 minutes. Heart rate, blood pressure, and respiration also return quickly to normal.

About one-third of all women develop a widespread, thin coating of perspiration over the chest, back, thighs, and ankles during this phase, as the skin flush disappears. Heavy perspiration may appear over the entire

Figure 12.4   Female genitalia in preexcitement state.

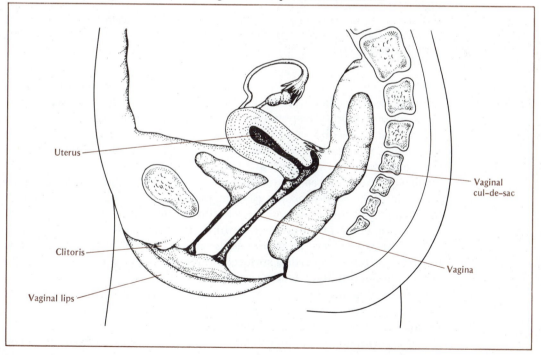

Uterus

Clitoris

Vaginal lips

Vaginal cul-de-sac

Vagina

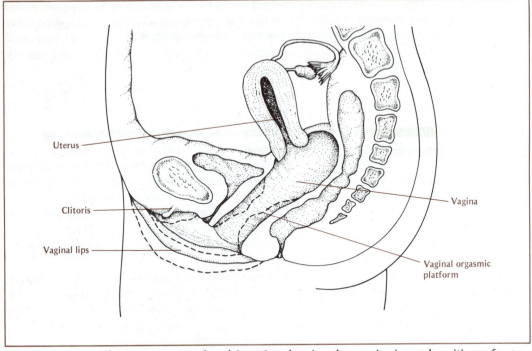

Figure 12.5 Female pelvic region showing changes in size and positions of organs and tissues with increasing sexual excitement and orgasmic response. Note ballooning and tenting effect of inner portion of vagina. Dotted lines show organ positions during orgasm.

body but especially on the forehead, upper lip, and underarms. These reactions are unrelated to the physical activity in the first three phases. The extent of perspiratory response parallels the strength of orgasm.

Within 10 seconds after the orgasmic contractions of the vagina cease, the clitoris returns to its normal position. Vasocongestion of the clitoral glans and shaft may remain 5 to 10 minutes after orgasm and occasionally persists for as long as 30 minutes. Vasocongestion that produced the orgasmic platform during the plateau phase rapidly disappears, causing the diameter of the outer one-third of the vagina to return to normal size. The tenting effect of the inner two-thirds is rather slowly and irregularly lost as the vagina reverts to its usual collapsed state. The vaginal barrel reverts to its rough, wrinkled surface and the tissue loses its dark hue. This process frequently lasts as long as 10 to 15 minutes.

Uterine contractions cease, and the elevated organ rapidly resumes its usual position. As vasocongestion disappears, the uterus reverts to normal size, although it remains somewhat enlarged—for 10 to 20 minutes. If orgasm does not occur, increased uterine size may persist for 60 minutes or longer. Immediately following orgasm there is a slight dilation of the cervical opening, which continues for 5 to 10 minutes. (Contrary to earlier scientific opinion, recent investigations demonstrate that this dilation does not aid sperm transportation, and there is no sucking process in the uterus at the time of orgasm.)

The major lips return to normal size faster in women who have not had children. The lips return rather quickly to their midline position, which partially covers the vaginal outlet. In women who have had children, engorgement of the major lips may persist for 2 to 3 hours before complete detumescence (subsidence of swelling).

Even in cases of pronounced color change, the minor lips return within 2 minutes (often within 10 to 15 seconds) to the light pink color of their preexcitement state. Return to normalcy in this phase occurs in the reverse order that changes took place during the first two phases. Discoloration fades, then vascular tension disappears. With detumescence, the labia minora return to their midline position.

It will be noted that no mention has been made of reactions by the ovaries and fallopian tubes. No direct observations have been made of these organs during the sexual response cycle, so their reactions are not known. It is believed, however, that the ovaries enlarge during the first two phases because of vasocongestion, then shrink to normal size after orgasm.

The Male Sexual Response Cycle

Excitement Phase

About 60% of men experience nipple erection during the sexual response cycle, usually during the late excitement phase and continuing through the other phases. The measleslike sex flush appears on about 25% of sexually responding men as compared with 75% of sexually responding women. In men, however, the flush does not usually appear until late in the excitement phase or in the plateau phase. It is usually first observed on the stomach, then spreads to the chest, then to the neck and face.

Muscular tension becomes clinically observable in the latter part of the excitement phase, although it is more pronounced during the plateau phase. At this point contractions primarily involve the voluntary muscles, as evidenced by both restless and purposeful movements. Involuntary muscular contractions are more typical during the late part of this phase, and are responsible for elevating the testes toward the perineum. Leg, arm, and abdominal muscles tend to tense voluntarily or involuntarily, according to coital position.

As sexual tension increases, there is a corresponding increase in heart rate and blood pressure (Fig. 12.6).

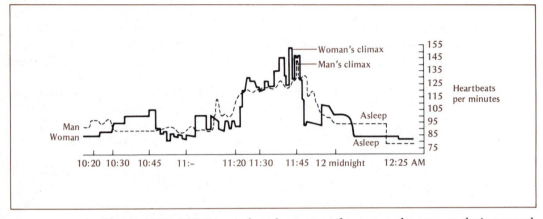

Figure 12.6   Variations in heartbeat rates of a man and a woman during sexual activity.

With effective stimulation, the three spongy cylindrical bodies of the penis become engorged with blood, producing erection. The urethral opening or meatus widens as the phase progresses. Penile erection may subside and be regained many times during a prolonged excitement phase. It may also be impaired in both the excitement and plateau phases by adverse stimuli, such as sudden loud noises, noticeable changes in lighting or temperature, fear, pain, and anxiety.

With mounting sexual tension comes smooth-muscle contraction and vasocongestion of the scrotal tissue, pulling the scrotal sac toward the body and markedly restricting testicular movement. The cremasteric musculature (spermatic cord) shortens, elevating the testes. Despite penile erection, a prolonged excitement phase (lasting more than 5 to 10 minutes) may cause the cremasteric musculature and scrotal sac to relax perhaps several times, each time returning the testes to their original low-scrotal position, before plateau-level sexual tensions establish complete elevation. The Cowper's glands and the secondary sex organs—the prostate, vas deferens, and seminal vesicles—show no noticeable changes at this time.

Plateau Phase

Both voluntary and involuntary muscular tensions increase during the plateau phase. Strong muscular contractions of the face (especially around the mouth), neck, and abdomen may occur. A man may also demonstrate carpopedal spasm, indicating a high level of sexual excitement. As orgasm nears there may be clutching, clawing, grasping movements of the hands, curling of the toes, and arching of the feet.

Heightened sexual tension increases respiratory rate. Heart rate rises to between 100 and 175 beats per minute. Blood pressure elevates to perhaps 180/110—somewhat higher in some cases. As with women, the rise in heart rate and blood pressure parallels the buildup in sexual tension.

The corona of the penile glans becomes more tumescent, and coloration of the glans and the area just below the corona may deepen. The urethral bulb (base of the urethra) increases to three times its normal size. Its additional distension late in the phase is indicative of impending orgasm.

The testes must undergo elevation before a man can experience a full ejaculatory sequence. (Partial elevation will result in ejaculation, to be sure, but there will be a significant reduction in force.) Once the testes become positioned next to the perineum, the orgasmic phase will inevitably follow if effective sexual stimulation is maintained. In nearly all men, one testicle hangs slightly lower than the other, which in about 85% of all men is the left one. The two testicles often react to sexual stimulation independently of one another. The right may elevate completely in the late excitement or early plateau phase, while the left may not do so until just before ejaculation.

A vasocongestive reaction in the testes increases their size over the unstimulated state by approximately 50%. The increase is as much as 100% in some men. Generally speaking, the more protracted the plateau phase, the more marked the vasocongestion and increase in testicular size.

The Cowper's glands secrete two or three drops of preejaculatory mucoid fluid during this phase.

Orgasmic Phase

The sex flush, when present, parallels the intensity of orgasm. There is loss of voluntary muscle control plus severe involuntary-muscle tension throughout the body. The total body is involved.

Respiratory rate frequently rises to 40 breaths per minute and the heartbeat to 110 to 180 beats (or more). Blood pressure rises even higher than in the previous phase, in some cases to 220/130 or more. The lower the nonstimulated heart rate and blood pressure, the smaller the rise, usually, during sexual stimulation.

The rapid distension of the urethral bulb signals that orgasm is imminent. Immediately before ejaculation, seminal fluid collects in the ejaculatory ducts and secondary sexual organs. Contractions in the latter appear to begin in the vasa efferentia (the tubes leading from the testicles to the epididymis), continue through the epididymis, the vas deferens, the seminal vesicles, and, finally, the ejaculatory ducts, which pass through the prostate. The systolic action of the prostate forces the seminal fluid into and through the urethra with contractions of varying force. Intervals between contractions are roughly the same as those of the vagina during orgasm—0.8 seconds between the first three or four major responses. Intervals between subsequent contractions lengthen until the final one lasts perhaps several seconds. Rectal sphincter muscles usually contract during orgasm only two to four times. For a comparison of the male genitalia in preexcitement through orgasmic phases, see Figs. 12.7 and 12.8.

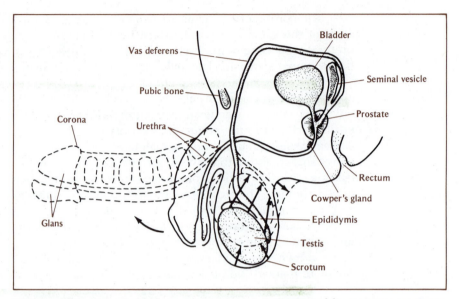

Figure 12.7 Male genitalia in preexcitement state. Dotted lines represent organ positions in excitement and plateau phases. Note that testis and scrotum move up, toward body cavity.

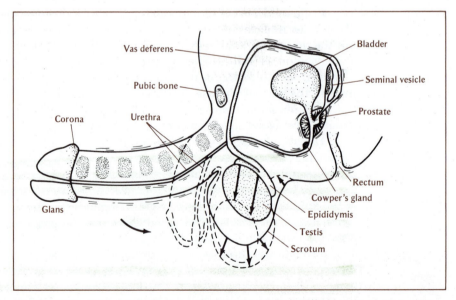

Figure 12.8 Male genitalia in orgasmic phase. Dotted lines represent positions after resolution phase. Note that testis and scrotum move down, away from body cavity, during resolution phase.

Resolution Phase

Men, like women, demonstrate a rapid reversal of the tissue and organ changes that occurred in the first three phases. If no further sexual stimulation occurs, the sex flush and muscular tension almost always dissipate within 5 minutes. Heart rate, respiratory rate, and blood pressure rapidly return to normal. However, nipple erection may not disappear for up to an hour after ejaculation. About 33% of men have a perspiratory reaction immediately after ejaculation. As with women, it may involve the entire body; but the reaction in men is usually confined to the hands and feet. The response is unrelated to the strong physical exertion or sex flush of earlier phases.

Penile detumescence occurs in two stages. The primary loss of erection occurs early in the refractory period, at which time the fully erect penis reduces to a size 50% larger than its usual flaccid state. This early loss is rapid. The secondary stage of detumescence persists for a much longer time, especially when there is residual sexual tension.

On the whole, the manner and duration of sexual stimulation experienced during the excitement and plateau phases determine the time required for the penis to revert to its normal flaccid dimensions. But penile involution may be speeded up by sufficiently intense external asexual stimuli. If a man removes his penis from the vagina shortly after orgasm, and, more particularly, if he does something unrelated to sexual activity—walking about, urinating, reading, or smoking—both stages of detumescence will occur rapidly.

The urethra and its broadened opening revert to their usual dimensions shortly after ejaculation.

In 25% of men, the scrotum is slow to return to its nonstimulated state. In the remaining 75%, loss of congestion is rapid, and retrogression to the normal loosely wrinkled appearance of the scrotum is equally rapid.

The testes undergo loss of vasocongestion and reduction in size in an involutional pattern similar to that of the scrotal sac. The process can be swift or protracted. Generally speaking, the longer the plateau phase persists, the longer the testicles take to reduce to normal size during the resolution phase.

Sexual competency or a satisfying relationship does not depend on orgasm accompanying each sexual experience. Sexual response to the point of orgasm is highly desirable because of the great physical and emotional pleasure and release involved (Beigel 1963). And because if affords relief from tension and anxiety, it can also be called therapeutic (Kassel 1976). But overemphasizing orgasm can lead to conflicts that are damaging to the enjoyment of coition and the emotional relationship between a couple (Beigel 1963).

The desirability of simultaneous orgasms has long been the subject of speculation (Ellis 1960). Naturally, if both partners prefer orgasms at the same time, and many couples do, they should strive for this goal. However, some aspects of sexual response should be considered prior to embarking upon the uneven struggle toward simultaneous orgasm, or before accepting the premise that it offers the ultimate in coital achievement.

Essential to rewarding sexual activity is the effort to give one's partner the fullest measure of pleasure and satisfaction. If either person is primarily concerned with self-gratification or is caught up in his/her own impending orgasm, full attention cannot be given to the partner. Similarly, if too much attention is being devoted to the partner's gratification, appropriate concentration on one's own response and pleasure is impossible.

Furthermore, men and women react quite differently in bodily movements at the time of orgasm. The man's tendency is to plunge into the vagina as deeply as possible at the moment of orgasm and to hold this position for a length of time, to be followed perhaps by one or two deep, deliberate thrusts. The woman's tendency, on the other hand, is to have the same stroking, plunging movements of the excitement and plateau phases continued during the orgasmic reaction, with perhaps an acceleration of the thrusts and an increase of pressure in the vulval area. These two highly pleasurable patterns of movement are obviously incompatible. Since both cannot be executed at the same time, whichever pattern is carried out during simultaneous orgasm must of necessity detract from the full pleasure of one of the partners.

The arguments, therefore, would appear to be stronger against than for simultaneous orgasm. It is easier for a man to reach orgasm, but he is usually capable of only one. It would therefore seem sensible for the man to delay his own pleasure until his partner is fully satisfied. The couple can devote full attention to giving the woman as many orgasmic responses as she wishes. Then they can both concentrate wholly on providing the man with as satisfying an orgasm as possible.

Several studies reveal that 50% to 60% of women pretend—fake— orgasm from time to time (Butler 1976; Hite 1976). The reasons given include fear of appearing "less a woman"; an attitude of "let's get this over with"; a wish to protect the man's ego; and an effort to ensure that the man will not seek another sexual partner. (These women also report that when they do have orgasms, their partners are aware of it 90% of the time.) Specifically, women realize that many men place great value on their ability to bring their partners to orgasm in practically every coital encounter. Women are therefore often willing to make the pretext even though, in fact, they may not be even close to having an orgasm. The wish to end a particular sex act by pretending orgasm may also stem from dissatisfaction with it, or to hide orgasmic difficulties (Rosenbaum 1970). Whatever the motivation, women who usually experience orgasm are considerably more likely to pretend to have one when they actually did not than women who seldom or never experience orgasm (Shope 1968b). When women do pretend, they are usually successful in misleading their partners.

Whether or not a woman should ever pretend to climax is a topic of much debate (Ottenheimer *et al.* 1971). It is fairly clear, however, that she should not do so on a regular basis, for pretense accomplishes nothing more than a perpetuation of the difficulty. A more sensible approach is to search for the cause and to correct the problem—through psychotherapy if necessary.

Women frequently report that they achieve sexual satisfaction in a sex act even though they fail to reach a climax. Investigation has shown, however, that on such occasions they are much more aware of sexual tension than when they reach orgasm. This finding tends to support the argument that, although emotional satisfaction from coitus can be gained without climax, relief from sexual tension cannot. Such residual tension can spill over into other areas of a woman's life and sometimes cause problems without discernible cause (Shope 1968a).

Orgasmic responses vary more in individual men (Beigel 1963; Hite 1976). And although reasonable consideration should be given to the matter, there should be no great anxiety if a woman does not respond as intensely as either partner had hoped. Because of earlier sexual involvement with partners of profound coital desire and response, some persons are led to believe that their present partners should respond to them with the same frequency and intensity. What these men and women fail to realize is that the very strength of their previous partners' sex drive, not necessarily a deep emotional commitment, perhaps impelled them into sexual involvements. Their present partner may simply not possess such strong sexual needs. The inference therefore cannot be drawn that the present partner, because of a less intense sexual drive, is any the less loving or concerned for the welfare of the relationship.

It cannot be overstressed that, although the material in this chapter has focused on the physiological considerations of human sexuality, one cannot infer that the emotional aspects of sexuality are of less importance. A close human relationship and emotional involvement—love, deep affection, commitment—are of paramount importance to a complete and fulfilling sexual experience. Physiological sexual needs can be relieved without love, closeness, or even understanding. But no one can really attain complete emotional, physical, and sexual satisfaction, in all its fulfillment, without those elements.

Summary

Orgasm is an intensely pleasurable, tension-relieving experience that leads to physical and emotional gratification for both sexes. While orgasmic sensations and responses appear to be essentially the same for both men and women, one dissimilarity is the phenomenon of ejaculation, which accompanies male orgasm. Although the emphasis of this chapter is on the physical aspects of orgasm, emotional intimacy, tenderness, closeness, and sharing of deep feelings are also important and can be fulfilling in themselves in a sexual relationship, and certainly enhance orgasm if it occurs.

The methods that most readily lead to orgasm for women are the use of electric vibrators, and oral-genital or manual stimulation of the clitoris. Recent research indicates that stimulation of the anterior wall of the vagina may be highly pleasurable for many women. In contrast, most men report they find it easier and more satisfying to achieve orgasm through coitus. Although most women do not reach orgasm as easily as men, they are more capable of experiencing multiple orgasms and the sustained orgasmic response known as *status orgasmus*. Emotional factors such as guilt, anxiety, anger, or indifference play an important part in affecting the orgasmic capacity of both women and men.

A few ejaculatory and orgasmic problems are found in some men. Men who have *retrograde ejaculations* experience a backward ejaculation of the semen into the bladder rather than through the penis. Prostatic surgery, accident, or disease may result in this condition. Those men who have *ejaculatory anhedonia* experience ejaculation with little pleasure or sensation. Such diminished orgasmic pleasure is usually psychological in origin.

Women tend to report more variability in the subjective quality of their orgasms than do men. The ease with which women reach orgasm may be thought of as arranged along a continuum, with one extreme being reaching orgasm through erotic fantasy alone to the extreme at which orgasmic response is totally inhibited. Most women find they respond somewhere in the middle of this continuum with varying degrees of nongenital and genital stimulation being required to reach orgasm. The vast majority of women are orgasmic most easily and regularly through masturbation. In contrast, less than half of women appear to achieve orgasm regularly through coitus and through oral-genital stimulation. But, whether they achieve orgasm or not, most women like the experience of vaginal penetration.

The human sexual response may be conceptualized as being divided into four phases: excitement, plateau, orgasmic, and resolution. Of these, the excitement and resolution phases are the two most protracted phases, while the plateau and orgasmic phases are intense but of shorter duration. These four phases are similar in both sexes except that after orgasm, men enter a refractory period (a state of temporary resistance to sexual stimulation). Women do not usually enter such a period and generally remain capable of returning to earlier phases of the cycle. Scientific instruments exist to help determine the intensity of sexual arousal or orgasmic response in men and women.

The female sexual response cycle is characterized by the following: (1) In the excitement phase breasts enlarge and the nipples become erect, the maculopapular sex flush appears in many women, the body muscles tense, blood pressure and heart rate increase, the clitoris enlarges, there is lubrication in the vaginal barrel, the vagina lengthens and dilates, the vagina darkens in coloration, the uterus increases in size and pulls upward in the lower abdomen, and the labia minora and labia majora enlarge. (2) In the plateau phase the breasts become their fullest, the sex flush is most intense, muscular tension increases and *carpopedal spasms* occur, heart rate and blood pressure continue to increase, breathing becomes heavier, the clitoral body and glans pull back beneath the foreskin, the orgasmic platform becomes observable, the uterus elevates to its maximum potential and uterine fibrillation intensifies, and coloration of the minor lips becomes more evident. (3) In the orgasmic phase involuntary contractions of the sphincter muscles of the rectum may occur, heart rate and blood pressure become further elevated, breathing rate increases, the orgasmic platform contracts, and uterine contractions begin. (4) In the resolution phase the sex flush disappears, there is a loss of nipple erection and slow decrease in breast size, muscular tension disappears, heart rate and blood pressure and breathing return to normal, perspiration may appear, the clitoris returns to its normal position, vasocongestion disappears, the vagina returns to normal size, coloration of the sex skin lessens, uterine contractions cease and the organ returns to normal position and size, and the major and minor lips return to usual size.

The male sexual response cycle is characterized by the following: (1) In the excitement phase 60% of men experience nipple erection and 25% of men experience a measleslike sex flush, muscular tension becomes observable, the testes elevate toward the perineum, heart rate and blood pressure increase, and the penis becomes erect. (2) In the plateau phase voluntary and involuntary muscular tensions become more apparent, breathing rate increases, heart rate and blood pressure continue to rise, the corona of the penile glans becomes more tumescent and coloration of the glans may deepen, the testes become positioned next to the perineum and the testes increase in size, and the Cowper's glands secrete a few drops of preejaculatory mucoid fluid. (3) In the orgasmic phase there is intense muscular tension throughout the body, breathing rate increases, heart rate and blood pressure increase, the urethral bulb becomes distended, seminal fluid collects in the ejaculatory ducts and secondary sexual organs, the systolic action of the prostate forces the seminal fluid into the urethra with contractions of varying force, and the sphincter muscles of the rectum contract. (4) In the resolution phase the sex flush and muscular tension dissipate, breathing rate, heart rate, and blood pressure quickly return to normal, a perspiratory reaction may occur, penile detumescence occurs, the urethra and its opening revert to usual size, the scrotum returns to its loose wrinkled state, and the testes reduce in size.

The experience of orgasm leads to a release of sexual tension for both men and women, although overconcern with simultaneous orgasms, the intensity of orgasms, or the faking of orgasms can lessen pleasure and lead to problems in sexual relationships. Once again, it is important to emphasize that the emotional aspects of human relationships are intermingled with the physical aspects, and affect the degree of gratification that can be obtained in sexual interactions.

Annotated Bibliography

Ellis, Albert and Wolfe, Janet. The vaginal-clitoral orgasm controversy re-examined. In *The new sex education*, ed. H. Otto. Chicago: Follett, 1978.

> This article examines the controversial notion that women experience both clitoral and vaginal orgasm types. The authors review literature relevant to the myth of vaginal-clitoral orgasm, discuss its bases and implications for sexual satisfaction, and present an argument against the use of terms "vaginal" and "clitoral" to refer to orgasm in women.

Hite, Shere. *The Hite report: A nationwide study on female sexuality.* New York: Macmillan, 1976.

> This book reports results of a national survey of female sexuality, exploring women's sexual attitudes, feelings, experiences, and behavior. Topics include masturbation, orgasm, intercourse, sexual slavery, the sexual revolution, and aging and sexuality. Dispelling many myths related to female sexuality, this book would be of interest to the general reader.

McCary, James Leslie. *Freedom and growth in marriage (2nd ed.).* New York: John Wiley and Sons, 1980.

> This book for the student and general reader considers various aspects of marriage, dating and mate selection, focusing on implications for individual growth and freedom within the marriage relationship. The past and future of marriage are discussed, as well as relevant contemporary issues, alternatives to marriage, the nature of love, aspects of human sexuality, marital adjustment, and other topics.

Nowinski, Joseph. *Becoming satisfied: A man's guide to sexual fulfillment.* Englewood Cliffs, New Jersey: Prentice-Hall, 1980.

> This book is a practical guide for men who have sexual concerns. The book is designed to enhance understanding of sexuality and to aid in dealing with erectile problems, overcoming sexual tension and fear of women, learning to relax, learning to delay or accelerate orgasm, and other problems.

Raley, Patricia E. *Making love: How to be your own sex therapist.* New York: The Dial Press, 1976.

> This well-illustrated sexual self-help guide is intended for the adult reader of any sexual orientation who is interested in maximizing satisfaction in relationships. Systematic guidelines are provided for exploring sex history, sexual fantasy, sexual attitudes, sexual anatomy, arousal, orgasm, sexual communication, relationships with self and others, and other significant aspects of erotic life.

Rosenberg, Jack Lee. *Total orgasm (2nd ed.).* New York: Random House, 1975.

> This practical book describes various techniques to increase orgasmic pleasure, such as breathing and movement exercises with and without a partner, and masturbation. A special chapter deals with spirituality and sexuality, discussing teachings of "Kundalini" yoga. A chart summarizes relevant exercises.

Sandler, Jack, Myerson, Marilyn, and Kinder, Bill N. *Human sexuality: Current perspectives.* Tampa, Florida: Mariner, 1980.

> This text presents a comprehensive perspective of the field of human sexuality. A wide range of topics is covered, including sexual anatomy and sexual response, aphrodisiacs and anaphrodisiacs, past and current sexual attitudes and behavior, sexual diseases and disorders, sexual dysfunctions, birth control, sexual health, and sex and the law. Though designed for the student, this book would serve as a valuable general reference.

Witters, Weldon and Jones-Witters, Patrica. *Human sexuality: A biological perspective.* New York: D. Van Nostrand, 1980.

> This text approaches the various aspects of human sexuality from the biological standpoint. Topics of special interest include genetic engineering, hormonal control of sexuality, drugs affecting sexual function, surrogate parenthood, artificial insemination, cloning, and sex selection. The text is well illustrated and contains student performance objectives, but its appeal extends beyond the classroom.

Birth Control

Nearly 30 centuries of recorded evidence attest to the desire of humans to control their powers of reproduction and their conscious efforts to do so. As N.E. Himes (1963) said, "Human beings have always longed for both fertility and sterility, each at its appointed time and its chosen circumstances."

The term **birth control** was coined by Margaret Sanger, founder of the planned parenthood movement in the United States, in her efforts to popularize the idea of contraception. (As we shall see, contraception is actually only one form of birth control.) Working as a nurse among the very poor in New York, Sanger was personal witness to the coexistence of poverty and uncontrolled childbearing, as well as high rates of infant and maternal mortality. As a feminist and sensitive human being she strongly supported a woman's right to determine the size of her family, and devoted herself to removing legal barriers to the distribution of birth-control information.

In the U.S. as well as in other countries, birth control has passed through successive periods of active opposition, permissiveness, and open support as governments came to recognize the severe hindrance to social and economic progress created by uncurbed population growth.

279

The U.S. birthrate has steadily declined, to be sure, in the past 175 years—7.0 births per woman in 1800 vs. 2.3 in 1974 and 1.8 in 1977. The year 1980 closed with the U.S. population numbering almost 227 million citizens. The Bureau of the Census predicts future population increases of 1 million Americans each year.

Despite a decline in birthrate in many nations—due to the wider availability of birth-control devices—the world's population jumped by 90 million during 1976, to a total of about 4.3 billion people. If growth were to continue at this rate, the population of the world would double by the year 2007. The majority of population experts continue to believe that resources will be inadequate to sustain the needs of this burgeoning population.

Birth control is the only plausible solution to the problems caused by haphazard pregnancy. The primary purposes of fertility limitation, aside from curbing an unsupportable growth in population, are listed below.

1. *To further certain physical and socioeconomic objectives.* Spacing the arrival of children or limiting the number of them allows a couple to give full consideration to the mother's health and to the couple's economic circumstances. Excessive childbearing can leave the mother with certain undesirable physical conditions, such as high blood pressure, varicose veins, and relaxed vaginal tissue. It has been claimed that when births are only one year apart, the death rate for babies is about 50% higher than when births are two years apart (Guttmacher 1947). Furthermore, the chance of infant mortality increases with each additional child borne by the same mother after the birth of the second child.

Women are often reluctant to spend all their young and energetic adult lives caring for a child. Those who choose to have their children during the first few years of marriage are thereby free in their later years to commit themselves to a profession or community affairs.

A child's success in later life, incidentally, appears to be related to the size of its family. Of the adult men in this country, twice as many "only" children complete high school as those who have three or more siblings. Economic considerations also play a role. Yet impoverished adults of working age have twice as many children to provide for as do adults with adequate incomes. In other words, those who can least afford children seem to have the most (Chilman 1968).

2. *To aid in early sexual adjustment in marriage.* During the inevitable period of marital adjustment, sexual compatibility may be reached earlier and in a more satisfactory manner if fear of pregnancy is removed. It has also been shown that a woman's sexual responsiveness is directly related to the degree that both she and her partner are satisfied with their present method of contraception (Adams 1966).

3. *To prevent unwanted pregnancy among the unmarried.* The sociological problems and personal distress to all concerned in an unwanted pregnancy are legion.

4. *To avoid aggravation of existing illnesses or diseases.* Many illnesses and diseases—tuberculosis, heart and kidney disease, an advanced stage of diabetes (especially when complicated by damaged blood vessels), emotional disorders, nervous afflictions, recent surgery for cancer—raise questions about the advisability of pregnancy.

5. *To curb inherited diseases.* Inherited diseases can obviously be best controlled by preventing the pregnancy of an afflicted woman or a woman married to an afflicted man.

The probability of conception resulting from a single act of sexual intercourse in which no protection against pregnancy is employed is only 2% to 4% (Tietze 1960). It has been established, however, that if coitus occurs two days before ovulation, the probability of pregnancy is 5%; one day before ovulation, the probability rises to 30%; on the day of ovulation, 50%; one day after ovulation, the probability drops to 5% (Lachenbruch 1967).

Birth control and contraception are often discussed as if they were the same, but they are not. **Contraception** may be defined as any means or device permitting coitus between fertile partners that prevents conception. Contraception is, however, only one form of birth control. Methods of birth control fall into four major categories: abstinence, sterilization, abortion, and contraception.

Abstinence

Dictionaries define **abstinence** as "self-denial; an abstaining from the gratification of appetite." Clearly, sexual abstinence should be mutually agreeable to the partners; otherwise, it becomes merely partner-denial.

Some advocates of abstinence base their arguments on Freud's theory of sublimation. However, no empirical evidence exists to indicate that biological drives can really be sublimated. As a matter of fact, a conscious attempt to sublimate sexual urges and to direct sexual energies into other areas of life can result in such psychological malfunctions as lack of sexual desire, inability to concentrate, irritability, and insomnia, or in such physical problems as premature ejaculation, difficulty in achieving erection, prostatitis, ovarian and vulval congestion (H. S. Kaplan 1979). It should be pointed out, however, that voluntary abstinence is less damaging to the normal functioning of the organism than involuntary abstinence.

There are, of course, occasions when abstinence becomes a matter of consideration of one's partner or oneself—for example, during an illness, during late pregnancy, immediately after childbirth, or when one wishes to avoid contracting or spreading VD. Even in these cases, either partner or both may wish to have some sexual outlet, whether through oral or manual stimulation or masturbation.

In the context of human sexuality, not much can really be said for abstinence except that it is profoundly successful as a birth-control technique.

Sterilization

Sterilization is a surgical procedure rendering a person incapable of reproducing. By 1960, an estimated 5.6% of white women in the U.S. between the ages of 18 and 39, or their husbands, had undergone voluntary sterilization. By 1970, it ranked second only to the Pill as the birth-control method of choice among married couples. Since 1973, it has become the leading means when the wife is over 30 (Brody 1976). Although the true incidence of voluntary sterilization is not known absolutely, it is estimated that 11.5 million adults in the U.S. use sterilization and that for married couples over 30 years of age, it is the most common form of birth control (Hatcher *et al.* 1980). The U.S. Agency for International Development (AID) had estimated that by mid-1976 sterilization had become the world's leading birth-control technique; 65 million couples were dependent upon it, as opposed to 3 million in 1950.

Aside from family limitation, there are other reasons for sterilization, which fall chiefly into two categories:

1. *Therapeutic reasons.* Sterilization is sometimes performed when certain pathological conditions exist: tuberculosis, cancer, cardio-renal-vascular diseases, hypertension and high blood pressure, and kidney disorders; or when there are certain Rh blood incompatibilities (Russell 1961).
2. *Eugenic reasons.* Sterilization is performed as a means of protecting the physical or mental well-being of the next generation. Three types of persons have been considered likely subjects for eugenic sterilization.

   The habitual criminal. The rationale for sterilizing a habitual criminal is based on the theory that the "criminal mind" is inherited. Fortunately the Supreme Court has ruled that sterilization in these cases is "cruel and unusual punishment." In any event, there is little scientific evidence to support the role of heredity in criminal behavior.

   The sex offender. Sterilization is unlikely to benefit either offenders or society, inasmuch as these people are often driven to their behavior by complicated psychological problems. Only a vengeful public or the offender's unconscious desire for punishment is served by such punitive measures.

   The person with a hereditary mental disease or deficiency. In some states it is required that citizens with marked intellectual deficiencies and certain mental diseases, especially those thought to be inheritable, be sterilized.

Young to middle-aged couples who voluntarily seek sterilization are advised to consider other methods of birth control if they have any serious doubts or misgivings about becoming sterile. While approximately 80% of sterilized persons are glad they became sterilized, 20% express some form of dissatisfaction or regret. Generally speaking, persons over 30 years of age who have at least two children, who are emotionally stable, and who have carefully thought through their options are the best candidates for voluntary sterilization (Bernstein 1980).

Sterilization Methods in Women

There are two principal methods of sterilization: **tubal ligation,** or **partial salpingectomy,** and **laparoscopic sterilization.** In the first procedure, the fallopian tubes are cut and tied so that the two ends do not meet, thus keeping sperm and ova from contacting one another (Fig. 13.1). Tubal ligation may be accomplished by abdominal incision or through the vagina.

Vaginal tubal ligation offers the advantages over abdominal surgery of less postoperative discomfort, shorter hospital stay (hence less expense), and absence of visible scars. From the doctor's view, it is a more difficult procedure. Further, there is greater danger of infection than in the abdominal incision, because bacteria can enter the abdominal cavity from the vaginal canal (DeLora & Warren 1977). Reconnecting the fallopian tubes after ligation is about 50% successful. But the risk of tubal pregnancy rises after such surgery is performed.

In laparoscopic sterilization, the second method, two tiny punctures (sometimes only one) are made in the abdomen. This operation is performed under general or local anesthetic. Through one incision a bright heatless light, the laparoscope, is passed. Through the other, an electrical instrument is inserted, with which the fallopian tubes are cauterized or cut. the procedure is usually performed on an outpatient basis and is relatively inexpensive. Only Band-Aids are needed to cover the incisions, hence the popular description "Band-Aid sterilization" (*Williams Obstetrics* 1976).

The failure rate in all techniques of abdominal tubal ligation is about 0.8% (Hatcher *et al.* 1976). Attempts at purposeful rejoining of the tubes after laparoscope sterilization have been about 70% successful with the advent of microsurgical techniques (Hatcher *et al.* 1980). The woman considering laparoscopy, however, should consider it to be a permanent decision rather than a reversible one. Women's sex drive is not likely to be impaired following sterilization. On the contrary, because fear of pregnancy is permanently removed, there may be renewed sexual interest.

The following three operative procedures obviously leave a woman

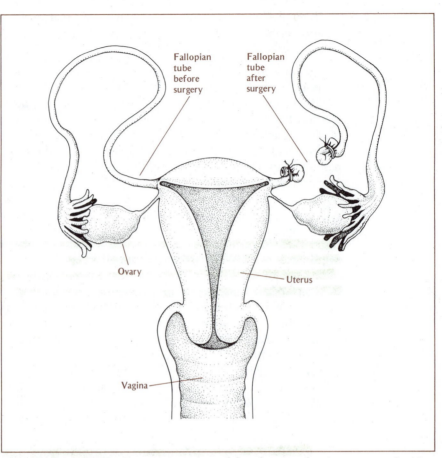

Figure 13.1   Schematic representation of female reproductive system, showing effects of tubal ligation. In actual sterilization, of course, surgery is performed on both sides of body.

permanently sterile. They are not ordinarily used for the purpose of sterilization alone, but to correct certain abnormalities or malignancies. **Oophorectomy,** the surgical removal of the ovaries, brings ovulation permanently to a halt. **Total salpingectomy** involves removal of the fallopian tubes. **Hysterectomy** is the surgical removal of the uterus, a procedure that may or may not include removal of the uterine tubes and ovaries. Estrogen replacement therapy may be helpful if a woman's hormonal balance is affected by such procedures. A woman's level of sexual desire and capacity to be sexually responsive also need not be adversely affected. Appropriate information and counseling may alleviate many of the sexual and emotional concerns present in a woman following sterilization procedures (Martin 1980).

Sterilization Methods in Men

Two major types of sterilization are available to men, vasectomy and castration. Vasectomy is now a commonly performed procedure; current estimates indicate that 1 million men undergo this form of sterilization each year (Lewis & Lewis 1980b). **Vasectomy** is a surgical procedure whereby the semen-carrying ducts, the vas deferens, are cut and tied. A small incision is made in the scrotum, and the vas is lifted out so that about an inch can be cut away. The ends are then tied, blocking the passage of the sperm from the testicles to the ejaculatory ducts (Fig. 13.2). The site of the incision is well away from the testicles and in no way disturbs them or

Figure 13.2 Schematic representation of male reproductive system, showing effects of vasectomy. Note that in actual sterilization, surgery is performed on both sides of body.

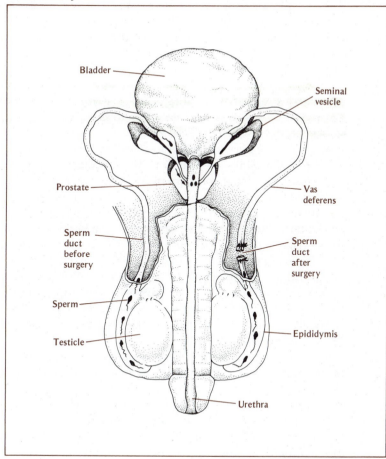

their functioning. The vasectomized man remains potent but sterile. The sperm he now produces are simply absorbed by his body.

A vasectomy is a simple operation. It is less expensive than the woman's tubal ligation, and can usually be performed in about 20 minutes on an outpatient basis under general or local anesthetic (*Williams Obstetrics* 1976). Afterward, the patient is usually required to remain relatively inactive for about 48 hours. The doctor will probably advise the use of a support for several weeks to prevent any pulling of the testicles and to minimize soreness during the healing process.

The patient remains fertile for a certain time following vasectomy because the first 10 to 20 ejaculations often will contain residual sperm. In fact, sperm have been found in as late as the 32nd ejaculate after surgery (DeLora & Warren 1977). The vasectomized man is advised to have two consecutive sperm-free semen evaluations before he assumes he is sterile (*Williams Obstetrics* 1976; Zinsser 1976).

Of 1500 vasectomy patients surveyed in one study, 5% suffered from some aftereffects—minor stitch abscesses, slight scrotal bleeding, or a tiny clump of sperm at the cut ends of the tubes. These conditions usually respond to conservative treatment, with or without antibiotics (Klapproth 1976).

A promising new nonsurgical alternative to vasectomy is a process called **vas sclerosing.** In this procedure, the wall of the vas deferens is injected with small quantities of material that produce scarring, thus blocking the passageway of the vas. The technique greatly reduces the risks inherent in any surgical process, as well as overcoming the psychological objections that many men have to any cutting in the genital area.

Despite the skill and care of the surgeon, vasectomy failures occur at the rate of about 3 per 2000 persons, usually because of recanalization (spontaneous reconnection of the tubes) or unprotected coitus before the reproductive tract is cleared of sperm (Hatcher *et al.* 1976). In rare cases, an unsuspected third (or more) vas exists. Search of the literature reveals a worldwide incidence of somewhat less than 1% of spontaneous recanalization (Klapproth 1976). Whatever the cause, pregnancy following a vasectomy can be the source of severe misunderstanding and discord between a couple. It is therefore well, when vasectomy is the birth-control measure of choice, to understand beforehand that the surgical procedure is not always successful.

Success in reversing vasectomy surgically has been reported as high as 70%, but a more realistic figure may be as low as 5% (Hatcher *et al.* 1980). Willscher (1980) reports that use of microscopic surgical techniques helps to achieve a more precise connection of the previously severed vas. Willscher estimates that success in reversing vasectomy surgically can be such that 50% of the males may impregnate their mates. Some sperm may pass through the tubes after the reversal operation in up to 90% of the cases, but for one reason or another (too low a sperm count, diminished sperm viability, and antibodies created by the surgery itself), a lesser percentage of the men are able to impregnate after reversal. Few men ever seek corrective surgery, however. Out of approximately 11.5 million vasectomies performed in India, as an example, there were fewer than 10 requests for reversal surgery (Chase 1969). Other researchers estimate that as many as one out of 2000 vasectomized men seek reversal surgery (Lewis & Lewis 1980b).

Sperm banks offer another solution for the man who might change his mind after a vasectomy, but only if he anticipates the possibility. Before surgery he need only store a sample of his ejaculate, to be used later in artificial insemination. At least four centers for freezing and storing semen presently exist in the U.S., although the long-term viability of stored sperm has not yet been demonstrated (*Williams Obstetrics* 1976).

Despite the fact that they know a vasectomy does not decrease sex drive or the ability to satisfy it, men are nevertheless often reluctant to have the operation. In an investigation of 151 subjects who had been vasectomized, 17.9% reported an increase in sexual appetite, 74.2% showed no change, and only 7.9% reported a slight diminishing of desire (Russell 1961). Other investigators suggest that two-thirds of men who undergo vasectomies may experience enhanced sexual enjoyment during coitus (Lewis & Lewis 1980b). The increase in sexual drive is probably a consequence of psychological factors, such as reduction of anxiety because the fear of causing pregnancy has been removed.

Other factors also seem implicated in the reluctance to undergo vasectomy, as revealed by an investigation of a group of vasectomized men and their wives by means of personal interviews and psychological testing (Ziegler *et al.* 1966). In the personal interviews—in which, of course, only conscious beliefs were expressed—the parties voiced unanimous satisfaction with the operation. In the psychological testing, however, in which unconscious feelings were revealed, both husbands and wives showed more anxiety, greater vulnerability to actual or imagined physical ailments, and a greater degree of overall sexual maladjustment than the control subjects did. The husbands also manifested more concern about masculinity than a control group did. Four years later, a follow-up study revealed that the differences in anxiety levels between the study and control groups had largely disappeared (Ziegler *et al.* 1969).

Castration, the second type of male sterilization, has been known and used since ancient times. If the man is an adult, castration—in which both testicles are surgically removed—does not necessarily lead to impotence. But there is a gradual loss of sexual desire with the passage of time because of loss of testicular hormones. This hormonal deficit may also cause such physiological changes as an increase in voice pitch, decrease in beard growth, and excess fat. Fortunately, the undesirable changes following castration can often be corrected with proper hormone therapy. Needless to say, almost no men voluntarily seek castration as a method of sterilization.

Abortion

Abortion is the spontaneous or induced expulsion from the uterus of an embryo before it has reached a point of development sufficient for its survival, generally considered to be the 28th week of gestation (Neumann 1961).

Spontaneous abortion is medical terminology for a miscarriage that occurs prior to the third month of fetal life. It is not a form of birth control. **Induced abortion** is a term used for expulsion of the embryo because of an intentional effort to terminate a pregnancy. Because it is a deliberate act to control pregnancy, it is considered a form of birth control.

Spontaneous Abortion

Spontaneous abortions, also called **miscarriages,** occur at a much higher rate than many people realize. It has been estimated that about 33% of all fertilized eggs abort before the next menstrual period is overdue. In these cases most women never realize that they are—or were—pregnant. An additional 25% of all pregnancies miscarry between the time of fertilization and labor, meaning that almost 60% of all pregnancies end before a viable birth occurs. These abortions and miscarriages occur, of course, without any human intervention (W. H. James 1970).

Some of the factors related to a high incidence of spontaneous abortion are of interest. For example, white women have only half the number of miscarriages that black women do. Fetal death rate is lower when the mothers are 20 to 24 years old than when they are under 20. Among women older than 24, fetal mortality rises rapidly with advancing age. There are 97 fetal deaths per 1000 pregnancies among mothers in the 20 to 24 age group, in comparison with 219 deaths per 1000 pregnancies among mothers 35 and older (Kiser *et al.* 1968).

Controlling for the age factor, miscarriage risk in a first pregnancy is lower than it is in subsequent pregnancies. And the risk rises in each additional conception: the risk is about twice as high in a fourth pregnancy as in a first. Furthermore, if a woman has already had one miscarriage, she runs twice the risk of other women that she will miscarry a second time. In multiple births, the fetal death risk rises in direct proportion to the number of babies conceived. There are 15 fetal deaths per 1000 pregnancies in single births, 42 per 1000 in twin births, and 61 per 1000 in triplet births (Westoff & Westoff 1971).

Induced Abortion

The subject of elective abortion appears throughout history in social, economic, political, and religious contexts. The Chinese are said to possess the oldest method of abortion, a procedure described in a manuscript over 4000 years ago.

One of the strongest opponents to abortion is the Roman Catholic Church. Yet the Church's position in the matter has shifted several times over the centuries. The earliest Christians called abortion infanticide. Later theologians debated the issue of the animation of the fetus; at which point of development might it be considered a living being, and its purposeful destruction murder? By the 12th century the penalty of excommunication was generally withdrawn in cases of abortion—provided that the fetus, if male, was less than 40 days old (80 days for females!). This position remained largely unchanged until 1588, when Pope Sixtus V declared that all abortions were a form of murder. Three years later his successor, Pope Gregory XIV, withdrew all penalties against those involved in an abortion, except when it was performed after 40 days of pregnancy. This decree held until 1869, at which time Pope Pius XI condemned all abortion, regardless of circumstance and length of pregnancy. The Church's present attitude toward abortion was thus established slightly over 100 years ago (Westoff & Westoff 1971). Recent remarks by Pope John Paul II reaffirm the Church's strong antiabortion stance (Houston 1979).

In ancient Greece opinion was divided on abortion. Hippocrates rejected the concept as a means of population control. He concluded in the Hippocratic Oath still taken by physicians today a pledge not to give a woman an abortive agent, which he considered an interference with nature. But his opinion was actually a minority one. Aristotle considered birth control the best method of population control, and he regarded abortion as an acceptable alternative when other methods failed (Neumann 1961).

To the Romans, abortion was simply the removal of a portion of the body, like an arm or leg. The idea that it might be murder did not occur to them. Here again, considerations of population control predominated, although abortion came to be practiced so extensively among the ruling classes that the ratio of citizens to slaves became a matter of political concern. As a result, efforts were made to outlaw abortion, but they met with only partial success.

The 1973 Supreme Court decision that permitted American women to have abortions on demand led to the formation of many anti-abortionist groups. The most prominent of these is the National Right to Life Committee, which claims 2800 chapters. The group is headed not by a Catholic but by

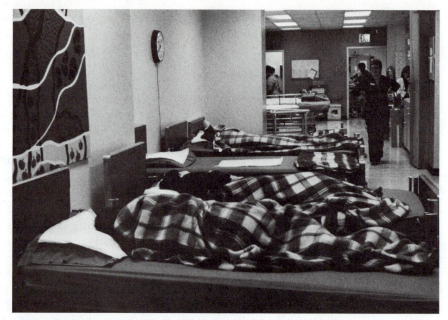

A scene from an abortion clinic (Erika Stone)

a black Methodist female surgeon, whose interest stems from the belief that legalized abortion is a genocide movement against minorities and the poor (Klemesrud 1976).

Generally speaking, the higher a woman's education, the more receptive she is to the idea of abortion. White women tend to be more in favor of abortion than black women at all levels of education. Yet the highest incidence of actual abortion is among the black poor. The group most favorable to abortion appears to be white non-Catholic college graduates; the group least favorable, white Catholic college graduates, 30% of whom reject all grounds for abortion (Westoff & Westoff 1971).

In a recent Gallup survey, 25% believed abortion should be legal under all circumstances, while 18% believed abortion should be illegal under all circumstances (The Gallup Opinion Index 1980). Over half believed abortion should be legal under certain circumstances. Interestingly, public opinion on abortion appears to have changed very little since the 1973 Supreme Court ruling.

The incidence of induced abortion.   Authorities differ on the incidence of ''criminal'' abortion prior to the easing of American law, but a reasonable estimate was 1 million a year (Hatcher *et al.* 1976). In the first six months following the liberalization of New York's abortion laws, 75,000 legal abortions were performed in New York City alone (Westoff & Westoff 1971). After two years, 334,865 had been performed, two-thirds on out-of-state residents, and 26% on women younger than 19. In the U.S. in 1976 the incidence of legalized abortions rose to 1,115,000, an 8% increase over the year before ("Legal Abortions Up" 1977). While married women seeking abortions were once said to outnumber single women 4 to 1, the ratio between married and single women dropped to about 50-50 immediately after legalization of abortion. In 1976 the ratio dropped still further: 4 single women to 1 married woman ("Legal Abortions Up" 1977).

Abortion remains today the principal method of population control in some countries and among certain primitive tribes. In certain Middle European countries, the incidence of legal abortion appears to be greater than that of live births. In Hungary, as an example, there are about 150 abortions per 100 births. In Belgrade alone, there are 4 abortions for every child born. In the U.S., too, abortions exceed live births for teen-agers below age 15; in 1976 this group had 15,000 abortions compared with 12,642 live births ("Legal Abortions Up" 1977).

In 1971 the World Health Organization reported that throughout the world there occur from 3 to 4 maternal deaths per 100,000 abortions, compared with 20 maternal deaths per 100,000 births in countries with good obstetric services (Associated Press 1971). In the one-year period following legalized abortion in New York State in 1970, pregnancy-related deaths declined by 56% (United Press International 1971b). Deaths associated with legal abortions numbered 2.6 per 100,000 in 1975, down from 4.1 per 100,000 three years earlier. Both figures are considerably below the death

Table 13.1. Maternal Mortality Associated with Pregnancy/Childbirth and Four Common Birth-Control Methods (after Tietze et al. 1976)

Age Group	Pregnancy and Childbirth Deaths*	Induced Abortion Deaths†	Pill Deaths‡	IUD Deaths‡	Tubal Sterilization Deaths§
15–19	10.8	2.3	1.3	1.0	—
20–24	8.5	1.9	1.3	1.0	—
25–29	12.1	1.9	1.3	1.0	10.0–20.0
30–34	25.1	4.2	4.8	1.0	10.0–20.0
35–39	41.0	9.2	6.9	1.0	12.5–25.0
40–44	69.1**	10.1	24.5	1.0	15.0–30.0

* Ratio per 100,000 live births.
† Ratio per 100,000 first-trimester abortions.
‡ Ratio per 100,000 users per year.
§ Ratio per 100,000 operations at beginning of age category.
** Ratio for *all* women over 40: 78.5 per 100,000 live births.

rate from complications of childbirth—11.2 per 100,000 live births (Vital Statistics 1979). When abortions are performed by unskilled persons and under nonsterile conditions, the incidence of severe complications and death is understandably high.

There is, of course, some risk involved in almost all birth-control techniques. But the incidence of death relative to the major reversible forms of birth control, whether abortion or contraceptive use (with the exception of the Pill after age 40), is very low in comparison with pregnancy and childbirth mortalities (Table 13.1).

Methods of Inducing Abortion

Abortion, among the oldest forms of folk medicine, has been attempted in many ways. Primitive efforts include jumping on the woman's abdomen; probing the uterus with sticks; potions made from animal secretions, dung, herbs, and seawater; and recourse to magic and mystical incantations. Self-induced abortion has been attempted through medications such as pills and injections, spraying the uterus with chemicals, and violent physical exercise. When abortion is not legal, there remains the illegal abortionist, who more often than not is a dangerous amateur. The most common procedure in these illegal abortions is a form of dilatation and curettage of the womb, which is most often done by the woman's partner or an abortionist who inserts some sort of instrument into the uterus and scrapes away the embryo. Abortionists' fees vary according to the socioeconomic status of the patient and, perhaps, of the abortionist as well: the higher the status of either, the higher the cost.

These are the indignities, dangers, and stresses women must undergo to obtain an abortion if one is not readily, legally, and safely available. *And no law prohibiting abortions has kept a woman from getting one, no matter how unsafe, if she really wants one.* Investigations into the medical and legal problems of abortion reveal that "abortion in itself is a safe, simple procedure without clinically significant psychiatric sequelae, but it becomes an emotionally traumatic experience because of medico-legal obstacles" (Fleck 1970). There are, to be sure, more legal abortions performed now than in the recent past. Even so, far too many women are still denied the right to have a legal abortion whenever they want one.

The vast majority of legal abortions are done on an outpatient basis, under local anesthetic, and using a suction technique. Several insurance companies cover abortions for single women and dependent children. City hospitals perform the operation on minors without parental consent if the patient is at least 17 years old and married, or, if she is unmarried, self-supporting, and living away from home (Westoff & Westoff 1971). A 1980 decision by the Supreme Court banning federal financing of abortions is likely to change the incidence of legal and illegal abortions in the near future ("Supreme Court" 1980).

Therapeutic or elective abortion. Hatcher *et al.* (1980) point out that the safety of abortion depends on three factors: prompt diagnosis of pregnancy, early referral, and prompt action by the gynecologist. The safest period for an abortion is the first trimester, especially between the 8th and 10th weeks. Abortions taking place after the 13th week of pregnancy are 3 or 4 times more risky than those performed earlier. An important aspect of liberalized abortion laws is that a woman can obtain an abortion quickly. Under restrictive laws, she is often forced to delay the abortion because she is unsure how to find someone to perform it, or how to raise the money for it (Tietze & Lewit 1972).

Therapeutic abortions are usually recommended when certain pathologic conditions exist. The most common are serious cardiac conditions, tuberculosis, certain malignancies, diabetes, some kidney diseases, certain mental diseases, German measles during the first trimester of pregnancy, and advanced hypertensive heart disease. They are also frequently recommended when pregnancy has resulted from rape or incest, or if the fetus is in danger of serious mental deficiency or physical abnormality (*Williams Obstetrics* 1976).

Therapeutic or elective abortions can be performed in several ways. **Menstrual extraction** is a common method, used when the menses is only a few days late. It is a suction technique, in which a thin flexible plastic tube is inserted into the uterus without the necessity of cervical dilation. Parts of the uterine lining and menstrual fluids that have been building up during the month are extracted, including a fertilized ovum if one happens to be present. The process requires a minimum of medication, takes only a few minutes to perform, can be done on an outpatient basis at relatively low cost, and has no troublesome aftereffects. Menstrual extraction is performed within the first two weeks of a missed period, which is too soon after ovaluation for laboratory tests to make an accurate diagnosis of pregnancy. The procedure therefore has the additional advantage of the woman's never knowing if she was actually pregnant, an important consideration for one who might be disturbed by undergoing an abortion.

Suction abortion or **vacuum curettage** can be used up to the 12th week of pregnancy when the woman knows she is pregnant. After that, the uterus is too soft and the fetus too large for this procedure ("Abortion in Two Minutes" 1972). In a recent 2-year period in New York City there were 1.5 maternal deaths per 100,000 suction abortions (Cherniak & Feingold 1973). Suction abortion differs from menstrual extraction in that the cervix is dilated, the inserted tube larger, and the suction stronger (DeLora & Warren 1977).

A **dilatation and curettage (D&C)** is frequently performed if pregnancy has not progressed beyond the 12th or 13th week. This procedure is performed in a hospital with the patient under anesthesia. The cervix is dilated by inserting graduated sizes of instruments to stretch the opening, the largest dilator being about the size and shape of a small cigar (Fig. 13.3). Or a seaweed (*Laminaria*) plug is inserted, which in 8 to 24 hours will have swollen sufficiently to dilate the cervix, permitting an easy D&C after its removal (*Williams Obstetrics* 1976). Once dilation is accomplished, a spoon-like instrument, a curette, is used to scrape the implanted embryo or early fetus from the uterus. The conceptus is usually broken up into small pieces in the process of raking out the uterine material. Care must be taken not to perforate the uterine wall.

Saline abortion, widely used in Japan after World War II but now abandoned there because of postabortion complications and death, has gained popularity in the U.S. in cases of pregnancy advanced beyond the 14th week (*Williams Obstetrics* 1976). A needle is inserted through the abdominal and uterine walls and a certain amount (usually 200 cc) of amniotic fluid is withdrawn. The fluid is then replaced with an identical

Figure 13.3   Lateral view of female reproductive system, showing dilatation and curettement. Dilator opens the cervix, through which curette is inserted to scrape uterine lining.

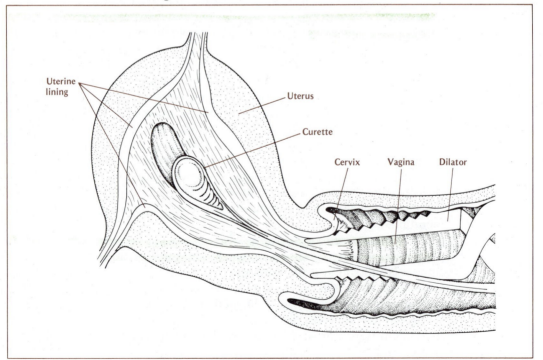

amount of saline solution. Within 6 to 48 hours, abortion occurs spontaneously. The procedure is more difficult, psychologically and physically, than vacuum curettage, which bolsters the case for performing an abortion in the first trimester of pregnancy (Cherniak & Feingold 1973). Mortality rate is about the same as in normal childbirth, and morbidity (medical complications) rate is 26.3 per 100 women (Hatcher *et al.* 1976). Other compounds, namely, urea and prostaglandins, are also being injected for abortions.

Hysterotomy is also a method used when pregnancy has advanced beyond 12 weeks (*Williams Obstetrics* 1976). One hysterotomic technique is actually a small caesarean section, a procedure used because the fetus is too large for usual methods of removal. In another technique, a vaginal incision is made near the cervix, and a slit is made in the lower part of the uterus, through which the fetus is removed. Since hysterotomy involves all the disadvantages of a major abdominal surgical procedure and has a morbidity rate of 23.1 per 100 women, its use is restricted (Hatcher *et al.* 1976).

The relative risk of the various types of abortion procedures, based upon the 1972–1976 death to case rate in the United States, is as follows: D&C, 1.0; saline abortion (including other infusion fluids), 9.1; hysterotomy and hysterectomy, 24.9; other methods, 5.8 (Hatcher *et al.* 1980, p. 149).

Contraception

In the long search for effective forms of birth control other than abortion and infanticide, primitive people evolved some curious contraceptive techniques. Some are effective, most ineffective, and many quite dangerous. In the attempt to cope with imperfectly understood biological processes, these people often brought religious beliefs, superstition, and magic into their efforts to control fertility.

An ancient Chinese belief, for example, held that a woman would not become pregnant if she remained completely passive during coitus. The philosophy underlying this belief was that a woman's enjoyment of intercourse was evil and merited punishment, pregnancy apparently being a form of it (Finch & Green 1963). Even today some women persist in the false belief that if they do not have an orgasm simultaneously with their partner, they will not become pregnant. Needless to say, holding back from orgasm will not prevent impregnation. The best proof is the fact that a woman can be made pregnant through artifical insemination, at which time no orgasm occurs at all.

The oldest medical prescription for a contraceptive, in about 1850 B.C., is found in the Egyptian Petri Papyrus. Women were advised to use a vaginal suppository concocted of crocodile dung and honey. The pastelike substance was apparently expected to prevent the sperm from entering the cervix (C. Allen 1968). Over the centuries some incredible substances and techniques have been tried—mouse dung, amulets, and induced sneezing, as examples. Some methods were at least partially effective; and when they were, a refinement of them occasionally led to a reasonably efficient contraceptive. The ancient Greeks, for instance, wrote that certain materials permeated with oil might constitute a workable contraceptive because oil slows down the movement of sperm. Thereafter, oil-saturated papers were inserted in the vagina to cover the cervix—a crude forerunner, perhaps, to today's diaphragm.

The 18th-century Italian adventurer Casanova is alleged to have placed a gold ball in the vagina to block the sperm's passage. He is also credited with using half a hollowed-out lemon as a diaphragm to cover the cervix. Perhaps the lemon shell did serve as an effective contraceptive, for citric acid can immobilize sperm. But if Casanova's reputation for sexual activity was deserved, and if in fact he managed not to impregnate any of his ladies (as he claimed), the most logical explanation is that his frequent ejaculations maintained his sperm count at such a low level that he was in effect sterile.

Just when the condom or penile sheath was first used is unclear. Some writers say that it has been used for centuries, perhaps even by the ancient Romans. The history of condoms includes the questionable story that a Dr. Condom in the court of England's King Charles II devised the contraceptive to help limit the number of the monarch's illegitimate offspring (Charles acknowledged 14 bastards). Or the word may come from the Latin *condus*, meaning receptacle, or the Persian *kendu* or *kondu*, meaning vessels for grain storage made from animal intestines. The 16th-century Italian anatomist Fallopius, who identified the female uterine tubes, recommended using linen condoms to prevent the spread of VD (Hatcher *et al.* 1974). Whatever its early history, the sheath was originally used more as a protection against VD than as a contraceptive (Tietze 1965).

The German scientist Graefenburg is generally credited with having introduced, in 1920, the use of foreign objects in the uterus to prevent pregnancy. This method is the forerunner of the **intrauterine device (IUD),** which is one of the most popular methods of present-day birth control. Instead of the plastic coil used today, Graefenburg used a coiled silver ring. Unfortunately, however, the metal often caused infection. But Graefenburg was not the first to use this technique. Centuries ago the Arabs put pebbles into the vagina or the uterus of female camels to keep them from becoming pregnant on long caravan treks across the desert (Westoff & Westoff 1971).

Despite the great technological advances of recent decades, the failproof contraceptive does not yet exist. And of all birth-control means, only these provide absolute safety from pregnancy: celibacy and the removal of the male or female gonads or the uterus. A contraceptive pill combining estrogen and progestin is not far behind in effectiveness. But despite the potential effectiveness of any birth-control technique, user error and inconsistency of use contribute far more to failure than faultiness in the method itself (Sandberg 1976).

Different investigators and organizations accord slightly different success-failure ratings to various methods, and they use different means to arrive at their totals. One system uses the term *woman-years*, and is calculated on the 13 menstrual cycles per year that a woman normally has. Fifteen failures of a particular technique per 100 woman-years means that 15 pregnancies occurred in 1300 cycles despite its use. Planned Parenthood Federation further defines success and failure according to *user* and *method*. User failure implies that a mistake, accident, or carelessness on the part of the user is involved. Method failure implies that the method was used correctly, and was used each time that coitus took place, yet pregnancy occurred anyway.

In 1955 it was estimated that 7 to 10 couples used some form of contraception (Westoff & Westoff 1971). By 1976 the number had risen to well over 8 in 10 (Ford 1978). When women who cannot conceive are excluded, the percentage who had used contraception, or expected to do so, rises to 97%. The major forms of contraception in use today are shown in Fig. 13.4.

Whether or not a couple uses contraceptives is directly related to educational level: the higher the education, the more likely they are to use some form (Freedman *et al.* 1959). One of the most important considerations in a couple's consistent use of a birth-control technique is their motivation to do so, motivation that is closely related to the acceptability of the technique.

Contraceptives Available with a Doctor's Prescription

With the exception of the condom and foam, the more reliable forms of contraception now available must be prescribed by a physician and should be used only with medical supervision.

The Diaphragm. A **diaphragm** is a thin, dome-shaped cup made of rubber or plastic, stretched over a collapsible rim, and designed to cover the entrance to the womb. In existence for over 100 years, it was the favorite birth-control device of women before the advent of the Pill and IUDs. To be effective, the diaphragm must always be used with a contraceptive cream or jelly; the device seals off the cervix while the cream or jelly inactivates the sperm. Neither interferes with the conduct or pleasure of intercourse.

The diaphragm must be fitted by a physician because of individual physiological differences in women. The physician will also show the patient how to insert it properly herself, and how to remove it. Having the correct size and shape is of vital importance, both for the wearer's comfort and for its effectiveness as a contraceptive. A woman cannot be fitted until her hymen is broken. Some physicians are therefore reluctant to prescribe a diaphragm until the woman has already engaged in coitus.

It is also a good idea to check the diaphragm occasionally for holes by holding it up to a light or filling it with water to see if there is any seepage. After use, it should be washed with soap and warm water and sprinkled with cornstarch (not talcum). It is important to dry the diaphragm thoroughly after it is washed and to make sure it is not stored in a rolled condition, which would damage it. It should not be stored in or near hot places. In addition, Vaseline or perfumed products can weaken the diaphragm rubber, and long, sharp fingernails can puncture the rubber if

Figure 13.4   The major contraceptive measures in use today.

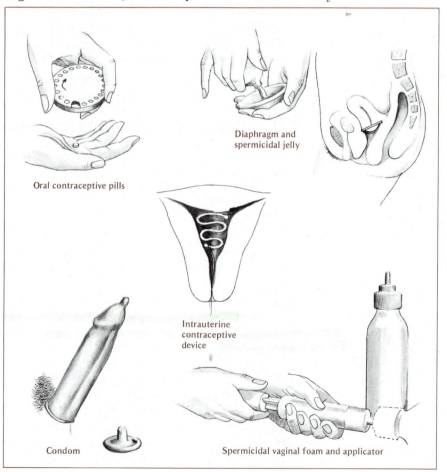

Oral contraceptive pills

Diaphragm and spermicidal jelly

Intrauterine contraceptive device

Condom

Spermicidal vaginal foam and applicator

Learning about birth control: A dimension in family planning. (Erika Stone)

proper care is not taken (Lane 1980; Lieberman & Peck 1975). A diaphragm usually must be refitted every year or two, and after each pregnancy, abortion, gynecological procedure, or weight change (10 lb or more) that might alter vaginal dimensions.

A diaphragm may be inserted several hours before coitus, or immediately preceding it. However, the spermicidal cream or jelly must be inserted not longer than 2 hours before intercourse, and additional cream or jelly added if coitus is repeated (Lieberman & Peck 1975). The device must not be removed until 6 hours after the final act of intercourse, and should not be left in place longer than 24 hours lest it encourage the growth of bacteria and lead to infection. If a woman wishes to douche, she must wait at least 6 hours following coitus to allow ample time for the spermicide to be fully effective.

One advantage of the diaphragm is that it can be used to hold the menstrual flow in the uterus for 24 hours. This makes coitus during menses more acceptable for some people (Hatcher 1976).

Diaphragms are considered by some to be inconvenient, uncomfortable, and difficult to use (Rodgers *et al.* 1965). And for some couples, the advance preparation interferes with spontaneity, which may detract from sexual pleasure. Another objection is that they can become dislodged in intercourse, especially in the woman-atop position (Hatcher *et al.* 1976).

Method failure is recorded at 2 to 4 per 100 woman-years; user failure, 10 to 20 per 100 woman-years.*

The Cervical Cap.   The **cervical cap** is a miniature diaphragm that fits over the cervix and is kept in place by suction. Cervical caps have been in use for many years (those made for use 20 to 40 years ago were often of silver and gold), but their effectiveness was not as good as the diaphragm. Estimates have indicated the failure rate at 8 per 100 woman-years. Caps manufactured in England are of soft rubber or impermeable plastic and are used in conjunction with a spermicide. Studies on the effectiveness of these new cervical caps are presently being done (Hatcher *et al.* 1980).

Oral Contraceptives.   It was demonstrated in 1937 that the administration of the ovarian hormone progesterone would inhibit ovulation in rabbits. Thereafter endocrinologists, biologists, chemists, and physicians, working together and separately, developed a method of contraception for human beings that appeared superior to any previously employed (Searle 1964).

In 1954 an **oral contraceptive** in the form of a pill was used in laboratory research; two years later well-controlled field tests were made in Puerto Rico and Haiti to determine its safety and effectiveness. The experiments were tremendously successful. Oral contraceptives were first licensed for use in the U.S. in 1960, and by 1974, 20% of women between 15 and 44 years were taking them (Goldzieher & Rudel 1974). Today the Pill, as oral contraceptives are popularly called, is used by perhaps 10 to 15 million American women (and 80 to 100 million women worldwide). The FDA has listed its failure rate as 0.01%. (A second type of birth control is recommended as a backup during the first month of taking the Pill, however.) Since their introduction, pharmaceutical houses have been working overtime to supply safer pills with fewer unpleasant side effects.

The Pill is a combination of synthetic hormones (progesterone and estrogen). When taken in adequate dosage, they prevent ovulation by mimicking the hormones produced naturally by the body during pregnancy. If no ovum is released, pregnancy obviously cannot occur. The Pill actually does several things to prevent pregnancy or make it extremely unlikely to occur (Trainer 1965). First, production of pituitary gonadotropin is inhibited. This interferes with the growth and development of the ovarian follicles. In addition, the uterine mucosa is affected in such a manner as to make

* Unless otherwise noted, effectiveness rates shown in this chapter are those of Planned Parenthood Federation of America, Inc., booklet No. 1253, "Basics of Birth Control."

implantation more difficult and early spontaneous abortion more likely if an egg were to be fertilized. The mucous plug of the cervix is thickened by the hormonal agents, thereby interfering with sperm's passage into the uterus. In 1980 about 30 different brands of contraceptive pills were available (Hatcher *et al.* 1980), most of them to be taken as follows:

Counting from the first day of her monthly menstrual period, a woman starts taking the pills on the fifth day. She must swallow one pill daily, and preferably at the same hour, for 20 days. Menstruation will start two to five days after the last pill is taken, although in about 3% of the cases it fails to begin. In the latter event, a physician usually advises the patient to begin a new round of 20 pills seven days after the last was taken, or alternate suggestions will be offered.

If a woman misses taking a Pill, she should take one immediately after she remembers it, then take the next Pill at the regular time. If she misses two, she should take two immediately after she thinks of it and two the next day. If three are missed, chances are that ovulation will occur; hence pregnancy is a real possibility. That packet of Pills should be thrown away and a backup birth-control method immediately used (Hatcher *et al.* 1980). Method failure with the combination Pill (estrogen-progesterone) is less than 1 per woman-year; user failure, 2 to 4. It should be noted that taking

The Pill. (Randy Matuson)

other drugs at the same time as oral contraceptives may decrease the efficacy of the contraceptives. Consultation with a physician or pharmacist about potential interaction effects is recommended.

Should a woman become pregnant while taking the Pill, some physicians recommend that she seek an abortion. Other physicians are not as concerned because the associated risks of having a malformed infant are only slightly increased when the Pill is taken during the first or second months of pregnancy (Hatcher *et al.* 1980).

Minipills have been in use since 1973. They are taken throughout the month, even during menses, eliminating the chore of counting pills and of stopping and restarting a series. Their use is indicated for those who have developed adverse estrogen-related symptoms, or might do so, from the combination Pill. The estrogenic component causes most of the Pill-associated complications. Containing progestin alone, Minipills do not necessarily inhibit ovulation, nor do they interfere with menstruation. Instead, they make the reproductive system resistant to sperm transport, ovum transport, or blastocyst implantation should fertilization take place. Their effectiveness is slightly less than that of the combination Pill, failure being highest during the first six months of use (Hatcher *et al.* 1980; *Williams Obstetrics* 1976). Method failure has been set at 2 to 3 per 100 woman-years; user failure, 2 to 4.

Like certain other medications, especially those taken for extended periods, the Pill is not an unmixed blessing. It creates certain unpleasant side effects in about 40% of women (Hatcher *et al.* 1980), and poses certain health risks. The most common symptoms, experienced primarily in the first months, are mild gastrointestinal disturbances, nausea, a bloated feeling and weight increase, and spotting and irregular bleeding. Other occasional negative effects are persistent cramping and painful swelling of the breasts (Trainer 1965). Presence of these side effects may dictate a switch to one of the Minipills. The Pill is definitely contraindicated in some women, especially those with certain clinical conditions, or who are over 40 years old, smokers, and overweight.

An analysis of inherent risks in various contraceptive means by the Population Council, released by the Planned Parenthood Federation in February 1976 (Tietze *et al.* 1976), confirmed the danger of the Pill for women over 40. The risk of death is 20 times greater than for younger women—25 per 100,000 users per year compared with 1.5 in women under 30. However, the council report pointed out that no method is without risk. (Risk is calculated not only on the basis of death caused by a contraceptive itself, but also from deaths linked to pregnancy resulting from contraceptive failures.)

The grave complications related to the Pill include pulmonary embolism, cerebral thrombosis, stroke, clotting disorders, and heart attack (DeLora & Warren 1977). A major study (Collaborative Group 1975) showed that Pill users of all ages incurred a fourfold risk over nonusers of strokes involving arterial blockage by blood clots. Another investigation, however, has suggested that fears concerning the Pill are exaggerated. New findings suggest that women who use the Pill do not have higher death rates and do not run greater risks of having circulatory problems or uterine, ovarian, or breast cancer than nonusers ("Reassessing the Pill's Risks" 1980). Women receiving placebos they thought were oral contraceptives also report a high incidence of side effects—a loss of sex drive (30%), headaches (16%), and nervousness (6%). Only one-third reported no side effects at all (Bragonier 1976).

It has been suggested that the Pill should not be used by girls who have not reached physical maturity—between 13 and 18 years, with the average being 16 years—because it can interfere with completion of normal growth and maturation (Cherniak & Feingold 1973). Further, since the Pill suppresses milk production, its use is not recommended during the period just after childbirth when a mother is nursing her baby. There is also evidence that if a mother takes the Pill while nursing a male child, the unusual combination of hormones in her body can enter the baby's bloodstream and have a feminizing effect on him (Curtis 1964).

Some women have expressed concern that taking the Pill will adversely affect their sex drive. Indeed, some authorities have warned women to expect some loss after protracted use of the Pill because of its interference with normal hormonal production (Trainer 1965). Masters and Johnson report that a reduction in women's sex drive occurs after taking the Pill for 18 to 36 months, and they suggest that other contraceptive methods be substituted from time to time, according to the advice of the individual woman's physician, so that the original hormonal balance can be restored (Masters & Johnson 1967). The Pill is also used to treat certain discomforts and disorders of the menstrual cycle, such as irregularity, too copious flow of blood, and discomfort before or during menstruation.

In a later critical review of the literature about claims for either positive or negative influences of the Pill on sexual responsiveness in women, Bragonier (1976) reports that it is unclear whether there is an increase or decrease in erotic drive. Women using the Pill do seem to have sexual intercourse more frequently than other women of the same age, race, religion, and education, and their coital rate increases with time.

All cautions about the Pill, however, should be weighed against the hazards of unwanted or dangerous pregnancies the Pill might have prevented. The following paragraphs set out some of the consequences of *not* using the Pill, although older women should consider statistics with their gynecologists to determine if an alternative contraceptive might not be advisable for them.

In their 1971 study of the 8.5 million women then using the Pill, whether strictly according to prescription or in a more casual way, Westoff and Westoff estimated that 340,000 pregnancies could be expected. If these same women had been using other forms of birth control, that expectation would jump to 2.5 million pregnancies. In the same sampling, 324 would have died of thromboembolic disease caused by the Pill. However, there would have been 1179 deaths if these same women had used other, less effective contraceptives, because of the typical complications arising from pregnancy, childbirth, and the postpartum period. It can therefore be estimated that the risk of dying was 3.5 times greater without the Pill than with it. Among women using no method of birth control, incidentally, the risk of maternal death is 7.5 times greater than it is among women taking the Pill (Hardin 1970). Perhaps the best summary of this discussion is found in *Williams Obstetrics* (1976):

> Concern has been rightfully raised for the safety of users of oral contraceptives. Fortunately, no major disasters have occurred and, in general, the use of oral contraceptives, when appropriately monitored, has proved to be safe for the great majority of women.

Other Hormonal Contraceptives.   Long-term (3-month) progesterone injections (called "The Shot") are now in use in 70 countries and are thought to be close to FDA approval in the U.S. The theoretical effectiveness rate is 0.25 per 100 woman-years. Contraindications to its use are the same as those applicable to the combination Pill. Also, the reversibility of infertility, once injections are stopped, needs further investigation (Hatcher *et al.* 1980).

Vaginal rings have been devised, which are impregnated with progestins. The rings are smaller than diaphragms but are used like them. They are inserted after the woman's menstrual flow is over and are left in place for 21 days, during which time the woman's body absorbs the slow-releasing progestins that serve to prevent pregnancy (Hatcher *et al.* 1976).

Intrauterine Devices (IUDs).   **IUDs are small plastic devices designed for insertion into the womb.** How the IUD prevents conception is not completely clear, but the best theory is that it makes the uterus resistant to ovum implantation. Technically, then, the method is not a form of contraception. It should more correctly be called contraimplantation.

IUDs have been used for 2000 years for many purposes, and have been made of wool, ivory, glass, and even diamond-studded platinum! Interest in them was rekindled in the late 1950s, and their present-day development was sparked by the Population Council (DeLora & Warren 1977).

The device must be selected and fitted in the uterus by a physician. Tiny plastic threads attached to the IUD protrude an inch or so into the vagina. If the threads cannot be felt with the fingers, the woman can assume that the IUD has been rejected. Or if the IUD itself is protruding from the cervix, it is ineffective. In both instances the woman must see a doctor and, in the meantime, use another form of birth control. Hatcher *et al.* (1976) recommends that backup contraception habitually be used midcycle (time of ovulation) and during the first four months after IUD insertion.

The IUD remains permanently in place until the woman wishes to become pregnant, at which time the doctor removes it (she or her partner should never attempt to extract the device). After the child is born, another IUD can be inserted. An IUD in no way affects the health of any children born to the woman or to her ability to conceive. The IUD is *not* recommended when there is pelvic or VD infection, uterine disorder or a too-small internal or external os; or when conditions such as severe dysmenorrhea, heavy menstrual bleeding, severe anemia, rheumatic fever, and impaired immune response are present (D. L. Cooper 1975). Even so, Pap smears (clinical tests made to detect cervical cancer) taken from thousands of IUD users reveal neither occurrence of cancer beyond its normal incidence in the female population nor evidence of other adverse effects that could be attributed to the devices.

There are certain disadvantages to using IUDs. Some women experience pain on insertion and cramping for several days afterward. Some have heavy menstrual bleeding and spotting, especially in the first months after insertion. In rare instances uterine perforation and pelvic infection have occurred (Sandberg 1976). Although further investigation is needed, some specialists have observed a significant increase in ectopic pregnancy among women who have used IUDs for longer than two years compared with those who have used them for a lesser period (*Williams Obstetrics* 1976).

The most bothersome problem with the IUD is undetected expulsion. It is estimated that spontaneous expulsion is experienced by 8–10% of women (Boston Women's 1973), especially by those who have never been pregnant. Expulsion typically occurs in the first three months after insertion and during menstruation. But about 40% who do expel the device manage to retain it once it is reinserted (Westoff & Westoff 1971). After menses, the woman or her partner should check for the tiny threads, a check that should be repeated once a week between periods.

Failure rate is estimated at 2 to 4 per 100 woman-years. When pregnancy does occur, the spontaneous abortion rate is 25% if the device is removed, about 50% if it is not (DeLora & Warren 1977; *Williams Obstetrics* 1976).

The shapes and materials of IUDs are many. Perhaps the most widely known are the Lippes Loop, the Copper 7 (small, made of plastic, and wound around with 89 mg of copper wire), the Copper T, and the Saf-T Coil (*Williams Obstetrics* 1976). Another T-shaped device, called Progestasert, is an important recent addition to the group. A small flexible unit, it is the first hormone-enhanced IUD on the market. It releases small continuous doses of the natural female hormone progesterone. It thus combines the effects of an IUD and hormonal inhibition of blastocyst implantation (not ovulation). The hormone also acts to thicken cervical mucus, which impedes sperm passage (Connell 1975). An additional advantage is that Progestasert seems less likely than most IUDs to cause cramping. It must be replaced every year, however, because it loses its hormonal effectiveness. The Copper T and Copper 7 must be replaced every 2 to 4 years for similar reasons (Brody 1980). Other types may remain in place indefinitely, until a pregnancy is desired.

In 1965 IUDs were the birth-control method of choice of only 1% of women. By 1977, the percentage had grown to 15%. Even so, 23% of users discontinue the IUD after the first year (DeLora & Warren 1977).

Contraceptives Available without a Doctor's Prescription

The Condom.   One of the most widely used contraceptive devices in the United States is the **condom,** also called a rubber, French letter, and prophylactic. Short of abstinence, it is one of only three effective male birth-control techniques demonstrated to date. There are about 1 billion condoms sold annually in this country (DeLora & Warren 1977). The flourishing market is probably a result of growing alarm about the dangers of the Pill and IUDs ("Birth Control: New Look at the Old" 1977), and of the ever-present concern about VD.

Condoms are made of strong thin rubber or sheep's intestine, their design and color often dazzling to the eye. They are cheap, simple to use, easily disposable; they are readily available in pharmacies and various men's restrooms, and have a shelf life of 2 years. The condom is a simple cylindrical sheath, with a rubber ring about 1.5 in. (3.6 cm) in diameter at the open end, and about 7.5 in. (19 cm) long. The closed end is usually plain, but some have a pocket to provide space for ejaculated semen. If there is no pocket, about 0.5 in. (1.5 cm) of the closed end should be pressed together when the condom is put on.

Since the FDA placed condoms under its control, the quality has been improved. The only problems preventing them from being totally effective are the possibility of breakage during use and of their slipping off during withdrawal after ejaculation, allowing semen to be spilled into the vagina. This second eventuality can be avoided if there is adequate vaginal lubrication and if the condom is held onto at the base of the penis while it is withdrawn.

Condoms should always be inspected before use by blowing air into them, and it is advisable afterward to fill them with water to be sure that no breakage has occurred. If a condom breaks in use, a contraceptive foam should be applied vaginally immediately. Once a condom has been used, it is best to throw it away and not try to re-use it.

Prior to the development of the vulcanization process, the French and English used sheep gut or the amniotic membrane of newborn lambs (Trainer 1965) to fashion fairly satisfactory condoms. In recent years, manufacturers have again begun producing gut condoms, which are aesthetically preferable because they interfere less with body warmth and other pleasurable sensations experienced during coitus. They appear to be as safe as the rubber ones.

Some men object to the condom because it dulls the pleasure of coitus. Its use may interfere with the natural progress of mounting sexual tension, because sex play must be interrupted to put it on. This objection may be overcome if the women makes rolling the condom onto the penis part of her love play (Hatcher *et al.* 1980).

The method failure of condoms is 2 to 4 per 100 woman-years; user failure is 10 to 20. These figures are no doubt reduced when the condom is used along with contraceptive foam. An added advantage of the condom is that, except for total abstinence, it is certainly the best (although certainly not an absolute) method of preventing the spread of VD. (Foam is also, to an extent, a barrier to VD infection.)

Foam, Creams, Jellies, and Other Chemical Methods. Contraceptive foam, which is introduced into the vagina with a plastic applicator, prevents conception in two ways. It blocks sperm from entering the cervix, and it contains an ingredient toxic to sperm. Creams and jellies are considered less effective than foam, but more effective than foam when used with a diaphragm.

A prescribed amount of foam is injected as deeply as possible in the vagina no later than 15 to 30 minutes before intercourse. The container should be shaken vigorously; the more bubbles, the greater the coverage. If coitus is repeated, an additional application must be used. If douching is desired (foam can be rather messy), at least 8 hours from the last ejaculation must have elapsed. It is a good idea to keep a spare container of foam on hand, because usually there is no way of knowing when the supply is running out.

One objection to foam is that it is unpleasant to the taste in cunnilingus. Interruption of sex play to insert foam is an objection in itself, although the man may use the insertion as part of his love play. The success of foam in preventing pregnancy is not spectacular—although method failure is 2 to 4 per 100 woman-years, user failure is 10 to 20 per 100. These failures occur primarily because not enough of the substance is used, or it is not used before every ejaculation, and douching is done too soon after the last ejaculation (DeLora & Warren 1977).

There are various other insertable spermicides—jellies, suppositories, tablets—but their effectiveness varies widely. One problem is that instructions for use are often unclear. Generally speaking, aerosol foams are the most successful of the chemical contraceptive agents (Hatcher *et al.* 1980).

Douches. Douching should *not* be considered a means of birth control; there is no medical support for its effectiveness. Its purpose is to flush seminal fluid from the vagina before it has a chance to enter the mouth of the womb. Actually, however, sperm move so quickly that the douche often fails to reach them, even if the woman leaps out of bed seconds after ejaculation. Further, douching can have the opposite effect; it can push sperm more quickly toward the cervix than they might otherwise travel (DeLora & Warren 1977).

Douching is actually unnecessary, because the natural secretions of a healthy woman keep her vaginal tract clean. But if douching after intercourse is desired for purely aesthetic reasons, water alone, or water to which vinegar, lemon juice, or alum is added, might be used. It should always be borne in mind, however, that frequent douching can destroy the colonies of beneficial bacteria that normally inhabit the vagina, thus leaving it vulnerable to organisms causing vaginitis. Commercial douche preparations can have the same effect.

Other Methods of Birth Prevention

Within the definition of contraception—which includes any agent or voluntary means of preventing conception—the following methods of birth control are commonly included. Since they do not involve mechanical or chemical methods, they are discussed separately.

Coitus Interruptus or Withdrawal.   **Coitus interruptus** requires the man to withdraw his penis from the woman's vagina before he reaches a climax. Many couples rely upon this technique of birth prevention for years with both success and satisfaction and without experiencing any of its alleged dangers to health. Certainly it is the oldest known form of contraception.

The popular misconception that prolonged reliance on this method will cause premature ejaculation is not supported by evidence. But there are certain disadvantages. Sexual intercourse cannot be enjoyed in a relaxed mood by either partner if the uppermost thought is withdrawal in the nick of time. For a woman slow to reach orgasm, preejaculatory withdrawal by her partner may not allow sufficient time for her to reach orgasm. In such cases the result may be congestion of blood in her genital organs, and, possibly, chronic pelvic pain and other gynecological complaints.

The first few drops of the ejaculate contain the great bulk of the male spermatozoa. Should the man be slow to withdraw, and should any of this first ejaculate enter the vagina, *coitus interruptus* can very easily fail. Furthermore, the secretion in the Cowper's glands of many men contain sperm cells that frequently ooze into the vagina even if no ejaculation follows (J. L. McCary 1966).

A distressing aspect of *coitus interruptus* is the man's responsibility to withdraw at the crucial moment. When ejaculation is about to occur, the typical male impulse is to drive the penis as deeply into the vagina as possible and to hold it there. The man should also time coital activity so that his withdrawal and ejaculation occur after his partner's climax. In addition, he would be most unwise to reenter the vagina for a considerable period of time after ejaculation, because of the presence of residual sperm in his urethra.

Generally speaking, those couples who use *coitus interruptus or* withdrawal extensively do not find it particularly undesirable; other couples despise the technique. In the absence of any other method, certainly it is better than nothing. The failure rate is 9–15 per 100 woman-years in consistent users and its overall failure rate, 20 to 25 (Hatcher *et al.* 1980).

Periodic-Abstinence Methods (Natural Birth Control). The **rhythm** or **calendar method** relies on timing coitus so that it occurs only when the woman is supposedly infertile. Authorities differ on the subject, but it is a generally accepted biological postulate that an ovum lives approximately 24 hours after ovulation unless it is fertilized (Landis & Landis 1963; Lehfeldt 1961b). Sperm released into the uterus remain alive and capable of fertilizing the egg for about 48 hours. This means that only during three days a month can a woman become pregnant. The difficulty, of course, is pinpointing the exact three days.

As a general rule, the average woman releases an ovum 14 to 16 days before her next menstrual period is due. If she menstruates every 28 days, she should ovulate midway between the two periods—about the 13th to 15th day after the first day of her period. In a 25-day cycle, ovulation should occur between the 10th and 12th day; if it is 35 days, between the 20th and 22nd days. About 70% of women ovulate between the 11th and 15th day of the cycle (Lachenbruch 1967).

Because different women menstruate on different schedules, a written menstrual record is usually kept for 12 consecutive months to determine the fertile ("unsafe") and infertile ("safe") days. Charts for this purpose are obtainable from family planning centers.

Only about a third of women are regular enough in menstruation to safely use the calendar method to avoid conception (Brayer *et al.* 1969). Women who vary as much as 10 days or more in the length of their cycles should have medical advice to determine their "safe" period. After childbirth the first few menstrual cycles may be very irregular, making the rhythm method particularly unreliable at that time.

The **temperature method** of birth control is based on the same biological postulation that rhythm is: the time of monthly ovulation. This technique does not rely merely on calendar observations of day 1 of menstruation. It is founded on the additional premise that there is a distinct correlation between changes in body temperature and the process of ovulation. A woman's temperature is usually relatively low during menstruation itself and for 8 days thereafter—13 days in all. At the time of ovulation, midway in the cycle, there is a dip in temperature and then a sharp rise of 0.5° to 0.7°. The elevation persists for the remainder of the cycle, then drops one or two days before the onset of the next period.

To achieve any sort of accuracy in predicting her "safe" period according to the temperature method, a woman must record her temperature, preferably upon awakening, every morning for 6 to 12 months. (Temperature kits can be bought at pharmacies without a prescription.) The primary difficulty in so determining a "safe" period for intercourse is that in some women the changes in temperature are not so pronounced or so consistent, although a doctor is much more skilled in interpreting temperature charts than the layperson. Another difficulty is that more than one ovum can mature during any one cycle. Furthermore, research (Buxton, Engle 1950) has indicated that the time interval between ovulation and the temperature rise can vary as much as four days.

Another variation of "natural birth control" has been called the **Billings method** (Billings *et al.* 1974). Rather than relying on a calendar, thermometer, or the cumulative information from several menstrual cycles, the Billings method is based on a specific symptom of approaching ovulation—namely, a cervical mucous discharge. The theory is that menstruation is typically followed by "dry days," in which there is a sensation of dryness in the genital region and during which time coitus is considered safe. Then a cloudy, sticky mucous discharge begins. (If there were no "dry days," mucous secretion is assumed to have begun after menstruation.) Clear mucus of the consistency of raw egg white, lasting a day or two, marks the peak of the symptom; ovulation immediately follows the peak. The mucus then becomes sticky and cloudy again, or disappears. The two days before and the three days following the peak are considered unsafe. The fourth day onward following the peak is considered an infertile period. Each cycle is judged individually, and charts are available to mark the sequence of events.

As the director of the Planned Parenthood Association has commented, the difficulty in this method is recognizing the onset of the mucous discharge. Yet preliminary reports of ongoing applications of this ovulation method in several countries show promising, though inconclusive, results (Wilson 1980). One study (Dolack 1980) indicated a 3.2 pregnancy rate per 100 woman-years in couples who were highly motivated to prevent pregnancy. This rate compares favorably with the diaphragm and is superior to some other popular methods of birth control.

Method failure in the periodic-abstinence techniques is 5 to 10 per 100 woman-years; user failure, 20 to 30.

Lactation as Birth Preventive. Lactation, especially when there is no supplemental feeding of the infant, does provide conception protection, for it usually suppresses ovulation. This is of special importance in developing countries. A study in Rwanda, for instance, showed that 50% of nonlactating mothers become pregnant within 4 months of delivery, whereas 50% of nursing mothers remain unpregnant for 18 months. Lactation's theoretical effectiveness is 15 per 100 woman-years of amenorrhea; actual effectiveness, 40 per 100 woman-years. Another important consideration in the matter of breastfeeding is that in Asia, as an example, if mothers ceased nursing their babies, a herd of 114 million cattle would be needed to make up the difference—a 40% increase over present numbers (Jelliffe & Jelliffe 1977; quoted in Hatcher *et al.* 1976).

According to estimates (Ryder 1973) the failure rates associated with commonly used birth-control techniques are these: the Pill, 6%; IUD, 12%, condom, 18%, diaphragm, 23%, foam, 31%, rhythm, 33%, and douche, 39%. At first glance these figures seem exceptionally high, but it bears repeating that carelessness in the proper use of a particular technique increases incidence of failure.

After-the-Fact Birth Prevention

A "morning-after Pill"—diethystilbestrol (DES)—can be used when unprotected coitus has occurred. It is often used after rape. Dosage must begin within 72 hours, preferably 24, and continue for 5 days. The possibility exists, however, of severe side effects—not only for the woman but for the infant, if one is already conceived. The baby may be malformed; and a female child may later develop vaginal carcinoma (Lieberman & Peck 1975). Because of these risks, the FDA has given approval for DES as an emergency measure only, and it is not to be thought of as a primary method of birth control. Also undergoing tests at present are the use of progestins and Ovral oral contraceptive tablets as morning-after pills. Although the initial results are encouraging, especially since they are safer than taking DES, the FDA has not yet given its approval.

Another after-the-event possibility is a next-morning IUD insertion, which may prevent the implantation of a fertilized ovum still on its journey to the uterus from the fallopian tube. The Copper 7 may be best for this purpose (Hatcher *et al.* 1980).

Birth-Control Techniques of the Future

There is considerable evidence that people need a much better method of fertility control than is now available. The side effects of the Pill, and fear of it, have caused many women to abandon its use. Other facts pointing to the need for more effective methods of birth control include the discomfort, expulsion rate, and occasional failure of IUDs; the high failure rate of most other contraceptives; and the great number of abortions and unwanted children. The 1971 book *From Now to Zero* (Westoff & Westoff) postulated that about 75% of all American women are sterile, pregnant, or trying to become pregnant; or they are using a birth-control technique that is relatively ineffective, inconvenient, messy, or incompatible with the natural, spontaneous enjoyment of intercourse. So scientists are turning their attention to new techniques and methods of birth control.

A technique involving a low dosage of progestin is currently being developed. A thin capsule 1 in. (2.5 cm) in length containing progestin is inserted into the woman's leg, arm, or groin by means of a hypodermic needle. The capsule releases just enough progestin at a constant rate to keep her from becoming pregnant. If she then decides to have a baby, it is necessary only to remove the capsule. Capsules capable of releasing progestin for as long as 1, 3, or 10 years—or even a lifetime—may be used.

It has been predicted that vaccines will be developed to immunize a woman against her partner's sperm, much as one is now vaccinated against smallpox, and to immunize a man with substances inhibitory to sperm production.

Scientists at the University of Georgia have identified a substance called DF (decapacitation factor) in the fluid surrounding human sperm cells. This substance, which protects the surface layer of sperm, must be removed if a sperm is to penetrate an ovum. The Georgia scientists believe that female enzymes act to destroy DF, thus making the sperm's penetration of the ovum possible. Fertilization might be prevented, they theorize, if destruction of the DF by these enzymes could be blocked off, or if DF could be biosynthesized and introduced into the fallopian tubes (Westoff & Westoff 1971).

Another possibility lies in the development of a contraceptive from natural sources, thus avoiding the potential harmful side effects of synthetic drugs. Scientists may have discovered a plant that, when brewed and drunk as a tea, can provide "morning-after" protection. Such a beverage would also have the advantages of ease of use and inexpensiveness, two factors particularly important in developing countries ("Contraception" 1980).

Biochemists continue to work on a hormonal birth-control technique for men designed to suppress production of the millions upon millions of sperm manufactured by a man in his reproductive life. In the view of most researchers, a workable technique is still several years away (Hatcher *et al.* 1980). To date, inhibition of spermatogenesis, by testosterone or progesterone, has caused complications. Hormonal interference is slow to act and affects the sex drive of some men. Fertility is slow to return and intake of alcohol may cause some abnormal reactions (Rubin 1961; Westoff & Westoff 1971). Further, testosterone and other androgens are critically linked with prostatic cancer and are associated as well with glaucoma and hardening of the arteries.

To arrive at a hormonal dosage low enough not to affect metabolic processes, yet effective enough to block spermatogenesis, demands an extremely delicate balance. A Pill that acts to prevent sperm from maturing may be more of a possibility (Westoff & Westoff 1971).

A device that measures the consistency of cervical fluid has been developed and is now being tested for effectiveness. Based on the principle that cervical fluid is thick and impenetrable by sperm except during the time around ovulation, the plastic device (called an ovutimer) is inserted into the vagina, where cervical fluid will cause two small plastic plates engraved with microscopic grooves to stick together or not, depending upon the woman's fertility that day. The developers of the device expect accuracy (and thus safety) within the range of the Pill ("Rhythm-linked" 1977).

Nothing in history matched the contraceptive revolution of the 1960s, sparked primarily by the introduction of the Pill, which demonstrated that improved technology can play a crucial role in combating unwanted pregnancy. Yet contraceptive failure has continued in "epidemic proportions." One U.S. survey of persons with low incomes revealed that less than half knew how to use a contraceptive effectively. This ignorance was particularly apparent among young people 15 to 18 years old (Speidel 1970). The problem is even more acute in underdeveloped countries, in which the techniques used are, as Harkavy and Maier (1973) point out, "too expensive, too complicated, too dependent on the medical profession" for pronounced success.

In Western cultures, at least, procreation and recreation are now recognized as two separate goals in sexual activity, neither of which need be subordinated to the other. The remaining problem relates to worldwide excess population growth. Fundamental research in future contraceptive technology apparently needs, therefore, to concentrate on the remaining mysteries of human reproduction.

Summary

Birth control has been an important topic in this country since the time of Margaret Sanger and the founding of the planned parenthood movement. Birth-control methods have been increasingly used as people have recognized the severe hindrance to social and economic development created by uncurbed population growth. Other purposes of fertility limitation have been to: (1) further certain physical and socioeconomic objectives; (2) aid early sexual adjustment in marriage; (3) prevent unwanted pregnancies among the unmarried; (4) avoid aggravation of existing illness or diseases; and (5) curb inherited diseases. Methods of birth control include abstinence, sterilization, abortion, and contraception.

Abstinence, though successful as a birth control technique, can lead to psychological malfunctions as well as physical problems. Voluntary abstinence is less damaging than involuntary abstinence. Some people may choose to abstain because of illness, discomfort during pregnancy or after childbirth, or concern about contracting or spreading VD.

Sterilization methods, or surgical procedures to render a person incapable of reproduction, have been employed to aid in limiting family size and for reasons that can be therapeutic or eugenic in nature. The two principal methods of female sterilization are tubal ligation, or cutting or tying the fallopian tubes, and laparoscopic sterilization, or "band-aid sterilization." When certain abnormalities or malignancies exist, operative procedures including oophorectomy, or removal of the ovaries, total salpingectomy, or removal of the fallopian tubes, and hysterectomy, removal of the uterus, may be performed. The two major types of male sterilization are vasectomy, or cutting and tying of the semen-carrying ducts, and castration, removal of the testicles. Vas sclerosing, a method of scarring the walls of the vas deferens to produce sterilization, may provide a promising alternative to vasectomy.

Abortion, or premature expulsion from the uterus of an embryo, can be a form of birth control. Spontaneous abortion, or miscarriage, is unintentional and thus is not considered a form of birth control. Induced abortion involves an intentional effort to terminate pregnancy and is thus considered a form of birth control. Legalized, induced abortions currently number over 1 million per year in the United States. The safest period for abortion is between the eighth and tenth week with techniques such as menstrual extraction, suction abortion, vacuum curettage, and dilatation and curettage (D&C), all of which may be performed within the first trimester of pregnancy. Saline abortion and hysterotomy are methods used when pregnancy has advanced beyond 12 or 13 weeks.

Effective contraceptive techniques have been developed, although the failproof contraceptive does not exist. Contraceptives can fail because the *user* does not properly use them or because the *method* does not work for some reason. Contraceptives that are available only with a doctor's prescription include: (1) the diaphragm, a dome-shaped cup that covers the entrance to the uterus; (2) the cervical cap, a miniature diaphragm that fits over the cervix; (3) birth control pills, containing a combination of synthetic progesterone and estrogen that prevents ovulation; (4) minipills, containing progestin alone that helps make the reproductive system resistant to sperm transport, ovum transport, or blastocyst implantation; (5) other hormonal contraceptives such as progesterone injections and vaginal rings; and (6) IUDs, or intrauterine devices, small devices designed for insertion in the womb. In general, those contraceptives prescribed by physicians can be highly effective and safe birth-control techniques when used properly.

Contraceptives that are available without a doctor's prescription include: (1) the condom, a cylindrical sheath that is rolled onto the penis before intercourse, and (2) foams, jellies, or creams, substances introduced into the vagina that keep sperm from entering the cervix or are toxic to sperm. Douching, sometimes used for birth control purposes, is not effective. Other methods of birth prevention are these: (1) coitus interruptus, which requires the man to withdraw his penis from his partner's vagina before he climaxes; (2) the rhythm or calendar method, which relies upon timing coitus so that it occurs during the woman's "safe" or infertile period; (3) the temperature method, which relies on detecting the time of a woman's ovulation by noting temperature changes that occur during her cycle; and (4) the Billings method, which relies on determining changes in cervical mucus that occur during a woman's cycle. Lactation may provide some minimal effectiveness as a contraceptive measure.

Possible after-the-fact measures include these: (1) diethystilbestrol (DES), a "morning-after Pill"; (2) other uses of progestins and oral contraceptive tablets as morning-after Pills; and (3) next-morning IUD insertion. Insertion of a progestin capsule into a woman's body, immunization of a man or woman with vaccines, manipulating or changing the substance DF that surrounds human sperm cells, development of contraceptive teas that can be drunk, a birth control pill for men, and development of more sophisticated devices to determine when a woman is fertile are among the birth-control techniques of the future.

Annotated Bibliography

Barker, Graham H. *Your search for fertility.* New York: William Morrow, 1980.
  Designed for the childless couple, this book answers in common language many questions related to fertility. Topics include tests of fertility, laparoscopy, miscarriage, induction of ovulation, sterilization reversal, artificial insemination, and test-tube babies. The book includes drawings and a useful glossary.
Guillebaud, John. *The pill.* New York: Oxford University Press, 1980.
  Written for the general consumer, this book attempts to dispel myths and fears concerning the use of oral contraceptives. The book answers many often-asked questions related to safety and effectiveness of birth control pills.
Hatcher, Robert A., Stewart, Gary K., Stewart, Felicia, Guest, Felicia, Schwartz, David W., and Jones, Stephanie A. *Contraceptive technology 1980–1981.* New York: Irvington Publishers, 1980.
  This book offers thorough, up-to-date information on various contraceptive techniques and issues related to contraception. Significant considerations regarding each technique are presented, including history, mechanism of action, effectiveness, contraindictions for use, side effects, cost, and special

instructions. This valuable general reference contains useful charts and tables and additional information on medical concerns and family planning services.

Hawkins, D. F. and Elder, M. G. *Human fertility control: Theory and practice.* Boston: Butterworth, 1979.

This text for family practitioners, obstetricians and gynecologists stresses the clinical procedures and methods of fertility control. Topics include hormonal contraception, barrier methods, intrauterine devices, legal abortion, sterilization, family planning and counseling, and future birth control techniques.

Hafez, E. S. E. *Human reproduction: Conception and contraception (2nd ed.)* New York: Harper and Row, 1980.

This comprehensive volume on human reproduction features articles by many leading authorities. General topics include male and female reproductive physiology, fertility and fertilization, and various contraceptive techniques. Important Appendices deal with identification of, potency of, characteristics and ingredients of, chemical formulas of, and side effects of many oral contraceptives.

Shapiro, Howard I. *The birth control book.* New York: Avon Books, 1978.

Written mainly for the practicing gynecologist, this book presents information on all types of birth control for men and women. Topics include the sponge diaphragm, vasectomy reversal, chemicals that have harmful interactions with the Pill, and considerations in choosing an abortion clinic. Of special value is a table of birth control pills by brand, ingredients, and possible side effects.

Silber, Sherman J. *How to get pregnant.* New York: Charles Scribner's Sons, 1980.

This book discusses in simple terms a wide range of topics related to conception and contraception. Some subject areas include male and female reproductive physiology, tests of fertility, treatment of conditions causing infertility, artificial insemination and sperm-banking, test-tube babies and cloning, and birth regulation and sterilization. This book is an excellent treatment of the topic for the general public.

Smith, Peggy B. Programs for sexually active teens. In *Adolescent pregnancy: Perspectives for the health professional,* ed. P. Smith and D. Mumford. Boston: G. K. Hall, 1980.

This article describes the formats and foci of social service delivery systems in communities, hospitals, schools, and agencies. The author discusses contraceptive services for males and stresses the need for family planning services for teens.

Wilson, Mercedes Arzu. *The ovulation method of birth regulation.* New York: Van Nostrand Reinhold, 1980.

Intended for family planning educators as well as the general public, this book describes a new, natural approach to birth control based on ovulation determination by mucous secretion. The book stresses the practical applications of the method and presents useful charts.

Wolman, Benjamin B. (Ed.) *Psychological aspects of gynecology and obstetrics.* Oradell, New Jersey: Medical Economics Company, 1978.

This book features articles by renowned contributors concerning psychological considerations in obstetrics and gynecology. Topics include changing roles, female sexual dysfunctions, puberty, contraception and fertility, the middle years and the climateric, pregnancy and complications, and many others. Special issues such as rape crisis and breast cancer are discussed. The book was written for students and medical practitioners, but many articles will appeal to the general audience.

Sex in the Later Years

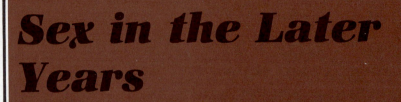

14

In past generations, society's failure to recognize the sexual needs of its older members was a serious matter. Today that failure has become critical. For in the early 1970s there were more than 35 million Americans 65 years of age or older. That figure is expected to approach 43 million by the year 2020. Many of these older men and women have living spouses; still others contract new marriges. (In the 1960s, for example, there were 35,000 marriages a year involving people 65 years old or older [Rubin 1965b].) With or without partners, all these people have sexual needs, and these needs are perfectly normal. It is unrealistic and unfair to accept the mythology that such a large segment of the population is incapable of sexual activity or uninterested in it—or, the most insidious fallacy, that it is "unseemly" for erotic yearnings to persist into venerable old age.

Psychosexual Aspects of Aging

At the base of the pyramid of misconceptions about sex among the aged is the essentially Victorian philosophy regarding human sexuality: that sexual activity is primarily a procreative function, and that those

319

beyond their reproductive years should practice self-denial. It is therefore "not quite nice" for older people to have sexual yearnings. Another attitude prevalent in our society that works against sexual expression in the older person is the idea that sex, love, and romance are provinces primarily of the young.

Unfortunately for the aging woman, our youth-oriented culture places undue value on youthful physical attractiveness. Most men make a subconscious split-second appraisal, based on these physical criteria, of all women they meet. Given the choice, most of them opt for the young and attractive. This culturally fostered preference frequently makes women unnecessary victims of the emotional burden of rejection as they grow older (Easley 1974).

The fear and anxiety associated with the aging process begin much earlier than many people think. Many late adolescents—especially girls—begin to fret because they are still unmarried. And the older the unmarried become, the greater the distress. For many women, aging means progressive sexual devaluation and disqualification. Men are not so troubled by aging anxiety. Many men at 40 are considered to be far more sexually attractive than they were 20 years earlier. Success, money, and power are accepted as sexually enhancing. By contrast, a woman who has succeeded in her profession is not similarly enhanced. In fact, her success would threaten or intimidate many men, certainly those who look at women as sex objects. A woman's sexual candidacy, then, generally remains active as long as she is young and attractive (and nonthreatening) (Sontag 1976).

The opinions revealed in a study of Brandeis University students, aged 17 to 23 years, may be typical of many young people's attitudes. They expressed the belief that sexual activity does not exist in the lives of most old people, or is unimportant to them (Golde & Kogan 1959). In another study (Pocs & Godow 1977), students were asked about their parents' sexuality. Many were reluctant even to consider the subject. Those who responded positively consistently rated the incidence of their parents' sexual activity below the national average in such matters as premarital intercourse and oral-genital sex. About 25% estimated that their parents no longer engaged in sex, or did so less than once a year.

The young often think that the elderly must abhor each other's aging bodies and therefore avoid physical contact. This anxiety of youth over the aging process is projected onto the elderly. Thus, for example, any sexual activity that in the value system of the young would "prove" the virility of a 25-year-old becomes lechery when the man happens to be 65 (Corbett 1981; Mozley 1974).

Small wonder, then, that older people are frequently perplexed by their sex drive and ashamed of it! The prevailing American attitude suggests that they should live in a sexual vacuum. Their children very likely hint, "Sex is for the young. Act your age." They may be further confounded when seeking advice from a physician on a sexual problem. For the doctor may, unfortunately, have his/her own sexual prejudices or be no better informed on sexual matters than the patients are. In such a case the doctor may only intensify the older person's feelings of guilt and bewilderment by answering any sex-related questions with: "Well, what do you expect at your age?" Even Freud was a victim of this faulty thinking. At the age of 41 he wrote to a friend complaining about his moods, adding: "Also, sexual excitation is of no more use to a person like me" (Fromm 1963).

Along these same lines, a 1977 study (LaTorre & Kear) showed that caretakers of the aged in nursing homes "have negative attitudes toward sex which are expressed toward the aged in their charge. . . ." The researchers concluded that "it will be necessary to change the beliefs and attitudes of people who care for the aged in order that they might understand and accept the aged individual's sexual problems, concerns, frustrations, and disappointments."

Older people typically enter the later stages of life with fear about new roles for which they have had very little preparation. Their children are gone from home, leading lives quite independent of their parents. One or both of the older couple may have been forced to retire from a job before physically or mentally ready to do so. Quite likely both have been shoved aside by the young in social and community affairs. From this enforced inactivity and society's indifference (if not prejudice) toward older people, there quite understandably develops the equation "Young is good; old is bad." And the aging person, along with everyone else, tends to internalize the concept that *old* is a dirty word.

Just how old is old? It is unjust—and unscientific—to establish that a person is old solely according to the number of years that he/she has lived, a criterion that Harry Benjamin has called "the tyrannical rule of the calendar" (Benjamin 1949). In terms of optimism, flexibility, and contribution, many people can be called old at 25. Conversely, a Marc Chagall, a Golda Meir, an Arthur Rubenstein, or a "Miss Lillian" Carter would be judged young at 80 or 90.

When does the aging process actually begin? It may be said with some justification that the science of geriatrics begins where the science of pediatrics leaves off. Aging is a gradual process: A person is not young one day and old the next. Aging is a sequence extending over a lifetime of subtle, often imperceptible change—just as daybreak blends into daylight, daylight into twilight, and twilight into darkness without a discernible shift (J. Weinberg 1971).

Old age and reaction to aging are largely determined by a person's perception and psychological "set." In an experiment, psychologist T. L. Smith of the University of Denver produced symptoms of senility in young men aged 18 to 22 years simply by having others treat them as if they were quite old. Other studies have shown that individuals who, for physical or attitudinal reasons, have a low sexual "set" abandon sexual activity at an earlier age than do those with a high sexual "set" (Comfort 1976).

Aging persons' lessened physical vigor and diminished social and professional status often damage a previously healthy self-concept. They begin to *feel* old, sometimes long before they have begun physiologically to age significantly. A good sexual relationship at this critical time of life can provide much-needed warmth and comfort, and can be a highly effective source of self-assurance.

Since there is so much to be gained from continued sexual activity in the later years, and since coitus (although not the only feasible sexual outlet) is almost always physiologically possible, why do so many older people shrink from it? For some, of course, sex has never been very important. The aging process provides a convenient excuse for giving up an activity that has always been, very likely, a source of anxiety. For many more, however, the popular belief that people past 50 have little interest in sex (or, if they *have* an interest, are sadly lacking in capability) becomes a self-fulfilling prophecy. Sensing disapproval or ridicule from younger segments of the population, older people develop guilt over sexual desires and seek to deny or extinguish their sexuality altogether. Once society's attitude has changed, older people will enjoy a fuller, healthier sex life. Fortunately, research is giving us a clearer, more compassionate understanding of the needs and capabilities of the aging. From this springs hope for us all.

Physiological Aspects of Aging

Physiosexual Changes in the Aging Woman

Women demonstrate few changes in the pattern of their sexual response as they grow older. Kinsey and other researchers have shown that a woman's sexual desire ordinarily continues undiminished until she is 60 years of age or older, after which its decline is very slow, if she remains sexually active (Kinsey *et al.* 1953; Masters & Johnson 1966; "Sex Behavior" 1966).

Certain physiological changes occur with the menopause, to be sure, and some of them can make coitus unpleasant. Thinning vaginal walls and diminished lubrication during sexual excitation make the vaginal vault less distensible and more liable to injury or pain, and uterine contractions during orgasm cause some women severe pain. But these problems are merely signals of postmenopausal hormone deficiency and can be circumvented by hormonal replacement, administered either orally or by suppository. Although a cancer scare arose in the mid 1970s, recent studies show that hormonal replacement, when used at a low-dosage level with judicious followup for a period of about a year, has not been shown to increase the risk of cancer (Greenblatt 1978; Landau 1979). Estrogen and progesterone otherwise have almost nothing to do with an older woman's libido or coital performance (Belliveau & Richter 1970; Corbett 1981; Kaplan & Sager 1971; Kinsey *et al.* 1953; Laury 1980a; Lief *et al.* 1968).

After about the age of 40, women may begin to experience a sharp decrease in the secretion of estrogen, a decrease that continues gradually for the remainder of their lives (Corbett 1981; LeWitter & Abarbanel 1961; Rubin 1966b). In the relatively unenlightened medical world of the 1800s, physicians reasoned that, since the ovaries dwindle in their production of estrogen at and after the menopause, a woman's sex drive would accordingly decrease. It is now known that a woman's sex drive often does not diminish even when the ovaries are surgically removed. In fact, removal of a woman's adrenal glands (which, in the female, produce androgen) has a far greater negative effect on her libido than ovariectomy (Martin 1980; Rubin 1965b).

A hysterectomy, like menopause, does not normally end a woman's sex drive. By definition, total hysterectomy involves the removal of the uterus, whereas panhysterectomy involves the removal of the uterus, fallopian tubes, and ovaries. In the first instance, there would not even be the reason of hormonal imbalance to account for loss of sex drive. If any change occurs, in fact, it might be in the direction of increased drive, since fear of pregnancy is removed. Hormonal changes will occur following a panhysterectomy, but again, the deficiency can be largely corrected. Given a sexually interested, active partner, the sex drive of a woman following menopause or hysterectomy will quite likely remain unimpaired (Daly 1968).

All women should take heart from Masters and Johnson's summary comment on sex and the older woman. Despite a reduction in both intensity of physiologic sexual response and the rapidity of it, they state that "the aging human female is fully capable of sexual performance at orgasmic response levels, particularly if she is exposed to regularity of effective sexual stimulation. . . . There seems to be no physiologic reason why the frequency of sexual expression found satisfactory for the younger woman should not be carried over into the postmenopausal years. . . . In short, there is no time limit drawn by the advancing years to female sexuality" (Masters & Johnson 1966). The small sample in this study, however, limits the generalizability of the results.

Physiosexual Changes in the Aging Man

As a man grows older, certain physical changes become evident. The size and firmness of the testicles diminish. They do not elevate to the same degree during sexual activity that they did when he was younger. The seminiferous tubules thicken and begin a degenerative process that, to an ever-increasing degree, inhibits the production of sperm. The prostate gland often enlarges, and its contractions during orgasm are weaker. The force of ejaculation weakens, and the seminal fluid is thinner and more scant. Orgasm is slower in coming and may not last as long as it once did. The intensity and duration of the sex flush during sexual excitation abate, and the involuntary muscular spasms accompanying orgasm decrease (Belliveau & Richter 1970; Corbett 1981; Masters & Johnson 1966). Even by age 40, the quality of a man's sexual pleasure may have begun changing noticeably. The shift is from the intense sensations localized in the genitals, as is common to the young, to a more generalized sensation diffused throughout the body (H. S. Kaplan 1974).

When he was young, a man may have required only a few seconds of stimulation to achieve erection; as an older man he may require several minutes. His erections are less vigorous and frequent. Objective investigations of male erectile responsiveness have shown that the response of men aged 19–30 years is 5.8 times faster than that of men aged 48–65 (Solnick & Birren 1977).

Despite these changes, however, the older man has certain advantages over the younger one because his ejaculatory control is much greater. He is able to maintain an erection for a considerably longer time without feeling the ejaculatory urgency that plagues the younger man (J. L. McCary 1973). Furthermore, a man who experiences problems with premature ejaculation in his younger years may find he is better able to control his ejaculation after reaching middle age. This greater control in turn may help him to become a happier and more adept lover (Laury 1980b).

The aging man may lose his erection rather rapidly after ejaculation and be unable to attain another for several hours, or even days. If he and his partner desire coitus more frequently than his erectile ability permits, there is a way around the problem. During coitus, the man should withdraw before he reaches orgasm. With minimal sexual stimulation he can easily attain another erection and then begin coitus anew. Although his ejaculatory capacity does not keep pace with his erectile ability, he now possesses the enviable faculty of prolonging intercourse indefinitely.

The sex drive of older men generally follows their overall pattern of health and physical performance. In a man of 30, secretion of the male sex hormone androgen is 55 units per 24 hours. It dwindles to about 8 units a day by the age of 60; the secretion remains fairly constant thereafter. The degree to which the sex drive of the individual man is affected by decreasing testosterone levels is not clear, and the subject is under investigation by the Gerontology Research Center (NIH). Another contributory factor in libidinal loss is the general loss of muscle tone and good physical condition (Harman 1975), yet another argument for sensible exercise programs.

Masters and Johnson emphasize the importance of the older man's accepting two physiological facts: (1) At no time in a man's life does he lose the capability of erection, except in extremely rare instances involving injury to or pathology of the central nervous system. (2) Loss of erectile ability, therefore, is not a natural part of the aging process (Masters & Johnson 1970).

The physical change causing the greatest difficulty in older men (although younger men can be similarly afflicted) involves the prostate gland. It is a wonder that an organ as small as the prostate, whose functions are not spectacular, should cause men so much trouble, to say nothing of anxiety. Yet the prostate in from 20% to 50% of all men in their middle and later years becomes enlarged, although only 35% of these cases will require surgery (Rubin 1965b).

Although **prostatitis**—inflammation of the prostate— is not uncommon among young men, **prostatectomy**, the surgical removal of all or part of the prostate, is far more common among men past 50. Even when surgery is required, however, the vast majority of men who were potent beforehand retain their potency afterward. The conclusion drawn in a study reported in the *Journal of the American Medical Association* was that a willing sexual partner is the most important factor in a man's retaining sexual ability after prostate surgery (Finkle *et al.* 1959). If a man ceases to function after surgery, the reason may well be that he was looking for an excuse to end his sexual life. He may want to be free of the marital obligation of intercourse or he may fear that intercourse will aggravate cardiac or other physical disabilities. In past attempts to find a sexual outlet he may have met with disapproval from his wife—or his children or neighbors may have expressed disapproval of sexuality in older people.

Anything that improves general health will also have a beneficial effect on sexual functioning. Especially after the age of 50, a man should consult a urologist regularly. He should be careful, however, to choose one who understands the need in a man for regular and frequent sexual outlet and who will do whatever is possible to ensure it. If the older man's physical problems are complicated by a defeatist attitude toward the future of his sex life, then consultation with a psychotherapist may be helpful.

Coital Capacity in Aging Men

Men's capacity for sexual intercourse is, of course, limited by potency— their ability to achieve and maintain an erection. Statistics on the subject of potency are revealing. The Kinsey researchers have shown that, among men aged 35 years, only 2% are impotent; of those aged 55, only 10%; and of those aged 75, 50%. Despite the last figure, the average frequency of coitus among all men over 65 is approximately four times a month (Kinsey *et al.* 1948). Other researchers also emphasize that there is no specific point in the aging process at which sexual activity dwindles and disappears. Rather, it decreases with advancing age at about the same rate it has been doing since young manhood (Bowers *et al.* 1963; Finkle *et al.* 1959; Freeman 1961; Masters & Johnson 1966, 1970; Newman & Nichols 1960; Rubin 1965b).

One study of older men ranging in age from 55 to 86 years revealed that, despite a gradual decline in sexual desire, 65% of those under 70 were still potent, and 33% of those over 70 were (Finkle *et al.* 1959). More than 75% of the men in another study, whose average age was 71 years, reported that they still felt sexual desire, and 55% reported that they were still capable sexually. The frequency of coital activity ranged from three or more times a week to once every two months (or less). Consistent with the findings of similar investigations, this study revealed that the sex drive of the older individual is directly related to the intensity of sex drive in youth. Men in whom the onset of sexual drive was early and strong in youth maintained the strongest desire and greatest capability in the advanced years (Freeman 1961; Newman & Nichols 1960; Rubin 1965b). These tendencies seem to hold true in many aspects of life. People are inclined to behave at 70 as they did at 30. If they were worriers earlier, they still worry; if they were insecure earlier, they still feel insecure; if they were socially oriented earlier, social contacts remain important to them; and if they were zestful and energetic in their earlier years, they are vigorous and full of fire in their later years (Maas & Kuypers 1974).

That an older man experiences erection during sleep and upon first awakening in the morning offers irrefutable evidence of his sexual capacity in later life, even though he may not actually be sexually active. Obviously the man capable of nocturnal or early-morning erections has no physiological barrier to erection. If he is incapable of penile erection in a sexual encounter, then the barrier is emotional and psychological.

Of men 75 years and older, 60% report that they still have involuntary morning erections, although the average declines from 4.9 times a week in youth to 1.8 times a week by the age of 65, and 0.9 at 75 (Kinsey *et al.* 1948, 1953; Laury 1980b; Rubin 1963). One study of men aged 70 to 96 years (average age 80.5) revealed that they continued to have erotic dreams productive of erection. Some 30% of these men, furthermore, whose average age was 75.6 years, demonstrated an erectile capability no different from that of much younger males (Kahn & Fisher 1969; Rubin 1970b).

Since the vast majority of older men—over 90% in one study—do not cite physical disability as a deterrent to sexual frequency (Tarail 1962), only one conclusion can be drawn. The agents working against continuing sexual performance are primarily psychological ones. Having had a venereal disease, however, does appear to affect sexual capacity in later years. One study of sexually potent men aged 60 to 74 showed that those with a history of VD engaged in coitus on an average of 14.1 times a year, while those who had never had VD averaged 24 times a year (Bowers *et al.* 1963).

Coitus in the Later Years

One of the best known and most detailed investigations on the subject of sex and older people compared the sexual activities, interests, and attitudes of 250 persons living in Durham, North Carolina (Newman & Nichols 1960). The subject population included married, single, divorced, and widowed men and women between the ages of 60 and 93 (average age 70). Both black and white subjects of various socioeconomic levels were included. The 149 married subjects were grouped into four classes according to age: 60–64 years, 65–69 years, 70–74 years, and 75 years and over.

The first three groups of married subjects contained about the same percentage of sexually active persons—60%. Of the group over 75, about 30% remained as sexually active as subjects in the other three. But the investigators were careful to point out that many of the subjects in the oldest group (or their spouses) were afflicted with chronic illnesses— arthritis, arteriosclerotic heart disease, and diabetes—that interfered with sexual activity (Newman & Nichols 1960).

The married women in this study reported less sexual activity than the married men did, possibly because they were more reluctant to disclose details of their sex lives. The more likely explanation, however, rests on the fact that women usually marry men older than they. The average age of the married women in this study was 70, and that of their husbands, 75. At this advanced age the husbands possibly lacked the interest or capacity for maintaining an active sex life with their younger wives (Newman & Nichols 1960).

Of the 101 subjects in this study without a marital partner, only 7% were sexually active. Of the 149 subjects still married and living with their spouses, 54% were active to some degree. These findings are supported by the results of other studies, especially those of Masters and Johnson, which point clearly to the fact that an essential factor in a continued and active sex life is a willing and cooperative sex partner (Friedfeld 1961; Masters & Johnson 1966, 1970).

The black subjects in the North Carolina study were significantly more active sexually than the whites (70% compared with 50%). But this observation is probably more indicative of socioeconomic differences than racial ones (Newman & Nichols 1960). Similar differences in degree of sexual activity exist when persons—no matter what their age—of the lowest socioeconomic stratum (in which blacks unfortunately predominate) are compared with those of the higher strata. The North Carolina investigators concluded, as have other researchers, that despite a gradual decline in sexual interest, capacity, and activity, older persons in reasonably good health with sexual partners whose health is also good can continue to be sexually active into their 70s, 80s, or even 90s.

Pfeiffer *et al.* (1973) did a series of studies on sex and the elderly. They concluded from one study of 254 subjects, aged 60 to 94 years, that decline in sexual interest and activity has its basis in middle age. In another study of 261 men and 241 women, whose ages ranged from 46 to 71, they found that 12% of the men and 44% of the women claimed they no longer engaged in sex; 6% of the men and 33% of the women were no longer even interested.

Overwhelmingly, the women placed responsibility for cessation on their husbands; the men blamed themselves (illness, inability, loss of interest). Interestingly, among both men and women, the oldest group (66–71) indicated more "moderate" or "strong" sexual interest than the next youngest group (61–65).

In a discussion of these findings, Stanley R. Dean (1973) emphasizes what Masters and Johnson (1966) and Kinsey *et al.* (1953) said before—that decline in women's activity or interest is related not to potential but to circumstance. Since society still forbids women the aggressiveness and freedom to pursue sexual contacts that men have, women simply resign themselves to a sexual vacuum. Ironically, this same male-dominated society perpetuates the custom of men marrying younger women, despite the disparity in male-female sexual survival. Wisdom—and physiology— would appear to dictate that the chronological tradition be reversed, with women marrying younger men. Such a reversal in ages at marriage would also make less likely a long widowhood, presently a statistical fact, since women now outlive men by about seven years. (And the 1977 Census Bureau prediction is that a girl born today will live 81 years and a boy 72.)

The question quite naturally arises why one elderly man should function satisfactorily while another does not. On the basis of their investigation into the sexual behavior of older males, Masters and Johnson (1966) describe six factors responsible for loss of sexual responsiveness in later life:

1. Monotony of a repetitive sexual relationship (usually translated into boredom with the partner, which the Kinsey group described as "psy-chologic fatigue").
2. Preoccupation with career or economic pursuits.
3. Physical or mental fatigue.
4. Overindulgence in food or drink.
5. Physical or mental infirmity of either spouse.
6. Fear of failure associated with or resulting from any of the former categories.

Fear of failure is especially devastating to a man. As Masters and Johnson point out, "Once impotent under any circumstance, many males withdraw voluntarily from any coital activity rather than face the ego-shattering experience of repeated episodes of sexual inadequacy" (Masters & Johnson 1966).

The Effects of Monotony

Coital monotony usually occurs when a couple allow sex to become a mechanical activity. A study of 100 consecutive cases of older men seeking treatment for impotence revealed that many were impotent only with their wives—very likely a result of sexual monotony (Wolbarst 1947).

But even when the excitement and stimulus of a new sexual partner provide a boost to fading virility, a man typically reverts to his previous level of potency in a relatively short time. This is especially so if the couple fail to make an effort to keep the new relationship exciting and novel (Rubin 1970b). One research project demonstrated that sexual adequacy in aging white rats increased when the animals had a chance to copulate with a number of females. As soon as the males had reached a certain age, however, the stimulating effect of variety became weaker and weaker, until copulation eventually ceased (Botwinick 1960; Rubin 1965b). It should be borne in mind, however, that lower animals are not as capable of introducing stimulative innovations into their sexual acts as humans are.

The sexual relationship in far too many upper-middle-class marriages can be accurately described as devitalized, despite the fact that the couple's financial affluence gives them the opportunity to vary the routine of their lives. Although many of these couples are still in their 40s, sex has become a predictable, brief encounter following a Saturday night social gathering at which both partners probably drank intemperately. Some of the wives in such marriages describe their sex life as "legal prostitution, not much better than masturbation." Many husbands refer to their wives as "legal, inexpensive, clean mechanisms for physical gratification" (Cuber with Harroff 1966; Rubin 1965b).

Many considerations enter into diminishing interest in sex in long-standing relationships (Oziel 1976). Among them are these:

1. Partners who have become less, often much less, sexually attractive to one another.
2. Decreasing intimacy on all levels of life together and shallow communication.
3. Monotony that develops when the partners have exhausted the few acceptable avenues of sexual exploration open to them.
4. An extramarital affair—as cause, not effect.
5. A lowered sex drive, especially in the male, related to psychological effects (preoccupation with career, general dissatisfaction) or physiological ones (illness, age-related debilitation).
6. Diminished self-esteem, when the person perceives him/herself as less physically attractive than in youth.
7. Situational and interpersonal relationship disturbances—forced early retirement, severe conflict with a child, financial worries.
8. Marital maladjustment.
9. Disorders of sexual function or the sexual system.
10. Organic disease (endocrine disturbance, brain tumor) and the depressive action of certain drugs (narcotics, alcohol).

Obviously many of these problems can be eliminated, or at least lessened, by appropriate psychological or medical measures, or by the simple rediscoveries made in open communication between the partners. Furthermore, despite these gloomy generalizations, there are many advantages to a long-standing relationship. Each partner knows what to expect from the other; each has adjusted, at least to a degree, to the other's foibles and peculiarities; and many of the rough edges that caused friction in the early years of the relationship have now worn smooth (Laury 1980a; Rubin 1965b). With concerted effort, a couple can learn to circumvent these pitfalls of a close relationship that may lead to boredom and monotony. As they grow older they can reap the rewards of enjoying one another and the warmth generated by a long, close relationship.

Sexual Outlets Other than Coitus

A major challenge to older people is finding the means to satisfy sexual needs when a spouse has died or is no longer interested in sexual acivity. Many have been counseled by experts in the marriage field to use masturbation to gain relief from erotic tensions. Those following this advice frequently find that maintaining some form of sexual expression helps to prevent depression, frustration, and hostility. It is an established fact that about 25% of men above 60—even those still enjoying coitus—masturbate regularly (Kinsey *et al.* 1948; Rubin 1963). Among older women, the actual or potential value of masturbation as a sexual oulet is particularly understandable. About 45% of all women between the ages of 65 and 74 are widows; among women past 75, the figure jumps to about 70%. Furthermore, the number of widows in our society increases at the rate of 100,000 each year—twice the annual increase in the year 1900 (Rubin 1965b).

About 59% of unmarried women between 50 and 70 years of age admit to masturbating. Approximately 30% of older women supplement marital coitus with masturbation (Kinsey *et al.* 1953). Older women remain capable of multiple orgasms, and indeed many frequently resort to various means, such as masturbation, to fulfill their needs and to keep their sex lives active and satisfying.

Heterosexual coitus and masturbation are not, of course, the only forms of sexual outlet available to the older person. Extended foreplay, petting, or sensate focus techniques can provide extremely rewarding experiences of intimacy and sexual stimulation for the older couple, even if intercourse is not possible (Laury 1980a). There can be great pleasure involved in emotionally and physically sharing an intimate sexual interaction without the accompanying pressures to perform or demands to experience orgasm. Elimination of the pressure to perform by just enjoying this extended foreplay can often result in renewed sexual vigor as well as a greater understanding and acceptance of one's sexual partner (Ficher 1979; Kirkendall 1980b).

Another outlet for some older people is homosexuality. From a study done of 1700 men whose average age was 64, over 6% had engaged in homosexual acts after they had reached the age of 60. Surprisingly, homosexual behavior had not been an important sexual outlet for them since they were teen-agers—in fact, the vast majority were either married or widowed. For most of their adulthood, then, they had lived an entirely heterosexual life (Calleja 1967).

Although this group included men from diverse backgrounds, ranging from agriculture to the professions, the researchers did not consider them strictly typical. Even so, that the homosexual pattern emerged after the age of 60 is most interesting. Why did these men turn to homosexuality? The men themselves, all in good physical and mental health, placed great emphasis on the empathy they felt for their male sexual companions. In fact, they felt that the sexual activity was perhaps of less importance than the warmth and sensitivity they found in their partners.

These men considered themselves quite masculine (and so did the researchers), and they likewise considered their partners to be very virile. In fact, they expressed a certain revulsion for effeminate men. Some stated that they had become practically impotent with women by this time of their lives, but found themselves fully potent with some of their homosexual partners. The overriding need, then, was for affection, something the subjects felt they were not getting in sufficient degree (for whatever reason) from their families. As people grow older, sometimes their need for affection also grows, and the need for sexual satisfaction may increase accordingly (Whiskin 1970).

Some of these men did feel guilty about their homosexual behavior because of religious and social disapproval. But they confessed that, guilty or not, they did not have inner resources strong enough to renounce the relationships. However, if the percentage revealed by this research is reasonably accurate, one can see that homosexuality constitutes a relatively minor mode of sexual expression among elderly men (Calleja 1967).

It cannot be emphasized strongly enough that a man's loss of sexual potency with advancing age is in almost all cases the outgrowth of psychological inhibitions rather than physical incapacity (Rubin 1964b). Indeed, loss of sexual vigor with age should be no greater than the loss of other physical capabilities. A man or woman of 60 is hardly capable of running 100 yards as quickly as he or she might have at 20. But the chances are excellent that the feat can still be accomplished by proceeding at a leisurely pace and feeling no anxiety about running less swiftly, or less often, than in the heyday of youth.

For all mature couples, be they 21 or 90, sexual interaction is best when it is an expression of the total personality of each individual. In addition to coitus, the sexual drive may find expression "in the need for continued closeness, affection, and intimacy, and in a continued cultural and intellectual interest in eroticism, or in the need for some romance in life" (Rubin 1965b). Indeed, sexual stimulation through caressing, massaging, and sensate focus exercises may be immensely pleasurable for older persons even if intercourse is not possible (Kirkendall 1980b; Laury 1980a).

A word should be addressed to the heart patient (young as well as old) who, understandably, may be hesitant about resuming his or her sex life after a coronary attack. Indeed, death has been known to occur because of the violent coronary response to sexual activity. Furthermore, heightened blood pressure can lead to rupture of blood vessels, particularly in older persons. These severe reactions are rare, however, and the warning to observe total (or near total) abstinence is not applicable to most heart patients. It is reserved for those with very serious coronary conditions.

Heart patients (and their partners) must understand that heartbeat and blood pressure will unquestionably rise during sexual activity, even if the patient plays a physically inactive role. This is not to say that he/she cannot engage in sensible sexual behavior and draw considerable benefit from it. The patient *is* warned, however, against prolonged coition, fatiguing sexual positions, and extended sex play. These factors may be especially hazardous if they take place too soon after a full meal, after a large amount of alcohol, with a new and vigorous partner, during periods of extremely hot or cold weather, during or immediately after an illness, or at a high altitude (about 5000 feet), especially if the patient has recently arrived at the high altitude and has not adjusted to the rarified air (Lewis & Lewis 1980c; Likoff 1977). As in other medical matters, the prescription (or proscription) of the physician must be rigidly observed.

Stresses posed by extramarital sex should be of particular concern to heart patients. One study of men with heart disease who died as a result of coitus revealed that 27 of the 34 deaths occurred during or after extramarital intercourse (Ueno 1963). Lewis and Lewis (1980c) likewise report that of those men who die during intercourse, eight out of ten are engaging in extramarital relations.

Holland (1980) reports that sexually active individuals burn up to 270 calories each hour during sex. Holland claims that this expenditure of energy is comparable to the energy required to walk at a rate of 2 miles an hour, to bicycle at a rate of 5 miles an hour, to dance, or to play golf. Assuming that a man or a woman is able to engage in these activities, it is likely that such a person will be able safely to engage in sex. Of course, sensible attention to good nutrition, rest, and exercise goes hand in hand with adequate sexual functioning. Regular medical follow-up of the older individual's physical condition is important to determine how vigorously the individual can engage in exercise or sexual activity.

Summary

Sex, love, and romance are not exclusively provinces of the young. In recent years there has been an increased sensitivity toward and understanding of the sexual needs of older people, so that the concept of old age and of one's reactions to aging are now viewed as being the result of a person's perceptions and psychological "set" rather than just physical factors. A good sexual relationship in the later years provides warmth, comfort, reassurance, and gratification for people who formerly might have been told that they were "over the hill" in sex as well as life.

Certain physiological changes occur in older women and men. Women may experience thinning of the vaginal walls, diminished vaginal lubrication, and decreases in estrogen secretion (perhaps due to menopause or a prior panhysterectomy), but these problems often can be circumvented by hormonal replacement. Men may experience changes in the size and firmness of their testicles; degeneration of seminiferous tubules may occur and sperm production may be inhibited. There may be enlargement of the prostate gland, a diminished force and consistency to ejaculation, less vigorous and less frequent erections, and an overall decrease in orgasmic response. However, for both women and men the sex drive and interest are closely tied to attitudinal or psychological factors. The important factors in continued sexual responsiveness and coital capacity of men in later life appear to be having a lifelong interest in sex plus a willing sexual partner.

Evidence indicates that older persons who are in reasonably good health and who have willing and cooperative sexual partners whose health is also good can continue active sex lives into their 70s, 80s, or 90s. Thus, when there is a loss of sexual responsiveness in later life, factors such as monotony, preoccupation with career or economic pursuits, fatigue, overindulgence in food or drink, infirmity, or fear of failure may be involved. Shallow communication, a lack of imagination or lack of a creative approach to sex, diminished self-esteem, financial worries, disorders of sexual functioning, and organic disease are other factors that may have adverse effects on long-standing sexual relationships.

Sexual outlets other than coitus that are rewarding to older people include masturbation, extended foreplay, petting, sensate focus techniques, caressing, and massaging. Some older people may even turn to homosexuality as a sexual outlet. If sensible attention is given to mental and physical health, good nutrition, rest, and exercise, most older people can enjoy the benefits of continuing active sex lives.

Annotated Bibliography

Berman, Ellen M. and Lief, Harold I. Sex and the aging process. In *Sex and the life cycle*, ed. W. Oaks, G. Melchiode, and I. Ficher. New York: Grune and Stratton, 1976.

> This article addresses several important topics related to sexuality and the elderly, including stresses common to aging, physiology of sex and aging, sex and the older married couple, sex and the older single person, and sexual dysfunctions among the aged.

Butler, Robert N. and Lewis, Myrna I. *Love and sex after sixty: A guide for men and women in their later years*. New York: Harper and Row, 1976.

> This book is a helpful practical guide for the older person interested in maximizing satisfaction in marriage and relationships. The book contains expert treatment of many medical problems related to sex, learning new lovemaking patterns, dating, remarriage and children, and where to go for help.

Calderone, Mary S. and Johnson, Eric W. *The family book about sexuality*. New York: Harper and Row, 1981.

> This creatively written sex education text for the family covers all significant topics related to human sexuality and relationships, including giving and receiving love, sexuality and aging, marriage and family planning, variant behavior, and sex education programs. Important features include a bibliography of additional family readings and a listing of family planning and counseling services.

Kuhn, Margaret E. Sexual myths surrounding the aged. In *Sex and the life cycle*, ed. W. Oaks, G. Melchiode, and I. Ficher. New York: Grune and Stratton, 1976.

> This chapter examines the problem of agism in society and attempts to debunk several myths related to sexuality and the aged. This article would illuminate the lay reader as well as the health care professional.

McCary, James Leslie. *Freedom and growth in marriage (2nd ed.)*. New York: John Wiley and Sons, 1980.

> This book for the student and general reader considers various aspects of marriage, dating and mate selection, focusing on implications for individual growth and freedom within the marriage relationship. The past and future of marriage are discussed, as well as relevant contemporary issues, alternatives to marriage, the nature of love, aspects of human sexuality, marital adjustment, and other topics.

Silny, Ann Johnson. Sexuality and aging. In *Handbook of human sexuality*, ed. B. Wolman and J. Money. Englewood Cliffs, New Jersey: Prentice-Hall, 1980.

> This essay reviews the research literature on sexuality and aging and discusses the changes in sex-related characteristics in men and women as they advance in age. The author outlines the main changes in sexual physiology, behavior, and attitudes among the elderly.

Witters, Weldon and Jones-Witters, Patricia. *Human sexuality: A biological perspective.* New York: D. Van Nostrand, 1980.

> This text approaches the various aspects of human sexuality from the biological standpoint. Topics of special interest include genetic engineering, hormonal control of sexuality, drugs affecting sexual function, surrogate parenthood, artifical insemination, cloning, and sex selection. The text is well illustrated and contains student performance objectives, but its appeal extends beyond the classroom.

COLLEGE OF
BUSINESS & PUBLIC
ADMINISTRATION

Part Four

Sexual Attitudes and Behavior in Today's Society

Every culture formulates its own sexual code, and the differences among various sexual ethics are often great. What is considered acceptable in one culture might be considered perverted in another. Many forces contribute to the formation of sexual attitudes. Some are based on sound moral and legal principles, and some are outgrowths of folklore and ignorance. However sexual attitudes become established, changes in them are slow to occur, no matter how unreasonable and costly they may be in terms of personal maladjustment.

Sexual attitudes set the stage for sexual behavior, and the evolution of such attitudes in Western society is examined in Chapter 15. Here we explain how prevailing sexual mores came to be and how they influence, for good or ill, our sexual behavior. The various forms of sexual activity common to Western cultures are discussed in Chapter 16 in terms of incidence and frequency of occurrence. We see what personal circumstances influence the differences found among individuals in the choice and frequency of sexual expression—education, religion, age, sex, area of residence, and marital status, as examples.

The variant forms of sexual expression, at least as delineated by our culture, are discussed in Chapters 17 and 18. The material in Chapter 17 shows that variation from normal sexual behavior in many instances does not create the sex fiend of popular fiction. Chapter 18 focuses on the subject of homosexuality and how it is viewed and dealt with in our society. It is hoped that Chapters 17 and 18 can help to create a more compassionate and understanding view of those whose sexual behavior is different from accepted norms in our society.

Finally, sex-related state and federal laws are discussed in Chapter 19 in terms of their relevance, fairness, and effectiveness. Of particular concern is the muddle of legislation relating to obscenity, pornography, abortion, illegitimacy, sterilization, and artificial insemination. Some behavior undeniably constitutes sexual offense or acts of aggression against the victim. These acts are also discussed, together with the characteristics of the person committing them. Attention is directed to model sex laws and the suggestions that have been made to improve standards of legal control of sexual behavior in American society.

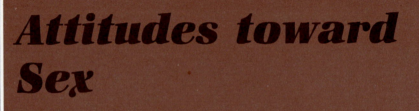

Attitudes toward Sex

15

Some psychotherapists hold that the way we think about or perceive events largely determines how we feel and act upon them. In other words, the way we "talk to ourselves" about life events determines how we will respond to those events. Indeed, the manner in which we think about sexual events or activities shapes whether we react in a normal, dysfunctional, or variant way.

Our sexual attitudes and behaviors are greatly influenced by our beliefs, thoughts, and perceptions regarding sex. When our sexual attitudes and behaviors are seriously out of phase, it may be because some irrational or misguided thought process is involved. In other cases, there may be a discrepancy between our attitudes and behaviors because there is a lag between changes in attitudes and beliefs and changes in behavior (Ellis & Harper 1976; Maultsby 1975; Zastrow 1979).

Of course, the demands and expectations of a particular culture, as well as differences within the culture, also produce a wide variety of attitudes toward sex. It may come as a surprise to many Americans to learn, for instance, that their disapproving views on premarital and postmarital sexual activity are not shared by the majority of the world's cultures. Of 158 societies investigated in one study, 70% were tolerant of premarital coitus, although such permissiveness did not include adulterous relationships (Ehrmann 1961). Indeed, many of the religious teachings and doctrines of the mystical sects of the East, Islam, Judaism, and segments of Christianity endorse the experiencing of sexual pleasure (Bullough 1980).

Anthropological investigations have consistently revealed that cultures encouraging women to be completely free in their sexual expression produce women whose reactions are as uninhibited and vigorous as those of men. Cultures in which there is approval of women having orgasms produce women who have orgasms. Cultures withholding such approval produce women who are incapable of orgasm (Kronhausen & Kronhausen 1965).

Women of emancipated modern societies are frequently troubled with menstrual difficulties of one sort or another. Yet Margaret Mead's anthropological studies of the women of Samoa (1928) uncovered only one woman in the entire population who even understood what was meant by pain or emotional upset during menstruation. That particular girl was in the employ of the island's white missionary family. In fact, the concept of menstrual pain struck Samoan women as "bizarre."

All cultures place specific restriction on the expression of sexuality. Yet if sexual needs are not expressed in one way, they *will* be in another. Much of a normal person's behavior is influenced by the inhibition and consequent displacement of sexual needs into other channels. For example, we are consciously disturbed by the thought of premarital or extramarital sexual relationships, yet are excessively interested in them. Consider how many of us express horror over the less than conventional behavior of certain luminaries in the entertainment world, yet voraciously consume every account of it, however exaggerated.

We satisfy our own desires, conscious or unconscious, by identifying with these people. At the same time, by pointing an accusing finger at them, we avoid self-guilt. Tensions accruing from the denial of our own desires are thus drained off through great interest, joking, and laughter (Ellis 1958). Certainly no sensible person suggests that control and appropriate expression of our sexual needs according to time and place are unnecessary. But to establish unrealistic and unreasonable prohibitions, whether directly or through the mechanism of guilt, is setting the stage for trouble now or later.

A Climate of Conflict and Change

There has been, to be sure, increased incidence of premarital coitus during recent years among both men and women, especially the latter. Yet the most significant change by far has been a growing liberalization of sexual *attitudes* and less adherence to the double standard (Bauman & Wilson 1976; Howat *et al.* 1979). The premarital sexual attitudes and behavior of young adult women and men have been converging since the 1960s, although women still lag somewhat behind.

Significant changes in human mores, behavior, laws, and social institutions occur gradually. Changes in what a culture considers acceptable sexual behavior are especially slow because the orientation and experiences of childhood impose such strong limitations on freedom of behavior in adulthood (British Council of Churches 1966; Ellis 1966; Rubin 1965a). And yet one can hardly have escaped noticing a change in sexual attitudes in recent years. Witness the freedom, almost unheard of 15 years ago, with which sexual topics are discussed today in the communication media, schools, churches, and government circles.

But many persons unaccustomed to casual conversation on sexual topics fail to understand that talk and actions are not necessarily one and the same. Attitudes (and the ease of discussing them) are not to be confused with behavior (Coombs 1968a). And inconsistency between sexual attitudes and behavior is *still* a characteristic of the American culture, despite the changes. Even those for whom a decision in the matter of a sexual ethic is most pertinent—today's young people—are bewildered and bedeviled by the dichotomy between prevailing attitudes and behavior. For example, a study involving sexually active lower-class delinquent girls, whose average age was 15.8 years, revealed that 91% of the girls, despite their behavior, believed premarital coitus to be wrong (Ball & Logan 1970).

In a survey published in 1960, Reiss (1960b) detailed the prevailing attitudes of American adults and of high school and college students toward premarital sex. The results of his survey are given in Table 15.1.

Table 15.1. **Approval of Petting and Full Sexual Relations by Stage of Relationship**

	Adults		Students	
	For Males	For Females	For Males	For Females
Petting:				
When engaged	60.8	56.1	85.0	81.8
In love	59.4	52.6	80.4	75.2
Strong affection	54.3	45.6	67.0	56.7
No affection	28.6	20.3	34.3	18.0
Full Sexual Relations:				
When engaged	19.5	16.9	52.2	44.0
In love	17.6	14.2	47.6	38.7
Strong affection	16.3	12.5	36.9	27.2
No affection	11.9	7.4	20.8	10.8
N	(1390)	(1411)	(811)	(806)

The fact that in both groups petting and coitus were more consistently approved of for males than for females gave evidence that some of the traditional double standard persisted. That approval of sexual involvement decreased as the level of emotional commitment in the relationship decreased was evidence of emerging permissiveness when affection exists, for both sexes. Even so, "a small (5%–15%) but not insignificant number of college women find full sexual intercourse acceptable even if there is no particular affection between the partners. For them, physical attraction, momentary impulse, or curiosity are enough to justify coitus" (K. E. Davis 1971).

A similar study reported in the mid-1970s (Hunt 1974) showed that, depending on the degree of a couple's affection or emotional involvement with one another, up to 84% of men thought premarital coitus was acceptable for males; and up to 81% considered it acceptable for women. Although less permissive, women (up to 73% of them) condoned male premarital coitus; up to 68% considered it acceptable for women. A 1969 Gallup poll showed that 68% of a national sample thought premarital sex was wrong; by 1973, only 48% were of that opinion, a decrease of 20% in four years.

Hunt's findings (1974) concerning the sexual attitudes of mid-1970 America present an interesting picture. Almost a third of the men and a fifth of the women see nothing wrong with mate-swapping. Almost 60% of both men and women see nothing wrong in anal intercourse. Four times as many women and twice as many men today as in the Kinsey era admit to being sexually aroused by erotically explicit material. Three-fourths of women who are not college-educated, and four-fifths who are, do not believe that fellatio is wrong; almost 90% of men and women under age 35 do not think cunnilingus is wrong. Of male white- and blue-collar workers aged 35 and older, 43% and 27%, respectively, and 65% and 41% under 35 years, think that homosexuality should be legal.

Larsen *et al.* (1980) have developed a scale to measure current attitudes of heterosexual college students toward homosexuality. These investigators have found that "being male, a business student, frequent church attender, responsive to negative peer attitudes, fundamentalist in religiosity, and authoritarian" are factors associated with antihomosexual attitudes. Conversely, women who are liberal arts students and nonfrequent church attenders tend to have more tolerant attitudes toward homosexuality. Positive peer attitudes, low religiosity, and low authoritarianism are also related to more tolerant views toward homosexuality.

Kinsey *et al.* (1953) found that women in his survey were less likely than men to demand virginity of their spouses at the time of marriage (23% vs. 40%). However, the double standard seems to be collapsing in the matter of virginity. A 1970 Gallup poll, conducted on 55 college campuses, revealed that men and women were then thinking very much alike on the subject;

75% of these students expressed the view that virginity in the person whom they marry is unimportant. The results of another study conducted about the same time (Christensen & Gregg 1970), however, indicate that the double standard continues to plague American college men. Although 55% of the sampling expressed approval of premarital coitus, 75% of them nevertheless stated that they would prefer to marry a girl without coital experience. Because both men and women tend to regard sexual conquests and experience as indications (however stereotyped) of masculinity in a man, many women prefer that a man not be a virgin (Burgess & Wallin 1953).

In a 1970 survey of college students (Frede), women listed religious or moral precepts as the main reason for restricting premarital coitus (60.8%). The men listed moral principles as the third most important reason (31.1%). Other reasons given were loss of self-respect (for women, the second most important reason; seventh for men); fear of endangering future marital relations (third for women, fourth for men); fear of pregnancy, for self or partner (fourth for women, second for men); and fear of loss of partner's respect (fifth for both). Men ranked lack of opportunity as the principal reason for restricting premarital coitus, a reason that ranked ninth among women.

The sexual attitudes and behavior of men and of women are converging today. Women expect the same sexual freedom that has traditionally been accorded only to men. Men, on the other hand, rather than moving in the direction of greater promiscuity, are slowly drifting toward the traditional female norm (Rubin 1971). Although several studies made in the 1970s revealed that only 65% to 75% of college males had actually experienced premarital coitus, up to 88% considered it acceptable behavior (Howat *et al.* 1979). Factors affecting this permissive attitude were race, age, semester in college, strength of religious beliefs, and region of the country. Older youths who had little religious conviction and were attending eastern, western, or southern colleges were more permissive than younger, religiously inclined midwesterners (K. E. Davis 1971). Although as many as 80% of college women approved of premarital coitus for themselves, less than 60% actually engaged in it (K. E. Davis 1971; Howat *et al.* 1979). In the Davis study, only 40% or less found premarital coitus acceptable under the less involved conditions of strong affection, if no exploitation existed. For college women, permissive sexual attitudes were related to having been in love two or more times and to being emotionally involved in a dating relationship (going steady, being pinned, or being engaged). Women's view of themselves as sexual beings still appears strongly related to feelings of romance, affection, and love (K. E. Davis 1971).

In recent years, attitudes appear to be much more predictive of behavior than they have been in the past. In 1958, 41% of the females and 65% of the males with premarital sexual experience held permissive sexual attitudes compared with 78% of the females and 82% of the males 10 years later. It is interesting to note that, as attitudes and behavior become less different, fewer males and females report negative reactions to first non-marital coital experience (Christensen & Johnson 1971).

Mid-1970 research data suggest that the sexual double standard may disappear during the late 1970s and 1980s. The question asked by college students today is not so much whether coitus should occur before marriage, but in which kind of relationship it should occur. A stable, affectionate dating relationship—today described as "going together" or living together—rather than a formal engagement, is the usually accepted norm for engaging in premarital coitus (King & Sobel 1975; Howat *et al.* 1979).

One of the most significant social changes to occur in recent years has been the emergence of women toward a position of equality in American society. The freedom and parity that women are demanding—and are increasingly enjoying—in the United States have had a profound effect on sexual attitudes. Most women today are unwilling to accept the notion that women and men are subject to different sexual standards. They expect pleasure from sexual activities as well as restraints to be equally applicable to both sexes (R. R. Bell 1971a; Poffenberger 1960). Despite recent liberalizing tendencies in the realm of women's rights, however, certain differences betweeen the sexual attitudes of the two sexes continue to be forged by such factors as childhood rearing, societal expectations, and certain phys-iological forces.

An interesting side effect of this struggle for equality is that the sexual attitudes of present-day American women are often considerably healthier than those of American men. Chroniclers of sexual histories, whether researchers or clinicians, have found that women are far more open and honest in supplying personal data. Some social scientists believe that, as a result of women's sexual liberation, men are increasingly fearful of female sexuality. Men may attempt through boasting to compensate for what they feel is a threat to their self-image. As a consequence, the data they provide are often unreliable (Maslow 1965).

Since the beginning of recorded history, older generations have been in a state of shock over the supposed immorality of the younger generation. About 2400 years ago Socrates wrote:

> Children now love luxury. They have bad manners, contempt for authority. They show disrespect for elders and love chatter in place of exercise. Children are now tyrants, not the servants of their household.

And in the 8th century B.C., the Greek poet Hesiod wrote:

> I see no hope for the future of our people if they are dependent on the frivolous youth of today, for certainly all youth are reckless beyond words.... When I was a boy, we were taught to be discreet and respectful of elders, but the present youth are exceedingly wise and impatient of restraint.

When young people do rebel against the values of older segments of the population, the older generations have to look at their own behavior for at least part of the answer. As long as those of us who are older continue in some of our own neurotic and self-defeating behavior patterns, we are not likely to get very far in persuading young people to listen to what we have to say.

Why should a youngster believe an adult about the dangers of say, smoking marijuana when that same adult smokes cigarettes from a package clearly labeled, "Warning: The Surgeon General Has Determined That Cigarette Smoking is Dangerous to Your Health"? The argument that smoking marijuana is illegal, while smoking tobacco is not, will quite likely be ignored. Young people of today are not thoroughly convinced of the value of laws, mainly because their parents frequently act in defiance of them—for instance, by driving 50 miles an hour in a 40-mile zone. The fact that there is little traffic does not change the existence of the law, or the requirement to obey it, any more than does the fact that many authorities question the dangers of marijuana justify smoking it. Because of the Vietnam war, business and political corruption, widespread dishonesty, and the older generation's poor record of marital stability, youth is no longer convinced of the wrongness of premarital sex or that marriage is an ultimately desirable goal ("Teen-age Sex" 1972).

Religious and Racial Influences on Sexual Attitudes

In the past, almost all studies showed that the intensity of religious belief greatly influences people's sexual attitudes and behavior. The influence of religion has been positive and beneficial for many people; yet in certain instances, such as the realm of sexuality, the influence of religion has at times been negative and detrimental. Larsen *et al.* (1980) have observed that intense religious doctrines often preach the benefits of love, understanding, and tolerance, while in fact these doctrines frequently practice rejection, punishment, and intolerance. Other investigations into this subject (Ogren 1974; Primeau 1977), however, have shown that it is not religion itself that influences sexual behavior, but sex-related guilt built up in certain individuals as a result of religious training and experiences. Some researchers have suggested that sexual anxiety, which may or may not be related to guilt, may be the important factor that influences behavior (Janda & O'Grady 1980). Whether the conceptualization is in terms of guilt or anxiety, however, it is of interest to note that those people who conduct their lives according to the philosophy of the Golden Rule rather than the dictates of the Ten Commandments have more mature, better adjusted, more fulfilling sex lives.

Research studies have consistently shown that blacks have a more active sex life before marriage, and begin it earlier, than whites (Rainwater 1966; Reiss 1970; Shah & Zelnik 1980). However, any person who is concerned about real or apparent differences between blacks and whites should never forget that it is next to impossible to isolate ethnic or racial factors as truly contributing forces in any measured difference. For example, Reiss (1974) carefully investigated apparent differences in the permissiveness regarding premarital sexuality said to exist between whites and blacks. He discovered that differences were related not to skin color, but to general attitudes of liberality or conservatism in other areas, such as politics, economics, religion, and marriage. A mid-1970 study (Delcampo *et al.* 1976) of university students in Virginia revealed that blacks and whites held quite similar attitudes toward premarital sexual permissiveness. (Both black and white males were less knowledgeable about contraception, yet more sexually lenient, than the female sampling of both races.) When proper controls are applied to investigations of sexual attitudes and behavior, alleged racial differences disappear and other causative factors emerge.

Attitude Formation in Young People

Many changes in sexual attitudes have their basis in the protracted period of adolescence imposed on present-day American youth. Our society requires longer periods of scholastic and vocational training than ever before, thus extending social adolescence. Yet today's young people become physically mature at a considerably earlier age than previous generations did. The period of social adolescence is now approximately twice as long as it was 100 years ago (R. R. Bell 1971a; Jones 1960).

During this prolonged preparation for adulthood, the two sexes begin to develop divergent attitudes toward premarital sexual activity. The natural feelings of insecurity bred by adolescence plus the accelerated physical drives typical of it, especially in boys, make the adolescent particularly susceptible to advertising extolling the supreme value of sex appeal in attaining popularity, success, admiration, security. Boys are influenced to believe that their masculinity (success as a *man*) depends on their success in seduction. The further they go with girls sexually, the more masculine they are in their own and their peer group's eyes.

Young girls are indoctrinated in the importance of being "sexy." They are lured to purchase an often ludicrous and useless assortment of products that are "guaranteed" to increase sexual attractiveness. A girl is indeed in a delicate position. She is told to appear and act "sexy" in order to attract as many boys and to have as many dates as possible—the symbols in her all-important peer group of popularity and social success. But at the same time she must hold the line of propriety, because otherwise she risks losing her "good girl" status and prestige. Girls—at least in their younger dating years—too often are favorably evaluated by their peer group only in terms of their popularity in dating (and the number of boys whom they cause to make open affectionate commitments), coupled with their ability to remain free of sexual involvements (R. R. Bell 1971a; Waller & Hill 1951).

The female sexual tease is a logical outcome of such attitudes. She may become what Albert Ellis terms a Donna Juanita, a female Don Juan, able to satisfy her needs only when she knows she has captured a man's attention and has made him desire her sexually. If she can accomplish this goal without coition, so much the better, for underlying this syndrome are pervading doubts about her sexual desirability and capability. Frequently she sees herself as being in competition with all women, so that the only male who can fulfill her needs is one already committed to another woman (Mathis 1970).

The dynamics behind such a girl's need to be appreciated for her physical attractiveness are easy to understand. When as a young child she wore a pretty dress and smiled sweetly, she gained considerable attention simply because of her looks. A small boy, however, does not win attention the same way. He must "do something" to prove his worth—flex his muscles, show how fast he can run, or boast that he can whip other boys in fights. An attractive physical appearance often becomes a woman's key to recognition, whereas physical power or success is the indicator of a male's desirability. Indeed, 82% of men report that sexual attraction was a distinct factor in their selection of a partner, whereas it figures in the choice of only 50% of women (B. L. Greene 1970).

These examples illustrate how our socialization processes breed sexist attitudes and behavior in males and females. Sexism is unfortunate for the individual, because rigid role assignments limit the possibilities of growth through identification and experience. But society as a whole is also the loser. It is deprived of the contributions a person might be capable of making in a role traditionally assigned to one of the opposite sex.

Younger teen-agers tend to accept the traditional sexual standards of their parents. But as they grow older and begin to think independently, they come to a progressively greater extent under the influence of outside values, particularly those of their peer group. They begin to adopt a more permissive sexual code of behavior (R. R. Bell 1971a; Reiss 1961a). Gradually learning from older adolescents that the preaching of their conscientious parents is not so fearsome as they had once believed, they begin to reject it. They no longer uncritically accept theological doctrine or traditional codes of ethics as guidelines for their behavior (Blaine 1967). Teen-agers also learn from their peers how to keep from being "found out" and thus avoid parental or societal wrath.

Another cultural influence on attitude formation in young people can be found in the daily commerce in sex that we are willingly or unwittingly subjected to—directly, as in "adult bookstore" sales; or indirectly, as in the sexual imagery of TV programming—which has effectively promoted the idea that sexual experimentation is not only acceptable but expected behavior. Some social scientists believe the inference already exists among boys and girls that if they do *not* participate in sexual experimentation, there is something wrong with them sexually (Menninger 1974).

Many youths lead well-behaved, moral lives simply because they fear the consequences of doing otherwise. When they reject their old patterns of behavior they often have no standard by which to conduct their lives, and are left to their impulses and strong sexual feelings (Frank 1963). Sensible parents should anticipate these possibilities and take proper steps to instill in their children a realistic code of ethical behavior.

A close, accepting, and loving family relationship is far more effective in controlling the sexual behavior of teen-agers than threats of punishment, eternal or temporal. Research both here and abroad shows that girls who get along well with their fathers and mothers are far less likely to be sexually experienced than those who do not. Daughters from unhappy homes have less stable and gratifying relationships with their male partners than girls from happy homes and, further, have more sex partners (Kirkendall & Libby 1969; Shah & Zelnik 1980; Uddenberg 1976). Even a happy home life, however, does not necessarily make it easy for youths to talk about sex with adults. Some college students were asked to play recordings of their own voices reading sexually explicit material in the presence of audiences of different ages. The students displayed the greatest discomfort when the listeners were middle-aged (Miller *et al.* 1976). When sex is the topic of discussion, apparently both young and old feel more comfortable with someone their own age.

Self-Defeating Behavior

Many girls in their mid-teens begin to feel (in spite of reality) that, in our society, the male is supposed to be strong and confident, and to offer security to his female. Not having the insight, tutelage, or experience to evaluate what constitutes genuine strength on the part of a boy or man and feeling inadequate themselves, many girls actually do not know what to look for by way of indicators of masculine strength, and may come to accept certain warped manifestations as qualities of manliness.

These are the girls who are often impressed by the anti-Establishment youth who is defiant of rules and of the society that makes them; the school dropout committed to drugs, tobacco, alcohol, and profanity, and to little else in life; the person who is as reckless of human life as he is of human sensibilities. These girls have no way of knowing that such behavior patterns may be attempts by the boys to mask marked feelings of inferiority which threaten to overwhelm them. The very things, therefore, that a young girl wishes to avoid—inadequacy and weakness in a man—are what she is unwittingly courting when she looks to the "tough guy" or "heel" as an ideal (Salzman *et al.* 1980). An unfortunate by-product of this twisted set of values is that the "nice" boy, who displays kindness and honesty in his dealings with others, is often ignored or regarded with downright contempt by such a girl.

Other factors enter into the emotional complexities of such girls. They are crossing the threshold into physical maturity and feel inadequate to cope with the accompanying social and sexual problems. Since such girls evaluate themselves as rather worthless and insufficient beings, the boys who behave decently and compassionately toward them cannot, they reason, have very good judgment. Or if the boys offer friendship so unselfishly, they must not be of much value themselves. It follows, then, that the boys who ignore or mistreat them are exhibiting good judgment, and are therefore the obviously strong masculine ones, the social or sexual worthies. Furthermore, these girls have normal sexual desires and wishes, but frequently feel guilty about them. It follows, in their thinking, that in our society guilt demands punishment. Therefore, by selecting one of the "tough guys," such a girl is able not only to satisfy her sexual desires, but at the same time assure her punishment because, unconsciously or otherwise, she realizes that, sooner or later, she will be mistreated or rejected by this boy.

While boys are more caught up in trying to prove their masculinity through sexual exploitations than they are in the sex-sin-punishment syndrome, they are still frequent victims of this pattern. For example, the very patterns of behavior a boy develops as "signs" of his masculinity— dropping out of school, use of alcohol, tobacco, and drugs—may be unconscious methods of punishing himself for sexual behavior that he engages in but cannot quite accept. Furthermore, males frequently become premature ejaculators and impotent as unconscious punishment for their unacceptable sexuality.

Both boys and girls often develop an unconscious feeling or attitude that good girls (mothers) and good boys (fathers) do not even think about sex, let alone engage in it. Yet at every turn these same young people observe that sex, although forbidden—certainly, at least, with decent partners—is really quite exciting and highly pleasurable. Thus, rather than being sexually aroused by decent, honest people, they are attracted to dishonest, unloving, and unlovable partners, the only ones with whom sex is "permissible." Unless this crooked thinking is worked out in young adolescence, boys and girls run the risk of being caught up in the Saint vs. Sinner syndrome, which can plague them all their lives (Layman 1976).

Teen-agers are not the only ones caught up in this complex sex-sin-punishment syndrome. It is found among adults of both sexes as well. It has long been recognized that some women are sexually attracted to men who have an element of the scoundrel in them. The moral training of a woman in these cases often explains why she makes unfortunate choices in men. Like men afflicted with the traditional princess-prostitute syndrome ("bad girls do, good girls don't"), certain women have been taught that sex is so dirty and improper that it should be dissociated from men they perceive as "good." Like those men who develop the unconscious feeling that sex cannot be enjoyed—must not be—with a princess (motherlike) figure, some women cannot associate sex with an honorable, reliable, loving (fatherlike) man. It is also a widely recognized phenomenon among psychotherapists and marriage counselors that many women marry "problem" men—for example, alcoholics—because they have an unconscious need to be punished.

The Home, Children, and Sexuality

Clinical observations and the results of empirical research have frequently underlined the marked discrepancy between what parents have themselves experienced (or are experiencing) by way of sexual activity, and the code of sexual ethics they profess to their children. It is also interesting that the parents' own attitude of sexual permissiveness is unrelated to the attitude of permissiveness held by the student son or daughter. However, how students perceive or interpret their parents' sexual permissiveness is related to their own permissiveness (Walsh 1972).

Fathers play an important part in their sons' sex-role identity and their perception of what is expected of men and masculinity. Mothers seem to play an even more important part in the development of the sexual attitudes of their daughters. For example, there may be real or merely perceived gaps in a mother's and her daughter's acceptance of premarital sexual behavior. In the matter of kissing, there is typically no misperception of the other's views. As the behavior becomes more involved or intense, not only is there a divergence in acceptance of that behavior (the mother, unsurprisingly, the more conservative), but each begins to misperceive the other's values—although the daughter always correctly identifies her mother's negative views toward premarital coitus (LoPiccolo 1973). Researchers suggest that, while open discussion between daughter and mother may clarify misconceptions of one another's attitudes toward various forms of premarital sexual activity, such discussions usually serve only to increase generational conflict.

In an interesting study by Wake (1969), 30% of the mothers interviewed admitted that they had experienced premarital coitus. But only 3% of them had a permissive attitude toward like behavior in their daughters, and 9%

toward their sons. Slightly over 50% of the fathers in this study reported that they had experienced premarital coition. But less than 10% expressed a permissive attitude toward their daughters' experiencing premarital coitus, and less than 20% toward their sons' doing so.

The 1974 *Redbook* survey of 100,000 women revealed far greater sexual freedom among women today than a generation ago. But, like other studies, it also showed that women's liberality sometimes does not include attitudes of sexual permissiveness for their children. The answers to two questions posed in the survey demonstrate that paradox: 12% of the women said they would object to premarital sex for their sons; 24% objected to the prospect for their daughters (Levin 1975).

The question naturally arises: Why is it that mothers have behaved in one way and felt no regret, yet expect their daughters to behave in a contrary manner? The explanation lies primarily in women's perception of the relationship between sexual attraction and emotional commitment (Ehrmann 1959).

Usually, a woman must have a strong emotional attachment before she allows herself to become sexually involved. She must be convinced that it is she, the person, who is important to the relationship, not simply her sexual potential (Vincent 1961). One investigation, for instance, demonstrated that women enter a university with conservative sexual attitudes, then shift later to more liberal ones, but *only* if they develop a deep emotional attachment or become engaged (Bell & Buerkle 1961). The liberalizing of their attitudes appears to be an outgrowth of emotional commitment.

A mother, then, in her own premarital sexual experiences may have had strong feelings regarding the significance of emotional involvement as a precedent to sexual contact, but cannot accept the fact that her daughter also recognizes the importance of this sequence. Furthermore, because she defied the sexual prohibitions of her own rearing by engaging in premarital coitus, the mother may now carry a residual guilt. This guilt can break through and be projected onto her maturing daughter in the form of disapproval of premarital sexual experience.

Psychotherapists have long observed more regret among women who remained virgins until marriage than among those women who did not. These clinical observations have been upheld by the results of several investigations (R. R. Bell 1971a; Burgess & Wallin 1953; Kinsey *et al.* 1953) showing that those women who have had premarital coition are not sorry. They maintain that they would repeat their behavior if they had it to do over again; but they expect their daughters to conform to a more conservative ethic. Essentially the same findings have been reported by Cuber and Harroff (1966), whose sampling was from a highly educated, influential, upper-middle-class group.

Through a national survey, Reiss (1971) appears to have uncovered the answer to the disparity in attitudes between older and younger people regarding premarital intercourse. When he merely compared the two groups as a whole, he found only an 8 or 9 percentage-point difference in attitudes between them (the older group being the more conservative, needless to say). However, when he divided all those in the older group of, say, 45 years of age into subgroups according to whether they were single, married without children, married with young children, or married with teen-age children, he found some radical differences. Acceptance of premarital intercourse spiraled significantly downward within the same age group from the single person to the married, to the married person with young children, to the one with teen-age children. Reiss concluded that these differences in attitude were based not on age, but on the individual's feelings of responsibility for the behavior of others, especially dependents.

This study also showed that, as siblings become older and assume a surrogate-parent role for younger children in the family, their permissiveness toward premarital intercourse declines. Between the ages of 10 and 20, the individual's acceptance of premarital sexual behavior increases markedly. Following marriage, however, it slowly decreases until the children born of the marriage reach the age of 20. A parent aged 40 and a 20-year-old daughter are crossing the opposite ends of the acceptance cycle, one at the low point, the other at the high. Despite these differences, however, almost 66% of the young people surveyed in one broad study expressed the belief that their sexual standards and those of their parents were similar (Reiss 1960a).

The sexually restrictive admonitions through which a mother attempts to indoctrinate her daugher quite likely will be no more effective than they were in her own generation. But the unfortunate consequence will be the same—generation after generation of women who tend to follow their emotional and sexual inclinations, but with guilt and shame, because they have violated the sexual ethic with which they were reared.

Parents stress to their daughters (and, to a lesser extent, to their sons) that love is an important aspect of happiness in boy-girl relationships. They thereby increase the likelihood that their children will engage in premarital sex, for research clearly indicates that love is a key motivation for girls' premarital coitus (Ehrmann 1959, 1961; Reiss 1968). The indications are that those girls who start dating, kissing, and other inceptive behavior at an early age are the ones most likely to have early intercourse (Kirkendall & Libby 1969).

The Role of Guilt

The strongest influential factor in developing sexual attitudes and behavior seems to be sexual guilt. A survey of the personal lives of professional psychologists revealed that it is sexual guilt far more than any other inhibitor that restricts sexual freedom (Primeau 1977). Similar findings have frequently emerged from investigations of laypeople (Mosher & Cross 1971). Even so, guilt itself is not necessarily an inhibitor of sexual behavior. For example, most young people gradually increase their sexual involvement, which tends to minimize whatever guilt they feel about premarital sexual activity. About 90% of women and 60% of men report that they eventually come to accept the sexual behavior that once made them feel guilty (Reiss 1960a, 1971).

In the beginning of a relationship, a couple may engage in kissing only, but feel some guilt about it. They then involve themselves in the kissing behavior again, but this time they do not feel so guilty. They continue the kissing episodes until the guilt disappears altogether. Next they move to a level of greater sexual intimacy—say, to petting. Again they feel guilty, but they overcome it by repeating the same behavior over and over again until the guilt disappears. They then move to another level of intimacy, and so on.

Ten steps may be involved in the progress from kissing to coitus. Although there is considerable distance between steps 1 and 10, there is likely to be no more distance between steps 9 and 10 than there was between steps 1 and 2. In new dating situations, furthermore, women quickly progress to the level of sexual activity they had reached in earlier relationships (Ehrmann 1959). Only the speed with which women move through the various levels of intimacy and the age at which they marry distinguish one from another. Thus a woman who marries early—say, at the age of 18—may not have moved through all 10 levels of sexual intimacy by the time she marries. But the woman who finishes college and does not marry until she is 22 or 23 has had more time in which to progress through the various levels. She is therefore less likely to be a virgin at the time of her marriage than the woman who marries at 18.

Slightly over 50% of teen-age girls admit to guilt feelings if they go "too far" in petting with their dates, while only 25% of the boys express similar guilt. These views stand in curious contrast to statements made by the other teen-agers in these samplings (33% of the girls and 75% of the boys) who are more conservative in their sexual conduct, yet indicate that they desire greater sexual intimacy on dates. Boys appear interested in petting and sexual intercourse on dates, while girls are willing to neck only (mild embracing and kissing limited to face and lips) (Bell & Blumberg 1960). As the relationship becomes more serious, however—from dating, to going steady, to engagement—sexual behavior becomes more intimate, and guilt becomes less for both sexes (Bell & Blumberg 1960; Christensen & Carpenter 1962a).

Patterns of guilt feelings undergo a change over a period of time in both sexes, especially among older unmarried groups. Clinicians have presented convincing arguments that many men are beset with considerably more guilt over sexual matters than women are. Their premise is that women, in nonmarital sex relationships especially, usually and understandably want reassurance that they are desired and respected for more than their sexual performance. Women also want assurance that the men will not "kiss and tell," and that they will maintain the same level of regard for them after coitus as before.

A man, on the other hand, feels that, as the instigator of the sex act, he is the "seducer," and that the responsibility for the woman's participation rests squarely upon his shoulders. To placate his own guilt or anxiety, therefore, he must feel either that there is love in the relationship, or that the woman is "bad." Furthermore, since he feels guilty about his "seduction" of the woman, he comes to regard her as the instigator of his guilt. He is then liable to project his self-anger by quarreling or fighting with her, speaking to her in a degrading manner, or otherwise manifesting his rejection of her—the very woman who thought enough of him to share with him the most intimate of human experiences.

It is important to human sexual enjoyment that sex-oriented guilt be reduced to a minimum. Studies have shown that the more guilt over sex one feels, the less one's desire for sex, the fewer orgasms one experiences, and the less sexually responsive one is (Kutner 1971; Leiman & Epstein 1961). Another researcher has also found that highly religious males and females are less likely to experience a wide array of sexual activities or behaviors (Mahoney 1980).

Because of unrealistic romantic ideals, many men and women are unprepared to accept the probability that there are thousands of persons whom they could love and to whom they could be satisfactorily married. For example, if a married man is attracted to another woman, he may interpret it as meaning that he no longer loves his wife. Because he thinks he can love only one woman at a time, he begins, consciously or unconsciously, to concentrate on the negative aspects of his wife and the positive ones of the other woman in order to make the new attraction acceptable (Vincent 1967). Or perhaps the husband falls in love with another woman and develops guilt feelings. If he were not married he would feel no guilt; therefore, he reasons unconsciously, his wife is the instigator of his guilt and deserves his hostility. He directs his negative feelings toward his wife, the only innocent party in the triangle. The same story can, of course, be told of a married woman.

Attitudes toward Nonmarital Sex

The evidence gathered from questionnaires completed by 20,000 politically liberal men and women—well educated, of high socioeconomic status, and predominantly under 30—revealed that only 1 of 10 advocated chastity until marriage. Over 50% felt that premarital sex equips people for more stable and happier marriages; about 75% had themselves experienced premarital coitus. About 80% of the total sample believed that extramarital sex might be acceptable under certain circumstances, although only about 40% of the men and 36% of the women had actually engaged in it (Athanasiou *et al.* 1970).

Ard (1974a) made a study of 161 married couples who had premarital coitus with one another and whose marriages were still viable 20 years later. The study revealed no correlation between premarital intimacy and deterioration of the relationship after marriage.

Adultery (intercourse between a man and woman, at least one of whom is married at the time to someone else) has been condemned in practically all Western cultures because of the threat it poses to the family unit. Furthermore, it is unequivocally condemned in Judeo-Christian theology. In the history of no culture, however, has men's extramarital coition been consistently controlled or severely punished, whereas women have universally been subjected to a much more stringent code of sexual ethics. These differences are primarily a result of the fact that, if women were to engage in extramarital coitus, it would threaten the economic stability of the entire society, would reflect on the masculinity and social prestige of their husbands, and, in the case of pregnancy, could raise the question of paternal responsibility (Harper 1961).

Wives at every social level are more tolerant of their husbands' extramarital affairs than husbands are of their wives' affairs. Only 27% of the women in Kinsey's sample said that they would consider their husbands' adultery sufficient grounds for seeking a divorce. But 51% of the men indicated they would regard infidelity by their wives as being totally destructive of the marriage (Kinsey *et al.* 1948, 1953). While the percentages have dropped among both sexes in recent years, men are still more unforgiving of their partners' infidelity than women are.

Perhaps husbands would be less upset by their wives' infidelity if they realized with what detachment some women can manage an extramarital affair, sexual or otherwise. A certain type of woman can "love and leave"; or have coitus with a man, and then attend to her obligations at home without remaining emotionally involved or carrying residuals of guilt. Neither does she necessarily compare her mate's sexual skills unfavorably with those of her lover, which an adulterous husband sometimes does. Tradition would have us believe that the man is the emotionally controlled and dispassionate one in a marriage. Yet in the majority of cases it is he who, upon the discovery of infidelity, rants, threatens, retaliates, divorces, or even kills one or both lovers (English 1971).

In *Extra-marital Relationships* (1969), Gerhard Neubeck has made a perceptive study of the motivation in adultery. The reasons most frequently given by men for sexual infidelity are these: desire for variety in sexual experience, retaliation, rebellion, new emotional satisfaction, the unexpected evolution of sexual involvement from friendship, the wife's encouragement, and the aging factor. The research cited by Neubeck suggests that marital infidelity (sexual or emotional) is not *necessarily* related to unsatisfactory or weak marital relationships or to neurotic inclinations or personalities.

It appears that in prolonged extramarital affairs, sexual fulfillment is not the overriding motivation. Most of these relationships endure primarily for reasons that fall somewhere between intellectual and sexual fulfillment. The relationships may last for 10, 15, even 20 years. Mistresses of middle-aged men are not the young, voluptuous women the stereotype would lead us to believe. They are, rather, near the age of the men involved, and they work to support themselves (Cuber 1969).

The ideal of lifelong, sexually exclusive, monogamous marriage apparently evolved over a period of several thousand years, during which time life expectancy climbed slowly from 20 to about 40 years. Because of the high maternal death rate, most men outlived two or three wives. A man might therefore be bound to sexual exclusivity with one woman for only a few years. Her death and his remarriage would then bring a new sexual partner into his life (Francoeur & Francoeur 1973). Matters are quite different today, when the average American male can expect to live about 67 years and the female, almost 75. Celebrations of 50th wedding anniversaries are not at all unusual.

So boredom in marriage is a real possibility today. And when men or women find romance and passion waning in their marriages, they are frequently propelled toward extramarital relationships. (Perhaps this pattern is more prevalent in America than in most other countries, where less value is placed on newness and experience-seeking [Whitehurst 1973].) Although extramarital affairs incur moral, legal, and social condemnation, and often create unique difficulties for one or both partners, the participants nonetheless frequently view their new attachment as an opportunity for love, excitement, adventure, romance, renewed vigor, enhanced ego, and return to youth—all the dreams marriage was supposed to fulfill but did not, or no longer does.

Americans have been persuaded by romantic novels, movies, and the like into the impossible expectation that marriage should serve all the needs of the spouses, especially the sexual ones. Continuing marital sexual relationships must retain, according to this mythology, the romance and passion of the courtship and honeymoon, and lovemaking must always be at a nerve-tingling orgasmic high. In no other area of human behavior is such unrealistic performance expected (Francoeur & Francoeur 1973). When the sexual expectations are not met, it is assumed that something is wrong (1) with the marriage; (2) with the mate and his/her interest in the partner or the marriage; or (3) with one's self. These anxieties are frequently complicated by a desire for extramarital sexual relationships, which the individual is unable to accept as being normal or ethical. Then follows a repression of these desires into the unconscious, where they become almost invariably associated with hostility toward the spouse (Bernard 1973).

Sexual Attitudes and Relational Adjustment

Finally, there must be an appreciation of the role that personality plays in the creation of sexual attitudes. In a particularly meaningful study by A. H. Maslow (1966b), the importance of emotions and of personality factors in relational happiness and sexual adjustment is clearly indicated.

In this study, Maslow found that women who rate high in dominance feelings (or high self-esteem) are considered to be self-confident and self-assured, and to possess a high evaluation of the self. They display feelings of superiority while showing a lack of shyness, self-consciousness, and embarrassment. Women who empirically rate low in dominance feeling (low self-esteem) show the opposite personality characteristics, while middle-dominance subjects fall about midway between the two extremes. Because dominance traits affect behavior as well as feelings, high-dominance women are much more likely than low-dominance subjects to masturbate, to have premarital sexual intercourse, to volunteer for sex research studies, not to shun pelvic examinations, and the like (Maslow 1966b).

Jewish women are generally found to be higher in both dominance feelings and dominance behavior than Catholic and Protestant women. Yet they show a higher percentage of virginity at marriage than either of the other two religious groups. Women who have *strong* religious feelings—whether Jewish, Catholic, or Protestant—are more likely to be virgins, not to masturbate, and to have lower ratings for "sex attitude" (a term used by Maslow to describe personal reactions to sexuality) than women with less pronounced feelings of religious guilt.

Women of low-dominance feelings avoid the upper position during intercourse while those with very high-dominance feelings frequently prefer that position. The low-dominance man or woman often dislikes or is afraid of sex. The most satisfactory relationships are those in which the man equals or is somewhat (but not markedly) superior to the woman in dominance feelings. On the other hand, if the woman has higher dominance feelings than the man, or if the man is markedly more dominant than the woman, social and sexual maladjustments are likely unless both are very secure persons. Moderately sexed women are more likely to reach orgasm during sexual activity if they feel loved and secure than if these components are weak or lacking entirely. In the matter of sheer sexual satisfaction, a monogamous state is preferable to a promiscuous choice of sexual partners, but monogamy does not satisfy the emotional needs of insecure people.

A high-dominance woman is usually attracted only to a high-dominance man and wants him to be straightforward, passionate, and somewhat violent or animalistic in his lovemaking. She wishes him to proceed quickly without prolonged wooing. The middle-dominance woman prefers gentle, prolonged wooing where sex, as such, is woven into a pattern of loving words, tenderness, soft music, and low lights. As Maslow put it, "The high-dominance woman unconsciously wants to be raped; the middle-dominance woman wants to be seduced" (1966a). He might have added that the low-dominance woman wishes to be left alone.

People who are rated high in "sex attitude" appreciate sex for its own sake and wholeheartedly approve of it. People who are rated very low are highly puritanical and inhibited in their sexual attitudes, and reject sex as something disgusting. A large portion of the high-dominance subjects like and engage in oral-genital activity; generally speaking, the higher the dominance rating (with ego security held constant), the more attractive they find the external genitalia of the sexual partner. In marriages of high-dominance people, the couples very frequently have experimented with almost every form of sexual activity known to sexologists. While these sexual acts would likely be considered pathological by low-dominance subjects, they contain no pathological connotation for high-dominance subjects.

Hunt (1974) found that, of his sampling, over 80% of men and women believe that women, no more nor less than men, should initiate coitus. In fact, less than 5% of men and women take a strong position that women should not be the initiator. Sexually conservative married couples are more likely than liberal ones to judge as obscene and offensive such sexual acts as unusual coital positions, oral sex, and masturbation (Byrne *et al.* 1974). Maslow (1966a) concludes: "It would appear that no single sexual act can *per se* be called abnormal or perverted. It is only abnormal or perverted individuals who can commit abnormal or perverted acts."

Although relational happiness depends to an important degree on sexual adjustment, the consistent observation of clinicians is that sexual adjustment is possible even when responsiveness is minimal. Conversely, when any significant nonsexual aspect of the relationship is unsatisfactory, a woman may be unhappy even though she may be highly responsive sexually (Adams 1966).

Gebhard (1966) discovered in his research that married women who reached orgasm 90% to 100% of the time in marital coitus were more often found in "very happy" marriages than in any others. Only 4% of women in "very happy" marriages never reached orgasm in coitus. This percentage gradually increased in the other marital-happiness categories, reaching 19% in marriages classified as "very unhappy." Researchers have concluded that marital happiness and female orgasm do correlate, but only in marriages at both extremes of the continuum.

The relationships between sexual satisfaction and relational satisfaction are complexly intertwined. A person's sex interest and responsiveness are directly related to his/her partner's sexual satisfaction, which in turn contributes to his/her relational satisfaction, which increases the sex interest and responsiveness of each, and so on (Udry 1968).

Summary

Our sexual attitudes and behaviors are greatly influenced by our beliefs, thoughts, and perceptions regarding sex. Cultural demands and expectations as well as religious teachings and doctrines also help shape our attitudes toward sex. One aim of growing up in a society is to learn how to express sexuality appropriately, without the burden of unreasonable prohibitions or excessive anxiety and guilt.

During the past two decades, there has been a growing liberalization of sexual attitudes and a decreasing adherence to the double standard. Thus, the marital sexual attitudes of young adult women and men are converging. Changes in attitude toward premarital coitus, mate-swapping, anal intercourse, erotically explicit material, oral-genital sex, and homosexuality have become evident. Particularly significant is the emergence of women in a more equal position in American society. Despite this revolution in attitudes and behavior, there appear to be few supporting reasons for the opinion of a growing moral decadence among today's young people.

Investigations of the impact of religious and social influences on sexual attitudes have shown that religion per se does not have a negative impact on sexual behavior, but that sex-related guilt acquired as a result of religious training and experience may affect behavior. Racial factors do not appear to have causative influence in the emergence of different sexual attitudes and behavior; however, political, economic, and religious factors appear to have such a causative effect.

The hawkings of Madison Avenue, the influence of the peer group, and the sexual imagery found on TV programs also influence attitude formation in young people. Young women grow up believing that attractive appearance is the key to recognition, while young men learn that physical power and/or success are the indicators of male desirability. By accepting these warped manifestations of masculinity and femininity, young people often get caught up in vicious cycles of self-defeating behavior. Parents can play a vital role in shaping their children's sexual attitudes and perceptions by promoting close, accepting, loving family relationships. However, parents sometimes go to the other extreme by expecting the children to conform to a sexual ethic even more conservative than that of the parents.

Human sexual enjoyment is negatively affected by sex-oriented guilt. This sexual guilt has been found to be the strongest factor influencing the development of sexual attitudes and behavior. Guilt also adversely affects one's sexual desires, responsiveness, and experiences. Evidence suggests that men have more guilt over sexual matters than women have. Although many people can resolve their guilt feelings with regard to petting and premarital coitus, attitudes toward extramarital coitus are more tenuous. Despite the persistent condemnation of adultery by society, a significant number of men and women are propelled toward extramarital relationships once they find romance and passion waning in their marriages. Not surprisingly, women are more forgiving of their partners' infidelity than men are.

Personality factors play an important role in the creation of sexual attitudes. One such factor is whether individuals have high dominance feelings, middle dominance feelings, or low dominance feelings; this affects the type of adjustment made in sexual and marital relationships. In general, the most satisfactory relationships were found to be those in which the man was equal to or slightly superior to the woman in dominance feelings. Although such findings might lead to the conclusion that it was the man's responsibility to begin sex, many men and women today believe women should take equal initiative in coitus. Overall, a person's sex interest and responsiveness appear to be directly related to the partner's sexual satisfaction, and this in turn contributes to his or her relational satisfaction, which increases the sex interest and responsiveness of both.

Annotated Bibliography

Bell, A. P. and Weinberg, M. S. *Homosexualities: A study of diversity among men and women*. New York: Simon and Schuster, 1978.

> This book presents a comprehensive exploration of homosexual behavior and life styles, exploding many myths. The authors review a wide range of topics pertinent to homosexuality, such as the gay sexual experience, problems of social adjustment, and the various psychological aspects. This book is important reading for persons who desire greater understanding of homosexuality.

DeLamater, J. and MacCorquodale, P. *Premarital sexuality: Attitudes, relationships, behavior*. Madison, Wisconsin: The University of Wisconsin Press, 1979.

> This book presents a comprehensive analysis of contemporary premarital sexuality based on results of a large-scale survey. Previous research related to sexual attitudes, relationships, and behavior is reviewed. This book would enlighten the general reader as well as the professional educator, clinician, and researcher.

Hass, Aaron. *Teenage sexuality: A survey of teenage sexual behavior.* New York: Macmillan, 1979.

> Reporting large-scale survey results, this book reveals teen attitudes, feelings, and experiences related to a wide range of topics in sexuality, including dating, masturbation, oral sex, intercourse, orgasm, sexual fantasy, homosexuality, pornography, parental attitudes, and performance anxieties. This book would be of interest to the lay reader as well as to the social and behavioral scientist.

Hite, Shere. *The Hite report: A nationwide study on female sexuality.* New York: Macmillan, 1976.

> This book reports results of a national survey of female sexuality, exploring women's sexual attitudes, feelings, experiences, and behavior. Topics include masturbation, orgasm, intercourse, sexual slavery, the sexual revolution, and aging and sexuality. Dispelling many myths related to female sexuality, this book would be of interest to the general reader.

Kuhn, Margaret E. Sexual myths surrounding the aged. In *Sex and the life cycle*, ed. W. Oaks, G. Melchiode, and I. Ficher. New York: Grune and Stratton, 1976.

> This chapter examines the problem of ageism in society and attempts to debunk several myths related to sexuality and the aged. This article would appeal to the lay reader as well as to the health care professional.

McCarthy, Barry. *What you (still) don't know about male sexuality.* New York: Thomas Y. Crowell Company, 1977.

> This book presents factual information related to the various aspects of male sexuality. The author stresses the need for deeper understanding of male sexuality among both men and women. Accurate information dispels misconceptions surrounding male sexual attitudes, feelings, and relationships.

Pietropinto, A. and Simenauer, J. *Beyond the male myth: A nationwide survey.* New York: Times Books, 1977.

> Based on results of a major survey of male sexuality, this book reveals the sexual views, preferences, attitudes, feelings, and experiences of the contemporary American male. The authors attempt to explode several prevalent myths related to male sexuality.

Sandler, Jack, Myerson, Marilyn, and Kinder, Bill N. *Human sexuality: Current perspectives.* Tampa, Florida: Mariner, 1980.

> This text presents a comprehensive perspective of the field of human sexuality. A wide range of topics is covered, including sexual anatomy and sexual response, aphrodisiacs and anaphrodisiacs, past and current sexual attitudes and behavior, sexual diseases and disorders, sexual dysfunctions, birth control, sexual health, and sex and the law. Though designed for the student, this book would serve as a valuable general reference.

Sexual Behavior
in Review

16

Now that the principal physiological, psychological, and social influences, good and bad, on sexuality have been discussed, we examine the more common forms of sexual expression: masturbation, nocturnal orgasm, heterosexual petting, homosexual relations, sexual contact with animals, and heterosexual intercourse (Kinsey *et al.* 1948, 1953). But first a word about sexual desire itself.

The Sex Drive

As has been said repeatedly, sex drive differs from person to person, as well as varying in the same person from time to time. The principal influences upon it are age, physical well-being, and psychological circumstances.

Awareness that certain shifts in sexual patterns occur in both men and women as they grow older is quite important to a solid understanding of human sexuality. A boy in his teens, for example, ordinarily has a very strong sex drive and is capable of almost instant erection; four to eight orgasms a day are not unusual. The refractory period after his first orgasm may last only seconds. He usually wants sexual release whether or not he has any emotional attachment to the sex object, and whether or not he is occupied with other matters, such as school or sports. If no sexual partner is available, he will achieve sexual release through masturbation and nocturnal emission.

As a man approaches his 30s he remains highly interested in sex, but the urgency is less acute and he is satisfied with fewer orgasms. Erections still occur quickly and detumescence is slow to take place. But by his late 30s a man's refractory period has lengthened to 30 minutes or more. Sexual slackening continues through the 40s. By the age of 50, the average man is satisfied with two orgasms a week and the refractory period is commonly 8 to 24 hours. At this age, the focus of sexual pleasure has usually shifted from an intense genitally centered sensation to a more generalized, sensuously diffused experience (Kaplan & Sager 1971).

The development of sexuality reveals far more individual variation among women. Women's sexual awakening is typically a slower process, not reaching its peak until the late 30s or early 40s. They do not appear to experience the same sexual urgency that men do. In their teens and 20s their orgasmic response is slower and less consistent than it is in their 40s. In their 30s, and frequently after childbirth, women begin to respond more intensely to sexual stimulation. They also initiate the sex act more frequently. The incidence of extramarital sex is greatest among women in their late 30s. Vaginal lubrication (the measure of female sexual response equivalent to male erection) occurs almost instantly for women in this age group, and many experience multiple orgasms.

Hite's (1976) sample of women was not grouped according to age, but the levels of sexual desire revealed are probably higher than most would have thought:

Those women wanting sex	
More than once daily	10%
Daily	20%
Three to five times weekly	15%
Two or three times weekly	15%
One or two times weekly	15%
One or two times monthly	3%
Those not wanting sex at all	<1%

Wilcox & Hager (1980) in their study of 69 married women also found that two-thirds of the women desired more frequent sexual relations than they were experiencing.

Some Definitions

It should be noted that, for the purposes of this discussion, the levels of educational achievement referred to are defined as follows:

> Grade school (low educational group)—8 years of schooling or less
> High school (middle educational group)—9 to 12 years of schooling
> College (high educational group)—13 years of schooling or more

Reference is also made to the incidence and frequency of the various patterns of sexual behavior. **Incidence** refers to the number of individuals in a sample population who have experienced a particular form of behavior, whether one time only or 1000 times. **Frequency** refers to the number of times the particular form of behavior has been engaged in by the same person (or by a percentage of the population).

Masturbation

The term **masturbation** (also called **autoeroticism**) is applied to any type of self-stimulation that produces erotic arousal (Kinsey *et al.* 1948). It is a common sexual practice among both males and females in premarital, marital, and postmarital states. Recent data indicate that males begin masturbating at earlier ages than females, apparently because young males have more opportunity to learn about masturbatory activity from peers (Cowart & Pollack 1979). However, many boys and girls begin masturbating at an early age; 13% of both sexes in Kinsey's sample had masturbated by their 10th birthday (Kinsey *et al.* 1953; Reevy 1961).

Males

The incidence of masturbation to the point of orgasm among men is generally fixed at about 95% of the total male population. The college group in Kinsey's study had the highest incidence (96%); those who had attended only high school, second highest (95%); and those who had attended only grade school, the lowest (89%). Slightly over 67% of all boys experience their first ejaculation through masturbation; about 75% learn how to masturbate from verbal or printed sources (R. R. Bell 1971a; Kinsey *et al.* 1948; Rubin 1963).

On the average, adolescent boys masturbate about 2.5 times a week, although 17% masturbate from 4 to 7 (or more) times a week. The incidence of masturbation in men declines progressively in postadolescent years, although some men, married or not, continue to masturbate on a sporadic basis throughout adult life (Ford & Beach 1966). Kinsey found that the average adult male under 35 years of age masturbated about 70 times per year, while those over 35 did so about 33 times. More recent estimates (Athanasiou 1976) place the figure for those under 35 at 75 to 100 times per year, and for those over 35, 33 to 50 times.

Kinsey's study (1948) showed that genital manipulation was by far the most common technique of masturbation among men (95%). In 72% of the cases, fantasy always accompanied masturbation; in another 17%, fantasy was present only occasionally. Hunt (1974) found almost no differences in incidence of masturbation, whether once or many times in a lifetime, among men who attend church regularly, sometimes, or not at all; the percentages were 92%, 92%, and 93%.

Females

According to Kinsey's findings (1953), masturbation ranks second only to heterosexual petting among the erotic activities of unmarried young women (comprising 37% to 85% of their total sexual outlet, depending upon the subcultural group), and second after coition among married women (about 10% of their total sexual outlet).

Of all types of sexual activity among women, masturbation ranks first as the most successful method of reaching orgasm—in 95% of its incidence, a climax is reached. Furthermore, women reach orgasm more quickly through masturbation than through any other sexual technique—75% in under 4 minutes (Hite 1976; Kinsey *et al.* 1953).

According to the figures of several investigations, 50% to 90% of all women masturbate at one time or another in their lives, whether or not they are aware of it. Many women do not recognize that indirect, pleasurable stimulation of the genitals, as in squeezing the thighs together or riding horseback, can be considered a form of masturbation. In the Kinsey study of females, 34% of the grade school sample, 59% of the high school, and 63% of the college graduates had masturbated. More recent studies (K. E. Davis 1971) indicate that these percentages have changed very little, while other investigations find significant increases. For example, Hite (1976) found that 82% of her sample of women masturbated regularly.

Frequency of masturbation in the Kinsey female sample ranged from once or twice in a lifetime to 100 orgasms an hour. Among women masturbating to orgasm, however, there was a striking similarity in frequency, regardless of age or marital status: once every two to four weeks. Current estimates (Athanasiou 1976) of frequency of female masturbation approximate those of Kinsey.

Most (57%) of the women in the Kinsey study accidentally discovered how to masturbate by exploring their own genitals. Another 40% learned through verbal or printed sources.

In contrast to men, among whom there is a decline in frequency of masturbation after the teen-age years, the incidence among women of self-stimulation to orgasm increases up to middle age, and remains fairly constant (Kinsey *et al.* 1953). Of the unmarried women between 50 and 70 years of age in one study, 59% admitted to autoeroticism, as compared with 30% of the married women in the same age group ("Sex Behavior of Older Women" 1966).

The majority of women (84%) in Kinsey's sample who stimulated themselves used genital manipulation, while a few others employed thigh pressure, muscular tension, or simply fantasy unattended by physical stimulation. Fantasy was an invariable accompaniment to masturbation for half the women who stimulated themselves, but only an occasional one for a few others (14%).

Among those women in the Kinsey sample who had never masturbated to orgasm before marriage, 31% to 37% failed to reach orgasm during coitus the first year of marriage, while of those who had previously masturbated to orgasm, less than 16% failed to have coital orgasm the first year. Incidence of masturbation was lower among the religiously devout, probably because of sexual guilt, than among the less devout. In Hunt's (1974) sample of women, 51% of regular churchgoers, 69% of irregular attenders, and 75% who do not attend church at all masturbated at some time in their lives.

Nocturnal Orgasm

It has long been recognized that men experience nocturnal emissions or "wet dreams." Although women obviously cannot have nocturnal emissions, it is nonetheless true that they too have erotic dreams which frequently culminate in orgasm. Curiously, however, this type of sexual outlet is persistently ignored in studies of female sexuality (Kinsey *et al.* 1953).

This form of sexual outlet is unique in that it is beyond conscious control. The incidence of nocturnal emission, therefore, bears little relationship to guilt feelings, religious affiliation, or strength of religious conviction.

Males

Almost 100% of men experience erotic dreams, and almost 85% have dreams that end in orgasm. Erotic dreams occur most frequently among young men in their teens and 20s, but half of all married men continue to have them.

The incidence of nocturnal emission in the Kinsey sampling was found to be considerably higher among college youths than among the less well educated, probably because college men do more petting not followed by orgasm, so that their sexual tensions are therefore more often at a high pitch at bedtime. Over 99% of the college men had had sexual dreams to orgasm at some time during their lives. But only 85% of those whose education had ended with high school, and 75% with a grade school education, had had nocturnal emissions.

Females

As many as 70% of all the women in Kinsey's sample (1953) had had dreams of sexual content, although only about half this number had had dreams culminating in orgasm. Because a woman, unlike a man, reveals no physical evidence that an orgasm did occur, some question the accuracy of data showing that 37% actually did dream to orgasm. However, there was no doubt in the minds of the women having the dreams that orgasm had occurred. It is of interest that, by contrast, only about 3% of the women in Hite's study (1976) reported dreaming to orgasm.

The incidence of sexual dreams to orgasm reaches a peak among the women in their 40s. Kinsey's research (1953) showed that women in all age groups, married or single, had an average of three or four such dreams a year. Over one-fourth of the married women (28%) and more than one-third of those previously married (38%) had had dreams to orgasm.

The Kinsey group found no correlation between frequency of nocturnal dreams to orgasm and a woman's religious or educational background, although fewer women of devout religious convictions than those of less serious commitment ever had such dreams.

Heterosexual Petting

The sexual outlet called **heterosexual petting** involves conscious, sexually oriented physical contact between persons of opposite sex that does not involve actual coitus (Kinsey *et al.* 1953). In this discussion, the significance of petting as a means of sexual expression is limited to premarital petting, inasmuch as petting in marriage is assumed to be a foreplay to intercourse or an outlet chosen by the partners in preference to coition as a means of achieving orgams.

Petting practices range from simple kissing to heavy petting, which is usually defined as genital stimulation—including cunnilingus and fellatio—while one or both partners are unclothed.

Males

A distinct correlation exists between frequency of petting and educational attainments. Those men with the lowest education pet the least; men of the middle group are next; and men with the highest education pet most of all.

Of the total male population in Kinsey's sample, almost 100% had engaged in simple kissing; 55% to 87% had engaged in deep kissing; 78% to 99% in manual manipulation of a woman's breasts; 36% to 93% in mouth-breast contact; 79% to 92% in manual manipulation of a woman's genitalia; and 9% to 18% of unmarried youths (4% of the less educated to 60% of the educated married men) in oral stimulation of their partner's genitalia. The two percentages cited in each instance refer to men at the two extremes of educational achievement (Kinsey *et al.* 1948, 1953).

In the past, educational achievement also correlated significantly with occurrence of petting to orgasm. According to the levels of schooling reached, the lowest educational group had achieved a climax through petting only 16% of the time, while the second group had done so 32% of the time; 61% of the petting in the college-level group had culminated in orgasm (R. R. Bell 1971a; Kinsey *et al.* 1948, 1953).

In the Kinsey studies (1938–1946), 15% of high-school and 43% of college-educated men had experienced fellatio in their marriages. The Hunt study some 35 years later (1974) showed that these figures had increased to 54% and 61%, respectively. Almost identical figures hold true for cunnilingus—15% and 45% in the Kinsey sampling, and 56% and 66% in the Hunt. In the latter study, over 90% of married couples under the age of 25, no matter what their educational level, had participated in oral-genital sex. In another study (Jacobs 1974), 65% of the men had had oral-genital contact with their wives and 45% had continued the stimulation to orgasm. Most husbands (75%) enjoyed cunnilingus, whether or not their wives reached orgasm.

An interesting study examining the relationship between sexual behavior and religiosity among college students has indicated that highly religious males are more likely to experience oral-genital sex before they experience sexual intercourse. Societal and peer pressures for males to obtain sexual experience apparently places highly religious males in a conflicting bind concerning how to express their sexuality and yet preserve their religious value systems. One solution to preserving virginity while at the same time gaining sexual experience is for highly religious males to engage in heterosexual activities that include oral-genital relations (Mahoney 1980).

Females

Almost 100% of all married women have had some sort of petting experience prior to their marriage, and 90% of the entire female population, whether or not they ever marry, engage in petting at one time or another.

Simple kissing is engaged in at one time or another by nearly all women at all educational levels. More sophisticated methods of petting, however, are directly related to educational achievement, decade of birth, and incidence and frequency of coitus. The more advanced the level of education, the more liberal the woman is in the types of petting she engages in.

Samplings made in the late 1960s show that a substantial majority of college women (60% to 90%) find intimate petting an acceptable form of sexual behavior. Approximately 28% of college women have experienced heavy petting with three or more partners, and over 50% have engaged in heavy petting with someone they did not love. Almost 60% of the college women in one sample had experienced heavy petting while still in high school (K. E. Davis 1971).

The type of petting more slowly accepted than others, because of social taboos, is oral-genital contact. This form of sexual stimulation, however, is apparently now rather widely accepted as an erotic outlet—and a normal, healthy one—by the majority in the higher socioeducational groups. Mahoney (1980) has found that highly religious college women are more likely to experience oral-genital sex before they experience coitus. However, this trend is not as pronounced among college women as it is among college men.

While the Hite survey (1976) did not specifically raise the question of the subjects' marital status, the manner in which they described their lives indicated that about half were single and half currently married. Approximately 1600 women answered the question regarding orgasm from cunnilingus. Only 3% stated that they had never experienced cunnilingus; of the other 97%, 75% reported that they do have orgasms from cunnilingus and 42%, that they do so regularly.

DeMartino's (1974) sample of intelligent women (single, married, and divorced) showed that the youngest group, 16–19 years, had the least experience in fellatio and cunnilingus (both 32%). Incidences in the other age groups (20–29; 30–39; 40–49; and 50–61) were remarkably similar: fellatio was 68% to 76%, and cunnilingus, 71% to 76%. In hand-genital petting, the percentages were slightly lower: 41% of the youngest group; 67% of the second group, 68% of the third, 58% of the fourth, and 47% of the oldest women.

With respect to marital fellatio, the 1938–1949 Kinsey studies showed that 46% of women of high-school background and 52% of the college-educated had participated. In the Hunt study (1974), the percentages were 52% and 72%. With respect to marital cunnilingus, of Kinsey's sample of high-school females, 50% had experienced it, and of the college-educated, 58%. The percentages in the Hunt study for the two groups were 58% and 72%. Like their husbands, over 90% of the 25-year-old and younger married women in the Hunt study had participated in both fellatio and cunnilingus.

In another study (Jacobs 1974), about half the wives declared fellatio to be an enjoyable experience, and 40% found it pleasant even when it continued to ejaculation.

Like most other forms of sexual behavior for women, petting is significantly related to religious background. The more pronounced the commitment, the more restricted the sexual behavior. Interestingly, however, religion ultimately had little influence, one way or the other, on frequency of petting to orgasm, even among the most religiously devout. Once devout women achieved orgasm through petting, they engaged in it as often as less devout women did. (R. R. Bell 1971a; Kinsey *et al.* 1953). The reason seemed to be that petting allowed a single woman sexual gratification without depriving her of her virginity.

Petting provides a higher percentage of total sexual outlet for women of all ages than it does for men of comparable age.

Sexual Contact with Animals

A taboo against sexual relations with animals is well established in the Old Testament and in the Talmud. Sexual contact between humans and infrahumans (also called bestiality) has occurred since early civilization, but is abhorrent to most people. The extent of such sexual activity among either men or women is extremely small. Its significance in a study of sexuality lies in its social impact, rather than in its importance as a sexual outlet (Kinsey *et al.* 1953).

Males

As would be expected, male contact with animals, whenever it exists, is found primarily among boys reared on farms. Between 40% and 50% of all farm boys in Kinsey's study (1948) had had some sexual contact with animals, but only 17% had experienced orgasm as a result of animal contact. About twice as many men (32%) as women (16%) were erotically aroused by seeing animals in copulation.

Sexual contacts with animals varied in frequency from once or twice in a lifetime to as high as eight times a week for some adolescent rural boys in the Kinsey survey (1948). The average was about twice weekly. Most sexual contact with animals occurred in preadolescence before the boy was capable of orgasm, and the episodes were usually limited to a two- or three-year period. Sexual contact with animals represented considerably less than 1% of the total sexual outlet for men in both urban and rural communities.

City boys had limited sexual experience with animals. Their contacts were customarily with household pets, and with animals on a farm they might visit during vacations.

Females

Very few women have sexual contact with animals. About 1.5% of Kinsey's female sample (1953) had had sexual contact with animals during pre-adolescence (usually as a result of accidental physical contact with a household pet), and only 3.6% had had sexual contact with animals after their adolescent years. Of those sexually precocious women who were able to have orgasms prior to adolescence, 1.7% had experienced their first orgasm in animal contact.

Out of the entire 5940 women in Kinsey's study, 29 had caused dogs or cats to stimulate their vulval area orally, and 2 had had coitus with dogs. In these histories, 25 women had been brought to orgasm by sexual contact with animals, and the method was primarily oral stimulation of their genitals. Of those women who had engaged in bestiality, half had had only a single experience, and a fourth had had six or more contacts.

Heterosexual Intercourse

The average man or woman is more interested in coitus with a member of the opposite sex than in any other type of sexual outlet. Coitus has been traditionally thought of in terms of a marital relationship. But three other forms are important to a discussion of the subject—premarital, extramarital, and postmarital intercourse.

Premarital Intercourse

Premarital heterosexual intercourse commonly refers to coition between two single persons, although one of the partners may be married (Ehrmann 1961). American culture still generally accords more latitude in sexual expression to men than to women. Premarital intercourse is the most controversial of these sexual outlets—the one most often considered in discussions concerning the double standard of morality. The degree to which the double standard has persisted in a 30-year period ending in 1975 can be judged from the research results regarding premarital coitus shown in Table 16.1 (Gunderson 1977).

American males are more sexually permissive and active than ever before; but the rate at which both their attitudes and behavior have relaxed

TABLE 16.1   Incidence of Premarital Intercourse among the College Educated Aged 18–22 (Gunderson 1977)

Researchers	Year	Location	Males %	Females %
Kinsey *et al.*	1948	Nationwide	49	—
Kinsey *et al.*	1953	Nationwide	—	25
Bell & Blumberg	1959	Temple U.	43	31
Ehrmann	1959	U. of Florida	65	13
Christensen &		Utah (Mormon)	39	9
Carpenter	1962b	Midwest	51	21
Landis & Landis	1963	11 colleges	—	10
Freedman	1965	Vassar	—	22
Grinder & Schmitt	1966	U. of Wisconsin	—	22
Freeman & Freeman	1966	Nationwide	—	55
Landis & Landis	1968	18 colleges	52	45
Packard	1968	21 colleges	57	43
		South	69	32
		West	62	46
		East	64	57
		Midwest	46	25
Robinson *et al.*	1968	U. of Georgia	—	29
Luckey & Nass	1969	21 colleges	58	43
K. E. Davis	1969	Kansas State U.	—	37
		U. of Colorado	—	56
Frede	1970	U. of Houston	72	42
Kaats & Davis	1970	U. of Colorado	60	41
Bell & Chaskes	1970	Temple U.	—	39
Christensen &		Utah (Mormon)	40	32
Gregg	1970	Midwest	52	34
Walsh	1972	U. of Illinois	—	39
Zuckerman *et al.*	1973	Delaware	66	63
Finger	1975	U. of Virginia	75	—

is considerably below that of American women. As can be seen in Table 16.2, the difference in incidence between male and female premarital sex has gradually—and, at times, dramatically—narrowed. That differences yet remain between the sexes is undoubtedly based on the fact that female sexuality is still suppressed, despite the social changes of the past several decades. However, if the present trend continues for another decade or so, over 95% of both men and women will have experienced premarital coitus, perhaps even causing premarital virginity to be "classified as 'sexual deviation'" (Zuckerman 1976).

Not only is there an increase in premarital coitus among both men and women, but the percentage of unmarried college men and women

TABLE 16.2   Percentages of Men and Women with Premarital Coital Experience by Decade at Which Maturity Was Reached*

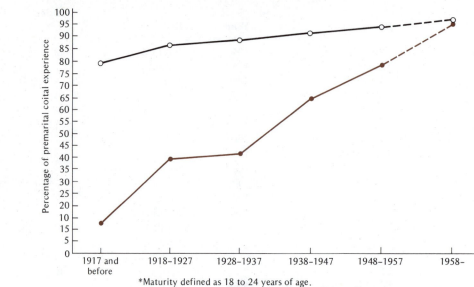

*Maturity defined as 18 to 24 years of age.
**Data through 1940s, after Kinsey (1948, 1953); data from 1950s through 1970s, after Hunt (1974); extrapolations, after Zuckerman (1976).

cohabiting (living with a person of the opposite sex to whom one is not married) is now quite high (Macklin 1974). The rate of cohabitation ranges from 36% at one large state-supported southwestern university to 9% at a small midwestern liberal arts college; the average is about 25%.

Males. Kinsey's studies (1948, 1953) indicated that, at some time or another before they were married, 98% of men who had attended only grade school, 84% of men who had attended only high school, and 67% of men with college education had had sexual intercourse. Studies conducted in the 1960s indicated that the incidence of premarital coitus for college men was from 58% to 65% (K. E. Davis 1971), approximating the earlier Kinsey figures. The decade in which men were born appeared to have little correlation with incidence of premarital coitus, in contrast to rather strong correlations between birth date and incidence among women.

Although the incidence of premarital intercourse among college men in many studies has not changed appreciably, its psychological and sociological aspects have. These men tend to have coition with a woman whom they love or care for deeply, rather than with a prostitute or casual pickup, as their fathers would have done. College men are now faced at a somewhat earlier time of life with the necessity for integrating their sexual attitudes and behavior, emotional feelings, and standards of appropriate conduct (K. E. Davis 1971).

Between the ages of 16 and 20, the grade-school group of men in Kinsey's sampling (1948) had had seven times greater frequency of sexual intercourse than the college group. This disparity in coital frequency lessened only slightly between the groups of older single men of the same educational levels. The unmarried college men were usually five or six years older than the unmarried men of lower educational levels when they first experienced intercourse.

Compared with earlier survey findings, Hunt's study (1974) revealed that premarital sexual experience has increased among college men. By age 17, for example, half those males who eventually went to college had experienced premarital sex, more than double the Kinsey figures (23.1%). Even among the noncollege men of this age group, there was an increase, although much smaller. Of course, since Kinsey's college sample experienced less premarital coitus than the noncollege men did, the greater increase would be expected in the first group.

Cuber's survey (1975) of a large state-supported midwestern university showed that 33% of the students were nonvirginal by the age of 17 (when they were usually still in high school). The proportion of nonvirgins increased progressively until 94% of the unmarried students were nonvirginal by age 24 (the men) to 26 (the women).

Later studies (K. E. Davis 1971) put the percentage of college men having coitus with prostitutes at 4.2% to 14%, most figures being lower than that of the 1948 Kinsey report (28%). At least two studies suggest a much higher incidence, however. One investigation of male students at a large southwestern state university revealed that 42% of the subjects had had coitus with prostitutes (Frede 1970). A similar investigation (L. G. Benson 1971) revealed that 43% of a college-student sampling had had sexual relations with a prostitute, 50% of that number having visited the prostitute with a group of other young males. As a matter of fact, 29% of the total sample of men in this study had participated in a form of "group sex" in which one woman (not necessarily a prostitute) and two or more men were involved.

The point should be made that the incidence of premarital intercourse among men may range from a single contact to 35 or more coitions a week (the latter pattern sometimes persisting for as long as five years or more). Many men, particularly those at the upper end of the social-educational scale, limit their premarital coition to one woman—often the woman they eventually marry. Other men, particularly at the lower end of the social-educational scale, may copulate with as many as several hundred women (Kinsey *et al.* 1948). In another study (Frede 1970) of the number of premarital sex partners college men have had, 14% reported only one partner; 25%, 2 or 3; 20%, 4 to 6; and 41%, 7 or more.

While a few single men have intercourse with older women—single, married, or divorced—almost all the coital experiences of single men are with single women, usually of their own age or slightly younger (Kinsey *et al.* 1948). Studies have shown that boys of a higher social stratum often sexually exploit girls of lower status, but that in college populations, young men and women customarily have their sexual experiences with persons of an equal social class (Ehrmann 1961; Hollingshead 1949). Of college men, 4% have engaged in coitus for such ulterior motives as money or to earn a favor (K. E. Davis 1971).

In Kinsey's study of men (1948), religion, at all socioeducational levels, bore a direct relationship to incidence and frequency of premarital intercourse. The greater the religious commitment, the less premarital sex. Hunt's study (1974) found that 88% of the married males under 35 years of age and 80% of those 35 and over who were regular churchgoers, compared with 78% of nonattenders, reported that intercourse during the past year had been "very pleasurable."

In one study (Burgess & Wallin 1953) of the effect premarital coitus has on the relationship between engaged couples, 92.6% of the men and 90.6% of the women felt it had been a strengthening force; 1.2% of the men and 5.4% of the women felt it had had a weakening effect; and the remainder were undecided.

Females. A rather noticeable change occurred in women's sexual behavior about 1920, affecting almost every aspect of their sexual lives. Of the women in Kinsey's study (1953), over twice as many of those born between 1900 and 1910 had had sexual intercourse before marriage as those born before 1900 (36% as compared with 14%). Another "sexual revolution" for women seems to have occurred in the 1960s. Between the late 1950s and early 1970s, the number of females having premarital coitus doubled (Zuckerman 1976).

The high percentage of women in Kinsey's study who had engaged in premarital coitus (almost 50%) surprised and disturbed many people. However, about half of these coitally active single women had had intercourse only with the men whom they eventually married. Furthermore, most of the women's premarital coition took place only during the year or so preceding marriage. Today, the marked increase among women in both incidence and frequency of premarital coitus causes far less surprise and shock among the general public than it did two decades ago. For example, little concern was expressed over a 1974 study (Levin 1975) of 100,000 women showing that 90% of those under age 25 had experienced premarital intercourse.

The frequency of premarital coitus among women as a group and individually often varied considerably in the Kinsey (1953) sampling. Coitally active single women under the age of 20 engaged in intercourse on an average of once every 5 to 10 weeks. About 20% of these women had coitus as often as 7 times a week (14 times for 7% in the same period). Some women who have premarital intercourse are capable of multiple orgasms from the very beginning of their coital experience (Kinsey *et al.* 1953; Masters & Johnson 1966, 1967; Terman 1938).

Of all the women in Kinsey's study (1953) who engaged in premarital coitus (whether or not they eventually married), 53% had one partner, 34% had 2 to 5 partners, and only 13% had 6 or more. Two studies (Frede 1970; Hunt 1974) that researched the number of premarital sex partners of women in the 1970s have revealed figures very similar to those reported by Kinsey. Of married women who had premarital coitus, 87% had at least some of their coital experience with the man they eventually married, and 46% had intercourse only with their future husband. Only 13% of these women had premarital coitus with men other than their future husband. A 1970 study of 200 newlyweds conducted in Pennsylvania revealed that 75% of the couples had had coitus with each other before marriage, and 30% of the women were pregnant when they married (Otto 1971).

The age at which marriage occurs has a significant impact on the incidence of premarital coition at the various educational levels. At first glance, Kinsey's 1953 findings would lead one to conclude that college-educated women were much more coitally active premaritally than women of the two lower educational groups. The data showed that 60% of the college-educated group, 47% of the high-school group, and 30% of those who had not gone beyond grade school had had premarital coitus. (These statistics, incidentally, stand in striking contrast to male experience: 67% of men with college education and 98% of those with only grade-school education were found to have had coitus prior to marriage [Kinsey *et al.* 1948].)

Despite the seemingly high incidence of premarital coition among college-educated women, certain facts should be borne in mind. Because women who are schooled only to grade-school or high-school level tend to marry considerably earlier than college women do, they have fewer premarital years in which to form attachments that might lead to intercourse. As Kinsey pointed out, among women within a given age group *after* the age of 20, no matter what their educational background, coital experience before marriage was about equal.

Women with little education tend to begin their coital experience at an earlier age than women with more education. Between the ages of 16 and 20, 38% of the grade-school group, 32% of the high-school group, and about 18% of the college group in Kinsey's sample (1953) had premarital coitus. Lower-class women also tend to engage in premarital coitus more frequently than middle-class women (Peretti 1969).

Investigations since the Kinsey group's have found that the incidence of premarital intercourse among college women is increasing. Various studies between 1945 and 1965 showed that about 25% to 30% of women students of all ages and class standings had premarital coitus, whereas studies conducted in the late 1960s and mid-1970s showed the rate to be about 35% to 60% (R. R. Bell 1971a; Kaats & Davis 1970; Zuckerman 1976). As expected, however, the percentage of premarital sexual experience was highest (55%) among women in certain liberal eastern colleges; the lows ranged from 19% in a southern university to 12% in a church-affiliated college (Packard 1968).

Studies in the 1970s by Hunt (1974) and by Levin (1975) also reveal a dramatic rise in premarital coital experience among women since the Kinsey data were published in 1953 (Table 16.3). Shah and Zelnik (1980) report that this trend of increased premarital intercourse among women is continuing. Furthermore, the age at which women first experience intercourse is dropping. A comparative study of never-married teen-agers in 1971 and 1976 revealed a 29% overall increase in premarital coitus in the five-year interval (Table 16.4). The percentage of increase ranged from 19.0% among the 16-year-olds to 53.8% among those 17 years of age. Francoeur and Hendrixson (1980) report data that over 50% of American adolescents between the ages of 15 and 19 are sexually active. Furthermore, one in ten of the young women in this age group became pregnant during 1979.

In 1958 most female students having premarital coitus were engaged to their partners. In 1968, however, the greatest number were merely dating

TABLE 16.3   **Premarital Coital Incidence among Females as Revealed in the Kinsey, Hunt, and Levin Surveys**

Age	Survey		
	Kinsey (1953)	*Hunt (1974)*	*Levin (1975)*
17 years	<10%	20% (now married)	
		33% (still single)	—
25 years	33%	<50% (now married)	
		75% (still single)	90%

TABLE 16.4   **Incidence of Premarital Coition among Never-Married Teen-age Females, 1971 and 1976***

Age	*1971*	*1976*
15 years	12%	17%
16	21	25
17	26	40
18	37	46
19	47	56

* Planned Parenthood figures.

or going steady with their partners. Coital rate among women students in both decades was lowest among Catholics and highest among Protestants, with Jews in between. But in this 10-year span, the rates went up proportionately in all three groups (Bell & Chaskes 1970). And the evidence is clear that there was considerably less guilt about premarital coitus among the 1968 subjects than among those questioned in 1958 (Table 16.5). In a 1967 study of freshman women at a state university, it was found that 7% were nonvirgins. A study of the same group in their senior year revealed that 39% had engaged in premarital coitus. Furthermore, data on freshman women entering the same university in 1970 showed that 15% had already engaged in premarital intercourse, more than double the 1967 figure (Walsh 1972). In the Kinsey study (1953), 3% of the white women subjects were nonvirgins at age 15, and 23% had had premarital coitus by age 21. In a similar survey made in 1971, 11% of the 15-year-olds were nonvirgins, and 50% of the single women had lost their virginity by age 19 (Reiss 1976; Zelnik & Kantner 1972).

TABLE 16.5 **Percentages of College Women Expressing Guilt over Premarital Coitus***

Relational Circumstance	1958	1968
Dating only	65%	36%
Going steady	61	30
Engaged	41	20

* After Bell & Chaskes, 1970.

TABLE 16.6 **Percentages of Premarital Sex Experience Relative to Religious Devoutness**

Survey	Strongly Religious	Nonreligious
Levin (1975)		
Women, under 25	75%	96%
Hunt (1974)		
Women under 35	55	90
Women over 35	27	62
Kanin & Howard (1957)		
Couples	28	61
Kinsey et al. (1953)		
Women under age 35		
Protestants	30	63
Catholics	24	55
Jews	25 (moderately devout)	60

The first coital experience of both men and women is usually with someone near their own age whom they have known for some time. Coitus generally occurs in the woman's home, her partner's home, or the home of a relative or friend and is remembered without regret (Lowry 1969; Shah & Zelnik 1980). Premarital coital experience for the women in Kinsey's sample (1953) was directly related to their degree of religious involvement, whatever the faith. Not surprisingly, women who were least religiously active were most likely to engage in premarital intercourse, the moderately devout next, and the devout the least of all. Once again, the figures in the Kinsey study were smaller than those found in other studies (see Table 16.6). It might be mentioned that only 53% of women in Hunt's 1974 sample who regularly attended church, as compared with 64% of those who did not do so regularly, claimed that coitus during the past year had been "very pleasurable."

Marital Intercourse

According to legal and moral codes of our Anglo-American culture, coitus between husband and wife is the one totally approved type of sexual activity (excepting, of course, erotic dreams). It is the sexual outlet most frequently utilized by married couples. Yet, as a conservative estimate, sexual relationships in about 33% of all marriages are somewhat unsatisfactory (R. R. Bell 1971a; Burgess & Wallin 1953; English 1957). Masters and Johnson (1970) have set the figure at 50%. An unsatisfactory sexual relationship in marriage usually generates other problems, partly because much is expected of sex.

Of all married couples who stated that sex has been about as important in marriage as they had anticipated, 66% rated their marriage "very happy," whereas 33% rated their marriage as "average" or "less than average" in happiness (R. R. Bell 1971a). After 20 years of marriage, however, most couples report they are less satisfied with every aspect of the marital state than they were during the earlier years (Pineo 1961). But Pietropinto (1980) reports evidence supporting the conclusion that "duration of marriage has little to do with coital frequency except for the first-year 'newlywed' phenomenon." Other evidence indicates that sexual closeness tends to lessen with the birth of each child unless the couple take conscious steps to maintain it (Feldman 1966).

The sex drive is usually somewhat greater in men than in women, especially during the early years of marriage, although each sex tends to misjudge the drive of the other (Burgess & Wallin 1953). A serious problem arises from this misjudgment. If their sex needs differ sharply, a husband and wife may work out some sort of compromise in frequency of sexual activity that, unfortunately, meets the needs of neither (R. R. Bell 1971a). As a group, husbands desire (or at least report they desire) sexual intercourse more frequently than their wives. A study (Levinger 1970) of middle-class couples, all parents in their late 30s whose marriages averaged 13.5 years in length, has supported this theory. Only 6% of the respondents reported that the wife's desire for intercourse exceeded that of her husband, although in actual fact the coital desire of 15% of the wives exceeded that of their husbands.

Marital coital frequency has increased in every age group in the past 20 or so years, according to estimates made by both male and female subjects in the Hunt and Kinsey studies (Table 16.7). Pietropinto (1980) also reports that his own recent research results indicate that the frequency of coital activity among married couples has continued to increase. The effects of the revolution in women's sexual behavior that occurred around 1910–1920 can be seen in the following statistical sequence. In a study made in the 1920s, two out of three married women reported that their sex drive was less strong than that of their husbands; very few women claimed to have a stronger drive (K. B. Davis 1929). In another study, conducted in the 1940s, 64% of the women reported satisfaction with the fequency of marital intercourse, while 16% said it occurred too frequently and 20%, too infrequently (Burgess & Wallin 1953). A third study later showed that 66% of the wives considered the frequency of marital coitus to be "about right," 2% said it was "too frequent," and 32% "too infrequent" (R. R. Bell 1971c).

In many women, unlike men, sex drive and needs tend to be periodic and to vary according to particular moods and situations. Even women who have had a very good sexual adjustment may be able to accept long periods of sexual deprivation without undue distress (Zehv 1968).

Males. Only an exceedingly small number of married men do not participate, at least occasionally, in marital coitus. Even among husbands in their late 50s, only 6% in Kinsey's sample refrained from marital intercourse. These statements, of course, do not mean that marital sexual activity is confined to marital coitus. Actually, Kinsey found that marital intercourse provided only 85% of the total sexual outlet for married men, the remaining

Table 16.7 **Marital Coitus: Weekly Frequency (Male and Female Estimates Combined) in Kinsey and Hunt Surveys (after Hunt, 1974)**

Kinsey (1948, 1953)		Hunt (1974)	
Age	*Median*	*Age*	*Median*
16–25	2.45	18–24	3.25
26–35	1.95	25–34	2.55
36–45	1.40	35–44	2.00
46–55	0.85	45–54	1.00
56–60	0.50	55 and over	1.00

15% coming from masturbation, nocturnal emissions, petting, homosexual activity, extramarital coitus, and, in some rural areas, animal contact (Kinsey *et al.* 1948).

Only 60% of American males are married at any one time, yet between adolescence and old age each 100 men average 231 orgasms a week. Correcting for the increased incidence of coition and total sexual outlet in marriage, one is led to conclude that only 106 orgasms a week per 100 men are from marital coitus (45.9% of their total sexual outlet). If 5% of the total outlet is accounted for in nocturnal emissions, then approximately 50% of men's total sexual outlet is obtained through other sources (Kinsey *et al.* 1948), which are or have been socially disapproved (oral sex) or illegal (homosexuality and nonmarital sex).

That differences exist among various subgroups in frequency of sexual intercourse has long been recognized. For Jews, the Talmud stipulates the conjugal obligations of men. Each man was advised to perform according to his strength and occupation. Those who have constant leisure could copulate nightly; workers employed in the city, twice a week; workers employed out of the city, once a week; donkey drivers, once a week; camel drivers, once every 30 days; sailors, once every 6 months; scholars, once a week (and it was customary for a scholar to be intimate with his wife on Friday night).

A study (Pearlman 1972) of 2655 married males revealed new information concerning the "normal" frequency of sexual intercourse (Table 16.8). An interesting contrast in incidence of marital intercourse in relation to total outlet for men at the various educational levels was revealed in Kinsey's findings. Among lower educational groups, about 80% of the total outlet in the early years of marriage was provided by marital coitus, the incidence for this group increasing to 90% as the marriages continued.

For the college-educated man, marital coitus provided 85% of the total outlet during the early part of marriage, but by the time he had reached the age of 55, only 62% of his total sexual outlet was provided by marital coitus.

Table 16.8 Frequency of Intercourse among Married Men (after Pearlman, 1972)

Age	3–4 Times per Week	1–2 Times per Week	1 Time per Week	3 Times per Month	2 Times per Month	1 Time or Less per Month	None
20–29	45.2%	29.6%	18.3%	0.9%	4.0%	0.3%	2.3%
30–39	26.5	29.5	25.6	3.7	8.4	4.9	1.2
40–49	13.6	28.1	28.3	5.0	11.8	8.9	4.2
50–59	5.2	16.2	27.1	4.1	17.4	19.0	11.0
60–69	0.9	6.0	19.0	2.2	13.7	25.0	33.2
70–79	0.4	3.6	6.7	1.2	8.8	21.8	57.0

The assumption is that these college-educated men had reevaluated the moral restraints placed on them during their early life, finding them less constrictive and threatening than formerly. They had come to the conclusion that they should have the sexual experiences they wished, or felt they had missed earlier in their lives. However, it should be emphasized that half the remaining 38% of their total sexual activity other than marital coitus was not with another woman (or man), but consisted of the solitary act of masturbation or nocturnal emissions (Kinsey *et al.* 1948).

Petting in marriage is usually considered to be only an introduction to intercourse. As we have seen, educational achievement exerts considerable influence on attitudes toward precoital stimulation. About half the total population, especially those with less education, are uninterested in prolonging the sexual act. They want to proceed with coition as quickly as possible to achieve orgasm in the shortest period of time. The man with a low level of education may limit his precoital activity to a simple kiss without causing any upset to his wife. Similar perfunctory behavior on the part of the college-educated husband, however, would be interpreted by his wife as rejection or a lack of interest.

Once coitus is under way, the college-educated husband will attempt, more often than a man of lower education, to delay orgasm (although 75% of Kinsey's total male sample reached orgasm within 2 minutes). About 90% of college-educated men prefer to have intercourse in the nude, but only half as many of the grade-school group have ever had intercourse without being clothed. Because college-educated men are in general thought capable of a higher level of abstraction than men with only grade-school and high-school educations, they can probably be more excited by external erotic stimulation. Consequently, they prefer to have intercourse in a lighted room where they can observe the nude body of the partner and the act of coition itself (Kinsey *et al.* 1948).

Precoital techniques of petting in marriage are similar to premarital ones. Since marital coition is readily available, however, the length of time devoted to petting is usually not as protracted within marriage. Among Kinsey's sample population, precoital marital petting was limited to less than 3 minutes in 11% of marriages, 4 to 10 minutes in a third of them, and 11 to 20 minutes in another third. About 22% of couples—primarily in the groups with higher education—extended petting beyond 20 minutes (occasionally for as long as an hour or more).

For many women, as has been noted, the need for cuddling and closeness is of considerably greater importance than the need for coitus itself. In fact, some women lure their partners into sexual intercourse just to satisfy this very real need to be held or cuddled. They are willing to barter coitus for close body contact, which tends to reduce their anxieties and to promote relaxation and feelings of security (Hollender 1971).

The belief still exists among the lower, less well-educated social classes that men are much more highly sexed than women and that a woman's sexual gratification is of less importance than a man's. College-educated women and increasing numbers of others today hold that they have as much right to sexual fulfillment as men. These women are consequently more satisfied with their sex lives than less-educated women. In contrast to men with less education, highly educated men are sensitive to the sexual needs of women. For example, the research of Masters and Johnson (1966) showed that 82% of men with some college education expressed concern for their partner's satisfaction, in contrast to a mere 14% of men with no college education. Lower-class males feel less total involvement in sex at any given time than higher-class males do, and their interest in sex decreases more rapidly with the passage of time than that of higher-class men (R. R. Bell 1970, 1971c; Rainwater 1968).

Because marital coitus is the only sexual outlet totally sanctioned by all religious groups, one would expect the frequency of marital coition to be greater among the religiously devout than among the religiously inactive—or that, at the very least, there should be no differences in frequency between the two groups. The frequency of marital intercourse, however, was lower among the religiously active Protestants in Kinsey's sampling (1948) than among the inactive Protestants. (Insufficient data on Catholic and Jewish groups prevented similar comparisons.) It is difficult to escape the conclusion that the strict early religious training of devout Protestants carries over into marriage and continues to inhibit sexual expression, despite the couples' conscious acceptance of the "rightness" of marital coitus.

Females.   Practically all married women participate in intercourse, although there is a gradual decline in frequency after the first two years of marriage. Men too, it will be remembered, experience marital coitus less frequently in the later years of life, but the decline among women is somewhat steeper. Kinsey found that the incidence in his sampling of those still engaging in coitus at the age of 50 was 97% of the men and 93% of the women; at the age of 60, the percentages were 94% and 84%, respectively. Curiously, marital coition is the only form of sexual outlet among women that undergoes such a decline with advancing age (Kinsey *et al.* 1948, 1953).

Bell and Bell (1972) questioned 2372 married women at all educational levels about various aspects of their marriages, the average length of which was 13.2 years. Coital frequency, by age groups, was given as:

26–30 years	9.4 times monthly
31–40	7.4
41–50	6.1
Over 50	4.1

The subjective evaluation of the women's sex life was also correlated with coital frequency.

"Very good" sex life	10 times monthly
"Good"	8.6
"Fair"	6.3
"Poor"	5.1
"Very poor"	2.3

Of all aspects of sexual activity, these women found the greatest satisfaction from:

Closeness or feeling of oneness with partner	22%
Orgasm	21%
Coitus	20%
Foreplay (petting)	19%
"Everything"	9%
Oral-genital contact	7%
Other responses	2%

The aspects of sex life least liked were:

Anal or oral sex	21%
"Messiness" after coitus	17%
Lack of orgasm	16%
Routine or ritual nature of sex	12%
Excessive or rough foreplay	12%
"Nothing"	9%
Coitus	6%
"Not enough sex"	4%
Other responses	3%

The decline in female coital frequency is rather puzzling in light of Kinsey's findings that women reach their peak of sexual desire between the ages of 31 and 40. However, since men's sexual drive peaks between the late teens and the age of 25 and thereafter shows a decline, it is probably the aging of men that causes the decrease in women's marital coital frequency (Armstrong 1963; Kinsey *et al.* 1953). During the first year of marriage, 75% of all women studied attained orgasm at least once during coitus. The percentage gradually increased to 90% after 20 years of marriage (Kinsey *et al.* 1953).

It should be remembered that the decline in frequency of marital coitus after the first two years of marriage does not necessarily imply declining interest in other forms of sexual activity. Kinsey showed that the incidence of female masturbation and nocturnal dreams involving orgasm increases after marriage, then remains fairly steady at its maximum level until women become 60 years of age or even older. Between the ages of 21 and 25, 89% of a married woman's total sexual outlet is derived from marital coition. After the age of 25 there is a gradual but consistent decline, so that by the time a woman reaches the age of 70, only 72% of total sexual outlet is provided by marital coitus (Kinsey *et al.* 1953).

A decline in satisfaction with marital sex was noted in the Levin and Levin (1975) survey. Women rated marital sex as "good" or "very good" in these percentages, according to the number of years they had been married:

Less than 1 year	82%
1 to 4 years	68%
5 to 10 years	67%
More than 10 years	67%

Pietropinto (1980) reports research that supports the percentages in the above survey. It is noteworthy that main drop in satisfaction with marital sex occurs in the early years of marriage and then apparently levels off.

According to the Kinsey study (1953), women capable of achieving climax in marital coitus did so in about 75% of their coital experiences. During the later years of marriage, the incidence of female orgasm in coition increased for all educational levels, although the incidence was consistently greater among the more educated groups.

As previously noted, the incidences of masturbation, premarital petting, and premarital coitus are inversely related to a woman's religious devoutness. It has also been noted, however, that once a woman had had these experiences, the frequency of her sexual activity continued, bearing little or no relationship to her religious background. The same sequence was found in marital coitus. A pattern of frequent coition was somewhat slower to develop among the more devout women; but once the frequency was established, no further relationship to the degree of religious involvement existed (in contrast to the findings concerning Protestant males). A correlation did exist, however, between the percentage of total sexual outlet provided by marital coitus and a woman's devotion to her religion (Kinsey *et al.* 1953). The more devout women experienced 4%–12% more of their total outlet in marital coition than did the women who were religiously inactive. There were no differences in the incidence of intercourse leading to orgasm, except that devout Catholic women were less likely to have orgasms during marital coitus than women of the other religious groups. This tendency probably stems from a fear of pregnancy that would affect Catholic women more than others, because of their church's stand against certain birth-control measures. Kinsey (1953) and Terman (1938) found that almost 15% of all the women in their samples regularly responded with multiple orgasms. Masters and Johnson (1966) conclude from their investigations that the percentage is somewhat higher, saying further that "woman is naturally multiple-orgasmic in capacity" (Masters & Johnson 1967).

Extramarital Behavior

The phrase extramarital sexual behavior customarily means adultery in some people's thinking. However, many sexual outlets other than coition are technically implied in the total scope of extramarital behavior. In this discussion, unless otherwise indicated, extramarital sex relations will refer to extramarital coition only—that is, coitus between a man and woman, at least one of whom is married at the time to someone else.

For men, the frequency of extramarital coitus, as with other types of sexual activity, decreases with age. For women, in keeping with certain other forms of sexual activity, both the frequency of extramarital coitus and the percentage of total sexual experience it represents increase with age (Harper 1966). Recent research indicates, however, that the incidence of extramarital coitus has increased for young women under age 25 (Williams 1980). Because of society's attitude toward extramarital affairs, the participants will usually go to rather extreme lengths to hide or deny their adultery. As a result, it is difficult to arrive at the true incidence and frequency of extramarital coition. The experience of psychotherapists confirms this secretiveness. They find their patients reluctant to admit to adulterous conduct, despite an extended time in therapy and the confidential nature of the therapeutic relationship.

In one survey of 750 case histories, 30% of the subjects had initially reported having taken part in extramarital coitus. After a period of intensive psychotherapy, during which the patients had gained confidence in the therapist-examiner, an additional 30% revealed secret affairs (Greene *et al.* 1974). Various reasons were given for extramarital coitus. *Sexual frustration* (70% of the subjects) was cited twice as frequently by men as by women. *Curiosity* was cited by 50% of the respondents, at the rate of 3 men to 2 women. *Revenge* and *boredom* were listed by 40% of the men and 30% of the women, while 20% of both sexes gave *need for acceptance and recognition* as the reason. Salzman (1980) points out that extramarital coitus may also occur under atypical circumstances, such as when one's sexual partner is temporarily absent. Furthermore, aging individuals may seek extramarital outlets to allay fears or doubts concerning sexual desirability or functioning. Availability of sexual partners in certain social contexts, overreaction to job pressures or situational difficulties, and even susceptibility to physical disorders or medical conditions may underlie isolated instances in which some individuals become involved in extramarital relations.

One must recognize that complex unconscious motives are much more basic to behavior than conscious ones. Despite the conscious or unconscious motivations in infidelity, both men and women generally rate marital sex as being more pleasurable than extramarital sex, though both rate extramarital coitus as pleasurable. Inexperience, guilt, or anxiety may lead individuals to perceive extramarital sex as being less satisfying than marital sex (Williams 1980). Many investigators believe women experience orgasms in marital sex much more often than they do in extramarital affairs (Hunt 1974). Others believe that extramarital coitus leads to orgasms in women at about the same or higher frequency as marital coitus (Butler 1976). Differences in these viewpoints are probably related to the length of the extramarital affair, the depth of emotional involvement, and many other similar variables.

The shift in present-day ethical values suggests that society views both premarital and extramarital sexual activity with greater leniency than in the past. Yet social, religious, and even legal condemnation remains strong enough that adultery is often destructive to a marriage (Harper 1961; Williams 1980). A large sample of college students at a midwestern university during the 1970s continues to express negative and conservative attitudes toward extramarital coitus, indicating that a revolution with respect to this sexual behavior is not likely to occur in the near future (Howat *et al.* 1979).

Males.   Most married men admit to at least an occasional desire to have an extramarital affair, and a conservative estimate is that from 50% to 75% of them actually do so at some point during their marriage (Ellis 1972; Kinsey *et al.* 1948; Terman 1938). Of the men in Hunt's sample (1974), only 41% admitted they had ever had extramarital coitus. He estimated that the cumulative incidence would probably approach but not exceed 50%. Still, one must take into account the fact that many people conceal secret affairs.

Men of the lowest educational group in Kinsey's sample had had more extramarital coitus during the early years of marriage (as well as more premarital coition) than men of the other educational levels. College men, who had had less premarital coitus, also had less extramarital coitus during the early years of marriage than other educational groups. As marriages continued, extramarital involvements decreased for the less educated groups and rose for the college-educated (Table 16.9).

Between the ages of 16 and 20, men of lower education had over 10 times (10.4) as much extramarital coitus as college men of the same age. Laborers and semiskilled workmen aged 16–20 had almost 17 times (16.5) more extramarital intercourse than young men of the same age who later entered the professions (Kinsey *et al.* 1948). Men frequently become promiscuous in their nonmarital sexual behavior, whether it involves premarital coition, extramarital coition, or homosexual contacts. The married men in Kinsey's sample (1948) derived 5%–10% of all their orgasms

Table 16.9 **Incidence of Male Extramarital Coitus at Various Ages and According to Education**

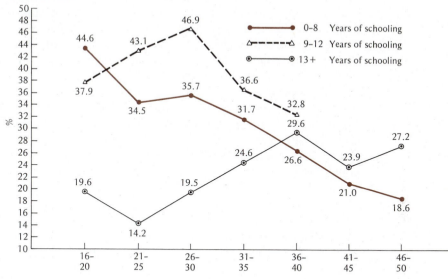

from extramarital coition, intercourse with prostitutes comprising 8%–15% of these sexual contacts.

Females. Kinsey's study (1953) showed that, among white American married women, 7% had extramarital sexual intercourse by the age of 26, and 26% by the age of 40.

While it is generally accepted that the incidence of extramarital coitus among married women has increased significantly since Kinsey's time—perhaps doubling his figure of 26% (Athanasiou *et al.* 1970)—the incidence found varies considerably from study to study. Again, whether or not one will admit to extramarital sexual experience depends largely on the confidence the person has in the therapist or researcher.

The 1974 *Redbook* survey reported that 30% of the married women in its sample had had extramarital coitus. There is a positive correlation, the study showed, between length of marriage and likelihood of extramarital sex. Only 12% of those married for less than a year had been involved, compared with 38% of women married more than 10 years (Levin 1975). *Redbook* also noted a predictable correlation between how a woman passes her time and extramarital activity. Of those who stay at home, only 27% have affairs; of those who do volunteer work, 32%; of full-time wage-earners, 47%. About half those having affairs reported being happy with their marriages and with marital sex (Levin 1975).

In 1979 *McCall's* survey found that one out of three of their female respondents acknowledged having been "unfaithful." Furthermore, many of these women expressed the opinion that their extramarital affairs had actually had the effect of strengthening their marital relationships. Still, 60% of the women in the *McCall's* survey endorsed the belief that sexual fidelity is extremely important in relationships. In general, most of the respondents indicated that the emotional issues revolving around home, family, and satisfying companionships were more important than sex alone in judging the quality of their relationships (Gittelson 1980).

Kinsey's findings (1953) showed that of those women who experienced extramarital coitus, 68% had also had premarital intercourse (in contrast to 50% of his total female sample who had had premarital sex). Of those women who had not experienced extramarital coitus, 83% stated they had no expectations of doing so, while only 44% of those who had extramarital intercourse stated that they did not expect to renew their activity.

The notion is almost universal that men customarily prefer sexual intercourse with somewhat younger partners. But the evidence shows that men frequently prefer coition with middle-aged or older women. The reason appears to be that, since the sex drive in women reaches its peak between the ages of 35 and 40, a woman of that age or older is ordinarily more responsive than a younger woman. Furthermore, she is more experienced sexually and has a better knowledge of sexual techniques. She has also thrown off many of the taboos and inhibitions that plague younger women, making her a freer and more responsive partner.

Education, decade of birth, and religious factors had a direct bearing on extramarital coitus among the women of Kinsey's study. Nearly a third (31%) of the college-level women had had extramarital intercourse by the age of 40, as compared with about 24% of those in the same age group who had had only grade-school or high-school education. *Redbook* found that college graduates are less likely to have extramarital sex than the high-school group—until they reach the age of 40, after which they are more likely to do so (Levin 1975).

In every age group in the Kinsey sample (1953), the lowest incidence of extramarital intercourse was among the religiously devout. By the age of 30, for example, 7% of religiously active Protestant women had had extramarital intercourse, as compared with 28% of religiously inactive Protestant women. In the *Redbook* survey, most women engaging in extramarital affairs claimed to have weak religious convictions. These experiences were twice as likely to occur among the minimally religious as among the strongly religious (Levin 1975).

About 41% of the women in Kinsey's study who had had extramarital affairs had limited their activity to a single partner. Another 40% had had 2 to 5 partners; 16% had had between 5 and 20 partners; and 3%, more than 20. Figures reported by Hunt (1974) on the number of extramarital partners were almost identical to those published by Kinsey. Up to the date their histories were taken, about 33% of the women in Kinsey's sample had had extramarital coitus 10 times or less. About 42% had been involved in their extramarital relationships 1 year or less; about 25% had had affairs over a 2- to 3-year period; and about 33% had continued for a period of 4 years or longer.

In the Kinsey study, 40% of the women who had had extramarital coitus believed their husbands knew of it, and an additional 9% thought they suspected it. When these figures are added to the percentage of women whose husbands had no suspicion whatever of their affairs, it indicates that for 71% of these women no marital difficulty had yet developed on this ground. In 42% of the instances in which the husbands knew or suspected the relationship, no retaliatory action was taken. In fact, some of these men had encouraged their wives to have affairs. Some wished to provide themselves with an excuse for their own extramarital affairs, but more commonly the encouragement stemmed from a desire to allow the women the "opportunity for additional sexual satisfaction" (Kinsey *et al.* 1953).

In yet another study, Bell and Peltz (1974) surveyed the incidence of women's extramarital coitus by questionnaire, collecting 2372 usable reports from 38 states. For the most part, the subjects were working and had higher than average education. The most significant finding was the far smaller increase in extramarital coitus over the Kinsey (1953) figures than the public commonly believes or than other studies have shown. In fact, the percentages revealed by this study and those of Kinsey are remarkably similar.

Generally, the findings in this 1974 survey show that the women most likely to have extramarital coitus are those who first had premarital sex at age 17 or younger; do not attend church; are generally dissatisfied or unhappy most of the time; rate their marriage as "poor" or "very poor"; evaluate coitus in their marriage as occurring too often or too infrequently; consider the sexual aspect of the marital relationship "poor" or "very poor"; are nonorgasmic in marital sex; masturbate frequently; have seen pornographic films that sexually arouse them; have used various artificial devices in sex play; and believe there must be a high degree of giving and receiving in marriage. At least, women who had had extramarital coitus expressed these opinions more frequently than women who had not engaged in extramarital sex.

Postmarital Behavior

Little research has been done on the subject of postmarital sex—that is, of men and women who are separated, divorced, or widowed (S-D-W). Most of the existing studies were conducted among men and women who were quite old and therefore do not reflect the accurate incidence of postmarital sexual behavior in the general population. In one study of S-D-W women, carried out by the Kinsey Institute (Gebhard *et al.* 1958), 76% of the separated, 73% of the divorced, and 72% of the widowed reported continuing coitus after their marriages terminated. Such sexual patterns, therefore, seem to be the rule rather than the exception. Given the liberalization of sexual attitudes and behavior in recent years, it is expected that today the S-D-W persons—especially the younger groups—will continue their sexual activity on a regular basis after a reasonable period of adjustment to their new roles. Furthermore, since most divorces occur during the early years of marriage, it is likely that many people are opting for postmarital sexual experiences (Glick 1980). The incidence of postmarital coitus and other sexual activity in the S-D-W population today is undoubtedly well over the 90% level.

Summary

The common forms of sexual expression include **masturbation, nocturnal orgasm, heterosexual petting, homosexual relations, sexual contact with animals,** and **heterosexual intercourse.** The degree of sex drive differs from person to person and depends upon factors such as age, physical well being, and psychological circumstances. Men experience the peak of their sex drive in the late teens or early 20s with a gradual decline in sex drive thereafter. Women typically do not reach the peak of their sex drive until the late 30s or early 40s.

Masturbation, or autoeroticism, is a common sexual practice among both males and females in premarital, marital, or postmarital states. An overwhelming majority of men masturbate at some time during their lives, although the incidence of masturbation declines in postadolescent years. Most women masturbate at one time or another in their lives and, in contrast to men, the incidence of self-stimulation to orgasm increases up to middle age and remains fairly constant thereafter. A common method used in masturbation by both males and females is genital stimulation, and such stimulation is often accompanied by fantasy.

Erotic dreams, often accompanied by nocturnal orgasm, is another form of sexual outlet for men and women. Together with orgasm, men experience nocturnal emissions or "wet dreams." Women also report having dreams that culminate in orgasm.

Heterosexual petting is a form of sexual expression enjoyed at one time or another by most men and women. Petting practices vary, ranging from kissing to breast manipulation to manual stimulation of the genitals to oral-genital stimulation. Interestingly, petting provides a greater percentage of total sexual outlet for women of all ages than it does for men of comparable ages.

Sexual contact with animals, or bestiality, is not practiced extensively by either men or women. Male contact with animals occurs primarily among boys who have been reared on farms, while very few women, urban or rural, have sexual contact with animals. The significance of bestiality in the study of human sexuality lies primarily in its social impact rather than its importance as a sexual outlet.

Heterosexual intercourse—whether it is premarital, extramarital, or post-marital—is the sexual outlet of greatest interest to both men and women. Premarital heterosexual intercourse—coition between two single persons—has increased in the U.S. American males are more sexually permissive and active than ever before, but the difference in incidence between male and female premarital sexuality has narrowed, indicating that the sexual per-missiveness and activity of females has increased at an even more rapid rate. This increase in premarital coitus among both sexes has been accompanied by an increase in the rate of cohabitation among college men and women. Men today more frequently choose to have coition with a woman whom they love or care for deeply rather than with a prostitute or casual pickup. Women are more sexually active than before, in part as a result of the "sexual revolution" that seems to have occurred in the 1960s. Socio-educational and other factors influence the degree of premarital sexual activity in both sexes. Religious commitment particularly affects sexual activity for both men and women. There is an inverse relationship between religion and sexual activity—the greater the religious commitment the less premarital sex that person has.

Heterosexual intercourse within marriage is an approved type of sexual activity according to the legal and moral codes of our culture. Nevertheless, it is estimated that up to 50% of marital sexual relationships are unsatis-factory. Typically, husbands desire intercourse more frequently than their wives while women need cuddling and closeness more than coitus. Highly educated men tend to be more sensitive to the sexual needs of their mates than less-educated men. Both sexes experience marital coitus less frequently in later life, with a steeper decline among women. Since they reach the peak of their sexual desire between the ages of 31 and 40 while men reach their peak between the late teens and age 25, it is probably the aging of men that leads to this decrease in women's marital coital frequency. The incidence of nocturnal dreams involving orgasm and masturbation increases after marriage for women, remaining fairly steady until they become 60 years of age or older.

Extramarital sexual intercourse, or adultery, refers to coitus between a man and a woman, at least one of whom is married at the time to someone else. Generally, the frequency of extramarital coitus decreases with age for men while it increases with age for women. While the social, religious, and legal condemnation of adultery is still prevalent, perhaps 50% of men and 25% to 33% of women become involved in extramarital sexual intercourse at some point in their marital lives.

Postmarital sexual activity, or the continuation of sexual activity by men and women who are separated, divorced, or widowed, is common—especially since the liberalization of sexual attitudes and behavior in recent years. Probably over 90% of separated, divorced, or widowed people engage in postmarital coitus or other sexual activities.

Annotated Bibliography

Bell, A. P. and Weinberg, M. S. *Homosexualities: A study of diversity among men and women.* New York: Simon and Schuster, 1978.

> This book presents a comprehensive exploration of homosexual behavior and life styles, exploding many myths. The authors review a wide range of topics pertinent to homosexuality, such as the gay sexual experience, problems of social adjustment, and the various psychological aspects. This book is important reading for persons who desire greater understanding of homosexuality.

DeLamater, J. and MacCorquodale, P. *Premarital sexuality: Attitudes, relationships, behavior.* Madison, Wisconsin: The Universtity of Wisconsin Press, 1979.

> This book presents a comprehensive analysis of contemporary premarital sexuality based on results of a large-scale survey. Previous research related to sexual attitudes, relationships, and behavior is reviewed. This book would enlighten the general reader as well as the professional educator, clinician, and researcher.

Hass, Aaron. *Teenage sexuality: A survey of teenage sexual behavior.* New York: Macmillan, 1979.

> Reporting large-scale survey results, this book reveals teen attitudes, feelings, and experiences related to a wide range of topics in sexuality, including dating, masturbation, oral sex, intercourse, orgasm, sexual fantasy, homosexuality, pornography, parental attitudes, and performance anxieties. This book would be of interest to the lay reader as well as to the social and behavioral scientist.

Hite, Shere. *The Hite report: A nationwide study on female sexuality.* New York: Macmillan, 1976.

> This book reports results of a national survey of female sexuality, exploring women's sexual attitudes, feelings, experiences, and behavior. Topics include

masturbation, orgasm, intercourse, sexual slavery, the sexual revolution, and aging and sexuality. Dispelling many myths related to female sexuality, this book would be of interest to the general reader.

Morrison, E. S., Starks, K., Hyndman, C. and Ronzis, N. *Growing up sexual.* New York: D. Van Nostrand, 1980.

Based on anonymous autobiographical papers by students, this unique book tells in students' own words their feelings, thoughts, and experiences of sexual development. Topics include learning about sex, first sexual experiences, family styles, sex roles, self-image, contraceptive use, sexual exploitation, and personal sexual values. The young person particularly will benefit from this book, which has special applicability as a sex education tool.

Myers, Lonny. Extramarital sex: Is the neglect of its positive aspects justified? In *Sex and the life cycle,* ed. W. Oaks, G. Melchiode, and I. Ficher. New York: Grune and Stratton, 1976.

This article reviews the medical and nonmedical literature concerning various aspects of extramarital sex, stressing the positive. The author's main contention is that the literature has a strong bias against adultery, which may be healthy for some individuals. The author directs his comments toward the more sophisticated general reader.

Pietropinto, A. and Simenauer, J. *Beyond the male myth: A nationwide survey.* New York: Times Books, 1977.

Based on results of a major survey of male sexuality, this book reveals the sexual views, preferences, attitudes, feelings, and experiences of the contemporary American male. The authors attempt to explode several prevalent myths related to male sexuality.

Sandler, Jack, Myerson, Marilyn, and Kinder, Bill N. *Human sexuality: Current perspectives.* Tampa, Florida: Mariner, 1980.

This text presents a comprehensive perspective of the field of human sexuality. A wide range of topics is covered, including sexual anatomy and sexual response, aphrodisiacs and anaphrodisiacs, past and current sexual attitudes and behavior, sexual diseases and disorders, sexual dysfunctions, birth control, sexual health, and sex and the law. Though designed for the student, this book would serve as a valuable general reference.

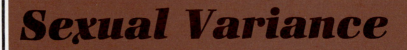

Sexual Variance

Variance in Methods of Functioning and Quality of Sexual Striving
  Sadism
  Masochism
  Exhibitionism
  Voyeurism and Scopophilia
  Nudism
  Troilism
  Transvestism
  Transsexualism
  Transgenderism
  Gender Identity Disorders of Childhood
  Sexual Analism
Variance in Choice of Sexual Partner or Object
  Pedophilia
  Bestiality
  Necrophilia
  Pornography and Obscenity
  Fetishism
  Frottage
  Saliromania
  Gerontosexuality
  Incest
  Mate-Swapping
  Klismaphilia
Variance in Degree and Strength of Sexual Drive
  Nymphomania
  Satyriasis
  Promiscuity
  Prostitution
  Rape

One of the major problems in the field of sexology today—and, indeed, in the whole realm of mental health—centers on the question of what is normal sexual behavior and what is abnormal.

Too many people are ready to stigmatize any sexual activity that deviates from their own behavior as aberrant or perverted. Yet, in the course of human history, sexual practices and ethics have varied within and among different cultures. What is usual in one culture may be unusual in another, and thus may become branded as abnormal, although unusual sexual behavior is not perverted simply because it is out of the ordinary for a given culture. Indeed, as Marmor (1971) points out, "our attitudes concerning nudity, virginity, fidelity, love, marriage, and proper sexual behavior are meaningful only within the context of our own cultural and religious mores." In discussing the differences between healthy and unhealthy sexual behavior, he says further:

> In our culture, a key distinguishing factor between what is regarded as healthy or unhealthy sexual behavior is whether such behavior is motivated by feelings of love or whether it becomes a vehicle for the discharge of anxiety, hostility, or guilt. Healthy sexuality seeks erotic pleasure in the context of tenderness and affection; pathologic sexuality is motivated by needs for reassurance or relief from nonsexual sources of tension. Healthy sexuality seeks both to give and receive pleasure; neurotic forms are unbalanced toward excessive giving and taking. Healthy sexuality is discriminating as to partner; neurotic patterns often tend to be nondiscriminating. The periodicity of healthy sexuality is determined primarily by recurrent erotic tensions in the context of affection. Neurotic sexual drives, on the other hand, are triggered less by erotic needs than by nonerotic tensions and are therefore more apt to be compulsive in their patterns of occurrence.

Many terms are used to describe sexual behavior that differs from the cultural norm: sexual abnormality, deviation, aberration, perversion, variance. Mental health practitioners also use the term paraphilia to describe disorders in which "unusual or bizarre imagery or acts are necessary for sexual excitement" (DSM III 1980). It is apparent, however, that true sexual abnormality is difficult to define and pinpoint. The term *variance* may be the fairest word to use for the purposes of this chapter, since it is the one that seems least emotionally charged or suggestive of disapproval.

It is possible for individuals to label themselves as perverted simply because they lack basic knowledge of what normal sexual behavior really is. They believe that their fantasies and behavior, or the frequency of either, deviate markedly from the public norm (Everett 1971). When humans do engage in truly abnormal sexual behavior on a continuing, compulsive basis, the behavior is typically unrelated to sexual needs. Rather, it is a symbolic, ongoing attempt to solve deep-seated personal problems (Auerback 1970).

Sociologists and other behavioral scientists have recently begun to view sexual variance as a social process rather than a social disease (Denfeld & Gordon 1970). As Becker (1963) observed:

> We ought not to view it [variant behavior] as something special, as depraved or in some magical way better than other kinds of behavior.

We ought to see it simply as a kind of behavior some disapprove of and others value, studying the process by which either or both perspectives are built up and maintained.

Generally speaking, a particular form of sexual behavior should be considered acceptable, whether or not others would care to participate in it, if three conditions are met: that it is not harmful to the participants; that it is carried out by consenting adults (adults who are willing to assume all responsibility for their acts) without any sort of coercion; and that it is out of sight and sound of unwilling observers. These conditions would also serve as valid criteria for judging what is and is not variant behavior (Ellis 1958).

Sexual variance may be said to fall into three categories: (1) method of functioning and quality of sexual striving; (2) choice of sexual partner or object; and (3) degree and strength of sexual drive (Thorpe *et al.* 1961).

Variance in Methods of Functioning and Quality of Sexual Striving

Sadism

Sadism is a sexual variance wherein sexual gratification, or at least sexual pleasure, is derived by inflicting either physical or psychological pain on the partner. The aggressive act serves no purpose except to secure sexual gratification (DSM III 1980). The word *sadism* comes from the name of a French writer, the Marquis de Sade (1740–1814). This man wrote extensively of his erotic exploits, which included several marriages, imprisonment for cruel acts in houses of prostitution, luring a shopkeeper's wife into a house where he horsewhipped her at gunpoint, administering poisonous "aphrodisiac" drugs to guests, and inflicting hundreds of scalpel wounds upon a woman whom he confined in a house.

Whipping, biting, pinching, and slapping are typical acts of the sadist. Sadism is expressed verbally in the form of sarcastic, belittling, threatening, teasing, or bullying remarks. Sadistic aggressiveness, however, may be unconscious and expressed indirectly or deviously, as well as through conscious and direct actions. (One must remember, however, that causing minimal pain—for example, lightly biting the partner's earlobe during sex play—is usually quite normal and can add pleasure to sexual activity.)

The causes of sadism are as varied as the means of expressing it. A person may have been taught, consciously or unconsciously, to have disgust for anything sexual. Because normal sexuality is unacceptable, the acts of cruelty are a punishment of the partner for engaging in something shameful.

In a man, another cause of sadism is a fear of castration (feelings of inferiority). The sadistic acts reassure the sadist that he is more powerful than his partner, and therefore need have no fear. Until the sadist convinces himself that he plays the superior role in the sexual relationship, his partner remains overwhelmingly threatening to him. In other cases, the sadist's behavior is merely a method of acting out repressed hostility toward parents (Coleman 1972; Moore 1969; Thorpe *et al.* 1961).

It should not cause surprise that some people are sexually aroused by giving or receiving pain. Our culture accepts as its basis the dominance-submission relationship, and aggressiveness is highly valued socially. Furthermore, television, movies, newspapers, and other mass media link violence and sex as their primary pleasure package (Gebhard 1976). When consciously expressed in extreme forms, however, sadism—and masochism—are considered pathological variances even if carried out between consenting adults. Our culture sees the need to protect even "consenting" victims from aggravated assault (Gadpaille 1972).

Hunt (1974) found that about 5% of the males and 2% of the females in his sampling had at one time or another received sexual pleasure from inflicting pain on a sexual partner. The incidence among men and women under 35 was double that of those over 35, and it was five times greater among single men than among married men.

Lust murder is the extreme of sadistic sexual abnormality, as the victim must be murdered and mutilated in order to provide sexual gratification. In true lust murders, no coitus occurs; orgasm is the outcome of the act of murder and mutilation. At least at the time of the act, such a person's mental illness is at psychotic level.

Masochism

Masochism is the mirror image of sadism. The masochist receives sexual pleasure or gratification from being hurt, physically or mentally, by the sexual partner (DSM III 1980). This disorder also derives its name from a historical figure, the Austrian novelist Leopold von Sacher-Masoch (1836–1895). A Doctor of Law at the age of 19, he experienced a long career of masochistic involvements. His first love, an older woman who insulted and victimized him at every turn, finally left him for a Russian adventurer. He then met a princess who compelled him to serve as her valet and secretary until she tired of him. After affairs with two baronesses, the second a lesbian, he married an extremely ugly woman who satisfied his craving for punishment and eventually deserted him.

Masochism is a much more common phenomenon than sadism, perhaps because our society and religion do not sanction injuring another person, or perhaps because masochism implies relief from the guilt generated by sex (erotic pleasure must be punished). Pain itself is not what the masochist seeks—nor, generally, is it what the sadist wants. To the masochist, accidental pain is neither sexual nor pleasurable; it must be "planned pain." In sadomasochism (S/M) an elaborate script is typically followed in which one partner has allegedly done something for which he or she must be punished. The confrontation of "evildoing" is followed by a period of threat and suspense, then by punishment (Gebhard 1976).

Masochism, like sadism, develops from an attitude of shame and disgust toward heterosexual relationships. Masochists use the pain and punishment inflicted on them to wash away the guilt associated with sexual desires. In other cases, they dominate their partners with their ability to endure punishment, which in their thinking proclaims their strength and superiority, and which also serves to make them the center of attention. Often, their sexual partners are identified with parent figures who dominated them during childhood. For example, the masochist may remember experiencing sexual excitement in childhood while being beaten, a sensation centered in the erogenous zones of the skin and muscles about the buttocks.

Many sexologists believe that the masochist does not actually wish to suffer pain, but merely wants to signify acquiescence to the partner by willingness to submit to physical or mental maltreatment. In any event, it appears that the masochist is so fearful of rejection that he or she is willing to be subjected to almost any humiliation or punishment that will please the partner and win affection and acceptance (Coleman 1972; Moore 1969).

In Hunt's sampling (1974), 2.5% of the males and 4.6% of the females reported experiencing pleasure from having pain inflicted on them by their sexual partner. For both sexes, by far the greater number who professed to enjoy these masochistic encounters were under 35. Five times more single than married women reported experiencing such pleasure.

Exhibitionism

In **exhibitionism,** sexual gratification is derived from exhibiting the genitals to unwitting (and typically unwilling) observers. Occasionally an individual will masturbate while exhibiting himself (DSM III 1980). Its pathology lies in the fact that satisfaction is gained in a vicarious manner rather than through straightforward sexual experience. A relatively common sexual problem, it is involved in 35% of all arrests for sexual violations (C. Allen 1961; DSM III 1980). Far more men than women are exhibitionists, although just how many women do actually exhibit themselves is impossible to determine. The public has a far different attitude toward the exposed bodies of women than of men, and women found exposing themselves would probably not be reported by the viewer.

This behavior begins, classically, in feelings of insignificance or inadequacy. The exhibitionist hopes to gain attention. Some psychoanalysts believe this deviancy in men stems from a fear of castration, the exposure of self being explained as an attempt to disprove castration. Others claim that exhibitionism is an extreme form of autoeroticism based on narcissistic (self-love) impulses.

The male exhibitionist is usually a quiet, timid, submissive person who lacks normal aggressiveness and who is beset with feelings of inadequacy and insecurity. He is often described as "nice" but immature. He characteristically was reared in a cultural atmosphere of overstrict and puritanical attitudes toward sex, and his formative years were dominated by a powerful, engulfing mother. The most common age for the onset of exhibitionism is during a man's early or mid-20s. Later onset of exhibitions may reflect major emotional disturbances such as dementia, psychosis, alcoholism, or depression (Bastani 1980; DSM III 1980). Despite the fact that most male exhibitionists are married, the sexual relationship with their wives is likely to be a poor one. All these influences work to create in exhibitionists pervading doubts and fears concerning their masculinity (Coleman 1972). Indeed, when one applies such criteria as frequency of coitus with spouse or lover, degree of impotence, number of coital partners, and age at which coitus first occurred, the typical exhibitionist must be described as undersexed (Mathis 1969).

Since the male exhibitionist obviously hopes his genital exposure will profoundly shock the viewer, a woman who responds hysterically to his behavior merely feeds the illness. Confronted by an exhibitionist, her most sensible approach is calmy to ignore the act and to suggest that he stands in need of psychological help and can benefit from it.

It should be remembered that the male exhibitionist is more of a nuisance than a menace. He rarely becomes involved in more serious crimes; and when he does, his criminality is classically of a nonsexual nature. The exhibitionist seldom exposes himself while he is close to his victim. He chooses, rather, to remain at a safe distance—usually 6 to 60 feet away (Gebhard *et al.* 1965).

Exhibitionism is frequently linked with a compulsive pattern of behavior wherein the display occurs in the same place and usually at the same time of day, indicating the exhibitionist's desire or need to be apprehended. In these linkage cases, the prognosis is fairly good. The factors involved in their exhibitionistic tendencies are more easily made clear and intelligible to these patients. Understanding the causes of their difficulties, they appear to feel that a serious effort on their part will lead to a more healthy sexual adjustment.

Pseudoexhibitionism is often confused with true exhibitionism. In this syndrome, heterosexual relations are not available and the persons exhibit themselves only as a poor substitute for preferred sexual intercourse.

Voyeurism and Scopophilia

Voyeurism and **scopophilia** (also called *scoptophilia*) are disturbances in which the viewer of sexual acts and erotic things derives unusual sensual pleasure and gratification. Behaviorists refer to scopophilia as meaning sexual pleasure gained from observing sexual acts and genitalia, and voyeurism as simply the scrutinizing of nudes. But the terms are often used interchangeably, voyeurism being the more popular (Karpman 1954).

In the case of the voyeur (commonly called a "Peeping Tom"), the viewing is usually done secretly. In an effort to observe sexual activity the voyeur often peers hopefully through windows, or goes to such lengths as to bore peepholes through walls and doors of toilets, dressing rooms, and guest rooms. Only a small number of women are known to be voyeurs or scopophiliacs. According to FBI reports, nine men to one woman are arrested on charges of "peeping."

Like other variant behavior, these phenomena are believed to develop as defense mechanisms against what the individual feels is a threat to self-evaluation. By merely *looking*, the voyeur guards against any personal failure in sexual activity, and at the same time enjoys a feeling of superiority over those secretly observed. According to psychoanalytic interpretation, fixations relating to certain events witnessed as a child, such as seeing parents in the act of intercourse, underlie voyeurism. Little appears in scientific reports on the subject of voyeurism. In an exhaustive review of the literature, R. S. Smith (1976) found no texts and only 15 articles dealing specifically with voyeurism. And in none of these investigations had the usual experimental research methods been used.

The desire to view the naked body of one's sexual partner or the act of coitus itself is certainly normal; so is the pleasure a couple experience in viewing themselves in mirrors during sexual activity. Viewing becomes abnormal only when it is consistently preferred to petting or intercourse, or when it becomes a compulsive act (DSM III 1980).

Nudism

Nudism is regarded by some as a variance because they erroneously link it with exhibitionism. Social nudism, however, is not a sexual deviation. As a matter of fact, the overall atmosphere in most nudist camps is, because of rigidly enforced rules of behavior, more suggestive of asexuality than of sexual permissiveness (M. S. Weinberg 1971).

The average nudist is also the average citizen, although he or she may have become free of certain taboos still clinging to the rest of us. The male nudist, in company with almost all men, prefers watching a woman undress to finding her already nude. The vast majority of both male and female nudists report that their coital frequency remains unchanged as a result of practicing nudism, although over 33% of them express the opinion that nudism has contributed positively to their sexual happiness (Hartman *et al.* 1969).

Troilism

Troilism (also *triolism*) is the sharing of a sexual partner with another person who looks on. It may involve two couples having sexual relations at the same time in sight of each other. In the traditional view, the troilist cannot perform the sex act unless he or she is partaking in the "sharing" experience (Branson 1960). Threesomes usually involve two members of one sex and one member of the other sex, but homosexual triangles have been known. Even in predominantly heterosexual threesomes, however, bisexuality may be involved. Perhaps the most significant problem that can arise in threesomes centers on the feelings of isolation and jealousy that may occur in the individual who is temporarily excluded from the interaction (Frank 1980).

Many sexologists see elements of voyeurism and exhibitionism in troilism. Others believe it is an expression of latent or disguised homosexuality, since the troilist may identify with the marital partner during these erotic activities. However, the premise that troilism is sexually variant must be reexamined in the light of recent preliminary research findings concerning mate-swappers (pp. 344, 427). In any case, troilism is far more prevalent among men than among women: men usually instigate the behavior pattern and derive the greatest pleasure from it—at least initially.

Transvestism

Transvestism, or **cross-dressing,** refers to excitement or gratification, either emotional or sexual, derived from dressing in the clothes of the opposite sex (D. G. Brown 1961; DSM III 1980). The practice usually begins in early childhood and is often brought about by parental rejection of the child's sex. The "petticoat punishment" of attempting to humiliate a young boy by forcing him to dress in girls' clothing may backfire and instead cause him to pursue cross-dressing. Sometimes the practice of cross-dressing does not begin until adolescence, at which time it is done without parental rejection or reinforcement and out of the sight or knowledge of others (DSM III 1980; Krueger 1980). Most transvestites engage only in normal and acceptable sexual activities; their cross-dressing habits, reserved for "special occasions," are their only variance. Most transvestites are able to adjust satisfactorily to sex and marriage, especially when the partner is understanding and cooperative.

Authorities agree that the majority of transvestites are decidedly *not* homosexual. In fact, 74% of the 272 transvestites surveyed in one study (Benjamin 1967) were married, and 69% had fathered children; only 25% admitted having any homosexual experience at all. This last figure is especially interesting, since Kinsey found that 37% of all men have had at least one homosexual contact to the point of orgasm in their lives. Other investigators also report that the majority of transvestites are heterosexual males who are typically married and often fathers (Krueger 1980; Wise & Meyer 1980). Estimates vary, but transvestism exists today in possibly 1% to 3% of the population. The difficulty in making a more accurate estimate lies in the secrecy with which perhaps 90% of transvestites indulge in their habits (D. G. Brown 1961; Krueger 1980).

The difference between the homosexual and the transvestite is that transvestism is typically a secret pursuit involving only one individual, whereas homosexuality obviously must involve two people. Furthermore, to attract a partner, the homosexual must reveal him/herself as being gay. The transvestite might be said to possess two personalities, one male and the other female, which alternately assert themselves. By contrast, the homosexual is always a homosexual. There is nothing in the present-day understanding of genetics to support the contention that transvestism results from an inborn, instinctive predisposition toward it.

The pattern of cross-dressing varies among male transvestites. In one instance, women's apparel is worn only periodically. In another, the man has a fetishlike fondness for a particular article of women's clothing—panties or a brassiere—which he habitually wears under his own clothing. In yet another, the yearning to wear women's finery may be so deeply ingrained that the transvestite discards men's clothing to embark upon a lifelong masquerade as a woman.

Transvestites typically attest to a sense of pleasure and relaxation when wearing the clothing of the opposite sex. They relish the feel of the cloth and seeing themselves thus attired in the mirror. A man's cross-dressing allows him to express the gentle, graceful, sensuous side of his nature, a part of him that has somehow become identified with the feminine gender and that society does not permit him to express as a man.

Treatment of this variant behavior includes psychotherapy (especially the use of aversive conditioning techniques) and the administration of hormones (hormonal treatment is quite useless if the purpose is to bolster the man's masculine interests and behavior). Wise & Meyer (1980) note, however, that the majority of transvestites do not seek treatment, and that those who do often do not gain much from the therapeutic experience. Behavior therapy techniques may prove to be the treatment of choice when individuals wish to attempt to change this behavior.

Transsexualism

Also called **sex-role inversion, transsexualism** is a condition in which an individual's anatomy and sex-role orientation (*gender identity*) are incompatible (Green & Money 1969). The large majority of persons with this problem are male, although there are female transsexualists as well. Since the majority are male, for the purpose of this discussion we shall consider the phenomenon from the point of view of a man who is physiologically male, but whose psychological inclinations are female. With rare exceptions, the transsexualist has the genetic and anatomical characteristics of a man. His sex-chromosome pair is XY, designating the male sex; he possesses normal male genitals, internally and externally; and he is capable of impregnating a woman.

Nowhere is the difference between the sex assigned by nature and the gender identity acquired through social conditioning (discussed more fully in the next section) more dramatically demonstrated than in the transsexual. The man knows he is a male, yet he rejects his maleness. Not content with dressing as a female, as the transvestite is, he wishes to live the life of a woman—emotionally, physically, sexually. The male sex organs become such hated objects that attempts at self-castration or suicide are not uncommon among transsexuals. As Harry Benjamin—an endocrinologist and a recognized authority on transsexualism—puts it, the transsexual views his sex organs as a deformity (Buckley 1967). Transsexuals may have a previous sex history that is asexual, homosexual, or heterosexual in character. Those transsexuals with previous homosexual experiences or arousal patterns may claim, however, that their sexual behavior was really heterosexual since they were women in their mind-set. Other transsexuals

Dr. Richard Raskind before sex change operation. (Wide World Photos) Dr. Rene Richards after sex change operation. (United Press International)

have never had any intense sexual feelings, and still others have had extensive heterosexual experience (DSM III 1980).

Typically, a man will undergo transsexual surgery because he wants to be perceived as and/or loved as a woman by a "straight" man. He does not wish to be loved by a homosexual, whose love-sex object is another man. The transsexual is firmly convinced that some cruel caprice of nature has imposed upon him the body of a male and the emotionality and mentality of a woman. It should be pointed out that transsexuals are not hermaphrodites—that is, they do not possess, even to a limited degree, the physical characteristics of both sexes. The problem is at the other end of the body. In his mind, the transsexual is convinced that he was given the wrong body.

The causative factors in transsexuality appear to be much the same as those in transvestism and homosexuality. The transsexualist's mother is typically an unhappy woman, who clutches her son to her bosom—literally and figuratively—entering into an intensely close relationship with him from which the father and the other children of the family are excluded. Thus, one of the most common predisposing factors to transsexualism is a troubled parent-child relationship (DSM III 1980; R. Green 1969).

There are an estimated 10,000 transsexuals in the U.S. Perhaps from 3000 to 4000 have undergone sex-reassignment surgery, although, for obvious reasons, the identities of very few are known. Until recently, American transsexuals had to go to Europe or Casablanca for a sex-change operation. However, fostered by the interest of Harry Benjamin (1966), American medicine has in recent years given reluctant consideration to the dilemma of the transsexual.

Many doctors shrink from what is to them a mutilation of the human body. But, as Benjamin (1967) has pointed out, all forms of psychotherapy have been singularly unsuccessful in helping these people who, in company with the transvestite and homosexual, are notably resistant to change. Since the transsexual's mind cannot be made to adjust to his body, Benjamin contends, the only sensible and humane course is to make the body adjust to the mind.

The U.S. hospitals and clinics that perform such operations do so only after exhaustive consideration of each applicant. Primary requirements for consideration are that the individual has lived as a member of the opposite sex for a considerable time and has undergone hormonal treatment. It is significant that persons approaching such operations—which involve, in a man, the removal of testicles and penis, leaving sufficient skin to form an artificial vagina—have not been known to get "cold feet" and back out.

The surgical technique for male-to-female sex reassignment has been perfected fairly well, although follow-up surgery may be needed in some cases to correct residual problems. On the other hand, the female-to-male surgical technique presents many problems that have not been overcome.

For example, the construction of a penis from grafted skin is possible only after several operations, and once surgically installed, it is insensitive and cannot become erect. Female-to-male transsexuals may retain the capacity for orgasm, however, as the clitoris remains unaffected by the surgery. The outcome of hormonal sex reassignment is satisfactory for both transsexuals (Money & Wiedeking 1980).

Transgenderism

Transgenderism is a relatively new term in the field of sexology, one meant to describe a variance falling at some point between transvestism and transsexualism. As such, it is a variance not yet accepted by all workers in the field.

The male transgenderist identifies himself powerfully with the female gender. He may consistently cross-dress and assume the female role in daily life, yet he does not wish to have the transsexual surgery that would transform him into a woman. Dressing, acting, and looking like a woman— assuming the female gender identity as completely as possible—is apparently enough for him. The male transgenderist may take female hormones (even at the expense of his sex drive) for softer skin and less facial hair, and may have breast-enlargement surgery. These steps do not remove him from transgenderism into transsexualism, but they do place him closer to it (Slavitz 1976).

Gender refers to genetic sex, male or female, which is irreversibly fixed at the moment of conception by the pairing of the 23rd, or sex-determining, chromosomes (XX or XY). Hence gender is biologically determined. Identity, on the other hand, is environmentally or psychologically determined, the product of how one views the self, whether one associates oneself, subjectively, more logically or comfortably with one sex than the other— whether one *feels* feminine or masculine, a girl or a boy, a woman or a man. Put another way, a male is always a male, and a female is always a female, but a *man* can become a *woman*, or a *woman* a *man*. And this process of identifying oneself with one sex or the other, which is occasionally out of phase with genetic sex, is typically completed in the first three years of life. The problems referred to by most authorities when they speak of **gender disorders** are hermaphroditism, homosexuality, transvestism, transsexualism, and transgenderism.

Gender Identity Disorders of Childhood

A child who expresses an extreme distaste for his or her sexual identity will often identify strongly with the other sex. Such a child may deny or repudiate his or her sexual organs and insist that he or she will grow up to be the other sex. Not unexpectedly, such a child will often experience social conflicts and ostracism by his or her peers. A boy who exhibits this disorder may only be interested in playing with dolls or dressing up in girls' clothing; a girl who exhibits this disorder may be interested in playing only sports or in identifying with traditional male roles.

Excessive emotional and physical closeness between a male infant and his mother, with the relative lack or absence of a father figure, may lead to this gender identity problem for a boy. Lack of or absence of a mother figure in the early life of a female infant may cause her to excessively identify with her father and thus lead to a gender identity problem for a girl. While gender identity disorders of childhood appear to be rare, such disorders, when they do occur, initially manifest themselves before a child's fourth birthday (DSM III 1980).

Sexual Analism

Sexual analism refers to the use of the anus (rectum) for copulation. **Sodomy** is another term for it, although the legal interpretation of sodomy may encompass a much wider range of sexual variance. Because of its prevalence in the sexual practices of American men and women, it is questionable whether anal intercourse should be included in a chapter on sexual variance.

Either the incidence and frequency of anal intercourse have increased markedly in recent years, or couples are more honest about engaging in it. Studies in the 1960s (Gebhard *et al.* 1965; Storr 1964) suggested that only about 3% of married men and women had ever engaged in anal intercourse, and at that, only once or twice on an experimental basis. Kinsey (1948) observed that anal activity among heterosexuals was too infrequent to permit an accurate estimate of its incidence. Hunt (1974) found that about 15% of heterosexuals between 35 and 44, and about 25% of those under 35, had copulated anally in the year preceding his sampling. Although most said they rarely practiced analism, over 6% of those under 35 reported that they did so "sometimes" or "often."

About 50% of currently active homosexual males practice anal intercourse, although only 18% to 20% of all males with any homosexual experience have engaged in it (Carrier 1971; Hunt 1974; Kinsey *et al.* 1948). Recent evidence indicates that the incidence of anal sex may be as high as 90 percent for homosexual males (Lewis & Lewis 1980a).

Hite (1976) reported that about half the women in her sample enjoyed anal contact. About 40% of those who did so preferred simply being touched anally, about 30% preferred anal penetration by finger, and 30%, penile-anal penetration. Masters and Johnson (1970) state that the most persistent organism invading and infecting a woman's vaginal tract originates in the bowel. Following anal intercourse, if a man were to penetrate the vagina, he might infect it by his bacterially contaminated penis. A woman wishing to avoid certain vaginal infections should insist that her partner not penetrate both rectum and vagina during a single sexual encounter. Venereal diseases, viral infections, parasitic infections, and sexual problems such as prostatitis may result if appropriate attention is not given to hygiene during anal intercourse (Lewis & Lewis 1980a).

Homosexuals and, to a lesser extent, heterosexuals make use of other body parts in sexual relations—for example, using the space between the thighs, which is an act called *interfemoral sexual intercourse.* Scientific opinion is that there is nothing physcially or psychologically wrong or abnormal with nonvaginal methods of coitus.

Variance in Choice of Sexual Partner or Object

Pedophilia

Pedophilia is a form of sexual variation in which adults derive erotic pleasure from relationships of one form or another with children. Pedophilic practices include exposure of the genitals to the child and manipulation and possible penetration of the child. One study (Jaffe 1976) showed that 85% of child molestation involved such behavior as indecent exposure, genital manipulation, obscene language, and physical advances. In 11% of the cases, such offenses as vaginal intercourse, anal penetration, and rape were involved. Of all sex offenders, about 30% are classed as pedophiles, most of them men (Ellis & Brancale 1956). This group is usually less aggressive and forceful than rapists, although public outrage against them is often stronger.

Many child molesters are mentally dull, psychotic, alcoholic, and asocial. Most fall within the age range of 30 to 40 years, the average age being 37 (Coleman 1972; DSM III 1980; McCaghy 1971; Revitch & Weiss 1962). Older offenders seek out very young children, while younger offenders appear to concentrate on adolescent girls. The child molester is typically branded as a "sex fiend," "sex maniac," "dirty old man," or "pervert." Yet severe physical violence occurs in probably no more than 3% of all cases of sexual molestation; and only about 15% of all adult-child sexual contacts involve any kind of coercion, including threats (McCaghy 1971).

Child molesters direct their sexual interests toward opposite-sex children twice as frequently as toward same-sex children. The heterosexually oriented child molester, almost always male, usually prefers girls in the 8-to-10-year age range. Typically the sexual activity is limited to noncoital acts such as touching or looking. The homosexually oriented child molester, once again almost always male, tends to engage older children in sexual activity. A child molester who seeks both heterosexual and homosexual contacts may look to younger children (DSM III 1980).

It is interesting that these offenders have, otherwise, a Victorian attitude toward sex. They believe in the double standard, assess women as either "good" or "bad," insist that their brides be virgins, and so forth (Gebhard *et al.* 1965; Rubin 1966a). It is both curious and disquieting that imprisoned sex offenders in general exhibit strong religious convictions. They see themselves as devout, practice religious rituals faithfully, respect the ministry, read the Bible regularly, and take part in long and self-centered prayers that they believe can cure their illnesses.

These same men, however, are overly concerned about sexual matters, feel guilty and doomed, think that life has been unfair to them, and are painfully pulled in the opposite directions of sex and rigid piety. About 90% of all sex offenders admit to having received religious training in childhood (G. H. Allen 1966), yet only 0% to 33% (depending on the type of sex offense) report that their sex education came from their fathers or mothers (Gebhard *et al.* 1965).

Typically, the child molester is not a stranger lurking in the shadows, as so many parents think; from 50% to 80% of all child molestation is committed by family friends, relatives, or acquaintances. Although the Kinsey statistics show that 80% of girls who had been molested were "emotionally upset or frightened," the upset was, generally speaking, about as great as if the child had been frightened by a spider or a snake (McCaghy 1971). Any lingering effects from the experience were probably caused by the hysterical reaction of parents or other adults to the incident. Most psychologists agree that sexual experiences at the hands of a pedophile are less traumatic to the child than to the parents. If parents can deal with such unfortunate occurrences in a controlled manner, the child will usually suffer no residual trauma.

Child molesting in one form or another is more common than most people realize. Kinsey and his co-workers found that 20% to 25% of their middle-class female sample had been directly approached between the ages of 4 and 13 by adult males (or males at least five years older than they were) who made or attempted to make sexual contacts. Such experiences are even more common among lower-class females. Among college students studied, 30% of the men and 35% of the women reported they had had some form of experience during childhood. Among the women, 50% of these experiences involved exhibitionists, and among the men almost 85% involved homosexual overtures. In many such cases the children are "collaborative" victims (McCaghy 1971).

This deviation usually develops as an attempt on the part of the pedophile to cope with a fear of failure in normal interpersonal and heterosexual relationships, especially with a sexually experienced adult; or as an attempt to satisfy a narcissistic love of himself as a child (Kopp 1962). Efforts to rehabilitate pedophiles through psychotherapy have shown promising results, although some become recidivists (relapsed offenders or criminals). The rate of recidivism among homosexually oriented child molesters is between 13% and 28%, while the rate of recidivism among heterosexually oriented child molesters is about half as great (DSM III 1980). Although a prison sentence apparently does little to alter the subsequent behavior of sexual deviates, society is, of course, protected from them during their term of imprisonment (Coleman 1972).

Not all men charged as sex offenders against children are disturbed or sick; some have simply been trapped. It is a sad truth that our culture places an inordinate emphasis on physical beauty. Advertisements incessantly stress the advantages of being sexually attractive. As a consequence, many girls in the 12- to 15-year-old age bracket, especially those who have been poorly guided by their parents in the matter of healthy self-evaluation, feel inadequate because of their youth. They turn to cosmetics and sophisticated clothing and conduct in an effort to give the appearance of being older than they really are. Unable to judge such a girl's true age men sometimes get caught in the legal trap of statutory rape (coitus with someone under legal age of consent) (Gebhard *et al.* 1965).

Bestiality

Bestiality is sexual gratification obtained by engaging in sexual relations with animals. The Kinsey investigators (1948) reported that 17% of men reared on farms have reached orgasm through sexual relations with animals, and many others probably have had some sort of sexual contact with them.

Only when the pattern of behavior becomes fixed can bestiality be considered a mechanism to avoid feared failure with the opposite sex. Or it may be a means of avoiding distress or threat because relations with any woman suggest incest with the mother. In many cases the individual shows his hostility or contempt toward women by identifying them with animals, or by choosing animals in preference to them. *Zoophilia* is an unnatural love for animals, although the term is usually used interchangeably with bestiality.

Necrophilia

Necrophilia is a rare sexual deviation and signifies profound emotional disturbance, almost always of psychotic proportions. Sexual gratification comes from looking at a corpse, or actually having intercourse with it, sometimes followed by mutilation of it (Thorpe *et al.* 1961). The necrophile may kill to provide himself with a corpse, have sexual relations with it, mutilate it, and even cannibalize it. This rare but obviously severe form of sexual deviation may be explained as an attempt by the individual to dominate someone, even if it is a cadaver (Coleman 1972). Most professionals view necrophilia as the most deviant of all sexual aberrations.

Pornography and Obscenity

Pornography (from the Greek words for *harlot* and *writing*, assumed to mean the advertisements of prostitutes) is written or pictorial material deliberately designed to arouse sexual excitement (Gebhard *et al.* 1965). The material may be obscene, but the responsibility of so labeling it lies with the courts. **Obscenity** consists of utterances, gestures, sketches, and the like that are judged repugnant according to the mores of a society. Most obscene behavior, such as crude writing on the walls, telephone calls (usually anonymous), or public remarks, is assaultive in nature. The subject of sex is no doubt chosen because of its almost certain shock effect, or because the behavior is indicative of actual fantasy. People often are confused by definitions, and sometimes label inoffensive material "obscene" when it is merely sexually arousing (Primeau 1977).

By frightening or shocking his victim, the person making an obscene telephone call, like the exhibitionist, is attempting to deny (at least unconsciously) a deep-seated, morbid fear of sexual inadequacy. The anonymity of the telephone protects him from being evaluated as he sees himself—as an uninspiring, physically laughable creature. Usually an immature person, severely deficient in self-esteem and meaningful interpersonal relationships, the offender attempts to satisfy narcissistic needs through the reactions of shock from others (Nadler 1968).

The attitude of Americans toward pornography is varied indeed. Many consider it informative or entertaining. Others believe that it leads to rape or moral breakdown; or that it improves a couple's sexual relationship and leads to innovation in their coital techniques; or that it eventually becomes only boring; or that it causes men to lose respect for women; or that it serves to satisfy normal curiosity.

More people than not report that the effects on themselves of erotica have been beneficial. Those who judge pornography dangerous tend to see it harming others, not themselves. Those with a passion for purity and a determination to control the moral behavior of others typically cite two reasons why someone (usually themselves) should sit in judgment on what others may or may not read: (1) children's minds are corrupted by such material, and (2) it provokes sexual criminality or other sexual acting-out.

The first question that immediately arises is just what constitutes pornography. No matter how many laws are passed, lechery, like beauty, remains in the eye of the beholder. A massive Rubens nude will evoke admiration for its artistic merit in one person, some degree of sexual arousal in another, and moral indignation in a third. The same nude might evoke in a fourth only thoughts of the local reducing salon. Is the Bible pornographic? Is Shakespeare? Chaucer? St. Augustine? John Donne? Benjamin Franklin? All have, amazingly, been subjected to censorship, which is an indispensable tool in the business of purification. Ridiculous? Of course.

But because censorship is almost always based on false premises and administered by the unenlightened or overzealous, it almost inevitably goes to ridiculous or dangerous extremes.

Does Pornography Harm Children? Young people, it is generally assumed, are particularly vulnerable to the arousal of strong sexual desires as a result of reading prurient material. But the contention that pornography has a degenerative effect on them—or even on young children—is highly debatable. Certainly there is no research or clinical data to support the argument. In the most recent refutation, the President's Commission on Obscenity and Pornography—a 19-man team of experts conducting a two-year study—stated among its preliminary conclusions in August 1970: "There is no evidence to suggest that exposure of youngsters to pornography has a detrimental impact upon moral character, sexual orientation, or attitudes."

Sex-Related Criminality and Pornography. The consensus of such professionals as psychiatrists, psychologists, sex educators, social workers, and marriage counselors is that sexual materials cause neither adults nor adolescents any harm. Yet the argument persists that pornography stimulates people to commit criminal sex acts. And when making an arrest for a sex offense, law-enforcement officers may, true enough, find the back seat of the culprit's car sagging under a collection of "dirty" books and magazines. However, the age-old chicken-or-egg quandary immediately arises: Which came first, interest in pornography or tendency toward sex-related crime?

As with the allegation that pornography harms children, there is no scientific evidence supporting a link between pornography and sexual criminality. The preliminary report of the presidential commission (1970) contains this statement:

> Research indicates that erotic materials do not contribute to the development of character defects, nor operate as a significant factor in antisocial behavior or in crime. In sum, there is no evidence that exposure to pornography operates as a cause of misconduct in either youths or adults.

Rather, a careful examination of imprisoned sex offenders shows that they "have histories of sexual repression as youngsters growing up in strict families," suggesting that this repression, "not stimulation by pornography, is what leads them to sex crimes."

The Kinsey group's 25-year study of sex offense shows that pornography has quite a different effect from what it is commonly believed to have. Of its entire sample of 2721 men, of whom less than half were imprisoned sex offenders, only 14 had never been exposed to pornography. This almost universal exposure provides a valid basis for drawing certain conclusions about the effects of pornographic material on an adult (Gebhard *et al.* 1965).

For a man to respond strongly to pornography, two conditions are important: youthfulness and imagination, both characteristically lacking in sex offenders. As a group, they are not youthful, and, as they are poorly educated, their imaginativeness and ability to project, to "put themselves in somebody's else's shoes," are limited. Their response to pornography is accordingly blunted. The Kinsey researchers suggest that a typical reaction of a sex offender might be, "Why get worked up about a picture? You can't do nothing with a picture." Not only did the Kinsey group reject the premise that pornography is a spur to sexual criminality, but it went on to suggest that a man's *inability* to attain vicarious sexual pleasure through some form of erotica may possibly cause him to break out into a display of unacceptable sexual behavior. While this view was once judged as simply the thoughtful speculation of researchers who have spent a great many years studying sex offenders, it has recently received empirical support from a much-publicized experiment in Denmark, a subject examined more fully in Chapter 19, Sex and the Law.

A survey of New Jersey psychologists and psychiatrists revealed that practically none had ever seen a normal patient with a history of delinquency whose delinquent behavior had been prompted by pornography. Two-thirds of these professionals thought, as a matter of fact, that such "literature" would reduce delinquent acts by providng substitute outlets (Katzman 1969).

The University of Chicago Department of Psychiatry polled some 3400 psychiatrists and psychologists as part of a research project to determine what relationship (if any) they had seen between pornography and such asocial sexual behavior as rape. It is obviously difficult to measure the long-term effects of pornography experimentally; this research therefore focused on the clinical experience of professionals dealing with disordered human behavior. Only 7.4% of these therapists reported cases in which they were "somewhat convinced" of the linkage between pornography and sexual acting-out; 80% said they had never encountered such a case. An even larger number—83.7%—were convinced that the person exposed to pornography was no more likely than the unexposed person to commit an act of sexual aggression. Furthermore, 86.1% of these therapists thought that people intent on stamping out pornography are frequently bedeviled by their own unresolved sexual problems. Two-thirds of the clinicians polled in this study opposed censorship because of the climate of oppression it creates, and because of the inhibitions it imposes on human creativity (Rubin 1970a).

Pornography and Sexual Acting-Out. The President's Commission (1970) concluded from its investigation, according to its preliminary report, that during the 24 hours following the viewing of highly erotic material there may be some sexual arousal and, in some cases, increased sexual activity. But, the commission observed, basic attitudes and sexual patterns do not change because of it. In several experiments reported by the group, a large number of men and women watched pornographic films. It was found that 90% of the couples 20 to 25 years old, and from 30% to 60% of those 40 to 50 years of age, were aroused by what they saw (women as well as men, it should be pointed out). The commission's report contained the comment that "there are no recorded instances of sexual aggression, homosexuality, lesbianism, exhibitionism, or sexual abuse of children attributable to reading or receiving erotic stimuli among several hundred participants in the 12 experiments reviewed."

As a result of exposure to erotica, the masturbatory or coital behavior of some individuals does, in fact, increase. For a few others, it decreases. The majority report no change in form or frequency of sexual activity after exposure to erotica. If the increased activity is masturbatory, it typically occurs among those individuals with established masturbatory habits or among those who would prefer an established sexual partner who happens not to be available. An increase in coital frequency following exposure to erotica generally occurs among sexually experienced persons with an established and available sexual partner.

In one study, middle-aged married couples reported that both frequency and variety of coital performance increased in the 24-hour period after they viewed erotic films, although there was no *overall* increase in sexual activity after viewing pornography. When there was an increase, it was short-lived, generally disappearing after the night the films were shown (M. Brown *et al.* 1976; Primeau 1977). Furthermore, following erotic exposure, people show greater tolerance toward others' sexual behavior than they did before, although their own standards do not change (Commission on Obscenity 1970). Subjects classifed as "prudes" (those "anti-sex" subjects who object to pornography) and "pornophiles" ("pro-sex") are aroused to an equal degree by erotic films. However, it is interesting to note that after viewing erotic material, there was increased sexual activity among the prudes, but not among the pornophiles (Fisher & Byrne 1976).

Certain physiological changes following a person's exposure to pornography have been recorded. For example, levels of urinary acid phosphatase have been noted to increase following sexual arousal (Barclay 1970). The rise is rather pronounced on the first day of exposure, but gradually drops with repeated viewing of the same material. With the presentation of new material after several days of exposure to the old, acid-phosphatase secretion again increases. People, especially males, appear to become bored with the same erotica, but show renewed interest in new material.

In summary, no one denies that the young are more vulnerable to what they read than those who are older, more sophisticated, and more critical. However, by extrapolating from Mayor Jimmy Walker's observation that no girl was ever ruined by a book, one can safely say that pornography has a negative effect only on the mind that was disordered to begin with.

As Gebhard *et al.* (1965) summed it up: "Pornography collections follow the preexisting interest of the collector. Men make the collections, collections do not make the men."

Does Pornography Have Any Value?

A surprising detail revealed by the report of the President's Commission is the purely educational value of pornography. From the evidence it appears that pornography can enlighten the ignorant—assuming, of course, that the information contained in it is factual—and that it fosters less inhibited attitudes toward sex. When a healthy and informed attitude toward sexuality exists, pornography is not a significant source of information about sexual behavior. But when sexual ignorance prevails, pornographic material does have a positive value for both adolescents and adults. Over half the adult patrons of hard-core pornographic films surveyed in one study reported that a significant factor underlying their attendance was a search for information (Berger *et al.* 1970; Winick 1970).

One might also argue that pornography does add some spice to what would otherwise be the completely dull and lackluster sex life of some unfortunate men. It is highly doubtful that perusing pornographic material will psychologically hinder such a man when he eventually attempts to establish a normal social relationship with a woman. In the meantime it is possible that obscene material serves as a harmless sexual release and that it might psychologically help those who are sexually repressed. There is little clinical or empirical evidence to prove either contention (Stokes *et al.* 1963). However, in a recent canvass of a large group of psychologists concerning their opinions of pornography and their experience with it, 66.5% stated that watching erotic films had been personally beneficial (Primeau 1977).

Who Are the Patrons of Pornography?

Approximately 85% of adult men and 70% of adult women in the United States have been exposed at some time during their lives to material of explicitly sexual content in either visual or written form. Individual exposure to erotica does not appear to be an ongoing phenomenon, however; that is, only about 40% of adult males and 26% of females report having seen graphic depictions of coitus during a given two-year period (Commission on Obscenity 1972).

Many factors appear related to the incidence of individual exposure to erotica. Men are more likely to be exposed to it than women, young adults more likely than older ones, and people with more education more likely than the less well educated. People who read a broad assortment of books, magazines, and newspapers and who see a general range of films search out and come upon more erotica than those whose exposure to these media is more limited. The more socially and politically active have greater exposure than those who are less active. Those who attend religious services often are less likely to have contact with erotic material than those whose attendance is less regular (Commission on Obscenity 1972).

Most Americans have their first taste of explicit sexual material during adolescence—about 75% before the age of 21. Adult males report retrospectively that their adolescent experience was not an isolated incident or two, but tended to be both extensive and intensive. Several recent studies of high-school and college-age youths confirmed that minors today have considerable exposure to erotica, much of it in preadolescent and adolescent years. More than 50% of the boys were so exposed by the age of 15, and the girls, a year or two later. By the time they reach the age of 18, roughly 80% of boys and 70% of girls have seen pictures of coitus or have read descriptions of it. Substantial numbers of adolescents have had more than a casual exposure, although the incidence does not in the least indicate an obsession with erotica (Commission on Obscenity 1972).

Exposure to specific sexual material, either in pictorial or written form, has been studied. More striking than the number of adults so exposed (85% of the men and 70% of the women) was the number of young people who had been. Between the ages of 15 and 20, 49% of the boys and 45% of the girls reported having seen as least five or more such depictions (Commission on Obscenity 1972).

Women in the past have not been as much interested in explicit erotic material as men. Or they have simply not seen or read as much of it, or claimed not to have an interest in it (Commission on Obscenity 1970; Kinsey *et al.* 1948, 1953). The evidence is growing, however, that women are increasingly interested in the same erotica that once was assumed to appeal only to men, and that they respond to it similarly (Athanasiou 1980). For example, men and women alike are sexually aroused by seeing movies of members of the opposite sex masturbate (Schmidt 1975). (They are not much turned on by watching members of their own sex masturbate; and men are actually repulsed by it.) Women as well as men reported physiological reactions to erotic material (Heiman 1975; Schmidt & Sigusch 1970; Schmidt *et al.* 1973); over 25% of both sexes experienced genital responses, for example. Male and female college students do not differ in their reactions to erotica, or the degree of arousal to it, whether the material is hard-core porno or a tender love story. Another investigation (Heiman 1975) shows that women have as vivid and self-arousing sexual fantasies as men do.

Patrons of so-called "adult" bookstores and cinemas are predominantly white, middle-class, middle-aged, married males. The men typically dress in business suits or neat casual attire; they usually attend the film alone, perhaps on an impulse while out shopping. Almost no one under 21 is observed in these establishments, even when it is legal for them to be there. The average patron appears to have had fewer than average sex-related experiences during adolescence, but to be more sexually oriented as an adult than the average male adult (Commission on Obscenity 1972).

Most "for-adults-only" books are written expressly for heterosexual males. But an increasing number are directed toward the male homosexual market and a small number for males with fetishistic tastes. Virtually none is intended exclusively for female consumption.

The college-educated, religiously inactive, and sexually experienced are more likely to be aroused by erotica than religiously active persons of less education and sexual experience. Not surprisingly, young persons are more likely to be aroused by erotica than older ones. In general, persons who are older, less well educated, and who have no great experience with erotica, and persons who are religiously active or who feel guilty about sex, are most likely to judge a given erotic stimulus as obscene (Commission on Obscenity 1972). A 15-day experiment using saturation exposure to erotica demonstrated that repeated exposure to such material resulted in a marked decrease in its capacity to generate sexual arousal and interest (Commission on Obscenity 1970).

Social scientists have long recognized that people with a sense of self-satisfaction feel secure enough to regulate their lives according to flexible rather than rigid rules. Self-satisfied people have been shown to respond favorably to pornography. Furthermore, as Athanasiou (1980) concludes, there is virtually no scientific evidence which indicates a causal connection between exposure to pornography and antisocial behavior. Exposure to erotica does not appear to present any significant danger to society.

Factors in Individual Judgments of Obscenity. One study, involving a large number of subjects, investigated the factors leading an individual to judge pictures or books obscene. These determinants appear related more to the individual's psychological makeup, occupation, and particular socioeconomic and educational milieu than to the sexual act seen or read about. The subjects of this study were asked to view two sets of photographs. One, of women in various poses, was of the type found in popular magazines; the other set had been confiscated by the police. The subjects were asked to rate the pictures according to their erotic properties and obscenity. Persons of lower socioeconomic status rated nudity as obscene, even if no genitalia were shown. They were more likely than subjects of higher socioeconomic and educational strata to regard any nude photo as being sexually exciting (Higgins & Katzman 1969).

Black-and-white photos were judged more obscene than color photos; pictures of poor photographic quality more obscene than those of higher quality; unattractive models more obscene than pretty ones, regardless of the pose; and erotic scenes in an indoor setting more obscene than those in an outdoor setting.

The reaction of sexual liberals and conservatives to the same erotic slides is interesting. Liberals considered the most arousing pictures to be also the most entertaining. Conservatives rated them as being the least entertaining and the most offensive. Both groups were sexually aroused, so the conclusion can be drawn that sexual guilt aroused in the conservatives was converted into disgust. Sexual guilt limits a person's ability to respond positively to pornographic material. Not only did the conservatives more frequently rate erotic stories and pictures as pornographic than the liberals did, but they also favored government censorship, which the liberals opposed (Byrne *et al.* 1974; Ogren 1974; Wallace & Wehmer 1972).

Aggression and violence are known to stimulate sexual arousal (Barclay 1971b). Rape, for example, is sometimes fantasized by both sexes as a means of becoming sexually aroused. When a film depicting a girl being assaulted by several men was shown to a group of men and women, both sexes were quite aroused. Yet the film had the concomitant negative effects of arousing guilt feelings in the men and a sense of helplessness in the women (Schmidt 1975).

The researcher's own attitude toward obscenity has been shown to exert a significant influence on the judgment of his/her subjects as to what is or is not obscene. Researchers with sexual conflicts involving obscenity will unconsciously inject their bias into any instructions given their subject population. If they project the view, consciously or unconsciously, that sex is bad, more of the subjects will rate the pictorial matter of the investigation as obscene than if the attitude is projected that sex is pleasurable.

No one denies that genuine pornography and obscenity exist. However, apart from their presenting sex often unrealistically, and sometimes as something ugly, the chief objection must lie in their literary, theatrical, or pictorial worthlessness, rather than in their power to corrupt. Classics scholars point out that ancient pornography was created by the most enlightened and cultured of the community, and was the source of pleasure and delight. The difference between it and American porno is that most of the latter is cheaply done, debasing, and vulgar, created to turn a fast buck ("The Porno Plague" 1976).

Any legal curbs on pornography and obscenity, however, imply the imposition of censorship—an eventuality that any thinking person would wish to avoid. As early as 1644, John Milton—a Puritan among Puritans—addressed Parliament in opposition to censorship, which he regarded as the handmaiden of tyranny. He argued that reading everything one wishes is the means of gaining knowledge of the good and evil, the ugly and beautiful, that flourish indiscriminately in the world. Corrupting forces, he said, are everywhere present, and they can be met only by building up an inner discipline and *the ability of rational choice*. Censorship serves no such purpose.

But even some of those who oppose censorship object to the apparent no-holds-barred attitude in the current wave of both hard- and soft-core porno. They see in it a brutalizing of sexuality and a dehumanizing of both sexes, particularly of women. While they do not feel that they have the right to interfere with what others do in private, they *do* object to what they see as an invasion of their own privacy in the blatant porno encountered on all sides. They fear that if some sort of brake is not applied, censorship (which they seriously oppose) is inevitably not far behind ("The Porno Plague" 1976).

"If the purpose of pornography is to excite sexual desire," says Malcolm Muggeridge (formerly editor of *Punch*), "it is unnecessary for the young, inconvenient for the middle-aged, and unseemly for the old" ("The New Pornography" 1965). No one admires or wishes to encourage pornography (except, of course, the writers or purveyors thereof). But the alternative to it is censorship—which would mean that the Song of Solomon is in as much danger of oblivion as a magazine called *Screw*.

Fetishism

Fetishism is defined as a psychosexual abnormality in which an individual's sexual impulses become fixated on a sexual symbol, a fetish, that is substituted for the basic love object. Fetishes are not limited to articles of female attire and do not include sexually stimulating objects such as vibrators (Caprio 1955; DSM III 1980). Usually articles that are the focus of the fetish are fondled, gazed upon, or made part of masturbatory activities. They may be articles of underclothing, hats, shoes (especially high-heeled shoes), or gloves. (For some unexplained reason, rubber has a very strong appeal to the fetishist.) Or the object may be a bodily part of the opposite sex, such as hair, hands, thighs, feet, ears, or eyes. The fetishist is almost always male, and in acquiring his sex symbols he often commits burglary or even assault (Karpman 1954).

Gebhard (1976) has defined a practical continuum of fetishistic behavior. At one end are persons who express a slight preference for a fetish object; next are those holding a "strong preference"; next, those who must have the fetish to function sexually; and last, those who substitute the fetish for a human sexual partner. Gebhard believes that statistical normalcy ends and deviance begins approximately at the point where strong preference is expressed.

Fetishism is actually an intensification of the normal tendencies existing in almost all people. Men, for example, find certain objects more sexually exciting than others—sweaters, hair, breasts, buttocks, or legs. They often jokingly refer to themselves as being "breast men," or "leg men," or "fanny men." Women are frequently attracted by a male's hairy chest, buttocks, or broad shoulders. It is therefore understandable that the symbol of the basic love object can become the love object itself in certain personality structures.

The fetishist obtains sexual gratification from a particular object or bodily part because of its unique relationship to some childhood conditioning. The particular fetish somehow became associated with sexual excitement or with the love and acceptance the fetishist once received from a meaningful person, such as the mother or perhaps a former schoolteacher (Caprio 1955; DSM III 1980). Childhood experiences and habits, then, reinforced by later unsatisfactory interpersonal relationships, are the most frequent reasons for seeking comfort and sexual pleasure in objects rather than in people (Dickes 1970).

Two fetishistic patterns that deserve special attention are kleptomania and pyromania. **Kleptomania** is compulsive stealing, usually of an object that is of no value to the thief except for its sexual symbolism or its association with sexual gratification. The kleptomaniac is typically an emotionally disturbed woman beset with feelings of being unloved and unwanted (Alexander 1965b). Occasionally the thief is a boy or young man who takes women's undergarments (particularly panties) in order to achieve erotic stimulation through the symbolic nature of the clothing, and through the excitement and suspense of the act of stealing (Coleman 1972).

Pyromania is compulsive firesetting that often has sexual overtones. The relationship between fire and sex is apparent from such terms as "in heat" and "becoming hot" for someone. The pyromaniac typically experiences mounting tension, restlessness, and an urge for motion as the first symptoms of an oncoming act of pyromania. Sexual excitement and gratification in the form of tension release usually occur as the person— always a man and usually young—sets the fire or watches the early stages of the conflagration (Robbins *et al.* 1969).

Once orgasm occurs, the individual usually feels guilty and frequently steps forward to help extinguish the fire (Coleman 1972; Gold 1962). Many pyromaniacs can give no reason for their impulse to set fires; others claim revenge as their motive. A large number of these fetishists are psychotic (Stiller 1964), and about half are mentally defective or of subnormal intelligence. The nonpsychotic arsonist is usually acting in a framework of frustration, anger, loneliness, and desperation (Robbins *et al.* 1969).

Frottage

Frottage is the act of obtaining sexual pleasure from rubbing or pressing against the desired person, and the person who performs such acts is called a frotteur. Such conduct often passes unnoticed, as it may be performed in crowded public places, such as a subway or elevator. The dynamics behind this behavior are probably similar to those of exhibitionism. At worst, the frotteur is an unappealing, sexually inadequate man who would probably be frightened of the opportunity for sexual intercourse with an adequate, adult woman.

Saliromania

Saliromania is a sexual disorder found primarily in men characterized by the desire to damage or soil the body or clothes of a woman or a representation of a woman. These men frequently have marked feelings of sexual inadequacy or associate strong aggressive impulses with sex, the latter frequently being a consequence of unreasonable guilt feelings surrounding normal desires. The hostility often is expressed symbolically by the throwing of acid, tar, ink, or the like on a strange woman or a statue; by cutting and tearing women's clothing; or by defacing or disfiguring a painting or statue. The beheading a few years ago of the famous mermaid statue in Copenhagen's harbor and the disfigurement of Michelangelo's *Pièta* were very likely acts of such disordered men. Saliromaniacs usually become sexually excited to the point of erection and perhaps ejaculation during their acts of destruction.

Gerontosexuality

Gerontosexuality is a variance in which a young person has a distinct preference for an elderly person as the object of sexual interest. The economic considerations of a marriage between a person who is quite old and one who is very young may well be more important than the sexual aspects (C. Allen 1961). However, when there is an actual sexual preference for a person of advanced years, there may be an indication of a sexual desire for a parent substitute.

Incest

Incest is sexual intercourse between two persons, married or not, who are too closely related by blood or affinity to be legally married. Laws relating to incest bear little uniformity from state to state and are often highly confusing (Sherwin 1961). When marriage is involved, for instance, certain states have legislated separate penalties for the marriage itself and for the sex act.

Incest does not often come before the courts. Of those convicted of sex offenses, only 6% or 7% are charged with incest (Cutter 1963). While the number of reported cases of incest in the United States is very low in the general population each year, the act of incest nonetheless probably occurs far more frequently than statistics reveal or the average citizen realizes. Since it is an intrafamilial experience, it is difficult for an outsider to detect; and the shame and guilt felt by family members often cause them to hide and deny it (Cavallin 1966). The offense is more likely to occur in families of low socioeconomic levels than in others (Cutter 1963).

The person who commits incest against children usually has a sordid home background, is preoccupied with sex, drinks heavily, and is often unemployed, giving ample opportunity to be at home with the children. The incest offender with adults is typically "conservative, moralistic, restrained, religiously devout, traditional and uneducated" (Gebhard *et al.* 1965; Rubin 1966a).

The most common form of incest is probably brother-sister, especially in poor families where children of both sexes must share a bedroom. The next most common form, and the type most frequently reported to legal sources, is father-daughter incest (Coleman 1972; Bernstein 1979). In many instances of adult father-daughter incest, the daughter is a voluntary participant. Sometimes the daughter does not report the relationship because she craves parental attention and affection and interprets her father's advances as being an indication of love or caring. In other cases, the daughter may remain quiet because she fears retaliation or because of fears that the family unit will be disrupted. The father in such relationships is often experiencing sexual maladjustment with his wife. He is usually in his 30s or early 40s and he frequently has unconscious homosexual strivings, psychopathic tendencies, and noticeable paranoid traits (Cavallin 1966; Bernstein 1979).

Brownmiller (1975) suggests that the incidence of father-daughter incest, which she calls "father rape," is impossible to calculate because of the silence imposed by the patriarchal system of sexual private property, wherein women are chattel and children "wholly owned subsidiaries." The Code of Hammurabi, for instance, merely banished from the city a man who "knew" his own daughter; the penalty was death if he took the virginity of another man's child. Mother-son incest appears to be rare; its incidence may be somewhat higher than is suspected, however, because neither party is likely to report it.

Many psychotherapists believe that a child is less affected by actual incest than by a parent's seductive behavior that never culminates in any manifest sexual activity. One theory is that actual incest will not have such a deleterious effect on the child because parental approval is implicit. The child, therefore, will have little residual guilt—except later, perhaps, when he/she grows older and reads and listens to the opinions of others in the matter of incest (R. E. L. Masters 1963).

Incest is not universally a taboo. Most cultures, however, both primitive and modern, are of the opinion that family and subculture survival depends upon expansion through marriage outside the immediate family. Only recently has the interest of scientists been directed toward this ancient problem, although novelists, poets, and scholars have often probed the subject and have contributed much to our understanding of it (R. E. L. Masters 1963). Sexologists are now attempting to determine the real and measurable effects of incest on the contemporary world, without regard to the biases of ancient societies.

In Japan about 5% of all marriages are between first cousins. A study of children conceived or born to these marriages, in comparison to other Japanese children, revealed a significantly above-average fetal loss and neonatal mortality; surviving children are smaller physically, have lower IQs, develop more slowly in auditory and visual acuity, and are slower to talk and walk (Schull & Neel 1965).

Mate-Swapping

Mate-swapping (also called **swinging**) has been defined as "the sexual exchange of partners among two or more married couples" (R. R. Bell 1971b). That the phenomenon is not as rare as most people believe can be judged by the estimate that in 1970 approximately 1 million Americans regularly engaged in mate-swapping (Bartell 1971). Fang (1976), however, showed that swinging is on the decline, perhaps well on its way to becoming an outmoded form of sexual diversion. The *Redbook* survey of 100,000 women (Levin 1975) revealed that less than 4% (3600) admitted to having engaged in group sex. And this figure held whether the women were married, single, or divorced, or separated. Other estimates have indicated that 1% to 5% of Americans have engaged in mate-swapping and that as many as 1% to 2% have done so on a regular basis (Karlen 1980).

Because people tend to become bored by routine sex with one partner, some social scientists think an acceptable solution to the need for novelty must be found. Prostitution was once thought to fulfill the need for novelty for men without threat to the marriage, because the risk of romantic involvement with a prostitute was slim (K. Davis 1966). Later, pornography was regarded as serving the same purpose (Polsky 1967). More recently, according to these behaviorists, mate-swapping has been adopted as the means of providing sexual variety, allegedly without damage to the marital relationship; the big difference is that the woman's sexual needs are taken into account as well as her partner's (Denfeld & Gordon 1970). Indeed, with the development of improved contraceptive methods and with greater knowledge concerning VD and issues of personal hygiene, women can now indulge in their sexual desires with more freedom and pleasure than ever before (Karlen 1980; Rosen 1971). Subjective assessment of marital happiness revealed no difference between swingers and nonswingers. There was no difference in the reported personal habits of the two groups, nor in their emotional health, although childhood relationships with parents had been less gratifying for swingers than for nonswingers (Gilmartin & Kusisto 1973).

Mate-swappers frown on an extramarital affair unless all the marriage partners involved are fully aware of it. "Swingers" believe that the real danger to marriage in extramarital sex lies in the risk of romantic involvement with another person and the dishonesty inherent in a secret affair. Swappers maintain they engage in swinging to improve and support their marriage as well as to add sexual variety and fun to their lives. Issues of sexual jealousy and risks of emotional attachment to other sexual partners certainly exist when mate-swapping occurs, but many swingers are apparently able to take care of or resolve these concerns (Karlen 1980; Rosen 1971).

Most mate-swappers appear to be conservative, conventional, hard-working individuals who lead normal or ordinary lives in other respects. While quite unconventional swinging clubs or circles do exist, most mate-swappers are found within the more traditional occupations such as shopowners, housewives, physicians, or stockbrokers. The evidence suggests that swingers just tend to be more interested in and desirous of sexual activity than nonswingers (Karlen 1980). In most cases, the husband is the one who first suggests mate-swapping. But once the idea is proposed, the wife offers less resistance to the prospect than the husband does. Conclusions drawn from what little research has been done into the psychodynamics of mate-swapping suggest that swingers are not sexual perverts; nor are they mentally or emotionally disturbed (Karlen 1980; Rosen 1971).

Klismaphilia

Klismaphilia refers to erotic pleasure derived from taking enemas. It usually develops early in life as a result of a child's discovery of an erotic sensitivity in the lower bowels while being given an enema. Since an enema is typically administered by a caring person, quite likely the mother, it is understandable that the klismaphiliac may continue to associate it with being cared for by the mother (Denko 1976). Little research has been done on this subject.

Variance in Degree and Strength of Sexual Drive

Nymphomania

Nymphomania refers to the behavior of a woman whose abnormally voracious sexual hunger overshadows all her other activities. It is sometimes, although rarely, the outgrowth of certain physical disorders. More often the basis is psychological (Auerback 1968).

Characteristically, true nymphomania involves an uncontrollable sexual desire that must be fulfilled when aroused, no matter what the consequences. The sexual craving is unquenchable regardless of the number of orgasms and the pleasure received from them. Nymphomania is compulsive sexual behavior in the true sense of the term, driving the victim to irrational and self-defeating activities with all the stresses and problems that any compulsion causes (Ellis & Sagarin 1964).

It must be stressed, however, that few words in our language are as misapplied as "nymphomania." It is bandied about by the man on the street; it is a popular theme in grade-B films and a frequent topic of discussion in fraternity houses. Everyone from the minister to the mailman claims to know at least a half-dozen such women. Yet, as a sexual disorder, nymphomania is quite rare.

Most men are sexually fulfilled after one orgasm and care very little about continuing sexual activity afterwards. Sexually mature women, however, may not be satisfied with one climax. (Many women during masturbation may experience 5 to 20 orgasms, or more, during one episode [Masters & Johnson 1962, 1965a].) Men who do not understand this normal sexual need are likely to believe they are involved with a sensual freak who refuses to recognize the end of a good thing. Such men often call a perfectly normal woman a nymphomaniac simply because she happens to have a healthy sexual appetite.

There is yet another type of man who, through ignorance, threat to masculinity, or, perhaps, cruelty, accuses his partner of nymphomania because she wants sex more often than he does. Because his own desire is satisfied by coitus two or three times a week, he is amazed that a woman might want it six or seven times a week, which is just as normal a level of sexual need as his own. If such a man has feelings of inferiority and uncertainty about his own masculinity, he is likely to be so threatened by such a woman that he must find some way to fight her. Hence he calls her a nymphomaniac; by branding her "abnormal," he preserves his self-image of "normalcy" by implication. The consensus of psychotherapists and marriage counselors is that most cases of alleged nymphomania that they see are actually not that at all. They are, rather, cases in which there is a pronounced and disturbing difference between husband and wife in strength of sex drive, both within the realm of normalcy in their sexual needs.

Psychological explanations for genuine nymphomania are that the woman may be attempting to compensate for sexual deprivation in adolescence and early adulthood, or that she is perhaps seeking a means for release of excessive emotional tensions. She may have fears of frigidity or latent homosexuality, which she seeks to disprove through her nymphomania, or she may be using the opposite sex as an unconscious means of revenge against her father (Thorpe *et al.* 1961). Probably the most frequent cause is an inordinate need to be loved and accepted, involving a carryover of early childhood emphasis on the value of the physical body as a tool to gain attention, recognition, and acceptance. A therapeutic program through which the patient can reevaluate herself is about the only successful method of treating nymphomania (J. L. McCary 1972).

Satyriasis

Satyriasis is an exaggerated desire for sexual gratification on the part of a man. Causative factors in this condition parallel those in nymphomania, or it may be an unconscious attempt to deny castration, or to reinforce a faltering self-view regarding masculinity and adequacy (Auerback 1968). One investigator has reported on a case of satyriasis in which a 24-year-old male stated he had sexual intercourse three times a day and in addition masturbated three or four times each day. The young man also experienced nocturnal emissions several times a week and had sexual fantasies that occasionally caused him to ejaculate. Reportedly, he also engaged in variant sexual activities, including frottage and voyeurism (Moore 1980).

The public does not show as much concern over men who are "oversexed" as it does over similarly "afflicted" women. As might be expected, this disparity in attitudes has its roots in the traditional sexual role of females. Women's deviation from the passive role assigned them by society is likely to be more noticeable. The incidence of true satyriasis and nymphomania is about the same—both are very rare disorders—and each can be successfully treated with psychotherapy.

Promiscuity

Promiscuity is generally defined as the participation in sexual intercourse with many people on a more or less casual basis. A person whose own sexual activity is limited in frequency and restricted in expression tends to condemn the more liberal sexual behavior of others as promiscuity. Thus, the term is often used more as a derogatory evaluation than as a widely recognized scientific label.

Studies involving personality and family backgrounds of promiscuous women indicate that they have generally made an uneven and perhaps incomplete progression to physical, emotional, intellectual, and social maturity. The investigations show that these women, before they left their parents' home, participated minimally in such group interaction as sports and other extracurricular activities. They neither entered into organized group experiences nor accepted the responsibility for their own behavior. Characteristically they blamed parents, husbands, and friends for their own failures and shortcomings. Their promiscuity was not caused by a strong sex drive; rather, it resulted from their attempt to use sex to cope with other emotional problems (Lion *et al.* 1945).

To a large extent, men follow the same behavioral patterns in their promiscuity (which has been called "Don Juanism"). In the case histories of almost all the men studied, promiscuous behavior proved to be the result of feelings of inadequacy, emotional conflicts, and other personality problems. There was no evidence that their sex drive, as such, was stronger than that of average men (Kirkendall 1961b; Safier 1949).

Several authors have pointed out that promiscuity in men and women is becoming more difficult to define and, as a result, a less meaningful term (Diamond & Karlen 1980; Sandler, Meyerson, & Kinder 1980). Changing standards of sexuality and great variety of individual differences have contributed to the difficulty in determining how much sexual activity constitutes excessive or promiscuous behavior. To be sure, there are individuals who engage compulsively in a variety of sexual encounters. But such activity may not be appropriately deemed hyperactive using as criteria arbitrary standards of "normal" sexual frequency. As Sandler, Myerson, and Kinder (1980) suggest, perhaps a more accurate criterion of promiscuity would be the degree to which frequent sexual activity harms other aspects of social functioning.

Prostitution

Prostitution is the participation in sexual activity for monetary rewards. Two elements are essential: First, sexual favors are offered for an immediate return of money or valuables; second, the selection of partners is relatively indiscriminate (Gebhard 1973).

Kinsey and his associates (Kinsey *et al.* 1948) found that 69% of white males had had some experience with prostitutes. However, over the past several decades there apparently has been a steady decrease in the number of professional prostitutes in America and in the frequency with which men consort with them. Supporting this viewpoint, Kinsey's 1948 study revealed that the first coital experience of some 20% of its college-educated sample was with a prostitute; in a comparative 1967 study, this figure had fallen to an estimated 2% to 7% (Rubin 1969a). As is typical of data-gathering in the social sciences, the part of the country in which the subjects live and other factors, such as religion and age, must be carefully considered before accurate comparisons can be attempted. For example, in 1968 Packard reported a 4% nationwide incidence among college men of premarital intercourse with prostitutes at least once; and in 1970 Kaats and Davis found a 14% incidence at the University of Colorado. Yet in another 1970 study involving a similar group in a large southwestern state-supported university, Frede found that 42% of her sample had experienced premarital coitus with prostitutes. Recent evidence indicates that college-age men are more likely to have sexual relations with young women in the context of an emotional relationship, while married middle-aged men are becoming the most frequent customers of prostitutes (Boles 1980).

Men visit prostitutes for many reasons. They may want variety. They may be too shy, too embarrassed, or too physically handicapped to find heterosexual outlets elsewhere. They may need to gratify variant sex urges, such as S/M or fetishistic tendencies, and can pay to have them satisfied. They may wish to have sexual activity without the obligations associated with less anonymous intercourse. Or perhaps their wives are pregnant, or a child has been born and they feel in competition with it for the wife's affection. In associating with prostitutes, however, men often forget that, since prostitution is illegal, they run the risk of blackmail, arrest, and scandal, to say nothing of the dangers of contracting VD or of being robbed.

The business of prostitution has traditionally operated in three ways. There is the brothel, a house in which several prostitutes live, presided over by an older woman (the madam), who has enough money and contacts to run the house. Second is the call-girl operation; the prostitute maintains her own apartment and her customers are sent to her by the operation's management, who do some screening of the clientele. Her status is therefore considered higher than that of the house girl. She is however, discouraged from making contacts of her own because she might not turn over the money earned. Third is the independent prostitute who depends on certain contacts for her clients or customers—hotel employees, taxi drivers, her pimp, and "the book." Books containing the names and phone numbers of long lists of men who are known to visit prostitutes are sold for large sums to women in the profession.

Very few women become prostitutes because they are highly sexed and actually enjoy most of the sexual experiences prostitution affords them. Most are not sexually responsive to their clients, although they may very well enjoy sex with their men friends or husbands (Gebhard 1969). Some become prostitutes because of a neurotic need to punish and degrade themselves, or as an act of rebellion against parents and society. Some prostitutes are mentally deficient, emotionally disturbed, lazy, or otherwise unable to engage in regular employment. However, the vast majority are motivated by money. Quick, easy money, and a great deal of it—or so they expect. Sometimes the pot of gold materializes; sometimes it does not. Pimps, corrupt city officials, and blackmailers often lurk in the shadows. A great many women enter the profession on a temporary basis. Once their financial situation improves, they return to their work as a salesperson, teacher, secretary, or housewife (Benjamin 1961). The more one reads about the types of women who become prostitutes, and why, the less valid any generalization becomes (Pierson & D'Antonio 1974).

The prostitute's attitude toward her clients is similar to that of anyone providing a service to customers: She likes some, dislikes others, and feels indifferent toward still others. Over 66% of those surveyed by Gebhard (1969) professed to have no regrets over entering the profession. Prostitutes are, however, subject to certain occupational hazards; about 66% of the Gebhard sampling, as an example, had contracted syphilis or, more commonly, gonorrhea. Yet contact with prostitutes accounts for only about 5% of VD cases in this country, despite their many customers (J. James 1976). In fact, uneducated, sexually active teen-agers are more likely to be transmitters of VD than prostitutes (Townley 1980).

Contrary to what many think, the incidence of lesbianism among prostitutes is not high. Neither is there a high incidence of drug use or addiction. Over 60% of Gebhard's sample (1969) had had no homosexual experience whatever, and only 24% had had pleasurable lesbian contacts 10 times or more. A scant 9% of the sample had ever experimented with or been addicted to hard drugs.

The male prostitute generally serves a male clientele, although from time to time brothels have been established for the pleasure of women. The award-winning film *Midnight Cowboy* is an excellent characterization of a young man attempting to earn money from sexual services to women. (A man's failure in this profession is no doubt attributable to his physiological inability to function beyond the point of sexual satiation, whereas a woman can function endlessly despite the absence of any erotic desire.) The "gigolo" is often thought of as a male prostitute; but he is usually employed more as a companion or escort than for sexual services (Hoffman 1972).

Some male prostitutes ("hustlers") are homosexual; most are not. A homophile seeking a male prostitute wants a "straight" partner. A hustler therefore attempts to magnify his masculine image by wearing a leather jacket, boots, and skin-tight bluejeans (Hoffman 1972). He allows himself to be picked up by men, usually older ones, in order to make some easy money. The hustler allows his male client to perform fellatio on him, for which privilege he receives money. There is rarely more to the relationship. It has been estimated (R. Lloyd 1976), and police do not dispute the figure, that some 100,000 boys aged 13 to 16 are actively engaged in homosexual prostitution, a sizeable number of their customers being older married men. These boys are, for the most part, runaways from working-class or welfare homes.

Rape

In the general consensus, **forcible rape** is defined as sexual intercourse forced on an unconsenting woman. The legal definition of rape includes cases in which the man or woman consents to intercourse only because of fear, force, or fraud, or who is incapable of rational consent because of mental retardation. Rape can also be charged if the woman is asleep, is unconscious from drugs or alcohol, or is tricked into coitus by a man pretending to be her husband (Czinner 1970). In legal theory, a man cannot be accused of forcing sexual union on his wife, as permanent consent to coitus has been considered part of the marriage contract (Brownmiller 1975). Recently, however, the problem of marital rape has come to the forefront of societal attention as some women have pressed legal charges against their husbands for rape. While marital rape is usually not reported, authorities estimate there may be as many as 2 million offenses per year (Groth & Gary 1981).

Statutory rape is another category of criminal intercourse. It implies coitus with a partner below the age of consent, which is usually 18. A man can be convicted and imprisoned on statutory rape charges even though the girl appeared old enough or lied about her age. Most rape convictions are based on statutory grounds (Slovenko 1971b).

Women can be convicted of rape if they are an accessory in forcing coitus on another woman, or in persuading an underaged girl to have intercourse. Women have also been convicted, although extremely rarely, of statutory rape involving an underaged boy and of forcible rape (even more rarely) involving an adult man (Oliver 1965). In every state rape is a felony.

Rape victims are usually between the ages of 18 and 25, although some are young children and old women. The male rapist is typically 20–24 years old, from a low-income, culturally deprived background, and of dull-normal intelligence. The convicted male rapist scores significantly lower on IQ tests than persons convicted of other violent crimes (Ruff *et al.* 1976). He is likely to have had emotionally unstable parents who imposed little supervision on him in his youth, or a weak, often alcoholic, father. The majority of rapists, however, come from broken homes. The male rapist is usually emotionally immature and frequently physically unattractive (Gebhard *et al.* 1965; Rubin 1966a). Rapists are strong believers in the double standard and place great value on a woman's virginity (Griffin 1976). A high percentage (30%–40%) are either married at the time they commit rape or have been married (50%–60%) at some time during their adulthood (Rada 1977). Others have several girlfriends and what appear to be satisfactory, nonviolent relationships with them. Nevertheless, most rapists report experiencing difficulties in being able to relate to women and in being able to form meaningful interpersonal interactions in general. Rapists often express feelings of inadequacy and low self-esteem (Pepitone-Rockwell 1980).

The histories of many male rapists reveal a wide variety of teen-age sexual offenses. They may progress from simple voyeurism to cruising in an automobile seeking solitary females before whom to exhibit their genitals and masturbate (Rada 1975). Alcohol plays a central role in sexual assault. With unusual consistency, the various studies of rape show that approximately 50% of rapists were drinking at the time of the attack (Rada 1975). Alcohol may serve any of several purposes—to give the rapist courage, to remove intellectual control over behavior, or to provide an after-the-fact excuse.

These generalizations do not rule out the possibility that a highly intelligent, otherwise respectable, handsome young person might become a rapist, because such is sometimes the case. One recent study of forcible rape (Amir 1971) suggests that rapists cannot be categorized as having a particular mental disturbance, nor can they be considered invariably more emotionally disturbed than comparable nonrapist control groups.

Rapists do, however, have a greater tendency to express violence and rage than other people do. Rape typically has little to do with uncontrollable lust. The rapist is motivated primarily by the wish to dominate and by hostility and aggression toward his victims (Groth & Gary 1981). The assault victim is often chosen by chance, and bears the brunt of the rapist's need at that moment to vent feelings of violence. Sometimes rape is committed almost incidentally in the course of another crime. Male homosexual rape in prison may not necessarily be associated with great sexual need. It may be an attempt to reaffirm the prisoner power structure. The prisoner may seek to reaffirm the sagging image of his masculinity by proving his ability to control others by force (Money & Bohmer 1980; Sagarin 1976).

Women's outrage at the ever-mounting incidence of rape is reflected in Susan Brownmiller's *Against Our Will* (1975), a thoughtful, carefully researched historical and sociological analysis of the crime. The author's contention is that rape is essentially an act of aggression, control, and degradation aimed at proving male superiority, not merely a random sexual gesture of a disturbed person. Historically, rape has been considered a "natural concomitant to war, the victor even in wars of religion exercising it as his reward. ..." (Brownmiller 1975). During riots, pogroms, and revolutions rape has also been considered the inevitable by-product of the hatreds that incited the clashes. Rules of chivalry in the Middle Ages were selective. High-born ladies must never be touched; peasant women were fair game. Being physically weaker than the male, woman from the beginning of time has accepted the domination of one man in exchange for protection from wholesale rape. Those accepting the burden of her protection— husband, brother, father, or clan—assumed it in exchange for her acceptance of chastity and monogamy, impositions of fidelity historically not required of men. Woman thus became chattel. The crime of rape was not committed against her; it was committed against the property of her protector.

The incidence of rape is increasing faster than any other crime of violence in America (FBI 1970). In 1974 well over 50,000 such assaults were reported, and it is generally thought that, for every reported case, between 5 and 10 go unreported. The incidence is higher in America than in other countries. In 1970 the incidence of forcible rape and assault to commit rape was 36 per 100,000 women. By comparison, incidence in Norway was less than one; in England, 3; in Poland, 7; in Japan, 12; and in Turkey, 14 (MacDonald 1973). More than half of all forcible rapes take place on weekends. From two to three times more rapes occur between 10 p.m. on Saturday and 4 a.m. on Sunday than at any other time of the week.

Group or gang rape (two or more rapists) has been estimated to comprise up to 70% of all rape cases (Steen & Price 1977). In Denver, 18.5% of such attacks were group rapes; in Philadelphia, 43%; in Toronto, 50%; in Denmark, 16%; and in Finland, 66%. Gang rape frequently occurs when a member of a group seeks ego-enhancement from his fellow members by challenging them to join him in a rape assault. In the Mentality of the Mob, there is safety in numbers; one can also shift responsibility for the attack from oneself onto the group (MacDonald 1974). Gang rape is planned ahead about 90% of the time (although the rapists do not usually know the victim), and the attacks of lone rapists, almost 60%. Curiously, three or more boys 15–19 years old are the most common perpetrators of gang rape, yet for solitary offenders that age bracket has the lowest incidence of rape (MacDonald 1974).

In the past, in some cultures, rape was considered so debasing to the family's image that the female victim was often beaten or murdered by her father or husband. Or, feeling that she had brought disgrace on her house, the victim committed suicide. Strong vestiges of the attitude that a woman is somehow responsible for her rape persist, and are reflected in the law and in judicial procedures following rape. Sexual assault is the only crime of violence in which the female victim must defend her part in it. Only recently have strenuous efforts been made to change this position. Nevertheless, the outrage of the woman's family (perhaps directed at her herself), the often inhumane attitude of the personnel in the hospital where she seeks treatment, and the humiliating questions posed by police investigators cause many rape victims not to press charges after the attack. The greatest injustice occurs, however, in the witness box, where the victim is frequently twisted into the posture of a defendant by the defending counsel: "She asked for it"; "She is of loose moral character anyway"; "She didn't fight hard enough." (One defense lawyer demanded of a one-armed woman raped at gunpoint why she hadn't tried to grab for the man's gun). The jury usually believes in much of the rape mythology and is often most reluctant to convict (Brownmiller 1975). Not infrequently, the victim is shattered emotionally by the treatment accorded her on the witness stand.

The respectability of the woman involved in rape cases has a curious effect on the public's attribution of blame. People's basic inclination is to believe in a just world; if something pleasant or unpleasant happens to someone, that person deserves it because he/she is intrinsically good or evil or because he/she must have done something specifically and directly to bring about the event (Lerner 1965). Thus, if disaster occurs and the victim is a respectable person, more fault is attributed to him or her than to someone less respected. In one study, rape victims were described as virgins, married women, or divorcees. It was hypothesized and confirmed that, since married women and virgins are considered more respectable than divorcees, the subjects would attribute more fault for the rape to the married women and virgins than to divorcees. The more respectable person is considered more likely to cause her own misfortune (by encouraging the man), because she did not deserve the misfortune owing to her intrinsically good character (Jones & Aronson 1973).

There are some grossly misleading myths about rape. The most classic is that all women secretly want to be raped, that they frequently provoke the assault. This fiction serves to ease the rapist's guilt feelings, of course. Another rapist may find pleasure in the vision of himself as a James Bond personality, whose great sexual power converts a resisting woman into a sexually satiated, purring kitten. But mythology it all is; statistics in the files of the Federal Commission on Crimes of Violence show that only 4% of reported rapes involve any provocative behavior on the woman's part.

As was pointed out earlier, men are by no means exempt from rape. Prison rape is seen as epidemic by penal authorities (Money & Bohmer 1980). One such authority commented:

> Virtually every slightly built young man is sexually approached within a day or two after his admission to prison. Many ... are repeatedly raped by gangs of inmates. Others, because of the threat of gang rape, seek protection by entering into a homosexual relationship with an individual tormentor. [Brownmiller 1975]

He added that, once the youth has been raped, that reputation follows him for the rest of his sentence, wherever he may be transferred. Many of these youths return to the outside world full of shame and hatred.

Every major U.S. city now has a rape crisis center to which victims may turn. These centers provide personal counseling, information on medical and legal procedures, and advice on rape prevention. The centers attempt, as well, to help make the victim's contact with hospital and police a more positive experience (Kollias & Tucker 1974).

Participants involved in training program designed to improve police investigations of rape. (Wide World Photos)

Personal counseling can help a victim deal with her reactions—both acute and long term—to rape. Acute reactions include physical injury (often serious), muscular tension, and gastrointestinal and urinary disturbances. Among the psychological reactions are severe anxiety, fear, and depression. In the long term, the victim may seek to escape by changing her residence; and she may suffer from recurring nightmares or exhibit phobic behavior (Burgess 1974). To avoid rape, women are advised (Kollias & Tucker 1974; Pepitone-Rockwell 1980) to observe the following precautions:

To carry a whistle so they can use it to attract attention if they are bothered

To own an attentive pet or watchdog

To exercise discretion in telephone directory listings of name and address

Not to go out alone on dark city streets

To walk in the middle of a sidewalk rather than close to building or curb where someone might be lurking

To avoid deserted areas, such as abandoned buildings and alleys

To ride a bus rather than a subway, and to hire or hail taxis only from a recognized company

To drive with windows up and doors locked

To lock the car when it is parked

Not to get into an elevator alone with a man or let a stranger into their apartments or homes for any reason

To use security locks on windows or doors in their apartments or homes

In order to avoid rape, women are advised to think through potential resistance methods they might use. Women can take courses in self-defense and assertiveness training to develop physical skills and self-confidence and thereby help reduce their vulnerability to rape. Women who are more self-assured and who take measures to prevent rape may thwart a potential rapist by not appearing to be weak, available, or easy prey (Pepitone-Rockwell 1980).

When attacked by a rapist a woman must decide whether to submit or resist. If severe bodily harm or her life is threatened by gun, knife, or sheer brawn, she may decide to submit. However, recent evidence indicates that a woman is more likely to escape if she actively resists her attacker. While fighting back may increase her chances for bruises or other minor injuries, a woman who resists does not appear at any greater risk of significant physical injuries than a woman who submits ("Active Rape Resistance" 1980). Certainly if a woman decides to resist, she should go about it as vigorously as possible. She should scream loud and long. (Someone suggests that shouting "Fire!" brings people to attention more quickly than calling for help.) She should kick the attacker in the groin or grab his testicles and squeeze as hard as possible. His reaction to severe pain will make him loosen his grip, giving her time to escape. If she cannot get at his genitals, she should attack his eyes. For instance, if she is pinned down she might place her hands gently at the sides of his face, pretending that she is going along with intercourse; then at the right time poke her thumbs in his eyes. She should bite, claw, and hit with any heavy object available. Squeamishness has no place in this desperate situation; self-protection is the only consideration (Kollias & Tucker 1974).

Summary

Sexual practices, ethics, and behavior vary widely within and among different cultures. What is usual or normal in one culture may be variant or abnormal in another culture. Generally, sexual behavior can be considered acceptable if three conditions are met: that it is not harmful to the participant; that it is carried out by consenting adults; and that it is out of sight and sound of unwilling observers. Sexual behavior may be variant or abnormal depending upon (1) the method of functioning and quality of sexual striving; (2) the choice of the sexual partner or object; and (3) the degree and strength of the sexual drive. Men typically reveal a greater tendency toward variant sexual behavior than do women.

One form of sexual variance is **sadism** wherein sexual gratification is derived by inflicting either physical or psychological pain on the sexual partner. **Lust murder** is the extreme of sadistic abnormality. **Masochism** is the mirror image of sadism because the masochist receives sexual pleasure or gratification from being hurt, physically or mentally, by the sexual partner. Figures indicate that 2 to 5% of men and women engage in sadistic behavior and 2 to 5% of men and women engage in masochistic behavior at some time in their sexual lives.

Exhibitionism involves sexual gratification that the individual, typically male, derives from exhibiting the genitals and occasionally masturbating before unwitting and unwilling observers. **Pseudoexhibitionism** may occur when heterosexual relations are not available and persons exhibit themselves only as a poor substitute for preferred sexual intercourse. **Scopophilia** or **scoptophilia** refers to sexual pleasure gained from observing sexual acts and genitalia. **Voyeurism** is the scrutinizing of nudes. **Social nudism** is not a sexual deviation, but it is regarded as a variance by some because it is erroneously linked to exhibitionism. **Troilism** involves the sharing of a sexual partner with another person or persons.

Transvestism, or **cross-dressing,** usually engaged in by heterosexual males, refers to emotional or sexual gratification that is derived from dressing in the clothes of the opposite sex. **Transsexualism,** or **sex-role**

inversion, refers to an obsession or compulsion to become a member of the opposite sex through surgical changes. **Transgenderism** involves a person who identifies strongly with the opposite sex and may cross-dress but does not wish to undergo transsexual surgery. **Gender identity disorders of childhood** involve a child who expresses an extreme distaste for his or her sexual identity and insists that he or she will grow up to be the other sex.

Sexual analism or **sodomy** (sometimes engaged in by heterosexuals and homosexuals) refers to the use of the anus or rectum for copulation. **Interfemoral sexual intercourse,** also engaged in by heterosexuals and homosexuals, involves using the space between the thighs as a nonvaginal method of coitus.

Pedophilia is a form of sexual variation in which the adult engages in or desires sexual activity with a child. **Bestiality** refers to sexual gratification obtained by engaging in sexual relations with animals and **zoophilia** (an unnatural love for animals) often is used synonymously. **Necrophilia** is a rare and severe form of sexual deviation wherein an individual has a morbid sexual attraction to corpses.

Pornography is written or pictorial material that is deliberately designed to arouse sexual excitement. **Obscenity** refers to utterances, gestures, sketches, and so on, that are judged abhorrent according to the mores of our society. No significant evidence exists showing that children's minds are corrupted by pornography or that pornography provokes sexual criminality or other sexual acting out. In fact, pornography may be of educational or informational value to those adults who are ignorant about sexual matters. Most men and women in the United States have been exposed at some time to material of explicitly sexual content, and there is no evidence that these individuals or society are harmed by such exposures to erotica. Whether sexually explicit material is judged obscene depends more upon the evaluating individual's psychological characteristics, occupation, and socioeconomic, political, and educational background. Curbs on pornography and obscenity through censorship often result in adverse consequences for society rather than the presumed benefits.

Fetishism is another sexual variance in which an individual's sexual impulses become fixated on a sexual symbol or object, such as an article of clothing or a bodily part such as hair, hands, thighs, feet, or eyes. **Kleptomania** is a fetishistic pattern that involves compulsive stealing, usually of an object that is of no value to the thief except for sexual symbolism. **Pyromania** is another fetishistic pattern that involves compulsive fire setting, often for reasons that have sexual overtones.

Frottage is a sexual variance in which an individual obtains sexual pleasure from rubbing or pressing against another person, such as in a subway or elevator. **Saliromania** is a disorder found primarily in men that is characterized by the desire to damage or soil the body or clothes of a woman or representation of a woman. **Gerontosexuality** is a variance in which a young person chooses a younger person as a subject of his or her sexual interest.

Incest involves sexual relations between close relatives, such as a brother and sister or father and daughter. **Mate-swapping,** or **swinging,** refers to the exchange of sexual partners between married couples. **Klismaphilia** is a form of erotic pleasure that a person derives from taking enemas.

Nymphomania, a rare disorder, refers to the uncontrollable or excessive sexual desire in a woman that must be fulfilled when she is aroused with no regard for the circumstances. **Satyriasis,** also rare, refers to the excessive or exaggerated desire for sexual gratification on the part of a man. **Promiscuity** refers to the participation in sexual relations with many people on a casual basis.

Prostitution involves the engagement of sexual activity for money or valuables. For the past several decades there has been a steady decrease in the number of professional prostitutes in America and in the frequency with which men consort with them. Now, college-age men appear to be seeking sexual relations with young women in the context of an emotional relationship, and as a result married middle-age men are the most frequent customers of prostitutes. The business of prostitution is usually carried out in a brothel, a call-girl operation, or by a woman working as an independent prostitute. The incidence of homosexuality and drug use or addiction does not appear unusually high among prostitutes. Male prostitutes generally serve a male clientele. A "gigolo," often thought of as a male prostitute, is usually employed more as a companion or escort than for sexual services.

Forcible rape involves sexual intercourse with a person who does not give consent or who offers resistance. **Statutory rape,** another category of criminal sexual relations, refers to coitus with an individual below the age of consent, which is usually 18. While women can be convicted of rape, most rapists are men beset with feelings of inadequacy and low self-esteem. Rapists are frequently under the influence of alcohol when they make their sexual attack. Rape is an act of aggression and has little to do with uncontrollable lust. Group or gang rape, usually by three or more young men, may be planned and perpetrated against an unsuspecting victim. Male homosexual rape in prisons is also known to occur.

Rape victims have at times been reluctant to press charges against rapists because of fears that their families, hospital staffs, or legal authority figures may be unsympathetic toward them. However, changes in societal attitudes and development of sources to which victims may turn, such as rape crisis centers, have led to a more understanding and sympathetic approach to the victim. Furthermore, women may learn how to lessen their chances of being raped by taking courses in self-defense and assertiveness training in order to develop their physical skills and self-confidence.

Annotated Bibliography

Barry, Kathleen. *Female sexual slavery.* Englewood Cliffs, New Jersey: Prentice-Hall, 1979.
> Based on research and interviews with victims and law enforcement personnel, this book explores the problem of forced prostitution and pornography, and other forms of sexual oppression in contemporary American society. Related historical, social, political, and economic issues are examined. Interesting book for the general reader.

Bullough, Vern L. *Sexual variance in society and history.* Chicago: University of Chicago Press, 1976.
> This scholarly volume examines historical and cross-cultural attitudes toward sexual behavior stigmatized as "deviant." Western society is emphasized in the discussion, which includes homosexuality as variant behavior. This book is written mainly for the student and sophisticated general reader.

Gosselin, Chris and Wilson, Glenn. *Sexual variations.* New York: Simon and Schuster, 1980.
> Based on interviews, case histories, and questionnaires, this book contributes to the understanding of backgrounds, preferences, and behavior of sexual variants, focusing on fetishism, sadomasochism, and transvestism. This book may be used by the professional as well as general reader.

Haslam, M. J. *Psychosexual disorders: A review.* Springfield, Illinois: Charles C. Thomas, 1979.
> This volume for the mental health specialist extensively reviews the literature on psychosexual disorders, providing historical perspective. Many significant aspects of the main sexual dysfunctions and the paraphilias are addressed, emphasizing surrounding legal and medical issues. In this book, discussion of homosexuality is included in a section covering behavioral anomalies.

Hursch, C. J. *The trouble with rape.* Chicago: Nelson-Hall, 1977.
> This book presents a comprehensive research-based analysis and description of the problem of rape. The author addresses resolution of legal, medical, sociological, and psychological problems and suggests new legislation and treatment of sex offenders. This is a valuable book for the general reader, and would be especially interesting to law enforcement personnel.

Justice, Blair and Justice, Rita. *The broken taboo.* New York: Human Sciences Press, 1979.
> This book presents an in-depth, research-based examination of the problem of incest, exploring its causes, dynamics, consequences, and cure. The authors attempt to dispel prevalent misconceptions related to incest. This book would appeal to the general reader.

Koranyi, Erwin K. (Ed.) *Transsexuality in the male: The spectrum of gender dysphoria.* Springfield, Illinois: Charles C. Thomas, 1980.

> Stressing the overlap between maleness and femaleness, contributors to this volume for medical and allied health personnel discuss historical, medical, and legal aspects of male transsexuality, especially as it relates to homosexuality and transvestism. Surgical treatment of transsexuality and legal complications surrounding sex reassignment surgery are considered.

Lederer, Laura (Ed.). *Take back the night: Women and pornography.* New York: William Morris, 1980.

> This book is a collection of articles by women on the history, ethics, politics, economics, and effects of pornography. This book is a product of the feminist effort to stop pornography, providing interesting perspective for the general reader.

Meiselman, Karin C. *Incest: A psychological study of causes and effects with treatment and recommendations.* San Francisco: Jossey-Bass, 1978.

> Integrating previous literature with the author's own findings, this book describes incest cases and discusses causes and effects of incest. Anthropological and sociological views of incest are presented, and research methodological issues are considered. This book would appeal to the mental health professional as well as to the general academic reader.

Rosen, Ismond (Ed.). *Sexual deviation (2nd ed.).* Oxford, England: Oxford University Press, 1979.

> This reference volume for the medical and allied health professional encompasses the historical, social, and legal aspects of sexual deviation and presents the latest reasearch on the etiology and treatment of perversion, fetishism, exhibitionism, scopophilia, voyeurism, and homosexuality. Drawing from their own clinical experience, the contributors to this volume discuss psychoanalytic approaches and techniques in treating sexual deviations, and the evaluation and outcome of behavior therapies.

Zuckerman, Marvin. Research on pornography. In *Sex and the life cycle*, ed. W. Oaks, G. Melchiode, and I. Ficher. New York: Grune and Stratton, 1976.

> This article reviews the findings of the Commission on Obscenity and Pornography as well as research relevant to pornography. Topics considered include reported arousal by visual stimuli, sex differences in reported arousal, factors in response to erotic stimuli, motivation and interest in seeing erotic stimuli, and associated personality variables.

Homosexuality

Homosexuality refers to sexual activity between same-sex partners. Sexual contact leading to orgasm is often but not always involved. In our society, homosexuality usually has been deplored as a mode of sexual activity, although legal and social sanctions are changing. Some sexologists regard the homosexual experience as being so diverse, and the psychological, social, and sexual aspects so varied, that to use the words *homosexual* or *homosexuality* to describe anything more than the individual's sexual choice at a particular time is misleading and inexact (A. P. Bell 1976).

At least as old as history, homosexuality was a well-known phenomenon in ancient Rome, where it was practiced openly and widely. Not only did the ancient Greeks regard homosexual behavior as natural (at least, for persons within certain intellectual ranks), but it was also a form of love more exalted than heterosexual affection. Male-female alliances represented practicality—an ordered household, a tax refuge, and a means of producing children. Homosexual love was more typically woven into the fabric of the philosophical, intellectual, and spiritual pursuits so prized by the Greeks (Karlen 1971).

Homosexuality is also known to exist in lower animals, sometimes in immature ones, or in those deprived of normal sexual outlets, such as those in captivity in zoos. Approximately 50% of the sex play among porpoises is among members of the same sex, and sodomy, exhibitionism, and "mutual masturbation" have all been noted in apes (C. Allen 1973). The behavior may be conditioned, but it also arises spontaneously. In her years of studying chimpanzees in their natural habitat, Jane van Lawick-Goodall observed sexual play between male chimps, but noted nothing she considered homosexuality (van Lawick-Goodall 1971). An earlier, comprehensive review by Beach (1947) noted masturbatory as well as homosexual activity among males and females in a wide variety of male and female mammals of several species (including chimpanzees), both in captivity and in the wild.

Many data exist on the subject of homosexuality, but one must remember that information coming from clinicians has often been gathered from homosexuals in treatment, and these data may represent a biased picture of homosexuality. To counteract what they consider distortions of their image, homosexuals have formed organizations (the Mattachine Society and the Daughters of Bilitis are the two oldest) to create a more accurate and favorable public opinion. In recent years, homosexuals also have formed political action groups to encourage changes in public policy that they think have worked unfairly against homosexuals.

Incidence

Kinsey and his co-workers (1948) established that homosexuality and heterosexuality are by no means absolute, and devised a seven-point continuum as a way to illustrate the degrees of homosexuality (Fig. 18.1). At one extreme is exclusive heterosexuality. This is followed by predominant heterosexuality with only incidental homosexuality. Then follows predominant heterosexuality, but with more than incidental homosexuality. At the mid-point, there is sexual function at equal levels. Still further along the continuum is predominant homosexuality, but with more than incidental homosexuality; then predominant homosexuality with only incidental heterosexuality; and, finally, exclusive homosexuality with no heterosexual leanings at all. Kinsey and his associates found that half of American males were classified somewhere between a score of 0 ("exclusively heterosexual") and a score of 6 ("exclusively homosexual"). Women also varied in their classification on this scale, although fewer women were found to be exclusively homosexual (Bell & Weinberg 1978). It should be noted that a person's classification on this scale refers to the degree of sexual responsiveness to others of the same and opposite sex.

To sum up the Kinsey findings, which are still pertinent today, 60% of males and 33% of females have engaged in at least one act of overtly

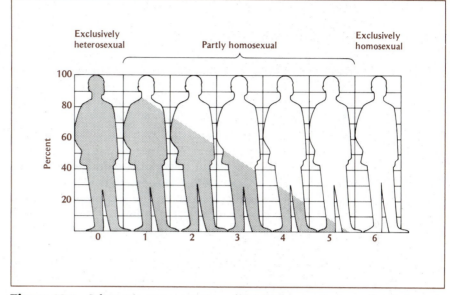

Figure 18.1 Schematic representation of the Kinsey continuum of male hetero-sexuality-homosexuality.

homosexual sex play by age 15. The researchers also found that 37% of the male and 13% of the female population engaged at least once in their lives in some form of homosexual activity to the point of orgasm. A study of 20,000 well-educated, liberal men and women of high socioeconomic status confirmed Kinsey's early conclusions that more than one-third of all men and nearly one-fifth of all women have had at least one homosexual experience involving orgasm. A substantial number of other women (22%) have considered engaging in homosexuality. Both homosexual men and women have their first *heterosexual* intercourse at an earlier age than heterosexuals. About 17% of the homosexual women and 18% of the homosexual men sampled had their first coitus before the age of 15, as compared with only 6% and 9%, respectively, of heterosexual women and men (Athanasiou *et al.* 1970; Kinsey *et al.* 1948, 1953). The average male homosexual has his first homosexual experience some time before age 14, and the average female homosexual at about 19 or 20 (Kaye 1971). In a 1976 study (Haynes & Oziel) of homosexuality at a large southern university, it was found that from 12% to 17% of the men and from 6% to 11% of the women had been involved in at least one homosexual act. Of the males, 6% reported that they were currently engaged in homophile activity, compared with 3% of the women.

The Kinsey figures may be somewhat misleading because many experiences included in the data involved only limited homosexual behavior, and early in life at that. On the basis of Kinsey's data and information from other sources, sociologist William Simon, a long-time research associate at the Kinsey Institute, has estimated that only 2%–3% of the male population have a long-term serious homosexual pattern; and an additional 7%–8% have casual or occasional homophile experiences. Therefore, the total would be about 10% of the male population who have had more than experimental or fleeting homosexual contacts in their lives (Karlen 1971). These figures were substantiated by Hunt (1974), who found that only 10% of his married subjects and 11% of the single ones had any homosexual experience at all after the age of 15.

The highly intelligent women studied by DeMartino (1974) showed differences among age groups in the incidence of past and probable future homosexual activity (Table 18.1). The percentage of the total group with past homosexual contact (21%) fell below that reported by Kinsey (28%). The findings of some investigations indicate that as many as 50% of all women have harbored "intense feelings" for another woman at some point in their lives. Most sexologists, however, agree with the more conservative conclusions of the Kinsey investigations that only 28% of women (compared with 50% of men) have experienced some sort of homosexual response (K. E. Davis 1971; Kinsey *et al.* 1948, 1953). Only about 1% to 3% of the female population between the ages of 20 and 35 in Kinsey's sample were exclusively homosexual, although an additional 2% to 6% in this age bracket were "more or less exclusively homosexual" (meaning that there might have been a rare heterosexual contact). Of all women who have engaged in any form of homosexual activity, Kinsey's study has indicated that about 33% have fewer than 10 experiences, and many have only 1 or 2 experiences.

Of the women participating in the Hite study (1976), 8% said they preferred sex with women, another 4% identified themselves as "bisexual," and an additional 5% claimed they had experienced sex with both men and women, but gave no preference. These figures are considerably higher than those reported in other surveys, and perhaps reflect a bias of the Hite sample from whom information was gathered. Consensus among authorities is that male homosexuals outnumber lesbians (female homosexuals) about

Table 18.1 Homosexuality among Intelligent American Women, Whether Married or Unmarried (after DeMartino, 1974)

Age Groups (Years)	Past Homosexual Experience	Anticipating Probable Future Experience
16–19	22%	12%
20–29	18	6
30–39	26	7
40–49	19	7
50–61	10	-0-

2 or 3 to 1, although the cause of this imbalance is frequently debated. It is extremely difficult, of course, to do more than estimate the true number of homosexuals in the United States, because most are still "in the closet"— that is, they keep their sexual preference hidden. A conservative estimate is that the country's gays number 5.5 million (about 2.5% of the population, based on the 220 million figure), while gay activists say that 22 million is a more accurate figure, which would mean 10% of the population. It is generally accepted by sexologists that about 4% of white males in the United States are exclusively homosexual throughout their sexual lives, 8% are exclusively homosexual for at least three years between the ages of 16 and 55, and 37% have experienced at least some form of overt homosexuality to the point of orgasm in their lifetimes. Furthermore, 10% of all men have some homosexual experience after marriage (Kinsey *et al.* 1948). Although these data apply to white males, it has been estimated that the percentages are equally pertinent to black American males (Cory 1961).

Generally speaking, the Kinsey study indicated that religious factors had a bearing on both incidence and frequency of homosexual contacts. The more intense an individual's commitment to religion, the less often he or she participated in homosexual activity. Certain other factors, however, tend to bias test results and lead to erroneous conclusions regarding religion and homosexuality. Religious gays may not be easily identifiable in scientific surveys because they are more worried about exposure. They are more likely than less religious men to identify with the heterosexual community (at least on the surface) and to deny their homosexuality. Religious gays also are more likely to believe that they were "born homosexual" and are less likely to experience all the common sexual practices of homosexuality (Weinberg & Williams 1976). In the Kinsey study (1948), educational levels bore a different relationship to incidence of homosexuality than to most other means of sexual expression. While the incidence of homosexuality among single men in the three educational groups was not significantly different, there was a great difference among the groups in the percentage of total outlet that homosexual practice constituted (see Table 18.2).

As indicated earlier, homosexuality is somewhat less common among women than among men. The occurrence of both exclusive and partial homosexuality among women is only two-thirds of that among men (Cory 1961). It is generally found, too, that most female homosexuals are bisexual. Either they have had heterosexual experiences, or they will have them in the future, or they will shift back and forth between homosexuality and heterosexuality. Only 33% of declared lesbians are exclusively homosexual (T. Bieber 1969; Peplau 1981). In one study of lesbians (Kaye 1971), 67% of those who declared themselves to be exclusively homosexual at the time of questioning reported earlier heterosexual relationships. Over 80% of Bell and Weinberg's (1978) lesbian sample reported previous heterosexual coitus,

Table 18.2 **Homosexual Incidence to Point of Orgasm and Percentage of Total Sexual Outlet among Men**

| Educational Level | Incidence to Point of Orgasm | | Homosexuality among Single Men Constituting Percentage of Total Sexual Outlet | | |
	Single to 35 Years of Age	Total Male Population	Ages 16–20	Ages 21–25	Ages 26–30
Grade school	50%	27%	6.85%	8.06%	14.04%
High school	58	39	10.81	16.31	25.95
College	47	34	2.43	3.72	8.82

but 33% denied orgasm as a result of such activity. Kinsey's study (1953) showed that female homosexuality is largely confined to single women and, to a lesser extent, to the previously married. Just over 30% of Masters and Johnson's (1979) lesbian sample had been previously married from less than 6 months to 13 years. Although 19% of Kinsey's total female sampling had had active homosexual contact by the age of 40, when the marital status of this group was considered the pattern of active homosexual incidence for the same age group shifted: 24% of the women had never been married, 9% had been previously married, and only 3% were married women. Hunt (1974) found that 9% of married women and 15% of the single ones in his sample had had at least one homosexual experience.

After a comprehensive study of homosexuality and an intensive review of the literature, Karlen (1971) concluded that no evidence since Kinsey's time supports the contention that the incidence of homosexuality has increased, although its visibility is indeed greater. In its 1974 survey of 100,000 women, *Redbook* magazine also found that, in the sexually permissive decade preceding its publication, the one female sexual behavior that has altered little is homosexuality (Levin 1975). According to official records, 20% of women prisoners practice lesbianism; prison staff members set the figure at 30% to 70%. Female inmates themselves estimate the incidence to be between 60% and 70% (Ward & Kassebaum 1964). Prison lesbian affairs are typically situational, since once women are released from custody, they resume heterosexual relationships. According to Kinsey's (1953) findings, the more devout adherents in three religious groups—Jews, Protestants, and Roman Catholics—had less homosexual contact to the point of orgasm than did the nondevout.

Of those women surveyed by Kinsey who had the most extensive homosexual experience, only 20% expressed definite regret. Almost 90% of all the women with homosexual experience themselves declared that they would keep as a friend any woman with a history of lesbianism. They were less accepting (74%) of male friends with a history of homosexuality.

Suggested Causes

Theories concerning the causes of homosexuality usually fall into three categories: hereditary tendencies, environmental tendencies, or hormonal imbalance.

Hereditary Theory

"Nativistic" theorists argue that homosexuality is inborn. They point out that most gays grow up in a culture that encourages heterosexuality and that they are usually ignorant of their homosexual tendencies until they reach pubescence and first encounter opportunities for homosexual attachments and expression. Therefore, these theorists reason, the homosexual tendencies must have been inborn and not learned. Even Freud believed that homosexuality had a genetic causality, and that the individual's early experiences either reinforce or extinguish the tendency.

Studies have indicated that the intelligence, interests, personality characteristics, and so on, of identical twins are often quite similar, regardless of whether the twins are reared together or apart (Bower 1979; Coleman 1972). The rationale behind such studies of identical twins is to find evidence to support the notion that human behavior is directly influenced by genetics. Previous reasoning went even a step further in suggesting that sexual orientation, in particular homosexuality, could be genetically determined. However, other conflicting evidence has seriously questioned the idea that there are direct genetic components underlying human behavior as complicated as homosexuality (Diamond & Karlen 1980).

Environmental Theory

There is more convincing evidence that homosexuality is the outgrowth of environmental pressures and other conditioning factors (Coleman 1972; Kinsey *et al.* 1948, 1953; Pomeroy 1966c; Thorpe *et al.* 1961). The individual may seek homosexual outlets, for instance, as the result of an accidental but pleasurable homosexual incident in childhood, or because of segregation with others of the same sex for long periods of time (such as in a boarding school or correctional institution).

The most likely explanation centers around factors in the home environment. One report (Saghir & Robins 1973) studying the childhood of adult male homosexuals revealed that 72%, compared with 12% of a control group of heterosexuals, had lost one or both parents before the age of 15. Furthermore, 50% of the gays but only 17% of the straights recounted that severe marital problems existed between their parents. Another study (Whitam 1977) found several "childhood indicators" of later adult male homosexuality. These indicators were: interest in dolls, cross-dressing, preference for company of girls rather than boys in games, preference for company of older women to older men, assessment by other boys as being a sissy, and sexual interest in other boys rather than girls in childhood sex play. Not only did adult homosexual males reveal a significantly higher number of childhood indicators than did the heterosexuals, but the stronger the homosexual orientation, the greater the number of childhood indicators exhibited.

Unhealthy patterns in homosexuals' family lives have often been noted. In one survey (Saghir & Robins 1973), 41% of the male homosexual respondents, in contrast to 23% of the heterosexuals, asserted that their mothers had overcontrolled them. Many other psychological pressures may act together or separately to veer a boy toward homosexuality, and similar forces influence a girl toward lesbianism. The father may have been weak, aloof, and an ineffectual force in his son's life, leaving the boy to develop an excessive mother attachment that he never outgrows. The more common father-son interaction that can culminate in the son's homosexuality, however, is the one in which the father is harsh, overly aggressive, and too much of a "tough guy" to allow his son to enter into a close relationship with him. The boy does not identify with his father and does not learn the masculine role in life. Frequently this sort of father attempts to teach his son to be a real "he-man" but he prevents the very thing he wants for his son by not establishing a healthy relationship rooted in tenderness, acceptance, understanding, and love. Thus, one comprehensive investigation revealed that 84% of the male homosexuals, as opposed to 18% of the male heterosexuals, felt that their fathers had been emotionally distant and indifferent (Saghir & Robins 1973).

Other environmental factors possibly productive of homosexuality are to be found in the home. A boy's parents, wanting a daughter, may have rejected his sex from birth. Or the child's sex education may have been so faulty and larded with guilt, or the relationship between his parents so bad, that homosexuality provides an escape from the feared and contemptible example of heterosexuality he or she witnessed in the home. Female homosexuality may result in the case of a girl who has a deep-seated hate of her father. Or, alienated from a cold mother, she may seek from another older woman the maternal love she was denied as a youngster. The evidence is strong that a heterosexual environment fraught with sexual taboos, threats, and fears favors the development of lesbianism (Kaye 1971).

The dynamics behind homosexuality are not generated solely in the home, however. Other sociological forces acting upon particularly vulnerable adolescents can be powerful. For example, a boy's relationship with girls may have been so unsatisfactory and threatening that he seeks the companionship of his own sex in order to avoid a repetition of his failures. Similarly, a sensitive girl who has been callously rejected by a boy she loves may decide never again to run the risk of another rejection, and turn to women for warmth and acceptance. Experiences such as these have led some behavioral scientists to conjecture that homosexuality is always associated with an unconscious fear of heterosexual relationships (Marmor 1965).

Hormonal Imbalance

According to the third theory, homosexuality is caused by an imbalance of sex hormones. The urine of a normal man or woman reveals hormones of both sexes; in others, the same-sex hormone dominates. It is suggested that if the dominance is reversed, homosexuality will result. This theory has alternately gained and lost support over the years, and while it is not usually considered significant in a study of homosexuality, the sex research team of Masters and Johnson has recently revived interest in biological correlates. When testosterone and sperm-count levels of a group of 18- to 35-year-old homosexual and heterosexual males were compared, endocrine variants in bisexual homosexuals did not differ from those in heterosexuals. But those subjects who were predominantly or exclusively homosexual displayed "diminished plasma testosterone concentrations and impaired spermatogenesis" (Kolodny *et al.* 1971).

In a review of recent endocrine studies into the causes of homosexuality, Masters and Johnson (1979) cite several lines of investigation that have produced conflicting results. They point out that many such studies have methodological difficulties, that homosexuality is a diverse phenomenon (as is heterosexuality), and that the origins of heterosexuality are as obscure as those of homosexuality. Thus, researchers have been unable so far to determine whether the anomaly is testicular, pituitary, or hypothalamic in origin. They also warn that similar endocrine dysfunctioning has yet to be found in a majority of homosexuals. Even if such dysfunctioning were to exist, however, it might be primarily the result rather than the cause of homophile psychosexual orientation.

Homosexual Patterns and Practices

What homosexuals do when they have sexual relations is a mystery to many people. In fact, homosexual practices are the same as those of heterosexual couples; except for penile-vaginal coitus, there are no heterosexual practices that cannot be performed by a homosexual couple. Usually preceded by kissing and petting, these acts include oral-genital contact, mutual genital stimulation, anal intercourse, and interfemoral coitus. In the Masters and Johnson study (1979), it was found that committed homosexual couples differed consistently from their heterosexual counterparts in the amount of time spent in prolonged foreplay. The homosexuals took more time, appeared to be more relaxed, and were more completely and subjectively involved than were the heterosexual couples.

The sexual expressions of greatest importance to and most cherished by lesbians (in company with many heterosexual women) are embracing and close total body contact. Genital activity and orgasm frequently are of secondary importance (Bell & Weinberg 1978; Kaye 1971; Peplau 1981). Lesbians are more likely to reach orgasm than are heterosexual women, and are twice as likely to be multiorgasmic on each sexual occasion. These findings about women confirm the conclusions of Masters and Johnson that orgasm, multiple orgasm, and a greater intensity of response are all more likely through masturbation or digital manipulation than through intercourse (Athanasiou *et al.* 1970; Masters & Johnson 1966, 1979).

The sexual practices of American lesbians are limited only by the imagination of the particular couple. However, three seem more common than others: mutual manual-genital stimulation, cunnilingus, and *tribadism* (one woman atop the other, both making rhythmic pelvic thrusts to stimulate each other's clitoris and vulva). Positions may vary, of course, as they do among straight couples, and many sex acts common to lesbians are quite similar to practices of heterosexuals (Bell & Weinberg 1978; Lyon & Rosen 1974; Peplau 1981). Homosexual practices vary from one culture to another. For example, most American and English investigations suggest that oral intercourse is preferred to anal intercourse by most English and American male homosexuals (Bell & Weinberg 1978). In Mexico, however, 86% of the male homosexuals preferred anal intercourse and 90% practiced it. Furthermore, most of the Mexicans who engaged in oral-genital intercourse more than occasionally had done so with men from the United States (Carrier 1971).

As a matter of statistics, only about 15% of men with extensive homosexual experience and 5% of lesbians can be identified by appearance (Pomeroy 1966b). A high degree of effeminacy is evident in about 21% of male gays under age 26, the percentage dropping to about 7% as these men grow older. Effeminate characteristics are learned, and they can be unlearned. There are, to be sure, such stereotypes as limp-wristed, lisping, highly effeminate "queens." However, such "queens" represent a very small proportion of homophiles and tend to be shunned by the rest of the homosexual community. At the other extreme are homosexuals bent on presenting themselves as super-masculine. Theoretically, at least, they are attempting to attract those homophiles in search of a strong father-figure partner. As therapists have long recognized, a considerable number of weight-lifting "muscle-men" are homosexual. The public reacts differently to the gestures of different men. For example, a friendly slap on the fanny is usually interpreted quite differently when it is observed among players on a football field than among men working at jobs traditionally associated with women (Weinberg & Williams 1974).

It is typically thought that male homophiles play one of three roles in their sexual encounters: active, passive, or mixed. Homophiles themselves prefer to play no fixed role, changing it according to their partner's preferences and aggressiveness. That they tend to switch roles during a single sexual encounter further blurs the distinction between active and passive.

The life styles of lesbians—to the public eye, at least—appear to be less flamboyant and less promiscuous than those of male gays. They do not often go to gay bars searching for pickups. If they do go, it is with a friend, seeking sociability rather than social contacts. According to the study done by Bell and Weinberg (1978) in the San Francisco area, less than a fifth of the lesbians had visited a gay bar in search of a sexual partner during the previous year. More than two-thirds of the male homosexuals, on the other hand, had visited a gay bar to seek out a sexual partner or partners. Some men engage in homosexual practices with numerous partners. This seems to be because homosexual men do not ordinarily concern themselves with finding a steady or permanent partner until they reach the age of about 30. Prior to that, they seem intent upon seeking the satisfactions of the moment rather than establishing a lasting relationship (Peplau 1981; Sonenschein 1968).

Lesbians are much more likely than male gays to pair off and establish lasting relationships. This is easier for women than men because of the differences in society's role expectations. Lesbians melt into the community more easily and are subjected to far less harassment by the police. The duration of established lesbian relationships is comparable to that of heterosexual relationships. About 65% of the lesbians in one study (Rubin 1969b) had remained 1 to 9 years in a single partnership, and 17% had remained for 10 or more years. Bell and Weinberg (1978) found similar stability in their study. In comparison, Rubin (1969b) found 48% of the heterosexual women in his study had stayed for 1 to 9 years with one male partner, and 40% for 10 or more years. Although some clinical data suggest that the roles in a lesbian relationship are likely to be clearly defined, the Bell and Weinberg (1978) and Peplau (1981) data suggest it is rare to find a lesbian relationship in which one of the partners does all or even most of the "masculine" or "feminine" tasks. Public opinion to the contrary, most lesbians would not choose a man as a sexual partner in preference to a woman, no matter how great his charms and persuasiveness or his skill in making love. Bell and Weinberg (1978) found that nearly two-thirds of the lesbians in their sample expressed no regret over their homosexuality, nor had they ever seriously considered discontinuing homosexual activity. Most of those who did attempt to give up homosexuality did so only once, and few attempted marriage.

Many **bisexuals**—men and women who enjoy sex with members of both sexes—marry and adopt a life style that permits them to satisfy their dual sexual inclinations. A few lesbians (5%) and even fewer gay men (1%) marry a homosexual of the opposite sex for convenience or coverup, but the vast majority of gay women (66%) and men (83%) state they would not consider such a marriage under any circumstance. However, 87% of gay men and 95% of lesbians date members of the opposite sex, at least occasionally (Dank 1975), and 16% of the male homosexuals in the Bell and Weinberg study (1978) and 25% of the lesbians had experienced heterosexual coitus in the previous year.

Attitudes toward Homosexuality

Despite changes in public acceptance of homosexuality, the attitude of the average American toward gays and gay life styles is still quite negative and differs from that of many other cultures. A study of 76 primitive societies (Ford & Beach 1951) showed that 64% approved of homosexual relations. Another study of 193 societies throughout the world (Murdock 1934) showed that 28% accepted male homosexuality, at least to an extent, but only 11% accepted female homosexuality. Among 225 American Indian tribes, 53% accepted male homosexuality, again at least to some degree, but only 17% accepted female homosexuality (Pomeroy 1965). Erik Erikson (1963) noted that homosexuals in some American Indian tribes are assigned a special role within the community that is socially accepted. In the typical American community, however, the reverse of these acceptance patterns is generally true. Male homosexuality is severely denounced, often to the point of violence, while female homosexuality receives less restrictive disapproval.

There are regional differences in the acceptance of homosexuality. For example, in the Bay area around San Francisco the gay population is more accepted and therefore highly visible. Homophiles hold public office and are recruited by the police department, and there has not been a raid on a gay bar for nearly 20 years. In contrast, the Pennsylvania House of Representatives censured the governor in 1979 for proclaiming a "Gay Pride" week. And even in the same area there can be conflicting notions of acceptance. In the early summer of 1980, police in Houston raided a gay bar during Gay Pride week on the eve of the annual police-versus-gays softball game.

Some evidence, then, points to a recent change in public attitude toward homosexuality, a swing from almost total condemnation to a position of greater tolerance—at least toward gay civil rights, if not toward widespread acceptance of homosexuality as a life style. It was almost unheard of a generation ago for academicians, doctors, lawyers, and ministers to publicly identify themselves as members of a once despised and feared group. Yet over 70% of Americans still view homosexuals as sexually abnormal, perverted (50%), or mentally ill (40%) (Weinberg & Williams 1976). This same study, even when conducted in the San Francisco area, showed that 87% of those sampled expressed the same opinion: that homosexuals are psychologically disturbed.

In a reversal of its century-old position, the American Psychiatric Association in 1973 struck homosexuality from its list of mental disorders. "For a mental condition to be considered a psychiatric disorder," the decision reads, "it should regularly cause emotional distress or regularly be associated with generalized impairment of social functioning; homosexuality does not meet those criteria." Only those who are in conflict about their sexual orientation—or, rather, those whose conflict is great enough that they wish to change sexual directions—are considered disturbed, and hence in need of psychological help. In September 1976, the Council of Representatives of the American Psychological Association adopted a resolution that stated: "The sex, gender identity, or sexual orientation of natural parents, or of prospective adoptive or foster parents, should not be the sole or primary variable considered in custody or placement cases."

The 1980 edition of the American Psychiatric Association's *Diagnostic and Statistical Manual of Mental Disorders* further reflects the changing nature of homosexuality in that profession. In line with its 1973 position, homosexuality is not included as a separate diagnostic entity. The manual contains an entry for "Ego-dystonic Homosexuality" which refers to "... a desire to acquire or increase heterosexual arousal so that heterosexual relationships can be initiated or maintained, and a sustained pattern of homosexual arousal that the individual explicitly states had been unwanted and a persistent source of distress" (DSM III 1980, p. 281). Civil rights groups and the homosexual community viewed these pronouncements as a great victory.

Although psychology, psychiatry, and the law have responded, at least to an extent, to the gays' plea for tolerance and understanding, why has society not been as generous? The answer is that the public's view is largely formed by the teachings of Christianity and Judaism, which hold that homosexual behavior is against the natural order of creation and therefore sinful. To be sure, several Protestant, Catholic, and Jewish groups, viewing the homosexual's dilemma with compassion and pastoral interest, have endorsed gay civil rights in matters of employment and housing. Others have been equally active in defeating such legislation.

Those who have "come out" maintain that it is harder to be a homophile than a black. Homosexuals identify with blacks as being a minority group, particularly in regard to discrimination. Yet there are differences. The prejudice based on a person's skin color is undeniably irrational, one might state, while the prejudice against homosexuality is for some not so mindless, even if the expression of this prejudice is often irrational and grossly unfair. In some minds there lingers the biblical condemnation of homosexuality; in others, a subconscious reminder of their own suppressed homosexual desires; in still others, the fear that children might be influenced toward homosexuality by adult models such as gay teachers.

As for employment, several major companies have lifted restrictions against hiring avowed gays—AT&T, NBC, IBM, and the Bank of America, for example. Of the largest corporations in the country represented by the Fortune 500, 122 have equal opportunity policies in regard to homosexual employees (Vetri 1980). The Civil Service Commission has similarly reexamined its employment practices, and no longer bars gays. This policy covers 90% of all federal jobs. Numerous court decisions have determined that termination of an employee solely because of homosexuality is not permitted. The alleged immoral and indecent conduct must be demonstrated to have a harmful effect on job efficiency. Such decisions have included cases involving civil service employees, public school teachers, university professors, and police officers (Vetri 1980). In both federal and industrial practice, however, a gay person frequently cannot obtain security clearance.

The military's traditionally rigid ban against homosexuals has not softened, despite the courageous efforts of several service personnel. USAF T/Sgt. Leonard Matlovich challenged the policy by openly declaring himself a homosexual and thus forcing a discharge hearing. He was considered to be a "perfect case" for such a confrontation because of his unblemished military record for 12 years—the lack of which has derailed other challenges. The military board that heard the case handed down a general discharge (less than honorable), which then often becomes a barrier to civilian employment and VA benefits, but a review board later upgraded the discharge to honorable. Thus the USAF—and the country—lost a dedicated public servant, once again leaving one to wonder how many potentially valuable public servants are lost because of their fear of exposure. In December 1978, the U.S. Court of Appeals, ruling in the case involving Matlovich, declared that the military cannot discharge gay persons without specific, appropriate reasons in addition to homosexuality.

Homosexuals can be as religious, moralistic, loyal to country or cause, inhibited, bigoted, or censorious of the other types of sexual variance as anyone else. They manifest no greater number of serious personality problems than is found in the general population (Hooker 1957, 1965). Nor are homosexuals more creative than heterosexuals, although it may seem to some that they are in the majority in the arts, letters, and fashion. The noted psychiatrist Samuel B. Hadden has offered this explanation: In his experience, homosexuals typically become aware early in their lives that they are "different." Their school years are lonely, so their mothers buy

Sgt. Leonard Matlovich, avowed homosexual, after his honorable discharge from the United States Air Force. (United Press International)

them a fiddle or paint box and send them off to take lessons; not being part of a group, they have plenty of time to practice. The prominence of homosexuals in the arts, then, does not reflect any special talent among them as a result of their homosexuality, but rather the fact that they were deprived of the rugged but distracting avocations of normal children and turned to the arts to attain some significance.

Homosexuality and Children

It is an unfortunate experience for a youngster between the ages of 7 and 16 to be seduced by a homosexual, but the effects are seldom permanent. These boys are no more liable to become homosexuals than boys who have not been seduced, and the evidence is that they later marry and lead quite normal lives ("From the Editor's Scrapbook" 1965). What of those cases in which there is close, frequent contact between a child and a homophile? Although a few local decisions have upheld the right of homosexuals to teach in the schools, parents are often apprehensive. Yet there is no evidence that a homosexual teacher will lure a child into the gay world, or that such a teacher is more likely than a heterosexual teacher to molest a child sexually. Some teachers *are* homosexual, without a doubt; but they keep their sexual preference to themselves, as do heterosexual teachers.

Nor does evidence exist that a homosexual parent will be less loving and effective than a heterosexual parent. Recently, several court decisions have given custody of children to lesbian mothers. In one case in California, the state supreme court awarded two lesbian mothers custody of their children, finding that their sexual preferences did not create a harmful child-raising environment (*Forum Newsfront*, 1979). Similarly, a New Jersey appeals court awarded custody of two girls to their lesbian mother instead of to the father. But in a complicated Florida case, a judge awarded custody of three preschool girls to their heterosexual father (who was living with his woman friend) rather than to the girls' mother (a bisexual) who had agreed not to live with her woman friend had she been awarded custody (*Forum Newsfront*, 1979). In adoption cases, an openly gay male couple recently has been permitted to adopt a child (Vetri 1980), and a homosexual minister has been granted the right to adopt a child in New York (*Forum Newsfront*, 1979). Still, the right of the professed homophile to have custody of children remains unsolved. As an example: responding to the plaintiff's plea not to let a child become the victim of "someone else's social experiment," a Dallas jury awarded custody of 9-year-old boy to his father. The mother, a nurse and an avowed lesbian who had been living with another woman since her divorce, was also ordered to pay part of the child's support.

It can be seen that many moral, ethical, attitudinal, and legal issues remain to be resolved within our society in regard to homosexuality. Certainly, homosexuality continues to be a sensitive subject for many people, and many of our values are brought into question when the straight world confronts and struggles to assimilate the gay community. Even the concrete provisions of the law are not so concrete when issues concerning homosexuality are heard in our courts. Our values and our laws concerning homosexuality continue to be in a state of flux, and our views of the gay community are constantly being reshaped and remolded.

Summary

Homosexuality refers to sexual attraction to or sexual activity with members of one's own sex. Homosexuality is not unique to modern society as history records that it was practiced in ancient Rome and Greece. Nor is homosexuality unique to humans—it also exists in lower animals. Today, attitudes, values, and perceptions toward homosexuality are changing, and homosexuals are forming organizations and political action groups to protect and enhance their public image.

Homosexuality and heterosexuality are not necessarily totally separate and distinct human behaviors. Kinsey and his co-workers devised a seven-point continuum indicating that sexual behavior varies from exclusive heterosexuality at one extreme to a combination of heterosexual and homosexual behavior to exclusive homosexuality at the other extreme. That much overlap exists in the expression of human sexual behavior is demonstrated by evidence indicating that more than one-third of all men and nearly one-fifth of all women have at least one homosexual experience involving orgasm. While probably 10% or less of men and women have had extensive homosexual experience, perhaps over 50% of men and women have had homosexual feelings or some sort of homosexual response at some point in their lives. Male homosexuals outnumber female homosexuals by 2 or 3 to 1, and it is noteworthy that most female homosexuals are bisexual. Devoutly religious individuals appear less likely to engage in homosexual activity than less devout individuals. While homosexuality has increased in its visibility in recent years, there is no evidence to support the contention that the incidence of homosexuality has increased.

Contrasting theories exist to account for the supposed causes of homosexuality. One of these theories is that homosexuality has a hereditary basis and is based on one's genes. The environmental theory suggests that homosexuality develops as a result of the psychological pressures and conditioning factors coming from the home and family. A third theory postulates that homosexuality is caused by an imbalance of sex hormones.

Regardless of the causes of homosexuality, evidence indicates that homosexual practices are the same as those of heterosexual couples, except for penile-vaginal coitus. Kissing and petting, oral-genital contact, mutual genital stimulation, and anal intercourse, interfemoral coitus, and rhythmic pelvic thrusts such as those involved in tribadism are among the practices of homosexuals. The majority of homosexuals cannot be identified by their appearance, although certainly the effeminate "queens" or super-masculine appearing males or females can be found in the homosexual community. **Lesbians** (female homosexuals) do tend to be less flamboyant and less promiscuous than male gays, however, and are more likely to pair off and establish lasting relationships. Rather than having exclusively homosexual relationships, some men and women opt for bisexual relationships in which sex can be enjoyed with members of both sexes. Many homosexual men and women occasionally date members of the opposite sex.

Despite the changes in public acceptance of homosexuality, most Americans still maintain a negative attitude toward this form of human sexual expression. In our society male homosexuality is severely denounced while female homosexuality receives less restrictive disapproval. The American Psychiatric Association and the American Psychological Association have adopted positions that no longer view homosexuality as a mental disorder, but the teachings of Christianity and Judaism have influenced the public by their view that homosexual behavior is against the natural order of creation and therefore is sinful. Private industry, the federal government, and the military have become more tolerant of homosexuals among their ranks, but not without legal battles and public resistance. Homosexuals continue to meet opposition and public condemnation even though they are similar to heterosexuals in everything except their mode of sexual preference.

It is unfortunate when a young person is seduced by a homosexual, but even in such instances few if any of the potentially negative effects are permanent. Homosexuals are no more inclined to seduce children than are heterosexuals. Many homosexuals are loving and affectionate parents, and recently some courts have allowed homosexuals to gain custody or adopt children. Homosexuality is still a sensitive subject in our society with many moral, ethical, attitudinal, and legal issues to be resolved.

Annotated Bibliography

Bell, A. P. and Weinberg, M. S. *Homosexualities: A study of diversity among men and women.* New York: Simon and Schuster, 1978.

> This book presents a comprehensive exploration of homosexual behavior and life styles, exploding many myths. The authors review a wide range of topics pertinent to homosexuality, such as the gay sexual experience, problems of social adjustment, and the various psychological aspects. This book is important reading for persons who desire greater understanding of homosexuality.

Kirkpatrick, M. (Ed.). *Women's sexual development: Explorations of inner space.* New York: Plenum Press, 1980.

> Articles in this volume discuss various significant topics related to female sexuality, including history of female sexuality, female sexual physiology, femininity, masturbation, lesbianism, father-daughter relationships, and sexual self-help. The book would appeal to a wide audience.

Marmor, Judd (Ed.) *Homosexual behavior: A modern reappraisal.* New York: Basic Books, 1980.

> This book is a collection of articles examining homosexual behavior from biological, social, and clinical viewpoints. Advances in understanding homosexuality are appraised and many issues are examined, including development of sexual identity, the stigma of the homosexual label, homosexuality and

aging, genetics in homosexual etiology, gay culture, and cross-cultural approaches. This book would be read profitably by a wide audience.

Masters, William H. and Johnson, Virginia E. *Homosexuality in perspective.* Boston: Little, Brown, 1979.

Based on the authors' research and clinical experience, this book attempts to dispel the many myths surrounding homosexuality and to establish a better understanding of homosexual behavior. The authors discuss treatment of sexual dysfunctions among homosexuals and report results of treatment of conversion or reversion. This book will be of interest to the lay reader as well as the professional.

Plummer, Ken. Men in love: Observations on male homosexual couples. In *The couple*, ed. M. Corbin. New York: Penguin Books, 1978.

Based on observations and interviews with several male homosexual couples, this insightful article explores what it means to be gay. The article focuses on the social context of homosexuality and issues and problems faced by male homosexuals in forming and maintaining gay relationships. Also, the future of gay relationships is discussed.

Rowan, Robert L. and Gillette, Paul J. *The gay health guide.* Boston: Little, Brown, 1978.

This medical guide for homosexual men and women focuses on the identification, transmission, diagnosis and treatment of venereal diseases and how to avoid them. The guide also deals with problems of sexual performance and emotional considerations. Of special value is a listing of gay health clinics.

Silverstein, Charles. *Man to man: Gay couples in America.* New York: Simon and Schuster, 1981.

This book presents a personal examination of the lives and experiences of a number of gay men based on the author's personal interviews. Many important issues faced by gay couples are addressed, including religion and gay love and coming out. This book would appeal to a wide variety of readers, irrespective of sexual orientation.

Wolf, Deborah Goleman. *The lesbian community.* Berkeley: University of California Press, 1980.

This book describes the development of a lesbian community in San Francisco and presents the socio-historical background of the gay liberation movement and lesbian-feminism. The general reader will likely gain an increased understanding of female homosexuality.

Woodman, Natalie Jane and Lenna, Harry R. *Counseling with gay men and women.* San Francisco: Jossey-Bass, 1980.

This sensitive book addresses clearly and concisely the social and cultural context of homosexuality and the difficulties experienced by homosexual men and women in developing positive attitudes, life styles, and relationships. This book is intended to facilitate the work of the helping professional.

Sex and the Law

Societies have always attempted to keep the sexual behavior of their individual members in conformity with prevailing mores. Means used to exert control have included religious codes, group pressure, and, as a last resort, the law. More often than not, a substantial gulf exists between the sexual ethics of one society and those of another. Further, the standards set for different groups within the same society are often at variance—those pertaining to men and women, for example.

Most societies agree on the need for measures to control such offenses as murder, assault, and theft. But the need for laws to regulate sexual behavior is less clear-cut. Consequently, such laws vary enormously and generate much conflict. Unlike other laws, they are designed not so much to reform or punish the individual as to keep others, through the harsh punishment involved, from deviating from the particular society's sexual ethics, real or imagined (Schwartz 1973).

Laws regulating sex chiefly concern two kinds of offenses: those in which sex is forced on an unwilling partner, and those committed in privacy by willing partners. The latter category causes the greatest controversy; enforcement of pertinent laws is an almost hopeless task, often involving such undesirable police techniques as entrapment.

Just how far the community pursues prosecution in these "victimless crimes" depends upon the degree of outrage that certain citizens feel. And, as research has shown, outrage is proportionate to the ignorance and sexual guilt of those vocal few who feel compelled to march on City Hall or the district attorney's office.

If it were not for the tragedy involved, one of the greatest farces of American history would be the laws designed to control sexual behavior. Even a cursory examination of legislation attempting to regulate sexual expression reveals amazing vagueness and inconsistency among the various states (and frequently within the same state). Much of this confusion can be accounted for historically. Over the past 50 years, the nation's laws have undergone constant scrutiny and change, but this flexibility and review have as yet barely touched legislation governing sexual matters (Sherwin 1961). Not long ago, a man in North Carolina was convicted and sentenced to 30 years' imprisonment for homosexuality, "the abominable and detestable crime against nature, not to be mentioned among Christians." Upon appeal, the United States district judge who heard the case suggested it was time that the state legislature redraft this criminal statute, since the law was first enacted over 300 years ago (Beigel 1965).

The Legacy of Anthony Comstock

Much of America's overly rigid legislation relating to sexual matters owes its beginnings to a professional moralist from New York, one Anthony Comstock (1844–1915). This zealot's unflagging efforts against vice resulted in the passage in his own state, as well as others, of excessively severe, unrealistic legislation governing "obscenity." Not content with these successes, he eventually pressed his campaign onto the floor of the U.S. Congress.

Early in life Comstock developed a hatred for alcohol, and dedicated several years to the eradication of this "evil" from the world. His attitude on the subject of alcohol was honeylike, however, in comparison with his venomous attitude toward obscenity. On his own initiative, he began personal investigations of alleged violations of New York statutes against "immoral works." He was the inspiring force in the formation of the Commission for Suppression of Vice, through which he worked for passage of federal legislation against obscenity (Commission on Obscenity and Pornography 1970). On March 3, 1873, Comstock's lobbying efforts came to fruition. Congress passed the Obscenity Act, legislation unreasonable in its restrictions and a tribute to obscurity in its definitions. As noted earlier, birth-control information was classed as obscenity, and sending it through the mails a punishable offense. The Tariff Act of 1890 prohibited importation from abroad, or by interstate shipment, of information or devices. Further, incredible penalties were stipulated for the distribution of anything that an active imagination (or a twisted one) could construe as obscene.

With passage of the bill into law, Comstock was made a special agent of the Post Office, in charge of enforcing the federal law. He now held the legal right to open other people's mail. He began to employ trickery to entrap people whom he believed to be involved in obscenity (which, naturally, he defined with considerable latitude). Although Anthony Comstock the man is no longer with us, the spirit of his attitudes lives on in the legislation he influenced and the deprivation of personal liberties for which he established many precedents.

Resistance to changing laws governing sexual behavior stems, of course, from the anxieties of the nation's citizenry when it must deal with anything sexual. It is the result, as well, of every lawmaker's reluctance to do anything that might cause uneasy constituents to view his/her attitudes on sex, punishment, or morality as lax.

In addition, the administration and enforcement of laws pertaining to sexual matters are in discord. It is well known that the ratio of enforcement to violation is very low (Ellis 1961c; Ellis & Brancale 1956; Sherwin 1961). For example, millions of homosexual acts are performed in America for every one conviction. On the whole, homosexual behavior is punished only when it occurs in public (Slovenko 1971a). Yet the laws condemning such behavior both in public and in private remain on many statute books. Oral or anal intercourse between individuals of opposite sex is viewed as a crime in most states ("Abominable & Detestable Crime" 1968; Dolgin & Dolgin 1980), but few law-enforcing agencies bother to prosecute. Many states have statutes making voluntary coition between unmarried adults a criminal act. Yet they license and support a variety of services for unwed mothers, who undeniably have violated the statutes on fornication. Prosecution of these women for their "criminal" act is rare, of course (Vincent 1968c).

Inconsistencies in the enforcement of sex laws often relate directly to the religious beliefs and social attitudes of the judge and law enforcement officers. Inconsistency also stems from confusion over what specific acts a law is intended to define as sexual offenses. Furthermore, Dolgin and Dolgin (1980) observe that legal and judicial rulings tend to reflect the social and moral concerns of the previous generation, since the judges who make the rulings are typically financially secure, male, over 60, and members of the American Bar Association. The whole enforcement picture is muddied even further by the great disparity in penalties for the same offense in various jurisdictions (Caprio 1955; Dolgin & Dolgin 1980), and by the application of a double standard of justice within one jurisdiction. A well-documented 1967 study of sentencing practices in the state of Maryland, for instance, revealed that the average sentence of a black man convicted of raping a white woman (not including those receiving a death or life sentence) was 15.4 years; for a black man raping a black woman, the figure fell to 3.18 years. For white men raping a white woman, sentences averaged 3.67 years and for raping a black woman, 4.6 years ("From the Editor's Scrapbook" 1968a).

The extent to which some of our present laws are at odds with reality is shown by the fact that premarital, extramarital, oral-genital and anal sex, homosexual acts, and sexual relations with a prostitute or with animals are legally prohibited in most states. Although it is not likely, a married couple *can* be arrested for many of the sexual acts typically conducted in the privacy of the bedroom other than the insertion of the penis into the vagina. According to the fuzzy laws of most states, 95% of adult American men and a large percentage of American women have experienced orgasm in an illegal manner (Beigel 1965; Dolgin & Dolgin 1980; Ellis 1961c; Kinsey *et al.* 1953). Illinois was the first state to attempt to eliminate from its criminal code all sexual acts occurring privately between consenting adults.

The constitutionality of archaic sex legislation is coming more and more under attack. In 1965 the U.S. Supreme Court (in *Griswold* v. *Connecticut*) declared unconstitutional Connecticut's law prohibiting the use of birth-control devices, holding that married couples have a substantial right to marital privacy ("Abominable & Detestable Crime" 1968). The dispensing of contraceptives and their use—by married couples, at least—are now legal in all 50 states (Guttmacher 1971). Statutes that give only physicians and pharmacists the right to prescribe and distribute contraceptives have often been challenged in the courts on the ground that such legislation violates the individual's right to privacy and serves no justifiable public interest. The challenge has consistently failed, however. In June 1967 the Supreme Court struck down state laws banning interracial marriage (such legislation still remaining at that time on the statute books of at least 16 states). And in 1968 the U.S. Seventh Circuit Court of Appeals reversed a sodomy conviction in Indiana, citing the 1965 Supreme Court decision mentioned above: "The import of the *Griswold* decision is that private, consensual, marital relations are protected from regulation by the state" ("Abominable & Detestable Crime" 1968).

In recent years the Supreme Court has handed down many decisions establishing the constitutional right to sexual privacy in many areas—notably contraception, abortion, and possession of obscene material. But this right is not yet extended to sexual deviates, which homosexuals are legally considered to be. We have a long way to go.

Obscenity and Pornography

One area of sex legislation considered by many to be a matter of private morality concerns laws on obscenity and pornography. Because they are ambiguous, such laws are subject to a variety of interpretations and frequently appear to be used in the course of legal prosecution largely to satisfy the unconscious needs and desires of the accuser rather than to protect society from the accused. The American culture reacts to the subject of sex with such intense emotion that almost any literary or pictorial representation of sexual interaction is liable to be objectionable to *someone*, hence open to the charge of being obscene (Honigmann 1963). Negative reactions to pornography are often unfounded because, as Athanasiou (1980) points out, there is no evidence to indicate that exposure to erotica "represents a clear and present danger to society in the way that, say, alcohol and tobacco do."

Despite the fact that the U.S. Supreme Court has been called upon several times recently to settle questions of law regarding obscenity, there remains much ambiguity over what is and is not legally obscene and pornographic (Kirkendall 1965). Such ambiguity, as a matter of fact, has led in the past to the censorship or restriction of sale of such classics as *Alice in Wonderland, Huckleberry Finn, Adventures of Sherlock Holmes, Robinson Crusoe, On the Origin of Species,* and *The Scarlet Letter.* Two 1957 U.S. Supreme Court rulings indicate the difficulty in defining what is and is not obscene. The Court held that, while the First and Fourteenth Amendments give no one the right to purvey obscene material, the Constitution does not restrict any material "having even the slightest redeeming social importance . . . ," however unpopular the ideas therein contained. The Court did hold as obscene any material "utterly without redeeming social importance . . .

The legal dilemma: What is pornographic and what is obscene? (Charles Gatewood)

in which to the average person, applying contemporary community standards, the dominant theme of the material taken as a whole appeals to prurient interest."

The 1957 rulings generated enormous confusion and many court battles in the attempt to define what is obscene. In 1973 the U.S. Supreme Court again attempted to resolve the problem by further elaborating upon its 1957 opinions. The latest definition states that the offense of obscenity must be limited to "works, which taken as a whole, appeal to the prurient interest in sex, which portray sexual conduct in a patently offensive way, and which do not have any serious literary, artistic, political, or scientific value." The Supreme Court's decision also dispensed with the concept of a national standard and placed the burden of definition of obscenity on "contemporary community standard." There is little evidence that these recent opinions have clarified or simplified anything. The responsibility for a precise definition has merely been shifted from the Supreme Court to the states and local courts. One can see the endless possibilities for divergent evaluation of the same piece of material, since it is now the responsibility of each township, county, or state to determine the obscenity (or lack of it) in a particular work. What might not cause an eye to widen in Greenwich Village could cause apoplexy in some small midwestern town.

In 1969 Denmark abolished all laws forbidding the sale of pornography. One notable result was the sharp decline in sales of pornographic materials. But the most significant consequence was a 31% drop during 1969, in comparison with 1968 figures, in the overall number of sex crimes committed in Denmark. The greatest decrease was in homosexual offenses, exhibitionism, and child molestation; rape and attempted rape also decreased, although by a smaller margin (Lipton 1971). Furthermore, Danish school officials state that the relaxation of the law has not increased children's contact with obscene material ("Pornography" 1969).

The Kinsey researchers' 25-year study of sex offenders (Gebhard *et al.* 1965) may have uncovered an explanation for the Danish experience in pornography's relevance (or lack of it) to violent sex crimes. The Kinsey group asserted that rapists and other male sexual aggressors are motivated by other factors and are unlikely to be affected by sexually stimulating writing. The sexual aggressor is essentially a psychopath, taking whatever he wants when he wants it. A sexual assault, then, is merely part of his general criminality. His is a socially disordered mind, not a sexually variant one, upon which pornography might act as a trigger.

The relationship between the availability of erotic material and the commission of sex crimes in America appears to present a more complex picture than that in Denmark. In recent years, as pornography has become much easier to buy in this country, the incidence of certain sex crimes (such as forcible rape) has increased, whereas the incidence of others (such as overall juvenile sex-related criminality) has declined. Among juveniles, the number of arrests for sex crimes decreased, although arrest for nonsexual crimes increased by more than 100%. Among adults, arrests for sex offenses increased slightly more than arrests for other offenses (Commission on Obscenity and Pornography 1970). The conclusion must be, therefore, that the relationship between freer availability of erotica and current shifts in the incidence of sex crimes can be neither proved nor disproved. But it is known that no massive overall increase in sex-related criminality has occurred as the result of the large quantities of pornography available in the marketplace today.

The President's Commission on Obscenity and Pornography, which made its report in August 1970, found no scientific evidence that exposure to pornography acts as a cause of misconduct in either youths or adults. The two sociologists on the commission concluded, in fact, that all existing federal, state, and local statutes regarding obscenity, including those restricting juveniles' access to pornographic materials, should be repealed. In recommending repeal, the sociologists declared: "Advocating repeal is not advocating anarchy, for we believe that informal social controls will work better without the confusion of ambiguous and arbitrarily administered laws. With improvements in sex education and better understanding of human sexual behavior, society can more effectively handle, without legislation, the distribution of material deemed by some to be offensive to juveniles or adults" (Commission on Obscenity and Pornography 1970).

Despite the rationality of these views and the relaxation in the 1960s and early 1970s in anxiety over pornography, the late 1970s witnessed a swing back toward conservatism. Antipornography activity once again became evident in many communities and on court dockets. For instance, the publisher of a national sexually oriented magazine (*The Hustler*) was convicted of violating obscenity laws and given a prison term.

The Sex Offender

Psychotherapists speak of sexual variance, deviance, or perversion, but the law considers only *offenses*. The **sex offender** is an individual who commits an act designated by law as a sexual offense and hence a crime (Sadoff 1969). Periodic public clamor for stricter laws for sex crimes has received the support of such personages as the late J. Edgar Hoover, who, when testifying before the House Appropriations Subcommittee, advocated fingerprinting all teachers; he considered them potentially dangerous sex offenders! (To support his position, Hoover cited one instance of a child's having been molested by a teacher [Falk 1965].) On the other hand, many scientific investigators contend there has been no drastic increase in sex crimes in recent years, despite an increase in the number of arrests and in public outcry. They say, further, that what is really needed is a more objective attitude toward sex offenders, more understanding and treatment rather than punishment (Beigel 1965; Ellis 1961c; Ellis & Brancale 1956; Falk 1965; Gebhard *et al.* 1965; Money & Bohmer 1980; Sherwin 1961).

The sex offender is rarely involved in nonsexual crimes. Rather than progressing through a sequence of unacceptable or illegal sexual acts to more serious and diversified criminality, he usually (not always, of course) becomes relatively fixed in variant erotic behavior (Coleman 1972). Few convicted sex offenders resemble the "sex fiend" of popular fiction; most are rather harmless minor deviants (Ellis 1961c; Ellis & Brancale 1956; Gebhard *et al.* 1965; Rubin 1966a). The sex offender who is arrested is usually found to be suffering from personality disturbances. In a study of 300 typical sex offenders at a New Jersey diagnostic center, only 14% were psychologically "normal"; 29% were classified as mildly neurotic, 35% as severely neurotic, 8% as borderline psychotic, 5% as organically brain-damaged, 4% as mentally deficient, 3% as psychopathic, and 2% as psychotic (Ellis & Brancale 1956).

The majority of apprehended sex offenders come from low socio-economic backgrounds, are poorly educated, and fall well below average in intellectual capacity. Subnormal intelligence is more typical of offenders convicted of statutory rape, bestiality, incestuous relations, and sexually aggressive acts against little girls than of offenders convicted of forcible rape, exhibitory acts, homosexuality, and the dissemination of "obscene" material (Ellis 1961c; Ellis & Brancale 1956; Gebhard *et al.* 1965). Few sex criminals take narcotics or are under the influence of drugs at the time of the offense. However, many convicted sex offenders are under the influence of alcohol or other drugs when they commit crimes involving sexual assaults and incestuous relations with children (Ellis 1961c; Ellis & Brancale 1956; Gebhard *et al.* 1965; Bernstein 1979). Contrary to popular notion, the typical convicted sex offender is undersexed rather than oversexed. He is quite likely to be afraid of sexual contact with adult females and to be severely inhibited sexually (except when the crime is statutory rape or incestuous acts against minors). The less emotionally disturbed the sex offender, the less sexually inhibited he tends to be (Caprio 1955; Ellis & Brancale 1956; Gebhard *et al.* 1965).

A popular and often tragic misconception is that the sex offender is typically an elderly person. One of the most compassionate statements ever made on this subject—and certainly an accurate one—came from Dr. Frederick E. Whiskin of the Harvard Medical School. He termed the old man alleged to be a sex offender the most maligned person in our society: a "benign and impotent" creature, whose actions typically are not genital in origin but spring from tragic loneliness (Rubin 1970b). There is special pathos in the plight of the older man charged with a sexual offense. Many old people, in their loneliness and emotional starvation, reach out to a child for warmth and affection (Corbett 1981). If an elderly woman caresses a child, the act is regarded as normal and natural. If an elderly man does so, his simple gesture—which rarely bears any sexual overtones—may well meet with a hysterical cry: "Molester!"

The Kinsey data (Gebhard *et al.* 1965) flatly disprove the popular image of the sex offender as a "dirty old man." The average age of child molesters is 35! Only one-sixth of all men arrested on charges of child molestation are past the age of 50. A comparative study in Pennsylvania of all paroled sex offenders according to age groups heaps further discredit on this popular misconception. Only 4.58% of these offenders were past 60, although men in this age group constituted nearly 20% of the state's total male population. The largest number of sex offenders (23%) fell in the age range of 20 to 24 years, yet men in this age group comprised only 8% of the male population of Pennsylvania ("Dangerous Sex Offender" 1963).

Most convicted offenders are the "losers" of our society. They are usually so inept and severely disturbed emotionally that all their activities, sexual offenses included, are probably executed in a stupid or indiscreet manner. They are, consequently, quite liable to be found out—in contrast to intelligent sex offenders, who are not, and even if discovered, are less likely to be convicted (Ellis 1961c; Gebhard *et al.* 1965). Because of his emotional problems, the sex offender may well repeat his offense unless he receives psychotherapy (Ellis 1961c). Even so, the recidivism rate among convicted sex offenders is lower than that of other criminals. During one 13-year span, less than 10% of 4000 convicted sex offenders studied and treated at New Jersey's Menlo Park Diagnostic Center were known recidivists. Attention centers, unfortunately, on the 10% who do become recidivists rather than on the 90% who never do ("Sex Offenders Good Parole Risk" 1963).

Investigators generally divide sex offenses into two broad categories (Ellis & Brancale 1956; Gebhard *et al.* 1965). The first involves more or less normal behavior, which does not deviate very far from that of the general populace. Transgressions falling in this category (for example, the man who occasionally becomes a Peeping Tom) do little or no psychological damage to the people involved, and have no adverse effect on social organization. For various reasons, however, the conduct is considered by society as sufficiently inappropriate to warrant punishment. Since society is not harmed by these offenses, punishment should not be severe. Effort is more appropriately directed toward helping offenders make a better adjustment to their life situation.

The second class of sex offense is uncommon. Here the behavior is truly unacceptable and is motivated by abnormal personality traits. The offenses may constitute a public nuisance, be socially disruptive, and cause psychological damage to those involved. It is toward this category of sex offenders that attention and money should be spent for detection, research, and treatment. Several states now, fortunately, have sexual psychopathy statutes, which provide for the commitment and treatment of those whose commission of sexual offenses stems from mental disorders.

Homosexuality

Homosexual contact is considered a crime in most states, and punishment ranges from a fine to life imprisonment. As of 1980, only 21 states had ended the criminalization of consensual sodomy by adults in private (Vetri 1980). Respondents in various national polls have been more consistent in their ranking of homosexuality as deviant than they have been in their ranking of any other sexual act among the 200 listed. Homosexuality has been regarded (according to various surveys) as a greater menace to society than abortion, prostitution, or adultery. It has been ranked third (after the sale of salacious literature and teen-age sex relations) in a list of elements considered most detrimental to society. In still another poll, only communism and atheism outweighed homosexuality as the greatest threat to the nation (Weinberg & Williams 1974). Although increasing numbers of thoughtful people dispute the view that homosexual behavior among consenting adults should be considered a crime (or even a misdemeanor), a 1977 Gallup poll showed that 43% of Americans still do not favor decriminalization of it.

Is the public justified in its strong distrust of homosexuals? Their sexual proclivities notwithstanding, homophiles hardly present the picture of men and women who are in any way a detriment to their community. Of all sex offenders, they have the highest socioeconomic status and are the best educated. Drugs and drink are not factors in their behavior. They are least likely of all to deny guilt when faced with legal charges of homosexuality. The number of homophiles convicted of offenses other than sexual ones is the smallest of all sex offenders in the Kinsey study (Gebhard *et al.* 1965). The Kinsey investigators concluded that homosexuals are neither dangerous nor criminal. "They do not damage society; they merely do not fit into it" ("Homosexuality" 1969).

Under the sponsorship of the National Institute of Mental Health, a 14-member panel (led by Dr. Evelyn Hooker of UCLA, a leading authority on homosexuality) completed a far-reaching study of homosexuality. The panel concluded that the hostility and suspicions harbored by so many Americans toward homophiles are unfounded, that they pose no threat to public morals and decorum. The report said further that the widespread infamy and contempt attached to homosexuality do more social harm than good.

The report continues: "Homosexuality presents a major problem for our society largely because of the amount of injustice and suffering entailed in it, not only for the homosexual, but also for those concerned about him" ("Homosexuality" 1969). The report went on to recommend that the United States follow the example of England, which in 1968 made legal any homosexual act performed discreetly between consenting adults. There have been no discernible ill effects suffered by the British public. (Any forcible homosexual contact or one involving minors remains, of course, a criminal act.) The implication of the Hooker report is that we have jeopardized the mental health of homophiles by driving them underground into a life shrouded by fear of discovery and the ever-present danger of blackmail. The techniques of entrapment used by the police are degrading. The homosexual is discriminated against in government and private industry jobs, although most are good citizens and productive members of society. Homosexuality is an undesirable way of life to members of the "straight" world. But this in no way implies that all homosexuals are undesirable members of society—or that heterosexuals are more desirable because they are "straight."

The suggestion that homosexuals in top-level government jobs are poor security risks and should therefore be fired upon discovery may be well taken—but not for the reasons usually offered to support it. Because the homosexual's preferences are different from those of the average heterosexual, the homophile is judged to have a flawed character, and to be lacking in the virtues of trustworthiness and loyalty. It is assumed, therefore, that at the first opportunity—or at least with little pressure—homophiles are ready to betray their country. Knowing that the revelation of their homosexuality will bring shame to their families, loss of their job, and perhaps legal prosecution, homosexuals understandably might yield to threat and commit acts of disloyalty rather than face public exposure. It is the threat of blackmail that makes the homosexual somewhat vulnerable to corrupt pressures, rather than an innate tendency to disloyalty. Recent data (Bell & Weinberg 1978) indicate, however, that very few homosexuals any longer worry about having their homosexuality exposed.

It seems that reasonable, decent people would want—in fact, demand—equal rights for all citizens. Most Americans would no doubt agree that a person's behavior is acceptable as long as it harms no one else. But in the matter of homosexuality, the American public is not so sure. Even the proposed, beleaguered ERA amendment would bar discrimination against sex, not sexual preference. Many opponents of the decriminalization of homosexuality concede that there is not any more danger of youngsters being sexually seduced by homosexuals than by heterosexuals. Their opposition is based on the contention that making homosexuality legal and removing discriminatory policies provides tacit approval of homosexuality as a sanctioned option for youngsters to consider. They see particular dangers, then, in permitting homosexuals to teach in public schools, for instance, because they fear that the teacher might provide an undesirable role model.

Prostitution

The prevailing American attitude is that prostitution is a social and moral evil and a threat to health, and that legal controls should be leveled against it.

Despite the laws against it, prostitution continues to flourish (as it has from time immemorial), and efforts to abolish it have largely been ineffective. The act of prostitution is outlawed in 38 states; 44 prohibit solicitation; and 6 punish prostitutes under antivagrancy laws. Some states—notably California—have sought to remove the act of prostitution from their penal codes, but with little success to date. Postitution is legal in only one state (Nevada). Efforts at controlling it in the other 49 have met with uneven success, depending upon the size of the city or village, strength of local laws, and determination of the enforcement agents. Further, when prostitutes are arrested, the penalty is typically a fine, not imprisonment. Such penalties are small deterrents to prostitution, and might be viewed as a form of excise tax that will ultimately be passed on to the customer. Incidentally, the customer is rarely arrested.

Legal control of prostitution in other Western countries is about as muddled as it is in America. It is permitted in Germany, although strictly regulated. England's Wolfenden Report (1957) recommended that, while prostitution should not be illegalized, legislation should be passed "to drive it off the streets" on the ground that public solicitation is a nuisance. Laws to decriminalize prostitution have also been formulated in France, Sweden, Denmark, and the Netherlands (Townley 1980).

As an example of the ineffectiveness of much prostitution legislation, a law passed in Italy in 1958, aimed at stamping out prostitution and "freeing" the inhabitants of brothels, had precisely the opposite effect. By 1965 the number of Italian prostitutes had increased from 18,000 to an estimated 200,000, the latter figure including part-time practitioners. Within a year of the 1958 legislation, furthermore, the incidence of syphilis in Italy had risen by 25%, and by 1961, the country's VD rate had become the highest in Europe ("From the Editor's Scrapbook" 1966).

Abortion

In January 1973, the U.S. Supreme Court ruled (7 to 2) that the decision to have an abortion in the first trimester of pregnancy is a personal judgment to be made by the pregnant woman and her physician without interference from the law. And under special circumstances it may be performed during the second or even the third trimester. It is required that a physician perform the abortion, and criminal statutes are enforceable against non-physicians. This ruling invalidated almost all existing state laws, many of which contradicted one another. The Court further ruled that state statutes requiring the consent of the husband or the parents, in the case of unmarried minors, are unconstitutional. The woman must, however, be mentally competent to make the decision to have an abortion.

In June 1977, the same Supreme Court ruled that no state is obliged to pay for an abortion, even though matching federal funds are available. As dissenting Justice Harry Blackmun observed, the Court has now freed the individual states to do indirectly what they could not do directly after the 1973 decision—to deny abortion to anyone who cannot pay for it. More affluent women remain free to go to private physicians and hospitals for an abortion. Poor women, typically the ones most desirous and in need of abortions, apparently can go elsewhere—an implication in the ruling reminiscent of Anatole France's comment in the 19th century, "The law in its majestic equality forbids the rich as well as the poor to sleep under bridges."

Three years later, in 1980, the Supreme Court further ruled in a 5 to 4 vote to uphold the ban by Congress on federal funding of the majority of welfare abortions. The Supreme Court also said that states are not obliged to provide money for abortions, since the Congressional Hyde Amendment withdraws federal financing of abortions. The effect of the Supreme Court decision is to eliminate funding for Medicaid abortions. Federal funding will be allowed only in cases where the woman's life is in jeopardy or in special cases where pregnancy results from incest or rape ("Supreme Court" 1980). The result inevitably will be dark and dirty abortion attempts, do-it-yourself and otherwise, or the addition of thousands to the ranks of unwanted children. Even the economic considerations implicit in the Court's ruling are questionable. The cost to the public through Medicaid is about $150 for an abortion; the cost to taxpayers of supporting a child in just its first year of life is $2200 (Fraker *et al.* 1977; Morrow 1977).

Some objections to abortion hinge on the possible psychological damage it may cause the woman. But when scientific research is used as an index rather than personal opinion, doubt is cast on the possibilities of such harm. Women tend to show few negative emotional reactions on a result of abortion. In fact, emotional benefit appears to accrue to those women whose request for abortion was granted in comparison with those whose request was refused (Hook 1963; Osofsky & Osofsky 1972).

Despite varying opinions on abortion legislation and practice, the moral as well as legal problems are clearly profound. They revolve around the question of when the conceptus becomes a human being and hence capable of being murdered. To those who believe that human life begins the moment the sperm enters the ovum, any abortion constitutes murder, no matter how great the therapeutic or eugenic justification. Indeed, the zygote does contain the full component of its chromosomal inheritance from the moment of conception. As a human being, this group argues, the fetus comes under the protection of the Constitution and has the right to life. Others view the embryo as nothing more than a cell mass or an organic part of the mother until it becomes capable of living apart from her (generally considered to be about the 25th week of prenatal life). A fetus under 20 weeks old usually does not require burial or a death certificate. They argue that an embryo, as a part of the mother, is subject to her will—and that a woman has the fundamental right to choose whether or not to bear a child.

Because personal convictions regarding abortion differ vastly, one is left with the doubt that a consensus among doctors, lawyers, lawmakers, and the general public can ever be reached. What, for example, are the legal rights of the unborn child? Certain court rulings in the United States have established the inheritance rights of the unborn child, and its right to recover damages if it receives injuries prior to birth. What about the right of the unborn to be born? How sacred is that right? If a group of lawmakers decrees that the right to birth is not absolute, to what degree is the mother's health, sanity, and well-being superior to the right of the infant? In those cases in which there is good reason to suspect that the child conceived will be born with serious defects, what considerations justify legislation to terminate the pregnancy?

If abortion is right under special circumstances, what are they? At what fetal age does it become wrong? Is it, in fact, a legal question at all, or should the decision be left to the person most concerned in the matter— the woman involved in the unwanted pregnancy?

Despite the incredible advances in techniques of birth control, will it ever be possible to prevent all pregnancies except those a woman desires? Public conscience appears to be moving gradually toward the following view, as expressed in a *Time* magazine essay:

> Along with poverty, ignorance and moral strictures against birth control, the unpredictability of human sexual practices makes un- wanted pregnancy inevitable. The way to deal with the problem forthrightly is on terms that permit the individual, guided by con- science and intelligence, to make a choice unhampered by archaic and hypocritical concepts and statutes. ["Desperate Dilemma of Abortion" 1967]

Illegitimacy

Unwanted pregnancies and high illegitimacy rates continue to be matters of great concern. Increased sexual activity among young people accom- panied by inconsistent use of contraceptives has inevitably led to increased pregnancy rates, particularly among teen-agers (Hacker 1980). Of the 60 million women in the world who became mothers in 1975, 20% were teen-agers. Each year about 10% of all American female teen-agers—more than 1 million—between 15 and 19 become pregnant, and over half give birth. Two-thirds (about 625,000) of these pregnancies are conceived outside marriage. Furthermore, 30,000 girls *younger* than 15 become pregnant annually. Of those teen-age mothers whose babies are born out of wedlock, 87% keep the child, 5% allow it to live with others (usually relatives), and 8% place it for adoption (Alan Guttmacher Institute 1976).

Americans have traditionally regarded illegitimacy as a moral evil, for which both mother and child have been subjected to social disapproval and, in the past, legal punishment (R. R. Bell 1971a). However, attitudes have relaxed since the 1960s, at least legally. Many states now grant protection to the illegitimate child comparable to that given the legitimate one. In the matter of paternal support, however, court awards are less generous to the illegitimate child than to the legitimate one. The illegitimate child still cannot inherit in most states should the father die without a valid

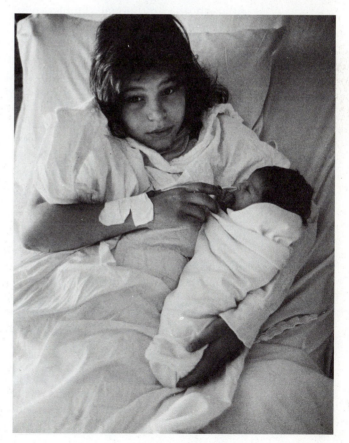

Unmarried teenage mother with her child (Mary Ellen Mark/Magnum Photos, Inc.)

will (Vincent 1973). The child of the unwed mother in the United States has the same inheritance rights to her property that her legitimate children do, although in most states the child does not automatically inherit from her relatives. In only a very few states are *all* children considered legitimate and accorded equal rights (R. R. Bell 1971a).

Financial support of the illegitimate child is a frequent matter of public controversy. The fact that Aid to Dependent Children (ADC) benefits are not based on legitimacy has raised the ire of many Americans, who see ADC as motivating financially needy women to produce illegitimate children. Some states have gone so far as attempting to pass laws requiring compulsive sterilization of women having more than one illegal pregnancy. The actual fact is that less than 10% of illegitimate children receive ADC (Vincent 1973). Furthermore, it would take a strange woman to go through the ordeal of giving birth and rearing a child just to obtain the small amount of financial support available in such cases.

The social, emotional, and financial consequences of an illegitimate birth continue to be grim for both mother and child. Attitudes toward sexual activity appear more tolerant than was the case several decades ago, although the traditional double standard of judgment still applies to illegitimate mothers and illegitimate fathers (Shah & Zelnik 1980). The illegitimate mother continues to be judged severely, perhaps because she has obviously had "illicit sex" and is seen as a threat by women who may doubt their own sexual desirability or whose marriages are shaky. The unmarried father carries with him no physical evidence of his unacceptable premarital sexual behavior. His violation of the moral standards of the community is therefore less obvious than that of the unwed mother. Even within marriage, the woman is more often blamed for an unwanted pregnancy. This attitude carries over into public thinking in the matter of illegitimate pregnancies, and is perhaps responsible for legislation in some states carrying the suggestion that after several nonmarital pregnancies, a woman be sterilized. These laws make no mention of the fathers.

Whatever the burdens faced by the illegitimate mother and the illegitimate father, it seems clear that it is the illegitimate child who is affected most by the circumstances surrounding his/her birth. Little can be done to correct society's prejudice against the illegitimate child until the laws are changed to protect that child fully. It seems only fair, and it is certainly sound insofar as the mental health of the population is concerned, that the states should establish more adequate laws to protect the illegitimate child (Landis & Landis 1963). Here are some of the ways in which this goal might best be accomplished:

1. Birth certificates should be so worded that the data in them regarding paternity do not reveal illegitimacy. Birth data are public records and in most states are available at the county seat of a baby's birthplace; anyone who cares to look can do so.

2. The state should be made responsible for attempting to establish paternity, since the mother is often unable (or unwilling) to do so. As matters presently stand, if the mother does not institute legal proceedings, there is no pressure on the father to support the child.
3. Adequate prenatal care should be available to every expectant mother, regardless of whether her pregnancy is legitimate or illegitimate.
4. All needy children should be given adequate financial aid by the state.
5. From the pulpit, home, and school should come sincere efforts to remold the public's view of the illegitimate child. For if blame for illegitimacy must be ascribed, it should be to the parents and not to the child, who is innocent of any wrongdoing.

Sterilization

Sterilization for eugenic reasons is sanctioned in some American states, particularly in tax-supported institutions. In these instances a doctor is free to perform sterilizing operations without concern for any legal consequences. If the operation is done purely for reasons of health, however, the doctor's legal position is less secure. As a consequence, many doctors are reluctant to perform sterilization at a patient's request.

In this area, too, there are no uniform laws among the various states. In California, malpractice suits resulting from surgery for sterilization are not usually covered by insurance companies. Written consent by the patient affords the physician some measure of safety, but is no guarantee against a subsequent suit or even prosecution in a court of criminal law. All states hold that sterilization is legal in cases of severe medical necessity and for socioeconomic reasons, although Utah prohibits sterilization of institutionalized persons (Guttmacher 1971; Pilpel 1971).

Artificial Insemination

The use of semen from a donor to impregnate a woman whose husband is infertile has an uncertain legal status. Some jurists have declared artificial insemination to be adultery and the children born as a result of it illegitimate. Others have deemed it a legal procedure, producing legitimate children.

At least seven states (Georgia, Oklahoma, Arkansas, California, Kansas, Maryland, and North Carolina) and one municipality (New York City) have taken action to bring order out of this chaos by passing statutes legalizing artificial insemination by donor, provided both husband and wife sign their consent. Actually only the Georgia, Kansas, and Oklahoma statutes provide for the rights of all parties involved: father, mother, child, physician, and donor. The others merely protect the child by declaring it legitimate.

Model Sex Laws

It seems reasonable to suppose that the purpose of laws concerning sexual conduct is to protect the individual from coercion, to protect the young against the unwholesome designs of adults who would take advantage of them, to protect the public from flagrant displays of sexual acts that may be disruptive of the peace, and to protect the institutions of family and marriage. The purpose of such laws should not be to determine and enforce standards of morality (Cory & LeRoy 1964). These were the principles set forth in the early 1960s by the Illinois and Chicago Bar Associations. In their formulation of a legal code governing sexual behavior, they suggested that these principles would adequately and realistically meet the needs of a modern society. The two groups of lawyers propounded and had accepted by the Illinois state legislature what is probably the most sensible and enforceable set of sex laws ever found in America (Cory & LeRoy 1964).

Under the Illinois code, for example, the legal definition of rape no longer includes "statutory" or "nonviolent" rape. A sexual act is not rape unless the male uses force against the female. If she gives her consent but is not of legal age, the offense is handled under that section of the penal code dealing with "contributing to the sexual delinquency of a child."

Furthermore, no offense is committed under the Illinois code for engaging in bestiality. Acts of sexual gratification involving the sex organs of one person and the mouth or anus of another are no longer punishable, unless such acts are brought about by force, threat, or violence, or unless one participant is underage, or unless the act offends public decency. Such acts performed by consenting adults, whether heterosexual or homosexual, if conducted in private, are not punishable.

Punishment for incest in Illinois now takes into consideration the closeness of the relationship between the parties and their ages. Aggravated incest, which incurs the most severe punishment, is defined as coitus or an act of deviant sexual conduct between a man and his daughter, no matter what her age. Other forbidden sexual contact involves father-stepdaughter and father-foster daughter, if the girl is under the age of 18. The strictness of this law is based on the strong position that the father often holds in the family, and the influence he can exert on a daughter.

Public indecency or public exposure, according to the Illinois law, relates to the place where the sex act is carried out. A public place is "any place where the conduct may reasonably be expected to be viewed by others." Thus, while a boy and a girl may be permitted to engage in light petting on a park bench, two men could not expect to get by with similar activity. However, a man would not be punished for suggesting to another man that they engage in such acts in private.

The Illinois law punishes men and women alike for prostitution, solicitation for a prostitute, operating a place for prostitution, and patronizing a prostitute. While the law defines prostitution as accepting money for sexual intercourse or deviant sexual conduct, it does not define as prostitution the acceptance of nonmonetary gifts (such as jewelry) for sexual favors.

In May 1967, the President's Crime Commission recommended removing from the domain of criminal law many sexual acts now considered crimes, contending that these matters are often social ills and should be treated as such. In an effort to cope more realistically with the sexual activity of their citizenry, seven other states have adopted the Illinois approach. In the matter of state control of sexual activity, the remaining 42 states are positioned at various points along a wide spectrum. Marked differences remain in both definition of acts classified as crimes and penalties provided for them.

Legislative bodies are giving renewed attention to laws pertaining to rape. In June 1977, the U.S. Supreme Court ruled that the death penalty for rape is cruel and unusual punishment (except when the victim is murdered) and is therefore unconstitutional. There are also indications that many states are in the process of making much-needed changes in their rape laws. The new approach is to treat rape as violent assault, which it is. In the past, trials seemed to be of the rape victim rather than the accused. Cross-examinations about the victim's sex life are typically demeaning and humiliating, aimed at establishing that she is an unchaste woman of poor character. Some victims commented that the rape was bad enough, but the trial was worse. Dolgin and Dolgin (1980) report that only a small percentage—estimated at between 5% and 20%—of rape victims go to the police or legal authorities after being raped. Perhaps the fear of being blamed or somehow being held responsible for the rape has kept women from reporting the crime.

Changes that might reverse this trend include these:

1. Barring defense attorneys from delving into the sexual history of the victim, except with respect to the defendant, and then only upon a written motion heard outside the hearing of the jury.
2. Doing away with the 17th-century "Lord Hale instructions," required in many states to be read to rape juries by the presiding judge, which state that rape is the "easiest charge to make and the most difficult to prove."
3. Doing away with the necessity for corroborating testimony—an eyewitness or other evidence that the woman put up a struggle.

As long ago as 1960, legal experts from all over the world met in an attempt to bring order and equity to the chaos of existing criminal law. The Fourth International Convention on Criminology, held in The Hague, attended by over 600 governmental representatives and criminal law professors from almost every nation on the globe, adopted various resolutions to correct inequities in and misuse of sex laws. They called for:

1. Removal of fornication and adultery from the list of criminal offenses.
2. More liberal interpretation and lenient punishment of acts of incest.
3. More liberal laws concerning birth control, abortion, and artificial insemination.
4. Extension of equal rights and freedom to homosexuals.
5. Tougher laws concerning nonsupport of wives and children. [Mueller 1965]

Since the first Kinsey reports, the thinking of many experts in the legal, psychological, and sociological fields has been that laws pertaining to sex should be limited to those sex acts that (1) involve the use of force or threat of force, (2) involve minors, or (3) are performed in public. By concentrating on these aspects, many problems are bypassed—especially those created by laws that are unenforceable, useless, antiquated, inapplicable, or simply not within the province of law enforcement. In addition to these three basic criteria, other measures geared to prevent potential sex offenses and to provide better care and treatment of acknowledged offenders have been suggested by Albert Ellis (1961c), who has been prominent in the study of the psychology of sex offenders:

All laws pertaining to sexual behavior should be rewritten in more definitive and meaningful terminology.

Before the accused is sentenced, a complete psychological examination should be performed to determine whether he is sexually or psychologically abnormal, or is psychopathic.

Psychological treatment should be provided for offenders in their own community while they are on probation. If confinement is ordered, it should be in a mental hospital or similar institution that affords specific psychotherapy for sex offenders. In the event of institutionalization, protective custody should be maintained for as long as the patient is judged to be a menace to society.

Sex offenders should be offered help and understanding, rather than contempt and punishment.

If a preventive approach is to be effective, there must be wider dissemination of accurate sex information. Through such education, children will gain a more scientific and objective understanding of human sexuality.

Money and Bohmer (1980) point out that it does not make sense to confine sex offenders in an environment that may actually encourage continued offenses. These investigators suggest that some form of conjugal visitation or perhaps even family living arrangements may be a more logical course of action, especially in light of the coercive sexual acts and rampant homosexuality that currently appear to exist in many prisons. New efforts by prison authorities to protect prisoners from sexual assault would seemingly aid in the rehabilitation of these individuals.

When a society refuses to seek improvement of the condition of its sick and downtrodden, and when overly severe punishment is meted out to transgressors, something is assuredly wrong. Psychological evaluation of those members of society who would maltreat the unfortunate will quite likely reveal personal hostilities and conflicts rather than an altruistic desire to protect the community.

If legislation governing sexual affairs is to be improved, society must gain a clearer understanding of the character of the sex offender. Implicit in this understanding is an insight into the significant roles played by guilt and conflict in sexual difficulties. Guilt regarding sexual matters begins early in childhood when a child engaging in sexual exploration is censured, or when questions concerning sex are avoided by parents. At such moments, the youngster's sexual acts and desires, such as they are, begin to be tinged with guilt; the ability to respond normally and naturally to his or her sex drive becomes impaired. Out of this guilt spring almost endless possibilities for psychosexual disturbances. A denial of sexuality and deviant or furtive methods of expressing sexuality are among the potential aberrations that can result from defective sexual training.

It can be hoped that we are finding our way out of the morass of sexual ignorance and guilt. Perhaps the next decade will bring a better understanding of human sexuality, and with it more realistic approaches to social problems.

Summary

Religious codes, group pressure, and the law all have been used to influence individuals to conform with the prevailing societal mores. Examination of those laws regulating sexual behavior shows that they are often vague or inconsistent and sometimes have been the outgrowth of ignorance and guilt rather than the result of reason and emotional objectivity. While those laws regulating sex forced on an unwilling partner seem acceptable or at least understandable, those laws regulating sexual acts committed in privacy by willing partners have generated much controversy.

Today's overly rigid legislation on sexual matters derives from the efforts of Anthony Comstock over a century ago. Comstock was the prevailing force toward passage of federal legislation against obscenity, and the resultant deprivation of personal liberties grew out of this influence. Today, inconsistencies exist in the enforcement of sex laws because there often is confusion over what specific acts a law defines as sexual offenses. As a result, 95% of American men and a large percentage of American women have experienced orgasm in an illegal manner, although the likelihood of arrest and prosecution for these "deviant" sex acts is slim. The Supreme Court rulings such as the 1965 *Griswold* vs. *Connecticut* decision have gone a long way toward re-establishing constitutional rights to privacy.

The laws on obscenity and pornography are good examples of the problems involved in the legislation of sexuality because these laws have been subjected to a variety of interpretations. While these laws have come on the books primarily because of the general public's fears of societal decay, it appears that such negative reactions to pornography often are unfounded because no evidence exists indicating that exposure to erotica causes danger to society. Two 1957 U.S. Supreme Court rulings and a later 1973 ruling have attempted to clarify the definition of obscenity, but questions still exist as to what constitutes obscenity. Currently, the definition of obscenity rests on the "contemporary community standards"; thus variations exist in different towns, counties, or states on whether a given piece of material is obscene. It should be noted that no massive increase in sex-related criminality in America has resulted from the availability of pornography. Nevertheless, the current trend toward conservatism had led to increased efforts against pornography in many communities.

Sex offenders are defined as those individuals who engage in acts designated by law as sex offenses and hence are crimes. One category of sex offenses includes relatively minor sex offenses (e.g., voyeurism) and another category of sex offenses stems from mental disorders. While individuals in the second class of sex offenses require special attention and treatment, the typical convicted sex offender (male) is undersexed rather than oversexed and is often afraid of sexual contact with an adult female. Most sex offenders are relatively young and could be classified as the "losers" in our society.

Homosexual contact is considered a crime in most states. Many people consider it to be a menace to society. In contrast to these fears, homosexuals pose no threat to public morals or decorum, but they still suffer societal and legal injustices. Nevertheless, many homosexuals continue to be productive members of society; of all sex offenders they have the highest socioeconomic status, are the best educated, and drug and drink are seldom factors in their behavior. Those who oppose the decriminalization of homosexuality contend that making homosexuality legal and encouraging its acceptance by society would provide tacit approval of homosexuality as a sanctioned option for youngsters to consider. The legal and social issues surrounding homosexuality remain a subject for further debate.

Prostitution is illegal in most states in the U.S. although the legal efforts to abolish it have largely been ineffective. Prostitution in the U.S. is legal only in Nevada, but laws to decriminalize prostitution have been enacted or formulated in other Western countries. Some of the past efforts to control prostitution through legislation were found to have backfired.

Abortions have been more readily available to women since the U.S. Supreme Court ruled in 1973 that the decision to have an abortion in the first trimester of the pregnancy is a personal judgment to be made by the woman and her physician. A more conservative national attitude appears to be developing toward the subject of abortion and more recent court rulings may make abortions less available to women because of financial reasons. While more affluent women will probably go to private physicians and hospitals if they want abortions, poor women will have to bear unwanted children. This may happen despite findings showing that many women have derived emotional benefits when they have had the option of terminating their unwanted pregnancies. Moral and legal questions revolving around the rights of the unborn child and the right of a woman to choose whether or not to bear her child complicate the issue of abortion.

Prime matters of concern today are the unwanted pregnancies and high illegitimacy rate prevalent among teenagers. The social, emotional, and financial consequencies of an illegitimate birth continue to be grim, particularly for the mother and the child, with the father being judged less severely. While many states now grant protection to the illegitimate child, there are still instances when the illegitimate child does not have the same inheritance or other rights that the legitimate child has. Changes in laws to protect the illegitimate child appear especially pertinent.

Sterilization, for eugenic reasons as well as for purely health reasons, is often performed in the United States. State laws are not uniform with regard to sterilization, although all 50 hold sterilization to be legal in cases of severe medical necessity and for socioeconomic reasons. Artificial insemination also has a lack of uniformity in legal status from state to state. Some of the states do have statutes providing for the rights of all parties involved.

Model sex laws such as those formulated by the Illinois State Legislature have led to a more sensible and enforceable approach to sexual issues including rape, bestiality, oral-genital sex, incest, public indecency or public exposure, and prostitution. Other legislative bodies are changing rape laws to recognize that rape is an act of violent assault and thus take a more sympathetic and understanding approach to the rape victim. At the same time, a more sensitive and sympathetic approach to the plights of sex offenders have been advocated by legal and health authorities. Efforts to eliminate sexual guilt and ignorance in the general population have been recommended by mental health professionals. In this way, legislation governing sexual affairs can be made more sensitive to the needs of today's society.

Annotated Bibliography

Athanasiou, Robert. Pornography: A review of research. In *Handbook of human sexuality*, ed. B. Wolman and J. Money. Englewood Cliffs, New Jersey: Prentice-Hall, 1980.
> This article surveys studies concerning the effects of pornography, physiological response to pornography, the effects of pornography on social behavior and personality, and social and sex differences in response to erotica. The variety of definitions of pornography with respect to local statutes is considered.

Barry, Kathleen. *Female sexual slavery*. Englewood Cliffs, New Jersey: Prentice-Hall, 1979.
> Based on research and interviews with victims and law enforcement personnel, this book explores the problem of forced prostitution and sexual oppression in contemporary American society. Related historical, social, political, and economic issues are examined. This book would be interesting reading for the general public.

Dolgin, Janet L. and Dolgin, Barbara L. Sex and the law. In *Handbook of human sexuality*, ed. B. Wolman and J. Money. Englewood Cliffs, New Jersey: Prentice-Hall, 1980.
> This article studies the application of law to sexual activity and the interrelationship between law and sex. Citing relevant court decisions, the authors consider such matters as sex discrimination, contraception, homosexuality, obscenity, abortion, prostitution, consensual sodomy, and rape. Appendices include purposes and definitions concerning sex and treatment of rape under New York penal law.

Faust, Beatrice. *Women, sex, and pornography*. New York: MacMillan, 1980.
> This book analyzes the issue of pornography from the perspective of women, focusing on differences in male and female sexuality. This book offers provocative reading for a lay audience.

Heilman, Madeline. Sex discrimination. In *Handbook of human sexuality*, ed. B. Wolman and J. Money. Englewood Cliffs, New Jersey: Prentice-Hall, 1980.
> This essay examines the historical and cultural stereotypes concerning women as the basis for sex discrimination. Findings and implications of research related to sex discriminatory behavior are discussed.

Hursch, C. J. *The trouble with rape*. Chicago: Nelson-Hall, 1977.
> This book presents a comprehensive research-based analysis and description of the problem of rape. The author addresses resolution of legal, medical, sociological, and psychological problems and suggests new legislation and treatment of sex offenders. This is a valuable book for the general reader, and would be especially interesting to law enforcement personnel.

Lederer, Laura (Ed.). *Take back the night: Women and pornography.* New York: William Morris, 1980.

> This book is a collection of articles by women on the history, ethics, politics, economics, and effects of pornography. This book is a product of the feminist effort to stop pornography, providing interesting perspective for the general reader.

MacKinnon, Catherine A. *Sexual harassment of working women.* New Haven: Yale University Press, 1979.

> Written by a lawyer especially for lawyers, this book examines the social problem of sexual harassment of women in the employment setting. The argument is advanced that sexual harassment is actually discrimination based on sex. The general public would find this book interesting.

Sandler, Jack, Myerson, Marilyn, and Kinder, Bill N. *Human sexuality: Current perspectives.* Tampa, Florida: Mariner, 1980.

> This text presents a comprehensive perspective of the field of human sexuality. A wide range of topics is covered, including sexual anatomy and sexual response, aphrodisiacs and anaphrodisiacs, past and current sexual attitudes and behavior, sexual diseases and disorders, sexual dysfunctions, birth control, sexual health, and sex and the law. Though designed for the student, this book would serve as a valuable general reference.

Witters, Weldon and Jones-Witters, Patrica. *Human sexuality: A biological perspective.* New York: D. Van Nostrand, 1980.

> This text approaches the various aspects of human sexuality from the biological standpoint. Topics of special interest include genetic engineering, hormonal control of sexuality, drugs affecting sexual function, surrogate parenthood, artificial insemination, cloning, and sex selection. The text is well illustrated and contains student performance objectives, but its appeal extends beyond the classroom.

Zuckerman, Marvin. Research on pornography. In *Sex and the life cycle*, ed. W. Oaks, G. Melchiode, and I. Ficher. New York: Grune and Stratton, 1976.

> This article reviews the findings of the Commission on Obscenity and Pornography as well as research relevant to pornography. Topics include reported arousal by visual stimuli, sex differences in reported arousal, factors in response to erotic stimuli, motivation and interest in seeing erotic stimuli, and personality variables associated with viewing pornography.

79 GEFESSELTER PROMETHEUS 1946.

Part Five
Sexual Complications

Despite the efforts and good intentions of schools, parents, churches, social scientists, and other mental health professionals to educate or otherwise help people toward sexual understanding and adjustment, sexual problems continue to be a major obstacle in smoothly functioning human relationships. Some of these problems are physical; a disease or anatomical disorder in the reproductive system exists. Some have to do with psychological problems or conflicts that may interfere with certain individuals' ability to function sexually in a manner satisfactory to themselves or their partners.

Whatever the difficulty may be, it can create much misery in the lives of the persons affected by it, as well as their sexual partners. Further, it is important to recognize that sex-related diseases, disorders, and dysfunctions are more prevalent than one might think.

The material in Part Five is presented so that the reader may better understand the number and extent of various types of sexual complications and their underlying causes. Chapter 20 provides information about training programs designed to correct sexual dysfunctioning. Through the efforts of a few dedicated scientists and institutions in recent years, help is now available to persons thus affected. The material in Chapter 21 is intended to alert readers to the critical problem of venereal disease. The causes and symptoms of VD as well as the other diseases and disorders of the sexual system are discussed, together with the therapeutic measures used to treat them.

20

Sexual Dysfunctions

The assertion that at least 50% of American marriages are flawed by some form of sexual maladjustment or dysfunction is a gloomy commentary on one of mankind's oldest institutions (Lehrman 1970; Masters & Johnson 1970). The entire structure of a marriage is usually affected by sexual problems, because the distress experienced by one partner directly affects the other. Masters and Johnson (1970) have repeatedly emphasized that no matter what form the difficulty takes there is "no such entity as an uninvolved partner contending with any form of sexual inadequacy." Indeed, relationships with every other family member are affected as well. (It should be noted, however, that some couples whose sexual relationship is poor may nonetheless have a good, loving relationship in other areas.) Often sex reflects a couple's feelings and behavior in the overall relationship—but not always (Sager 1976).

One survey revealed that the average physician encounters about three cases a week in which problems of sexual maladjustment exist (Mace 1971a). The actual number of patients with sexual problems is undoubtedly considerably higher than this survey indicates. Many

493

physicians do not routinely inquire into the sexual aspect of their patients' lives for the obvious reason that their medical specialty precludes it. A more compelling reason is that they may be beset with sexual problems themselves and uncomfortable discussing sex with their patients. Studies have consistently shown that the physician who asks patients specifically about their sexual adjustment will uncover far more sexual problems than the physician who waits for them to volunteer such information (Pauly & Goldstein 1970). Psychiatrists, psychologists, social workers, and other specialists in human behavior report that as many as 75% of their patients have sexual problems that require help (Wiener 1969).

The overwhelming majority of complaints to physicians about sexual difficulties come from married women. They are distressed that they cannot achieve orgasm easily, or are lacking in sexual desire. They are distressed because they feel no affection for their husbands. Or they complain they find sex too overwhelming an experience, or that it is physically uncomfortable, if not painful. The questions married men most frequently ask their doctors concern impotence or premature ejaculation, the infidelity of their wives, and the frequency with which coitus should normally occur (Mace 1971a).

Because sexual dysfunctions vary from case to case, different remedial approaches are obviously required. Further, the complexity of cause is directly related to the ease or difficulty of treatment and its enduring success (H. S. Kaplan 1975). In many instances the basis of the problem lies in simple ignorance about sexual techniques, or in general misinformation about sexuality, which can easily be corrected with sex counseling. In other instances, the causality is more complicated. Persons can become impaired in their sexual functioning by *fear of failure*, a need to remain under *conscious control* during sexual activity, or a distressing *fear of rejection* if they do not perform adequately. These patients can usually be helped by brief sex therapy aimed primarily at opening up the couple's ability to communicate.

Patients in yet another group also suffer from performance anxiety and fear of rejection, but are more difficult to treat. Still other patients are unconsciously "fearful of romantic or sexual success" (H. S. Kaplan 1979). Their sexual problems are associated with negative thoughts and attitudes toward themselves and internal feelings of conflict and profound insecurity. Sex therapy must be directed toward alleviating a basically disturbed relationship between the sexes and problems of fragile self-esteem and guilt following the pleasures of sex. The therapist must be able to recognize the psychodynamics of unconscious conflict and motivation. He/she must have good enough clinical judgment to determine when to attempt to resolve the basic conflicts and when to bypass them with simple support against anxiety. The therapist must know when to shift from sex therapy to psychotherapy, and he/she must be able to provide both methods of treatment or recognize when referral is appropriate (H. S. Kaplan 1975, 1979).

A final group of patients are not at all appropriate candidates for brief sex therapy. Their problems involve profound personal psychopathology, such as deep depression, pervasive paranoia, and marked hostility in relationships. Or the patients have built such rigid defenses against personal interrelationships that they need extensive psychotherapy before they can begin to benefit from sex therapy (H. S. Kaplan 1974, 1979). Fortunately, persons in this category rarely present themselves for treatment of sexual dysfunction alone.

In isolated cases, sexual dysfunction is the result of some physical disorder—birth defect, trauma, diabetes. However, the vast majority of sexual inadequacies are the by-products of early conditioning—in or outside the home—or the result of simple ignorance in sexual matters and human relationships. These problems often surface in persons who have no psychological difficulties in other spheres of their lives (H. S. Kaplan 1974). In practically all instances, psychogenic sexual dysfunction could have been circumvented had the individual received an adequate, well-timed sex education (Blazer 1964; Masters & Johnson 1970).

Studies of sexual inadequacy have been limited primarily to middle-class men and women of better-than-average education. This choice of subject population has been determined by several circumstances. First of all, those of poorer education and of lower income cannot afford the financial burden of professional assistance with their emotional problems. They are consequently seldom seen. Second, even when lower-income patients do seek psychological help, the attending therapist seldom refers them to specialists in the field of sexual dysfunctioning.

Third, the double standard is more entrenched among the less well educated than among those with a better education. Lower-class women therefore do not expect to experience orgasm in the marital relationship. And men tend to deny their own contributory sexual inadequacy, for such an admission would constitute an unfavorable reflection on their masculine self-image. Less well educated men, for example, do not ordinarily regard premature ejaculation as a problem. Rather, it is the expected standard of performance, because neither they nor their partners recognize the importance of female orgasm. Last, people of low socioeconomic status do not appear to be affected with the variety or severity of sexual problems that frequently beset those of higher status.

Cooperative interaction between partners is essential to good sexual performance, just as it is essential, on a mental and emotional level, to the maintenance of a good overall relationship. When conditions exist that prevent easy synchronization of mental signals with bodily movements, sexual difficulties will inevitably follow. And the condition underlying most instances of sexual failure or malfunction is fear.

General Causative Factors and Therapeutic Approaches

Human sexual response depends upon a series of autonomic (spontaneous; nonvolitional) reflexes, which work successfully in people who abandon themselves to erotic experiences, do not attempt consciously to monitor their actions, and are in a calm emotional state. It is well known that such negative factors as fear and stress have a detrimental effect upon one's ability, even desire, to function sexually. In the autonomic nervous system there are two subsystems, the sympathetic and the parasympathetic.

The *sympathetic system* places us in battle-alert condition by releasing adrenalin, which in turn propels us into action to meet danger or threat, or to run away from it—to fight or to flee. The male sympathetic system controls the physiological events associated with ejaculation. In women, the sympathetic system probably is responsible for the motor aspects of orgasm (the orgasmic platform). In both sexes the *parasympathetic system* governs those quiet, recuperative states during which blood pressure is lowered, heart rate slowed, and muscles relaxed. It controls digestion, rest, and sleep; it also governs certain aspects of sexual response—erection, vaginal lubrication and vasocongestion, and the sensory aspect of orgasm.

Under normal circumstances the two systems work in concert, or one works effectively alone with the second system assuming control from time to time, as circumstances dictate. It is when one system interferes with a bodily function for which it is not suited, or when there is an inappropriate interaction between the two, that difficulties arise. For example, the parasympathetic system can successfully mediate a man's attaining and maintaining an erection if he is free of anxiety. But if he carries anxiety to bed with him, or develops worry or stress while there, the sympathetic system overpowers the parasympathetic, making the relaxation necessary for adequate function difficult, if not impossible. The more concerned the man becomes, the more powerful is the interference of the sympathetic system and the greater the amount of adrenalin pumped into his system. And adrenalin collapses an erection as surely as water extinguishes fire.

Unfortunately a single sexual failure can set the stage for future failure. Fear of future failure can become a self-fulfilling prophecy. Another causative factor in almost all sexual inadequacies is rigid religious conformity. "Unequivocally, absolutely, religious orthodoxy is responsible for a significant degree of sexual dysfunction. And it doesn't matter which of the three major religions is involved" (Lehrman 1970). Another investigator has reported evidence indicating that highly religious men and women have more limited or restrictive sexual experiences and behaviors (Mahoney 1980). Men and women with sexual difficulties are almost invariably the victims of negative sexual conditioning during their formative years. In general, therefore, therapy should in part be directed toward assisting patients to (1) abandon or alter the negative aspects of their sexual value system; (2) retain and elaborate upon the positive ones; and (3) add new, positive experiences and develop new values that will aid in the success of the ongoing relationship. The primary aim in treating sexual inadequacy is "to restore sex to its natural context, so that it functions, as it should, like breathing—spontaneously, and without conscious effort" (Lehrman 1970).

Some therapists believe this goal is more easily achieved by a therapy team consisting of a man and a woman, because no man can thoroughly understand female sexuality—and conversely. Others believe that many problems can be just as effectively treated by one therapist working with both partners (H. S. Kaplan 1974). Still others hold that self-treatment following a prescribed program setting for the dos, don'ts, and how-tos can be quite beneficial. In an important book, *Sexual Awareness*, Barry McCarthy and colleagues (1975) have formulated useful techniques for increasing sexual sensitivity in both men and women, together with detailed instructions for self-treatment of various inadequacies. Similarly effective methods for treating various sexual dysfunctions and for increasing sexual awareness have been recorded on cassette tapes and filmstrips for use by both therapists and patients (LoPiccolo & Heiman 1976; Neiger 1973; Zussman & Zussman 1977). Hypnotic techniques also have been used by therapists to help patients become more aware, relaxed, or self-confident and to resolve sexual problems and concomitant emotional conflicts (Brown & Chaves 1980; Crasilneck & Hall 1975).

The team therapeutic approach offers each partner—especially the woman—the opportunity of having a sympathetic therapist of the same sex who can interpret his or her feelings and symptoms for the partner. An additional asset in this approach is that the patients do not feel that they must somehow win the approval of the counselor of the opposite sex (Lehrman 1970; Masters & Johnson 1970).

Before treating any couple, a therapist should take a thorough history, which, in a very real sense, also serves as a psychological examination. The therapist must rely heavily on a "sensitive and empathetic assessment of the couple's *sexual experience*," as they relate it, to perceive the symptoms, signs, and causes of their present difficulties (H. S. Kaplan 1975). This history will aid the therapist immeasurably in determining what arouses each partner and what supresses feelings—what fantasies, unconscious thoughts, hopes, and fears affect responsiveness. For thorough evaluation and effective treatment, the therapist must know exactly what happens when the couple make love. It must be determined that there are no medical or physical factors causing the dysfunction. And the psychological evaluation must reveal the presence of any significant emotional problems in either partner, and the nature of them; the effect they might have on the couple's sexual function; and the quality of their relationship.

In the sexual function interrogation, the therapist will pose such questions as these to the couple, sometimes together, sometimes separately:

Did your sexuality develop normally? Do you recall any specific event that you think affected your sex life? When do you remember first having sexual thoughts? Sexual feelings? When did you first masturbate? How did you feel about it? What things were you told about masturbation? How was each of the many aspects of sex discussed in the family? What was your first sexual experience? What were your feelings about it? What homosexual experiences did you have as a child? How did you feel about them? What has excited you in the past? What excites you sexually now? What stirs up sexual guilt or shame in you now? Under what circumstances can you function satisfactorily now? What circumstances cause you *not* to function satisfactorily? How do you achieve orgasm? How do you feel about clitoral stimulation? Oral sex? How do you account for these feelings? How do you feel about ejaculation during oral sex? How do you feel about a woman's genital odor? Your partner's genital odor? Vaginal secretion? What do you think excites her (him) the most? How do you feel about doing it? Why? How do you feel about your body? Do you think you or your partner takes too long or too short a time to climax? Must his (your) penis be stimulated physically to become erect? How much pressure? How do you feel when he is (you are) slow to get an erection, or cannot do so at all? How do you feel if she (he) fails to reach orgasm? How do you feel if you do not? How do you feel, knowing that she (he) can masturbate to orgasm but cannot respond to orgasm with you? How do you feel about the size of his (your) penis, her (your) vagina, her (your) breasts? How do you feel about multiple orgasms?

It is undoubtedly true that every 3-year-old has pleasurable, positive sensations and attitudes relating to sex. Before the child reaches the teens, however, these normal reactions typically have been distorted by the prevailing attitude that sex is dirty and evil. Added to this negativism are the fears, ignorance, and misinformation concerning sex that young people so easily absorb from their environment.

Part of the Masters and Johnson program for sexually inadequate patients is to reestablish the positive, pleasurable sensations and attitudes naturally present in early childhood. Their chief therapeutic tool is what they call **sensate focus** (Helen Kaplan prefers the term **pleasuring**), the keystone of which is the sense of touch. By touching, feeling, caressing, and exploring all the skin surfaces of the partner's body with fingers and palms, the patient is brought back into contact with sensory reactions. Patients can thus be taught to revert to the uninhibited sensual responses of early childhood. Each is removed, furthermore, from the role of mere spectator in sexual activity, and is placed in a position of effective communication with the sexual partner through giving and receiving pleasure. In addition, anxiety diminishes as the two become more natural with one another and fear of failure dissipates. Masters and Johnson begin their treatment with exercises in sensate focus. Kaplan (1974) and others prescribe pleasuring only when the specific dysfunction seems to warrant it and according to the psychodynamics of the particular case.

Learning the art of pleasuring or sensate focus is usually carried out as a three-step program. In phase I, purposeful erotic arousal—genital stimulation—is carefully avoided. Tender and gentle stroking is used instead, not only to reestablish contact with sensory reactions and to remove fear of failure, but also to increase intimacy and mutual involvement. The partners are freed of the burden of delivering a sexually adequate performance, either for self or partner. For example, in the problem of impotence the man is not required to have an erection, and the responsibility for inducing one is not placed on the woman. In fact, neither effort is permitted at this stage (H. S. Kaplan 1975).

Instructions for those beginning pleasuring exercises vary from couple to couple, according to their particular problem, anxiety level, and cultural background. In all cases, however, the therapists should be well trained, relaxed, and free of sexual conflicts themselves, especially in the matter of touching. They might guide their patients, whom we shall call Ed and Carol, in this way:

> In the early part of this program, I want you to avoid direct sexual stimulation, intercourse, and orgasm altogether. Strange as that may sound, there are important reasons. Basically, we are trying to reestablish the small child's means of communicating—touching and caressing—which we all used once but which have somehow disappeared from our lives over the years. As you practice this approach, you will begin to discover certain joys and excitement—perhaps for the first time. Anyway, I want you to try it for the next few days to see how much closer it brings you sexually.
>
> Tonight when you have all the chores done, the kids are tucked away for the night, and you have both bathed, I want you to go to bed completely nude. You can have the lights on, soft music playing, or even incense burning if you want. But we're not really interested in those senses; we are concerned with the sense of touch. I want you to touch and caress each other—first one and then the other. [*It usually makes no difference who is to give and to receive first. But if the therapists, from the couple's history, decide that a certain sequence is important, they will so indicate.*]
>
> Ed, suppose you caress Carol first. Carol, you lie flat on your back with your arms extended slightly away from your body and your legs

slightly apart. Ed, you sit or kneel at her side, or between her legs, whichever is easiest and most comfortable. If your hands are roughened, use some nonsticky lotion or cream so that the stroking or caressing will be easy on the skin. I want you to gently caress, touch, stroke Carol's body from hairline to genitals, then go to the feet and begin to stroke upwards toward the genitals. But I want you to carefully avoid touching the genitals or any part of her body that is erogenous. For example, if touching Carol's breasts ordinarily causes her to become sexually aroused, avoid touching them altogether. Move your hands around and between them, but avoid touching them, especially the nipples.

Use your fingertips, fingers, and hands to touch every inch of Carol's body as you gradually move toward her genitals. Touch every curve and mound of her body—eyes, nose, neck, chest, abdomen. I want you to use advance–and–retreat stroking, meaning that you will return from time to time to caress once more an area that you've already touched; but generally you are to move toward the genitals.

Once you reach the pubic hair, be careful not to touch the genitals, but move on to touch the hips and insides of her legs. Then go to the feet and stroke them. Afterwards, begin your caressing movements upwards toward the genitals. Stroke the top, outside and inside of the legs in the same sensuous manner as before; but again, be careful not to touch the genitals.

This part of the sensate-focus technique is not to produce direct sexual arousal; we want arousal to evolve from the caresses, from this "new-old" way of communicating physically. Also, you should both remember that caressing is just that—light stroking and touching. Avoid massage at this point. That is fine later on; but what we want now is to stimulate the skin surface, not the muscles below.

Now, Ed, as you stroke or caress, I want you to concentrate on the pleasure you receive from touching Carol's body. Always keep that in mind. And, Carol, you are to concentrate on the pleasurable sensations you are experiencing as he glides his hands over your body.

On the first two or three occasions, it usually takes 25 or 30 minutes to caress the front side of the body. Then Carol is to turn on her stomach and, Ed, you caress her back in the same way, which should take about the same length of time.

Next, you simply change places. Ed, you can first lie on your stomach while Carol strokes, touches, and caresses you in the same way you did her, taking about the same amount of time. Not only do you change places physically, but, of course, you shift the focus of your concentration. Ed, you think hard about the pleasure you are receiving and, Carol, about the gratification you receive from giving this pleasure.

> Both of you should remember one thing: Don't worry that your partner may be getting tired or bored. Be a little selfish. Think of the pleasant feelings you are receiving.
>
> Communicate verbally when you want to. Tell the other when something feels especially good, or merely tickles, or if the pace is too fast or too slow. Also, I have suggested that each of you spend 25 to 30 minutes on each side, which is about 2 hours and may be too long for you. If it is, shorten it to meet your preferences. However, the first 2 or 3 days is a learning period, and couples usually find it beneficial to spend a full two hours in this "exercise."

It is important that the therapist receive feedback from the couple in the first few days, especially after their first attempt at the exercises. Open discussion will help establish free, authentic communication between the couple, and will help clarify for the therapist and the couple the emotional and behavioral aspects of the encounter. Discussion of fantasies the partners experience during the pleasuring period often provides clues that each can follow in the future to bring about the fullest measure of arousal for the other. Such discussion frequently gives, as well, valuable insight into unconscious needs and motivations (H. S. Kaplan 1975).

Phase II of sensate focus normally follows phase I, although in some cases (such as premature ejaculation) the therapist may begin training with the second phase. In either case, the couple are instructed in genital pleasuring, which involves gentle, tantalizing stimulation of the genitals. The intent is to produce sexual arousal, but not orgasm, at least not in this phase of training or by this method (H. S. Kaplan 1974, 1975). Part of the discussion now, if it has not occurred earlier, concerns the couple's feelings about oral-genital sex. Oral-genital stimulation is not integral to treatment of sexual problems; success can certainly be achieved without it. But if both parties enjoy this type of stimulation, it can serve as a pleasurable and successful adjunct to treatment. Couples inhibited about this kind of sex often find their inhibitions dissolve in the course of treatment, and discover both giving and receiving such stimulation can be exquisitely exciting and fulfilling. Most problems relative to oral-genital contact arise when one partner ardently desires it and the other is just as ardently opposed to it. In such cases it is typically unwise to attempt such stimulation until the opposing partner has sufficiently worked through the inhibition, at least to the extent of willingness to try it (H. S. Kaplan 1974, 1975).

Typical instructions for phase II of sensate-focus therapy are these:

> I want you to take turns in giving the other as much exquisite genital pleasure as you can. At first take turns, and later you can give and receive simultaneously. I want you to take turns in the beginning so that you can experience as much pleasure as possible alternately from

receiving and giving. If you are caught up in the erotic sensations of both at the same time, you are often not able to separate your feelings and thoughts to concentrate sufficiently on either.

Carol, suppose you start by giving Ed as much body caressing as required to arouse him. Do whatever it takes to get him sexually excited. Stroke his penis, gently play with his testicles, stimulate the area around his anus and between the anus and scrotum, nibble on his ear, rub the head of his penis, take his penis in your mouth (if acceptable) and gently suck on it, rolling your tongue around its head. Play with his nipples, run your tongue rapidly and softly back and forth across them. Do whatever you can to arouse him. [*Refer to Chapter 9, "Techniques in Sexual Arousal," for further details.*]

Get his penis erect if you can, but don't worry if nothing happens; the stimulation itself will be pleasurable to him. Once you get him erect, caress other parts of his body and then let the erection subside. Then repeat it all to get him erect again. Ed, you relax and enjoy the stimulation. Try not to think of anything else. Just surrender to the pleasure and exctement as completely as possible and stay with those feelings. Both of you concentrate on the pleasure you are experiencing at the moment.

When you both feel that you've gained a reasonable amount of satisfaction—that you've had enough—exchange roles. Ed, now you stimulate Carol. First, caress and fondle her whole body. Do what you can to please her. Gradually work her up sexually. Follow her leads; do whatever she tells you to do, and when you feel she is ready to move to another level of stimulation, do so. Play with her breasts, kiss and suck her nipples, kiss her ears, her lips, her neck, and back to her nipples. All this time, let your hands play around and over her body, gradually moving toward her genitals. Lightly brush your fingertips around her clitoris, but don't touch it directly yet. Move your fingers around the vaginal opening, then lightly stroke or tickle the area between her anus and vagina. Now lightly touch the minor lips, spread them apart, and insert a fingertip just barely into the vaginal opening. Then remove it to stimulate the clitoris more and more directly, which her mounting excitement will now make acceptable.

Carol, you should verbalize to Ed what feels good and exciting to you, what you want him to do next. Women can observe an erect penis and know that a man is sexually excited. But men have no way of knowing definitely that what they are doing is sexually arousing to a woman. Ed, remember that the purpose of stimulation at this point is to generate sexual pleasure, not orgasm. Do those things that will bring about her full arousal and will maintain her at that point. Remember to vary what you do; too much pressure or too lengthy stimulation of one area can defeat your purpose.

When a couple's (or the affected partner's) response to genital pleasuring is positive, they are ready to proceed to the next step, which is to produce orgasm by noncoital or coital means. If the response to genital pleasuring has been negative, it may be that anxiety has been generated in one or both parties, perhaps requiring psychotherapy before further sexual stimulation is attempted. In some cases the negative response may be overcome by merely repeating the sequence of genital pleasuring.

As part of the training in touching and feeling, special consideration must often be given to the inhibitions that many people have concerning the coital fluids—the man's seminal fluid and the woman's vaginal secretions. Masters and Johnson have had a special lotion concocted, which has a texture somewhat like that of these bodily secretions and which also softens the hands. By using this lotion the patient not only applies a smoother, softer, more sensitive touch to the partner, but may begin to lose inhibitions about sexual fluids in the process.

The Nature of Sexual Dysfunction

In both males and females, sexual response consists of two distinct and somewhat independent components. First is genital vasocongestion, which produces penile erection and vaginal lubrication and swelling of vaginal and labial tissue. Second is the reflex or involuntary clonic (alternating tensing and relaxing) muscle contractions involved in both male and female orgasm (H. S. Kaplan 1974, 1975). Thus in the male, potency and ejaculatory disorders are controlled by different parts of the autonomic nervous system and are different clinical entities. Similar differences are found in women, in that sexual dysfunctions involve general sexual inhibitions and/or specific orgasmic problems.

There are six forms of sexual dysfunction, three affecting each sex. In the male, **inhibited sexual excitement** (also known by the names **erectile dysfunction** and **impotence**) implies that erectile ability is impaired, with the inhibition limited to vasocongestive aspects of sexual response. The second and third forms of sexual dysfunction in the male are composed of two types of ejaculatory dysfunctions. The first is **premature ejaculation,** in which a man is unable to exercise proper voluntary control over his orgasmic reflex. The result is that he climaxes before he wishes. The second type is **retarded ejaculation** (also known as **inhibited male orgasm** and **ejaculatory incompetence**), in which the male is troubled with involuntary overcontrol, causing his ejaculatory reflex to be excessively delayed, if it occurs at all, despite the fact that he receives what ordinarily would be considered adequate stimulation.

The first form of female dysfunction is **sexual unresponsiveness** (with alternate names of **inhibited sexual excitement** and **general sexual dysfunction**), in which the woman derives little erotic pleasure from sexual contact. This condition roughly parallels male erectile dysfunction, in that vaginal vasocongestion and lubrication fail to occur. The second form, **orgasmic dysfunction** or **inhibited female orgasm,** occurs when a woman, although sexually responsive otherwise, experiences difficulty in achieving orgasm. This condition is not unlike male retarded ejaculation. The third form, **vaginismus,** has no counterpart in the male. Muscles ringing the vaginal opening go into spasmlike contractions when penetration is attempted, making coitus impossible (DSM III 1980; H. S. Kaplan 1974, 1975). Helen Kaplan (1974) also discusses **sexual anesthesia** in women as a fourth type of sexual disturbance, although she considers the problem a disorder rather than a dysfunction. In sexual anesthesia, a woman suffers from a hysterical conversion neurosis, as a result of which she "feels nothing" when sexual stimulation is attempted, even though she may enjoy the warmth and pleasure of the physical closeness it affords. Clitoral stimulation produces nothing more than a sensation of touch, and she may be unable to discern when the penis enters the vagina.

Male Sexual Dysfunction

Erectile Dysfunction (Impotence)

In the context of sexual dysfunction, erectile dysfunction or impotence (from the Latin: without power) can be defined as a man's inability to attain or maintain an erection of sufficient strength to enable him to perform the act of intercourse. Three types are recognized: organic, functional, and psychogenic (Kelly 1961).

The first of these, *organic impotence,* is relatively rare and is caused by some anatomical defect in the reproductive or central nervous system. *Functional impotence* involves physiological difficulties, in that erection and other functions of the sexual system depend upon adequate hormonal activity, a satisfactory vascular supply, and an intact, properly functioning nervous system. Anomalies in any one of these areas can result in defective potency (H. S. Kaplan 1975). Specifically, functional impotence may be caused by a nervous disorder, excessive use of alcohol or certain drugs, circulatory problems, the aging process, or physical exhaustion.

Psychogenic impotence is by far the type most frequently encountered, accounting for about 85% of the known cases in America (Harper 1965; H. S. Kaplan 1975). This malfunctioning is usually caused by emotional inhibitions that block or interfere with certain impulses from the brain that act upon the neural centers of the spinal cord controlling erection.

There are, of course, no absolutes in judging male erotic drive and capacity. The strength of individual capability falls, in fact, anywhere along an 11-point continuum (Ciociola 1962), as follows:

1. A total absence of both desire and capacity for erection.
2. The presence of erotic desires unaccompanied by a physical capability for erection.
3. Ability to attain partial erections through special types of stimulation.
4. Strong erections and ability to have sexual intercourse if tumescence can be instigated and maintained through special methods of stimulation.
5. Spontaneous morning erections, but none at other times of the day, no matter which stimulative technique is employed.
6. Weak erections under almost any circumstance, but firm erections and vaginal penetration possible only after extensive caressing of the penis.
7. Erections occurring from caresses of the body and other erotic stimuli.
8. Spontaneous erections if the nontactile erotic stimulus is strong.
9. Spontaneous, immediate erections even though the erotic stimulus is very mild.
10. Strong, vigorous, spontaneous erections, accompanied by a strong sex drive.
11. Very strong and vigorous erections and a powerful sex drive. A man with this degree of potency can have many and prolonged acts of intercourse during one sexual contact, with or without ejaculation, and he may have two or more climaxes without loss of erection.

Masters and Johnson have classified psychogenic impotence as being either primary or secondary.

Primary impotence implies that the man has *never* been able to achieve or maintain an erection of sufficient firmness to engage in coitus. Research and clinical observation have consistently revealed that the causes most frequently underlying primary impotence are the family, especially untoward maternal influences; severe religious orthodoxy, which hampered the individual's psychosocial development; homosexual involvement; or an emotionally scarring experience with a prostitute. Despite a relatively stable religious, family, and personal background, if a man's first sexual encounter was singularly squalid and dehumanizing, he may have been unable to function sexually then or thereafter with anyone else. Early indoctrination into homosexual practices, especially when the homophile alliance lasted a year or more, can also produce primary impotence even though the man now has a conscious desire to function heterosexually. In other men the psychodynamics of the dysfunction lie in a complex interaction of many factors in their background. But, regardless of the specific cause, Masters and Johnson consistently observed two characteristics in all the cases of primary impotence treated by them: fear, and an unusual sensitivity to unknown psychological influences that apparently would not have caused primary impotence in another man.

Secondary impotence is defined as a sexual dysfunction in which the man has had at least one successful coital experience, but is now incapable of it. This man is typically successful in his first attempt at coition, and continues to be coitally effective dozens or perhaps thousands of times thereafter. But the day arrives when, for one of many reasons, he fails to achieve erection. A single failure, of course, in no way means impotence. Virtually all men on one occasion or another, particularly when upset or very tired, are unable to attain an erection or maintain it long enough for penetration (Ellis 1963; Laury 1980b). In fact, approximately 50% of all men experience transient periods of impotence. Further, erectile difficulties occur in men of all ages (H. S. Kaplan 1974) (Fig. 20.1).

Anxiety typically sets the stage for secondary impotence—a man's anxiety, for example, over his adequacy and his partner's satisfaction; fear of rejection by her; guilt over the sexual encounter (or his enjoyment of it); or anticipation of failure because of recent erectile difficulties, however isolated (H. S. Kaplan 1974, 1975). When a man fails to achieve penile erection in 25% of his sexual attempts, the condition may be correctly diagnosed as secondary impotence (Masters & Johnson 1970).

As has been stated, men are often led to believe they have grown too old to function sexually. They are so strongly convinced of this fallacy that

Figure 20.1   Schematic representation of the incidence of impotence in men. The shaded areas indicate the average percentage of men who usually suffer from impotence at various ages.

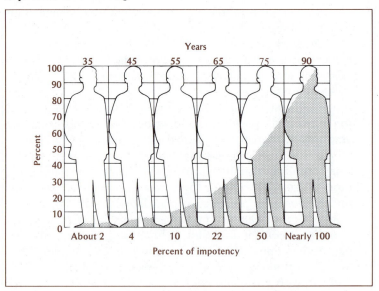

they do indeed become impotent, despite the fact that they continue to have erections during sleep and upon awakening. The one fact which emerges clearly is that a man with a morning erection *is* capable of having an erecton; any failure at other times has psychological rather than physical causality (Harper 1965). Almost all men have erections every 60 to 80 minutes during sleep (and sleeping women develop vaginal lubrication at about the same time intervals), whether or not they are capable of erections during waking state (Fisher *et al.* 1965; Masters & Johnson 1971).

Masters and Johnson have listed these causes of secondary impotence, in descending order of frequency: a history of premature ejaculation, intemperate alcoholic consumption, excessive maternal or paternal domination in childhood, inhibitory religious orthodoxy, homosexual conflict, inadequate sexual counseling, and certain physiological inhibitors (Lehrman 1970). In those cases in which premature ejaculation is the herald of impotence, the evolution of the problem typically follows this course: the man regularly ejaculates prematurely, and at first his partner is tolerant. But as time passes she complains more and more. The man, who perhaps has been insensitive to the severity of his partner's sexual frustration, finally internalizes her accusations. He now views himself as a grossly inadequate lover and decides that at all costs he must learn to delay ejaculation. He tries all manner of techniques to take his mind off the pleasurable sensations of coitus, but he succeeds only in blocking his full emotional involvement. In his anxiety, and not wishing to risk additional failure, he begins to avoid coition altogether. Sooner or later, however, his partner approaches him sexually and he discovers to his horror that he does not respond with an erection. He is now struck with the thought that he has a problem of considerably greater magnitude than premature ejaculation—that he is now incapable of coitus. Thus failure generates fear, and fear generates further failure (Masters & Johnson 1970). (About 15 years before Masters and Johnson popularized their "performance anxiety" concept as the principal culprit in erectile failure, Tuthill [1955] presented a similar argument.)

Alcohol figures prominently in the life of a man whose impotence is related to immoderate use of it—martinis at business luncheons, highballs for relaxation before dinner, and a parade of evening business or social gatherings at which spirits flow freely. Despite the man's greater-than-average consumption of alcohol over the years, his sexual functioning has remained satisfactory. Then some incident involving too much alcohol occurs that alters everything. Perhaps he somehow angers his partner in the course of an evening during which he has had many drinks. He decides to make amends by making love to her. To his dismay, he cannot achieve an erection. A day or so later the man finds himself pondering this sexual failure. He determines to accomplish that night what he failed to do two nights before. Evening comes; there are several drinks "to relax" and a heavy meal with wine. But erection once again fails to occur. This failure is almost inevitable because the burden of anxiety and fear bred by the first failure has been complicated by a heavy intake of alcohol and food. In attempting to "will an erection," the man has effectively ensured a second failure

Secondary impotence in some men stems from unhealthy mother-son relationships, which may have bred unconscious incestuous desires or association of all women with the mother image. Some men become sexually incapable because of conscious or unconscious disgust, anger, or hostility toward their wives.

The ills resulting from inadequate sexual counseling have already been firmly established. Suffice it to say here that guilt and shame, usually relating to some childhood experience or stemming from faulty sex education, are common contributors to sexual inadequacies.

The Treatment of Erectile Dysfunction.   Although general therapy procedures have been described earlier in this chapter, it is useful to discuss specific techniques according to the particular dysfunction.

Of primary importance in initial treatment of impotence is avoiding a direct attack on the problem of inadequate erection. The impotent man must instead be convinced that he does not have to be *taught* to have an erection. He must learn to relax and enjoy the physical pleasures of body contact and the emotional interaction with his sexual partner without feeling compelled to achieve a firm erection. The couple must become attuned—and responsive—to one another's needs, for only in giving pleasure does one achieve it (Masters & Johnson 1970).

The main therapeutic goals in treating impotence are: (1) removing the man's fear of failure; (2) divesting him of a spectator's role in sexual activity by reorienting his emotions and sensations toward active, involved participation; and (3) removing the woman's fear of the man's impotence. Both must recognize that fear is causing the problem in the first place.

The importance of the woman's role cannot be overemphasized. Betraying disappointment rather than showing compassion over his failure only increases his anxiety and guilt feelings, thus intensifying his inhibitions. From a review of the literature, A. J. Cooper (1971) concludes that when a man's partner is included in the therapy, the outcome is significantly better than when she is not. The treatment program in impotence or erectile dysfunction usually follows, in general, the sensate-focus technique, and consists of five steps:

1. Pleasuring without direct attempt to produce an erection
2. Penile erection through genital pleasuring
3. Extravaginal orgasm
4. Penetration without orgasm
5. Full coitus with orgasm

Following sensate-focus or pleasuring techniques, the couple learns to relax and to give erotic pleasure in order to receive it. Erection is not the specific goal at first; it will occur in time because neither feels compelled to produce it. And once it does occur, they are encouraged to let the penis become flaccid, then stimulate it into erection again, repeating the cycle several times. Both parties are able to observe that if the man has one erection, he can have another one, and that the loss of penile firmness is not necessarily a permanent one (Lehrman 1970).

Once the man gains confidence (steps 1 and 2), his partner is encouraged to produce an extravaginal orgasm by such means as manual or oral stimulation (step 3). This deflects his concern over effective coital functioning, and serves to further diminish his anxiety. It is often recommended, as well, that at this point in therapy the man bring the woman to orgasm extravaginally. Thus stress is further diminished because both partners recognize that he can give her orgasmic pleasure by means under his voluntary control, that they are not totally dependent on his erectile ability, over which he has no voluntary control (H.S. Kaplan 1975).

Masters and Johnson insist that the couple refrain from attempting intercourse during the early days of therapy, no matter how ready or confident the man feels. After about 10 days, the woman is instructed to initiate the first attempt at coitus (step 4). The man lies on his back and the woman assumes the female-superior position (Fig. 20.2). She manipulates his penis into an erection and, still manipulating, guides it into her vagina as she adjusts her hips to the best angle. If the penis becomes soft after insertion, it is withdrawn; the woman again manipulates it into an erection and reinserts it. If it again becomes flaccid the couple are instructed to desist from further sex play at that particular time. Once the penis can remain firm after intromission, it is usually better at first for the woman to

Figure 20.2   Female-superior coital position.

remain still and allow the man to do the pelvic thrusting. In the final days of treatment, both share the pelvic movements. Even though the man is able to maintain his erection following insertion, he is instructed to withdraw before ejaculation. They allow the erection to subside and the woman again fondles his penis to erection and once more guides it back into the vagina. Either or both may now make coital thrusts, but the man again withdraws before ejaculating. At the stage when he does ejaculate, he should do so extravaginally in order to minimize anxiety. Ejaculation and orgasm will follow (step 5) if the response is not forced (Lehrman 1970; Masters & Johnson 1970).

It is important to keep anxiety minimal even at this final phase of treatment. The man is now told that if he feels capable of vaginal ejaculation, and if he wants it, excellent. But if he does not want it, or has any fears about his ability, he should withdraw and climax extravaginally as before. (In the presence of his partner he has been instructed to be "selfish" at this point of the treatment.) But if he ejaculates extravaginally, he should bring his partner to noncoital orgasm, as he did earlier in treatment (H. S. Kaplan 1975).

In treating cases of primary impotence, Masters and Johnson report a success rate of 59.4%, and in cases of secondary impotence, 73.8%. It should be remembered that, if the success achieved through the prescribed treatment is not maintained for at least five years, the therapy is considered a failure (Masters & Johnson 1970).

Joseph Wolpe (1958) attacks erectile dysfunction through the technique of **systematic desensitization.** The patient is instructed by the therapist to fantasize certain sexual situations that, in previous therapy sessions, have been determined to be anxiety-provoking. The patient dwells first on the least threatening one, until he can fantasize it without arousing fear, anxiety, or disgust. He signals the therapist nonverbally, then moves to the next most stressful imaginary scene, and so on. No new situation is fantasized until the less stressful ones can be handled without anxiety. And if anxiety occurs at any level of fantasy, the patient gives a nonverbal signal and returns to an earlier one that no longer causes threat.

Wolpe's treatment also requires that the patient inform his sexual partner of his sexual fears, patently absurd or unreasonable though they may appear, which with her help he feels he can overcome. This help involves her being with him in close sexual contact on several occasions without expecting intercourse. She is to be patient, affectionate, and noncritical. They lie nude in bed as relaxed as possible, doing only what he feels comfortable in doing and *absolutely nothing more.* No performance is required. From one sexual encounter to the next, anxiety gradually subsides and sexual excitement increases.

For men suffering from impotence induced by disease or injury, surgery offers new hope. The procedure involves implantation of an inflatable penile prosthesis. The miniature hydraulic system consists of two elastic silicone tubes that are inserted in the penis, a thumb-sized pump in the scrotal sac, and a fluid reservoir under the abdominal muscles (Fig. 20.3). Erection is achieved by pressing the pump several times, forcing liquid into the tubing, thus forming a framework to support the penis during intromission. After coitus, a valve permits the fluid to flow back into the reservoir and the penis to revert to its flaccid state (Furlow 1976). Of 150 such operations performed by a Baylor College of Medicine urology team— after a careful screening of the patients (diabetes victims constituted a major percentage)—90% reported great satisfaction with the results ("Penis Prosthesis" 1976).

Figure 20.3   The inflatable penile prosthesis. Illustration courtesy of American Medical Systems, Minneapolis, Minnesota.

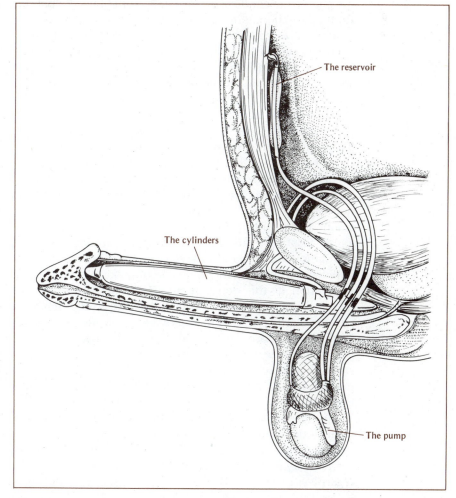

The hydraulic-system implant is only one of many attempts over the years to give assistance to men who are troubled by erectile problems. The U.S. Patent Office has issued over 100 individual patents for devices to aid and improve male sexual performance (Lutz 1976). Nevertheless, psychotherapy combined with sex therapy may be a more effective treatment for those men suffering from other severe medical illnesses, psychological conditions such as depression, marital conflicts or problems, or undiagnosed or psychogenic impotence (Olsson 1979).

Ejaculatory Dysfunction

Premature Ejaculation.   Premature ejaculation occurs in men at all socioeconomic levels, and there seems to be no correlation between it and any specific sexual conflicts or particular from of psychopathology (H. S. Kaplan 1974). Many people assume premature ejaculation is primarily the result of a physical condition, such as a penis made abnormally sensitive by circumcision. Neurological and clinical testing of sensitivity to touch has failed, however, to reveal any difference in the sensitivity of a circumcised and an uncircumcised penis. Even in those cases in which the prepuce does not fully retract, the response to stimulation of the penis, circumcised or uncircumcised, is the same.

From the outset of this discussion, however, it is well to settle the question of what premature ejaculation is and is not.

Some authorities declare arbitrarily that ejaculation is premature if it occurs before penetration or within 10 seconds thereafter. They say, further, that ejaculation occurring any time after 10 seconds of intromission, but not within the man's conscious control, must be considered "early ejaculation." Other authorities state that a man who cannot control his ejaculation for at least one full minute after penetration suffers from premature ejaculation (Kinsey *et al.* 1948; Mozes 1963). Others believe that the number of pelvic thrusts a man is capable of making after penetration and before ejaculation is the determinant (H. S. Kaplan 1974). Still others define premature ejaculation in terms of the sexual requirements of the individual partners, and are not concerned about specific periods of time. Prominent in this group are Masters and Johnson, who designate ejaculation as premature if the man cannot delay it long enough after penetration to satisfy his sexual partner in at least half of their acts of intercourse. For many reasons, none of these definitions is completely satisfactory. For example, is the man a premature ejaculator if he can delay his climax only 25 minutes while his partner requires 30 minutes of coital stimulation? And what of the man who cannot last longer than 60 seconds of intromission, yet whose partner climaxes after only 30 seconds? The crucial measure of prematurity is "the absence of voluntary control over the ejaculatory reflex, regardless of whether this occurs after two thrusts or five, whether it occurs before the female reaches orgasm or not" (H. S. Kaplan 1974).

In any discussion of premature ejaculation, a word of caution must be injected. It is important to understand that at one time or another every man has ejaculated more quickly than he or his partner would have liked. The essential thing is that the man not become anxious over possible future failures. Otherwise, what is a normal situational occurrence may become a chronic problem.

Helen Kaplan (1975) hypothesizes that the man who ejaculates prematurely has not learned to control his ejaculation because he fails to identify the sensations immediately preceding orgasm. The anxiety he has experienced in the past during this brief period has interfered with his learning process. Unlike erection, which cannot be brought under voluntary control, ejaculation and orgasm can be. With proper training men can learn to detect the sensations that herald orgasm and then learn to control ejaculation.

As with erection, the penis does not control ejaculation, premature or otherwise: The brain does. And the psychological forces involved are legion. An element of revenge is often present in premature ejaculation—toward the particular woman or toward women in general. Or the man may be unduly tense, tired, or lacking in self-confidence in his sexual abilities. Intercourse may have been preceded by an overlong period of sexual abstinence; or the man may have undergone a prolonged period of sexual excitement, because of foreplay, before intromission was attempted (Thorne 1943). Young men of today typically have their first sexual encounter with girls of their peer group. Often, these experiences take place in a parked car, in imminent danger of being discovered by the police; or on a couch in the girl's living room, where at any moment her father is liable to come into the room. The anxiety thus generated serves to condition many younger men to the pattern of quick ejaculation. Certainly anxiety is a major factor in blocking a man's perception of the sensations that signal impending ejaculation.

Another common form of teen-age behavior can also condition premature ejaculation. After extensive petting, the youth, possibly fully clothed, lies atop the girl, rubbing his penis over her vulval region by moving his body back and forth, as is done in intercourse, until he ejaculates. Thus the youth is conditoned to ejaculate through rubbing and body pressure rather than from prolonged penetration. (Aside from the unfortunate conditioning of the male, the girl's unrelieved sexual tensions, and additional cleaning bills, about all one can say of this technique is that it usually prevents unwanted pregnancies, preserves that girl's virginity, and affords the lad some sexual release.)

Other men who have had wide sexual experience as teen-agers develop in the process a near-total lack of regard for women. The female exists, in their thinking, solely for male gratification, an instrument for sexual release. Her needs and welfare are of no concern. In fact, this utter disregard for their partners' sexual satisfaction was Masters and Johnson's most consistent and significant finding in their study of the early sexual histories of men who ejaculate too soon.

Only rarely does premature ejaculation have a physical basis, as has been pointed out. The glans may be abnormally sensitive because of, say, a chemical irritation. Or the prostate or the verumontanum (a part of the urethra) may be infected. But beyond these rare incidents, premature ejaculation is usually caused by emotional or psychological factors.

The Treatment of Premature Ejaculation.   Premature ejaculation is a reversible phenomenon and, as mentioned earlier, the technique of delaying orgasm *can* be learned. Self-treatment is possible; but since the problem is a shared one, the best chance for success lies when both partners consult a psychotherapist or counselor knowledgeable in treating sexual problems. The principal purpose of the therapy is learning to recognize the signs of imminent orgasm (H. S. Kaplan 1975). A lubricant is often useful in manual penile stimulation. If, however, the man finds its use too arousing, it should be abandoned in the first few sexual encounters. Once he learns to control his urgency without lubricant, its use may be reintroduced.

The woman stimulates the man until he feels early sensations of "ejaculatory inevitability" (the point at which he senses imminent ejaculation of seminal fluid, and feels that he can no longer control it). At that moment he signals her to cease all stimulation to allow the ejaculatory urge to subside. Once it has abated, the partner renews stimulation. This "start-stop" sequence, first developed by James Semans (1956), is repeated several times; Kaplan (1975) suggests four. The man is then allowed to ejaculate.

Masters and Johnson prescribe a "squeeze technique" in treating this condition. When the man signals his partner to stop, she not only ceases manual penile stimulation but also applies immediate pressure to the penile glans by placing her thumb below the frenulum and two fingers above, one just forward of the coronal rim and one just behind, on the shaft (Fig. 20.4). Rather strong pressure, short of pain, should be applied for several seconds, until the erection has largely collapsed. This alternating stimulation and squeezing should proceed through four trials, each lasting perhaps 15 to 20 minutes (Masters & Johnson 1970). The man is permitted to ejaculate on the last trial of each training session.

After four or five successful stimulation-stop sessions the couple is ready for coitus, which proceeds in the same sequence followed in manual penile manipulation. With the woman's help, the man now inserts his penis into her vagina as she sits astride him (see Fig. 20.2). When the man senses impending orgasm, he halts movement to allow the ejaculatory urgency to subside. They then begin the sequence anew, repeating it several times before he is permitted to ejaculate.

If the squeeze technique is used, the man withdraws immediately that he feels the key signs of ejaculatory inevitability approaching, and the

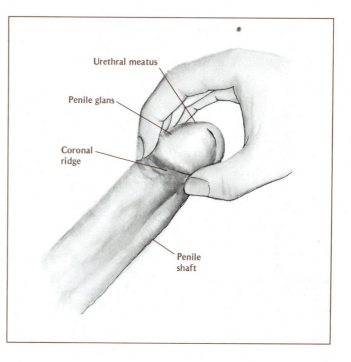

Urethral meatus

Penile glans

Coronal
ridge

Penile
shaft

Figure 20.4 Demonstration of the
"squeeze technique" in treatment of
premature ejaculation.

woman once more squeezes the penis to stop ejaculation. Use of these
techniques is continued in further sexual encounters until, progressively,
the man is capable of prolonged sexual intercourse, in any position, without
ejaculating sooner than he wishes.

Masters and Johnson sound two notes of caution: First, the technique
will be unavailing or, at the very least, less effective if the man himself
applies the pressure to his penis; and, second, the couple must not treat
this new skill as a game and overdo it. Used immoderately, the technique
may eventually render the man insensitive to the stimulation and he might
be unable to respond to it. He may then very easily develop new fears, this
time about his potency, thus running the risk of developing secondary
impotence. Masters and Johnson (1970) report a 97.8% success rate in the
treatment of premature ejaculation.

Some counselors (Aycock 1949; Kelly 1961) recommend that a local
anesthetic (such as Nupercainal) be applied to the penile glans—care being
taken not to smear any on the woman's vulva—a few minutes before
intercourse. The assumption is that the deadening effect of the anesthetic
will decrease the sensitivity of the penis, thus delaying ejaculation. Others
prescribe the wearing of one or more condoms to reduce the stimulation
generated by the friction, warmth, and moisture within the vagina. Since
muscular tension is a notorious catalyst in ejaculation, the man's lying
beneath the woman and thus taking a more passive role in coitus is believed
by many to be helpful. Muscular tension that terminates in early response

for the man is one of the reasons (along with fear of detection) that sexual intercourse in the cramped confines of an automobile is unsatisfactory.

Some men also find taking a drink or two before coitus helps, since alcohol is a deterrent in all physiological functioning. Other men claim similar success through concentrating on singularly unsexy thoughts. Despite some writers' out-of-hand condemnaton of these methods, most psychotherapists who work with problems of ejaculation control find them useful at times and with certain patients.

Having an orgasm and, after a short rest, attaining another erection often permit a man to experience a more prolonged act of coitus the second time. Some men masturbate shortly before they expect to have sexual intercourse. Because their sex drive will thereby be decreased, they can then prolong intercourse. Usually, however, treatment of premature ejaculation is more complicated than this.

Retarded Ejaculation.   Retarded ejaculation or ejaculatory overcontrol is a relatively rare form of sexual inadequacy in which a man has difficulty ejaculating while his penis is in a woman's vagina. He may, however, be able to ejaculate by masturbating, or during a homosexual encounter, or, in the case of some married men, with a woman to whom he is not married (Masters & Johnson 1970). Or he may not be able to ejaculate at all (Ovesey & Meyers 1970).

Sometimes a man with a quite satisfactory, normal ejaculatory ability loses it because of a psychologically traumatic experience. In other cases, the dysfunction is rooted in his distaste for his partner. The failure to ejaculate is merely a means of rejecting her. In other instances, fear of impregnating, the partner's known infidelity, and the danger of interruption during coitus can cause a man, consciously or unconsciously, to withhold his ejaculate.

It is interesting that the same fears, performance anxiety, and minimal commitment to the sexual partner will cause impotence or erectile difficulties in one man and retarded ejaculation in another. The overcontrolled man puts unconscious reins on his ejaculation, thus avoiding anxiety, while in men totally or partially incapable of erection, anxiety is so pervasive that erection is extremely difficult or impossible (H. S. Kaplan 1975).

Men who do not ejaculate clearly possess sexual "staying power," thus providing their partners with such prolonged sexual intercourse that multiple orgasms frequently result. Nevertheless, it is often the woman who seeks help in correcting her partner's ejaculatory incompetence—because she wants a child, or feels that her partner is not sexually normal, or suspects that she herself is not an adequate sexual partner.

The Treatment of Retarded Ejaculation.   Because retarded ejaculation is the direct opposite of premature ejaculation, the treatment is quite different. The woman is instructed to use manual or oral manipulative techniques or artificial aids (a cream or lotion having the consistency of vaginal secretions) to stimulate the man to orgasm extravaginally. Once he does ejaculate, no matter how long it takes, the couple have overcome a major psychological hurdle. "When she has brought him pleasure, he identifies her (not infrequently for the first time in the marriage) as a pleasure symbol rather than as an objectionable, perhaps contaminated, sexual image" (Masters & Johnson 1970).

The orgasm brought about by the woman's efforts not only gives the man pleasure and constitutes the first step in overcoming his ejaculatory dysfunction, but allows her to demonstrate to him the happiness she feels in pleasing him. This is invaluable in recementing a crumbling sexual relationship. (It should be pointed out that many quite normal men occasionally ejaculate without realizing that they have done so, especially if they are excessively fatigued or under great conflict. In such cases there is usually a seepage of seminal fluid without the accompanying orgasmic sensations [H. S. Kaplan 1974].)

Some men can reach orgasm only if they are alone. Desensitization therapy, involving both partners, is often successful. The man is instructed to masturbate behind locked doors, using his favorite lubricant and concentrating on his favorite fantasy, while the woman remains in another part of the house. Once orgasm is reached in these circumstances, he masturbates on the next occasion with the woman in the adjacent room. Next, she stays in the same room with him and observes the masturbatory activity. As the next step, they engage in coitus until the woman is sexually fulfilled; the man then withdraws and masturbates to orgasm. The purpose of this procedure is to establish a firm association between heterosexual coitus and orgasm. The man's partner, using a lubricant, then manually stimulates him to orgasm. After this stage is reached, the man is prohibited from further lone orgasm by masturbation.

At this point the *male bridge maneuver* is used. The woman stimulates the man to the point of orgasm, at which time he enters her and begins coital thrusts while she continues stimulating his penis with her hand. When he reaches the point just before ejaculation, he signals her to stop the stimulation He then proceeds to use coital thrusts alone to produce orgasm (H. S. Kaplan 1975). Once ejaculation occurs intravaginally, much of the man's unconscious stress and conflict seem to disappear. After several successful encounters of this sort, less and less precoital play is necessary and orgasm occurs normally during intromission. Using this technique, Masters and Johnson report a success rate of 82.4% in treating retarded ejaculation (or ejaculatory incompetency, as they term it).

Female Sexual Dysfunction

The nation's leading sex therapists, Masters and Johnson (1970) and Helen Kaplan (1974, 1975), use somewhat different classifications to describe sexual dysfunctions in women. For example, the former have discarded the term "frigidity" in favor of *female orgasmic dysfunction*. They argue that frigidity has different meanings for different people and more precise terminology is needed. A man desiring coitus seven times a week may consider his partner frigid because she wants it, or is orgasmic, only three times; the man who desires coitus three times weekly would consider her sex drive perfectly normal. Kaplan tends to use the terms *frigidity*, *general sexual dysfunction*, and *female sexual unresponsiveness* interchangeably, and includes the dysfunction as one of her four classifications of female sexual dysfunctions.

Despite these differences in classification, there is a general agreement among sex therapists regarding the nature, cause, and treatment of the various forms of female dysfunctioning (Ard 1974b; Hartman & Fithian 1972; H. S. Kaplan 1974, 1975; Masters & Johnson 1970; McCarthy *et al.* 1975). For present purposes, Kaplan's terminology (1974) will be used: (1) female sexual unresponsiveness (also called general sexual dysfunction); (2) orgasmic dysfunction; and (3) vaginismus.

Causative factors in a woman's sexual difficulties may be organic, relational or psychological (Ellis 1961b). *Organic causes* include injuries to or constitutional deficiencies in the sexual apparatus, hormonal imbalance, disorders of the nervous system, inflammation or lesions of the internal or external genitalia and surrounding areas, excessive use of drugs or alcohol, and the aging process.

Relational factors suggest that the man may also be suffering from some sexual dysfunction or problem and contributes to his partner's feeling of revulsion toward sex. Resentment, for whatever reason, can inhibit or destroy sexual functioning. So can a number of other forces, realistic or unrealistic. A common cause is a woman's inability to accept her mate. She may find him sexually unattractive or undesirable; he may be a poor provider; or he may not be the man she wanted to marry. For whatever reason, he does not fit her concept of "the right man" (Masters & Johnson 1970). Because, typically, a woman is aware that sexual relations are important to a man, she can, by withholding her sexual response, express her conscious or unconscious hostility toward him (McGuire & Steinhilber 1970). As said before, it is also sometimes true that women cannot function sexually if feelings of love, concern, and closeness are not involved.

The most common and by far the most important causes of female sexual dysfunctioning are *psychological*, typically such emotional problems as shame, guilt, and fear. In women who have conflicting feelings about sex, erotic feelings arouse anxiety. These women's defense against sexual anxiety is not only to avoid sexual stimulation, but also to build defenses that will prevent them from becoming aroused. Typically, these women have been indoctrinated in a negative sexual value system based on the implication that sex is bad, whether in or out of marriage (Masters & Johnson 1970). Even if they cannot avoid sexual activity on the physical plane, they can minimize their participation by refusing to become involved in the inter-action of sexual response.

Other factors responsible for a woman's unresponsiveness are many and varied. She may expect physical pain in coitus and therefore dread it. She may fear rejection or condemnation by her lover if she lets herself go sexually; she may be frightened of becoming pregnant. She may have homosexual tendencies, be too emotionally tied to her father, or bear a repressed hostility toward men in general (Ellis 1960, 1961b).

Sexual Unresponsiveness

Sexually unresponsive women vary considerably in their capacity for erotic sensation or sexual pleasure. Some are completely devoid of desire and consider sexual contact an unbearable ordeal; some find coitus disgusting or frightening, and endure it only to preserve the relationship; some find no erotic pleasure in the act, but derive distinct emotional fulfillment from the physical closeness of coitus.

In classifying female sexual unresponsiveness and orgasmic dysfunc-tion as separate entities, Helen Kaplan (1974) points out that some women have no erotic feelings in sex play, show no physiological signs of arousal, and are "dry and tight"; yet they may respond to orgasm rather easily once coitus is initiated.

The most inhibited woman is the most difficult to treat, quite naturally. The prognosis is considerably brighter if the patient currently has a modicum of responsiveness, or if she has been responsive in the past, but now is not because of some situational circumstance.

A five-year study (Fischer 1973) of the sexual responsiveness of 300 middle-class married women in Syracuse, New York, failed to confirm many previously held beliefs about female sexuality. For example, Fischer found no relationship between a woman's orgasmic responsiveness and the man's sexual technique, her source of sex education, her parents' attitudes toward sex, or her religiosity, femininity, general mental health, traumatic sexual experiences (or lack of them), sensitivity to stimulation, or premarital and marital experience. Fischer's findings confirm other research showing that women who experience orgasm through vaginal penetration are no more emotionally mature than those who achieve it through direct clitoral stimulation. In fact, about 66% of the women stated that, of the two, they prefer clitoral stimulation. Probably the most interesting of Fischer's findings is that highly orgasmic women are more likely than others to have been reared by fathers who were dependable, caring, demanding men who were "insistent that their daughters meet certain moral standards and expecta-tions."

The Treatment of Sexual Unresponsiveness. Albert Ellis (1960, 1961b) recommends dealing with female unresponsiveness through self-therapy in conjunction with any medical or psychological treatment that seems advisable. These are some of his suggestions:

Select a suitable time for sexual activity, *e.g.,* when the woman is rested and as free from immediate troubles as possible.

There should be a minimum of disharmony between the partners at the time chosen.

Kindness, consideration, and expressions of love usually prove more effective than rough treatment.

The man should acquaint himself with the parts of his partner's body that are especially responsive to stimulation, and they should be caressed.

It is often effective to take brief periods of rest between efforts at arousal.

Genital, particularly clitoral, stimulation should precede intromission.

Mild stimulants are sometimes useful.

The woman's focusing on sexually stimulating fantasy is helpful, while the man can offer encouragement through using terms of endearment and emphasizing his distinct interest and pleasure in her. Sexually arousing conversation often is of benefit.

If arousal is attainable but the woman is to an extent sexually insensitive, then one or more of the following procedures are recommended: steady and rhythmic pressure, intermittent or forceful strokings, and verbal encouragements. A woman's stimulating herself is often a valuable aid to her partner's attempts at arousing her.

Self-exploration and masturbation have been demonstrated to be valuable techniques in developing a woman's sexual responsiveness. She thereby learns which parts of her body are most sensitive to stimulation, and which movements and pressures the most pleasurable—information that can be passed on to her sexual partner (Heiman *et al.* 1976).

The therapist dealing with female insensitivity will emphasize such basic tools as open communication about sexual feelings and desires. The couple can be taught means of creating an affectionate, nondemanding, sensuous atmosphere during lovemaking, which will allow the sexual response to unfold naturally. The woman is encouraged to abandon herself to the erotic experience, although psychotherapy may be required to remove the guilt and fears blocking natural sexual response. Pleasuring or sensate-focus techniques are integral to treatment. After sensate-focus stimulation has aroused sensuous and erotic feelings in the woman, her lover should proceed to light, teasing genital play by gently and slowly caressing her nipples, clitoral region, and vaginal opening. A lubricant might be useful. The love-play should not be oriented toward orgasm because the woman might sense an implicit demand that she "perform" and thus be turned off. There must be no compulsion to produce orgasm.

Most therapists believe that woman superior is the most favorable position at this point, as it allows the woman to direct coitus to her best advantage. After intromission she halts movement to experience the sensation of the erect penis in her vagina. Slow and gentle thrusts are recommended over hard and rapid ones. Women often find that contracting the pubococcygeal muscles (according to the method discussed in Chapter 5) while thrusting produces erotic sensations they perhaps have never before experienced (H. S. Kaplan 1975).

The woman is encouraged to be "selfish" by not concerning herself at this point about her partner. Her movements and experimentation should be geared solely to her own pleasure. If her partner becomes too excited, they should rest quietly until he gains control. During this period of rest, the man may stimulate her clitoris or she may do so herself, or she may rely on penetration and pelvic thrusts for arousal. All depends upon what is most effective for the woman at that particular time. The exercise is halted when the woman is tired or feels she has succeeded in learning a new, satisfying means of achieving vaginal stimulation. The man is then brought to orgasm by whatever method pleases them both (H. S. Kaplan 1975).

Nondemanding, pleasure-oriented sexual experiences have several advantages. First, they are not likely to mobilize the anxiety and defenses that block a woman's erotic response. Second, the acts are designed specifically for *her* erotic pleasure. Third, both the woman and her lover become more perceptive of the other's needs and responses. She sees that he enjoys making her happy and does not reject her when she seeks sexual pleasure.

Orgasmic Dysfunction

The sexual dysfunction women most commonly complain of is orgasmic difficulty: (1) the inability to achieve orgasm; or (2) the ability to achieve orgasm by means other than coitus, but not through coitus; or (3) coital orgasms that are slower to achieve than either they or their partners like.

Female orgasmic dysfunction is classified as either primary or situational. The woman in the *primary* category has never achieved an orgasm through any method of sexual stimulation. The woman in the *situational* category has managed to achieve at least one orgasm in her experience, whether by coitus, masturbation, or some other form of stimulation, but no longer does so (Masters & Johnson 1970).

The causes of orgasmic dysfunction are much the same as those involved in sexual unresponsiveness. Further, orgasm may have acquired some symbolic meaning, signifying to the woman submission to the male or loss of self-control; or the intensity of the orgasmic experience frightens her. Whatever the cause, the physiological result is an involuntary inhibition of the orgasmic reflex (H. S. Kaplan 1974). The woman is afraid to "let herself go," and she unconsciously reinforces the control because it also holds her sexual anxieties at bay. The syndrome becomes so automatic that the woman is unable to climax even when she loves her partner, is calm, sexually aroused, and wants to experience orgasm.

The Treatment of Orgasmic Dysfunction. Various forms of psychotherapy and counseling are of excellent use in these cases, the objective being to free the woman from the involuntary overcontrol of her orgasmic response. She is taught to focus attention on sensations associated with mounting sexual excitement. She learns not to inhibit them but to allow them to flow freely to their natural conclusion. Through psychotherapy she is made aware of her sexual conflicts and helped to resolve them. Through behavior modification she learns how to cease interfering with the natural progression of sexual events that culminate in orgasm (H. S. Kaplan 1974). Through group therapy treatment programs, she gains insights and information into how to experience orgasms more readily and how to employ different methods to enhance sexual responsiveness (Barbach & Flaherty 1980).

Treatment involves having the woman first achieve orgasm by masturbation, then through clitoral stimulation by her partner, and finally by coitus. As Helen Kaplan (1975) states, "The main principle of achieving orgasm is simple: Maximize the stimulation and minimize the inhibition." This objective is best accomplished by removing any existing guilt and shame concerning masturbation, after which the woman stimulates herself to orgasm, manually or with an electric vibrator, when she is alone and under no pressure.

Psychotherapy frequently reveals that these women do not know what to expect of orgasm. They may be afraid of losing control, of dying, or of liking it so much that they will become promiscuous. Or they may think they should be in love before it is right to have an orgasm (H. S. Kaplan 1975).

Early in treatment, the anorgasmic woman should be told what an orgasm is like—details of the build-up and response itself should be carefully explained (see Chapter 12). She is encouraged to use her most exciting fantasies during self-stimulation and try various "tricks" to bring about orgasm. Some women can hurry an orgasm by relaxing stomach and buttock muscles; others, by "bearing down" or alternately tightening and relaxing the vaginal muscles; still others, by rapid panting or active pelvic thrusts. It is sometimes helpful to allow sexual arousal to mount to a certain point, stop and allow the arousal to subside, then start anew.

Once the woman can achieve orgasm alone, she begins the second stage of conditioning, which includes her partner. Sometimes the approach must be gradual, such as achieving orgasm through masturbation while he is just outside the bedroom, then while he is in the same bedroom, then beside the bed, then in bed with her, perhaps observing her masturbate to orgasm. Finally, he holds the vibrator or manually stimulates her to orgasm.

The woman continues to use whatever fantasy or physical action aided her in the first phase.

As the third step of treating the anorgasmic woman, phases I and II of sensate-focus and nondemand coitus are followed by a crucial technique called the *female bridge maneuver*. Once the woman has experienced pleasurable vaginal sensations, her partner penetrates her so that the position of their bodies permits either or both to stimulate her clitoris manually or with a vibrator without losing penile contact (Fig. 20.5). Additionally, the woman is again encouraged to use erotic fantasy and to continue coital body movements until she feels orgasm coming. Direct clitoral stimulation is now halted and attention directed to active pelvic thrusts.

This shift in stimulation sometimes causes a woman's arousal to dissipate, especially at first. When it does happen, the couple should start the combined coitus–direct clitoral stimulation anew, proceeding to the point just before orgasm. Once more they should stop direct clitoral stimulation and rely on quick-paced coital thrusts to stimulate the clitoris

Figure 20.5 Use of a vibrator in clitoral stimulation.

between their two pubic bones. This technique almost always produces an orgasm—unless the woman is unusually conflicted about penetration itself, in which case psychotherapy is indicated (H. S. Kaplan 1975; Witkin 1980).

During any coital activity, it is recommended that the couple take several "breaks" and lie in each other's arms, quietly caressing one another. This quietude gives the woman an opportunity to concentrate on sensual feelings, something not often possible during actual coition. A key to ultimately achieving an orgasm is to enjoy quiet, unhurried sensate pleasure and to guard against the attempt to force or *will* an orgasm. Coital mobility is very important, but movement uninhibited by any conscious thought processes is probably of greater importance. It has been found that women who can consciously control their movements at the height of intercourse are not so likely to reach orgasm as are those who lose control of their movements (Shope 1968b). For full sexual pleasure during intercourse, it is often desirable or even necessary to shift coital positions. Masters and Johnson (1970) describe in detail the steps to be taken in shifting from the female-superior position to the lateral coital position. (Compare Fig. 20.2 with Fig. 20.6.) Masters and Johnson report 83.4% success in their treatment of primary orgasmic dysfunction and 77.2% in situational cases—an 80.7% overall rate of success.

Both research results and clinical findings differ in their assessment of women's orgasmic capabilities. Estimates vary, but 90% or more of all American women are able to achieve orgasm by one means or another, although perhaps less than 50% of women reach orgasm regularly during coitus without additional clitoral stimulation (H. S. Kaplan 1974; Wilcox & Hager 1980). Recent research indicates that many women may be orgasmic with proper stimulation of the anterior wall of the vagina (Hoch 1980).

Figure 20.6   Lateral coital position.

That a woman does not receive optimally effective clitoral stimulation from coitus is widely recognized. Yet the emotional rewards from the warmth and closeness of coitus are so great that many, if not most, women quite naturally want the experience of orgasm in the course of it (H. S. Kaplan 1975; Masters & Johnson 1970). Certain women do not wish to have orgasms coitally, or are unable to. They should be assured that they are in no way neurotic, maladjusted, or sexually inadequate, nor is the partner inadequate or a poor lover. In her study of 3019 women aged 14–78, Hite (1976) found that only 30% regularly achieve orgasm through coitus; another 22 % are successful only occasionally; and another 19% require simultaneous manual stimulation. Some women who reach coital orgasm easily none-theless prefer manual, vibrator, water-spray, or oral stimulation. Some people prefer vanilla ice cream; others prefer chocolate; the rationale is the same.

Vaginismus

Vaginismus is an extremely powerful and often exceedingly painful con-traction of the muscles surrounding the vaginal tract, which may persist for long periods of time (Fig. 20.7). In severe cases even the attempt to introduce the penis into the vagina will produce agonizing pain, making penetration impossible. In less severe cases, vaginal spasms merely delay intromission

Figure 20.7 Schematic representation of the vagina, showing vaginal muscles relaxed (left) and contracted (right) in spasms of vaginismus.

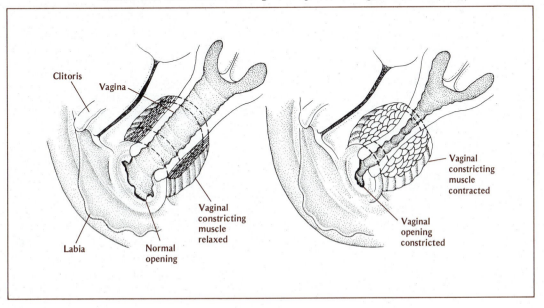

or make it difficult. Vaginismus is considered a sexual dysfunction only when it is so acute that penetration is not possible (Wabrek & Wabrek 1976).

Masters and Johnson assert that the chief cause of vaginismus is an impotent male whose repeated attempts at intercourse followed by failure have so frustrated his partner that she protects herself subconsciously by closing the vaginal doors. Other important causes are anticipated pain of first penile penetration; fear or guilt concerning coitus; inhibitions formed by emotionally traumatic experiences, such as rape; conflict growing out of homosexual tendencies; and physical abnormalities that make intercourse extremely painful (Masters & Johnson 1970).

The noted marriage counselor David Mace has suggested an additional dimension in the problem of vaginismus. He theorizes that in some instances the woman is saying to her partner in effect, "I am afraid to let you come fully into my life by opening myself freely and trustfully to you" (Mace 1971b).

Men as well as women must understand the dynamics behind vaginismus in order to avoid any behavior that will produce discomfort for either partner. A selfish, inconsiderate, and brutal man can do irreparable damage to the relationship by continuing his attempts at intercourse when his partner is suffering these muscular spasms.

Vaginismus seldom occurs in women of the lower socioeconomic and educational strata. It is an affliction almost exclusively of women in the upper levels of these groups (Kelly 1959).

The Treatment of Vaginismus.   Sometimes the application of local anesthetics to the vulva, vagina, and hymenal area before intromission is successful in reducing the pain of vaginismus. But professional assistance is usually required, starting with the therapist's explaining the causes to the couple and showing the man that the insertion of even a finger into a vagina constricted in these spasms will cause great distress.

In another approach, the woman is encouraged to relax as thoroughly as possible, mentally and physically, by taking a long soak in a tub of hot water. She should then retire to bed, alone, where she leisurely strokes and caresses her body until she feels ready to experiment with her genitals. First, she studies her vaginal opening with a mirror, then she places a fingertip in it, carefully noting her sensations as she does. During therapy she discusses in detail her feelings and what they meant to her.

Once she can insert a fingertip without discomfort, she is instructed to insert the entire finger. She is then to contract the vaginal muscles against her finger as hard as possible, the purpose of the exercise being to teach her control over these muscles. Once she has learned to contract the muscles at will, she will also have learned to relax them as well. When the patient can accommodate one finger, she experiments with two fingers, then three. She will then recognize that, if she can introduce three fingers without discomfort, she can quite likely accommodate a penis without difficulty.

Her sexual partner is now included in the therapy. He is instructed to examine her vaginal opening in full light and to insert a lubricated fingertip in it. He then inserts, one, two, then three fingers into the vagina, as she herself did earlier in treatment. When no muscular spasms occur, the couple are ready for first penile penetration. This first intromission is very important. The penis should be well lubricated; the man slowly inserts it while the woman guides it. He rests quietly within her a few minutes and then slowly withdraws. They hold each other warmly and talk about the experience, learning what they can do to make the next penetration easier and more pleasurable.

In an alternate therapeutic approach, the patient is given several dilators to use in stretching the vaginal muscles so that she can comfortably accommodate a penis (Shaw 1954). After the largest dilator can be inserted without stress or pain, she is encouraged to retain it for several hours each night—perhaps to sleep with it in place throughout the night. Use of dilators for a 3- to 5-day period is usually highly successful in helping to relieve the involuntary spasms of vaginismus (Masters & Johnson 1970). But because most causes of vaginismus are psychological, physical efforts at overcoming it are sometimes unavailing, and psychotherapy is indicated. The treatment of vaginismus as outlined is usually successful, almost all cases being corrected in a relatively short period of time (Masters & Johnson 1970).

Dyspareunia

A sexual problem often associated with vaginismus is **dyspareunia,** or painful coitus. It can strike both men and women, although women are affected far more frequently than men. Men sometimes experience acute pain at the time of erection, but that is not actually dyspareunia. Men suffer from dyspareunia only when orgasm causes severe, jabbing pain. The pain is commonly the result of congestion of the prostate, seminal vesicles, or ejaculatory ducts, or an inflamed verumontanum. In other cases, the pain may be caused by an irritation of the glans penis in the uncircumcised male arising from poor hygienic habits. Peyronie's disease (see Chapter 21) can also make coitus painful for a man. Otherwise, dyspareunia in men is extremely rare.

Dyspareunia in women frequently has its inception in tension, fear, or anxiety over initial sexual intercourse, and the pain can involve vagina, cervix, uterus, or bladder. The vaginal muscles become taut and coitus can be painful, especially if the man is clumsy or insensitive. Furthermore, depending upon the type and thickness of the hymen, pain may be experienced when the tissue is ruptured by penile penetration (Ellis 1960; H. S. Kaplan 1979; Kelly 1959; Netter 1961).

Coitus may be painful because of lesions or scar tissue formed in the vaginal opening as a result of an episiotomy, a crude nonprofessional abortion, or rape, especially gang rape (the last two quite predictably capable of causing as much emotional as physical trauma). Some women suffer considerable pain when the cervix is touched and moved by the penis during sexual intercourse; coitus, in fact, becomes impossible at times.

Dyspareunia in postmenopausal women frequently occurs because the mucous membrane of the vagina has become fragile and thin, sometimes shrinking to a fraction of its former thickness. It does not secrete sufficient lubrication for easy penile intromission. Vaginal creams are frequently prescribed in such cases to act as a lubricant and to stimulate the mucous membrane. Estrogen therapy may help in certain instances to make the vagina a more comfortable or relaxed sexual organ (Clark 1956b; Martin 1980; Rubin 1966b).

A displaced or prolapsed uterus is another persistent cause of painful coitus in women. So also are polyps, cysts, and tumors of the reproductive system. Some women suffer pain during intercourse because the vaginal barrel is irritated by the chemicals contained in contraceptive creams, foams, jellies, or suppositories. Other women experience pain because of reaction to the rubber or plastic in condoms and diaphragms or because of douching with harsh chemicals. Still other women produce insufficient vaginal lubrication during coition, so that coital movements produce a painful or burning sensation. (In this case, coital discomfort can be avoided by using a commercial lubricant.)

Medical opinion is that if dyspareunia persists over a period of time, small undetected lesions in the vagina (which cause 85% of the cases) are to be suspected (Kleegman 1959). Furthermore, any infections of the vagina, uterus, bladder, or surrounding areas can obviously make intercourse painful for a woman. Medical and surgical remedies are clearly of great value in many cases of dyspareunia. Nevertheless, the benefits of psychotherapy should not be overlooked when the foundations of the disorder appear to lie in emotional blocks and fears.

The Unconsummated Marriage

It should be mentioned here that emotional barriers are sometimes so overwhelming that a woman refuses to attempt sexual intercourse even though she is married. Several scientific investigations have been made into the causes and nature of unconsummated marriages. One of the most extensive of these studies concerned 1000 American Caucasian females ranging in age from 17 to 47 years (average age, 29 years) (Blazer 1964). The length of marriage—and period of nonconsummation—ranged from 1 to

21 years (average length of marriage, 8 years), with 98% of the women having been married for more than 3 years. Of the sample, 76% had married between the ages of 20 and 29.

All of the 1000 were deemed physically capable of intercourse. A gynecologist examined each of the subjects, and if there was any doubt about a woman's being virginal, she was excluded from the sample. Although none of the women had engaged in coitus, about 25% of them did participate in mutual masturbation with their husbands.

The reasons given by these 1000 wives for their sexual abstinence fell into the following categories:

Fear of pain in the initial intercourse—203 (20.3%).
Opinion that the sex act is nasty or wicked—178 (17.8%).
Impotent husband—117 (11.7%).
Fear of pregnancy or childbirth—102 (10.2%).
Small size of the vagina—82 (8.2%). (Physical examinations revealed that neither husbands' nor wives' genitals were beyond the range of normalcy.)
The couple's ignorance regarding the exact location of the wife's sex organs—52 (5.2%).
Preference for a female partner—52 (5.2%).
Extreme dislike of the penis—46 (4.6%).
Deep objection to intercourse unless impregnation is intended—39 (3.9%).
Dislike of contraceptives—33 (3.3%).
Belief that submission of woman to man implies inferiority—31 (3.1%). (Reasons given by these women for entering marriage included "the thing to do," "fear of being an 'old maid,'" and "security.")
General dislike of men—30 (3.0%).
Desire only to "mother" their husbands—14 (1.4%).
Fear of damaging husband's penis—12 (1.2%).
Fear of semen—9 (0.9%).

The conclusion drawn by the researchers was that, if these psychosexually disturbed women had been given appropriate sex education at an early age, the sexual problems of at least 80%–85% of them very likely would not have existed—or persisted. Psychotherapeutic treatment of married virgins is reported to be about 70% successful.

Inhibitions of Sexual Desire

Sexual dysfunctions can be understood within the framework of a biphasic model of human sexual response. This model allows for sexual dysfunctions to be viewed as resulting from problems in the excitement or orgasmic phases. For example, impotence in males and general sexual dysfunction in females can be described as excitement phase disorders, and premature ejaculation in males and orgasmic dysfunction in females can be described as orgasmic phase disorders. Behavioral treatments and brief, supportive psychotherapeutic techniques, as discussed in this chapter, often lead to quick and successful resolutions of such disorders.

Helen Kaplan (1979) has recently emphasized, however, that a triphasic model is necessary in order to more fully take into account the complete range of human sexual response. The model recognizes the existence of the excitement and orgasmic phases and, in addition, notes the importance that a third phase, the *desire* phase, plays in human sexual response. The triphasic model thus leads to a more comprehensive understanding of human sexuality, especially in the area of dysfunctions, by recognizing the roles played by all phases.

The importance of having the third category in this triphasic model is seen in estimates suggesting that up to 40% of all sexual problems in males and females may result from inhibitions in the desire phase. The sexual conflicts that arise out of desire phase disorders are often deep seated, and require intensive psychotherapeutic and psychosexual treatment. Anger, fear of failure, performance anxiety, sexual phobias, maladaptive communication patterns, fears of sexual success, and fears of intimacy may be at the root of desire phase disorders.

Kaplan's term for this third class of disorders is **inhibitions of sexual desire (ISD).** She has found that the success rate for treatment is substantially less than the rate using the briefer therapies for excitement and orgasmic phase disorders. Nevertheless, there is hope for improving the success rate as increasingly sophisticated treatment strategies—including desensitization techniques, sensate-focus exercises, insight-oriented psychotherapy, and sometimes medication—are specifically developed for the desire phase disorders. This will occur once desire phase disorders become more fully recognized and understood (H. S. Kaplan 1979).

Since the 1970 publication of Masters and Johnson's pioneering work, *Human Sexual Inadequacy*, concerning the treatment of sexual dysfunction, clinics and counselors have multiplied throughout the country. Some are, of course, professionally qualified. Many others are not. And, whether inspired by good intentions or by greed and their own personal problems, the latter have found it easy to prey on a gullible public who are anxiously seeking solutions to sexual problems. Needless to say, an untrained person passing him- or herself off as a sex therapist or counselor may only aggravate the patient's problems.

Recognizing the need for special training and certification of sex therapists, the American Association of Sex Educators, Counselors, and Therapists (AASECT) took steps in 1973 to protect the public. It appointed a group of the nation's most highly qualified professionals to establish guidelines* for the training of sex counselors and therapists. Having established these strict professional guidelines, AASECT appointed a committee to review the qualifications of persons wishing to specialize in sex therapy. As a result, AASECT has become the best-known, although unofficial, organization of certification for sex therapists. Persons seeking the names of qualified professionals in their part of the country should address inquiries to: AASECT, 600 Maryland Avenue, S.W., Washington, D.C. 20024.

Summary

Psychiatrists, psychologists, social workers, and other specialists who study human sexual behavior have asserted that at least 50% of American marriages are flawed by some form of sexual maladjustment. Some sexual problems stem from ignorance about sexual techniques, whereas other problems are rooted in fears of failure, fears of rejection, or performance anxiety. Other sexual problems are more complicated, and the individuals affected may require both sex therapy and psychotherapy. Those individuals affected by profound personal psychopathology require intensive psychotherapy rather than sex therapy. Despite these complicated groupings, many sexual dysfunctions or problems are amenable to treatment as the affected individuals are often middle-class men and women of better-than-average education. For such individuals, the emotion underlying most of their sexual failures or malfunctions is fear.

Physiology and emotions are intimately intertwined in the human being. Recognition of this relationship is important to an understanding of why an individual does or does not experience a satisfactory sexual response. Adequate and satisfying sexual functioning depend on the *sympathetic* and *parasympathetic* systems of the *autonomic nervous system* working in concert. Fear and other emotional interferences prevent such harmonious functioning. The moderation of such emotional factors (such as the fear of sexual failure and overly rigid religious conformity) often leads to a resolution of the sexual dysfunction.

Programs to treat sexual dysfunctions are of various types: They may involve a man and a woman therapy team, an individual therapist, or sometimes educational self-treatment techniques. The foundation of sex therapy programs to help sexually inadequate or disturbed individuals is the use of *sensate focus* or *pleasuring techniques*, which key on developing the

---

* *The Professional Training and Preparation of Sex Counselors* (Washington, D.C.: American Association of Sex Educators, Counselors and Therapists, 1973).

sense of touch. Learning the art of pleasuring or sensate focus is typically carried out in a three step program: (1) The couple is encouraged to spend time stroking or touching each other without any genital stimulation; (2) the couple is instructed to engage in genital pleasuring with the intent of producing sexual arousal but not orgasms; and (3) the couple are allowed to produce orgasm by noncoital or coital means. Such step-by-step sex therapy programs have been found to be effective in helping couples overcome their sexual fears and anxieties and thus experience a positive and satisfying sexual interaction.

Sex therapy programs have been used to treat sexual dysfunctions in both sexes. Those forms of sexual dysfunctions that affect men are: (1) *inhibited sexual excitement*, also known as *erectile dysfunction* or *impotence;* (2) *premature ejaculation;* and (3) *retarded ejaculation*, also known as *inhibited male orgasm* or *ejaculatory incompetence.* Those forms of sexual dysfunction that affect women are: (1) *sexual unresponsiveness*, also known as *inhibited sexual excitement* or *general sexual dysfunction;* (2) *orgasmic dysfunction* or *inhibited female orgasm;* and (3) *vaginismus. Sexual anesthesia* is also a type of sexual disturbance or disorder that affects some women.

Erectile dysfunction or impotence refers to a man's inability to attain or maintain an erection of sufficient strength to enable him to perform the act of intercourse. Three forms of impotence exist: (1) *organic impotence*, caused by some anatomical defect in the reproductive system or central nervous system; (2) *functional impotence*, caused by a nervous disorder, the excessive use of alcohol or drugs, circulatory problems, the aging process, or exhaustion; and (3) *psychogenic impotence*, caused by emotional inhibitions that block or interfere with sexual response. Psychogenic impotence is further classified as either *primary* (which implies that the man has never been able to achieve or maintain an erection to engage in coitus) or *secondary* (which indicates that the man has had at least one successful coital experience but is now incapable of it). Anxiety, guilt, or the anticipation of failure often underlie the problem of impotence. The main therapeutic goals in treating impotence include: (1) removing the man's fear of failure; (2) reorienting the man toward active, involved sexual activities; and (3) removing the woman's fear of the man's impotency. The treatment program, which includes the man's partner, typically consists of five steps: (1) pleasuring without a direct attempt to produce an erection; (2) penile erection through genital pleasuring; (3) extravaginal orgasm; (4) penetration without orgasm; and (5) coitus with orgasm. Other therapeutic techniques, such as *systematic desensitization* and surgical techniques, for example, the implantation of an inflatable penile prosthesis, are alternatives in the treatment of impotence.

Premature ejaculation refers to ejaculation prior to, just at, or soon after intromission. Different definitions establish different guidelines for what is considered premature ejaculation based on time of intromission, the number of pelvic thrusts, or the sexual requirements of the individual's partner. Only rarely does premature ejaculation have a physical basis. More often, it is the psychological forces (including anxiety) that act to block a man's perception of the sensations that lead up to orgasm. The treatment for premature ejaculation involves having the man learn to detect the sensations of "ejaculatory inevitability" and then, with the help of his sexual partner, learning to control ejaculation through the "start-stop" sequence or the "squeeze technique." Some counselors also recommend that the man use a local anesthetic on the penile glans, wear one or more condoms, take a more passive role in coitus by lying beneath the woman, take a drink or two of alcohol before coitus, or have an orgasm a short period before they expect to have coitus in order to help control ejaculation and thus prolong intercourse.

Retarded ejaculation is a form of sexual inadequacy in which a man has difficulty ejaculating while his penis is in a woman's vagina. Fear, performance anxiety, or minimal commitment to the woman are often underlying factors in this sexual dysfunction. An important step in the treatment of retarded ejaculation is for the woman to stimulate the man to orgasm extravaginally. Desensitization therapy may also be included as part of the treatment process. When the man is ready, the *male bridge maneuver*, which includes manual and coital stimulation, can be used to help the man experience orgasm intravaginally.

Three types of female sexual dysfunction, according to the terminology of Helen Kaplan, are: (1) *female sexual unresponsiveness* or *general sexual dysfunction*; (2) *orgasmic dysfunction*; and (3) *vaginismus*. Organic, relational, and more commonly, psychological causes are contributing factors in female sexual dysfunctions. Additionally, factors such as the expectation of pain in coitus, the fear of rejection, fears of becoming pregnant, or the harboring of hostility toward men in general can also be responsible for the unresponsiveness of a woman.

Women who experience female sexual unresponsiveness may be devoid of desire entirely. On the other hand, they may find coitus disgusting or frightening or they may find no erotic pleasure during coitus although they derive emotional fulfillment. The treatment of sexual unresponsiveness often includes the use of self-therapy in conjunction with medical or psychological treatments. These women are encouraged to engage in self-exploration and masturbation in order to develop their sexual responsivity. Their therapists often emphasize that these unresponsive women learn to communicate their sexual feelings openly and use pleasuring or sensate focus techniques with their sex partners. The woman may be encouraged to use the woman-superior coital position and to contract their pubococcygeal muscles during thrusting to produce erotic sensations. The aim of the nondemanding, pleasure-oriented sexual experiences is to lower anxiety and defensiveness. The woman learns to participate in acts designed for her erotic pleasure and, with her lover, gains a fuller understanding of what each of the sex partner's needs and responses may be.

The sexual dysfunction women most commonly complain of is orgasmic difficulty. Female orgasmic dysfunction is classified as *primary* if the woman has never achieved orgasm through any method of stimulation and as *situational* if the woman has managed to achieve at least one orgasm through coital or noncoital means but no longer does so. Treatment of orgasmic dysfunction may include various forms of psychotherapy and counseling, behavior modification techniques, and group therapy treatment programs. Treatment often involves the woman first achieving orgasm through masturbation, then through clitoral stimulation by her partner, and finally, through coitus. Manual and electric vibrator stimulation and later oral-genital stimulation are frequently effective methods for women to experience orgasm. The *female bridge maneuver,* using a combination of direct clitoral stimulation and coitus, can be quite effective in helping the woman to experience orgasm during intercourse. Recent research indicates that many women may be orgasmic with appropriate stimulation of the anterior wall of the vagina. The key to a woman achieving orgasm, however, is for her to enjoy quiet, unhurried sensate pleasure and not to try to force or will an orgasm.

Vaginismus refers to the presence of strong muscular contractions within the vagina which make penile penetration impossible. The causes of vaginismus include a fear of pain associated with penile penetration, fear, guilt, frustration concerning coitus, inhibitions formed by emotionally traumatic experiences, conflicts growing out of homosexual tendencies, and physical problems that make intercourse painful. Interestingly, vaginismus occurs most commonly in women who are in the upper socioeconomic and educational strata. Treatment may include the application of local anesthetics to the vulval area before intromission. More commonly, the use of relaxation techniques as well as the use of fingers or dilators to stretch the vaginal muscles are effective in treating cases of vaginismus. Psychotherapy also may be employed.

Dyspareunia, a sexual problem often associated with vaginismus, is painful or difficult coitus. Men may suffer from dyspareunia, although women are more frequently affected. Emotional factors, physical traumas, disorders, diseases, infections of the reproductive system, and insufficient vaginal lubrication are among the factors that can cause dyspareunia in women. Medical and surgical techniques as well as psychotherapy are treatment modalities for this sexual problem.

Because of emotional barriers, some couples do not attempt sexual intercourse even though they are married. Reasons given by women for their unconsummated marriages are that they fear pain in intercourse, they have negative opinions of the sex act, they or their husbands have a physical disorder or sexual dysfunction, they fear becoming pregnant, they are ignorant about physiology, they have homosexual preferences, or they have a general dislike of men. Appropriate sex education or psychotherapeutic treatment can often alleviate or eliminate concerns about marital coitus.

Recent evidence indicates that a triphasic model of human sexual response may exist and that a more comprehensive understanding of human sexuality may be gained by recognizing the roles played by the desire, excitement, and orgasmic phases of this model. This triphasic model has the particular strength of allowing for a clearer understanding of inhibitions of sexual desire (ISD). As a result, increasingly sophisticated and effective treatment strategies are being developed that soon may improve the success rate in treating the heretofore misunderstood or ignored desire phase disorders.

Annotated Bibliography

Berman, Ellen M. and Lief, Harold I. Sex and the aging process. In *Sex and the life cycle*, ed. W. Oaks, G. Melchiode, and I. Ficher. New York: Grune and Stratton, 1976.
> This article addresses several important topics related to sexuality and the elderly, including stresses common to aging, physiology of sex and aging, sex and the older married couple, sex and the older single person, and sexual dysfunctions among the aged.

Fischer, J. and Gochros, H. J. *Handbook of behavior therapy with sexual problems (Vols. I & II)*. New York: Pergamon Press, 1977.
> This handbook is a practical volume for clinicians and educators of diverse theoretical orientations. Volume I describes specific behavioral techniques and gives indications for their use with sexual dysfunctions and problem sexual behaviors. Volume II covers a wide range of sexual problems and includes reviews of relevant research, descriptive and empirical articles, and case studies.

Kaplan, Helen Singer. *The new sex therapy*. Volume II: *Disorders of sexual desire*. New York: Brunner/Mazel, 1979.
> The author uses detailed case studies drawn from her own experience as a clinician to demonstrate treatment of various sexual dysfunctions, especially problems of desire. Included in the Appendix are valuable tables covering the effects of drugs and physical illness on sexuality and the physical causes of dyspareunia. This is an excellent volume for the clinician.

LoPiccolo, J. and LoPiccolo, L. (Eds.) *Handbook of sex therapy.* New York: Plenum Press, 1978.

> This outstanding volume provides comprehensive coverage of the etiology and treatment of male and female sexual dysfunctions and professional and ethical issues in sex therapy. Especially interesting is a section devoted to sex therapy for special populations such as heart patients and the elderly. Though intended as a source book for clinicians, articles in the Handbook would also appeal to lay readers.

Masters, William H. and Johnson, Virginia E. *Homosexuality in perspective.* Boston: Little, Brown, 1979.

> Based on the authors' research and clinical experience, this book attempts to dispel the many myths surrounding homosexuality and to establish a better understanding of homosexual behavior. The authors discuss treatment of sexual dysfunctions among homosexuals and report results of treatment of conversion or reversion. This book would be of interest to the lay reader as well as the professional reader.

Masters, William H., Johnson, Virginia E., Kolodney, Robert C. and Weems, Sarah M. (Eds.) *Ethical issues in sex therapy and research (Vol. II).* Boston: Little, Brown, 1980.

> This comprehensive volume for the professional sex therapist and researcher presents contributions by leading authorities regarding six fundamental issues: informed consent, problems of consent, privacy and confidentiality, sex research involving children and the mentally retarded, value imperialism and exploitation in sex therapy, and training and accreditation of sex therapists.

Murjack, D. J. and Oziel, L. J. *Sexual medicine and counseling in office practice.* Boston: Little, Brown, 1980.

> This book offers specific information for medical and allied health professionals on diagnosis and evaluation, counseling, and management of patients with sexual problems. The book also addresses the issue of how and when to refer patients who require lengthy or more expert treatment.

Nowinski, Joseph. *Becoming satisfied: A man's guide to sexual fulfillment.* Englewood Cliffs, New Jersey: Prentice-Hall, 1980.

> This book is a practical guide for men who have sexual concerns. This book is designed to enhance understanding of sexuality and to aid in dealing with erectile problems, overcoming sexual tension and fear of women, learning to relax, learning to delay or accelerate orgasm, and other problems.

Raley, Patricia E. *Making love: How to be your own sex therapist.* New York: The Dial Press, 1976.

> This well-illustrated sexual self-help guide is intended for the adult reader of any sexual orientation who is interested in maximizing satisfaction in relationships. Systematic guidelines are provided for exploring sex history, sexual fantasy, sexual attitudes, sexual anatomy, arousal, orgasm, sexual communication, relationships with self and others, and other significant aspects of erotic life.

Sandler, Jack, Myerson, Marilyn, and Kinder, Bill N. *Human sexuality: Current perspectives.* Tampa, Florida: Mariner, 1980.

> This text presents a comprehensive perspective of the field of human sexuality. A wide range of topics is covered, including sexual anatomy and sexual response, aphrodisiacs and anaphrodisiacs, past and current sexual attitudes and behavior, sexual diseases and disorders, sexual dysfunctions, birth control, sexual health, and sex and the law. Though designed for the student, this book would serve as a valuable general reference.

Sarrel, Lorna J. and Sarrel, Phillip M. *Sexual unfolding: Sexual development and sex therapies in late adolescence.* Boston: Little, Brown, 1980.

> The authors describe the process of sexual development in late adolescence as an interaction of social, biological, and psychological factors. Clinical work with young people who have sexual problems is discussed. An important reference for the professional, this book would also be beneficial to parents and young people.

Witkin, Mildred Hope. Sex therapy: A holistic approach. In *Handbook of human sexuality*, ed. B. Wolman and J. Money. Englewood Cliffs, New Jersey: Prentice-Hall, 1980.

> This article describes a holistic approach to treating sexual dysfunctions, based on the central role occupied by sex in human functioning. The process and implications of sex therapy for dyadic and family treatment are discussed. This article would be read profitably by the student as well as the professional sex therapist.

Witters, Weldon and Jones-Witters, Patricia. *Human sexuality: A biological perspective.* New York: D. Van Nostrand, 1980.

> This text approaches the various aspects of human sexuality from the biological standpoint. Topics of special interest include genetic engineering, hormonal control of sexuality, drugs affecting sexual function, surrogate parenthood, artificial insemination, cloning, and sex selection. The text is well illustrated and contains student performance objectives, but its appeal extends beyond the classroom.

Sexual Diseases and Disorders

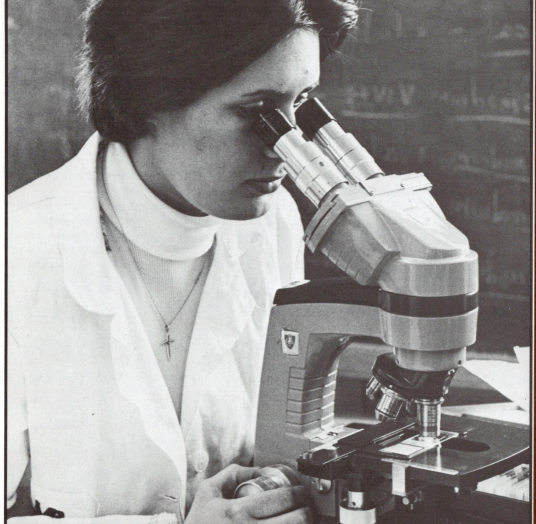

Venereal Diseases
    Gonorrhea
    Syphilis
    Chancroid
    Granuloma Inguinale
    Lymphogranuloma Venereum
    Venereal Warts
    Genital Herpes
Nonvenereal Diseases
    Nonvenereal Syphilis
    Leukorrhea
    Trichomoniasis
    Candidiasis or Moniliasis
    Peyronie's Disease
    Tuberculosis
    Carcinoma
    Elephantiasis
    Infectious Mononucleosis
    Dermatoses
    Inflammation of Internal and External Genitalia
Sexual Disorders
    Disorders Affecting Males
    Disorders Affecting Females
    Other Sex-Related Disorders

The relationship between the word *venereal* (from the Latin *venus:* love or sexual desire) and the usual source of venereal disease (VD), sexual contact, is not difficult to see. The causative organisms of VD are ordinarily found only in human beings, and they cannot live long outside the human body. The diseases, therefore, are almost always acquired by direct sexual contact.

These diseases attack men, women, and children throughout the world, and are considered among the most serious afflictions of humankind. The discovery of penicillin and other antibiotic drugs gave hope that control or even elimination of VD would be possible. Now, however, complete eradication is no longer considered a realistic goal, at least not until new techniques of treating and monitoring sexual contacts are developed. Yet, fortunately, scientists continue to expend great effort in seeking solutions to the problem of VD. For example, under USPHS and other sponsorship as well, microbiologists at the Florida Institute of Technology are working on an experimental vaccine for syphilis, and have succeeded for the first time in growing the causative spirochete, or bacterium, in a test tube (Jones *et al.* 1976).

Controlling VD is difficult for many reasons. Physicians are reluctant to report new cases in private patients to public health officials, especially when the patients are adolescents, among whom the increase has been the greatest in recent years. As a result, persons who infected the adolescents—and those, in turn, whom the adolescents have infected—are not contacted and treated. Recent statistics show that 20% of the total reported new cases of gonorrhea occurred in the 15- to 19-year-old age group. In this same age group were also found 17% of the new cases of syphilis (Najem 1976). Another explanation for lack of better VD control is that hospital testing for syphilis, for example, is haphazard at best. If such screening were routinely performed, it would help to identify some of the estimated half-million undetected cases of the disease in the country today.

Public funds necessary to assist medical authorities in searching out and treating infectious contacts are rarely adequate. The legal problems in controlling VD are legion, for it is impossible to legislate effectively against human behavior leading to the spread of VD. Further, there is a natural reluctance on the part of both adults and teen-agers to divulge the identity of their contacts (or even to seek treatment, in many cases). Most young people do not feel free to turn to their parents with a problem of this nature, nor do they often have ready access to physicians in whom they can confide. (Even when they do, teen-agers are more reticent than adults to divulge the full history of their sexual behavior.) The difficulties involved in accurately judging the number of cases of VD active at any one time are thus all too obvious. The American Social Health Association estimates that the incidence is perhaps four times greater than reported (Smartt & Lighter 1971).

Although progress has been made toward the eradication of syphilis, there has been a rampant rise in the incidence of gonorrhea in the United States and many other parts of the world—growth that has now reached epidemic proportions. Methods that have shown some success in curbing syphilis are not suitable to the treatment of gonorrhea. Because the incubation of syphilis is relatively long—about three weeks—contacts can be sought out and treated before they reach the infectious stage. Gonorrhea, by contrast, has an incubation period of two to eight days. Public health officials therefore lack a sufficient period of grace to find the sexual contacts of the newly diagnosed gonorrheal patient before the disease becomes manifest in contacts who in turn may have transmitted it to still other persons (Quinn 1971).

Between 1963 and 1970 the number of reported cases of gonorrhea increased by 75%. The current rate of increase per year is about 15% (Quinn 1971; Smartt & Lighter 1971); in 1975 over 100,000 new cases were reported.

And there is, unfortunately, no indication that this pestilence will abate in the next few years.

Prompted into action by the increasing number of adolescent cases of VD, public health agencies have made various studies to determine what sort of teen-ager becomes infected. Which stratum of society does he/she come from; to what extent are ethnic, religious, and similar factors involved; and what unique pressures, if any, impel a 20th-century American adolescent toward premarital sexual experimentation, which too often ends with a venereal infection? The incidence of syphilis and gonorrhea by age and sex is shown in Table 21.1. Incidence of both diseases is highest among the 20- to 24-year-old group; of those affected, 60% of the females and 80% of the males are single.

The studies have revealed no "typical" teen-ager who is more likely than another to contract VD. The infected young people studied were of all personality types and represented the whole spectrum of American society. Of the cases treated at VD clinics, the majority, as might be expected, came from low-income minority-group families. The other infected youngsters were no doubt treated by private physicians. Otherwise, the statistics showed that, although most of those infected had begun high school, only about 15% had graduated. A few were attending college. About 25% attended religious services, while 50% of their parents did so (Deschin 1963).

The incidence of gonorrhea is thought to be somewhat higher among men than among women, although in 1974 the rise was greater in women

Table 21.1   Venereal Disease Rates per 100,000 Population, 1973

Age	Male	Female	Total
	Primary and Secondary Syphilis		
15–19	18.7	19.7	19.2
20–24	56.3	27.6	41.3
25–29	53.9	17.6	35.2
30–39	35.0	10.3	22.2
40–49	14.4	3.9	9.0
50 +	2.7	0.5	1.5
	Gonorrhea		
15–19	1075.2	1234.5	1155.0
20–24	2479.4	1406.7	1918.2
25–29	1461.6	565.8	1000.9
30–39	546.2	176.5	354.8
40–49	145.2	37.3	89.5
50 +	25.9	5.9	14.9

SOURCE: U.S. Department of Health, Education, and Welfare, *Venereal Disease Statistical Letter 120*, August 1974, pp. 15, 16.

than in men—9.5% vs 4.9%, according to the USPHS. About 80% of women (and a few men) have no clinical signs or symptoms of gonorrheal infection and therefore do not suspect that they are diseased. These individuals constitute to a large extent the nucleus of ongoing gonorrheal infection, since they infect their sex partners unknowingly (Smartt & Lighter 1971).

One of the segments of the population showing the greatest increase in VD in recent years has been the male homosexual group (Ginsberg 1980; Tarr & Lugar 1960; Trice *et al.* 1960). Studies have revealed an extremely high rate of VD among male homosexuals, but an insignificant incidence among lesbians. Only 3% of men infected with gonorrhea name another man as the infectious contact, whereas from 12% to 18% of syphilitic males contract the disease from another male (Ketterer 1971). The same venereal infections are seen in the homosexual population that are found among heterosexuals, although the sites of infection may be different (Unger 1975).

Factors other than heightened or more indiscriminate sexual activity in the general populace have also contributed significantly to the rise in VD in recent years. First, with the growing popularity of other birth-control techniques, use of the condom, which offers protection against pregnancy and VD alike, has not kept pace with the growing increase of coitus. Second, several strains of gonococcus have demonstrated a measure of resistance to the usual dosage of penicillin, the treatment of choice, while at least one strain is altogether unaffected by it. Third, asymptomatic gonorrheal infection in both men and women is on the rise, which leads to unwitting infection of others. A fourth factor has been the general ineffectiveness of public health agencies in tracking down sexual contacts of infected persons; and fifth, certain diseases (such as herpes) that were previously considered nonvenereal have now been added to the roster of VD infections (Piemme 1974).

Promiscuity is definitely linked to VD. Strong sexual drive, however, is not of itself a cause of promiscuous behavior. People are promiscuous because relationships encompassing mutual understanding and confidence have been absent from their lives. VD patients frequently see themselves as worthless, unlovable victims of some force over which they have no control. When seriously depressed by these feelings, they seek relief in irresponsible sexual relations. The traditional American attitude that associates security with love, and love with sex, brings about their misguided attempts to solve emotional problems through sexual acting-out behavior.

Society must face the fact of VD when it appears. When there is even the slightest suspicion that one's partner or oneself may have VD, prophylactics should be used during intercourse. The simplest and best prophylactic for men, if they suspect their partner is infected, is the condom, followed by a thorough soap-and-water cleansing of the genitalia after coitus. If a woman is going to have intercourse with a partner of unknown hygiene, she should insist that he use a condom; and if there is any suspicion that VD is present, she should use an antiseptic douche, followed by a soap-and-water cleansing of the genitalia.

Venereal Diseases

Now follows a discussion of a variety of venereal diseases, both the well known and obscure. It is presented in the belief that sex instruction is dangerously incomplete without such information. It also rests on the conviction, supported by research, that knowledge can help curb promiscuity as well as the spread of VD itself.

Gonorrhea

Gonorrhea (from the Greek: flow of seed) is the most ancient, and most prevalent, of all venereal diseases. It is second only to the common cold in incidence of communicable diseases in the United States. Chinese writings as early as 2637 B.C., as well as the unmistakable references in the Bible to gonorrhea, attest to its existence for many centuries (Blau 1961; Fiumara 1971). The word *gonorrhea* was first used by the Greek physician Galen in A.D. 130 to describe the disease; however, the causative organism was not identified until 1839, at which time it was given the name *gonococcus*. Until the advent in 1943 of the "miracle drugs," notably penicillin, and their remarkable effect on the organisms of VD, gonorrhea was not easily cured, and complications often resulted in ailments requiring specialized treatment. Following the discovery of penicillin, gonorrhea became relatively easy to treat. Now certain strains have demonstrated resistance to penicillin, making the disease more difficult to cure. A new strain of gonococcus, called "Super Gon" by some VD-control authorities, had been identified in several states by early 1977. It appears not only resistant to penicillin, but also actually to thrive on it. To complicate matters, it exhibits resistance as well to the backup antibacterial treatment, spectinomycin.

Primarily a disease of the young, gonorrhea's highest incidence today is among those 20–24 years old. Its second highest incidence is among 15-to 19-year-olds. Of those infected 25% are under 20, and 65% are under 25. After 25 the incidence declines steadily. Among men 50 and older, the incidence is about the same as it is among boys 14 and younger (W. J. Brown 1972; U.S. Department of Health, Education, and Welfare 1970). However, one investigator estimates that gonorrhea is as prevalent in homosexual males over age 40 as it is in males under age 20 (Ginsberg 1980).

Gonorrhea is almost always contracted during intercourse with an infected person. Curiously, however, a study of United States Navy personnel in the Philippines revealed that, even without the use of prophylaxis, the risk of acquiring gonorrhea by sexual contact with an infected female is only about 20% to 30% after one or two acts of coitus (Holmes 1975a; Holmes *et al.* 1970). The gonococcus usually restricts its attack to the genitourinary area, although the rectum may become infected during anal intercourse or, in the case of women, by spreading from the genitals (Blair 1961; Oill & Guze 1980). Homosexual males and heterosexual females who engage in fellatio and have gonorrhea in another body location have a pharyngeal infection in approximately 20% of cases (Ginsberg 1980). Gonococcus has been known to involve the skin, joints, and, much more rarely, the brain and blood system.

Gonorrhea in a man usually manifests itself first by acute *urethritis* (inflammation of the urethra). A thin watery discharge from the penis commences from 2 to 7 days following the date of infectious sexual contact, usually becoming thicker and greenish-yellow in color within another day or so. The patient typically feels an urgent and frequent need to urinate. The act of urination is accompanied by a burning sensation at the tip of the penis, which is now swollen and inflamed.

Painful complications, which are sometimes serious, commonly result from gonorrhea. One of the most agonizing is *epididymitis*, characterized by swelling of the maturation chamber connecting the testes and vas deferens. The testes sometimes become as large as oranges and extremely painful. Other complications include arthritis—the leading cause of acute arthritis in young adults is gonorrhea (Eschenbach 1976)—iritis, conjunctivitis, skin infections, and, more rarely, endocarditis and meningitis. Gonorrheal infection of the prostate can become chronic, causing a man to remain infectious for a considerable length of time. Urethral stricture is another common and serious complication. The obstruction thus produced predisposes the patient to attacks of *pyelonephritis* (inflammation of the kidney) and kidney damage (Blau 1961; *Dorland's Illustrated Medical Dictionary* 1957). These complications, which are typically accompanied by fever, malaise, and marked debility, repeatedly caused the death of gonorrheal victims prior to the introduction of antibiotic drugs.

It is a medical axiom that most cases of gonorrhea in males reveal clinical signs or symptoms, while infected females remain largely asymptomatic. Perhaps only 10% to 20% of men with penile gonorrhea develop no symptoms (70% with rectal gonorrhea are asymptomatic). Although estimates of asymptomatic women range from 15% to 90%, the most common figure is 80% (Ginsberg 1980; Handsfield 1974; Taub 1976). The majority of men and women with rectal gonorrhea are asymptomatic, but it is possible for moderate to severe symptoms to develop. Symptoms associated with rectal gonorrhea may range from anal itching, discomfort, or irritation to severe burning and pain, anal discharges, or even mucopus or blood in the bowel movements (Oill & Guze 1980).

Laboratory tests reveal the cervix as the most common site of infection in women. Combined cervix and urethral cultures are positive in about 75% of female gonorrheal patients. *Neisseria gonorrhoeae*, the causative organism, can be isolated from the anal canal of 35%; and in 10% of them, it can be isolated from the pharynx. In the latter instance, the percentage rises to 19% among female victims who have had oral-genital sex, or who demonstrate sore throats (Eschenbach 1976; Ginsberg 1980). Although women do not develop a precise symptom comparable to urethritis in men to signal infection, at least 20% of all infected women develop severe symptomatic complications. An additional number reveal uncomplicated symptoms of local infection, which are disregarded or ascribed to other conditions (Eschenbach 1976). These women often do not seek therapy for their mild, transient symptoms, and soon revert to the status of "asymptomatic" carriers who, it is hoped, are later identified as sexual contacts by men with symptomatic gonorrhea.

When the disease does manifest itself distinctly in women, the first evidence appears 2 to 7 days after infectious contact. The vulva becomes red, raw, and irritated. There is an urgent and frequent need to urinate, and urination is accompanied by pain and a scalding sensation. Gonorrheal complications in women are considerably more common and severe than in men, because women are so often unaware of infection, or tend to ignore a vaginal discharge or attribute it to other causes. Further, diagnosis and treatment of the disease in women is more difficult than in men (Fletcher & Landes 1970).

Two major complications that women can develop are inflammation of the Bartholin's glands *(bartholinitis)*, and inflammation of the fallopian tubes *(salpingitis)*. In bartholinitis, the gland on one or both sides of the vulva swells and becomes tender and painful. An abscess or a cyst sometimes forms in the affected gland, requiring medical or occasionally surgical attention (Ball 1957; Blau 1961; TeLinde 1953). Acute salpingitis often produces severe lower abdominal pain on one or both sides of the body, accompanied by fever and malaise. A tubal abscess can form on either or both sides, depending on the extent of inflammation of the fallopian tubes. These conditions frequently cause severe colicky abdominal pain, menstrual irregularity, chronic invalidism, and sterility. Surgical treatment is often required if the conditions are to be properly corrected (TeLinde 1953). It has been observed that patients with gonorrhea-induced salpingitis and tubal or ovarian abscesses usually had been exposed to the disease during their menstrual flow, or soon thereafter. During those times the epithelial tissue of the internal genitalia is thin, providing an excellent medium for the growth of the organism (Goss 1971).

The treatment of choice for men is a single intramuscular injection of 2.4 million units of penicillin. The recommended dosage for women (and men with anal gonorrhea) is double that, or 4.8 million units; the dosage is divided into two injections, given during a single visit to a clinic. Ampicillin or tetracycline may be substituted when the patient is allergic to penicillin. Spectinomycin may be used when the gonococcal strain is penicillin-resistant (W. J. Brown *et al.* 1971; Ginsberg 1980; Oill & Guze 1980). Any complications stemming from the original infection will, of course, require special treatment.

Children are sometimes accidentally infected with gonorrhea, although such an occurrence is uncommon, since the source of the infection is almost always coitus. Children have been infected through mutual masturbation, sexual exploration and experimentation, and sexual assault. At one time, nearly 33% of all blindness in children was the result of gonococcal ophthalmia (inflammation of the conjunctiva or membrane lining the eyelid), which the newborn acquires in the birth process from its infected mother. This affliction has now been almost eradicated by treating the eyes of all newborn babies with a silver-nitrate or penicillin solution (Blau 1961).

In men, gonorrhea is commonly diagnosed through microscopic examination of a smear of urethral discharge. In women, a gonococcus culture is usually required. A modern method of diagnosis known as the "fluorescent antibody technique" has been found effective in detecting the organism in patients who show no clinical signs of infection, but this diagnostic technique is not widely available.

Nongonococcal urethritis (NGU) is common in men, with *Chlamydia trachomatis* being the causative agent in 30% to 50% of cases. One-third or more of women who are contacts of NGU-infected men have *Chlamydia trachomatis* associated with their cervical infections. The symptoms of NGU are similar to those of gonorrhea, although it is not ordinarily considered a venereal disease. The primary difference between them is that in nongonococcal urethritis no gram-negative cocci are found in a smear of the urethral exudate (discharge). Antimicrobial medication is the usual treatment. But if the physician discovers that the urethritis is caused by trichomonads, bacteria, fungi, or other infectious agents, he will treat the infection according to the causal agent (McCormack 1976; Oriel 1980).

Syphilis

The physician Fracastoro in 1530 published a poem, which achieved wide popularity, about a shepherd named Syphilis who had been stricken with a disease that, until then, had been known as "the great pox." The disease has been known ever since as **syphilis.**

It is still debated whether Columbus and his crew brought syphilis to America from Europe, or whether they contracted the disease from West Indian women and then carried it to Europe. Indeed, study of the bones of American Indians has revealed evidence that syphilis existed in America at least 500 years before Columbus's voyages ("News of the Month" 1961a). But whichever the direction, syphilis spread in epidemic proportions across the known world within a few years after Columbus and his men returned to Europe. Columbus himself probably died, in 1506, from general paresis, one of the neurological disorders resulting from syphilitic infection (Coleman 1972). It was about 400 years later, in 1905, that the causative organism of syphilis was discovered. A short time later, the relationship between syphilis and paresis was recognized.

The cause of syphilis was found to be a corkscrew-shaped spirochete, or bacterium, known as *Treponema pallidum*. It is a cylindrical body with 8 to 14 rigid spirals best seen with the aid of a dark-field microscope. Subsequently, in 1913, the scientists Noguchi and Moore found this same spirochete in the cerebral cortex of patients dying of general paresis. Once the spirochete had been identified, extensive studies were made of the disease, and effective methods of diagnosis were developed (the Wassermann test, for example).

Despite the fact that penicillin has been universally used in the treatment of a broad spectrum of infectious diseases since 1943, *Treponema pallidum* has not become immune to it and remains vulnerable to its antibiotic action. The recommended dosage is 2.4 million units of benzathine penicillin G given intramuscularly during a single visit to a treatment center. A penicillin-sensitive patient can be treated with tetracycline or erythromycin (W. J. Brown *et al.* 1971).

Early Syphilis. Early syphilis is subdivided into *primary* and *secondary* stages of infection. It is important to recognize the disease during its early phase (the two years following infection) because it can be most easily cured then; irreversible tissue damage has not yet occurred. This is also the period when the patient is most infectious and is the greatest menace to public health.

The *primary* stage of syphilis is easily identified by a lesion or a chancre (sore) that usually appears in the anal-genital area 10 to 40 days after sexual contact with a diseased person. In about 10% of the cases, the chancre may appear in the mouth or on the tonsils or lips, and the infection may be extragenital in origin (Eagle 1952). The chancre begins as a small red papule (circumscribed elevation of the skin) that becomes eroded and moist. The only other sign of infection at this stage is a painlessly swollen lymph gland at the site of the regional lymph drainage. For example, if the chancre is on the penis or labia minora, the glandular swelling will be in the groin. During the early primary stage, the invading microorganisms leave the bloodstream and enter other tissues of the body, usually causing the lesions characteristic of the secondary stage of syphilis. If the disease is adequately treated in its primary stage, a cure is easily effected and the danger of transmission removed. Without treatment, the primary chancre heals in 4 to 10 weeks. The surface warning signal is thus removed, but the danger of internal damage remains.

During this primary stage, a dark-field microscopic examination of serum from suspected areas is a valuable diagnostic tool, especially in the case of men, in whom the chancre is usually quite detectable. For a more definitive diagnosis, a blood test should be made for antibodies produced against the spirochetes 6 to 8 weeks after suspected infection. A blood test is especially important for women who suspect infection because the syphilitic lesions and chancres may be internal or otherwise hidden from view. Once treatment is undertaken or completed, blood tests to check the titer levels (concentration levels) will reveal whether the disease has been arrested or not.

The *secondary* stage is characterized by a non-itching eruption (giving rise to the name "great pox" to distinguish the disease from smallpox) or rash on the skin, usually on the trunk of the body. The rash—which begins after 6 weeks and usually within 3 months—is sometimes so indistinct as to escape notice (Lewis 1955). Other symptoms appear at this time, but their significance is usually recognized only by a competent physician: glandular enlargement, throat infection, headaches, malaise, and a low-grade fever. There may also be a loss of eyelashes and eyebrows, and bald spots on the scalp, giving it a "moth-eaten" appearance ("Secondary Syphilis" 1971). Secondary lesions then heal, without treatment and without leaving scar formation, within a few weeks or months—possibly a year.

Although coitus is by far the most common means of transmitting syphilis, it is not the only means. The progress of syphilitic infection in the secondary stage of infection may induce eruptions in the mucous membrane of the mouth, causing the saliva to swarm with spirochetes. It is obvious, therefore, that the contagion can be passed on to another person by kissing, especially if there is a break in the skin in or around the mouth (Clark 1970c).

The Latent Period.   The third stage of untreated syphilis (also called the latent period) begins from 6 months to 2 years after the initial infection. The disease is termed *early latent* when the patient has been infected less than 4 years or is under 25 years of age (Lewis 1955). Syphilis is considered to be *late latent* when infection has persisted longer than 4 years or when the patient is over 25 years old. The latent period is dangerously deceptive; all symptoms associated with syphilis disappear, and the latency may last for months or years. It was at this stage during the great syphilis epidemic of the 15th century that the disease was thought to be cured. During latency, syphilitics do not infect contacts, but the results of a blood serology test are always positive. Such a test is the only reliable method of diagnosis. Without treatment, the disease can now progress to the destructive stage of late syphilis.

Late Syphilis. The fourth stage—called *late syphilis*—may manifest itself in any organ, in the central nervous system and cardiovascular system, and, particularly, on the skin. These symptoms can appear as late as 30 years after the initial infection. Late lesions may appear in the mouth and throat and on the tongue, usually accompanied by thickening of the tissue or destructive ulcers. These late lesions are responsible for the crippling, disabling, and disfiguring effects of syphilis. A chronic inflammatory process may develop in this late stage, involving bones, joints, eyes and other organs, and especially the cardiovascular system.

Although the disease still rages, modern methods of diagnosis and treatment have eliminated syphilis as "the great scourge." In 1975, for example, some 26,000 new primary and secondary cases were reported in the U.S. (up from 20,000 in 1970). However, it is estimated that some 70,000 to 75,000 persons were actually infected—small figures, nonetheless, when they are compared with those of new gonorrheal infections.

The estimate is that only half those exposed to syphilis contract the disease (Taub 1976). And in about 50% of those persons who do contract the disease and receive no treatment, there is no disability or discomfort. Another 25% will have some residual evidence of the disease, but will suffer no disability or shortening of life (Blau 1961). The reason that such a high proportion of untreated syphilitics suffer few or no ill effects from the disease is not known, but some speculate that resistance to the disease is built up because of the administration of penicillin and other antibiotics in the treatment of earlier illnesses. Yet syphilis still cannot be classified as benign because of the very serious effects in 25% of untreated cases.

The incidence of **congenital syphilis** (syphilis existing at birth) has greatly diminished in recent years because of improved routine prenatal care and treatment of mothers. In 1941 there were 13,600 cases of congenital syphilis diagnosed in children under 1 year of age. By 1970 that figure had dropped to 300. A syphilitic mother usually transmits the disease to any child she conceives during the first 2 years of her infection. If she is treated before the fourth month of pregnancy, the child is usually born nonsyphilitic. In these instances, only 1 infant in 11 is born with the disease (Pund & Von Haam 1957). Treatment of the mother after the fourth month may help the fetus but it may still show signs of congenital syphilis.

Undetected congenital syphilis usually manifests itself early in life by certain pathological symptoms, although the symptoms may not appear until the victim is 10 to 15 years of age, sometimes not even until he or she is as old as 30. The course of congenital syphilis is similar to that of the second and third stages in the contracted form of the disease. Pupillary signs are frequently the only indication of congenital syphilis. More often, presence of the disease is manifested in various degrees of mental defect ranging from mild to severe deficiency. There are sometimes cerebral developmental defects as well.

Untreated syphilis may produce certain severely disabling disorders, the two most common being neurosyphilis and general paresis. In the past, about 5% of all untreated cases progressed to general paresis. Recently the figure has dropped to about 3%, although the reason for this decrease is not known (Coleman 1972). Neurosyphilis occurs in from about 10% to 25% of untreated cases of syphilis. Blood and cerebrospinal fluid serology tests are frequently required to diagnose the disease. Neurosyphilis can affect every part of the cerebrospinal system in several forms (or a combination) of the disease: syphilitic meningitis, meningovascular neurosyphilis, parenchymatous neurosyphilis, paresis, and tabes dorsalis. Individuals who may not be inclined toward establishing long-term or stable emotional and sexual relationships, such as some male homosexuals or military personnel, may be particularly at high risk for the disease (Greenwood 1980; Pund & Von Haam 1957).

Clinical signs of neurosyphilis are many. Whether they are mild or severe, acute or chronic, depends on such circumstances as onset, rate of progress, and extent of the affliction. There may be headache, dizziness, nausea, various subjective pains, numbness, attacks of unconsciousness, or epilepticlike convulsions. The list of personality disorders that may accompany neurospyhilis is also lengthy: restlessness, dullness, irritability, apathy, anxiety, depression, defective memory, mild or severe delirium, dementia, and so forth. On the other hand, the disease can exist without any clinical indices.

General paresis is a chronic progressive syphilitic disease with which certain physical symptoms are associated, as well as the better-known psychological indications of psychosis and progressive mental deterioration (Coleman 1972; Greenwood 1980). The disease usually makes its appearance 10 to 20 years (occasionally longer) after the primary syphilitic lesion. It is commonly observed between the ages of 30 and 50, more frequently in men than in women, and is often fatal.

General paresis may affect any and all areas of the nervous system, and is frequently confused with functional psychotic illnesses. Pupillary changes and a positive serology test are often the only factors calling attention to the actual nature of the disease. The symptoms, typically of psychotic proportions, may range from sudden manic or depressive reactions to a more complex syndrome—anxiety, insomnia, hypochondria, fatigue, irritability, loss of interest, and a loss of power to concentrate. Because its symptoms resemble those of various psychological illnesses, general paresis is sometimes referred to as "the great imitator."

Juvenile general paresis usually manifests itself at some point between the age of 10 and adolescence. The symptoms typically involve delusional trends, depression or excitement, defective memory, general loss of interest, and disorderly conduct. These reactions are frequently masked by pronounced mental deficiency or convulsions. Juvenile paresis progresses more slowly and in a less clear-cut manner than adult forms of the disease do, although the physical symptoms of the two are the same. The disease is rarely found today because of prophylactic measures taken with syphilitic pregnant women (Ball 1957; Coleman 1972).

Chancroid

Chancroid (caused by the streptobacillus of Ducrey) is a highly painful, contagious disease typically spread through intercourse. It is characterized by ulcerations, usually at the points of physical contact, and by local lymph-gland swelling. The first sign of chancroid appears about 12 to 16 hours after infectious sexual intercourse has taken place. It usually takes the form of an inflamed papule or pustule, which soon breaks down to become a ragged-edged ulcer filled with dead tissue. The ulcer varies in size, but may become extremely large and destructive of the skin affected (Ball 1957; Blau 1961).

Ordinarily the discharge from the ulcer will infect the surrounding area on a man's prepuce, frenum, or penile shaft. In a woman, the ulcer usually forms on the labia majora, vestibule, or clitoris. Occasionally the lymph glands of the groin may swell, cause pain, and rupture. If not treated, chancroid ulcerations can drain for months. The adverse effects of this disease are considerably greater in women than in men (Pund & Von Haam 1957).

Chancroid may be contracted in conjunction with other venereal diseases. Accurate diagnosis and treatment therefore require expert clinical and laboratory techniques. Sulfonamides, which are the drugs commonly chosen to combat chancroid infection, usually effect a cure in 3 to 8 days (Blau 1961).

Granuloma Inguinale

Granuloma inguinale, a chronic disease, is unique primarily because of its extensive ulceration and scarring of skin and subcutaneous tissues. The disease is more prevalent in temperate and tropical zones than in colder climates. The genitals are a special mark for attack, but extragenital sites can also be invaded (Blau 1961). The disease is infectious—the incubation period is thought to be 2 to 12 weeks (Gerwels & Beckett 1975)—but it is not necessarily contracted through intercourse. "Venereal" is not, therefore, a wholly appropriate label (Blau 1961).

At the onset of granuloma inguinale, a small red papule appears, ordinarily on the penis or labia, but occasionally on other parts of the body, such as the face, neck, anus, rectum, or groin. Lesions enlarge and spread, and the ulcerations grow together to form a larger area of infection. The tissue degenerates into a red, moist, malodorous, granulated, and frequently bleeding mass. Spontaneous healing does not ordinarily occur. Slow extension of the ulceration is capable of destroying much of the tissue of the entire genital region, which then becomes replaced by thick scar tissue.

The absence of lymph-node involvement is a marked feature of the disease and is an excellent diagnostic aid. The organism itself is difficult to isolate, even in scrapings from active lesions. Identification must usually be made by microscopic examination of stained slides. The disease can be cured by careful treatment with antibiotic drugs of the mycin family (Ball 1957; Blau 1961; TeLinde 1953).

Lymphogranuloma Venereum

Lymphogranuloma venereum is a systemic disease that invades tissues in the anal-genital and inguinal areas. *Chlamydia trachomatis* is the causal agent. Lymphogranuloma venereum is clinically observed more frequently in men than in women. The most serious problem associated with this disease is that it has an insidious onset, and its destruction of body tissue can be silent and painless (Felman 1980).

The primary lesion can manifest itself within a week after sexual contact in the form of a small blister that soon ruptures to form a shallow ulcer with clear-cut edges surrounded by reddened skin. The blister is painless and heals rapidly without leaving a scar. The initial lesion may appear on the glans, prepuce, vulva, vaginal walls, or cervix, or in the urethra or anal region. If the virus is contracted during cunnilingus, it can cause the tongue to blister and swell, a reaction often followed by swelling in the neck glands (Blau 1961; Felman 1980).

Approximately 2 weeks after the primary lesion, the disease progresses to a secondary stage, characterized by pain in the anal-genital region followed by visible enlargement of the lymph nodes, which are very tender. Further complications, such as elephantiasis of the penis, scrotum, or vulva, may develop as the disease progresses (Felman 1980).

The LGN complement-fixation test can be performed in diagnosing this disease. When lymphogranuloma venereum is diagnosed, the preferred treatment is 500 mg of tetracycline to be taken four times daily for three weeks. Sulfisoxazole can be used in treatment if pregnancy or unusual circumstances dictate against the use of tetracycline (Felman 1980). If begun during the acute stage of infection, treatment usually lasts 3 to 6 weeks. But if it is delayed until the chronic stage, it may require several months (Duncan 1976).

Venereal Warts

Venereal warts are actually benign tumors. They are probably the result of a filtrable (capable of passing through a filter that blocks ordinary bacteria) viral infection. In a man, they usually appear around the base of the glans and develop quickly in the moist environment of a tight prepuce. A woman may develop venereal warts on the labia and perineum; the growths can spread to cover the entire area. Venereal warts may be transmittted to other persons or to other parts of one's own body.

A study of 97 patients who had had coitus with partners known to be infected with venereal warts showed that 62 became similarly infected. The incubation periods ranged from 3 weeks to 8 months, the average being 2.8 months (Blank & Rake 1955; Netter 1961; Oriel 1971). Treatment should be directed by a physician since medication (topical application of 10% or 25% podophyllin in spirit) must be carefully controlled; toxic effects from absorption of the drug are a danger. Cauterization by electric needle, curettage, and the use of liquid nitrogen are other modes of treatment (Felman 1980; Oriel 1973).

Genital Herpes

Herpes is an acute skin disease caused by the herpes simplex virus, which has two forms, Type I and Type II. Herpes Type I generally appears above the waist, typically as cold sores or fever blisters affecting the mouth, lips or nose. The Type II infection, or genital herpes, is commonly found below the waistline. The sites most commonly affected in men are the penis and urethra, and in women the cervix, vagina, and vulva. Because of the growing practice of fellatio and cunnilingus in recent years, however, a mixture of the two herpes types is being found with increasing frequency in both facial and genital regions (Fiumara 1980). Type II is usually sexually transmitted; Type I is not.

Until about 1965, Type II herpes was almost never seen by physicians in this country. But since that time its incidence has increased dramatically, so that it now ranks second only to gonorrhea in venereal incidence and accounts for about 13% of all sexually related or transmitted disease in the United States (Amstey 1974; Blough & Giuntoli 1979). Two serious problems are linked to herpes Type II, both related to the infection in women. First, genital herpes during pregnancy may have serious consequences for the fetus, ranging from spontaneous abortion to premature delivery. Or in the process of birth through a herpes-infected vagina, the baby may itself contract the infection, from which it can develop a crippling or fatal form of meningitis. Second, there is increasing evidence that herpes Type II is related to cancer of the cervix (Blough & Giuntoli 1979; National Institute of Allergy and Infectious Diseases 1976; Reyner 1975).

The sores of genital herpes, which look like blisters or small bumps, can rupture to form open sores, or ulcers, which are often quite painful. Other possible symptoms include fever, enlarged lymph nodes, and generalized symptoms of infection. Patients in extreme discomfort may require analgesics. The disease can spread on the body through autoinfection and may, for example, involve the entire external genitalia (Fiumara 1976). Pain during urination is the most distressing symptom reported by women. To relieve the burning, doctors often prescribe application of lidocaine (Xylocaine) to the affected area. If the treatment is not successful, patients may be instructed to urinate while sitting in a pan of water or while spraying the vulval area with cold water from a plastic spray bottle (Chang 1974; Fiumara 1980).

Effective cures for herpes infections have been difficult to find and to develop. Some physicians have reported success in treating the lesions by painting them with light-absorbing dye and then shining a fluorescent light on them. The virus becomes hypersensitive to light and can be inactivated by exposure to it (Kaufman *et al.* 1973). More recently, physicians and medical researchers have begun to report success in treating herpes infections with chemotherapeutic agents such as 2-Deoxy-D-glucose, vidarabine, and acyclovis (Blough & Giuntoli 1979; Check 1977; Gunby 1980).

Nonvenereal Diseases

Many diseases, infections, and inflammations affecting the male and female sexual systems may have no relationship to sexual activity. But in each instance some part of the internal or external genitalia is affected and may possibly be aggravated by sexual contact.

Nonvenereal Syphilis

Nonvenereal syphilis, an endemic infection acquired in infancy, is caused by an invasion of a parasitic organism closely related to the treponemal organism causing venereal syphilis. The disease is frequently referred to as "yaws" or "pinta." It affects many people in widely separated parts of the world, and typically thrives in warm, moist climates and in conditions of filth. Penicillin has been used successfully in many countries in mass eradication campaigns conducted by the World Health Organization (Blau 1961).

Leukorrhea

Leukorrhea is excessive vaginal mucous discharge caused by a chemical, physical, or infectious agent. Its pathogenesis is varied, and it is not a disease entity in itself. Women taking the Pill, for instance, especially one with high estrogen content, frequently suffer from it, as do those infected with such diseases as trichomoniasis or moniliasis. Some vaginal discharge is, of course, to be expected under certain normal circumstances. Sexual excitement causes vaginal secretions to increase, and the mucous discharge of most women is greater than average just before the menses and throughout pregnancy. The discharge can be considered abnormal when it stains the clothing, causes local symptoms, or has an offensive odor (Fiumara 1976).

When the Pill is responsible for leukorrhea, the discharge is clear and odorless. But if it is annoying, the condition can be corrected by special douching to balance the vaginal pH, or by taking a Pill of different hormonal content. Foreign bodies—forgotten tampons, diaphragms, IUDs, or pessaries—often cause leukorrhea. In these cases the discharge may be purulent, blood-tinged or brown, and malodorous. The foreign bodies must be removed, of course (Fiumara 1976).

Trichomoniasis

Trichomoniasis, the most common of the minor gynecological diseases, afflicts approximately 25% of all women. That trichomoniasis is a common disorder is further reflected in estimates such as 1977 data indicating the occurrence of 2.5 million cases of the disorder in the United States. Both men and women may suffer from this infection, although men seldom experience the copious discharges, itching, and burning symptomatic of the ailment in many women. Furthermore, a nagging odor is often associated with trichomoniasis for women that makes the infection even more annoying (Cibley 1980; Felman 1980; Netter 1961; Shafer 1966).

Trichomoniasis is caused by a minute one-celled animal, *Trichomonas vaginalis.* A flagellated parasite approximately the shape and size of a paramecium, the organism propels itself by thrashing small whips at one end of its body. Thousands of these organisms can be seen when a bit of infected vaginal secretion is examined under a microscope.

Trichomonads normally limit their attack to the vagina and perhaps the cervix, living on the surface of the membranes but not invading them. The first indication of infection is usually a white or yellowish vaginal discharge, accompanied by itching and burning. In many women this discharge causes constant inflammation and soreness of the vulva. A separation of the inflamed labia commonly reveals a thick, smelly, bubbly discharge in the vestibule.

In other women, trichomoniasis tends to cause severe itching rather than soreness. Practically all women who have had this infection report that their underclothing is quickly soiled by the discharge, which, together with the irritation or itching, seems to worsen immediately before and after menstruation. Some women experience severe symptoms; others, mild ones. Why some women are more susceptible than others to trichomoniasis remains a perplexing gynecological question. Whether the symptoms are mild or severe, a doctor should be consulted immediately if there is the slightest indication of infection.

Ordinarily an infected man has no symptoms except for a slight, thin, whitish discharge; occasionally urination causes an itching and burning in his urethral tract. If one partner is found to be infected with trichomoniasis, the other should be examined also. Nothing is accomplished by curing one partner only to have him or her reinfected by the other. Careful examination reveals that 60% of the husbands of infected women also have the infection ("Medical Science Notes" 1961d). It is possible for a couple to pass these infectious parasites back and forth for many years, especially since a man frequently does not realize he is infected. If a man is aware that he is infected and uses a condom while engaging in sexual activity over a three- to four-month period, the parasites will most likely die and end the reinfection occurrences (Cibley 1980). Trichomonads house themselves under the foreskin of a man's uncircumcised penis; in severe cases, they may also invade the prostate. Furthermore, 15% of men seeking treatment for urethritis present evidence of being infected with trichomonads (Tanowitz 1974). The mild urethritis that men sometimes experience as the result of trichomoniasis can, if untreated, proceed to more serious disorders such as balanitis, epididymitis, prostatitis, and even sterility (Felman 1980).

It is not known just where these microscopic animals come from, or precisely how one contracts the disease (other than from an infected sexual partner). Many gynecologists state that there is a similarity between the trichomonads of the vagina and those found in the bowels. However, parasitologists maintain that the two types are actually quite different. They further claim that trichomoniasis is a venereal infection in that it is transmitted only by intercourse. Trichomoniasis is only rarely transmitted by anal intercourse and it does not appear to be transmitted at all through oral-genital sex relations (Cibley 1980). Still other scientists believe the infection is not necessarily a venereal one, because it can be contracted in a swimming pool or a bathtub, where the organism may rather easily gain entry into the vaginal tract. A 20% incidence of the infection has been found in women isolated from sexual contact in mental institutions (Parsons & Sommers 1962). Trichomoniasis is easily transmitted in the sexual contacts that occur among homosexual females (Cibley 1980). However contracted, the incubation period is thought to be 4 to 28 days (Felman 1980; Tanowitz 1974).

The most effective therapy is systemic administration of the drug metronidazole (Flagyl), which has a success rate of well over 85%. When a cure is not achieved with this drug, the fault usually lies with the patient's failure to complete the full course of medication, or with the affected partner, who has not been treated as well (Tanowitz 1974). Obtainable by prescription only, the drug effects a cure within 10 to 14 days for both men and women. If for one reason or another the drug cannot be used, some other form of medication can be applied to the vaginal area, and antiseptic douches are recommended. A note of caution: Patients under treatment with metronidazole are advised against drinking alcohol during treatment, since the combination may produce unpleasant side effects. It may also suppress the activity of white blood cells, which seem to cooperate with antibiotics in killing the bacteria causing the disease (Holmes 1975b). Furthermore, metronidazole is often not recommended for use during pregnancy (Cibley 1980; Felman 1980).Trichomoniasis may be complicated by its association with other infections. For example, trichomoniasis may be complicated by an association with a gonorrhea infection (Cibley 1980; Felman 1980). Trichomoniasis is often complicated by monilia and perhaps by one or several other various associated pathogenic bacteria. Treatment of trichomoniasis and any accompanying bacterial infection should be rigorously pursued, for although the disease is not considered serious, it can be tormenting and sexually inhibiting.

Candidiasis or Moniliasis

Candidiasis, or **moniliasis,** (commonly called **monilia**) is a fungus infection of the genital region, affecting women primarily, that can cause acute discomfort. The monilia organism has the power to lie dormant for long periods of time—in a woman's vagina or under the foreskin of a man's penis—until circumstances become favorable for its activation. More frequently than not, monilia accompanies other infectious organisms, such as trichomonads (Netter 1961; Shafer 1966).

Examination of a genital area afflicted with monilia reveals white cheesy spots on the vulva, in the vagina, and on the cervix. Minute ulcerations of the labia minora may also be present, accompanied in some instances by a thick or watery vaginal discharge. All these symptoms can eventually lead to a raw, bleeding surface if treatment is not prompt and careful.

Most organisms causing infection and irritation in the vagina thrive on menstrual blood. Therefore, women who are harboring such a fungus as monilia commonly complain of the greatest discomfort and distress just before and just after menstruation.

Monilia is sometimes found in children. It is quite likely to afflict women who have diabetes or who have been overtreated with antibiotic vaginal suppositories, which can kill off the native protective bacilli in the vaginal tract. It is also likely to affect women who are suffering from malnutrition, endocrine imbalance, or obesity. Women who are pregnant and those who are on the Pill are also easy victims of the disease. A cure can be obtained, however, with persistent and adequate treatment under the direction of a gynecologist (Felman 1980; Fiumara 1976).

Peyronie's Disease

Peyronie's disease affects only men. Fibrous tissue develops in the space above and between the two large spongy bodies (corpora cavernosa) of the penis (Fig. 21.1). In about 20% of the cases calcium deposits develop in the

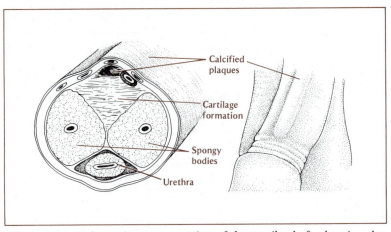

Figure 21.1   Schematic representation of the penile shaft, showing the effects of Peyronie's disease. Note abnormal formation of calcium along top of the penis between the spongy bodies.

fibrous tissue, and occasionally the affected tissue hardens into cartilage and bone.

The symptom marking the early stages of Peyronie's disease is pain during erection, caused by stretching of inflamed penile tissue. There is rarely pain when the penis is flaccid. As the disease progresses, inflammation abates and pain subsides. Then fibrosis develops, causing the penis to become deviated to the left, right, or upward. This deviation is the most distressing aspect of the disease, especially since coitus sometimes becomes impossible (Bruskewitz 1980; Netter 1961; Poutasse 1975; K. Walker 1963).

Some specialists recommend X-ray therapy in the treatment of Peyronie's disease (Duggan 1964). However, such treatment may result in penile and testicular tissue damage, rendering the patient sterile. When medication is the treatment of choice, improvement can be expected in 75% of the cases. Interestingly, the history of a sample of 12 patients showed that, without any treatment, 9 showed improvement and 3, complete remission, in an average period of 4 years. Given these findings, many doctors reject X-ray therapy as the preferred mode of treatment (McDonald 1974).

Vitamin E and potassium para-aminobenzoate are two popular remedies prescribed by physicians to treat Peyronie's disease. Ultrasound, steroid therapy, and drugs such as potassium iodide also have been employed. When surgical techniques are called for, skin grafts and penile prostheses are often utilized in removing calcified plaques and in straightening the curved penis (Bruskewitz 1980).

Tuberculosis

Tuberculosis of various genital areas sometimes occurs in both men and women. Tuberculous prostatitis is not a common disease, but it is found in about 12% of all terminal cases of tuberculosis. Although the normal glandular tissue of the prostate is replaced by a crumbly fibrous growth and calcification as the disease progresses, tuberculous prostatitis is almost always painless. The infection can also invade the epididymides and testicles. In all instances, these infections are secondary to a primary active tubercular infection outside the urogenital tract, especially in the lungs.

Among women, tuberculosis constitutes about 2% of all diseases of the upper genital tract. The fallopian tubes and uterus are typically affected. Only rarely are other reproductive organs involved (Ball 1957; Netter 1961; TeLinde 1953).

Carcinoma

Carcinoma (cancer) can strike any part, or related part, of the sexual system. Its symptoms are diverse, and one should immediately consult a physician upon recognizing any suspicious signal, such as the seven general symptoms outlined by the American Cancer Society:

Unusual bleeding or discharge
A lump or thickening in breast or elsewhere
A sore that does not heal
Change in bowel or bladder habits
Persistent hoarseness or cough
Persistent indigestion or difficulty in swallowing
Change in size or color of a wart or mole

All sensible precautions against cancer should be taken. The lives of thousands of women could be saved every year if they had regular—at least annual—gynecological examinations that include breast examination and a Pap smear test. A simple and painless procedure, the Pap test involves taking a sample of cervical fluid by means of a cotton swab and examining the fluid for the presence of cancer cells. Cancer cells in deep tissue work their way to the surface and will appear in the smear taken from the surface of the cervix.

The evidence is increasingly strong that there is a more than casual relationship between cancer in specific areas of the body and certain physical, social, and environmental factors. For example, both penile and cervical cancers are thought by some researchers to bear a direct relationship to whether or not a man has been circumcised. There is no consensus on this subject, however. In any case, meticulous penile cleanliness would accomplish the same hygienic end as circumcision. The theory is that smegma and other impurities, which can collect under the prepuce of an uncircumcised penis, predispose a man to penile cancer. Furthermore, the theory continues, the same impurities under a man's prepuce predispose his partner to cervical cancer (Ball 1957; Licklider 1961; Netter 1961).

Recent studies of Lebanese Christians and Moslems fail to support this theory, however. These studies revealed no relationship between cervical cancer in Lebanese women and the fact that their husbands were circumcised (as Moslems are, early in life) or were not circumcised (Lebanese Christians rarely are). The low incidence of cervical cancer among Jewish women appears to be related to factors other than the circumcision of their husbands (Abou-David 1967; Rosato & Kleger 1970).

The age at which a woman first has intercourse and the number of her sexual partners seem to bear some relationship to the risk of her later developing cervical cancer. Women who begin coitus early in life and continue to engage in it on a regular basis thereafter are more liable to develop cancer of the cervix than women who marry later in life (Christopherson & Parker 1965; "Reassessing the Pill's Risks" 1980; Rotkin 1967; Sebastian 1980).

The possible presence of cervical cancer (there were 19,000 new cases in 1974 and 7800 deaths) should be checked through regular Pap smear tests. The American Cancer Society recommends that these tests be made from the time a woman is 20—even earlier for women who have already begun sexual activity (Naughton 1974). It should be noted, as well, that an association has been made between cancer and herpes Type II, antibodies of which have been found in 83% of cervical carcinoma patients (Blough & Guintoli 1979; Reyner 1975).

Whether the explanation for the correlation between coitus and cervical cancer lies with the frequency of sexual intercourse, the strength of the sex drive, personality factors, or the increased possibility for contact with men whose genitalia are unclean or diseased is not known (Pereyra 1961). Further support for observations concerning cervical cancer and the promiscuous woman comes, perhaps strangely, from the fact that nuns have a considerably lower incidence of cervical cancer than is found in the general population. However, nuns have cancer of the uterus, ovaries, and breasts as frequently as women in the general population ("Science Notes" 1969).

It might be mentioned that those women who for medical reasons must undergo a clitoridectomy can take solace from present-day knowledge of the physiology of sexual response. The woman who was sexually responsive prior to having a vulvectomy, a much more radical surgical procedure than a clitoridectomy, usually remains capable of orgasm once sexual intercourse is resumed (Melody 1970).

Breast cancer, representing 28% of all the cancers, is responsible for 20% of cancer-related deaths in women. Breast cancer is thus a leading cancer killer among women; its incidence surpasses that of cancer-related deaths resulting from pelvic malignancy. Carcinoma of the breast is the most frequent cause of death for women in the 40- to 50-year-old age group, so gynecological examinations become especially relevant once women reach their middle years. The questions associated with breast cancer are how most effectively to detect it, and how to treat the malignancy. In the first instance there is manual examination and, more recently, thermography, a technique of heat-sensitivity scanning of the breast. There is also the X-ray technique called mammography, said to pinpoint minute lesions undetectable in other examination techniques (Marchant 1980).

In the matter of treatment, radical mastectomy has been the traditional approach—the removal not only of the breast, but also of the lymph glands in the armpit and the muscles of the chest wall. The resulting disfigurement is an added psychological trauma for many women. Emotional swings, intense feelings of depression, and a temporary regression to a psychological state of dependency may be evidenced by some women who experience the loss of a breast (Witkin 1979). Today some doctors are opting for less radical measures, arguing that, by the time the disease is detected, the cancer has already spread and will recur no matter what form of surgery is done. Destruction of the primary cancer is therefore the best that doctors can do, they maintain, and this can be accomplished by radiation as effectively as by surgery.

Prostatic cancer represents 10% of all malignancies occurring in men, and showed a 20% increase in the 22-year period, ending in 1969, surveyed by the American Cancer Society in 1975. Mazur (1980) cites American Cancer Society statistics indicating that prostatic cancer claims approximately 22,000 lives each year. Surgery in the case of a cancerous prostate is a far more radical procedure than in noncancerous cases, since tissues around the prostate also must be removed as a safety measure. Furthermore, advanced prostatic cancer, even when metastasized throughout the body (it typically spreads to the bones of the pelvis and spine before the patient is aware that anything is wrong), may be controlled dramatically when castration is performed or the patient is treated with female hormones. Both treatments, of course, are unfavorable to the patient's retaining his potency.

Typically a "silent" cancer, prostatic cancer claims the lives of more men past 50 than any other form of cancer. Many of these deaths could be avoided if men would take the simple precaution of undergoing an annual prostatic examination by a urologist. It is a brief and painless examination in which the physician seeks signs of cancer, such as hard lumps, in the prostate. He can also catch nonmalignant prostatic difficulties before they become serious. The examination for possible colorectal cancer can also be done at the same time as the prostatic examination (Mazur 1980; Shafer 1968).

Testicular cancer kills only a relatively small number of men each year, but it is a disease that primarily affects young men in their early twenties. Testicular lumps do not necessarily cause pain in the affected testicle, but symptoms such as pain in the nipples or breasts and fluid accumulation or painful swelling of the scrotum may be indicative of this form of cancer. Medical treatment, including chemotherapy, is available to help make this disease a preventable fatality. Also, men can be shown by their physicians how to make testicular self-examinations (TSE) so that detection of unusual or possibly malignant lumps can be made early (Mazur 1980).

Elephantiasis

Elephantiasis involves a marked growth of subcutaneous tissues and epidermis, producing an enlargement varying from slight to monstrous. In extreme cases an infected scrotum, a favorite target in men, may touch the ground and weigh as much as 200 pounds. In women, elephantiasis may manifest itself in excessive growth of the labia majora. Ordinarily indigenous to tropical regions, this disease is only rarely found in the United States.

Infectious Mononucleosis

Infectious mononucleosis is neither a venereal disease nor a sexual disorder in the sense that the terms are used in this book. Its inclusion in this section rests with its popular name, "the kissing disease." It is an acute infectious disease of the lymph glands, characterized by the sudden onset of fever, marked fatigue, chills, sweating, headache, sore throat, and loss of appetite (Blank & Rake 1955; *Dorland's Illustrated Medical Dictionary* 1957; "Medical Science Notes" 1961c). Because severe and even fatal complications occasionally occur, all instructions of the attending physician must be rigidly followed.

How the disease (which is caused by a filtrable virus) is transmitted has not been definitely determined, although many authorities suspect deep kissing with an infected person. One study found that 71 of 73 "mono" patients had engaged in deep kissing at the exact time the incubation period for mononucleosis would have begun for them ("Medical Science Notes" 1961c). In the course of the disease, fever usually subsides after 5 days. Other acute symptoms abate within 3 weeks, although some symptoms may persist for months.

Dermatoses

Dermatoses (or skin diseases) of the genital region are fairly common, and the causative organisms and substances are legion. Men occasionally develop a sensitivity reaction to their partner's vaginal secretions (J. H. Kaplan 1975). Chemicals—such as those contained in soap that is not rinsed off properly after a shower—can collect in the sensitive areas of the genitalia and produce irritation or burns (Corsini 1965). The difficulty may be compounded by attempting a cure with medication too strong for the distressed area. Unfortunately, many people adopt the premise that if a little medicine is good, a lot will be even better.

Tinea cruris, or **jock itch,** is a fungus infection of the genital region. Its initial symptoms are reddish, scaly patches that may develop into large, highly inflamed zones with stressful itching and considerable pain. The affliction has a striking similarity to athlete's foot. Sweating, tight clothing, and inadequate drying of the genitalia after a bath provide a favorable environment for the development of this infection (Netter 1961).

Scabies and **pediculosis (crabs)** are two forms of dermatoses caused by parasites that can invade the genital and other areas, such as hands, wrists, elbows, feet, chest, buttocks (Ellis 1960; Netter 1961; Newcomer 1976; Schneidman 1980). Scabies is a highly contagious skin disorder in which a female mite (*Sarcoptes scabiei*) burrows between the layers of skin and deposits her eggs. Little vesicles housing the mite and her eggs appear on the skin surface and soon develop into papules, pustules, and a rash that itches formidably, especially at night.

In *pediculosis pubis* the pubic hair is infested with crab lice (*Phthirus pubis*), the bites of which cause an itchy skin irritation. Scratching produces further irritation, and a brownish discoloration of the skin may develop. The crab louse usually buries its head in the follicles of the pubic hair and attaches its body to the hair itself. These parasites commonly pass from one person to another through sexual contact with an infected partner, although they may also be picked up from a toilet seat or bed. Medical treatment is available that kills the pediculi that may be on the skin and hair of the pubic region. Shaving the pubic hair serves no value in getting rid of the lice (Ellis 1960; Netter 1961; Schneidman 1980).

Psoriasis is a disease of the skin characterized by scaly red patches. It may attack the genital region as well as other parts of the body. Excruciating itching called *pruritus* typically accompanies psoriasis and other skin diseases. Medication usually provides relief for the itching, and treatment is often successful in controlling the skin condition (Netter 1961).

Folliculitis is an inflammation at the opening of the hair follicles that is precipitated by various sorts of infection, including staphylococci. The infection finds a suitable environment in which to flourish when the skin is not kept clean, clothing is too tight, and bodily resistance is generally low (Netter 1961).

Inflammation of Internal and External Genitalia

The suffix *-itis* added to the name of an organ indicates inflammation of that organ. Many disorders of the internal and external genitalia of both men and women fall into this grouping.

Vaginitis, or vaginal irritation, is fairly common and may be caused by such conditions as bacterial invasion, the introduction of foreign objects into the canal, and the use of strong chemicals. Children, especially, inject small objects (coins, marbles, pins, sticks) into the vagina, possibly in a clumsy attempt at masturbation. Douching with too high a concentration of chemicals, overmedication, and tampons that are inserted and then forgotten can all cause inflammation of the vaginal tract. Furthermore, a general impairment of health can reduce bodily resistance to contagion, making one more susceptible to low-grade infections such as vaginitis. Nonspecific vaginitis is an affliction considered gynecology's most perplexing unsolved problem. Intercourse when such conditions exist may be the source of even further irritation in the vaginal tract (Netter 1961; Shafer 1966).

Excessive douching or the use of overly strong solutions is the basic evil in many instances of vaginitis, because such douching destroys nature's protective organisms, *Doderlein's bacilli,* which normally inhabit the vagina. When this happens, the acid condition of the vagina is reduced and hostile bacteria find a suitable place for development; any of various vaginal maladies can be the consequence.

All too often, women—especially the young and newly married ones—are overly concerned about feminine hygiene. They apparently feel that if a little douching is good, more must be better. They therefore increase the strength of the solution and the frequency of its use; the results in the long run are often distressing. A study of prison women showed that daily douching with water, or with a mild vinegar or alkaline solution, did not produce the changes in the vaginal lining or any other ill effects claimed by some gynecologists ("Science Notes" 1964). The real danger, then, would seem to come from douching with harsh chemicals.

One form of vaginitis, known as *Haemophilus vaginalis,* or *Corynebacterium vaginale,* occurs primarily during the reproductive years and affects an estimated 10% to 20% of women in this age group. The true incidence of this form of vaginitis is unknown, however. It apparently is transmitted by the man during coitus, although he is asymptomatic. In one study of 101 infected women, the causal organism was found in the urethral cultures of 91 of the husbands, whereas it was found in only one culture from a group of 38 medical students. Caused by a bacillus, *C vaginale,* this disease has the potential to be associated with serious medical problems such as carcinoma. The disease typically appears to be one of the mildest of all common vaginal infections. The only symptom many women consider troublesome is an excessive vaginal discharge with an unpleasant odor. Treatment with drugs such as ampicillin or cephradine under the direction of a gynecologist will usually solve the problem. But to prevent reinfection from the same sex partner—the ping-pong effect—the partner must be treated simultaneously and successfully (Felman 1980; Kaufman 1976).

Other, similar problems for women occur during and following menopause, when the lining of the vagina undergoes a marked change. Diminished hormonal production causes the membrane to become much thinner—perhaps 25% of its former thickness. While this change should in no way decrease a woman's sexual desire or ability, the tissue of her vagina does become more fragile, and she is more easily made uncomfortable, or even injured, by sexual activity. These difficulties can be solved through the administration of female hormones, but they must be carefully evaluated by a physician (Clark 1965b; Martin 1980; Rubin 1966b). In fact, every woman should have a checkup by a gynecologist at least once a year.

Other causes of vaginitis include penile penetration before adequate vaginal lubrication has occurred; failure to douche out a contraceptive foam, to which the woman is particularly sensitive, within 6 to 8 hours after use; a diaphragm left in place 2 or 3 days at a time, to which several applications of a spermacidal agent are added; seepage of spermicidal gels, creams, or jellies, which may irritate the external genitalia; sensitivity to the rubber of condoms, especially when they are used in conjunction with the lubricant petrolatum (sometimes they combine poorly); and even pinworms (Pierson 1975). Finally, psychosexual tensions must be considered, since unresolved guilt, anger, or stress over sexual roles and identity can produce psychosomatic disorders of the vagina and vulva. Vaginitis is a common physical manifestation of psychosexual tension (Jorgensen 1975).

Cystitis refers to inflammation of the bladder, a disorder that may occur in a variety of ways (Netter 1961; TeLinde 1953). Symptoms usually include a severe burning sensation in the urethra during urination, a frequent need to urinate, and sharp pain in the lower abdomen. Women who have inflammation of the bladder often report that the pain is especially severe when they have sexual intercourse, and that they must often discontinue coition because of the pain (Ellis 1960).

The bladder may become infected when lowered bodily resistance precipitates an attack of existing internal bacteria, or when infective organisms from the perineal area enter the bladder via the urethra. Irritation of a woman's bladder may occur as a result of frequent intercourse, because the bladder tends to become somewhat displaced by the pressure of the penis against both it and the urethra through the vaginal walls. In fact, the highest incidence of lower urinary-tract infection in women develops 24 to 48 hours after sexual activity (Marshall 1974). This condition occurs not infrequently during honeymoons, giving it the rather graphic name of "honeymoon cystitis" (Rowan 1964).

Bladder inflammation can be better controlled when the body is otherwise healthy. Furthermore, good personal hygiene will do much to combat the problem once it occurs. Treatment should include high fluid intake as a means of flushing the urinary tract of bacteria, and thorough cleansing of the external genitalia as well as of the urethral opening. Showering in the evening is recommended if coitus typically takes place then (Marshall 1974). In addition, a woman will be more comfortable if she empties her bladder before intercourse, and if she uses a lubricating jelly. Both measures will decrease pressure on the abdominal organs during coitus.

Like vaginitis, cystitis can have emotional as well as organic causes. As with all diseases and disorders discussed here, a physician should be consulted at the first signs of infection, for with early treatment the patient may avoid serious complications.

Epididymitis is a common sexual disorder that affects over 600,000 men yearly in the United States. It involves inflammation of the epididymis, that important structure closely attached to each testicle. Sexually transmitted diseases such as gonorrhea, urinary tract abnormalities and infections, or tuberculosis may be predisposing conditions leading to epididymitis. Less frequently, the onset of epididymitis is related to physical straining or heavy lifting.

There are degrees of this infection, both in duration and in severity of symptoms. Mild cases involve only slight swelling and tenderness, which respond readily to treatment. In severe cases the entire testicular structure may be greatly swollen and painful. The disease can lead to growths and strictures, possibly resulting in sterility, that only surgery may be able to correct. Some cases of chronic epididymitis persist for years. Nonsurgical treatment involves extensive use of drugs, a balanced and wholesome diet, scrotal support or elevation, bed rest, and a warm climate (Berger 1980; Netter 1961).

Prostatitis, an inflammation of the prostate gland, is a common problem among men (far more so among older ones). The condition may be either acute or chronic. Since the discovery of antibiotics, however, acute prostatitis is rare. In the past it frequently accompanied gonorrhea but is now seen only occasionally, usually as the result of staphylococci infection following catheterization (Ellis 1960; Netter 1961). Chronic prostatitis may be caused by infection, such as bacteria invading the prostate; or by congestion of the prostate gland, believed to be caused in most instances by too infrequent ejaculation (Mobley 1975). Chronic prostatitis can lead to an eventual enlargement of the prostate. A clear relationship exists, however, between infrequent sexual activity and the temporary enlargement of the prostate that typically accompanies chronic prostatitis. It can also follow prolonged infection in other parts of the body. It is estimated that from 30% to 40% of American men in the 20- to 40-year-old age group suffer from chronic prostatitis (Brosman 1976; Finkle 1967; Stiller 1963).

In either acute or chronic prostatitis, symptoms may include a thin mucous discharge, especially in the morning. There may be pain in the lower back, testicles, perineum, posterior scrotum, and, perhaps, in the tip of the penis (Cawood 1971). Prostatitis can also lead to painful or inadequate erection, premature and sometimes bloody ejaculation, impotence, and sterility. In addition, many patients reveal collateral emotional stress and hypochondriacal complaints far out of proportion to the severity of the disease.

A urologist typically recommends prostatic massage, antibiotics, and prolonged warm baths to clear up prostatic infection and to bring about drainage of the congested gland. However, it is somewhat difficult to eradicate the infection completely because the ductwork of the sexual system is so complex. Most physicians recommend that sexual stimulation of any sort be rigidly avoided during an attack of acute prostatitis (Davis & Mininberg 1976).

The prostate tends to enlarge as a man grows older—about 20% of all men are so affected after middle age. (For further discussion of this subject, see Chapter 14.) It is not definitely known what causes this enlargement, although the most widely accepted theory is that an excess of the male hormone androgen is responsible. If the condition is not corrected, the man may experience difficulty or pain in urination or incomplete emptying of the bladder. In severe cases it can eventually cause total urinary retention. Such secondary complications as serious bladder infection, kidney stones, and uremic poisoning often follow. Hormone therapy is often successfully used to correct an enlarged prostate (Geller 1964), but surgery to remove all or part of it (prostatectomy) is sometimes indicated.

The surgical approach in prostatectomy can be made via the abdomen, or through the penis (a process called transurethral prostatectomy), or from a point between the anus and strotum (a perineal prostatectomy). But what of sexual potency after the removal of a noncancerous prostate? A recent study on the effects of the three major types of prostatic surgery in patients who had been potent before surgery revealed that 95% who had undergone transurethral surgery, 87% who had undergone abdominal surgery, and 71% who had undergone the perineal incision retained their potency. The reduced percentage in the third instance is attributed to the surgical approach having been made through sex-related nerve centers, involving greater risk to the nerves controlling erection. Selection of the operative procedure is dictated primarily by the seriousness of the case, as well as the age and physical condition of the patient (Finkle 1968).

When the prostate is cancerous, the possibilities of a man's retaining his potency after prostatectomy are not so favorable. But about 80% of prostatectomies are, fortunately, performed to correct nonmalignant growths, and these patients have every reason to expect to retain their sexual vigor. When potency is lost following a prostate operation, one has to question whether the cause was truly physical, or whether negative psychological forces were at work. Did the man *expect* to lose his potency, thereby almost guaranteeing its loss? Did his surgeon fail to discuss the sex-functioning aspects of the operation with him? Or, worse, did the doctor perhaps compound the patient's silent fears by having him sign a paper relieving the doctor of responsibility in the event impotency followed the surgery? Had the man's sexual relationship with his partner prior to the operation become so dreary and unsatisfying that he welcomed an excuse to abandon it? Had his partner not properly understood the effects of a prostatectomy and, expecting impotency, appeared to reject him, thus precipitating impotency? Or was she afraid to resume intercourse because she feared it might in some way endanger his health?

Another matter that concerns men facing a prostatectomy is whether they will continue to enjoy intercourse even if potency is preserved. Because the structures within the prostate, notably the ejaculatory ducts emptying into the urethra, are as a rule unavoidably damaged (although less frequently with the transurethral than with the open approaches), it is no longer possible for the man to ejaculate normally. Instead of being expelled through and out the penis, the ejaculate may flow backward into the bladder in what is called a **retrograde** or **dry ejaculation.** (The semen is later discharged in the urine, and there is no harmful effect whatever on the man.) In other cases the surgery prevents ejaculation altogether. Some men miss the pleasant sensation of ejaculatory pulsation, which decreases or is missing altogether after prostatic surgery. But this is a loss to which they quickly become adjusted (Trainer 1965).

Hemospermia (also called **hematospermia**) is a condition in which blood appears in the ejaculate as a result of an inflamed prostate or seminal vesicles or, perhaps, tuberculosis, venereal infection, and bladder-neck obstruction. The discoloration may be black, brown, rust, or red, depending upon how long the blood has been in the seminal tract before ejaculation. Hemospermia is seldom serious, and if any treatment is required it typically consists of prostatic massage followed by appropriate medication (Burkholder 1975; Carson 1980).

Peritonitis is an infection of the peritoneum, the membrane lining the abdominal walls. In women it is frequently caused by pus draining from the fallopian tubes into the peritoneal cavity. The infection may be generalized, or it may be localized in the specific area where the drainage collects. The type and area of infection, the resistance of the patient, and the timing and type of treatment all affect the mildness or severity of peritonitis, as well as its potential danger. Even after the condition abates, adhesions can cause organs in the cavity (such as the uterus and rectum) to change their fixed position. Backaches, pain during elimination, and distressful copulation are typical secondary symptoms. Diathermy, medication, and occasionally surgery are methods of treatment (Netter 1961; TeLinde 1953).

Balanitis and **balanoposthitis** exist when there is an inflammation of the penile glans and prepuce. Chemicals, drugs, irritations, infections, sexually transmitted diseases, lesions, and neoplasms may act singly or together to produce this problem. Circumcision may provide relief, and early medical attention is advisable (Netter 1961; Persky 1980).

Sexual Disorders

Sexual disorders are customarily considered to be physical anomalies of the genitalia caused by hereditary, constitutional, or postnatal factors.

Disorders Affecting Males

Hypospadia, occurring once in every 500 births, is the second most common malformation (after club foot) in male babies at the time of delivery. It is a congenital defect, although apparently no hereditary factor is involved. Because the genital fold fails to close completely during prenatal development, the urethral opening is on the underside of the penis rather than at its tip. In glandular hypospadia, the urethral meatus is slightly below and to the back of the normal site of the opening. In penile hypospadia, the opening is somewhere along the lower part of the penile shaft.

Plastic surgery should be performed as soon as possible on any child with this anomaly to ensure that the urethra and corpora cavernosa will develop properly and in straight alignment. Men in whom this condition is never corrected usually remain capable of engaging in coitus. If the meatus is sufficiently recessed on the penile shaft, however, these men will obviously have difficulty impregnating their partners (Netter 1961; Stiller 1966). A similar anomaly occurs in women, in which the urethra opens into the vagina; but it is rarely troublesome.

Epispadia is much more rare than hypospadia and is usually associated with a congenital malformation of the bladder. In this disorder, the urethral opening is on the dorsum (top) of the penis. The epispadiac penis typically curves upward, is deformed, and requires early plastic surgery (Netter 1961; Stiller 1966). About 50% of these patients are partially or totally incontinent. Surgical treatment is usually deferred until the status of urinary control is determined, which often is not possible until the patient is about 3 years old (Culp 1974).

Chordee, frequently associated with hypospadia or the result of urethral infection, is a downward curvature of the penis requiring corrective surgery. The ideal age for this plastic surgery is approximately 18 months, although for various reasons the patient is usually not presented for treatment until he is considerably older (Culp 1974).

Phimosis is an anomaly in which the penile prepuce is abnormally long and cannot be pulled back or retracted from over the glans (Levie 1965). Fibrous growths sometimes attach the prepuce to the glans, making even the attempt to draw it back quite painful (Netter 1961). Smegma may collect, leading to ulceration or inflammation of the penis. Surgery, usually in the form of circumcision, can correct this difficulty.

Hydrocele, a fairly common male birth malformation (9th in frequency) involves a collection of fluid within the two layers of tissue making up the *tunica vaginalis* (membranes covering the testes). As the testes descend from their abdominal position (usually at the 7th month of prenatal life), they carry with them two layers of the peritoneum. Any abnormality in these layers of tissue can provide a natural environment for a variety of hydrocele conditions. Hydroceles can also follow physical trauma, operations, infection of the epididymis or other areas, gonorrhea, and tuberculosis. Suspending the scrotum and surgically removing the fluid and distressed portion of the tunica vaginalis are suggested methods of treatment. In some cases the fluid is drawn off with a hollow needle, although this procedure always introduces the possibility of infection (Clark 1962; Netter 1961; "Sex in the News" 1963; Stiller 1966).

Spermatocele is a soft swelling on either side of the scrotum, the result of an intrascrotal cyst. The cyst obstructs the tubular structure between the testicles and epididymis, causing a blockage of sperm and a collection of fluid. The fluid has a milky coloration because of the millions of sperm and lipids trapped there. Surgery is the usual method of treatment (Clark 1962; Netter 1961).

Varicocele is a swelling of the veins that lead to the testicles. In 99% of such cases, the varicocele develops on the left side of the testicles; only 1% develop bilaterally. Perhaps 1 man in 10 has some degree of spermatic vein dilation. There can be rather severe pain, accompanied by a sensation of pulling and tugging at the testicles, the symptoms tending to disappear when the patient lies down and allows the blood to flow out of the veins. A suspensory can relieve the discomfort of the excessive weight, and cold baths may temporarily alleviate swelling and pain, but a surgical procedure is usually required to correct the condition (Clark 1962; Netter 1961).

Hematocele is an accumulation of blood in the tunica vaginalis, usually resulting from an injury. Spontaneous hematocele may be a result of syphilis, arteriosclerosis, diabetes, or an inflammatory condition within the scrotum. Surgery is the treatment of choice (Clark 1962; Netter 1961).

Edema (abnormal amount of fluid in intercellular tissue) **of the scrotum** results from inflammation or other disturbances in the vascular or lymphatic system. Such occurrences as physical trauma, allergic states, and insect bites may produce an edematous reaction, which, because of the loose and elastic nature of scrotal tissue, causes the scrotum to swell to near basketball-size proportions (Netter 1961). Penile edema can also result from physical trauma, allergic states, irritation, or infective sources. Penile edema is often associated with sexually transmitted diseases such as syphilis, herpes, gonorrhea, NGU, or scabies (Chapel 1980).

Torsion of the testicle is an abnormal rotation of the testicle causing a blockage of the blood supply to that organ. The rotation is precipitated by any of several physiological conditions. The amount of damage varies, depending upon the degree of torsion and how long the condition persists. If severe torsion is allowed to continue for as long as a few hours, necrosis of testicular tissue or even complete gangrene in the area can result. Survival of the testicle depends upon prompt diagnosis and appropriate corrective procedures, such as untwisting the spermatic cord. Manual efforts to correct the torsion without opening the scrotum are unsuccessful; the condition must be rectified by surgery (Berger 1980; Netter 1961).

Undescended testes (cryptorchidism) are found in about 1 boy in 50 at the age of puberty, but this ratio dwindles to approximately 1 in 500 among adult men. The delay in the descent can be caused by an inadequate gonadotropic hormone secretion; a congenital defect in the gonadal germ cells, or the absence of them altogether; or physiological failure in the structure, such as a malformed inguinal ring, through which the testes pass from the abdomen to the scrotum (Ellis 1960; Engel 1981; Netter 1961).

Testes that remain undescended after puberty will progressively degenerate, and eunuchoidal (having only partial external genital structure) symptoms will develop, especially if both testicles are involved. Hormonal treatment will often effect a successful descent of the testicles. When physical defects block what would otherwise be a normal descent, or when some cosmetic repair is desirable, surgery is indicated. Some surgeons perform operations to correct problems associated with undescended testes on male children when they are as young as 1 or 2 years. Other surgeons may delay surgery until the affected children are 4 or 5 years old (Engel 1981; Sperling 1980). In some instances the descent of the testes is faulty because they enter foreign areas and lodge there. These ectopic testes require surgery to effect proper placement in the scrotum (Garrett 1964). Since there appears to be a correlation between testicular cancer and undescended testes, early and appropriate medical attention to the problems associated with cryptorchidism is advisable (Mazur 1980).

Monorchism is the condition of having only one testicle in the scrotum, an anomaly that only a physician can confirm after a thorough examination. Monorchism is of no clinical significance, inasmuch as the existing testicle produces sufficient quantities of both hormones and sperm for normal physiological and sexual functioning. The condition nevertheless causes feelings of sexual inadequacy in certain men (Wershub 1968). Sometimes cosmetic surgery involving placement of a prosthetic testicle in the scrotum can help affected male children and adult men deal more effectively with such feelings and issues related to body image (Sperling 1980). In other males, one testicle is significantly smaller than the other. This inequality is not monorchism, however, since two testicles are present and both are functional.

Anorchism is the congenital lack of both testicles. The condition is extremely rare, but when it does exist it is characterized, predictably, by the lack of sexual desire. The man is, furthermore, incapable of erection and emission. And he possesses such feminine characteristics as scanty facial hair, narrow shoulders, wide hips, and a high-pitched voice (Wershub 1968). Hormone therapy and prosthetic testicular replacement may be called for to help bring about puberty and to promote the appearance of secondary sex characteristics (Sperling 1980).

Testicular failure may involve the interstitial cells that produce male hormones, the spermatic tubes where sperm develop, or both. In almost all instances, failure of the interstitial cells involves failure of the spermatic tubes, although the reverse is not necessarily true. **Hypogonadism** (insufficient secretion of the gonads) produces eunuchoidal characteristics, sometimes involving excessive growth of the long bones. The afflicted boy, although shorter in stature than others his age, will have proportionately very long arms and legs. Approximately 75% of eunuchoidal boys are underweight because of poorly developed muscles and bones. But even so, these boys commonly develop excess fat over the abdomen, around the mammary glands, above the pubis, and on the buttocks (Netter 1961). External genitals are extraordinarily small and poorly developed, and the prostate and seminal vesicles may also be markedly underdeveloped. Secondary sexual characteristics are typically feminine in appearance.

Testicular failure may be intrinsic, or it may manifest itself at any of the different stages of a boy's development and growth. Treatment usually consists of endocrine therapy and meets with rather good success. Testicular failure can also manifest itself in sterility without the presence of any overt signs of changes in the external genitalia.

Priapism is a continual and pathological erection of the penis. There is usually an erection of the corpora cavernosa without an accompanying erection of the glans of the penis or the corpus spongiosum (the small lower spongy body). The onset of priapism is sudden, painful, and unaccompanied by sexual desire (K. Walker 1963). The origin of this disorder may be an inflammation of the genitourinary system, leukemia, or tumors and inflammation of the central nervous system. However, it most typically occurs without an identifiable cause.

Although priapism is found in all racial groups, its incidence is highest among blacks because of their liability to sickle-cell disease and the poor venous drainage related to it (LaRocque & Cosgrove 1976). If erection persists for two days or more, thrombosis of the large spongy bodies occurs, followed by the possibility of a gristlelike replacement of the spongy bodies, rendering future erection impossible (Netter 1961). In recent years shunt operations have been rather effective in improving venous flow from the penile corpora; 60% of patients were sexually potent thereafter (LaRocque & Cosgrove 1976).

Disorders Affecting Females

Congenital anomalies of the vagina, uterus, and fallopian tubes are more common than many realize. For example, the vagina may be closed (**gynatresia**) or missing entirely. (In the latter case, an artificial vagina that is functional for intercourse can be surgically constructed.) Double vaginas also occur; one is usually considerably larger than the other, or the vagina may be divided into two parts by a septum, as the nose is. Similar anomalies are also found occasionally in the uterus (rudimentary, double, divided) and in the tubes (rudimentary, extra ampullae, blocked opening). And the uterus or tubes may be missing altogether. If the organs exist even in a malformed state, they may or may not be functional, depending upon how extensively they are affected. Such congenital anomalies are usually a result of the failure of the müllerian ducts to fuse completely or properly during prenatal development (Ball 1957; Masters & Johnson 1966; Netter 1961; TeLinde 1953).

Atrophic conditions of the vulva involve loss of fatty tissue in the mons pubis and labia majora; reduction in size of the clitoris and labia minora; loss of elasticity of the skin; inflammation, abrasions, and fissures of the vulva; and development of a leatherlike condition of the vulval tissue. Atrophic conditions of the vagina include a reduction or loss of its wrinkled surface; shrinking of the mucous membrane; narrowing of the canal, especially at the apex; formation of adhesions; and an ill-smelling, irritating discharge. Causality may be related to aging, removal of ovaries, X-ray, or fungal invasion (Netter 1961; Shafer 1966). Varicose veins of the vulva usually arise during pregnancy when intrapelvic pressure retards venous flow. An aching, "dragging" sensation may be felt in the pelvic region. The symptoms may be more severe while the woman is standing, then tend to disappear when she is lying down. Surgery can correct this and other circulatory disorders of the vulval region (Netter 1961).

An **imperforate hymen** is a condition wherein the vagina is sealed off by a solid mass of hymenal tissue. The condition may go unnoticed until the onset of menstruation. Unless the hymen is punctured at the menarche, however, the menstrual fluid is retained in the vagina, and the uterus must enlarge in order to contain the flow. Incision of the hymen corrects the condition easily and quickly. A **fibrous hymen** is not a common occurrence, however often the condition is discussed in medical writings. The hymenal tissue in this instance is inordinately thick and tough. It must be surgically incised before penile penetration is possible (Netter 1961; Shaw 1954; TeLinde 1953).

Vaginal fistulae are pipelike openings that may develop between the bladder and vagina, urethra and vagina, or rectum and vagina. The etiology may be congenital, as in hypospadia (in which the urethra empties into the vaginal tract); or traumatic, as from obstetrical or surgical injury. Malignant tumors can also produce these unwelcome fistulae. Urinary incontinence and severe infection are only two of the possible consequences of such anomalies. Surgical treatment is difficult and complicated. Recent advances in operative methods now used in the investigation and correction of pelvic disorders make prognosis more favorable than formerly (Ball 1957; Netter 1961; Shaw 1954; TeLinde 1953).

Abnormal uterine bleeding is the most frequent gynecological complaint encountered by physicians. The term *functional uterine bleeding* refers to hemorrhages not precipitated by detectable anomalies. If ovulation should not occur, too little or no progesterone is secreted, yet the secretion of estrogen continues. The result in some instances—although not all—is that the proliferation or growth phase of the menstrual cycle persists, and with it comes a thickening of the uterine mucosa (endometrium).

In these circumstances there is no growth stimulation of the ovarian follicles because ovarian estrogen inhibits the release of FSH (the follicle-stimulating hormone) from the pituitary gland. The uterine lining therefore thrives under the continued flow of estrogen, and the nonstimulated and unruptured follicles gradually convert into cystic structures. This process reduces the level of estrogen, which causes some FSH production and hence the development of some *new* follicles. The growth process of the endometrium is repeated, eventually producing both gross and microscopic changes in the endometrium itself. The irregular hormonal interplay produces unnatural growth in the uterine tissue; abnormal bleeding (abnormal both in frequency and amount) from the uterus may result. In about 66% of the cases of functional uterine bleeding, **endometrial hyperplasia** (that is, excessive growth of the uterine lining) is present.

Endometrial hyperplasia may be induced simply by the presence of polyps, or by the more serious conditions of uterine carcinoma, pregnancy disorders, or psychogenic states. (Birth-control pills inhibit ovulation, but they do not cause a disturbance in hormone balance; they therefore act to prevent malfunctions of this nature.) Women should not delay in consulting a gynecologist when any unusual or abnormal complex of symptoms pertaining to the reproductive system manifests itself (Ball 1957; Netter 1961; Shaw 1954; TeLinde 1953).

Menstrual cramps may have a physical basis, as when caused by a tilted or infantile uterus, inadequate dilation or blockage of the cervical os, endometrial disorders, and similar anomalies. Frequently, there is no precise, specific, known physical cause, and psychological factors are sometimes at the root of the problem (Clark 1963a; Dingfelder 1980; Mead 1928; Melzack 1961).

Endometriosis involves the ectopic or aberrant growth of the endometrium (uterine mucosa). Symptoms of the disorder may include sterility (32%–53% of the time), dysmenorrhea, backaches, and painful intercourse.

While the condition can exist as long as the ovaries produce hormones, it is most often found in women in their 30s. The tissue can commence growth in any of various parts of the body—the cervix, abdominal walls, intestines, Bartholin's glands, vulva; even the umbilicus may be invaded by ectopic endometrium. But the tissue always retains the histologic and biologic characteristics of uterine mucosa. Treatment depends upon the severity of the symptoms, but may involve conservative or radical surgery.

Cervical erosion is in most cases due to congenital defects or childbirth injuries. The usual symptoms are red granular tissue in the area in and around the external cervical opening or os. Any break in the cervical tissue, such as unhealed lacerations caused by childbirth, or any unusual exposure of the cervical mucous glands to the bacteria inhabiting the vaginal tract, makes the cervix susceptible to infection, which is usually chronic and low-grade. Infection of this area may lead to erosion and ulceration of the cervical tissue, correction of which may require a partial excision of the cervix (*Dorland's Illustrated Medical Dictionary* 1957; Netter 1961; Shaw 1954; TeLinde 1953).

Displacement of the uterus is said to exist when the womb becomes fixed in an abnormal position. The usual uterine position in a woman standing erect is approximately at right angles to the axis of the vagina, putting the uterus in an almost horizontal plane above the bladder. For various reasons, the ligaments supporting the uterus may become too taut or too loose, and the organ shifts to an unusual position, exhibiting a slight to great degree of deviation. The shift frequently causes painful menstruation, backaches, and pelvic congestion and makes sexual intercourse uncomfortable. If there is no pain connected with uterine displacement, there is no necessity to correct the condition. The displacement does not seem to interfere with the possibility of pregnancy, and properly positioning the uterus apparently does not increase the chances for pregnancy (Netter 1961; TeLinde 1953).

Prolapse of the uterus means that the supportive uterine ligaments have relaxed to such an extent that the uterus protrudes into the vaginal canal. The degree of prolapse can be slight, wherein the supporting tissue relaxes minimally to permit only a small portion of the uterus to drop into the vagina; or second degree, wherein the cervix actually protrudes from the vagina; or complete, in which the entire uterus protrudes from the vaginal barrel. Prolapse of the uterus usually pulls down the bladder as well, and there is often an accompanying cystocele. Functional bleeding, backaches, a "bearing-down" feeling, and difficulties in elimination are typical symptoms. Surgery is usually required to correct the condition, especially if the prolapse is second degree or complete (Ball 1957; Netter 1961; Shaw 1954; TeLinde 1953).

Cystocele is a hernial protrusion of the bladder through the vaginal wall. It is especially common, though in varying degrees of severity, among women who have had children. The muscles supporting the vagina become torn or considerably weakened, allowing the bladder to push through. A sensation of dragging or tugging in the lower abdomen, frequent urination, incontinence, and infection are common symptoms. Sometimes pessaries may help correct the less severe of these conditions, but more often surgical repair is required. Rupture of the perineal area, or damage to it, may produce **rectoceles,** wherein the vagina becomes closed by a bulging rectum (Netter 1961; TeLinde 1953).

Uterine myomata or **fibroid tumors,** found in 4% to 11% of women, vary greatly in size and position. The description "fibroid" is something of a misnomer, in that these tumors form from muscle cells, not from fibrous tissue. Their incidence is greatest among women in their 50s, although women considerably younger may develop uterine tumors. It is thought that hormonal imbalance of some sort produces fibroid tumors, since it has been established that existing ones either shrink or remain static in their dimensions after menopause. In about 50% of the cases, excessive bleeding is a symptom, and eventual calcification in a fibroid tumor is not unusual. A gynecologist can easily determine in each case the most suitable method of treatment (Ball 1957; Netter 1961; Shaw 1954; TeLinde 1953).

Other Sex-Related Disorders

Chromosomal Anomalies.   Chromosomal anomalies are of several kinds. Since early in this century, it had been thought that man's cellular structure contains 48 chromosomes (from the Latin, *chromo:* color; and *soma:* body; so called because they become visible if put in special dyes). Recently, however, careful research revealed that there are normally only 46, represented by 44 autosomes (nonsex chromosomes) and an additional pair of sex chromosomes, labeled XX in the female and XY in the male.

It was first observed in 1938, and has since been studied in detail, that certain congenital sexual disorders are related to an abnormal karyotype, a term used to indicate an arrangement of chromosomes (Briggs 1963; Turner 1938). Faulty splitting of the 23 pairs of chromosomes in the process of spermatogenesis or oogenesis may produce a sperm or ovum containing no sex-determining chromosomes at all, or a gamete that contains one (perhaps more) too many. Among the most widely recognized of conditions caused by such chromosomal abnormalities are Turner's syndrome and Klinefelter's syndrome.

In **Turner's syndrome,** an ovum containing only 22 autosomes is fertilized by an X-bearing sperm, thus creating an XO sex karyotype rather than the normal XX. The full complement of chromosomes is therefore 45 instead of the normal 46. (A YO karyotype created by the union of an atypical ovum and a Y-bearing sperm leads to certain death of the zygote.) The result is a female whose primary external sex structure is female, although poorly developed, but who has no ovaries. Besides the deficiencies in the primary and secondary sex characteristics, other typical indications of this disorder are a short stature, winglike folds of skin extending from the base of the skull to an area over the clavicle, and a broad, stocky chest. Deafness, urinary infections as the result of renal anomalies, cardiac defects, and mental deficiency are also fairly common (Netter 1961; Scott 1980; Shaffer 1963). Anabolic agents to stimulate growth and estrogen-progestogen compounds, such as found in oral contraceptives, to aid in feminization can be used in treatment of individuals with Turner's syndrome. It is estimated that about one in 3000 females is born with Turner's syndrome (Scott 1980).

In **Klinefelter's syndrome** a 24-chromosome ovum is fertilized by a Y-bearing sperm, creating an XXY karyotype and making a total of 47 chromosomes. This additional female sex chromosome produces a man of incomplete virilization and distinctly feminine appearance. The testicles are small and incapable of producing mature sperm, and breast development is prominent. These men, furthermore, show a tendency toward mental impairment, and a large number can be characterized as having inadequate personalities. Predictably, their sex drive is low (Money 1968b). About one male in 500 is thought to be born with Klinefelter's syndrome (Winchester 1973).

Both Turner's and Klinefelter's syndromes can be caused by the union of a similarly abnormal sperm and a normal ovum (Winchester 1973).

A third form of chromosomal anomaly, discovered in certain men, has attracted considerable attention. It involves extra Y chromosomes (XYY, XYYY, or even XYYYY karyotypes). Some investigators have speculated that the disorder creates a "supermale," one more prone than the average man to undisciplined, aggressive, criminal, or sociopathic behavior. Indeed, appeal against the death penalty for the convicted murderer of eight young nurses in Chicago was based on this premise, although repeated tests later showed that his chromosomal pattern was the normal XY (Okie 1976). In a few studies made of the effects of a man's possessing an extra Y chromosome, consensus among the investigators has by no means been reached. Nevertheless, results of 11 studies of this phenomenon reveal a significantly higher proportion of XYY males in prison populations (1.8% to 12.0%) than in the general population (0.14% to 0.38%), suggesting some relationship between sociopathic behavior and this chromosomal abnormality (Gardner & Neu 1972).

Geneticists also speculate that maternal age is associated with a child's having one too many chromosomes (**trisomy**). As the mother's age advances beyond 30 years, the incidence of trisomy doubles for every 5 years of her age. Paternal age seems associated with the XO karyotype (Turner's syndrome) (Lenz *et al.* 1967). Similar abnormal karyotypes are created when normal ova are fertilized by sperm having 22 or 24 (or more) chromosomes.

As more precise scientific instruments are developed and techniques for investigation are refined, new discoveries in the field of chromosome structure continue to be made. For example, individuals with XXXY, XXXXY, and XXYY karyotypes have recently been identified (Briggs 1963; C. W. Lloyd 1964).

Hermaphroditism.   **Hermaphroditism** is a rare congenital condition in which an individual cannot be clearly defined as exclusively male or female (Fig. 21.2). Historically, the classifications of hermaphroditism that have been recognized are true hermaphroditism, male hermaphroditism, and female hermaphroditism. A fourth classification, dysgenetic hermaphroditism, has recently been discussed in the scientific literature (Money 1980b; Money & Ehrhardt 1972). Hermaphroditic classification is not determined by sex chromosome constitution. Rather, classification is ordinarily based on the form and structure of the gonads.

    True hermaphroditism is the very rare structural condition of sexual ambiguity in which an individual has the gonads of both sexes. That is, the true hermaphrodite possesses at least some ovarian and some testicular

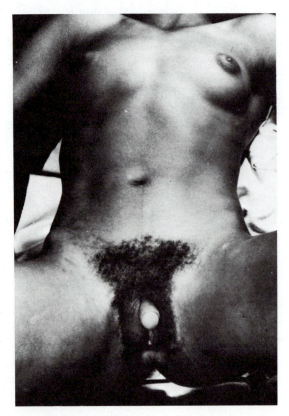

Figure 21.2 Photograph of a true hermaphrodite with a left ovary, a right testis, and 44-plus-XX chromosome count. The subject always lived as a male and was married and a stepfather. From Money, *Sex Errors of the Body*. Baltimore: The Johns Hopkins University Press, 1968.

tissue (Money 1968b, 1980b; Money & Ehrhardt 1972). At puberty the true hermaphrodite may develop a body that is ambiguous. Usually, however, the body of the true hermaphrodite becomes predominantly male or predominantly female in appearance (Money & Ehrhardt 1972).

Male hermaphroditism and **female hermaphroditism,** formerly called **psuedohermaphroditism,** are believed to be much more common disorders than true hermaphroditism, although there are no reliable statistics to indicate their actual incidence. The male hermaphrodite has gonads that are testes, at least from an anatomical standpoint, but the external genitalia are either ambiguous or feminine in appearance (Money 1968b; Money & Ehrhardt 1972). The gonads of the female hermaphrodite are ovaries, but the external genitalia are either ambiguous or masculine in appearance, even a penis and an empty scrotum. The male hermaphrodite sometimes develops a totally feminine body at puberty, irrespective of attempted treatment; the female hermaphrodite, untreated, may develop a totally male body at puberty.

Dysgenetic hermaphroditism occurs in the case of an individual who fails to develop completely the gonads of either sex and thus cannot be classified as either a true male or true female hermaphrodite.

One factor known to cause female hermaphroditism is the presence of androgen, the male sex hormone, during a critical stage in prenatal development. In the XX female fetus, the adrenal cortical glands may erroneously produce androgen, instead of the correct hormone, cortisol. This is the **androgenital syndrome,** characterized by varying degrees of masculinization of the female sexual anatomy. The androgenital syndrome is caused by the transmission of a recessive gene (Mazur & Money 1980; Money 1968b, 1980b; Money & Ehrhardt 1972). Androgenital girls may in some cases be sex assigned and reared as boys. The disorder, however, may be diagnosed at birth and may be corrected successfully with corti-costeroid injections throughout life (Mazur & Money 1980), together with surgical feminization of the genitalia.

The **androgen-insensitivity syndrome,** also genetically transmitted, occurs in XY male individuals. Cellular insensitivity to androgen in the prenatal environment may result in near or complete feminization of the sex organs (Mazur & Money 1980; Money 1968b, 1980b; Money & Ehrhardt 1972). In the complete form of the syndrome, the affected babies are indistinguishable in external appearance from normal females and are sex assigned and reared as girls. The disorder may remain undetected until puberty, when it is noticed that the onset of menstruation fails to take place. The condition may need no further treatment unless **gonadectomy,** surgical removal of the gonads, is decided upon. In that case, hormonal replacement therapy with estrogen is essential to prevent a postsurgical menopause.

There are other forms of male hermaphroditism not characterized by androgen insensitivity. The sex to which these individuals are assigned and the legal, social and pronoun status are decided on the basis of how well the genitals can be surgically reconstructed to function during coitus as either female or male. The hormonal control of puberty is therapeutically regulated.

Childhood influences quite naturally predispose the individual to assume the interests, attitudes, and sexual behavior of one sex, however much his somatic characteristics may be those of the opposite one—another indication of the superiority of psychological over physiological factors in sexual matters (Money 1965). In animals lower than primates, sexual behavior is primarily a process of biological stimulus and response. Sexual control and, indeed, sexual behavior in humans are based more on conscious effort, desire, and patterns learned from past experience than they are in lower animals. The learning process is therefore especially important in sexual functioning. That is why biological and psychic sex identity can be two different things in the same individual. Psychological sex, or gender-role identification, is not established until a child becomes verbal, usually between 18 and 36 months of age.

If parents or doctors have made an error in correctly identifying the child's biological sex, but recognize this error before the 30th month and treat the child accordingly thereafter, little psychic damage will result. But if the parents attempt to assign a different gender role after this age, the child may never accomplish the psychological switchover—at least, not without severe emotional stress and conflict—and hormonal treatment will be of little or no avail. Thus training and the learning process, not biological instinct, govern sexual orientation and account for the great diversity of sexual expression found among humans (Barclay 1971a; Bing & Rudikoff 1970).

When external somatic characteristics are in any way ambiguous regarding the sex of a newborn child, it is essential that parents seek advice of specialists at once. Sometimes surgery is indicated, not only to alter the sexual characteristics of the child, but also to alleviate or prevent the emotional problems that typically accompany such anomalies (Money 1965).

Other Problems.   Sexual tissues may become congested if a woman or man engages in prolonged, sexually stimulating petting for which there is no culminating release through orgasm. As it is a common occurrence during an engagement period, the term "engagement ovaries" is frequently used. Protracted but unrelieved sexual tensions cause blood to concentrate in the ovaries and other areas of the internal genitalia, producing swelling and congestion of the tissues, which are the source of pain. A woman's vulva may also become painfully congested for the same reason. In men, protracted sexual excitement without orgasmic relief gives rise to a concentration of blood in the testicles, which creates conditions of swelling, pain, and aching, popularly called "stone-ache" (Masters & Johnson 1966; Menaker 1961).

Congenital and acquired anomalies of the breast are found in both men and women. The most frequent of these disorders among men is **gynecomastia,** in which there is a feminization and abnormal increase in breast size. Studies of armed services personnel have reported that 7 to 13 cases of gynecomastia are discovered in every 100,000 men. Other medical authorities, however, consider these figures unrealistically high (Rector 1970).

Gynecomastia may have its inception in adolescence when an endocrine change ordinarily takes place. It may also occur in adulthood as a result of endocrine disorders, or because estrogenic substances have been medically prescribed to combat certain ailments, such as prostatic carcinoma. Endocrine medication to shrink excessive tissue, or simply surgery to remove it, are the most popular methods of treatment.

Gynecomastia has also been found in young men 22 to 26 years old who are heavy users of marijuana—and by heavy use the Harvard medical-school investigators mean 1 to 3 hours of smoking a day, 3 or 4 times a week (Harmon & Aliapoulios 1972). The young men not only experienced painfully enlarged breasts, but their nipples discharged a milky substance. Three required surgery to reduce breast size. The doctors see a distinct similarity between an ingredient in marijuana (delta ninetetrahydrocannabinol) and a female hormone, estradiol.

Women may possess one or more extra breasts (**polymastia**), supernumerary nipples (**polythelia**), or an abnormally enlarged breast or breasts (**mammary hypertrophy** or **macromastia**). Even more rarely, the nipple or areola may be missing altogether. These conditions are usually all congenital anomalies. Extra breasts and nipples usually follow the milk line, which starts under the arm, then extends through the breasts and down both sides of the abdomen in a line to the lips of the vulva, terminating in the inner thighs. Plastic surgery can correct these abnormalities once the enlargement has formed (*Dorland's Illustrated Medical Dictionary* 1957; Goin & Goin 1980; Netter 1961). Any unusual growth, pain, or change in the feel, function, or appearance of the breast should be investigated immediately by a physician.

Sexual precocity may have its origins in a premature development of hypothalamic centers, in which event the disorder is said to be of the cerebral type. Certain dysfunctions of the adrenal cortex or the interstitial cells of the testes cause the endocrine type of disorder. Primary and secondary sex characteristics are prematurely well developed in young boys so affected. They may have the appearance of a small adult (endocrine type); or their physique may be inordinately muscular and their bone structure mature, although they maintain other boyish characteristics, and development of the central nervous system is normal (cerebral type). Similar manifestations in girls are **neoplasms of the ovaries,** growths on or within the ovaries, sometimes affecting the hormonal output of these organs so greatly that marked changes in secondary sex characteristics take place. Some feminizing neoplasms develop in prepubertal girls, typically resulting in rapid and premature enlargement of the breasts, premature development of the genitalia, and early growth of pubic hair. Estimated ratios of female to male rates of precocious puberty range from 4.1 to 7.8 girls to each boy (Johnson 1980; Netter 1961).

Masculinizing ovarian neoplasms cause such changes in physical characteristics as hirsutism (abnormal hairiness), enlargement of the clitoris, overdevelopment of muscles, and a masculine lowering of the voice. The condition can also induce such defeminizing changes as sterility, amenorrhea, and decrease in breast size. Most incidences of masculinizing neoplasms occur in women 25 to 45 years old, although girls as young as 15 and women as old as 65 have been affected. Other endocrine changes may result from abnormal growths in hormone-producing glands, such as the adrenal or the pituitary (Netter 1961; Shaw 1954).

Polyps are pedunculated (stemlike) growths that arise from the mucosa and extend into the lumen or opening of any body cavity. They are true tumors, the inception of which is a morbid enlargement of the mucous membrane. Polyps may be found in any bodily area where there is mucous tissue. In the male genitalia, the tumors are benign and are usually found within the penile meatus. Urinary disturbances, such as painful, difficult, and urgent urination, as well as difficulties in sexual functioning are the usual symptoms of this disorder. Minor surgery is ordinarily sufficient to correct the problem (Netter 1961; Shaw 1954; TeLinde 1953).

Cysts are sacs, containing a liquid or semisolid substance, that develop abnormally in some part of the body. They may appear in the bladder or urinary tract, in the prostate, Cowper's glands, or scrotum, and in the vagina, uterus, vulva, or Bartholin's glands, causing inordinate retention of urine and various sexual malfunctionings. The size of cysts varies considerably. The method of treatment depends upon a number of factors, such as the cyst's location, size, and rate of growth (Ball 1957; Netter 1961; Shaw 1954; TeLinde 1953).

Summary

The causative organisms of veneral disease (VD) are ordinarily found only in human beings and are almost always acquired by direct sexual contact. Progress has been made toward the control of syphilis, but the incidence of gonorrhea in the U.S. has risen sharply. The incidence of VD is particularly high among teen-agers and young adults in their twenties. Young people infected with VD are of all personality types and represent the whole spectrum of American society. Gonorrhea is difficult to control because 80% of women have no clinical signs or symptoms of infection and thus do not know that they may be transmitters of the disease. Promiscuity, both heterosexual and homosexual, is definitely linked to VD, and there has been a great increase of VD in recent years among the male homosexual group. Men and women who suspect that they or their sexual partners may have VD can control the spread of infection by using prophylactics and paying close attention to personal hygiene after coitus.

Gonorrhea is the most ancient and prevalent of the veneral diseases. The causative organism (the *gonococcus*) usually attacks the genitourinary area, although rectal infections, pharyngeal infection, and infections of the skin, joints, brain, and blood system can occur. In the male, gonorrhea is experienced through an urgent and frequent need to urinate accompanied by a burning sensation at the tip of the penis. The complications resulting from gonorrhea include epididymitis, arthritis, iritis, conjunctivitis, skin infections, urethral stricture, and accompanying kidney difficulties. Most cases of gonorrhea in men reveal clinical signs and symptoms, while cases of gonorrhea in women remain asymptomatic. The majority of men and women with rectal gonorrhea are asymptomatic. Symptoms of gonorrhea in the female, when present, are usually shown through an urgent and frequent need to urinate accompanied by pain and a scalding sensation. Complications of gonorrhea include bartholinitis and salpingitis. For both sexes, penicilin is the treatment of choice for gonorrhea, although other drugs occasionally need to be substituted. Silver-nitrate or penicillin solutions are put in the eyes of all newborn babies to help protect babies from the possibility of gonorrheal infection acquired in the birth process from an infected mother. Diagnosis of gonorrhea is by microscopic exam-ination of the smear of urethral discharge and gonococcus cultures from women. *Nongonococcal urethritis* (NGU), a common infection with symp-toms similar to those of gonorrhea, is differentiated from gonorrhea by the fact that in NGU no gram-negative cocci are found in the smear of the urethral discharge.

Syphilis is a disease caused by a corkscrew-shaped spirochete, or bacterium, known as *Treponema pallidum*. Penicillin, or drugs such as tetracycline or erythromycin, is used to treat syphilis. Early syphilis is divided into a primary stage, identified by a lesion or a chancre usually in the anal-genital area together with a swollen but painless lymph gland, and a secondary stage, characterized by a nonitching eruption or rash on the skin. Micro-scopic examination and blood tests are used in the diagnosis of syphilis. Latent syphilis, which commences six months to two years after the initial infection, is dangerously deceptive. During this period all symptoms associated with syphilis disappear for months or years. Late syphilis may manifest itself in any organ, in the central nervous system and cardiovascular system, and on the skin. Symptoms can appear as late as 30 years after infection, although it is noteworthy that a high proportion of untreated syphilitics show few or no ill effects from the disease. Congenital syphilis, or syphilis existing at birth, can occur when a syphilitic mother transmits the disease to any child she conceives during the first two years of her infection. Untreated syphilis may produce *neurosyphilis*, a syphilitic infection of the nervous system, or *general paresis*, a progressive syphilitic disease that often includes the psychological indicators of psychosis and mental deterioration.

Chancroid is a painful, contagious disease that is typically spread through intercourse, characterized by ulcerations at the points of physical contact and by local lymph-gland swelling. Sulfonamides are the drugs commonly used to treat chancroid infection. *Granuloma inguinale*, a disease typically affecting the genitals, is characterized by widespread ulcerations and scarring of the skin and underlying tissues. The absence of lymph-node involvement is a marked feature of the disease. Antibiotic drugs are used in the treatment of granuloma inguinale. *Lymphogranuloma venereum* is a systemic disease that typically affects tissues in the anal-genital and inguinal areas. In the primary stage of the disease a small, painless blister ruptures into a shallow ulcer with clear-cut edges. In the secondary stage, pain occurs in the anal-genital area followed by enlargement of the lymph nodes. Tetracycline is the preferred treatment for lymphogranuloma venereum.

Venereal warts are benign tumors that are found in the genital area and that may be transmitted to other persons or to other parts of one's own body. Treatment for venereal warts may include medication or cauterization by electric needle, curettage, and use of liquid nitrogen. *Herpes* is an acute skin disease caused by a virus that has two forms, Type I and Type II. Herpes Type I generally appears above the waist, while herpes Type II (usually sexually transmitted) is commonly found below the waist line. Occasionally a mixture of the two types is found. The incidence of herpes Type II has increased dramatically since the mid-1960s and can lead to serious problems for affected women. The sores from genital herpes look like blisters or small bumps and can be painful. Effective cures for herpes infections have not yet been developed, although medical treatments are available to alleviate the symptoms.

Nonvenereal diseases also affect the male and female sexual systems that may have no direct relationship to sexual activity. *Nonvenereal syphilis*, also referred to as "yaws" or "pinta," is a parasitic organism related to the organism causing venereal syphilis. It typically thrives in warm, moist climates and in conditions of filth. *Leukorrhea* is excessive vaginal mucous discharge caused by a chemical, physical, or infectious agent. *Trichomoniasis*, the most common of the minor gynecological diseases, often causes copious discharges, itching, burning, and a nagging odor for many women. Many men have only mild or no symptoms of trichomoniasis, although they can carry the parasites and pass them to (or back and forth with) their sexual partner. Flagyl is an effective drug used in the treatment of trichomoniasis. *Candidiasis* or *moniliasis* is a fungus infection causing itching and inflammation of the vagina. This disease often accompanies other infections such as trichomoniasis.

Peyronie's disease is a condition in which a man's penis develops a fibrous ridge along the top or sides causing a curvature to the left, right, or upward. Vitamins, ultrasound, steroid therapy, drugs, and surgical techniques are used in treatment of this disease. *Tuberculosis* of various genital areas can occur in both men and women. Tuberculosis prostatitis can occur in men and tuberculosis of the fallopian tubes and uterus can occur in women.

Carcinoma, or cancer, can affect the sexual systems of both women and men. A knowledge of the general symptoms of the disease is important to its early diagnosis and treatment. Penile cancer can occur in men, and one theory suggests that the incidence of this form of cancer may depend on whether a man is circumcised or uncircumcised. In women, cervical cancer can be limited to early stages by taking regular Pap smear tests. Apparently, cervical cancer occurs most frequently in those women who begin coitus early in life and continue to engage in it on a regular basis. Breast cancer, representing 28% of all cancers, results in 20% of the cancer-related deaths of women. Manual examination of breasts, together with techniques such as thermography and mammography, can help in the detection of breast cancer. Mastectomy and radiation treatment are employed in treating breast cancer. Prostatic cancer, which can be detected in a brief and painless examination performed per rectum by the physician, represents 10% of all malignancies occurring in men. Surgery and treatment with hormones may help in controlling this form of cancer. Testicular cancer is a disease that primarily affects young men in their early twenties. Chemotherapy is available for testicular cancer, but men can learn how to make testicular self-examinations so that early detection of the disease is possible.

Elephantiasis involves a marked growth of subcutaneous tissues and epidermis, producing enlargements in the scrotums of men and labia majora of women. *Infectious mononucleosis* is an acute infectious disease of the lymph glands characterized by fever, fatigue, chills, sweating, headache, sore throat, and loss of appetite. Infectious mononucleosis, some symptoms of which persist for months, is believed to be transmitted by deep kissing with an infected person. *Dermatoses*, or skin diseases, of the genital region are fairly common and include problems such as tinea cruris (jock itch), scabies, pediculosis pubis (crabs), psoriasis and pruritus, and folliculitis. Inflammations of the internal and external genitalia may affect both men and women. *Vaginitis*, or vaginal irritation, is a fairly common disorder that may be caused by bacterial invasion, the introduction of foreign objects into the canal, and the use of strong chemicals. *Cystitis* refers to inflammation of the bladder—the symptoms usually include a severe burning sensation in the urethra during urination, a frequent need to urinate, and sharp pain in the lower abdomen. *Epididymitis* is a common disorder in men and involves inflammation of the epididymis. *Prostatitis*, the inflammation of the prostate gland, may be either acute or chronic. *Hemospermia* or *hematospermia* is a condition, seldom serious, in which blood appears in the ejaculate as a result of an inflamed prostate or seminal vesicles, or it may be because of various infections or obstructions. *Peritonitis* is an infection of the peritoneum, the membrane lining the abdominal walls. *Balanitis* and *balanoposthitis* refer to inflammations of the penile glans and prepuce. Medical treatments, including medication and surgery, are available to help control inflammations affecting the sexual organs.

Sexual disorders are physical anomalies of the genitalia. Those sexual disorders that affect males include: (1) *hypospadia*, a defect in which the urethral opening is on the underside of the penis rather than at its tip; (2) *epispadia*, a defect in which the urethral opening is on the top of the penis; (3) *chordee*, a downward curvature of the penis; (4) *phimosis*, a tightness of the penile prepuce so that it cannot be pulled back from the glans; (5) *hydrocele*, an accumulation of fluid in the scrotum; (6) *spermatocele*, a soft swelling on either side of the scrotum due to a cyst; (7) *varicocele*, a swelling of the veins in the spermatic cord; (8) *hematocele*, an accumulation of blood in the membranes covering the testes; (9) *edema of the scrotum* and *penile edema*, involving abnormal amounts of fluid in the intercellular tissue; (10) *torsion of the testicle*, an abnormal rotation of the testicle; (11) *cryptorchidism*, or undescended testes; (12) *monorchism*, a condition in which there is only one testicle in the scrotum; (13) *anorchism*, a congenital lack of both testicles; (14) *testicular failure* and *hypogonadism*, involving insufficient secretion of the gonads; and (15) *priapism*, a continual pathological erection of the penis. Surgical techniques or hormonal treatments are often employed in treating these physical anomalies of the male genitalia.

Sexual disorders that affect females include: (1) rudimentary, missing, extra, or divided vaginas, uteri, or fallopian tubes; (2) *atrophic condition* of the vulva or vagina; (3) *varicose veins of the vulva;* (4) *imperforate* and *fibrous hymens*, tissues that block or partly cover the external opening of the vagina; (5) *vaginal fistulae*, a pipelike opening that may develop between the bladder and vagina, urethra and vagina, or rectum and vagina; (6) *abnormal uterine bleeding* and functional uterine bleeding often caused by *endro-*

metrial hyperplasia or excessive growth of the uterine tissue; (7) *menstrual cramps* that may have a physical or psychological basis; (8) *endometriosis*, the aberrant growth of uterine tissue in other parts of the female pelvic cavity; (9) *cervical erosion*, because of infection, congenital defects or childbirth injuries; (10) *displacement of the uterus*, or abnormal positioning of the uterus; (11) *prolapse of the uterus*, or relaxing of supportive uterine ligaments so that the uterus protrudes into the vaginal canal; (12) *cystocele* or hernial protrusion of the bladder through the vaginal wall; and (13) *uterine myomata or fibroid tumors* that form from muscle cells. Surgical, hormonal, and other medical treatments exist to treat these anomalies of the female genitalia.

Chromosomal anomalies may occur such that an individual does not have the normal 46 chromosomes (represented by 44 autosomes and a pair of sex chromososmes). In *Turner's syndrome*, a disorder affecting females, one of the sex-determining pair (XX) of the chromosomes is missing, leaving 45 instead of 46 chromosomes. In *Klinefelter's syndrome*, a disorder affecting males, an extra X chromosome is contributed at the time of fertilization, creating an XXY karyotype and making a total of 47 chromosomes. Males with extra Y chromosomes (e.g., XYY, XYYY, or XYYYY) may be prone to behavior that gets them in trouble with the law. *Hermaphroditism* (which includes true hermaphroditism, male hermaphroditism, female herma-phroditism, and dysgenetic hermaphroditism), occurs when the development of the gonads or external genitalia are ambiguous or incomplete, often leading to problems in identifying whether the individual is male or female. If such determination is not made before age 3, an individual's identification with the traditional male and female societal role can be hampered, as both biological and psychological factors affect one's sex identity. Hormonal treatment, surgery, and even psychotherapeutic intervention may be employed in treating individuals with sex-related disorders.

Other problems that affect males and females are congested ovaries or testicles and congenital and acquired anomalies of the breast. *Gynecomastia*, an abnormal increase in breast size in men, *polymastia*, involving the presence of one or more extra breasts, *polythelia*, or supernumerary nipples, and *mammary hypertrophy* or *macromastia*, abnormally large breasts in women, are among the anomalies of the breast that may occur. *Sexual precocity* or premature sexual development may occur in girls and boys. *Neoplasms of the ovaries*, growths on or within the ovaries, can have feminizing or masculinizing effects on the development of a girl's secondary sex characteristics. *Polyps*, growths that arise from the mucosa, and *cysts*, sacs containing a liquid or semisolid substance, are also problems that may affect the sexual system. Endocrine medications and surgery may be employed to correct many of these problems.

Annotated Bibliography

Barlow, David. *Sexually transmitted diseases: The facts.* Oxford, England: Oxford University Press, 1979.

> This book contains detailed information for health care personnel on the etiology, diagnosis, and treatment of various sexually transmitted diseases and infections. Additional topics covered include sexual anatomy and function, history and development of treatment and control services, worldwide incidence of sexually transmitted diseases, and control of venereal disease. The book contains color plates, and would be useful as a reference for the lay reader.

Hart, Gavin. *Sexual maladjustment and disease: An introduction to modern venereology.* Chicago: Nelson-Hall, 1977.

> This volume for medical and allied health professionals covers a wide range of topics related to venereology, emphasizing the clinical features and various aspects of sexually transmitted diseases. Topics include sex education for health professionals, normal and abnormal sexual behavior, prevention and management of unwanted pregnancy, promiscuity and prostitution, and homosexual behavior.

Horton, Charles E. (Ed.) *Plastic and reconstructive surgery of the genital area.* Boston: Little, Brown, 1973.

> This well-illustrated, comprehensive source volume for plastic surgeons and other medical and allied health personnel covers psychological, developmental, and surgical aspects of genital surgery. Specific topics include history of genital surgery, embryology of male and female genitalia, genital anomalies, intersexuality and diagnosis of intersex problems, and surgical and psychiatric aspects of transsexualism.

Mazur, T. and Money, J. Prenatal influences and subsequent sexuality. In *Handbook of human sexuality,* ed. B. Wolman and J. Money. Englewood Cliffs: New Jersey: Prentice-Hall, 1980.

> This brief yet informative article discusses genetic and endocrinological influences in prenatal sexual development. Emphasis is placed on prenatal influences as they affect subsequent gender identity/role differentiation and development.

Money, John. *Love and love sickness: The science of sex, gender difference, and pair-bonding.* Baltimore: The Johns Hopkins University Press, 1980.

> This scholarly book encompasses a wide array of topics in human sexuality. Some general areas include the historical and cultural aspects of sexual behavior, factors influencing sexual orientation and pair-bonding, erotic sexuality, sexual taboos, and pornography. The author advances a new theory to guide understanding of sex differences based on the variety of factors contributing to gender identity and sex role. This book would appeal to the student, medical and allied health professional, and general academic reader.

Mumford, David M. and McCormick, Nancy. Venereal disease and the adolescent. In *Adolescent pregnancy: Perspectives for the health professional,* ed. P. B. Smith and D. M. Mumford. Boston: G. K. Hall, 1980.

This article discusses the incidence, types, characteristics, clinical features, and complications of various sexually transmitted diseases, especially among adolescents. Included in the discussion are gonorrhea, syphilis, herpes viruses, chancroid, and other venereal diseases. The article may be useful to the general reader as well as to the health professional.

Robertson, D., McMillan, A. and Young, H. *Clinical practice in sexually transmissible diseases.* Tunbridge Wells, Kent, Great Britain: Pitman Medical Limited, 1980.

This book for medical and health education readers covers the etiology, epidemiology, diagnosis, and treatment of various diseases and inflammations that are sexually transmitted. The book provides treatment of medically relevant issues such as background of sexual behavior, sexual habits of young people, and social impact of sexually transmissible diseases. Color plates are useful.

Rowan, Robert L. and Gillette, Paul J. *The gay health guide.* Boston: Little, Brown, 1978.

This medical guide for homosexual men and women focuses on the identification, transmission, diagnosis and treatment of venereal diseases and how to avoid them. The guide also deals with problems of sexual performance and emotional considerations. Of special value is a listing of gay health clinics.

Sandler, Jack, Myerson, Marilyn, and Kinder, Bill N. *Human sexuality: Current perspectives.* Tampa, Florida: Mariner, 1980.

This text presents a comprehensive perspective of the field of human sexuality. A wide range of topics is covered, including sexual anatomy and sexual response, aphrodisiacs and anaphrodisiacs, past and current sexual attitudes and behavior, sexual diseases and disorders, sexual dysfunctions, birth control, sexual health, and sex and the law. Though designed for the student, this book would serve as a valuable general reference.

Witters, Weldon and Jones-Witters, Patricia. *Human sexuality: A biological perspective.* New York: D. Van Nostrand, 1980.

This text approaches the various aspects of human sexuality from the biological standpoint. Topics of special interest include genetic engineering, hormonal control of sexuality, drugs affecting sexual function, surrogate parenthood, artificial insemination, cloning, and sex selection. The text is well illustrated and contains student performance objectives, but its appeal extends beyond the classroom.

References

Abelson, H., Cohen, R., Heaton, E., and Slider, C. Public attitudes toward and experience with erotic materials. *Technical reports of the Commission on Obscenity and Pornography*, Vol. 6. Washington, D.C.: U.S. Government Printing Office., 1970.

Abominable & detestable crime. *Time*, June 28, 1968.

Abortion in two minutes. *Family Health*, Oct. 1972, p. 8.

Abou-David, K. T. Epidemiology of carcinoma of the cervix uteri in Lebanese Christians and Moslems. *Cancer* 20 (1967): 1706.

Active rape resistance advisable, studies say. *The Houston Post*, Dec. 1, 1980.

Adams, C. R. An informal preliminary report on some factors relating to sexual responsiveness of certain college wives. In *Sexual behavior and personality characteristics*, ed. M. F. DeMartino. New York: Grove, 1966.

Addiego, F., Belzer, E., Comolli, J., Moger, W., Perry, J., and Whipple, B. Female ejaculation? *Med. Aspects. Hum. Sexuality*, Aug. 1980, pp. 99–103.

Alan Guttmacher Institute. *11 million teenagers: What can be done about the epidemic of adolescent pregnancies in the United States*. New York: Planned Parenthood Federation of America, 1976.

Alcohol and sex. *Parade*, Mar. 1, 1970.

Alexander, M. Is the nose a sex organ? *Sexology*, Nov. 1964, pp. 266–268.

    The overdue baby. *Sexology*, Jan. 1965a, pp. 410–412.

    Sex and stealing. *Sexology*, Apr. 1965b, pp. 636–640.

Allen, C. Perversions, Sexual. In *The encyclopedia of sexual behavior*, Vol. II. ed. A. Ellis and A. Abarbanel. New York: Hawthorn Bks, 1961.

    The long history of birth control. *Sexology*, Dec. 1968, pp. 276–278.

    Homosexuality. *Encyclopaedia Britannica*, 1973.

Allen, G. H. The damaging effects of prudery. *Sexology*, Feb. 1966, pp. 463–464.

Allen, G., and Martin, C. G. *Intimacy: Sensitivity, sex and the art of love*. Chicago: Cowles, 1971.

Amelar, R. D. *Infertility in men*. Philadelphia: Davis, 1966.

Amir, M. *Patterns in forcible rape*. Chicago: Univ. of Chicago Press, 1971.

Amstey, M. S. Herpes V.D.: A serious problem in pregnancy. *Med. Aspects Hum. Sexuality*, Aug. 1974, pp. 128–140.

Anderson, E. E. Gonadal failure in the male. *Med. Aspects Hum. Sexuality*, July 1970. pp. 114–121.

Answers to questions. *Sex. Behav.*, Feb. 1972, pp. 63–64.

Anthony R. *The teenager's guide to sexual awareness*. Tucson: Seymour Press, 1963.

Antibody's role in infertility studies. *J. Am. Med. Assoc.* 189 (1964): 32.

Ard, B. N., Jr. Premarital sexual experience: A longitudinal study. *J. Sex Res.* 10 (1974a): 32–39.

 Treating psychosexual dysfunction. New York: Aronson, 1974b.

Arey, L. B. *Developmental anatomy: A textbook and laboratory manual of embryology.* 7th ed. Philadelphia: Saunders, 1974.

Armstrong, E. B. The possibility of sexual happiness in old age. In *Advances in sex research*, ed. H. G. Beigel. New York: Harper, 1963.

Associated Press. Abortion is safer than birth. *Houston Chronicle*, Mar. 24, 1971.

Athanasiou, R. Frequency of masturbation in adult men and women. *Med. Aspects Hum. Sexuality*, Feb. 1976, pp. 121, 124.

 Pornography: A review of research. In *Handbook of human sexuality*, ed. B. B. Wolman and J. Money. Englewood Cliffs, New Jersey: Prentice-Hall, 1980.

Athanasiou, R., Shaver, P., and Travis, C. Sex. *Psychol. Today*, July 1970, pp. 39–52.

Auerback, A. Satyriasis and nymphomania. *Med. Aspects Hum. Sexuality*, Sept. 1968, pp. 39–45.

 Voyeuristic need. *Med. Aspects Hum. Sexuality*, Dec. 1970, p. 69.

Auerback, A., Hoffman, M., Newgard, K. W., Ramer, B. S., Terr, L., and McIlvenna, T. Symposium on "sexual idiosyncrasies." *Med. Aspects Hum. Sexuality*, Feb. 1976, pp. 70–99.

Aycock, L. The medical management of premature ejaculation. *J. Urol.* 62 (1949): 361–362

Babymaking: Dress them in blue. *Sci. News*, Jan. 12, 1974, pp. 20–21.

Bach, G. R., and Deutsch, R. M. Intimacy. In *Love, marriage, family: A developmental approach*, ed. M. E. Lasswell and T. E. Lasswell. Glenview, Ill.: Scott, 1973.

Baker, T. G. Primordial germ cells. In *Reproduction in mammals: Germ cells and fertilization*, ed. C. R. Austin and R. V. Short. New York: Cambridge Univ. Press, 1972.

Bakwin, H. Erotic feelings in infants and young children. *Med. Aspects Hum. Sexuality*, Oct. 1974, pp. 200–209.

Ball, J. C., and Logan, N. Early sexual behavior of lower-class deliquent girls. In *Studies in human sexual behavior: The American scene*, ed. A. Shiloh. Springfield, Ill.: C. C. Thomas, 1970.

Ball, T. L. *Gynecologic surgery and urology.* St. Louis: Mosby, 1957.

Barbach, L. G. *For yourself: The fulfillment of female sexuality.* New York: Anchor Bks, 1976.

Barbach, L., and Flaherty, M. Group treatment of situationally orgasmic women. *J. Sex Marital Therapy* 6 (1980): 19–29.

Barclay, A. M. Urinary acid phosphatase secretion in sexually aroused males. *J. Exp. Res. Pers.* 4 (1970): 233–238.

 Biopsychological perspectives on sexual behavior. In *Sexuality: A search for perspective*, ed. D. L. Grummon and A. M. Barclay. New York: Van Nostrand Reinhold, 1971a.

 Linking sexual and aggressive motives: Contributions of "irrelevant" arousals. *J. Pers.* 39 (1971b): 481–492.

Barfield, M. A study of relationships between sex information scores and selected personality variables, religious commitment, and biographical variables. Doctoral dissertation, University of Houston, 1971.

Barfield, M., and McCary, J. L. Why sex education. Paper presented at the annual meeting of the Texas Psychological Association, Dallas, Dec. 1969.

Baron, R. A., and Byrne, D. *Social psychology: Understanding human interaction*. 2d ed. Boston: Allyn, 1977.

Bartell, G. D. *Group sex*. New York: Wyden, 1971.

Bartz, W. R., and Rasor, R. A. Why people fall in and out of romantic love. In *Sexual behavior*, ed. L. Gross. Flushing, N.Y.: Spectrum Pubs, 1974.

Bastani, J. B. Counseling the exhibitionist and his family. *Med. Aspects Hum. Sexuality*, Oct. 1980, pp. 81–82.

Bauman, K. E., and Wilson, R. R. Premarital sexual attitudes of unmarried university students: 1968 vs. 1972. *Arch. Sex. Behav.* 5 (1976): 29–37.

Beach, F. A., A review of physiological and psychological studies of sexual behavior in animals. *Physiol. Rev.* 27 (1947): 240–307.

Becker, H. S. *Outsiders*. Glencoe, Ill.: Free Press, 1963.

Beigel, H. G. *Encyclopedia of sex education*. New York: Daye, 1952.

The danger of orgasm worship. *Sexology*, Nov. 1963, pp. 232–234.

False beliefs about reproduction. *Sexology*, Dec. 1964, pp. 334–336.

Outmoded sex laws should be changed. *Sexology*, Dec. 1965, pp. 341–343.

Bell, A. P. The homosexual as patient. In *Sex research: Studies from the Kinsey Institute*, ed. M. S. Weinberg. New York: Oxford Univ. Press, 1976.

Bell, A. P., and Weinberg, M. S. *Homosexualities: a study of diversities among men and women*. New York: Simon and Schuster, 1978.

Bell, R. R. Sex as a weapon and changing social roles. *Med. Aspects Hum. Sexuality*, June 1970, pp. 99–111.

Marriage and family interaction. 3d ed. Homewood, Ill.: Dorsey Press, 1971a.

"Swinging," the sexual exchange of marriage partners. *Sex. Behav.*, May 1971b, pp. 70–79.

Female sexual satisfaction as related to levels of education. *Sex. Behav.*, Nov. 1971c, pp. 8–14.

Bell, R. R., and Bell, P. L. Sexual satisfaction among married women. *Med. Aspects Hum. Sexuality*, Dec. 1972, pp. 136–144.

Bell, R. R., and Blumberg, L. Courtship intimacy and religious background. *Marriage Family Living* 21 (1959): 356–360.

Courtship stages and intimacy attitudes. *Family Life Coordinator*, Mar. 1960, pp. 60–63.

Bell, R. R., and Buerkle, J. V. Mother and daughter attitudes to premarital sexual behavior. *Marriage Family Living* 23 (1961): 390–392.

Bell, R. R., and Chaskes, J. B. Premarital sexual experience among coeds, 1958 and 1968. *J. Marriage Family* 32 (1970): 81–84.

Bell, R. R., and Peltz, D. Extramarital sex among women. *Med. Aspects Hum. Sexuality*, Mar. 1974, pp. 10–31.

Belliveau, F., and Richter, L. *Understanding human sexual inadequacy*. New York: Bantam, 1970.

Benjamin, H. Outline of a method to estimate the biological age with special reference to the role of sexual functions. *Intern. J. Sexol.*, Aug. 1949, pp. 34–37.

Prostitution. In *The encyclopedia of sexual behavior*, Vol. II, ed. A. Ellis and A. Abarbanel. New York: Hawthorn Bks, 1961.

The transsexual phenomenon. New York: Julian Press, 1966.

Transvestism and transsexualism in the male and female. *J. Sex Res.* 3 (1967): 107–127.

Bennett, S. M., and Dickinson, W. B. Student–parent rapport and parent involvement in sex, birth control, and venereal disease education. *J. Sex Res.* 16 (1980): 114–130.

Benson, L. *Images, heroes, and self-perceptions*. New York: Prentice-Hall, 1974.

Benson, L. G. *The family bond*. New York: Random House, 1971.

Berger, A. S., Gagnon, J. H., and Simon, W. Urban working-class adolescents and sexually explicit media. *Technical reports of the Commission on Obscenity and Pornography*, Vol. 9. Washington, D.C.: U.S. Government Printing Office, 1970.

Berger, R. E. Diagnosis and treatment of epididymitis. *Med. Aspects Hum. Sexuality*, Feb. 1980, pp. 131–132.

Bernard, J. Infidelity: Some moral and social issues. In *Renovating marriage*, ed. R. W. Libby and R. N. Whitehurst, Danville, Calif.: Consensus Pubs, 1973.

Bernstein, G. A. Physician management of incest situations. *Med. Aspects Hum. Sexuality*, Nov. 1979, pp. 66–87.

Bernstein, I. C. Sterilization: Social and psychiatric considerations. *Med. Aspects Hum. Sexuality*, March 1980, pp. 61–62.

Bieber, T. The lesbian patient. *Med. Aspects Hum. Sexuality*, Jan. 1969, pp. 6–12.

Billings, E. L., Billings, J. J., and Catarinich, M. *Atlas of the ovulation method*. Collegeville, Minn.: Liturgical Press, 1974.

Bing, E., and Rudikoff, E. Divergent ways of parental coping with hermaphrodite children. *Med. Aspects Hum. Sexuality*, Dec. 1970, pp. 73–88.

Birth control: New look at the old. *Time*, Jan. 10, 1977, p. 53.

Birth rate down as wives stay childless. *Houston Chronicle*, Feb. 8, 1981.

Blaine, G. B., Jr. Sex and the adolescent. *N.Y. J. Med.* 67 (1967): 1967–1975.

Blank, H., and Rake, G. *Viral and rickettsial diseases*. Boston: Little, 1955.

Blau, S. Venereal diseases, The. In *The encyclopedia of sexual behavior*, Vol. II, ed. A. Ellis and A. Abarbanel. New York: Hawthorn Bks, 1961.

Blazer, J. A. Married virgins—A study of unconsummated marriages. *J. Marriage Family* 26 (1964): 213–214.

Blough, H. A., and Giuntoli, R. L. Successful treatment of human genital herpes infections with 2-Deoxy-D-glucose. *J. Am. Med. Assoc.* 241 (1979): 2798–2801.

Boles, J. Age of prostitutes' customers. *Med. Aspects Hum. Sexuality*, July 1980, p. 67.

Boston Women's Health Book Collective. *Our bodies, ourselves*. New York: Simon & Schuster, 1973.

Botwinick, J. Drives, expectancies, and emotions. In *Handbook of aging and the individual*, ed. J. E. Birren. Chicago: Univ. of Chicago Press, 1960.

Böving, B. G. Embryology and development, Animal. *Encyclopaedia Britannica*, 1973.

Bower, T. G. R. *Human development*. San Francisco: Freeman, 1979.

Bowers, L. M., Cross, R. R., Jr., and Lloyd, F. A. Sexual function and urologic disease in the elderly male. *J. Am. Geriat. Soc.* 11 (1963): 647–652.

Bragonier, J. R. Influence of oral contraception on sexual response. *Med. Aspects Hum. Sexuality*, Oct. 1976, pp. 130–143.

Branson, H. K. Triolism: Sex on exhibition. *Sexology*, Jan. 1960, pp. 374–376.

How to handle pornography. *Sexology*, Dec. 1966, pp. 308–309.

Brayer, F. T., Chiazze, L., Jr., and Duffy, B. J. Calendar rhythm and menstrual cycle range. *Fertility Sterility* 20 (1969): 279–288.

Briggs, D. K. Chromosomal anomalies in hermaphroditism and other sexual disorders. In *Advances in sex research*, ed. H. G. Beigel. New York: Harper, 1963.

British Council of Churches. *Sex and morality*. London: S.C.M. Press, 1966.

Broderick, C. B. Preadolescent sexual behavior. *Med. Aspects Hum. Sexuality*, Jan. 1968, pp. 20–29.

Brody, J. E. New forms of IUD's promise improvements in safety. *Houston Chronicle*, Feb. 10, 1980.

    Sterilization is gaining acceptance in U.S. *International Herald Tribune*, May 10, 1976.

Brosman, S. A. How frequency of coitus affects prostate. *Med. Aspects Hum. Sexuality*, Mar. 1976, p. 143.

Brotman, H. The pleasures of orgasm: How men and women differ. *Sexology Today*, Nov. 1980, pp. 14–17.

Brown, D. G. Transvestism and sex-role inversion. In *The encyclopedia of sexual behavior*, Vol. II, ed. A. Ellis and A. Abarbanel. New York: Hawthorn Bks. 1961.

Brown, J. M. and Chaves, J. F. Hypnosis in the treatment of sexual dysfunctions. *J. Sex Marital Therapy* 6 (1980): 63–74.

Brown, M., Amoroso, D., and Ware, E. Behavioral effects of viewing pornography. *J. Soc. Psychol.* 98 (1976): 235–245.

Brown, W. J. The national VD problem. *Med. Aspects Hum. Sexuality*, Feb. 1972, pp. 152–178.

Brown, W. J., Lucas, J. B., Olansky, S., and Norins, L. C. Roundtable: Venereal disease. *Med. Aspects Hum. Sexuality*, Apr. 1971, pp. 74–97.

Brownmiller, S. *Against our will*. New York: Simon & Schuster, 1975.

Bruskewitz, R. Peyronie's disease. *Med. Aspects Hum. Sexuality*, Aug. 1980, pp. 77–78.

Buckley, T. The transsexual operation. *Esquire*, Apr. 1967, pp. 111–205.

Bullough, V. Sex, pleasure, and sin. *Sexology Today*, Dec. 1980, pp. 30–34.

Burgess, A. W. Persistent symptoms in rape victims. *Med. Aspects Hum. Sexuality*, Dec. 1974, p. 31.

Burgess, E. W., and Wallin, P. *Engagement and marriage*. Philadelphia: Lippincott, 1953.

Burkholder, G. V. Hematospermia. *Med. Aspects Hum. Sexuality*, Oct. 1975, p. 104.

Butler, C. A. New data about female sexual response. *J. Sex Marital Ther.* 2 (1976): 40–46.

Butler, N. R., and Goldstein, H. Smoking in pregnancy and subsequent child development. *Br. Med. J.* 4 (1973): 573–575.

Buxton, C. L., and Engle, E. T. Time of ovulation. *Am. J. Obstet. Gynecol.* 60 (1950): 3.

Buying precious time for baby: Approval for a new drug to curtail premature births. *Time*, June 30, 1980.

Byrne, D., Fisher, J. D., Lamberth, J., and Mitchell, H. E. Evaluations of erotica: Facts or feelings? *J. Pers. Soc. Psychol.* 29 (1974): 111–116.

Calderone, M. S. The Sex Information and Education Council of the U.S. *J. Marriage Family* 27 (1965): 533–534.

    Sex education for young people—and for their parents and teachers. In *An analysis of human sexual response*, ed. R. Brecher and E. Brecher. New York: New Am. Lib., 1966.

Sex education for children. *Sexology*, Apr. 1971, p. 71.

Love, sex, intimacy, and aging as a life style. In *Sex, love, and intimacy—whose life styles?* New York: SIECUS, 1972.

Calleja, M. A. Homosexual behavior in older men. *Sexology*, Aug. 1967, pp. 46–48.

Caprio, F. S. *Variations in sexual behavior*. New York: Grove, 1955.

The modern woman's guide to sexual maturity. New York: Grove, 1959.

Carbary, L. J. The fascinating facts about twins. *Sexology*, Feb. 1966, pp. 478–481.

Carrier, J. M. Participants in urban Mexican male homosexual encounters. *Arch. Sex. Behav.* 1 (1971): 279–291.

Carson, C. C., III. Hematospermia. *Med. Aspects Hum. Sexuality*, June 1980, pp. 138–139.

Cavallin, H. Incestuous fathers: A clinical report. *Am. J. Psychiat.* 122 (1966): 1132–1138.

Cavanagh, J. R. Rhythm of sexual desire in women. *Med. Aspects Hum. Sexuality*, Feb. 1969, pp. 29–39.

Cawood, C. D. Petting and prostatic engorgement. *Med. Aspects Hum. Sexuality*, Feb. 1971, pp. 204–218.

Cefalo, R. C. Toxemia of pregnancy. *Am. Family Phys.*, 19 (1979): 90–96.

Chang, Te-Wen. Relief of pain in women with genital herpes. *J. Am. Med. Assoc.* 229 (1974):641.

Chapel, T. A. Penile edema as a symptom of sexually transmitted disease. *Med. Aspects Hum. Sexuality*, Sept. 1980, p. 26.

Charny, C. W. The husband's sexual performance and the infertile couple. *J. Am. Med. Assoc.* 185, no. 2 (1963): 43.

Chase, L. Irrelevant worries. *Women's Med. News Service*, July 1969.

Check, W. Herpes encephalitis is successfully treated. *J. Am. Med. Assoc.* 238 (1977): 1121–1126.

Cherniak, D., and Feingold, A. *Birth control handbook*. Montreal: Montreal Health Press, 1973.

Chiazze, L., Jr., Brayer, F. T., Macisco, J. J., Jr., Parker, M. P., and Duffy, B. J. The length and variability of the human menstrual cycle. *J. Am. Med. Assoc.* 203 (1968): 377–380.

Chilman, C. S. Fertility and poverty in the United States: Some implications for family-planning programs, evaluation, and research. *J. Marriage Family* 30 (1968): 207–227.

Christensen, H. T., and Carpenter, G. R. Timing patterns in the development of sexual intimacy: An attitudinal report on three modern Western societies. *Marriage Family Living* 24 (1962a): 30–35.

Value-behavior discrepancies regarding premarital coitus in three Western cultures. *Am. Sociol. Rev.* 27 (1962b): 66–74.

Christensen, H. T., and Gregg, C. F. Changing sex norms in America and Scandinavia. *J. Marriage Family* 32 (1970): 616–627.

Christensen, H. T., and Johnson, K. P. *Marriage and the family*. New York: Ronald, 1971.

Christopherson, W. M., and Parker, J. E. Relation of cervical cancer to early marriage and childbearing. *New Eng. J. Med.* 273 (1965): 235–239.

Churchill, W. Do drugs increase sex drive? *Sexology*, Oct. 1968, pp. 164–167.

Cibley, L. J. Trichomonas Vaginalis vaginitis. *Med. Aspects Hum. Sexuality*, Mar. 1980, pp. 53–54.

Ciociola, G. Eleven kinds of virility. *Sexology*, Dec. 1962, pp. 299–301.

Clark, L. *Sex and you.* Indianapolis: Bobbs-Merrill, 1949.

    Sterility in the female. *Sexology,* Sept. 1959, pp. 308–314.

    Fluid tumors of the scrotum. *Sexology,* Sept. 1962, pp. 118–121.

    Your personal questions answered. *Sexology,* Oct. 1963a. p. 186.

    Your personal questions answered. *Sexology,* Nov. 1963b, pp. 251–260.

    Your personal questions answered. *Sexology,* July 1965a, p. 837.

    Painful intercourse. *Sexology,* Oct. 1965b, pp. 194–196.

    How long to make a baby? *Sexology,* Feb. 1967, pp. 478–481.

    Your personal questions answered. *Sexology,* Nov. 1969a, p. 36.

    The enjoyment of love in marriage. Reprint. New York: New Am. Lib., 1969b.

    Is there a difference between a clitoral and a vaginal orgasm? *J. Sex Res.:* 6 (1970a): 25–28.

    What gives women sex pleasure. *Sexology,* Jan. 1970b, pp. 46–49.

    Your personal questions answered. *Sexology,* Mar. 1970c, pp. 43–44.

Clarren, S. K., Alvord, E. C., Sumi, S. M., Streissguth, A. P., and Smith, D. W. Brain malformations related to prenatal exposure to ethanol. *J. Pediatrics* 92 (1978): 64–67.

Clarren, S. K., and Smith, D. W. The fetal alcohol syndrome. *New Eng. J. Med.* 298 (1978): 1063–1067.

Coleman, J. C. *Abnormal psychology and modern life.* 4th ed. Chicago: Scott, 1972.

Collaborative Group for the Study of Stroke in Young Women. Oral contraceptives and stroke in young women: Associated risk factors. *J. Am. Med. Assoc.* 231 (1975): 718–722.

Comfort, A. Anxiety over penile size. *Med. Aspects Hum. Sexuality,* Sept. 1980, pp. 121–130.

    The joy of sex. New York: Crown, 1972.

    Sexuality and aging. *SIECUS Rep.,* July 1976, pp. 1, 9.

Commission on Obscenity and Pornography. *The report of the Commission on Obscenity and Pornography.* New York: Bantam, 1970.

    Pornography: Patterns of exposure and patrons. In *The social dimension of human sexuality,* ed. R. R. Bell and M. Gordon. Boston: Little, 1972.

Conley, J. A., and O'Rourke, T. W. Attitudes of college students toward selected issues in human sexuality. *J. Sch. Health* 43 (1973): 286–292.

Connell, E. B. The uterine therapeutic system: A new approach to female contraception. *Contemp. OB/GYN,* Dec. 1975, pp. 49–55.

Contraception may just be a matter of a cup of tea, herbalist believes. *The Houston Post,* Aug. 23, 1980.

Coombs, R. H. Acquiring sex attitudes and information in our society. In *Human sexuality in medical education and practice,* ed. C. E. Vincent. Springfield, Ill.: C. C. Thomas, 1968a.

    Sex education in American medical colleges. In *Human sexuality in medical education and practice,* ed. C. E. Vincent, Springfield, Ill.: C. C. Thomas, 1968b.

Cooper, A. J. Treatment of male potency disorders: The present status. *Psychosomatics* 12 (1971): 235–244.

Cooper, D. L. The intrauterine device. *Med. Aspects Hum. Sexuality,* Aug. 1975, pp. 43–44.

Corbett, L. The last sexual taboo: Sex in old age. *Med. Aspects Hum. Sexuality,* Apr. 1981, pp. 117–131.

Corsini, R. J. Pruritis ani: An incident in psychotherapy. *Voices* 1, no. 1 (1965): 103–104.

Cory, D. W. Homosexuality. In *The encyclopedia of sexual behavior,* Vol. I, ed. A. Ellis and A. Abarbanel. New York: Hawthorn Bks, 1961.

Cory, D. W., and LeRoy, J. P. A radically new sex law. *Sexology,* Jan. 1964, pp. 374–376.

Coutts, R. L. *Love and intimacy: A psychological approach.* San Ramon, Calif.: Consensus Pubs, 1973.

Cowart, D. A., and Pollack, R. H. A Guttman scale of sexual experience. *J. Sex Educ. Ther.* 6 (1979): 3–6.

Crasilneck, H. B., and Hall, J. A. *Clinical hypnosis: Principles and applications.* New York: Grune and Stratton, 1975.

Cuber, J. F. The mistress in American society. *Med. Aspects Hum. Sexuality,* Sept. 1969, pp. 81–91.

＿＿＿ The natural history of sex in marriage. *Med. Aspects Hum. Sexuality,* July 1975, pp. 51–73.

Cuber, J. F., with Harroff, P. B. *The significant Americans.* New York: Appleton, 1966.

Culp, O. S. Anomalies of male genitalia. *Med. Aspects Hum. Sexuality,* Sept. 1974, pp. 126–147.

Curtis, E M. Oral-contraceptive feminization of a normal male infant. *Obstet. Gynecol.* 23 (1964): 295–296.

Cutter, F. The crime of incest. *Sexology,* June 1963, pp. 744–746.

Czinner, R. The many kinds of rape. *Sexology,* Jan. 1970, pp. 12–15.

Dager, E. Z., and Harper, G. Family life education in Indiana public schools: A preliminary report. *Marriage Family Living* 21 (1959): 385–388.

Dager, E Z., *et al.* Family life education in public high schools of Indiana: A survey report on course content. *Family Life Coordinator,* Apr. 1966, pp. 43–50.

Dailey, J. Help for the small or nonfunctioning penis. *Sexology Today,* Mar. 1980a, pp. 46–49.

＿＿＿ Women's most versatile muscle: The PC. *Sexology Today,* July 1980b, pp. 40–43.

Dalton, K. Menstruation and examinations. *Lancet,* Dec. 28, 1968, pp. 1386–1388.

Dalven, J. Bizarre menstrual bleeding. *Sexology,* May 1964, pp. 676–678.

Daly, M. J. Sexual attitudes in menopausal and postmenopausal women. *Med. Aspects Hum. Sexuality,* May 1968, pp. 48–53.

Danger zone (high-risk) pregnancies. *Human Sexuality Supplement to Current Health 2 and Current Lifestudies.* Curriculum Innovations, Inc., Dec. 1979.

Dangerous sex offender, The: A report of the panel of medical advisors on health and welfare to the joint state [Pennsylvania] *government commission.* Appendix to the legislative journal, May 1963, pp. 672–683.

Dank, B. M. Homosexuals who marry "for appearances." *Med. Aspects Hum. Sexuality,* Jan. 1975, p. 62.

Davis, J. E. and Mininberg, D. T. Prostatitis and sexual function. *Med. Aspects Hum. Sexuality,* Aug. 1976, pp. 32–40.

Davis, K. Sexual behavior. In *Contemporary social problems,* ed. R. Merton and R. Nisbet. New York: Harcourt, 1966.

Davis, K. B. *Factors in the sex life of twenty-two hundred women.* New York: Harper, 1929.

Davis, K. E. Sex on campus: Is there a revolution? *Med. Aspects Hum. Sexuality*, Jan. 1971, pp. 128–142.

Davis, M. E. Menopause. *Encyclopaedia Britannica*, 1973.

Dean, S. R. Discussion of "Sexual behavior in middle life" by E. Pfeiffer, A. Verwoerdt, and G. C. Davis. In *Sexual development and behavior: Selected readings*, ed. A. M. Juhasz. Homewood, Ill.: Dorsey Press, 1973.

Dearborn, L. W. Masturbation. In *Sexual behavior and personality characteristics*, ed. M. F. DeMartino. New York: Grove, 1966.

Dearth, P. B. Viable sex education in the schools: Expectations of students, parents, and experts. *J. Sch. Health* 44 (1974): 190–193.

Delcampo, R. L., Sporakowski, M. J., and Delcampo, D. S. Premarital sexual permissiveness and contraceptive knowledge: A biracial comparison of college students. *J. Sex Res.* 12 (1976): 180–192.

DeLora, J. S., and Warren, C. A. B. *Understanding sexual interaction*. Boston: Houghton, 1977.

DeMartino, M. F. Dominance-feeling, security—insecurity, and sexuality in women. In *Sexual behavior and personality characteristics*, ed. M. F. DeMartino. New York: Grove, 1966.

How women want men to make love. *Sexology*, Oct. 1970, pp. 4–7.

Sex and the intelligent woman. New York: Springer Pub., 1974.

de Moya, A., and de Moya, D. Viewpoints: What is the basis for the distinction many patients make between vaginal and clitoral orgasms? *Med. Aspects Hum. Sexuality*, Nov. 1973, pp. 84–103.

Denfeld, D., and Gordon, M. The sociology of mate swapping: Or the family that swings together clings together. *J. Sex Res.* 6 (1970): 85–100.

Dengrove, E. Myth of the captive penis. *Sexology*, Feb. 1965, pp. 447–449.

Denko, J. D. Erotic enemas. *Med. Aspects Hum. Sexuality*, Dec. 1976, pp. 37–38.

Deschin, C. S. Teenagers and venereal disease. *Pub. Health News* 43 (1962): 274.

Teen-agers and venereal disease: A sociological study of 600 teen-agers in NYC social hygiene clinics. *Am. J. Nurs.* 63 (1963): 63–67.

Desperate dilemma of abortion, The. *Time*, Oct. 13, 1967.

Devanesan, M. Type of clitoral stimulation women prefer. *Med. Aspects Hum. Sexuality*, July 1975, pp. 24–25.

Diamond, M., and Karlen, A. *Sexual decisions*. Boston: Little, Brown, 1980.

Dickes, R. Psychodynamics of fetishism. *Med. Aspects Hum. Sexuality*, Jan. 1970, pp. 39–52.

Dickinson, R. L. *Atlas of human sex anatomy*. Baltimore: Williams & Wilkins, 1949.

Dingfelder, J. R. Diagnosis and treatment of menstrual cramps. *Med. Aspects Hum. Sexuality*, Jan. 1980, pp. 117–118.

Dmowski, W. P., Luna, M., and Scommegna, A. Hormonal aspects of female sexual response. *Med. Aspects Hum. Sexuality*, June 1974, pp. 92–113.

Dolack, L. Study confirms values of ovulation method. Appendix 10 in M. A. Wilson, *The ovulation method of birth regulation*. New York: Van Nostrand Reinhold, 1980.

Dolgin, J. L. and Dolgin, B. L. Sex and the law. In *Handbook of human sexuality*, ed. B. B. Wolman and J. Money. Englewood Cliffs, New Jersey: Prentice-Hall, 1980.

Dorland's illustrated medical dictionary. 23d ed. Philadelphia: Saunders, 1957.

Dormont, P. Ejaculatory anhedonia. *Med. Aspects Hum. Sexuality*, Feb. 1975, pp. 32–43.

DSM III. *Diagnostic and statistical manual of mental disorders.* 3rd. ed. Washington, D.C.: American Psychiatric Association, 1980.

Duffy, J. Masturbation and clitoridectomy: A nineteenth-century view. *J. Am. Med. Assoc.* 186 (1963): 246–248.

  Masturbation and clitoris amputation. *Sexology*, May 1964, pp. 668–671.

Duggan, H. E. Effect of X-ray therapy on patients with Peyronie's disease. *J. Urol.* 91 (1964): 572–573.

Duncan, W. C. Lymphogranuloma venereum. *Med. Aspects Hum. Sexuality*, Dec. 1976, pp. 27–29.

Eagle, H. The spirochetes. In *Bacterial and mycotic infections of man*, ed. R. J. Dubos. Philadelphia: Lippincott, 1952.

Easley, E. B. Atrophic vaginitis and sexual relations. *Med. Aspects Hum. Sexuality*, Nov. 1974, pp. 32–47.

Eastman, N. J., and Hellman, L. M. *Williams obstetrics.* 12th ed. New York: Appleton, 1961.

Eddy, C. A. Detecting time of ovulation. *Med. Aspects Hum. Sexuality*, Dec. 1979, pp. 51–52.

Ehrmann, W. *Premarital dating behavior.* New York: Holt, 1959.

  Premarital sexual intercourse. In *The encyclopedia of sexual behavior*, Vol. II, ed. A. Ellis and A. Abarbanel. New York: Hawthorn Bks, 1961.

Eichenlaub, J. E. *The marriage art.* New York: Dell, 1961.

Elias, J. E. Exposure to erotic materials in adolescence. *Technical reports of the Commission on Obscenity and Pornography*, Vol. 9. Washington, D.C.: U.S. Government Printing Office, 1970.

Elias, S. Advising patients about genetic amniocentesis. *Med. Aspects Hum. Sexuality*, Aug. 1980, pp. 51–52.

Ellis, A. *Sex without guilt.* New York: Lyle Stuart, 1958.

  The art and science of love. New York: Lyle Stuart, 1960.

  The folklore of sex. New York: Grove, 1961a.

  Frigidity. In *The encyclopedia of sexual behavior*, Vol. I, ed. A. Ellis and A. Abarbanel. New York: Hawthorn Bks, 1961b.

  Sex offenders, The psychology of. In *The encyclopedia of sexual behavior*, Vol. II, ed. A. Ellis and A. Abarbanel. New York: Hawthorn Bks, 1961c.

  The American sexual tragedy. 2d ed., rev. New York: Lyle Stuart, 1962.

  Sex and the single man. New York: Lyle Stuart, 1963.

  The sex revolution. *Sexology*, May 1966, pp. 660–664.

  The civilized couple's guide to extramarital adventure. New York: Wyden, 1972.

Ellis, A., and Brancale, R. *The psychology of sex offenders.* Springfield, Ill.: C. C. Thomas, 1956.

Ellis, A., and Harper, R. *A new guide to rational living.* North Hollywood, California: Wilshire, 1976.

Ellis, A., and Sagarin, E. *Nymphomania.* New York: Gilbert Press, 1964.

Engel, R. M. E. Treatment of cryptorchidism. *Med. Aspects Hum. Sexuality*, Apr. 1981, pp. 51–52.

English, O. S. Sexual adjustment in marriage. In *Modern marriage and family living*, ed. M. Fishbein and R. Kennedy. New York: Oxford Univ. Press, 1957.

Positive values of the affair. In *The new sexuality*, ed. H. A. Otto. Palo Alto: Science & Behavior, 1971,

Erikson, E. H. *Childhood and society*. 2nd ed. New York: Norton, 1963.

Eschenbach, D. A. Myth of the woman with asymptomatic gonorrhea. *Med. Aspects Hum. Sexuality*, June 1976, pp. 118–126.

Even a late break from smoking could help fetus. *Med. World News*, Sept. 1979, pp. 48–49.

Everett, H. C. Competition in bed. *Med. Aspects Hum. Sexuality*, Apr. 1971, pp. 10–22.

Falk, G. J. The truth about sex offenders. *Sexology*, Nov. 1965, pp. 271–273.

Fang, B. Swinging: In retrospect. *J. Sex Res.* 12 (1976): 220–237.

Fawcett, D. W. Reproductive system. *Encyclopaedia Britannica*, 1963.

Federal Bureau of Investigation. *Uniform crime reports for the United States*. Washington, D.C.: U.S. Department of Justice, 1970.

Feldman, H. Sexual adjustment in early marriage. Address to the annual Groves conference on marriage and the family, Kansas City, Mo., Apr. 1966.

Fellman, S. Dry orgasm. *Med. Aspects Hum. Sexuality*, Feb. 1975, p. 88.

Felman, Y. M. Complications of some "minor" sexually transmitted diseases. *Med. Aspects Hum. Sexuality*, Sept. 1980, pp. 65–83.

Ficher, I. V. Value of extended foreplay. *Med. Aspects Hum. Sexuality*, Dec. 1979, pp. 12–23.

Fielding, J. E. Smoking and pregnancy. *New Eng. J. Med.* 298 (1978): 337–339.

Finch, B. E., and Green, H. *Contraception through the ages*. Springfield, Ill.: C. C. Thomas, 1963.

Finger, F. W. Changes in sex practices and beliefs of male college students: Over 30 years. *J. Sex Res.* 11 (1975): 305–317.

Finkle, A. L. The relationship of sexual habits to benign prostatic hypertrophy. *Med. Aspects Hum. Sexuality*, Oct. 1967, pp. 24–25.

Sex after prostatectomy. *Med. Aspects Hum. Sexuality*, Mar. 1968, pp. 40–41.

Finkle, A. L., Moyers, T. G., Tobenkin, M. I., and Karg, S. J. Sexual potency in aging males. I. Frequency of coitus among clinic patients. *J. Am. Med. Assoc.* 170 (1959): 1391–1393.

Fischer, S. *The female orgasm: Psychology, physiology, fantasy*. New York: Basic Bks, 1973.

Fisher, C., Gross, J., and Zuch, J. Cycle of penile erection synchronous with dreaming (REM) sleep. *Arch. Gen. Psychiat.* 12 (1965): 29–45.

Fisher, W. A., and Byrne, D. Individual differences in socialization to sex as mediators of responses to an erotic film. Paper presented at the Midwest Psychological Association, Chicago, May 1976.

Fiumara, N. J. Gonococcal pharyngitis. *Med. Aspects Hum. Sexuality*, May 1971, pp. 194–209.

Differential diagnosis and treatment of venereally transmitted urethritis and vaginitis. *Med. Aspects Hum. Sexuality*, Mar. 1976, pp. 41–42.

Sexual behavior and primary and recurrent herpes genitalis. *Med. Aspects Hum. Sexuality*, May 1980, pp. 151–152.

Fleck, S. Some psychiatric aspects of abortion. *J. Nerv. Ment. Dis.* 151 (1970): 42–50.

Fletcher, A., and Landes, R. R. Treatment of gonorrhea today. *Med. Aspects Hum. Sexuality*, Aug. 1970, pp. 50–61.

Ford, C. S., and Beach, F. A. *Patterns of sexual behavior.* New York: Harper, 1951.
    Self-stimulation. In *Sexual behavior and personality characteristics*, ed. M. F. DeMartino. New York: Grove, 1966.

Ford, K. Contraceptive use in the United States, 1973–1976. *Family Plann. Perspect.* 10 (1978): 264–269.

Forum Newsfront. *Playboy Magazine*, March 1979, p. 46.

Fox, C. A. Recent studies in human coital physiology. *Clin. Endocrinol. Metab.* 2 (1973): 527–543.

Fraker, S., Howard, L., and Sciolino, E. Abortion: Who pays? *Newsweek*, July 4, 1977.

Francoeur, R. T., and Francoeur, A. K. Hot and cool sex: Fidelity in marriage. In *Renovating marriage*, ed. R. W. Libby and R. N. Whitehurst. Danville, Calif.: Consensus Pubs, 1973.

Francoeur, R., and Hendrixson, L. The battle over sex education in New Jersey. *Sexology Today*, Sept. 1980, pp. 18–25.

Frank, L. K. *The conduct of sex.* New York: Grove, 1963.

Frank, M. How threesomes work. *Sexology Today*, Oct. 1980, pp. 22–27.

Frankl, V. E. *Man's search for meaning.* New York: Beacon Press, 1963.

Frede, M. C. Sexual attitudes and behavior of college students at a public university in the Southwest. Doctoral dissertation, University of Houston, 1970.

Freedman, M. B. The sexual behavior of American college women: An empirical study and an historical survey. *Merrill Palmer Quart.* 11 (1965): 33–48.

Freedman, R., Whelpton, P. K., and Campbell, A. A. *Family planning, sterility, and population growth.* New York: McGraw, 1959.

Freeman, J. T. Sexual capacities in the aging male. *Geriatrics* 16 (1961): 37–43.

Freeman, M., and Freeman, R. Senior college women: Their sexual standards and activity. II. Dating: Petting and coital practices. *J. National Assoc. Women Deans Counselors* 29 (1966): 136–143.

Friedfeld, L. Geriatrics, medicine, and rehabilitation. *J. Am. Med. Assoc.* 175 (1961): 595–598.

From the editor's scrapbook. *Sexology*, Jan. 1964, pp. 408–410.
    Sexology, Mar. 1965, pp. 536–538.
    Sexology, June 1966, p. 744.
    Sexology, Apr. 1968a, p. 588.
    Sexology, June 1968b, pp. 753–754.

Fromm, E. *The art of loving.* New York: Harper, 1956.
    Sigmund Freud's mission. New York: Grove, 1963.

Fujimoto, I. Intimacy: New interpretations—new life styles. In *Sex, love, and intimacy—whose life styles?* New York: SIECUS, 1972.

Furlow, W. L. Surgical management of impotence using the inflatable penile prosthesis. *Mayo Clin. Proc.* 51 (1976): 325–328.

Gabbe, S. G. New ideas on managing the pregnant diabetic patient. *Contemporary OB/GYN* 13 (1979): 109–113.

Gadpaille, W. J. Father's role in sex education of his son. *Sex. Behav.*, Apr. 1971, pp. 3–10.
    Sadomasochism. *Med. Aspects Hum. Sexuality*, Sept. 1972, pp. 155–156.

Gagnon, J. H. Sexuality and sexual learning in the child. *Psychiatry* 28 (1965): 212–228.
Talk about sex, sexual behavior, and sex research. Address to the annual Groves conference on marriage and the family, Kansas City, Mo., Apr. 1966.

Gallup Opinion Index, The Report No. 178. Princeton, New Jersey: The Gallup Poll, June, 1980.

Gardner, L. I., and Neu, R. L. Evidence linking an extra Y chromosome to sociopathic behavior. *Arch. Gen. Psychiat.* 26 (1972): 220–222.

Garrett, R. A. Treat undescended testicle by age six. *J. Am. Med. Assoc.* 188 (1964): 34.

Gebhard, P. H. Factors in marital orgasm. *J. Soc. Issues* 22, no. 2 (1966): 88–95.
Misconceptions about female prostitutes. *Med. Aspects Hum. Sexuality*, Mar. 1969, pp. 24–30.
Prostitution. *Encyclopaedia Britannica*, 1973.
Fetishism and sadomasochism. In *Sex research: Studies from the Kinsey Institute*, ed. M. S. Weinberg. New York: Oxford Univ. Press, 1976.

Gebhard, P. H., Gagnon, J. H., Pomeroy, W. B., and Christenson, C. V. *Sex offenders.* New York: Harper, Hoeber, 1965.

Gebhard, P. H., Pomeroy, W. B., Martin, C. E., and Christenson, C. V. *Pregnancy, birth, and abortion.* New York: Harper, 1958.

Geller, J. Progesterone drug may reduce benign prostatic hypertrophy. *J. Am. Med. Assoc.* 189 (1964): 32.

Genetic Engineering. *Human Sexuality Supplement to Current Health 2 and Current Lifestudies*, Curriculum Innovations, Inc., Feb. 1981.

Gerwels, J. W., and Beckett, J. Dermatologic manifestations of venereally transmitted diseases. *Med. Aspects Hum. Sexuality*, Oct. 1975, pp. 7–27.

Gibran, K. *The prophet.* New York: Knopf, 1923.

Gilmartin, B. G., and Kusisto, D. V. Some personal and social characteristics of mate-sharing swingers. In *Renovating marriage*, ed. R. W. Libby and R. N. Whitehurst. Danville, Calif.: Consensus Pubs, 1973.

Ginsberg, M. M. Gonorrhea among homosexuals. *Med. Aspects Hum. Sexuality*, Feb. 1980, pp. 45–46.

Gittelson, N. Marriage: What women expect and what they get. *McCall's*, Jan. 1980, pp. 87–89, 150–151.

Glick, P. C. Years of marriage most prone to divorce. *Med. Aspects Hum. Sexuality*, July 1980, p. 11.

Godow, A. G., and LaFave, F. E. The impact of a college course in human sexuality upon sexual attitudes and behavior. *Teaching of Psychology* 6 (1979): 164–167.

Goin, J. M., and Goin, M. K. Advising patients about breast reduction. *Med. Aspects Hum. Sexuality*, May 1980, pp. 91–92.

Gold, L. N. Psychiatric profile of a firesetter. *J. Sci.* 7(1962): 404.

Golde, P., and Kogan, N. A sentence completion procedure for assessing attitudes toward old people. *J. Gerontol.* 14 (1959): 355–363.

Goldstein, P. J. Diabetes and pregnancy. *Med. Aspects Hum. Sexuality*, March 1980, pp. 59–60.

Goldzieher, J. W., and Rudel, H. W. How the oral contraceptives came to be developed. *J. Am. Med. Assoc.* 230 (1974): 421–425.

Goss, D. A. Gonorrhea: Diagnosis, complications and treatment in the female. *South. Med. Bull.* 59, no. 2 (1971): 35–37.

Green, D. S., and Green, B. Double sex. *Sexology*, Mar. 1965, pp. 561–563.

Green, R. Change-of-sex. *Med. Aspects Hum. Sexuality*, Oct. 1969, pp. 96–113.

Green, R., and Money, J., eds. *Transsexualism and sex reassignment*. Baltimore: Johns Hopkins Univ. Press, 1969.

Greenbank, R. Are medical students learning psychiatry? *Penn. Med. J.* 64 (1961): 989–992.

Greenblat, B. R. *A doctor's marital guide for patients*. Chicago: Budlong Press, 1962.

Greenblatt, R. B., and Stoddard, L. D. The estrogen–cancer controversy. *J. Am. Ger. Soc.* 26 (1978): 1–8.

Greene, B. L. How valid is sex attraction in selecting a mate? *Med. Aspects Hum. Sexuality*, Jan. 1970, p. 23.

Greene, B. L., Lee, R. R., and Lustig, N. Conscious and unconscious factors in marital infidelity. *Med. Aspects Hum. Sexuality*, Sept. 1974, pp. 87–105.

Greenhill, J. P. What is the psychological significance of various coital positions? *Med. Aspects Hum. Sexuality*, Feb. 1971, pp. 8–16.

Greenwood, R. J. Diverse presenting symptoms of neurosyphilis. *Med. Aspects Hum. Sexuality*, April 1980, pp. 31–32.

Gregg, S., and Ismach, J. Beyond "VD." *Med. World News*, March 1980, pp. 49–63.

Griffin, S. Rape: The all-American crime. In *Sexuality today and tomorrow: Contemporary issues in human sexuality*, ed. S. Gordon and R. W. Libby. N. Scituate, Mass.: Duxbury Press, 1976.

Griffitt, W. Sexual experience and sexual responsiveness: Sex differences. *Arch. Sex. Behav.* 4 (1975): 529–540.

Grinder, R. E., and Schmitt, S. Coeds and contraceptive information. *J. Marriage Family* 28 (1966): 471–479.

Groth, A. N., and Gary, T. S. Marital rape. *Med. Aspects Hum. Sexuality*, March 1981, pp. 122–131.

Growing older—later. Editorial. *J. Am. Med. Assoc.* 191 (1965): 131.

Gunby, P. New anti-herpes virus drug being tested. *J. Am. Med. Assoc.* 243 (1980): 1315.

Gunderson, M. P. The effects of sex education on sex information, sexual attitudes and behavior. Master's thesis, University of Houston, 1976.

    The interrelationships between four sex variables (sex information and sexual guilt, attitudes and behaviors) and 16 personality factors. Doctoral dissertation proposal, University of Houston, 1977.

Guttmacher, A. F. The attitudes of 3,381 physicians towards contraception and the contraceptives they prescribe. *Hum. Biol.* 12 (1947): 1–12.

    How can we best combat illegitimacy? *Med. Aspects Hum. Sexuality*, Mar. 1969, pp. 48–61.

    Who owns fertility: the church, the state, or the individual? In *Sexuality: A search for perspective*, ed. D. L. Grummon and A. M. Barclay. New York: Van Nostrand Reinhold, 1971.

Hacker, S. S. Weapons for the sexual revolution. *J. Sex Educ. Ther.* 6 (1980): 47–50.

Halstead, L. S., Halstead, M. M., Salhoot, J. T., Stock, D. D., and Sparks, R. W. Human sexuality: An interdisciplinary program for health care professionals and the physically disabled. *South. Med. J.* 69 (1976): 1352–1355.

Hamilton, E. Emotions and sexuality in the woman. In *The new sexuality*, ed. H. A. Otto. Palo Alto: Science & Behavior, 1971.

Hammond, J. Reproduction. *Encyclopaedia Britannica,* 1973.

Handsfield, H. H. Incidence of asymptomatic gonorrhea. *Med. Aspects Hum. Sexuality,* Oct. 1974, p. 111.

Hanes, M. V. Ectopic pregnancy following total hysterectomy: Report of a case. *Obstet. Gynecol.* 23 (1964): 882–884.

Hanson, J. W., Streissguth, A. P., and Smith, D. W. The effects of moderate alcohol consumption during pregnancy on fetal growth and morphogenesis. *J. Pediatrics* 92 (1978): 457–460.

Hardin, G. *Birth control.* New York: Pegasus, 1970.

Haring, B. Conjugal love. Lecture presented at the conference on theology and sexuality, Yale University, New Haven, May 1967.

Harkavy, O., and Maier, J. Research in contraception and reproduction: A status report, 1973. *Fam. Plann. Perspect.* 5 (1973): 213–216.

Harlow, H. F., and Harlow, M. K. The effect of rearing conditions on behavior. In *Sex research: New developments,* ed. J. Money. New York: Holt, 1965.

Harman, S. M. Basis for decreased sexual desires in older men. *Med. Aspects Hum. Sexuality,* Dec. 1975, pp. 6–7.

Harmon, J., and Aliapoulios, M. A. Gynecomastia in marihuana users. *New Eng. J. Med.* 287 (1972): 936.

Harper, R. A. Extramarital sex relations. In *The encyclopedia of sexual behavior,* Vol. I, ed. A. Ellis and A. Abarbanel. New York: Hawthorn Bks, 1961.

    Overcoming impotence. *Sexology,* May 1965, pp. 680–682.

Harris, R., Yulis, S., and LaCoste, D. Relationships among sexual arousability, imagery ability, and introversion-extraversion. *J. Sex Res.* 16 (1980): 72–86.

Hartman, W. E., and Fithian, M. A. *Treatment of sexual dysfunction: A bio-psycho/ social approach.* Long Beach, Calif.: Center for Marital & Sexual Studies, 1972.

Hartman, W. E., Fithian, M. A., and Johnson, D. Sex in nudist camps. *Sexology,* Apr. 1969, pp. 580–586.

Hatcher, R. A. Postcoital measures to prevent pregnancy. *Med. Aspects Hum. Sexuality,* Sept. 1976, p. 121.

Hatcher, R. A., Stewart, G. K., Guest, F., Finkelstein, R., and Godwin, C. *Contraceptive technology 1976–1977.* 8th ed. New York: Irvington Pub., 1976.

Hatcher, R. A., Stewart, G. K., Stewart, F., Guest, F., Schwartz, D. W., and Jones, S. A. *Contraceptive technology 1980–1981.* New York: Irvington, 1980.

Hatcher, R. A., Stewart, G. K., Kline, R. W., and Moorehead, F. L. *Contraceptive technology.* Atlanta: Emory Univ. School of Med., 1974.

Haynes, S. N., and Oziel, L. J. Homosexuality: Behaviors and attitudes. *Arch. Sex. Behav.* 5 (1976): 283–289.

Heiman, J. R. The physiology of erotica: Women's sexual arousal. *Psychol. Today,* Apr. 1975, pp. 91–94.

Heiman, J., LoPiccolo, L., and LoPiccolo, J. *Becoming orgasmic: A sexual growth program for women.* Englewood Cliffs, N. J.: Prentice-Hall, 1976.

Hellman, L. M., and Pritchard, J. A. *Williams obstetrics.* 14th ed. New York: Appleton, 1971.

Henry, L. Some data on natural fertility. *Eugenics Quart.* 8 (1961): 81–91.

Herrick, E. H. Telegony. *Sexology,* Dec. 1959, pp. 316–319.

    Is virgin birth possible? *Sexology,* Apr. 1962, pp. 590–594.

Higgins, J. W., and Katzman, M. B. Determinants in the judgment of obscenity. *Am. J. Psychiat.* 125 (1969): 1733–1738.

Himes, N. E. *Medical history of contraception.* New York: Gamut Press, 1963.

Hirsch, E. W. *How to improve your sexual relations.* Chicago: Zeco, 1951.

Hite, S. *The Hite report: A nationwide study on female sexuality.* New York: Macmillan Pub. Co., 1976.

Hoch, Z. The sensory arm of the female orgasmic reflex. *J. Sex. Educ. Ther.* 6 (1980): 4–7.

Hoffman, M. The male prostitute. *Sex. Behav.,* Aug. 1972, pp. 16–21.

Holland, G. A. Living to be 120. *Sexology Today,* Aug. 1980, pp. 18–23.

Hollender, M. H. Women's wish to be held: Sexual and nonsexual aspects. *Med. Aspects Hum. Sexuality,* Oct. 1971, pp. 12–26.

Hollingshead, A. B. *Elmtown's youth.* New York: Wiley, 1949.

Holmes, K. K. Average risk of gonorrheal infection after exposure. *Med. Aspects Hum. Sexuality,* Feb. 1975a, p. 83.

⁣   Alcohol avoidance during VD treatment. *Med. Aspects Hum. Sexuality,* Nov. 1975b, p. 79.

Holmes, K. K., Johnson, D. W., and Trostle, H. J. An estimate of the risk of men acquiring gonorrhea by sexual contact with infected females. *Am. J. Epidemiol.* 91 (1970): 170–174.

Homosexuality: Coming to terms. *Time,* Oct. 24, 1969.

Honigmann, J. J. A cultural theory of obscenity. In *Sexual behavior and personality characteristics,* ed. M. F. DeMartino. New York: Grove, 1963.

Höök, K. Refused abortion. *Acta Psychiatr. Scand.* Suppl. 168 (1963): 1–156.

Hooker, E. The adjustment of the male overt homosexual. *J. Proj. Tech.* 21 (1957): 18–31.

⁣   An empirical study of some relations between sexual patterns and gender identity in male homosexuals. In *Sex research: New developments,* ed. J. Money. New York: Holt, 1965.

Hospital to open test-tube baby clinic. *The Houston Post,* Jan. 9, 1980.

Hotchkiss, R. S. How will an operation on the prostate affect a man's sex life? *Sex. Behav.,* Aug. 1971, p. 14.

Houston, J. The Pope's presence: Enough to sell his unpopular stand? *Christianity Today* 23 (1979): 64–69.

Howat, P. A., O'Rourke, T. W., and Rubinson, L. G. Trends in sexual attitudes and behavior among selected college students. *J. Sex Educ. Ther.* 6 (1979): 78–83.

Howe, R. L. *Herein is love.* Valley Forge, Pa.: Judson Press, 1961.

Hunt, M. *Sexual behavior in the seventies.* Chicago: Playboy Press, 1974.

Imber, G. Advising patients about the advisability and procedures involved in breast augmentation. *Med. Aspects Hum. Sexuality,* March 1980, pp. 25–26.

Infertility. *Human Sexuality Supplement to Current Health 2 and Current Lifestudies,* Curriculum Innovations, Inc., April 1979.

"J." *The sensuous woman.* New York: Lyle Stuart, 1969.

Jackson, R. Breast-feeding as contraceptive. *Med. Aspects Hum. Sexuality,* Nov. 1976, p. 137.

Jacobs, L. I. Comparison of men's vs. women's enjoyment of orogenital activity. *Med. Aspects Hum. Sexuality,* Aug. 1974, p. 49.

Jaffe, A. C. Child molestation. *Med. Aspects Hum. Sexuality,* Apr. 1976, pp. 73, 96.

James, B. E. Marriages in which the wife is the sexual initiator. *Med. Aspects Hum. Sexuality*, July 1980, pp. 16–24.

James, J. Prostitution: Arguments for change. In *Sexuality today and tomorrow: Contemporary issues in human sexuality*, ed. S. Gordon and R. W. Libby. N. Scituate, Mass.: Duxbury Press, 1976.

James, W. H. The incidence of spontaneous abortion. *Pop. Stud.* 24 (1970): 245.

Janda, L. H., and O'Grady, K. E. Development of a sex anxiety inventory. *J. Consult. Clin. Psychol.* 48 (1980): 169–175.

Javert, C. T. Role of the patient's activities in the occurrence of spontaneous abortion. *Fertility Sterility* 11 (1960): 550–558.

Jelliffe, D. B., and Jelliffe, E. F. P. *Human milk in the modern world.* New York: Oxford Univ. Press, 1977.

Jobaris, R., and Money, J. Duration of orgasm. *Med. Aspects Hum. Sexuality*, July 1976, pp. 7, 65.

Johnson, C. M. Sexual precocity: Male and female. *Med. Aspects Hum. Sexuality*, May 1980, pp. 52–66.

Jones, A. M., Zeigler, J. A., and Jones, R. H. Experimental syphilis vaccines in rabbits. I. Differentiation protection with an adjuvant spectrum. *Br. J. Vener. Dis.* 52 (1976): 9–17.

Jones, C., and Aronson, E. Attribution of fault to a rape victim as a function of respectability of the victim. *J. Pers. Soc. Psychol.* 26 (1973): 415–419.

Jones, H. E. Adolescence in our society. In *The adolescent*, ed. J. M. Seidman. New York: Holt, 1960.

Jorgensen, V. Vaginitis caused by psychosexual tensions. *Med. Aspects Hum. Sexuality*, May 1975, pp. 138–139.

Kaats, G. R., and Davis, K. E. The dynamics of sexual behavior of college students. *J. Marriage Family* 32 (1970): 390–399.

Kahn, E., and Fisher, C. REM sleep and sexuality in the aged. *J. Geriat. Psychiat.* 2 (1969): 181–199.

Kanin, E. J., and Howard, D. H. Postmarital consequences of premarital sex adjustment. *Am. Sociol. Rev.* 22 (1957): 197–204.

Kaplan, H. S. *The new sex therapy: Active treatment of sexual dysfunction.* New York: Quadrangle, 1974.

    The illustrated manual of sex therapy. New York: Quadrangle, 1975.

    The new sex therapy. Vol. II: Disorders of sexual desire. New York: Brunner/ Mazel, 1979.

Kaplan, H. S., and Sager, C. J. Sexual patterns at different ages. *Med. Aspects Hum. Sexuality*, June 1971, pp. 10–23.

Kaplan, J. H. Sensitivity reaction to vaginal secretions. *Med. Aspects Hum. Sexuality*, Feb. 1975, p. 87.

Karlen, A. *Sexuality and homosexuality.* New York: Norton, 1971

    Swingers: The conservative hedonists. *Sexology Today*, May, 1980, pp. 12–18.

Karpman, B. *The sexual offender and his offenses.* New York: Julian Press, 1954.

Kassel, V. Sex in nursing homes. *Med. Aspects Hum. Sexuality*, Mar. 1976, pp. 126–131.

Katzman, M. Obscenity and pornography. *Med. Aspects Hum. Sexuality*, July 1969, pp. 77–83.

Kaufman, R. H. Sexual transmission of *Haemophilus vaginalis*. *Med. Aspects Hum. Sexuality*, Nov. 1976, pp. 133–134.

Kaufman, R. H., Gardner, H. L., Brown, D., Wallis, C., Rawls, W. E., and Melnick, J. L. Herpes genitalis treated by photodynamic inactivation of virus. *Am. J. Obstet. Gynecol.* 117 (1973): 1144–1146.

Kaye, H. E. Lesbian relationships. *Sex. Behav.*, Apr. 1971, pp. 80–87.

Kegel, A. H. Letter to the editor. *J. Am. Med. Assoc.* 153 (1953): 1303–1304.

Keller, D. E. Women's attitudes regarding penis size. *Med. Aspects Hum. Sexuality*, Jan. 1976, pp. 178–179.

Kelly, G. L. *Sex manual.* Augusta, Ga.: Southern Medical Supply Co., 1959.

   Impotence. In *The encyclopedia of sexual behavior*, Vol. I, ed. A. Ellis and A. Abarbanel. New York: Hawthorn Bks, 1961.

Kerckhoff, A. C. Social class differences in sexual attitudes and behavior. *Med. Aspects Hum. Sexuality*, Nov. 1974, pp. 10–31.

Kernodle, R. W. Some implications of the homogamy-complementary needs theories for sociological research. *Soc. Forces* 38 (1959): 145.

Ketterer, W. A. Homosexuality and venereal disease. *Med. Aspects Human Sexuality*, Mar. 1971, pp. 114–129.

Keys, A. Experimental induction of psychoneuroses by starvation. In *Biology of mental health and disease* (27th annual conference of the Milbank Memorial Fund). New York: Harper, 1952.

Kiev, A., and Hackett, E. The chemotherapy of impotency and frigidity. *J. Sex Res.* 4 (1968): 220–224.

King, M., and Sobel, D. Sex on the college campus: Current attitudes and behavior. *J. Coll. Student Personnel* 16 (1975): 205–209.

Kinsey, A. C., Pomeroy, W. B., and Martin, C. E. *Sexual behavior in the human male.* Philadelphia: Saunders, 1948.

Kinsey, A. C., Pomeroy, W. B., Martin, C. E., and Gebhard, P. H. *Sexual behavior in the human female.* Philadelphia: Saunders, 1953.

Kirkendall, L. A. *Premarital intercourse and interpersonal relations.* New York: Julian Press, 1961a.

   Sex drive. In *The encyclopedia of sexual behavior*, Vol. II, ed. A. Ellis and A. Abarbanel. New York: Hawthorn Bks, 1961b.

   Obscenity and the U.S. Supreme Court. *Sexology*, Nov. 1965, pp. 242–245.

   Sex education. In *Human sexuality in medical education and practice*, ed. C. E. Vincent. Springfield, Ill.: C. C. Thomas, 1968.

   The importance of touch. *Sexology Today*, March 1980a, pp. 10–15.

   Sexual wisdom for the later years. *Sexology Today*, Aug. 1980b, pp. 14–17.

Kirkendall, L. A., and Libby, R. W. Sex and interpersonal relationships. In *The individual, sex, and society*, ed. C. B. Broderick and J. Bernard. Baltimore: Johns Hopkins Univ. Press, 1969.

Kirkpatrick, C. *The family: As process and institution.* 2d ed. New York: Ronald, 1963.

Kirsch, F. M. *Sex education and training in chastity.* New York: Benziger, 1930.

Kiser, C. V., Grabill, W. H., and Campbell, A. A. *Trends and variations in fertility in the United States.* Cambridge: Harvard Univ. Press, 1968.

Klapproth, H. J. Side effects of vasectomy. *Med. Aspects Hum. Sexuality*, Jan. 1976, pp. 169, 173.

Kleegman, S. J. Frigidity. *Quart Rev. Surg. Obstet. Gynecol.* 16 (1959): 243–248.

   Female sex problems. *Sexology*, Nov. 1964, pp. 226–229.

Kleegman, S., Amelar, R. D., Sherman, J. K., Hirschhorn, K., and Pilpel, H. Roundtable:

Artificial donor insemination. *Med. Aspects Hum. Sexuality*, May 1970, pp. 84–111.

Klemesrud, J. Surprising leader of U.S. anti-abortionists. *International Herald Tribune*, Mar. 4, 1976.

Knox, G. E., Reynolds, D. W., and Alford, C., Jr. Perinatal infections caused by rubella, hepatitis B, cytomegalovirus, and herpes simplex. In *Fetal and maternal medicine*, ed. E. J. Quilligan and N. Kretchmer. New York: Wiley, 1980.

Kollias, K., and Tucker, J. Interview: Women and rape. *Med. Aspects Hum. Sexuality*, May 1974, pp. 183–197.

Kolodny, R. C., Masters, W. H., Hendryx, B. S., and Toro, G. Plasma testosterone and semen analysis in male homosexuals. *New Eng. J. Med.* 285 (1971): 1170–1174.

Kolodny, R. C., Masters, W. H., Kolodner, R. M., and Toro, G. Depression of plasma testosterone levels after chronic intensive marihuana use. *New Eng. J. Med.* 290 (1974): 872–874.

Kopp, S. B. The character structure of sex offenders. *Am. J. Psychother.* 16 (1962): 64–70.

Krueger, D. W. Men who wear women's clothes. *Med. Aspects Hum. Sexuality*, Oct. 1980, pp. 16–63.

Kronhausen, P., and Kronhausen, E. *The sexually responsive woman*. New York: Ballantine, 1965.

Kushner, L. Sex and Judaism. In *Sexuality today and tomorrow: Contemporary issues in human sexuality*, ed. S. Gordon and R. W. Libby. N. Scituate, Mass.: Duxbury Press, 1976.

Kutner, S. J. Sex guilt and the sexual behavior sequence. *J. Sex Res.* 7 (1971): 107–115.

Labrum, A. H. Menopausal symptoms: Distinguishing psychogenic from physiological. *Med. Aspects Hum. Sexuality*, Feb. 1980, pp. 75–76.

Lachenbruch, P. A. Frequency and timing of intercourse: Its relation to the probability of conception. *Pop. Stud.* 21 (1967): 23–31.

Landau, R. L. Gonads, Disorders of. *Encyclopaedia Britannica*, 1963.
     What you should know about estrogens. *J. Am. Med. Assoc.* 241 (1979): 47–51.

Landis, J. T., and Landis, M. G. *Building a successful marriage.* 4th ed. Englewood Cliffs, N.J.: Prentice-Hall, 1963.
     Building a successful marriage. 5th ed. Englewood Cliffs, N.J.: Prentice-Hall, 1968.

Lane, M. E. Care and inspection of diaphragms. *Med. Aspects Hum. Sexuality*, August 1980, pp. 107–110.

Langmyhr, G. J. Varieties of coital positions: Advantages and disadvantages. *Med. Aspects Hum. Sexuality*, June 1976, pp. 128–139.

LaRocque, M. A., and Cosgrove, M. D. Priapism. *Med. Aspects Hum. Sexuality*, June 1976, pp. 69–70.

Larsen, K. S., Reed, M., and Hoffman, S. Attitudes of heterosexuals toward homosexuality: A Likert-type scale and construct validity. *J. Sex Res.* 16 (1980): 245–257.

LaTorre, R. A., and Kear, K. Attitudes toward sex in the aged. *Arch. Sex. Behav.* 6 (1977):203–213.

Laury, G. V. Sensual activities of the aging couple. *Med. Aspects Hum. Sexuality*, Jan. 1980a, pp. 32–36.
     Sex in men over forty. *Med. Aspects Hum. Sexuality*, Feb. 1980b, pp. 65–71.

Layman, W. A. The "saint or sinner" syndrome: separation of love and sex by women. *Med. Aspects Hum. Sexuality,* Aug. 1976, pp. 46–53.

Lear, H. Little ejaculatory sensation. *Med. Aspects Hum. Sexuality,* Aug. 1972, p. 106.

Leboyer, F. *Birth without violence.* New York: Knopf, 1975.

Lederer, W. J., and Jackson, D. D. *The mirages of marriage.* New York: Norton, 1968.

Ledger, W. J. Bacterial infections during pregnancy. In *Fetal and maternal medicine,* ed. E. J. Quilligan and N. Kretchmer. New York: Wiley, 1980.

Legal abortions up 8% in '76. *Houston Post,* June 14, 1977.

Legman, G. *An encyclopaedic outline of oral technique in genital excitation.* Quoted by "M," *The sensuous man.* New York: Lyle Stuart, 1971, p. 111.

Lehfeldt, H. Artificial insemination. In *The encyclopedia of sexual behavior,* Vol. I, ed. A. Ellis and A. Abarbanel, New York: Hawthorn Bks, 1961a.

    Contraception. In *The encyclopedia of sexual behavior,* Vol. I, ed. A. Ellis and A. Abarbanel. New York: Hawthorn Bks, 1961b.

Lehrman, N. *Masters and Johnson explained.* Chicago: Playboy Press, 1970.

Leiman, A. H., and Epstein, S. Thematic sexual responses as related to sexual drive and guilt. *J. Abnorm. Soc. Psychol.* 63 (1961): 169–175.

Lenz, W., Pfeiffer, R. A., and Tünte, W. Supernumerary chromosomes (trisomies) and maternal age. *Germ. Med. Monthly* 12 (1967): 27–30.

Lerner, M. J. Evaluation of performance as a function of performer's reward and attractiveness. *J. Pers. Soc. Psychol.* 1 (1965): 355–360.

Levie, L. H. Phimosis. *J. Sex Res.* 1 (1965): 189–200.

Levin, R. J. The Redbook report on premarital and extramarital sex. *Redbook,* Oct. 1975, pp. 38–44, 190.

Levin, R. J., and Levin, A. A Redbook report: Sexual pleasure. *Redbook,* Sept. 1975, pp. 51–58.

Levine, M. I. Sex education in the public elementary and high school curriculum. In *Human sexual development,* ed. D. L. Taylor. Philadelphia: Davis, 1970.

Levinger, G. Husbands' and wives' estimates of coital frequency. *Med. Aspects Hum. Sexuality,* Sept. 1970, pp. 42–57.

Levitt, E. E., and Brady, J. P. Sexual preferences in young adult males and some correlates. *J. Clin. Psychol.* 21 (1965): 347–354.

Lewis, G. M. *Practical dermatology for medical students and general practitioners.* Philadelphia: Saunders, 1955.

Lewis, H. R., and Lewis, M. E. Anal sex. *Sexology Today,* March 1980a, pp. 32–34.

    Vasectomy. *Sexology Today,* April 1980b, pp. 52–54.

    Sex and heart disease. *Sexology Today,* June 1980c, pp. 26–28.

LeWitter, M., and Abarbanel, A. Aging and sex. In *The encyclopedia of sexual behavior,* Vol. I, ed. A. Ellis and A. Abarbanel. New York: Hawthorn Bks, 1961.

Licklider, S. Jewish penile carcinoma. *J. Urol.* 86 (1961): 98.

Lieberman, E. J. Premarital coitus for upper- and lower-class women. *Med. Aspects Hum. Sexuality,* Feb. 1977, p. 16.

Lieberman, E. J., and Peck, E. *Sex and birth control: A guide for the young.* New York: Schocken, 1975.

Lief, H. I. Sex education in 106 medical schools. *Med. Aspects Hum. Sexuality,* Sept. 1974, p. 155.

Lief, H. I., and Ebert, R. K. Why sex education for medical students? In *Human sexuality: A health practitioner's text,* ed. R. Green. Baltimore: Williams & Wilkins, 1974.

Lief, H. I., Israel, S. L., Garcia, C. R., and Charny, C. W. Roundtable: Sex after 50. *Med. Aspects Hum. Sexuality,* Jan. 1968, pp. 41–47.

Liggins, G. C. The fetus and birth. In *Reproduction in mammals: Embryonic and fetal development,* ed. C. R. Austin and R. V. Short. New York: Cambridge Univ. Press, 1972.

Likoff, W. Coitus for cardiac patients at high altitudes. *Med. Aspects Hum. Sexuality,* Feb. 1977, p. 17.

Lindbergh, A. M. *Gift from the sea.* New York: Random House, 1965.

Lion, E. G., *et al. An experiment in the psychiatric treatment of promiscuous girls.* San Francisco: Dept. of Public Health, 1945.

Lipton, M. A. The "power" of pornography. *Psychiatry 1971.* New York: Medical World News, 1971.

Lloyd, C. W. *Human reproduction and sexual behavior.* Philadelphia: Lea, 1964.

Lloyd, J. A. Education about sex in medical schools. *Med. Aspects Hum. Sexuality,* June 1980, p. 131.

Lloyd, R. *For money or love: Boy prostitution in America.* New York: Vanguard, 1976.

LoPiccolo, J. Mothers and daughters: Perceived and real differences in sexual values. *J. Sex Res.* 9 (1973): 171–177.

LoPiccolo, L., and Heiman, J. Becoming orgasmic: A sexual growth program for women. (Films.) New York: Focus International, 1976.

Louria, D. B. Sexual use of amyl nitrite. *Med. Aspects Hum. Sexuality,* Jan. 1970, p. 89.

Lowry, T. P. First coitus. *Med. Aspects Hum. Sexuality,* May 1969, pp. 91–97.

Luciano, L. Birth control. *McCall's,* Aug. 1976, p. 37.

Luckey, E. B., and Nass, G. D. A comparison of sexual attitudes and behavior in an international sample. *J. Marriage Family* 31 (1969): 364–379.

Luffman, D., and Parcel, G. S. Adaptation of an instrument to measure premarital sexual permissiveness attitudes in young adolescents. *J. Sex Educ. Ther.* 6 (1979): 21–24.

Luttge, W. G. The role of gonadal hormones in the sexual behavior of the rhesus monkey and human: A literature survey. *Arch. Sex. Behav.* 1 (1971): 61–88.

Lutz, R. D. External penile prostheses. *Med. Aspects Hum. Sexuality,* Mar. 1976, pp. 123–125.

Lyon, P., and Rosen, D. H. Lesbian sex techniques. *Med. Aspects Hum. Sexuality,* Sept. 1974, p. 183.

"M." *The sensuous man.* New York: Lyle Stuart, 1971.

Maas, H. S., and Kuypers, J. A. *From thirty to seventy: A forty-year longitudinal study of adult life styles and personality.* San Francisco, Calif.: Jossey-Bass, 1974.

MacDonald, J. M. Comparative incidence of rape. *Med. Aspects Hum. Sexuality,* Jan. 1973, p. 185

    Group rape. *Med. Aspects Hum. Sexuality,* Feb. 1974, pp. 58–73.

MacDougald, D., Jr. Aphrodisiacs and anaphrodisiacs. In *The encyclopedia of sexual behavior,* Vol. I, ed. A. Ellis and A. Abarbanel, New York: Hawthorn Bks, 1961.

Mace, D. R. The danger of sex innocence. *Sexology,* Nov. 1970, pp. 50–52.

    The physician and marital sexual problems. *Med. Aspects Hum. Sexuality,* Feb. 1971a, pp. 50–62.

    Sex and marital enrichment. In *The new sexuality,* ed. H. A. Otto. Palo Alto: Science & Behavior, 1971b.

Emphasizing the positive in marriage. *Med. Aspects Hum. Sexuality*, July 1980, pp. 32–43.

Macklin, E. D. Cohabitation in college: Going very steady, *Psychol. Today*, Nov. 1974, pp. 53–59.

MacLean, P. D. New findings relevant to the evolution of psychosexual functions of the brain. In *Sex research: New developments*, ed. J. Money. New York: Holt, 1965.

Mahoney, E. R. Religiosity and sexual behavior among heterosexual college students. *J. Sex Res.* 16 (1980): 97–113.

Malcolm, A. H. Sex goes to college. *Today's Health*, Apr. 1971, pp. 26–29.

Mann, T. *The biochemistry of semen*. London: Methuen, 1954.

Marchant, D. J. Fundamentals of diagnosing breast disease. *Med. Aspects Hum. Sexuality*, July 1980, pp. 29–30.

Marmor, J. "Normal" and "deviant" sexual behavior. *J. Am. Med. Assoc.* 217 (1971): 165–170.

Marmor, J., ed. *Sexual inversion*. New York: Basic Bks, 1965.

Marmor, J., Finkle, A. L. Lazarus, A. A., Schumacher, S., Auerbach, A., Money, J., and Morris, N. Viewpoints: Why are some orgasms better than others? *Med. Aspects Hum. Sexuality*, Mar. 1971, pp. 12–23.

Marshall, S. Cystitis and urethritis in women related to sexual activity. *Med. Aspects Hum. Sexuality*, May 1974, pp. 165–168.

Martin, P. L. Sexual desire and response after oophorectomy. *Med. Aspects Hum. Sexuality*, July 1980, pp. 115–116.

Martinson, F. M. *Marriage and the American ideal*. New York: Dodd, Mead, 1960.

Maslow, A. H. *Motivation and personality*. New York: Harper, 1954.

Critique and discussion. In *Sex research: New developments*, ed. J. Money. New York: Holt, 1965.

Love in self-actualizing people. In *Sexual behavior and personality characteristics*, ed. M. F. DeMartino, New York: Grove, 1966a.

Self-esteem (dominance-feeling) and sexuality in women. In *Sexual behavior and personality characteristics*, ed. M. F. DeMartino, New York: Grove, 1966b.

Motivation and personality, 2d ed. New York: Harper, 1970.

Masters, R. E. L. *Patterns of incest*. New York: Julian Press, 1963.

Masters, W. H. The sexual response cycle of the human female: II. Vaginal lubrication. *Ann. N.Y. Acad. Sci.* 83 (1959): 301–317.

The sexual response cycle of the human female: I. Gross anatomic considerations. *Western J. Surg., Obstet. Gynecol.* 68 (1960): 57–72.

Masters, W. H., and Johnson, V. E. The human female: Anatomy of sexual response. *Minn. Med.* 43 (1960a): 31–36.

Vaginal pH: The influence of the male ejaculate. In *Report of the thirty-fifth Ross conference, endocrine dysfunction and infertility*. Columbus, Ohio: Ross Laboratories, 1960b.

Intravaginal environment: I. A lethal factor. *Fertility Sterility* 12 (1961a): 560–580.

Orgasm, Anatomy of the female. In *The encyclopedia of sexual behavior*, Vol. II, ed. A. Ellis and A. Abarbanel. New York: Hawthorn Bks, 1961b.

The physiology of the vaginal reproductive function. *Western J. Surg., Obstet. Gynecol.* 69 (1961c): 105–120.

The sexual response cycle of the human female: III. The clitoris: Anatomic and clinical considerations. *Western J. Surg., Obstet. Gynecol.* 70 (1962): 248–257.

The clitoris: An anatomic baseline for behavioral investigation. In *Determinants of human sexual behavior*, ed. G. W. Winokur. Springfield, Ill.: C. C. Thomas, 1963a.

The sexual response of the human male: I. Gross anatomic considerations. *Western J. Surg., Obstet. Gynecol.* 71 (1963b): 85–95.

Sexual response: Part II. Anatomy and physiology. In *Human reproduction and sexual behavior*, ed. C. W. Lloyd, Philadelphia: Lea, 1964.

The sexual response cycle of the human female: 2. The clitoris: Anatomic and clinical considerations. In *Sex research: New developments*, ed. J. Money. New York: Holt, 1965a.

The sexual response cycles of the human male and female: Comparative anatomy and physiology. In *Sex and behavior*, ed. F. A. Beach. New York: Wiley, 1965b.

Human sexual response. Boston: Little, 1966.

Major questions in human sexual response. A lecture presented to the Harris County Medical Society, Houston, Mar. 1967.

Human sexual inadequacy. Boston: Little, 1970.

Sexual values and sexual function. A paper delivered at the fortieth anniversary meeting of the Marriage Council of Philadelphia, Philadelphia, Dec. 1971.

The pleasure bond: A new look at sexuality and commitment. Boston: Little, 1975.

Homosexuality in perspective. Boston: Little, Brown, 1979.

Masterson, J. F. Adolescents and the sexual evolution. *Sex. Behav.*, June 1971, pp. 3–9.

Mathis, J. L. The exhibitionist. *Med. Aspects Hum. Sexuality*, June 1969, pp. 89–101.

The sexual tease. *Med. Aspects Hum. Sexuality*, Dec. 1970, pp. 21–25.

Maultsby, M. C., Jr., *Help yourself to happiness.* Boston: Marlborough House, 1975.

May, R. *Love and will.* New York: Norton, 1969.

Mazur, R. Men's sexual health: A radical approach. *Sexology Today*, Oct. 1980, pp. 44–49.

Mazur, T., and Money, J. Prenatal influences and subsequent sexuality. In *Handbook of human sexuality*, ed. B. B. Wolman and J. Money. Englewood Cliffs, New Jersey: Prentice-Hall, 1980.

McCaghy, C. H. Child molesting. *Sex. Behav.*, Aug. 1971, pp. 16–24.

McCarthy. B. W., Ryan, M., and Johnson, F. *Sexual awareness.* San Francisco: Boyd & Fraser, 1975.

McCary, J. L. *An introduction to sexology, a neglected subject.* Houston: Pierre St. Le Macs, 1966.

Sexual myths and fallacies. New York: Van Nostrand Reinhold, 1971.

Nymphomania: A case history. *Med. Aspects Hum. Sexuality*, Nov. 1972, pp. 192–202.

Sexual advantages of middle-aged men. *Med. Aspects Hum. Sexuality*, Dec. 1973, pp. 139–153.

Orgasm by nipple stimulation. *Med. Aspects Hum. Sexuality*, Sept. 1974, p. 190.

Freedom and growth in marriage. Santa Barbara, Calif.: Wiley, 1975.

Freedom and growth in marriage. 2nd ed. New York: Wiley, 1980.

McCary, J. L., and Copeland, D. R., eds. *Modern views of human sexual behavior.* Palo Alto, Calif.: Science Res. Assocs, 1976.

McCary, J. L., and Flake, M. H. The role of bibliotherapy and sex education in counseling for sexual problems. *Professional Psychol.* 2 (1971): 353–357.

McCary, J. L., and McElhaney, M. *The abbreviated Bible,* New York: Van Nostrand Reinhold, 1971.

McCary, S. P. The interrelationship between relevant sex variables and individuals' reported ages and sources of information for learning and experiencing sexual concepts. Doctoral dissertation, University of Houston, 1976.

Ages and sources of information for learning about and experiencing sexual concepts as reported by 43 university students. *J. Sex Educ. Ther.* 4 (1978): 50–53.

McCormack, W. M. Sexually transmitted urethritis in men. *Med. Aspects Hum. Sexuality,* Nov. 1976, pp. 124–129.

McDonald, D. F. Peyronie's disease. *Med. Aspects Hum. Sexuality,* Sept. 1974, pp. 155, 171.

McGinnis, T. C., and Ayres, J. U. *Open family living: A new approach to enriching your life together.* New York: Doubleday, 1976.

McGuire, T. F., and Steinhilber, R. M. Frigidity, the primary female sexual dysfunction. *Med. Aspects Hum. Sexuality,* Oct. 1970, pp. 108–123.

McLaren, A. The embryo. In *Reproduction in mammals: Embryonic and fetal development,* ed. C. R. Austin and R. V. Short. New York: Cambridge Univ. Press, 1972.

Mead, M. *Coming of age in Samoa.* New York: Morrow, 1928.

Medical science notes. *Sexology,* June 1961a, p. 790.

Sexology, July 1961b, p. 862.

Sexology, Aug. 1961c, p. 70.

Sexology, Oct. 1961d, p. 214.

Melody, G. F. Role of the clitoris. *Med. Aspects Hum. Sexuality,* June 1970, p. 116.

Melzack, R. The perception of pain. *Sci. Am.* 204 (1961): 41–49.

Menaker, J. S. "Engagement" ovaries. *Sexology,* Aug. 1961, pp. 49–53.

Mendelson, J. H. Marihuana and sex. *Med. Aspects Hum. Sexuality,* Nov. 1976, pp. 23–24.

Menninger, K. A., and Menninger, J. L. *Love against hate.* Reprint. New York: Harcourt, 1959.

Menninger, R. W. Decisions in sexuality: An act of impulse, conscience, or society? *Med. Aspects Hum. Sexuality,* June 1974, pp. 56–85.

Mestman, J. H. Thyroid and parathyroid diseases in pregnancy. In *Fetal and maternal medicine,* ed. E. J. Quilligan and N. Kretchmer. New York: Wiley, 1980.

Metz, C. W. Cytology. *Encyclopaedia Britannica,* 1963.

Miller, C., Byrne, D., Fisher, W. A., and White, L. Affective and attributional responses to communicating a sexual message. Paper presented at the Psychonomic Society Meeting, St. Louis, Mo., Nov. 1976.

Miller, M. A., and Leavell, L. C. *Kimber-Gray-Stackpole's anatomy and physiology.* 16th ed. New York: Macmillan Pub. Co., 1972.

Mobley, D. F. Relation of sexual habits to prostatitis. *Med. Aspects Hum. Sexuality,* Nov. 1975, p. 75.

Money, J. Phantom orgasm in the dreams of paraplegic men and women. *Arch. Gen. Psychiat.* 3 (1960): 373–382.

Psychosexual differentiation. In *Sex research: New developments,* ed. J. Money. New York: Holt, 1965.

Influence of hormones on psychosexual differentiation. *Med. Aspects Hum. Sexuality,* Nov. 1968a, pp. 32–42.

Sex errors of the body. Baltimore: Johns Hopkins Univ. Press, 1968b

Phantom orgasm in paraplegics. *Med. Aspects Hum. Sexuality,* Jan. 1970a, pp. 90–97.

Clitoral size and erotic sensation. *Med. Aspects Hum. Sexuality,* Mar. 1970b, p. 95.

The need for sex rehearsal play. *Sexology Today,* May 1980a, pp. 21–24.

Love and love sickness: The science of sex, gender difference, and pair-bonding. Baltimore: Johns Hopkins University Press, 1980b.

Money, J., and Alexander, D. Eroticism and sexual function in developmental anorchia and hyporchia with pubertal failure. *J. Sex Res.* 3 (1967): 31–47.

Money, J., and Bohmer, C. Prison sexuality: Two personal accounts of masturbation, homosexuality, and rape. *J. Sex Res.* 16 (1980): 258–266.

Money, J., and Ehrhardt, A. A. *Man and woman, boy and girl: The differentiation and dimorphism of gender identity from conception to maturity.* Baltimore: The Johns Hopkins University Press, 1972.

Money, J., and Wiedeking, C. Gender identity/role: Normal differentiation and its transpositions. In *Handbook of human sexuality,* ed. B. B. Wolman and J. Money. Englewood Cliffs, New Jersey: Prentice-Hall, 1980.

Money, J., and Yankowitz, R. The sympathetic-inhibiting effects of the drug Ismelin on human male eroticism, with a note on Mellaril. *J. Sex Res.* 3 (1967): 69–82.

Montagu, A. Smoking, pregnancy and sex. *Sexology,* Nov. 1963, pp. 220–222.

Sex made to order. *Sexology,* Jan. 1964, pp. 384–386.

Moore, J. E. Problematic sexual behavior. In *The individual, sex, and society,* ed. C. B. Broderick and J. Bernard. Baltimore: Johns Hopkins Univ. Press, 1969.

Moore, S. L. My most unusual sexual case: Satyriasis. *Med. Aspects Hum. Sexuality,* May 1980, pp. 110–111.

Morrow, L. Of abortion and the unfairness of life. *Time,* Aug. 1, 1977.

Mosher, D. L., and Cross, H. J. Sex guilt and premarital sexual experiences of college students. *J. Consult. Clin. Psychol.* 36 (1971): 27–32.

Mozes, E. B. The technique of wooing. *Sexology,* July 1959, pp. 756–760.

Premature ejaculation. *Sexology,* Nov. 1963, pp. 274–276.

Mozley, P. Devaluation of sex for older people. *Med. Aspects Hum. Sexuality,* Oct. 1974, pp. 126, 221.

Mudd, E. H. The couple as a unit: Sexual, social, and behavioral considerations to reproductive barriers. *J. Marital Fam. Ther.* 6 (1980): 23–28.

Mueller, G. O. W. Sex law reform. *Sexology,* June 1965, pp. 742–744.

Muller, H. J. Gene. *Encyclopaedia Britannica,* 1963.

Murdock, G. P. *Our primitive contemporaries.* New York: Macmillan, 1934.

Murstein, B. I. *Love, sex, and marriage through the ages.* New York: Springer, 1974.

Nadler, R. P. Approach to psychodynamics of obscene telephone calls. *Med. Aspects Hum. Sexuality,* Aug. 1968, pp. 28–33.

Najem, G. R. Incidence of VD among adolescents. *Med. Aspects Hum. Sexuality,* Oct. 1976, p. 117.

National Center for Health Statistics. *Age at menarche.* Series 11, No. 133. Washington, D.C.: Dept. of Health, Education and Welfare, 1974.

Natality. *Vital statistics of the United States, 1974.* Washington, D.C.: U.S. Government Printing Office, 1976.

National Institute of Allergy and Infectious Diseases. *Sexually transmitted diseases.* DHEW Publication No. (NIH) 76–909. Washington, D.C.: Government Printing Office, 1976.

Naughton, E. Cervical cancer. *Houston Post,* June 4, 1974.

Neiger, S. Increasing your sex pleasure. *Sexology,* May 1968a, pp. 656–659.

Sex positions. *Sexology,* June 1968b, pp. 730–733.

Overcoming sexual inadequacy. (Tapes.) Chicago: Human Dev. Institute, 1973.

Netter, F. H. *Reproductive system.* Summit. N.J.: CIBA Pharmaceutical Products, 1961.

Neu, C., and DiMascio, A. Variations in the menstrual cycle. *Med. Aspects Hum. Sexuality,* Feb. 1974, pp. 164–180.

Neubardt, S. *Contraception.* New York: Pocket Bks, 1968.

Neubeck, G. *Extra-marital relationships.* Englewood Cliffs, N.J.: Prentice-Hall, 1969.

Neumann, G. Abortion. In *The encyclopedia of sexual behavior,* Vol. I, ed. A. Ellis and A. Abarbanel. New York: Hawthorn Bks, 1961.

New English Bible, The. London: British and Foreign Bible Soc., 1972.

New forms of IUD's promise improvements in safety. *Houston Chronicle,* Feb. 10, 1980.

New pornography, The. *Time,* Apr. 16, 1965.

Newcomer, V. D. Scabies. *Med. Aspects Hum. Sexuality,* June 1976, pp. 67–68.

Newman. G., and Nichols, C. R. Sexual activities and attitudes in older persons. *J. Am. Med. Assoc.* 173 (1960): 33–35.

News of the month. *Sexology,* Oct. 1961a, p. 197.

Sexology, Dec. 1961b, p. 342.

Newth, D. R. Embryology and development, Animal. *Encyclopaedia Britannica,* 1973.

Ochsner, A. Adverse effect of smoking on sexuality. *Med. Aspects Hum. Sexuality,* Mar. 1976, p. 15.

O'Conner, L. R. *The photographic manual of sexual intercourse.* New York: Pent-R Bks, 1969.

Ogren, D. J. Sexual guilt, behavior, attitudes, and information. Doctoral dissertation, University of Houston, 1974.

Oill, P. A., and Guze, L. B. Diagnosis and treatment of anorectal gonorrhea. *Med. Aspects Hum. Sexuality,* June 1980, pp. 91–92.

Okie, S. The "supermale": Usually they're ordinary men. *International Herald Tribune,* Aug. 4, 1976.

Oliven, J. F. Youngest father on record. *Med. Aspects Hum. Sexuality,* Nov. 1974, p. 171.

Oliver, B. J., Jr. What the rapist is like. *Sexology*, July 1965, pp. 849–851.

Olsson, P. A. Penile prosthesis. *Med. Aspects Hum. Sexuality*, Nov. 1979, pp. 109–110.

O'Neill, N., and O'Neill, G. *Open marriage*, New York: Avon Bks, 1972.

Oriel, J. D. Chlamydial infections. *Med. Aspects Hum. Sexuality*, March 1980, p. 137.

Natural history of genital warts. *Br. J. Vener. Dis.* 47 (1971): 1–13.

Venereal transmission of genital warts. *Med. Aspects Hum. Sexuality*, Nov. 1973, p. 209.

Osofsky, J. D., and Osofsky, H. J. The psychological reaction of patients to legalized abortion. *Am. J. Orthopsychiat.* 42 (1972): 48–60.

Ottenheimer, L., Rosenbaum, S., Seidenberg, R., and Chernick, N. B. Should women ever pretend to climax? *Sex. Behav.*, Apr. 1971, pp. 11–13.

Otto, H. A. The new sexuality: An introduction. In *The new sexuality*, ed. H. A. Otto. Palo Alto: Science & Behavior, 1971.

Ovesey, L., and Meyers, H. Retarded ejaculation. *Med. Aspects Hum. Sexuality*, Nov. 1970, pp. 98–119.

Oziel, L. J. Revitalizing sexual relations after many years of marriage. *Med. Aspects Hum. Sexuality*, Aug. 1976, pp. 7–23.

Packard, V. *The sexual wilderness.* New York: McKay, 1968.

Paige, K. E. Women learn to sing the menstrual blues. *Psychol. Today*, Sept. 1973, pp. 41–46.

Parkes, A. S., and Bruce, H. M. Olfactory stimuli in mammalian reproduction. *Science* 134 (1961): 1049–1054.

Parlee, M. B. The premenstrual syndrome. *Psychol. Bull.* 80 (1973): 454–465.

Parsons, L., and Sommers, S. C. *Gynecology.* Philadelphia: Saunders, 1962.

Paulson, D. Hot tubs and reduced sperm counts. *Med. Aspects Hum. Sexuality*, Sept. 1980, p. 121.

Pauly, I. B., and Goldstein, S. G. Prevalence of significant sexual problems in medical practice. *Med. Aspects Hum. Sexuality*, Nov. 1970, pp. 48–63.

Pearlman, C. K. Frequency of intercourse in males at different ages. *Med. Aspects Hum. Sexuality*, Nov. 1972, pp. 92–113.

Penis prosthesis termed successful. *Houston Post*, Nov. 20, 1976.

Pepitone-Rockwell, F. Counseling women to be less vulnerable to rape. *Med. Aspects Hum. Sexuality*, Jan. 1980, pp. 145–146.

Peplau, L. A. What homosexuals want in relationships. *Psychology Today* 15 (1981): 28–38.

Pepmiller, E. G. How the handicapped make love. *Sexology Today*, Sept. 1980, pp. 30–34.

Peretti, P. O. Premarital sexual behavior between females and males of two middle-sized midwestern cities. *J. Sex Res.* 5 (1969): 218–225.

Pereyra, A. J. Relationship of sexual activities to cervical cancer. *Obstet. Gynecol.* 17 (1961): 154–159.

Persky, L. Sexual problems necessitating adult circumcision. *Med. Aspects Hum. Sexuality*, July 1975, p. 116.

Balanoposthitis. *Med. Aspects Hum. Sexuality*, Jan. 1980, pp. 105–106.

Pfeiffer, E., Verwoerdt, A., and Davis, G. C. Sexual behavior in middle life. In *Sexual development and behavior: Selected readings*, ed. A. M. Juhasz. Homewood, Ill.: Dorsey Press, 1973.

Piemme, T. E. Factors contributing to VD epidemic. *Med. Aspects Hum. Sexuality*, Aug. 1974, p. 117.

Pierson, E. C. Commentary on "Allergic reactions to contraceptives and douches" by A. A. Fisher. *Med. Aspects Hum. Sexuality*, Jan. 1975, pp. 121–125.

Pierson, E. C., and D'Antonio, W. V. *Female and male: Dimensions of human sexuality.* Philadelphia: Lippincott, 1974.

Pietropinto, A. P. Frequency of coitus after 20 years of marriage. *Med. Aspects Hum. Sexuality*, Sept. 1980, p. 5.

Pilpel, H. F. The voluntary approach: Population control. *Civil Liberties*, Nov. 1971.

Pineo, P. C. Disenchantment in the later years of marriage. *Marriage Family Living* 23 (1961): 3–11.

Pocs, O., and Godow, A. G. Can students view parents as sexual beings? *The Family Coordinator*, Jan. 1977, pp. 31–36.

   The shock of recognizing parents as sexual beings. In *Exploring human sexuality*, ed. D. Byrne and L. A. Byrne. New York: Crowell, 1977.

Poffenberger, T. Family life education in this scientific age. *Marriage Family Living* 21 (1959): 150–154.

   Individual choice in adolescent premarital sex behavior. *Marriage Family Living* 22 (1960): 324–330.

Pohlman, E. Premarital contraception: Research reports and problems. *J. Sex Res.* 5 (1969): 187–194.

Polsky, N. *Hustlers, beats and others.* Chicago: Aldine, 1967.

Pomeroy, W. B. Why we tolerate lesbians. *Sexology*, May 1965, pp. 652–654.

   The Masters-Johnson report and the Kinsey tradition. In *An analysis of human sexual response*, ed. R. Brecher and E. Brecher. New York: New Am. Lib., 1966a.

   Parents and homosexuality: I. *Sexology*, Mar. 1966b, pp. 508–511.

   Parents and homosexuality: II. *Sexology*, Apr. 1966c, pp. 588–590.

   Sexual myths of the 1970s. *Med. Aspects Hum. Sexuality*, Jan. 1977, pp. 62–74.

Porno plague, The. *Time*, Apr. 5, 1976.

Pornography: What is permitted is boring. *Time*, June 6, 1969.

Posner, L. B., Chidiac, J. E., and Posner, A. C. Pregnancy at age forty and over. *Obstet. Gynecol.* 17 (1961): 194–198.

Possible link studied between use of drug DES, sterility in sons. *The Houston Post*, Jan. 9, 1980.

Poutasse, E. F. Mechanism of pain in Peyronie's disease. *Med. Aspects Hum. Sexuality*, Feb. 1975, pp. 83, 87.

Pregnant women should not drink beverages with caffeine, FDA warns. *The Houston Post*, Sept. 5, 1980.

Primeau, C. Intercorrelations of sex variables among a selected group of psychologists. Doctoral dissertation, University of Houston, 1977.

Pritchard, J. A., and MacDonald, P. C. *Williams obstetrics*. 15th ed. New York: Appleton, 1976.

Proctor, E. B., Wagner, N. N., and Butler, J. C. The differentiation of male and female orgasm: An experimental study. In *Perspectives on human sexuality*, ed. N. Wagner. New York: Behavioral Pubs, 1974.

Pund, E. R., and Von Haam, E. Spirochetal and venereal diseases. In *Pathology*, ed. W. A. D. Anderson. St. Louis: Mosby, 1957.

Quality Educational Development, Inc. Sex education programs in the public schools of the United States. *Technical reports of the Commission on Obscenity and Pornography*, Vol. 10. Washington, D.C.: U.S. Government Printing Office, 1970.

Queenan, J. T. Erythroblatosis fetalis. In *Fetal and maternal medicine*, ed. E. J. Quilligan and N. Kretchmer. New York: Wiley, 1980.

Quinn, R. W. Epidemiology of gonorrhea. *South. Med. Bull.* 59, no. 2 (1971): 7–12.

Raboch, J. Will hormones increase your sex power? *Sexology*, May 1970a, pp. 9–12.

—— Penis size: An important new study. *Sexology*, June 1970b, pp. 16–18.

Rada, R. T. Alcohol and rape. *Med. Aspects Hum. Sexuality*, Mar. 1975, pp. 48–60.

—— Commonly asked questions about the rapist. *Med. Aspects Hum. Sexuality*, Jan. 1977, pp. 47–56.

Rainwater, L. Some aspects of lower class sexual behavior. *J. Soc. Issues* 22, no. 2 (1966): 96–108.

—— Some aspects of lower class sexual behavior. *Med. Aspects Hum. Sexuality*, Feb. 1968, pp. 15–25.

Ramey, E. Men's cycles (they have them too, you know). *Ms.*, Spring 1972, pp. 8–14.

Ramsey, G. The sex information of younger boys. *Am. J. Orthopsychiat.* 13 (1943): 347–352.

Reassessing the Pill's risks. *TIme*, June 30, 1980.

Rector, F. The unusual case of breast-feeding fathers. *Sexology*, July 1970, pp. 33–34.

Rees, B., and Zimmerman, S. The effects of formal sex education on the sexual behaviors and attitudes of college students. *J. Am. Coll. Health Assoc.* 22 (1974): 370–371.

Reevy, W. R. Child sexuality. In *The encyclopedia of sexual behavior*, Vol. I, ed. A. Ellis and A. Abarbanel. New York: Hawthorn Bks, 1961.

Reichlin, S. Relationship of the pituitary gland to human sexual behavior. *Med. Aspects Hum. Sexuality*, Feb. 1971, pp. 146–154.

Reiss, I. L. How and why America's sex standards are changing. *Trans-action* 5, no. 4 (1960a): 26–32.

—— *Premarital sexual standards in America*. Glencoe, Ill.: Free Press, 1960b.

—— Sexual codes in teen-age culture. *The Annals*, Nov. 1961a, pp. 53–62.

—— Standards of sexual behavior. In *The encyclopedia of sexual behavior*, Vol. II, ed. A. Ellis and A. Abarbanel. New York: Hawthorn Bks, 1961b.

—— Premarital sexual standards. In *Human sexuality in medical education and practice*, ed. C. E. Vincent. Springfield, Ill.: C. C. Thomas, 1968.

—— The influence of contraceptive knowledge on premarital sexuality. *Med. Aspects Hum. Sexuality*, Feb. 1970, pp. 71–86.

—— Premarital sex codes: The old and the new. In *Sexuality: A search for perspective*, ed. D. L. Grummon and A. M. Barclay. New York: Van Nostrand Reinhold, 1971.

—— Toward a sociology of the heterosexual love relationship. In *Love, marriage, family: A developmental approach*, ed. M. E. Lasswell and T. E. Laswell. Glenview, Ill.: Scott, 1973.

—— Heterosexual relationships. In *Human sexuality: A health practitioner's text*, ed. R. Green. Baltimore: Williams & Wilkins, 1974.

—— Adolescent sexuality. In *Sex and the life cycle*, ed. W. W. Oaks, G. A. Melchiode, and I. Ficher. New York: Grune, 1976.

Revitch, E., and Weiss, R. G. The pedophiliac offender. *Dis. Nerv. System* 23 (1962): 73–78.

Reyner, F. C. Venereal factor in cervical Ca. *Med. Aspects Hum. Sexuality*, Aug. 1975, p. 77.

Reyniak, J .V. Changes in breast size during menstrual cycle. *Med. Aspects Hum. Sexuality*, June 1976, pp. 81, 84.

Rhythm-linked birth control device unveiled. *Houston Chronicle*, June 30, 1977.

Riedman, S. R. Change of life. *Sexology*, July 1961, pp. 808–813.

Rizzo, J. M. How guilt got into sex. *Sexology*, Aug. 1968, pp. 64–67.

Robbins, E. S., Herman, M., and Robbins, L. Sex and arson: Is there a relationship? *Med. Aspects Hum. Sexuality*, Oct. 1969, pp. 57–64.

Robertson, W. B. Maternal-infant nutrition. In *Fetal and maternal medicine*, ed. E. J. Quilligan and N. Kretchmer. New York: Wiley, 1980.

Robinson, I., King, K., Dudley, C., and Clune, F. Changes in sexual behavior and attitudes of college students. *Family Coordinator* 16 (1968): 119–124.

Rodgers, D. A., Ziegler, F. J., Prentiss, R. J., and Martin, P. L. Comparisons of nine contraceptive procedures by couples changing to vasectomy or ovulation suppression medication. *J. Sex Res.* 1 (1965): 87–96.

Rosato, D. J., and Kleger, B. Is cervical cancer a venereally transmitted disease? *Med. Aspects Hum. Sexuality*, Mar. 1970, pp. 82–92.

Rosen, H. S. A survey of the sexual attitudes and behavior of mate-swappers in Houston, Texas. Master's thesis, University of Houston, 1971.

Rosen, L. R. Enjoying sex during pregnancy. *Sexology Today*, March 1980, pp. 50–53.

Rosenbaum, S. Pretended orgasm. *Med. Aspects Hum. Sexuality*, Apr. 1970, pp. 84–96.

Rothschild, Lord. X and Y spermatozoa. *Nature* 187 (1960): 253–254.

Rotkin, I. D. Epidemiology of cancer of the cervix: III. Sexual characteristics of a cervical cancer population. *Am. J. Public Health* 57 (1967): 815.

Rowan, R. L. "Honeymoon cystitis" and other bladder problems. *Sexology*, Sept. 1964, pp. 118–120.

Rubin, E., Lieber, C. S., Altman, K., Gordon, G. G., and Southren, A. L. Prolonged ethanol consumption increases testosterone metabolism in the liver. *Science* 191 (1976): 563–564.

Rubin, I. Birth control pills for men. *Sexology*, Aug. 1961, pp. 12–15.

    Sex over 65. In *Advances in sex research*, ed. H. G. Beigel. New York: Harper, 1963.

    Should students learn birth control? *Sexology*, Feb. 1964a, pp. 449–451.

    Sex needs after 65. *Sexology*, June 1964b, pp. 769–771.

    The electric vibrator and frigidity. *Sexology*, Oct. 1964c. pp. 156–158.

    Is there a sex revolution? *Sexology*, Nov. 1965a, pp. 220–222.

    Sexual life after sixty. New York: Basic Bks, 1965b.

    The new Kinsey report. *Sexology*, Feb. 1966a, pp. 443–446.

    Sex after forty—and after seventy. In *An analysis of human sexual response*, ed. R. Brecher and E. Brecher. New York: New Am. Lib., 1966b.

    Changing college sex: New Kinsey report. *Sexology*, June 1968, pp. 780–782.

    The prostitute and her customer. *Sexology*, June 1969a, pp. 785–787.

    New sex findings. *Sexology*, Nov. 1969b, pp. 65–66.

    New sex findings. *Sexology*, Jan. 1970a, pp. 67–68.

    Sexual life in the later years. SIECUS study guide no. 12. New York: SIECUS, 1970b.

New sex findings: Some trends and implications. In *The new sexuality*, ed. H. A. Otto. Palo Alto: Science & Behavior, 1971.

Ruff, C. F., Templer, D. I., and Ayers, J. L. The intelligence of rapists. *Arch. Sex. Behav.* 5 (1976): 327–329.

Russell, M. Sterilization. In *The encyclopedia of sexual behavior*, Vol. II, ed. A. Ellis and A. Abarbanel. New York: Hawthorn Bks, 1961.

Rutledge, A. L. Sex during pregnancy. *Sexology*, Feb. 1964, pp. 483–485.

Ryder, N. B. Contraceptive failure in the United States. *Fam. Plann. Perspect.* 5 (1973): 133–144.

Sadoff, R. L. Myths regarding the sex criminal. *Med. Aspects Hum. Sexuality*, July 1969, pp. 64–74.

Safier, B. *A psychiatric approach to the treatment of promiscuity*. New York: Am. Social Hygiene Assoc., 1949.

Sagarin, E. Prison homosexuality and its effect on post-prison sexual behavior. *Psychiatry* 39 (1976): 245–257.

Sager, C. J. Editorial. *J. Sex Marital Ther.* 2 (1976): 3–5.

Saghir, M. T., and Robins, E. *Male and female homosexuality: A comprehensive investigation*. Baltimore: Williams & Wilkins, 1973.

Salzman, L. Recently exploded sexual myths. *Med. Aspects Hum. Sexuality*, Sept. 1967, pp. 6–11.

Understanding adulterous behavior by men. *Med. Aspects Hum. Sexuality*, Aug. 1980, pp. 117–118.

Salzman, L., Meschan, R., Goldsmith, J., Lerner, H. E., and Steg, J. Viewpoints: Why do some women fall in love with men who are "heels"? *Med. Aspects Hum. Sexuality*, Sept. 1980, pp. 106–119.

Sandberg, E. C. Psychological aspects of contraception. In *The sexual experience*, ed. B. J. Sadock, H. I. Kaplan, and A. M. Freedman, Baltimore: Williams & Wilkins, 1976.

Sandler, J., Myerson, M., and Kinder, B. N. *Human sexuality: Current perspectives*. Tampa, Florida: Mariner, 1980.

Schering Corporation. *Sex endocrinology: A handbook for the medical and allied professions*. Bloomfield: Schering Corporation, Medical Research Division, 1944.

Schmidt, G. Male—female differences in sexual arousal and behavior during and after exposure to sexually explicit stimuli. *Arch. Sex. Behav.* 4 (1975): 353–364.

Schmidt, G., and Sigusch, V. Sex differences in responses to psychosexual stimulation by films and slides. *J. Sex Res.* 6 (1970): 268–283.

Schmidt, G., Sigusch, V., and Schäfer, S. Responses to reading erotic stories: Male—female differences. *Arch. Sex. Behav.* 2 (1973): 181–199.

Schneidman, H. Shaving pubic hair unnecessary for pediculosis pubis. *Med. Aspects Hum. Sexuality*, August 1980, pp. 6–11.

Schoenfeld, C. Effect of caffeine on sperm motility. *Med. Aspects Hum. Sexuality*, Feb. 1975, p. 82.

Schofield, M. G., *et al. The sexual behavior of young people*. London: Longmans, Ltd., 1965.

Schull, W. J., and Neel, J. V. *The effects of inbreeding on Japanese children*. New York: Harper, 1965.

Schuster, D. H., and Schuster, L. Speculative mechanisms affecting sex ratio. *J. Genet. Psychol.* 121 (1972):245–254.

Schwartz, L. B. Sexual behavior. *Encyclopaedia Britannica*, 1973.

Schwartz, M. F., Kolodny, R. C., and Masters, W. H. Plasma testosterone levels of sexually functional and dysfunctional men. *Arch. Sex. Beh.* 9 (1980): 355–365.

Science notes. *Sexology*, Oct, 1962, p. 214.

   Sexology, Nov. 1964, p. 281.

   Sexology, Sept. 1969, p. 14.

Scott, M. D. Turner's syndrome. *Med. Aspects Hum. Sexuality*, Sept. 1980, pp. 87–88.

Searle, G. D., and Co. *A prescription for family planning: The story of Enovid.* New York: G. D. Searle, 1964.

Sebastian, J. A. Cervical cancer a sexually transmitted disease. *Med. Aspects Hum. Sexuality*, October 1980, pp. 75–124.

Secondary syphilis. *Med. Aspects Hum. Sexuality*, July 1971, pp. 82–101.

Semans, J. H. Premature ejaculation: A new approach. *South. Med. J.* 49 (1956): 353–358.

Sentnor, M., and Hult, S. Erotic zones—Facts and superstitions. *Sexology*, Sept. 1961, pp. 76–81.

Settlage, D. S. F., Baroff, S., and Cooper, D. Sexual experience of younger teenage girls seeking contraceptive assistance for the first time. *Fam. Plann. Perspect.* 5 (1973): 223–226.

Sex behavior of older women. *Sexology*, June 1966, p. 734.

Sex in the news. *Sexology*, Oct. 1963, p. 209.

   Sexology, Jan. 1967, p. 421.

   Sexology, Nov. 1970, p. 7.

Sex offenders good parole risk. *Sexology*, June 1963, p. 768.

Sexual maturity and climate. *Sexology*, June 1961, p. 773.

Shafer, N. Vaginal discharges. *Sexology*, Mar. 1966, pp. 531–533.

   Catch prostate cancer early! *Sexology*, July 1968, pp. 823–826.

Shaffer, J. W. Masculinity—femininity and other personality traits in gonadal aplasia (Turner's syndrome). In *Advances in sex research*, ed. H. G. Beigel. New York: Harper, 1963.

Shah, F., and Zehrik, M. Sexuality in adolescence. In *Handbook of human sexuality*, ed. B. B. Wolman and J. Money. Englewood Cliffs, New Jersey: Prentice-Hall, 1980.

Shapiro, S. S. Artificial insemination. *Med. Aspects Hum. Sexuality*, May 1980, pp. 97–98.

Shaw, W. *Operative gynaecology*. Baltimore: Williams & Wilkins, 1954.

Shepard, T. H., and Lemire, R. J. Teratology. In *Fetal and maternal medicine*, ed. E. J. Quilligan and N. Kretchmer. New York: Wiley, 1980.

Sheppe, W. M., Jr. Physicians' preparedness to counsel for sex problems. *Med. Aspects Hum. Sexuality*, Mar. 1976, p. 8.

Sherman, J. K. Freezing human sperm. *Sexology*, July 1965, pp. 812–815.

Sherwin, R. V. Laws on sex crimes. In *The encyclopedia of sexual behavior*, Vol. II, ed. A. Ellis and A. Abarbanel. New York: Hawthorn Bks, 1961.

Shettles, L. B. Observations on human spermatozoa. *Bull. Sloane Hosp. Women* 6 (1960): 48.

   The great preponderance of human males conceived. *Am. J. Obstet. Gynecol.* 89 (1964): 130–133.

Predetermining children's sex. *Med. Aspects Hum. Sexuality*, June 1972, p. 172.

Shope, D. F. Orgasm in college girls. *Sexology*, May 1968a, pp. 711–715.

The orgastic responsiveness of selected college females. *J. Sex Res.* 4 (1968b): 206–219.

Short, R. V. Sex determination and differentiation. In *Reproduction in mammals: Embryonic and fetal development*, ed. C. R. Austin and R. V. Short. New York: Cambridge Univ. Press, 1972.

SIECUS. *Sexuality and man.* New York: Scribner, 1970.

Slavitz, H. Transsexualism: A radical crisis in gender identity. In *Sexuality today and tomorrow: Contemporary issues in human sexuality*, ed. S. Gordon and R. W. Libby. N. Scituate, Mass.: Duxbury Press, 1976.

Slovenko, R. Sex laws: Are they necessary? In *Sexuality: A search for perspective*, ed. D. L. Grummon and A. M. Barclay. New York: Van Nostrand Reinhold, 1971a.

Statutory rape. *Med. Aspects Hum. Sexuality*, Mar. 1971b, pp. 155–167.

Smartt, W. H., and Lighter, A. G. The gonorrhea epidemic and its control. *Med. Aspects Hum. Sexuality*, Jan. 1971, p. 96–115.

Smith, C. G. Effects of marijuana on male and female reproductive systems. *Med. Aspects Hum. Sexuality*, April 1980, pp. 10–15.

Smith, D. C., Prentice, R., Thompson, D. J., and Herrmann, W. L. Association of exogenous estrogen and endometrial carcinoma. *New Eng. J. Med.* 293 (1975): 1164–1167.

Smith, G. P. For unto us a child is—legally. *Am. Bar Assoc. J.* 56 (1970): 143–145.

Smith, L. Religion's response to the new sexuality. *SIECUS Rep.*, Nov. 1975, pp. 1, 14–15.

Smith, R. S. Voyeurism: A review of literature. *Arch. Sex. Behav.* 5 (1976): 585–608.

Smoking deters pregnancy. *Sexology*, Apr. 1968, p. 643.

Solnick, R. L., and Birren, J. E. Age and male erectile responsiveness. *Arch. Sex. Behav.* 6 (1977): 1–9.

Sonenschein, D. The ethnography of male homosexual relationships. *J. Sex Res.* 4 (1968): 69–83.

Sontag, S. The double standard of aging. In *Sexuality today and tomorrow: Contemporary issues in human sexuality*, ed. S. Gordon and R. W. Libby. N. Scituate, Mass.: Duxbury Press, 1976.

Sorenson, R. C. *Adolescent sexuality in contemporary America.* New York: World Pub., 1973.

Spanier, G. B. Formal and informal sex education as determinants of premarital sexual behavior. *Arch. Sex. Behav.* 5 (1976): 39–67.

Speidel, J. J. Knowledge of contraceptive techniques among a hospital population of low socio-economic status. *J. Sex Res.* 6 (1970): 284–306.

Sperling, E. Psychosexual development and cryptorchidism. *Med. Aspects Hum. Sexuality*, June 1980, pp. 93–94.

Spurr, G. A. Sex education and the handicapped. *J. Sex Educ. Ther.* 2, no. 2 (1976): 23–25.

Steen, E. B., and Montagu, A. *Anatomy and physiology*, Vol. 2. New York: Barnes & Noble, 1959.

Steen, E. B., and Price, J. H. *Human sex and sexuality.* New York: Wiley, 1977.

Steinhart, J. What women are learning about vibrators. *Sexology Today*, April 1980, pp. 17–21.

Steinhaus, A. H. *Toward an understanding of health and physical education.* Dubuque, Iowa: W. C. Brown, 1963.

Stiller, R. Electrically caused ejaculation. *Sexology,* Dec. 1962, pp. 321–322.

Common prostate problems. *Sexology,* July 1963, pp. 817–819.

The firebug and sex. *Sexology,* Nov. 1964, pp. 236–238.

Stiller, R., ed. *Illustrated sex dictionary.* New York: Health Publications, 1966.

Stokes, W. R., Montagu, A., Money, J., Rutledge, A. L., and Yoder, H. W. Is pornography harmful? *Sexology,* Aug. 1963, pp. 16–19.

Stone, A., and Stone, H. *A marriage manual.* New York: Simon & Schuster, 1952.

Storr, A. *Sexual deviation.* Baltimore: Penguin, 1964.

Story of the sperm. *Sexology,* Jan. 1965, pp. 379–381.

Sullivan, H. S. *Conceptions of modern psychiatry.* New York: Norton, 1953.

Sullivan, P. R. What is the role of fantasy in sex? *Med. Aspects Hum. Sexuality,* Apr. 1969, pp. 79–89.

Sullivan, W. Boys and girls are now maturing earlier. *New York Times,* Jan. 24, 1971.

Supreme Court agrees Congress can ban most welfare abortions. *The Houson Post,* July 1, 1980.

Tanner, J. M. *Growth at adolescence.* 2nd ed. Oxford: Blackwell Scientific Publications, 1962.

Growth and endocrinology of the adolescent. In *Endocrine and genetic diseases of childhood,* ed. L. Gardner. Philadelphia: Saunders, 1969.

Tanowitz, H. B. Parasitic gynecologic diseases. *Med. Aspects Hum. Sexuality,* Sept. 1974, pp. 45–63.

Tarail, M. Sex over 65. *Sexology,* Feb. 1962, pp. 440–443.

Tarr, J. D. F., and Lugar, R. R. Early infectious syphilis: Male homosexual relations as a mode of spread. *Calif. Med.* 93 (1960): 35–37.

Taub, W. Sex and infection: Venereal diseases. In *The sexual experience,* ed. B. J. Sadock, H. I. Kaplan, and A. M. Freedman. Baltimore: Williams & Wilkins, 1976.

Tauris, C. Good news about sex. *New York,* Dec. 6, 1976, pp. 51–67.

Teen-age sex: Letting the pendulum swing. *Time,* Aug. 21, 1972.

TeLinde, R. W. *Operative gynecology.* Philadelphia: Lippincott, 1953.

Terman, L. M. *Psychological factors in marital happiness.* New York: McGraw, 1938.

Thornburg, H. D. Age and first sources of sex information as reported by 88 college women. *J. Sch. Health* 40 (1970): 156–158.

Thorne, F. C. Ejaculatio praecox. *Dis. Nerv. System* 4 (1943): 273–275.

Thorpe, L. P., Katz, B., and Lewis, R. T. *The psychology of abnormal behavior.* New York: Ronald, 1961.

Tietze, C. Probability of pregnancy resulting from a single unprotected coitus. *Fertility Sterility* 11 (1960): 485–488.

History of contraceptive methods. *J. Sex Res.* 1 (1965): 69–85.

Fertility while breast feeding. *Med. Aspects Hum. Sexuality,* Nov. 1970, p. 90.

Tietze, C., Bongaarts, J., and Schearer, B. Mortality associated with the control of fertility. *Fam. Plann. Perspect.* 8 (1976): 6–13.

Tietze, C., and Lewit, S. Joint program for the study of abortion (JPSA): Early medical complications of legal abortion. *Stud. Fam. Plann.* 3 (1972): 97–122.

Townley, J. Prostitution: Should it be legalized? *Sexology Today,* May 1980 pp. 40–45.

Toxic shock illness cases rise. *The Houston Post,* August 29, 1980.

Trainer, J .B. *Physiologic foundations for marriage counseling.* St. Louis: Mosby, 1965.

Trice, E. R., Gayle, S., Jr., and Clark, F. A., Jr. The transmission of early infectious syphilis through homosexual practices. *Virginia Med. Monthly* 87 (1960): 132–134.

Turner, H. H. A syndrome of infantilism, congenital webbed neck and cubitus valgus. *Endocrinology* 23 (1938): 566.

Tuthill, J. F. Impotence. *Lancet* 1 (1955): 124–128.

Uddenberg, N. Mother—father and daughter—male relationships: A comparison. *Arch. Sex. Behav.* 5 (1976): 69–79.

Udry, J. R. *The social context of marriage*. Philadelphia: Lippincott, 1966.

Sex and family life. *Med. Aspects Hum. Sexuality*, Nov. 1968, pp. 66–82.

Ueno, M. The so-called coition death. *Jap. J. Legal Med.* 17 (1963): 535.

Unger, K. W. Medical problems caused by homosexual relations. *Med. Aspects Hum. Sexuality*, Feb. 1975, p. 152.

United Press International. Marijuana, impotency linked. *Houston Post*, Mar. 2, 1971a.

N.Y.C. pregnancy deaths decline. *Houston Post*, Apr. 27, 1971b.

Update: Smoking and pregnancy. *Family Health*, May 1979, p. 8.

U.S. Bureau of the Census. *Fertility indicators: 1970*. Current population reports, Series P-23, No. 36. Washington, D.C.: U.S. Government Printing Office, 1971.

U.S. Department of Health, Education and Welfare. Public Health Service. *Morbidity and mortality annual supplement summary 1969*. Public Health Service, Vol. 18, No. 54. Atlanta, Ga.: Center for Disease Control, 1970.

Venereal disease statistical letter 120, Aug. 1974.

Vance, E. B., and Wagner, N. N. Written descriptions of orgasm: A study of sex differences. *Arch. Sex. Beh.* 5 (1976): 87–94.

Van de Velde, T. H. *Ideal marriage: Its physiology and technique*. New York: Random House, 1957.

Van Den Haag, E. Love or marriage? In *Love, marriage, family: A developmental approach*, ed. M. E. Lasswell and T. E. Lasswell. Glenview, Ill.: Scott, 1973.

Van Emde Boas, C. Ten commandments for parents providing sex education. *J. Sex Educ. Ther.* 6 (1980): 19.

Van Lawick-Goodall, Jane. *In the shadow of man*. Boston: Houghton-Mifflin, 1971.

Vatsyayana. *The Kama sutra*. New York: Dutton, 1962.

Vaughan, V. C., and McKay, R. J., eds. *Nelson textbook of pediatrics*. 10th ed. Philadelphia: Saunders, 1975.

Vetri, D. The legal arena. Progress for gay civil rights. *J. of Homosexuality* 5 (1980): 25–34.

Vincent, C. E. *Unmarried mothers*. Glencoe, Ill.: Free Press, 1961.

The physician as counselor in postmarital and extramarital pregnancies. *Med. Aspects Hum. Sexuality*, Nov. 1967, pp. 34–41.

Unmarried mothers and pregnant brides. In *Human sexuality in medical education and practice*, ed. C. E. Vincent. Springfield, Ill.: C. C. Thomas, 1968.

Sex and the young married. *Med. Aspects Hum. Sex.*, Mar. 1969, pp. 13–23.

Illegitimacy. *Encyclopaedia Britannica*, 1973.

Vital Statistics Report. Final Mortality Statistics, 1977. NCHS, Vol. 28, No. 6 (Supplement), May 11, 1979.

Vizinczey, S. *In praise of older women*. London: Barrie & Rockliff, 1966.

Wabrek, A. J., and Wabrek, C. J. Vaginismus. *J. Sex Educ. Ther.* 2, no. 1 (1976): 21–24.

Wagner, N. N., and Solberg, D. A. Pregnancy and sexuality. *Med. Aspects Hum. Sexuality*, Mar. 1974, pp. 44–71.

Wake, F. R. Attitudes of parents towards the premarital sex behavior of their children and themsevles. *J. Sex Res.* 5 (1969): 170–177.

Walker, K. Erection disorders. *Sexology*, May 1963, pp. 696–698.

Wallace, D. H., and Wehmer, G. Evaluation of visual erotica by sexual liberals and conservatives. *J. Sex Res.* 8 (1972): 147–153.

Waller, W., and Hill, R. *The family*. New York: Dryden, 1951.

Walsh, R. H. The generation gap in sexual beliefs. *Sex. Behav.*, Jan. 1972, pp. 4–10.

Ward, D. A., and Kassebaum, G. G. Homosexuality: A mode of adaptation in a prison for women. *Soc. Problems* 12 (1964): 159–177.

Weaver, R. G. Scrotum and testes. *Med. Aspects Hum. Sexuality*, Oct. 1970, pp. 124–143.

Weideger, P. *Menstruation and menopause: The physiology and psychology, the myth and the reality*. New York: Knopf, 1976.

Weinberg, J. Sexuality in later life. *Med. Aspects Hum. Sexuality*, Apr. 1971, pp. 216–227.

Weinberg, M. S. Nudists. *Sex. Behav.*, Aug. 1971, pp. 51–55.

Weinberg, M. S., and Williams, C. J. *Male homosexuals: Their problems and adaptations*. New York: Oxford Univ. Press, 1974.

    Male homosexuals: Their problems and adaptations. In *Sex research: Studies from the Kinsey Institute*, ed. M. S. Weinberg. New York: Oxford Univ. Press, 1976.

Wershub, L. P. Male genital abnormalities which interfere with intercourse. *Med. Aspects Hum. Sexuality*, Sept. 1968, pp. 53–58.

Westoff, L. A., and Westoff, C. F. *From now to zero: Fertility, contraception and abortion in America*. Boston: Little, 1971.

Whiskin, F. E. The geriatric sex offender. *Med. Aspects Hum. Sexuality*, Apr. 1970, pp. 125–129.

Whitam, F. L. Childhood indicators of male homosexuality. *Arch. Sex. Behav.* 6 (1977): 89–96.

Whitehurst, R. N. Changing ground rules and emergent life-styles. In *Renovating marriage*, ed. R. W. Libby and R. N. Whitehurst. Danville, Calif.: Consensus Pubs, 1973.

Wiener, D. N. Sexual problems in clinical experience. In *The individual, sex, and society*, ed. C. B. Broderick and J. Bernard. Baltimore: Johns Hopkins Univ. Press, 1969.

Wilcox, D., and Hager, R. Toward realistic expectations for orgasmic response in women. *J. Sex Res.* 16 (1980): 162–179.

Williams, J. H. Sexuality in marriage. In *Handbook of human sexuality*, ed. B. B. Wolman and J. Money. Englewood Cliffs, New Jersey: Prentice-Hall, 1980.

Williams obstetrics. See Eastman and Hellman (1961); Hellman and Pritchard (1971); Pritchard and MacDonald (1976).

Williams, W. W. Semen variability. *Med. Aspects Hum. Sexuality*, Sept. 1974, pp. 67, 73.

Williamson, P. The erotic zones. *Sexology*, June 1961, pp. 740–743.

Willscher, M. K. Reversing vasectomy. *Med. Aspects Hum. Sexuality*, Aug. 1980, p. 6.

Wilson, M. A. *The ovulation method of birth regulation*. New York: Van Nostrand Reinhold, 1980.

Winchester, A. M. *The nature of human sexuality*. Columbus: Charles Merrill, 1973.

Winick, C. A study of consumers of explicitly sexual materials: Some functions served by adult movies. *Technical reports of the Commission on Obscenity and Pornography*, Vol. 4. Washington, D.C.: U.S. Government Printing Office, 1970.

Wise, T. N., and Meyer, J. K. Transvestism: Previous findings and new areas for inquiry. *J. Sex Marital Ther.*, 6 (1980): 116–128.

Witkin, M. H. Psychosexual myths and realities of mastectomy. *Med. Aspects Hum. Sexuality*, Dec. 1979, pp. 53–79.

Procedures to enhance female coital response. *Med. Aspects Hum. Sexuality*, Oct. 1980, pp. 87–88.

Wolbarst, A. L. The gynecic factor in the causation of male impotency. *N.Y. State J. Med.* 47 (1947): 1252–1255.

Wolchik, S. A., Beggs, V. E., Wincze, J. P., Sakheim, D. K., Barlow, D. H., and Mavissakalian, M. The effect of emotional arousal on subsequent sexual arousal in men. *J. Abnorm. Psychol.*, 89 (1980): 595–598.

Wolfenden, J. *Report of the committee on homosexual offenses and prostitution*. London: Her Majesty's Stationery Office, 1957.

Wolpe, J. *Psychotherapy by reciprocal inhibition*. Stanford: Stanford Univ. Press, 1958.

Wood, R. Popular sex superstitions. *Sexology*, June 1963, pp. 752–754.

Worley, R. J. Significance of 35-day menstrual cycles. *Med. Aspects Hum. Sexuality*, Aug. 1980, p. 11.

Wright, M. R., and McCary, J. L. Positive effects of sex education on emotional patterns of behavior. *J. Sex Res.* 5 (1969): 162–169.

Zarem, H. A. Breast augmentation. *Med. Aspects Hum. Sexuality*, May 1970, p. 145.

Zastrow, C. H. Self talk: A new theory to understanding and treating sexual problems. *J. Sex. Educ. Ther.* 6 (1979): 51–57.

Zehv, W. How men and women differ in sex. *Sexology*, May 1968, pp. 666–668.

Trying new positions in intercourse. *Sexology*, Jan. 1969, pp. 364–367.

Zelnik, M., and Kantner, J. F. Sexuality, contraception, and pregnancy among young unwed females in the United States. In Commission on Population Growth and the American Future, *Demographic and social aspects of population growth*. Washington, D.C.: U.S. Government Printing Office, 1972.

Sexual and contraceptive experience of young unmarried women in the United States, 1976 and 1971. *Fam. Plann. Perspect.* 9 (1977): 55–71.

Ziegler, F. J., Rodgers, D. A., and Kriegsman, S. A. Effect of vasectomy on psychological functioning. *Psychosomat. Med.* 28 (1966): 50–63.

Ziegler, F. J., Rodgers, D. A., and Prentiss, R. J. Psychosocial response to vasectomy. *Arch. Gen. Psychiat.* 31 (1969): 46–54.

Ziel, H. K., and Finkle, W. D. Increased risk of endometrial carcinoma among users of conjugated estrogens. *New Eng. J. Med.* 293 (1975): 1167–1170.

Zinsser, H. H. Sex and surgical procedures in the male. In *The sexual experience*, ed. B. J. Sadock, H. I. Kaplan, and A. M. Freedman. Baltimore: Williams & Wilkins, 1976.

Zuckerman, M. Sexual behavior of college students. In *Sex and the life cycle*, ed. W. W. Oaks, G. A. Melchiode, and I. Ficher. New York: Grune, 1976.

Zuckerman, M., Tushup, R., and Finner, S. Sexual attitudes and experience: Attitude and personality correlates and changes produced by a course in sexuality. *J. Consult. Clin. Psychol.* 44 (1976): 7–19.

Zuckerman, Z., Rodriguez-Rigau, L. J., Smith, K. D., and Steinberger, E. Frequency of distribution of sperm counts in fertile and infertile males. *Fertility Sterility* 28 (1977): 1310–1313.

Zussman, L., and Zussman, S. The Zussman lectures: Building sexual awareness. (Tapes and filmstrips.) New York: Focus International, 1977.

Glossary

Abdominal pregnancy   A type of displaced or ectopic pregnancy in which the embryo becomes attached to mislocated endometrial tissue in the abdominal wall.

Abortifacient   A drug or other agent that causes abortion.

Abortion   Premature expulsion from the uterus of the product of conception—a fertilized ovum, embryo, or nonviable fetus. Abortion can be *therapeutic*, indicating that a threat to the mother's life or possible fetal abnormality exists; or *elective*, indicating that it is performed at the request of the expectant parent(s). Either is termed *criminal* when performed contrary to existing laws. *Cf.* MISCARRIAGE.

Abstinence   A refraining from the use of or indulgence in certain foods, stimulants, or sexual intercourse.

Adolescence   The period of life between puberty (appearance of secondary sex characteristics) and adulthood (cessation of major body growth).

Adultery   Sexual intercourse between a married person and an individual other than his or her legal spouse.

Afterbirth   The placenta and fetal membranes expelled from the uterus following the birth of a child.

Agglutination test (or *clumping test*)   A popular pregnancy test in which the presence of the chorionic gonadotropic hormone is detected in the urine of the pregnant woman.

Amenorrhea   Absence of the menses (menstruation).

Amniocentesis (*amniotic tap*)   A procedure in which amniotic fluid is drawn from the amniotic sac surrounding the fetus and is subjected to microscopic analysis.

Amnion   A thin membrane forming the closed sac or "bag of waters" that surrounds the unborn child within the uterus and contains amniotic fluid in which the fetus is immersed.

Ampulla   A flasklike widening at the end of a tubular structure or canal.

Anal eroticism   Pleasurable sensations in the region of the anus.

Anaphrodisiac   A drug or medicine that reduces sexual desire.

Androgen   A steroid hormone producing masculine sex characteristics and having an influence on body and bone growth and on the sex drive.

Androgenital syndrome   Masculinization of the female anatomy because of the presence of androgen in the prenatal environment.

Androgen-insensitivity syndrome   Feminization of the male sex organs because of cellular insensitivity to androgen in the prenatal environment.

Anomaly   An irregularity or defect.

Anorchism   The congenital lack of both testicles.

Aphrodisiac   Anything, such as a drug or a perfume, that stimulates sexual desire.

Areola   The ring of darkened tissue surrounding the nipple of the breast.

Artificial insemination   Introduction of semen into the vagina or womb of a woman by artificial means.

Autoerotic   Pertaining to self-stimulation or erotic behavior directed toward one's self; frequently equated with masturbation.

Bartholin's glands   Two tiny glands in a female, located at either side of the entrance to the vagina.

Bestiality   A sexual deviation in which a person engages in sexual relations with an animal. *Cf.* ZOOPHILIA.

Birth canal   *See* VAGINA.

Birth control   Deliberate limitation of the number of children born—through such means as contraceptives, abstinence, the rhythm method, *coitus interruptus*, and the like.

Bisexual   Literally, having sex organs of both sexes, as in hermaphrodites; having a sexual interest in both sexes.

Blastocyst   The fertilized egg in the early stage of cell division when the cells form a hollow sphere.

Blastula   The embryonic stage of development in which the cells form a single-layered hollow sphere.

Body stalk   A complex connecting structure that attaches the embryo and placenta. It later develops into the umbilical cord.

Breech presentation   A birth position in which the baby is presented and delivered buttocks first.

Caesarean birth   (also *caesarean section*). Delivery of a child through a surgical incision in the abdominal and uterine walls.

Candidiasis   *See* MONILIASIS.

Carpopedal spasm   A spastic contraction of the hands and feet.

Castration   Removal of the gonads (sex glands)—the testicles in men, the ovaries in women.

Castration complex   In psychoanalytic theory, unconscious fears centering around injury or loss of the genitals as punishment for forbidden sexual desires; a male's anxiety about his manhood.

Celibacy   The state of being unmarried; abstention from sexual activity.

Cephalic presentation   A birth position in which the baby is presented and delivered head first.

Cervical cap   A contraceptive device shaped like a miniature diaphragm that fits over the cervix and is kept in place by suction.

Cervix   Neck; in the female, the narrow portion of the uterus or womb that forms its lower end and opens into the vagina.

Chancre   The sore or ulcer that is the first symptom of syphilis.

Chancroid   A highly contagious disease characterized by ulcerations at the points of physical contact and typically spread through sexual intercourse.

Change of life   *See* CLIMACTERIC, MENOPAUSE.

Chastity   Abstention from sexual intercourse.

Chordee   A downward curvature of the penis requiring corrective surgery; it may be associated with hypospadia or with urethral infection.

Chorion   The outermost envelope of the growing zygote (fertilized ovum), which later contributes to the formation of the placenta.

Chorionic gonadotropin (HCG)   A hormone released from the under-developed placenta within the fertilized egg that signals the corpus luteum to continue to secrete progesterone rather than degenerate. This continuation keeps the endometrium sensitized for blastocyst implantation.

Chromosomes   Rod-shaped bodies found in the nucleus of all cells that contain the genes, or hereditary factors. There are 22 pairs of *autosomal chromosomes*, which account for all the individual's hereditary characteristics. Sex is fixed by the 23rd or *sex-determining* chromosomal pair (X plus X or Y).

Circumcision   Surgical removal of the foreskin or prepuce of the penis.

Climacteric   The syndrome of physical and psychologic changes that occur at the termination of menstrual function (*i.e.*, reproductive capability) in the woman and reduction in sex-steroid production in both sexes; menopause; change of life.

Climax   *See* ORGASM.

Clitoris   (adj. *clitoral*). A small, highly sensitive nipple of flesh in the female, located just above the urethral opening in the upper triangle of the vulva.

Cloning   The exact duplication of a human being through genetic technology.

Coitus   Sexual intercourse between male and female, in which the penis in inserted into the vagina.

Coitus interruptus   (also *premature withdrawal*). The practice of withdrawing the penis from the vagina just before ejaculation.

Coitus reservatus   Prolonged coitus in which ejaculation is intentionally suppressed.

Colostrum   A thin, milky fluid secreted by the female breast just before and after childbirth.

Conception   The beginning of a new life, when an ovum (egg) is penetrated by a sperm, resulting in the development of an embryo; impregnation.

Condom   A contraceptive used by males consisting of a rubber or gut sheath that is drawn over the erect penis before coitus.

Congenital   Existing at birth, but not necessarily inherited.

Continence   A state of exercising self-restraint, especially in regard to the sex drive.

Contraception   The use of devices or drugs to prevent conception in sexual intercourse.

Coprophilia   A sexual deviation in which sexual gratification is associated with the act of defecation; a morbid interest in feces.

Copulation   Sexual intercourse; coitus.

Corona glandis   The rim surrounding the base of the glans penis in the male.

Corpus luteum   A yellow mass ("yellow body") that forms in the cavity of a ruptured graafian follicle within the ovary. It secretes the hormone progesterone.

Couvade   The practice among some cultures wherein the man suffers the same symptoms during pregnancy as those his partner, the pregnant mother, is experiencing.

Cowper's glands   Two glands in the male, one on each side of the urethra near the prostate, which secrete a mucoid material as part of the seminal fluid.

Crabs   *See* PEDICULOSIS PUBIS.

Cremaster   (adj. *cremasteric*). The muscles that elevate the testes.

Cryptorchidism   *See* UNDESCENDED TESTICLE.

Cul-de-sac   The "blind alley" ending of the vagina just beyond the opening into the womb (cervix).

Cunnilingus   The act of using the tongue or mouth in erotic play with the external female genitalia (vulva).

Cyst   A sac containing a liquid or semisolid substance that develops abnormally in some part of the body.

Cystitis   Inflammation of the bladder, usually characterized by a burning sensation during urination.

Cystocele   Hernial protrusion in women of the bladder through the vaginal wall.

Cytogenic   Forming or producing cells.

D&C   (**dilatation and curettage,** or **curettement**). A procedure in which the cervix is dilated and the lining of the uterus is scraped with a *curette*, a spoon-shaped medical instrument.

Defloration   The rupture of the hymen in a virgin's first experience of coitus, through vaginal examination, or through other means.

Detumescence   Subsidence of swelling; subsidence of erection in the genitals following orgasm.

Diaphragm   A rubber contraceptive, used by women, that is hemispherical in shape and fits like a cap over the neck of the uterus (cervix).

Diethystilbestrol (DES)   A drug that may be used for birth prevention when unprotected coitus has occurred. Because of possible severe side effects, the drug is typically used only in emergency and should not be considered a primary method of birth control. *Cf.* "MORNING-AFTER PILL."

Dildo   An artificial penis.

Doderlein's bacilli   The bacteria (germs) normally present in the vagina.

Dorsal   Pertaining to the back (as the back of the hand, of the whole body, or of the upper surface of the penis), as opposed to the *ventral* (front) side.

Douche   A stream of water or other liquid solution directed into the vagina for sanitary, medical, or contraceptive reasons.

Dry orgasm   Sexual climax in a male without any apparent ejaculation of semen; usually an instance of retrograde ejaculation, caused by some anomaly within the prostate, in which the semen is ejaculated backward into the posterior urethra and bladder rather than out through the penis. Removal of the prostate prevents production and ejaculation of semen, although capability for orgasm remains.

Ductless glands   (or *glands of internal secretion*) Glands of the endocrine system whose products, hormones, are secreted directly into the bloodstream.

Dysmenorrhea   Painful menstruation.

Dyspareunia   Coitus that is difficult or painful, especially for a woman.

Eclampsia   A condition of convulsions and coma that can occur in a woman during pregnancy or immediately following childbirth. *Cf.* TOXEMIA.

Ectoderm   The outermost of the three primitive or primary germ layers of the embryo, from which the nervous system, sense organs, mouth cavity, and skin eventually develop.

Ectopic   In an abnormal place, *e.g.*, an *ectopic pregnancy*, in which the unborn child develops outside the uterus, either in an ovary, the abdominal cavity, or a fallopian tube.

Edema   An abnormal amount of fluid in intercellular tissue, *e.g.*, edema of the scrotum.

Ejaculatio praecox   Premature ejaculation.

Ejaculation   The expulsion of semen, usually at the climax (orgasm) of the sexual act.

Ejaculatory anhedonia   Ejaculation not accompanied by orgasm; ejaculation with little pleasure or sensation; a difficulty usually of psychological origin.

Electra complex   Excessive emotional attachment of a daughter to her father.

Elephantiasis   A disease ordinarily found in tropical regions that involves a marked growth in subcutaneous tissues and epidermis, producing an enlargement varying from slight to monstrous.

Emasculate   To castrate; to deprive of manliness or masculine vigor.

Embryo   The unborn young in its early stage of development—in man, from one week following conception to the end of the second month.

Emission   Discharge of semen from the penis, especially when involuntary, as during sleep (nocturnal emission).

Endemic   Pertaining to or prevalent in a particular district or region; pertaining to a disease that has a low incidence but is constantly present in a given community.

Endocrine gland   *See* DUCTLESS GLANDS.

Endoderm   The innermost of the three primitive or primary germ layers of the embryo, from which the digestive and respiratory systems of the body develop.

Endometriosis   The aberrant presence of endometrial tissue (uterine lining) in other parts of the female pelvic cavity, such as in the fallopian tubes or in the ovaries, bladder, or intestines.

Endometrium   The mucous membrane that lines the cavity of the uterus in the female.

Epididymis   The network of tiny tubes in the male that connects the testicles with the sperm duct.

Epididymitis   Inflammation of the epididymis, a common disorder affecting men.

Episiotomy   Incision in a woman's perineum to facilitate the birth of a child.

Epispadia   A congenital defect in males in which the opening (meatus) of the urethra is on the upper surface of the penis instead of at its tip. *Cf.* HYPOSPADIA.

Epithelium   (adj. *epithelial*). The outer layer of cells covering the internal and external surfaces of the body.

Erection   The stiffening and enlargement of the penis (or clitoris), usually as a result of sexual excitement.

Erogenous zone   A sexually sensitive area of the body, such as the mouth, lips, breasts, nipples, buttocks, genitals, or anus.

Erotic   Pertaining to sexual love or sensation; sexually stimulating.

Estrogen   A steroid hormone producing female sex characteristics and affecting the functioning of the menstrual cycle.

Estrus   A recurrent period of sexual receptivity in female animals, marked by intense sexual urge.

Eugenics   A science that seeks to improve future generations through the control of hereditary factors.

Eunuch   A castrated male.

Eunuchoid   Having the physical characteristics of a eunuch without actually being castrated.

Excitement phase   The initial stage of the human sexual response cycle that follows effective sexual stimulation.

Exhibitionism   A sexual variance in which the individual—usually male—suffers from a compulsion to expose his genitals publicly.

Extragenital   Originating or lying outside the genital organs.

Extramarital   Literally, outside of marriage; usually used in reference to adulterous sexual intercourse.

Fallopian tube   The oviduct or egg-conducting tube that extends from each ovary to the uterus in the female.

Fecundity   The ability to produce offspring, especially in a rapid manner and in large numbers.

Fellatio   The act of taking the penis into the mouth and sucking it for erotic purposes.

Fertility   The state of being capable of producing young; the opposite of *sterility*.

Fertilization   The union of egg (ovum) and sperm (spermatozoon), which results in conception.

Fetal alcohol syndrome   A predictable syndrome of abnormalities, including central nervous system deficiencies, growth deficiencies, and facial disfigurements, that may appear in the babies of mothers who drink alcohol during pregnancy.

Fetishism   A sexual variance in which sexual gratification is achieved by means of an object, such as an article of clothing, that bears sexual symbolism for the individual.

Fetus   In humans, the unborn child from the third month after conception until birth.

Fibrillation   Spontaneous contraction of individual muscle fibers no longer under control of a motor nerve.

Follicle, ovarian   The small sac or vesicle near the surface of the ovary in the female that contains a developing egg cell (ovum).

Follicle-stimulating hormone (FSH)   A hormone secreted by the pituitary gland that stimulates, in the female, the growth and development of the ovarian follicles and, in the male, the production of sperm by the seminiferous tubules.

Foreplay   The preliminary stages of sexual intercourse, in which the partners usually stimulate each other by kissing, touching, and caressing.

Foreskin   The skin covering the tip of the penis or clitoris; prepuce.

Fornication   Sexual intercourse between two unmarried persons (as distinguished from *adultery*, which involves a person who is married to someone other than his or her coital partner).

Fourchette   The fold or mucous membrane at the posterior junction of the labia majora in the female.

Fraternal twins   Two offspring developed from two separate ova (eggs) usually fertilized at the same time.

Frenulum   A delicate, tissue-thin fold of skin that connects the foreskin with the under surface of the glans penis; frenum.

Frenum   *See* FRENULUM.

Frigidity   A common term for a form of female sexual dysfunction, implying coldness, indifference, or insensitivity on the part of a woman to sexual intercourse or sexual stimulation; inability to experience sexual pleasure or gratification.

Frottage   A sexual variance in which orgasm is induced by rubbing against an individual of the opposite sex, usually a stranger.

Fundus   The base or part of a hollow organ farthest from its mouth.

Gamete   The mature reproductive cell of either sex—sperm (male) or ovum (female).

Gastrula   The embryonic stage of development in which the cells form a double-layered hollow sphere.

Gender   One's genetic sex, biologically determined at the moment of conception by the pairing of the sex-determining chromosomes.

Gender identity   One's view of self as masculine or feminine; an environmentally or psychologically determined feature.

Gender identity disorder   The expression of distaste and disgust for one's own genetic sex and a preference for and strong identification with the other sex.

Gene   The basic carrier of hereditary traits, contained in the chromosomes.

Genital organs   (or *genitals* or *genitalia*). The sex or reproductive organs.

Germ cell   The sperm (spermatozoon) or egg (ovum).

Gerontosexuality   A sexual disorder in which a young person chooses an elderly person as the subject of his or her sexual interest.

Gestation   Pregnancy; the period from conception to birth.

Glans clitoridis   The head of the clitoris.

Glans penis   The head of the penis.

Gonad   A sex gland; a testicle (male) or ovary (female).

Gonadectomy   The surgical removal of all or part of the gonads (ovaries or testicles).

Gonadotropin   A substance having a stimulating effect on the gonads (sex glands).

Gonadotropin-releasing factor (GRF)   A hormone-like substance produced by the hypothalamus that controls the formation and release of the pituitary hormones concerned with sexual maturity and reproduction.

Gonorrhea   A venereal disease, transmitted chiefly through coitus, that is a contagious catarrhal inflammation of the genital mucous membrane.

Graafian follicle   A small sac or pocket in the ovary in which the egg (ovum) matures and from which it is discharged at ovulation.

Granuloma inguinale   A disease typically affecting the genitals, which is characterized by widespread ulceration and scarring of the skin and underlying tissues.

Gynecologist   A physician specializing in the treatment of the problems of the female sexual and reproductive organs.

Gynecomastia   Femalelike development of the male breasts.

Gynatresia   A congenital anomaly wherein the vagina is closed.

Heredity   The transmission of bodily traits and characteristics or of diseases from parents to offspring.

Hermaphrodite   An individual who, because of a rare congenital condition, cannot be clearly defined as either male or female.

Hermaphrodite, dysgenetic   An individual who fails to develop completely the gonads of either sex.

Hermaphrodite, female   An individual who possesses gonads that are ovaries but whose external genitalia are either ambiguous or masculine in appearance.

Hermaphrodite, male   An individual who possesses gonads that are testes but whose external genitalia are either ambiguous or feminine in appearance.

Hermaphrodite, true   An individual who possesses both male and female gonads (ovary and testicle) or gonadal tissue of both sexes.

Herpes   Clustered blisters on the surface of the skin or mucous membranes, caused by viral infection, which tend to spread and can be sexually transmitted.

Heterogeneous   Consisting of dissimilar elements; the opposite of *homogeneous.*

Heterosexuality   Sexual attraction to, or sexual activity with, members of the opposite sex; the opposite of *homosexuality.*

Hirsutism   Abnormal hairiness, especially in women.

Homologous   Corresponding in position, structure, or origin to another anatomical entity.

Homosexuality   Sexual attraction to, or sexual activity with, members of one's own sex; the opposite of *heterosexuality.*

Hormone   A chemical substance produced by an endocrine gland that has a specific effect on the activities of other organs in the body.

Hydrocele   An accumulation of fluid in the scrotum.

Hymen   The membranous fold that partly covers the external opening of the vagina in most virgin females; the maidenhead.

Hyperplasia   The abnormal multiplication or increase in the number of cells in a tissue. *Cf.* HYPERTROPHY.

Hypertrophy   An excessive enlargement or outgrowth of a bodily part or organ because of enlargement of its constituent elements.

Hypogonadism   Hormonal deprivation resulting in reduction or loss of sexual vigor and, perhaps, certain negative emotional reactions, such as depression.

Hypospadia   A congenital defect in males in which the opening (meatus) of the urethra is on the underside of the penis instead of at its tip. *Cf.* EPISPADIA.

Hypothalamus   A small portion of the brain that controls such vital bodily processes as visceral activities, temperature, and sleep.

Hysterectomy   Surgical removal of the uterus, either through the abdominal wall or through the vagina.

Hysterotomy   Incision into the uterus.

Identical twins   Two offspring developed from one fertilized ovum (egg).

Implantation   Embedding of the blastocyst (fertilized egg) in the mucous membrane, or endometrium, lining the uterus.

Impotence   Disturbance of sexual function in the male that precludes satisfactory coitus; more specifically, inability to achieve or maintain an erection sufficient for purposes of sexual intercourse.

Impregnation   The act of fertilization or fecundation; making pregnant.

Incest   Sexual relations between close relatives, such as father and daughter, mother and son, or brother and sister.

Infanticide   The murder of an infant.

Infectious mononucleosis   A virus-produced disease affecting the lymph glands.

Inguinal canal   The passageway from the abdominal cavity to the scrotum in the male through which the testicles descend shortly before birth or just after.

Inhibitions of Sexual Desire (ISD)   A category of sexual dysfunctions in which sexual desire for another person is missing or adversely affected.

Insemination   The deposit of semen within the vagina.

Intercourse, anal   A form of sexual intercourse in which the penis is inserted into the partner's anus; sometimes termed *sodomy*.

Intercourse, interfemoral   Nonvaginal method of coitus that uses the space between the thighs to hold the penis.

Intercourse, sexual   Sexual union of a male and a female, in which the penis is inserted into the vagina; coitus.

Interstitial cells   Specialized cells in the testicles that produce the male sex hormones.

Interstitial cell-stimulating hormone (ICSH)   A hormone secreted by the pituitary gland that stimulates, in the male, the maturation of the sperm cells.

Intrauterine device (IUD)   A small plastic or metal device that, when fitted into the uterus, prevents pregnancy. Also termed *intrauterine contraceptive device* (IUCD).

Intromission   The insertion of the penis into the vagina.

Invert   A homosexual; one who is sexually attracted to persons of his or her own sex.

Involution   An inward curvature; a shrinking or return to a former size, as of the uterus after childbirth; the regressive alterations in the body or its parts characteristic of the aging process.

Jock itch   *See* TINEA CRURIS.

Karyotype   All of the characteristics of the chromosomes of a cell—also, the arrangement of the chromosomes themselves.

Kleptomania   An irresistible compulsion to steal, usually without any use for the article stolen.

Klinefelter's syndrome (XXY)   An abnormality, afflicting males, in which the sex-determining chromosomes are XXY, instead of the normal XY, one gamete having somehow contributed an extra X at the time of fertilization. Symptoms of the condition include small testicles, sterility, and often a distinctly feminine physical appearance.

Klismaphilia   The erotic pleasure gained from taking enemas.

Labia majora   (sing. *labium majus*). The outer and larger pair of lips of the female external genitals (vulva).

Labia minora   (sing. *labium minus*). The inner and smaller pair of lips of the female external genitals (vulva).

Lactation   The manufacture and secretion of milk by the mammary glands in a mother's breasts.

Laparoscopic sterilization   (also *"Band-Aid" sterilization*). Sterilization accomplished by cutting or cauterizing the fallopian tubes through minute abdominal incision(s).

Lesbian   A female homosexual.

Leukorrhea   Excessive vaginal mucous discharge; not a disease entity in itself, but a condition caused by a chemical, physical, or infectious agent.

Libido   Sexual drive or urge.

Lochia   The discharge from the uterus and vagina that takes place during the first few weeks after childbirth.

Luteinizing hormone (LH)   A hormone secreted by the pituitary gland that stimulates, in the female, the formation of the corpus luteum.

Lymphogranuloma venereum   A virus-produced disease that affects the lymph glands in the genital region.

Macromastia   The condition of having an abnormally large breast or breasts.

Maculopapular   Spotted and raised or elevated.

Maidenhead   The hymen.

Masochism   A sexual variance in which an individual derives sexual gratification from having pain inflicted on him or her.

Mastectomy   The surgical removal of all or part of the breast(s).

Masturbation   Self-stimulation of the genitals through manipulation; autoeroticism.

Mate-swapping (also *swinging*)   A form of sexual variance in which two or more married couples exchange sexual partners.

Meatus   An opening, such as at the end of the urethral passage in the penis.

Meiosis   Cellular reduction division, as in spermatogenesis and oogenesis, in which daughter cells are produced containing half the number of chromosomes present in the original cell. *Cf.* MITOSIS.

Menarche   The onset of menstruation in the human female, occurring in late puberty and ushering in the period of adolescence.

Menopause   The period of cessation of menstruation in the human female, occurring usually between the ages of 45 and 55; climacteric; change of life.

Menstrual cramps   Pain experienced by a woman just before or during her menstrual period; the problem may have a physical or a psychological basis.

Menstrual cycle   The lapse of time from the first day of one menstrual flow to the day before the next one, typically between 24 and 32 days.

Menstrual extraction   A method of therapeutic or elective abortion, commonly performed within the first two weeks of a missed menstrual period, that involves the extraction of the uterine contents via suction through a thin flexible plastic tube.

Menstruation   The discharge of blood from the uterus through the vagina that normally recurs at approximately four-week intervals in women between the ages of puberty and menopause.

Menstruation, vicarious   The phenomenon of extragenital bleeding occurring during the menstrual flow, in which bleeding may take place from the nose or other anatomical structure.

Mesoderm   The middle layer of the three primitive or primary germ layers of the embryo, from which the muscular, skeletal, excretory, circulatory, and reproductive systems of the body develop.

Minipills   Birth-control pills containing small doses of progestin alone, as opposed to combination pills, which contain both progestin and estrogen.

Miscarriage   The premature, spontaneous expulsion of a fetus, especially between the fourth and seventh months of pregnancy.

Mitosis   Ordinary cell division involving nuclear and cytoplasmic fission and resulting in two new cells, each containing the full complement of 46 chromosomes. *Cf.* MEIOSIS.

Monilia   (or *moniliasis*). A yeastlike infective organism (fungus) causing itching and inflammation of the vagina; candidiasis.

Monogamy   Marriage between one man and one woman.

Mononucleosis   *See* INFECTIOUS MONONUCLEOSIS.

Monorchism   The condition of having only one testicle in the scrotum.

Mons veneris   (or *mons pubis*). A triangular mound of fat at the symphysis pubis of a woman, just above the vulval area.

"Morning-after Pill"   A birth prevention measure that may be used after unprotected coitus has occurred. Besides diethystilbestrol, the effectiveness of other drugs such as progestins and ovral contraceptive pills is still being tested. *Cf.* DIETHYSTILBESTROL.

Morula   Cell mass formed by cleavage of the ovum shortly after fertilization and before the blastocyst stage and implantation.

Mucoid   Resembling mucus.

Mucosa   A mucous membrane; a thin tissue whose surface is kept moist by the secretion of mucus.

Mucus   (adj. *mucous*). The thick, slippery fluid secreted by mucous membranes.

Müllerian ducts   The primitive genital ducts that, under hormonal influence, evolve into the female genitalia.

Multipara   (adj. *multiparous*). A woman who has given birth to two or more children.

Myoma   (pl. *myomas* or *myomata*). A tumor consisting of muscle tissue that grows in the wall of the uterus; also called *fibroid*.

Myotonia   Increased muscular tension.

Narcissism   Excessive self-love; sexual excitement through admiration of one's own body.

Natural childbirth A technique of childbirth that aims to minimize childbirth pain through programs of physical and psychological pain prior to delivery, rather than through reliance on drugs; educated childbirth.

Necrophilia A sexual variance in which an individual has a morbid sexual attraction to corpses.

Neonatal Pertaining or related to the first month of life.

Neural tube The epithelial tube that develops from the neural plate to form the embryo's central nervous system and from which the brain and spinal column develop.

Neurosyphilis Syphilitic infection of the nervous system.

Nidation The implantation of the blastocyst (fertilized ovum) in the lining of the uterus in pregnancy.

Nocturnal emission An involuntary male orgasm and ejaculation of semen during sleep; a "wet dream."

Nongonococcal urethritis (NGU) Inflammation of the urinary tract, usually by *Chlamydial Trachomatis*. Symptoms are similar to those of gonorrhea, but it ordinarily is not considered a venereal disease.

Nudism The social practice of those who prefer to discard their clothing. Often erroneously linked with exhibitionism, nudism is considered by some a sexual deviation. *Cf.* EXHIBITIONISM.

Nullipara (adj. *nulliparous*). A woman who has never borne a viable child.

Nymphomania Excessive sexual desire in a woman.

Obscene Disgusting, repulsive, filthy, shocking—that which is abhorrent according to accepted standards of morality.

Obsession A neurosis characterized by the persistent recurrence of some irrational thought or idea, or by an attachment to or fixation on a particular individual or object.

Obstetrician A physician specializing in the care of women during pregnancy, labor, and the period immediately following delivery.

Oedipus complex Excessive emotional attachment, involving conscious or unconscious incestuous desires, of a son in relation to his mother.

Onanism Withdrawl of the penis from the vagina before ejaculation; *coitus interruptus*.

Oocyte Ovum or egg in an immature stage of development.

Oophorectomy The surgical removal of an ovary or ovaries.

Oral eroticism Pleasurable sensations centered in the lips and mouth.

Orgasm The peak or climax of sexual excitement in sexual activity.

Orgasmic phase The third stage in the human sexual response cycle during which orgasm occurs.

Orgasmic platform The area comprising the outer third of the vagina and the labia minora, which displays marked vasocongestion in the plateau phase of the female sexual response cycle (term used by Masters and Johnson).

Os   A mouth or orifice, as the external os of the cervix (*os externum uteri*).

Ovary   The female sex gland, in which the ova are formed.

Oviduct   The fallopian or uterine tube through which the egg (ovum) travels from the ovary to the uterus.

Ovulation   The release of a mature, unimpregnated ovum from one of the graafian follicles of an ovary.

Ovum   (pl. *ova*). An egg, the female reproductive cell, corresponding to the male spermatozoon, that after fertilization develops into a new member of the same species.

Oxytocin   A hormone secreted by the pituitary gland that stimulates the muscles of the uterus to contract during childbirth.

Paraphilia   Sexual deviations; aberrant sexual activity.

Paresis   A chronic syphilitic inflammation of the brain and its enveloping membranes, characterized by progressive mental deterioration and a general paralysis that is sometimes fatal.

Parthenogenesis   Reproduction by the development of an egg without its being fertilized by a spermatozoon.

Parturition   Labor; the process of giving birth.

Pathogenic   Causing disease.

Pathological   Pertaining to a diseased or abnormal physical or mental condition.

Pederasty   Male sexual relations with a boy; also sexual intercourse via the anus.

Pediculosis pubis   An itchy skin irritation in the genital area caused by the minute bites of the crab louse.

Pedophilia   A sexual variance in which an adult engages in or desires sexual activity with a child.

Penis   (adj. *penile*). The male organ of copulation and urination.

Penis captivus   A condition in humans in which it is alleged that the shaft of the fully introduced penis is tightly encircled by the vagina during coitus and cannot be withdrawn. Most authorities say this condition occurs only in animals, notably the dog.

Penoscrotal raphe   The scar line on the underside of the penis, running from the anus to the glans. It is formed in male prenatal development from the fusion of the urogenital sinus that closes to form the tubular urethra within the penis.

Perineum   (adj. *perineal*). The area between the thighs, extending from the posterior wall of the vagina to the anus in the female and from the scrotum to the anus in the male.

Peritoneum   (adj. *peritoneal*). The strong, transparent membrane lining the abdominal cavity.

Perversion   Sexual deviation from normal; paraphilia.

Petting   Sexual contact that stops short of coitus.

Peyronie's disease   A condition, usually in men of middle age or older, in which the penis develops a fibrous ridge along its top or sides, causing curvature.

Phallus   The penis, usually the erect penis.

Phimosis   Tightness of the penile foreskin so that it cannot be drawn back from over the glans.

Pituitary   The "master gland," located in the head, that is responsible for the proper functioning of all the other glands, especially the sex glands, the thyroid, and the adrenals.

Pituitary gonadotropins   Hormones produced by the pituitary gland that stimulate the gonads (sex glands).

Placenta   The cakelike organ that connects the fetus to the uterus by means of the umbilical cord, and through which the fetus is fed and waste products are eliminated; the afterbirth.

Placenta previa   Low implantation of the blastocyst in the uterus that often results in miscarriage because of premature detachment of the placenta.

Plateau phase   The fully stimulated stage in the human sexual response cycle that immediately precedes orgasm.

Polyandry   The form of marriage in which one woman has more than one husband at one time.

Polygamy   The form of marriage in which a spouse of either sex may possess a plurality of mates at the same time.

Polygyny   The form of marriage in which one man has more than one wife at the same time.

Polymastia   The presence of one or more extra breasts.

Polyp   A stemlike growth that arises from the mucosa and extends into the lumen or opening of any body cavity.

Polythelia   The presence of supernumerary nipples.

Pornography   Sexually arousing material in literature, art, motion pictures, or other means of communication and expression.

Postpartum   Occurring after childbirth or after delivery.

Potent   Having the male capability to perform sexual intercourse; capable of erection.

Precocious sexuality   Awakening of sexual desire at a prematurely early age.

Precoital fluid   Alkaline fluid secreted by the Cowper's glands that lubricates the urethra for easy passage of semen.

Pregnancy   The condition of having a developing embryo or fetus in the body; the period from conception to birth or abortion.

Premature ejaculation   Ejaculation prior to, just at, or immediately after intromission; *ejaculatio praecox*.

Premenstrual syndrome   Discomfort or pain occurring before menstruation.

Prenatal   Existing or occurring before birth.

Prepuce   Foreskin.

Priapism   Persistent abnormal erection of the penis in males, usually without sexual desire.

Procreation   The producing of offspring.

Progesterone   (or *progestin*). The female hormone (known as the pregnancy hormone) that is produced in the yellow body or corpus luteum, and whose function is to prepare the uterus for the reception and development of a fertilized ovum.

Prolactin   A hormone secreted by the pituitary gland that stimulates the production of milk by the mammary glands in the breasts (lactation).

Promiscuous   Engaging in sexual intercourse with many persons; engaging in casual sexual relations.

Pronucleus, female   The nucleus of the secondary oocyte containing the maternal contribution of 23 chromosomes. At the time of fertilization, it is joined at the center of the ovum by the male pronucleus.

Pronucleus, male   Upon penetration into the ovum at the time of fertilization, the head of the sperm after its tail separates and disintegrates. It contains the paternal contribution of 23 chromosomes.

Prophylactic   A drug or device used for the prevention of disease, often specifically venereal disease.

Prostate   The gland in the male that surrounds the urethra and the neck of the bladder.

Prostatectomy   The surgical removal of all or part of the prostate.

Prostatic fluid   A highly alkaline, thin, milky fluid produced by the prostate gland that constitutes a major portion of the male's semen or ejaculatory fluid.

Prostatitis   Inflammation of the prostate gland, typically a disease of older men.

Prostitute   A person who engages in sexual relationships for payment.

Prudish   Extremely or falsely modest.

Pseudocyesis   False pregnancy.

Psychogenic   Of psychic or emotional origin; functional.

Puberty   (or *pubescence*). The stage of life at which a child turns into a young man or young woman: *i.e.*, the reproductive organs become functionally operative and secondary sex characteristics develop.

Pudendum   (pl. *pudenda*). The external genitalia, especially of the female (the mons pubis, labia majora, labia minora, and the vestibule of the vagina).

Pyromania   A compulsion, usually sexually oriented, to start fires.

Rape   Forcible sexual intercourse with a person who does not give consent or who offers resistance.

Rape, statutory   Coitus with a partner under the age of consent (usually 18).

Rectocele   A hernia in females in which part of the rectum protrudes into the vagina.

Rectum   The lower part of the large intestine, terminating at the anus.

Refractory period   A temporary state of psychophysiologic resistance to sexual stimulation immediately following an orgasmic experience (term used by Masters and Johnson).

Resolution phase   The last stage in the human sexual response cycle during which the sexual system retrogresses to its normal nonexcited state.

Retrograde ejaculation   Backward ejaculation in males into the posterior urethra and bladder, instead of into the anterior urethra and out through the meatus of the penis.

Retroversion   The tipping of an entire organ backward.

Rh factor   An element found in the blood of most people. People who have the Rh factor are Rh positive, and people who lack the Rh factor are Rh negative. Incompatibility in parents' Rh blood factors potentially can adversely affect fetal development.

Rhythm method   A method of birth control that relies on the so-called "safe period" or infertile days in a woman's menstrual cycle.

Rubella   German measles; a disease, which if contracted by a pregnant mother may result in birth defects.

Sadism   The achievement of sexual gratification by inflicting physical or psychological pain upon the sexual partner.

"Safe period"   The interval of the menstrual cycle when the female is presumably not ovulating.

Saline abortion   A method of therapeutic or elective abortion, sometimes used when pregnancy has advanced beyond the 14th week, that involves the removal of a small amount of amniotic fluid and replacement with an equal amount of saline solution. Abortion then occurs spontaneously usually within 48 hours.

Saliromania   A sexual variance, found primarily in men, that is characterized by the desire to damage or soil the body or clothes of a woman or a representation of a woman.

Salpingectomy   Surgical removal of a fallopian tube from a woman.

Satyriasis   Excessive sexual desire in a man.

Scabies   A highly contagious skin disorder caused by a mite that burrows into the skin to lay eggs. A rash results in affected areas.

Scopophilia   (or *scoptophilia*). A sexual variance in which a person achieves sexual gratification by observing sexual acts or the genitals of others. *Cf.* VOYEURISM.

Scrotum The pouch suspended from the groin that contains the male testicles and their accessory organs.

Secondary sex characteristics The physical characteristics—other than the external sex organs—that distinguish male from female.

Seduction Luring a female (sometimes a male) into sexual intercourse without the use of force.

Semen The secretion of the male reproductive organs that is ejaculated from the penis at orgasm and contains, in the fertile male, sperm cells.

Seminal emission (or *seminal fluid*). A fluid composed of sperm and secretions from the epididymis, seminal vesicles, prostate gland, and Cowper's glands. It is ejaculated by the male through the penis upon his reaching orgasm.

Seminal vesicles Two pouches in the male, one on each side of the prostate, behind the bladder, that are attached to and open into the sperm ducts.

Seminiferous tubules The tiny tubes or canals in each male testicle that produce sperm.

Sensate focus (also *pleasuring*). A therapeutic technique emphasizing the sense of touch, in which bodily surfaces are gently, manually explored by self or partner to reestablish the sensual reactions of childhood.

Serology The study of antigen and antibody reactions in blood-serum tests.

Sex drive Desire for sexual expression.

Sex flush The superficial vasocongestive skin response to increasing sexual tensions that begins in the plateau phase (term used by Masters and Johnson).

Sex gland A gonad; the testicle in the male and the ovary in the female.

Sex hormone A substance secreted by the sex glands directly into the bloodstream, *e.g.*, androgens (male) and estrogens (female).

Sex offender An individual who commits an act designated by law as a sexual offense and hence a crime.

Sex organs Commonly, the organs used in sexual intercourse—namely, the male's penis and the female's vagina.

Sex-skin The labia minora in the female, which show a discoloration response in the plateau phase of the sexual response cycle.

Sexual anesthesia An hysterical conversion neurosis causing a woman to "feel nothing" when sexual stimulation is undertaken.

Sexual inadequacy Any degree of sexual response that is not sufficient over a protracted period of time; frequent or total inability to experience orgasm.

Sexual intercourse *See* INTERCOURSE, SEXUAL.

Sexual outlet Any of the various ways by which sexual tension is released through orgasm.

Shaft, penile The body of the penis, composed of three cylindrical bodies and a network of blood vessels, which are encircled by a band of fibrous tissue and covered by skin.

Smegma A thick, cheesy, ill-smelling accumulation of secretions under the foreskin of the penis or around the clitoris.

Sodomy A form of paraphilia, variously defined by law to include sexual intercourse with animals and mouth-genital or anal contact between humans.

Somatic Pertaining to the body, as distinct from the psyche or mind: organic, as distinguished from functional or psychosomatic.

Spanish fly (*Cantharides*). A drug, widely considered to be an aphrodisiac, that is derived from the beetle, *Cantharis vesicatoria*. When ingested, the substance causes inflammation of the genitourinary tract and possibly erection in males; excessive doses may cause violent illness and death.

Sperm (or *spermatozoon*). The mature reproductive cell (or cells) capable of fertilizing the female egg and causing impregnation.

Sperm bank A center where a man's semen may be frozen and stored for later use in artificial insemination.

Sperm duct The tube or duct in males that conveys the sperm from the epididymis to the seminal vesicles and urethra; the vas deferens.

Spermatic cord The structure in males, by which the testicle is suspended, containing the sperm ducts, nerves, and veins.

Spermatocele A soft swelling on either side of the scrotum, the result of an intrascrotal cyst.

Spermatogenesis The process of sperm formation.

Spermatozoon (pl. *spermatozoa*). A mature male germ cell.

Spermicide An agent that destroys sperm.

Sphincter A ringlike muscle that closes a natural orifice.

Spirochete A corkscrew-shaped microorganism, one type of which causes syphilis.

Status orgasmus A sustained orgasmic response, experienced by some women, which lasts 20 seconds or longer.

Sterility The inability to produce offspring.

Sterilization Any procedure (usually surgical) by which an individal is made incapable of reproduction.

Stricture The abnormal narrowing of a canal, duct, or passage.

Suction abortion (*vacuum curettage*). A method of therapeutic or elective abortion usually performed up to the 12th week of pregnancy that involves removal of a fetus via suction through a large tube inserted into the uterus.

"Sweating" phenomenon The appearance of little droplets of fluid on the walls of the vagina early in the excitement phase of the female sexual response cycle.

Symphysis pubis The articulation between the pubic bones in the lower abdomen.

Syphilis   One of the most serious of venereal diseases. It is usually acquired by sexual intercourse with a person in the infectious stage of the disease and is caused by invasion of the spirochete *Treponema pallidum.*

Systemic   Spread throughout the body; affecting all body systems and organs.

Taboo   An absolute prohibition based on religion, tradition, social usage, or superstition.

Telegony   The alleged appearance in the offspring of one sire of characteristics derived from a previous sire or mate of the female.

Temperature method   A periodic-abstinence method of birth prevention that relies on the correlation between body temperature and the ovulation process to determine the woman's "safe period" or infertile days in her menstrual cycle.

Test tube baby   A baby who was conceived outside the woman's body via a laboratory procedure and was then later reimplanted in the woman's uterus for embryonic development to take place.

Testicle   The testis; the male sex gland.

Testis   (pl. ***testes***). The male sex gland or gonad, which produces spermatozoa.

Testosterone   The male testicular hormone that induces and maintains the male secondary sex characteristics.

Thrombosis   The clogging of a blood vessel as the result of the formation of a blood clot within the vessel itself.

Therapeutic abortion   Abortion performed when abnormal conditions threaten the well-being of the mother or the unborn child.

Tinea cruris   A fungus infection causing irritation to the skin in the genital region.

Toxemia   A disease state of pregnancy. The initial stage, preeclampsia, involves an increase in blood pressure and swelling of face and hands. It may progress further to eclampsia, symptomatized by dramatic blood pressure increases, coma, convulsions, and possibly death. *Cf.* ECLAMPSIA.

Toxic shock syndrome   A rare cluster of symptoms· in women (and sometimes men): vomiting, fever, diarrhea, a skin rash, and a rapid decrease in blood pressure, together with possible shock. A bacterium is suspected as the cause, whose growth may be made favorable by tampon usage.

Toxoplasmosis   A disease with symptoms similar to mononucleosis that can affect a pregnant woman and her unborn child. It may be contracted by consuming inadequately cooked meat or by poor personal hygiene.

Transgenderist   A person who identifies strongly with the opposite sex and may cross-dress, yet does not wish to undergo transsexual surgery.

Transsexualism   A compulsion or obsession to become a member of the opposite sex through surgical changes.

Transvestism   A sexual variance characterized by a compulsive desire to wear the garments of the opposite sex; cross-dressing.

Trichomoniasis   An infection of the vagina caused by infestation of the microorganism *Trichomonas* and characterized by inflammation, usually resulting in a vaginal discharge, itching, and burning.

Trimester   A period of three months; one of the three time divisions of a pregnancy.

Trisomy   Presence of an additional third chromosome of a particular chromosome pair, caused by improper splitting of the cell nucleus during cell division.

Troilism   (or *triolism*). A sexual variance in which, ordinarily, three people (two men and a woman or two women and a man) participate in a series of sexual practices.

Tubal ligation   A surgical procedure for sterilizing a female, in which the fallopian tubes are cut and tied.

Tubal pregnancy   A type of displaced or ectopic pregnancy in which the embryo fails to descend into the womb and instead develops in the fallopian tube.

Tumescence   The process of swelling or the condition of being swollen.

Turner's syndrome (XO)   An abnormality afflicting females, in which one of the sex-determining pair (XX) of chromosomes is missing, leaving a total of 45 rather than the normal 46 chromosomes. Symptoms of the condition include incomplete development of the ovaries, short stature, and often webbing of the neck.

Umbilical cord   The flexible structure connecting the fetus and the placenta; navel cord.

Undescended testicle   A developmental defect in males in which the testicles fail to descend into the scrotum; cryptorchidism.

Urethra   The duct through which the urine passes from the bladder and is excreted from the body.

Urethrocele   Protrusion in women of the urethra through the vaginal wall; a hernia.

Urologist   A physician specializing in the treatment of the diseases and disorders of the urinary tract of both sexes, as well as of the genital tract of the male.

Uterine tube   The fallopian tube, which extends from each ovary to the uterus in the female.

Uterus   The hollow, pear-shaped organ in females within which the fetus develops; the womb.

Vagina   The canal in the female, extending from the vulva to the cervix, that receives the penis during coitus and through which an infant passes at birth.

Vaginal barrel   The vaginal cavity in women.

Vaginal lubrication   A clear fluid (like sweat) that appears on the walls of the vaginal barrel within a few seconds after the onset of sexual stimulation.

Vaginal orgasm   A term of ambiguous meaning, apparently referring to an orgasm that a woman allegedly can achieve vaginally without any clitoral stimulation.

Vaginismus   Strong muscular contractions within the vagina, preventing intromission of the penis when intercourse is attempted.

Vaginitis   Inflammation of the vagina, usually as a result of infection.

Varicocele   A swelling or enlargement of the veins in the spermatic cord.

Vasa efferentia   The system of ducts in the male through which sperm are moved to the epididymis.

Vas deferens   (or *ductus deferens*). The sperm duct(s) in males, leading from the epididymis to the seminal vesicles and the urethra.

Vas sclerosing   Male sterilization wherein the vas deferens is blocked, preventing passage of sperm.

Vasectomy   A surgical procedure for sterilizing the male involving removal of the vas deferens, or a portion of it.

Vasocongestion   Congestion of the blood vessels, especially the veins in the genital area.

Vasospasm   Sudden decrease in the size of a blood vessel.

Venereal disease   A contagious disease communicated mainly by sexual intercourse, such as syphilis or gonorrhea.

Venereal warts   Benign tumors that may result from a viral infection. Growth is encouraged in moist parts of the body; infection can spread on oneself or be transmitted to others.

Verumontanum   A small mound in men in the portion of the urethra passing through the prostate, which contains the openings of the ejaculatory ducts.

Vestibule   The area surrounding and including the opening of the vagina in the female.

Virgin birth   *See* PARTHENOGENESIS.

Virginity   The physical state of a girl or woman before first intercourse.

Voyeurism   A sexual variance in which a person achieves sexual gratification by observing others in the nude or engaged in sexual activity. *Cf.* SCOPOPHILIA.

Vulva   The external sex organs of the female, including the mons veneris, the labia majora, the labia minora, the clitoris, and the vestibule.

Wassermann test   A blood test used to determine whether or not a person has syphilis.

Wet dream   *See* NOCTURNAL EMISSION.

Withdrawal   *See* COITUS INTERRUPTUS.

Wölffian ducts   The primitive genital ducts that, under hormonal influence, evolve into the male genitalia.

Womb   The uterus in the female.

X chromosome   A sex-determining chromosome present in all of a female's ova and in one-half of a male's sperm. The fertilization of an ovum by a sperm having an X chromosome will result in the conception of a female (XX).

Y chromosome   A sex-determining chromosome present in one-half of a male's sperm. The fertilization of an ovum by a sperm having a Y chromosome will result in the conception of a male (XY).

Zoophilia   A sexual variance that involves an abnormal degree of affection for animals. *Cf.* BESTIALITY.

Zygote   The single cell resulting from the union of two germ cells (sperm and egg) at conception; the fertilized egg (ovum).

Index